P9-DTM-892

SOMETHING ABOUT THE AUTHOR

AUTOBIOGRAPHY SERIES

ISSN 0885-6842

SOMETHING ABOUT THE AUTHOR

AUTOBIOGRAPHY SERIES

JOYCE NAKAMURA
EDITOR

VOLUME 7

GALE RESEARCH INC. • BOOK TOWER • DETROIT, MICHIGAN 48226

EDITORIAL STAFF

Joyce Nakamura, *Editor*
Carolyn Chafetz and Motoko Fujishiro Huthwaite, *Assistant Editors*
Shelly Andrews, *Research Assistant*

Mary Beth Trimper, *Production Manager*
Laura McKay, *External Production Assistant*

Art Chartow, *Art Director*

Vivian Tannenbaum, *Layout Artist*

Laura Bryant, *Internal Production Supervisor*
Louise Gagné, *Internal Production Associate*

Donald G. Dillaman, *Index Program Designer*

Library of Congress Catalog Card Number 86-641293
ISBN 0-8103-4456-4
ISSN 0885-6842

Contents

Preface

Each volume in the *Something about the Author Autobiography Series (SAAS)* presents an original collection of autobiographical essays written especially for the series by prominent authors and illustrators of books for children and young adults. This series takes its place beside other distinguished reference works on young people's literature published by Gale Research: *Children's Literature Review, Children's Book Review Index, Children's Literature Awards and Winners,* the biographical indexes *Children's Authors and Illustrators* and *Writers for Young Adults,* and particularly the highly acclaimed bio-bibliographical series *Something about the Author (SATA),* to which this *Autobiography Series* is a companion.

You may already be familiar with *SATA,* which has long been recognized as the only comprehensive ongoing reference series that deals with the lives and works of the people who create books for young readers. To complement *SATA*'s wide range of detailed information, *SAAS* presents a "close up" view of some of these fascinating people. In *SAAS* authors and illustrators are invited to write about themselves, especially for you, in the form of an extended essay. This is a new and exciting opportunity—for you, for the author, and for the publisher. A reference work that collects autobiographies of this kind has never existed before, and Gale is pleased to fill this information gap with the *SATA Autobiography Series.*

Purpose

This series is designed to be a place where young readers, as well as adults interested in young people's literature, can meet "in person" the men and women who create the books that children and young adults are reading today. Here you can learn about the people and events that influenced these writers' early lives, how they began their careers, what problems they faced in becoming established in their professions, what prompted them to write or illustrate particular books, what they now find most challenging or rewarding in their lives, and what advice they may have for young people interested in following in their footsteps, among many other subjects. In *SAAS* writers can talk directly to you on their own terms. They are free to choose what they will say to you, and the way they will say it. As a result, each essay highlights the individuality of its writer—that special quality that sets one creative person apart from another.

In *SAAS* young readers, adult students of children's literature, teachers, librarians, and parents can learn more about familiar authors and illustrators and make the first acquaintance of many others. Authors who may never write a full-length autobiography have the opportunity in *SAAS* to let their readers know how they see themselves and their work. Even writers who have already published full-length life stories have the opportunity in *SAAS* to bring their readers "up to date," or perhaps to take a different approach in the essay format. At the very least, these essays can help to satisfy every reader's natural curiosity about the "real" person behind the name on the book jacket. Each of these essays offers a distinctive view of the person who wrote it; taken together, the essays in this series offer a new window on young people's literature.

Even though the *SATA Autobiography Series* is still in its youth, we can look forward to what it will accomplish. The series expects to fill a significant information gap—the primary reason behind every reference book. But we expect *SAAS* to do even more: the original essays in these volumes will make *SAAS* a varied and rewarding anthology of contemporary writing for young people.

Scope

Like its parent series, *Something about the Author,* the *SATA Autobiography Series* aims to include writers and artists who produce all the types of books that young people read today. *SAAS* sets out to meet the needs and interests of a broad range of readers from upper elementary school through junior high school and high school. Each volume in the series provides about twenty essays by current writers whose work has special appeal for young readers. We consider it an extraordinary accomplishment that this many busy writers and artists are able to interrupt their writing, teaching, speaking, traveling, and other schedules to come together in print by a given deadline for any one volume. So it is not always possible to represent every area of young people's literature equally and uniformly in each volume of *SAAS.* About half of the twenty authors in Volume 7, for example, write in a variety of genres, including fiction, nonfiction, and poetry for children and young adults. The other writers in this volume concentrate in a particular area: three write nonfiction for children, one writes young adult fiction, and one specializes in fiction for children and young adults. In addition, three are illustrators. However, these categories do not begin to suggest the variety and vitality of their work. Many of the contributors to this volume have also written fiction and nonfiction for adults as well as worked for movies, television, radio, newspapers, and journals.

Format

Writers who contribute to *SAAS* are invited to write a "mini-autobiography" of approximately 10,000 words. We deliberately set no pattern for authors to follow in writing their essays, and we do not limit the essays to particular topics. This leaves the way open for the essayists to speak to you in the manner that is most natural and comfortable for each of them. Writers for *SAAS* are also asked to supply a selection of personal photographs, showing themselves at various ages, as well as important people and special moments in their lives. Our contributors have responded graciously and generously, sharing with us some of their most treasured mementoes, as you will see in this volume. This enticing combination of text and photographs makes *SAAS* the kind of reference book that even browsers will find irresistible.

A bibliography appears at the end of each essay, listing the writer's book-length works in chronological order of publication. Each entry in the bibliography includes the publication information for the book's first printing in the United States and Great Britain. Generally, the bibliography does not include later reprintings, new editions, or foreign translations. Also omitted from this bibliography are articles, reviews, and other contributions to magazines and journals. The bibliographies in this volume were compiled by members of the *SAAS* editorial staff from their research and the lists of writing that were provided by many of the authors. Each of the bibliographies was submitted to the author for review.

Each volume of *SAAS* includes a cumulative index that lists all the essayists in the series as well as the subjects mentioned in the essays: personal names, titles of works, geographical names, etc. The index format is designed to make these cumulating references as helpful and easy to use as possible. For every reference that appears *in more than one essay,* the name of the essayist is given before the volume and page number(s). For example, Franklin Delano Roosevelt is mentioned by several essayists in the series. The entry in the index allows you to identify the essay writers by name:

Roosevelt, Franklin Delano
Graham **5:** 126
Meltzer **1:** 210, 211
Peck **2:** 179
Sachs **2:** 198
Sterling **2:** 235
Turner **6:** 266
Uchida **1:** 271
Wells **1:** 281-82, 286
Wojciechowska **1:** 317

For references that appear *in only one essay,* the volume and page number(s) are given but the name of the essayist is omitted. For example:

Cromer, Guy **1:** 54, 56-59

Looking Ahead

All of the writers in this volume share a common goal—to tell you the tale of their lives. Yet each of these essays has a special character and point of view that set it apart from its companions in the collection. This small sampler from the essays ahead may hint at the unique flavor of these life stories.

William H. Armstrong, reflecting on valuable lessons learned: "... My mother's reading the Bible stores were just a part of every day. Whatever the importance was yet far away, unseen, undreamed. . . . Thirty years later when I was preparing to write a book. . . I would use the importance of leaving out rather than putting in. The importance of leaving out. . . by Old Testament writers had made me a part of the stories. Nothing was written about how Joseph felt when he was mistreated by his brothers, but as a reader I became part of the story—I was in Joseph's place. Joseph didn't utter a sound but I was crying out: 'Please don't leave me here to die: Please, please don't sell me to be lost forever in a strange land!' Thus it was that the book with the title of a dog named Sounder was written with wholesale omissions. If the boy's age was not given the reader could become a part of the story. . . . Place and time kept vague, no name or description of the boy. . . . And no names for the family. With names they would have represented one family; without names they became universal. . . . "

Marguerite Henry, describing the arrival of her famous filly: "The expressmen set down the crate just inside the stable and went off into the night. With hammer and wedge [my husband] Sid broke open the front of the crate. . . . I stared at an utterly strange pony. No golden coat, no golden eyelashes, no white map of the United States on her withers. She was all one color—the sooty gray of snow that has lain on the ground much too long. . . . Grandpa, I thought, had sent us the wrong pony. But that wasn't *her* fault. So we loved her anyway and called her Misty. . . . In the months that it took Misty to shed out, I groomed her story and Sid groomed her coat. He taught her to place her forefeet on a soapbox, and to shake hands like a politician running for the presidency. And when spring came her color returned in all its golden glory. Grandpa Beebe had sent the right pony after all!"

Mollie Hunter, reliving her childhood days in a small Scottish village: "The village street was our playground, especially in the long twilight that ends each summer day. . . —the 'gloaming', as we call it—when we would play the kind of games that involved much running and chasing and hiding. . . . From end to end of the village the cries would echo, sounding thin and eerie in that mysterious half light which has always seemed to me to be the ghost of the day that has passed. And listening from whatever hiding place I had chosen for myself, I would sometimes have the strangest feeling that I was hearing the voices of ghost children calling, calling. . . . Without my having the least awareness of what was happening, in fact, that childhood environment of mine was nurturing a whole range of feelings so essentially part of my nature that they were quite inevitably destined to become also an integral part of my writing."

Diana Wynne Jones, recalling her first encounter, as a young girl, with a "real" writer: ". . . Other mothers had taken the younger children to the lakeshore to play. . . . The noise they made disturbed the occupant of the houseboat out in the bay. He came rowing angrily across and ordered them off . . . and announced that he would come next morning to complain. He hated children. There was huge dismay among the mothers. Next morning I stood in the hall, watching them rush about trying to find coffee and biscuits . . . with which to soothe the great Arthur Ransome, and gathered I was about to set eyes on a real writer. I watched with great interest as a tubby man with a beard stamped past, obviously in a great fury. . . . I was very impressed to find he was real. Up to then I had thought books were made by machines in the back room of Woolworth's."

Robert Quackenbush, looking back on his first book illustration assignment: "The assignment was to illustrate, in woodcuts, Hans Christian Andersen's *The Steadfast Tin Soldier*. . . and [it] took several months to do. The project was a deep, emotional experience for me, and put me in touch with images and memories of my childhood that were buried in my unconscious. . . . I read *The Steadfast Tin Soldier* when I was nine, just after my father was killed in a tragic automobile accident. . . . What I was able to understand when I was at work on the illustrations. . . was why the story upset me so when I read it as a child. It was because I identified with the boy who threw the tin soldier in the fireplace. I believed, as many children do when a tragedy happens in a family, that somehow I had something to do with my father's death. When these early feelings surfaced, as I worked on the illustrations, I became a father to the child in me and came to terms with those feelings. . . . It was a truly liberating experience. . . . "

Joyce Carol Thomas, savoring the memory of delectable Southern foods: ". . . Sunday meals were different. A delight. . . . Dinner, most of it cooked on Saturday night, might be roast chicken and sage dressing, pan gravy, Kentucky Wonder string beans, Sunday yams, and 'monkey bread'—so called because these yeast rolls were so feathery light and buttery good you made a monkey of yourself eating too many of them. And the white coconut cake, moist, jump-in-the-mouth tender, was a mouth-watering delicacy with the blackberry jam filling the middle. . . . Out-of-town-guests? Then nothing would do but to add sweet-potato pies, peach and pear cobblers. . . . Many readers have commented about the importance of food in my novels. . . . I suppose the food's joyous inclusion and fragrant presence comes from having a mother who was known as the best cook in town. . . . Because in such a home food was another language for love, my books are redolent of sugar and spice, kale and collards."

These few examples can only suggest what unique stories the writers in this volume are ready to share with you. We invite you to treat yourself to an exceptional reading experience. Turn the page and see what these writers have to say just to you.

Acknowledgments

We wish to acknowledge our special gratitude to each of the authors in this volume. They all have been most kind and cooperative in contributing not only their talents but their enthusiasm and encouragement to this project.

Authors Forthcoming in *SAAS*

Donald Crews (picture book author and illustrator)—Two-time Caldecott honoree for his *Truck* and *Freight Train,* Crews celebrates the world of machines and other "things" with pop art that is both original and conceptual. Fusing brilliant color with sharp design, the author-illustrator creates new perspectives and delights for children.

Tomie de Paola (picture book writer and illustrator, and novelist)—Recognized as one of the most prolific and popular creators of children's books, de Paola illustrates his works so that children can "read the pictures." Subtle meanings and messages, conveyed by his precise and deliberate use of color, have helped create his award-winning *Strega Nona* and *The Clown of God.*

H. M. Hoover (author of books for young people)—Known for her unique approach to science fiction and fantasy, Hoover fills her futuristic novels, such as *The Children of Morrow* and *The Rains of Eridan,* with exotic surroundings and believable characters who face the same types of adolescent problems as do her readers.

Steven Kellogg (children's book writer and illustrator)—Marvelously detailed illustrations of fantasy mixed with everyday life abound in such Kellogg books as *The Mystery of the Missing Red Kitten* and *Can I Keep Him?* His "Pinkerton" stories have provided a new candidate for the list of classic characters in children's literature.

Hilary Knight (children's book writer and illustrator)—Knight's whimsical and highly stylized illustrations embellish such memorable children's books as *Eloise* by Kay Thompson and Betty MacDonald's *Mrs. Piggle-Wiggle.* He has also delighted readers by writing and illustrating several books of his own, including *Angels and Berries and Candy Canes* and *Where's Wallace?*

Jean Merrill (author of books for children, editor)—Merrill's talent for telling an engrossing story with a moral shines in *The Pushcart War* and *The Toothpaste Millionaire.* Her contemporary fables are rich in humor, satire, and wisdom.

Virginia Sorensen (author of books for children and adults)—A descendant of Mormon pioneers, Sorensen draws upon her heritage to create rich renderings of family life and customs in various historical periods. Her strong sense of community animates such books as *Plain Girl* and the Newbery Award-winning *Miracles on Maple Hill.*

Harvey Weiss (author and illustrator of books for young people)—A talented sculptor, Weiss is well known for writing and illustrating how-to books, like the award-winning *Pencil, Pen and Brush.*

Margot Zemach (children's book writer and illustrator)—At her touch, timeless tales come to life vibrantly in such books as *Nail Soup* and the award-winning *Duffy and the Devil.* Zemach seeks to match a story's meaning with the wit and beauty of her drawings.

SOMETHING ABOUT THE AUTHOR

AUTOBIOGRAPHY SERIES

William H. Armstrong

1914-

TOWARD THE GATES

William H. Armstrong

> *Before the gates of excellence*
> *the high gods have placed sweat.*
> —Hesiod

Every man's journey is the journey of Abraham of the Old Testament: "He looked for a city which had foundations whose builder and maker was God"—a lovely way of saying "a yearning for security in a fragile world."

And so it was with Homer's Ulysses's ten-year trial of sailing chartless seas and encountering the wrath of destroyers. This too was an experience of learning and a search for a familiar and secure harbor—the journey of every man.

Vergil's Aeneas—from the toppling walls of burning Troy toward the unknown—to build, far away in a strange land, a new city—again the same journey of every man—a place in the world.

How strange the journey, yet how certain the fateful misadventure and defeat, how uncertain the chance that the right road be taken toward "the gates of excellence" which simply is, without question, accepting one's lot and doing one's best at it. And this is happiness—the best moments, days, years separated out from failure and anxiety, and remembered.

On a September afternoon in Rockbridge County, Virginia, the journey began for William Howard Armstrong, the third child of farmer Howard Gratton Armstrong and Ida Morris Armstrong. The beginner of the journey is not aware of the moments of anxiety and pain and silent inward joy. Those involved and present remember always the hours, the great triumph of birth, the day, the moment, the weather, the signs.

Many would long remember that September afternoon, the fourteenth, at twenty minutes past four, when the midwife, Mrs. Beard, slapped the boy baby's behind, wiped the mucus from his mouth and nose, and said to the mother, "You can tell by the yelp it's a boy."

People would long remember that afternoon.

William, about 1915

The worst hailstorm and tornado in the memory of many swept across most of Rockbridge County.

And the mother wept with joy and fear. Joy that there was a boy, a helpmate for the father on the farm after two girls. Fear for the signs—born in the midst of the destroyer of much of summer's work. What omen but bad? What prophecy? What sign for the future?

The downstairs bedroom was used for birth and death and all sickness in between. Just outside the window there was a pear tree. Just across the road a field of corn, tall and full tasseled and heavy eared.

How many times my mother repeated the story: "I looked at you and I looked out the window, I smiled down at you and I cried for what I saw out the window. The pear tree had been bending from its load of fruit—almost ready to ripen. Now neither pear nor leaf left. Naked branches out of place—winter scene in summer. It was nearly dark when your father gathered the last of the fallen fruit and carried it to feed the hogs.

"The hail had stripped every blade from every stalk of corn. The ears now drooped as though the will to ripen was gone. The whole field reminded me of my own father's description of a corn field along Antietam Creek in Maryland on a September day in 1862 when bullets, like hail, stripped the stalks and made that September day the bloodiest single day in America's bloodiest war."

This then was William Howard Armstrong's welcome into the world. Years later, when I was old enough and my father would let me go to the store with him, I would hear arguments about the size of the hailstones in that great September storm. Where the lightning struck—how many cows were killed under one tree on Greever's farm. For a greeting, one neighbor, Mr. Millard Goodbar, always said, "How's the boy who brought the hail?" When I was grown and away at school he would say to my mother, "Is Billy stirring up a storm at that school?" By this time the ill omen of the storm had passed and my mother would smile and give him a report.

Like my parents with their meager one-room school education, Mr. Goodbar had a great interest in education for the young. His hardscrabble land, up the road near a second little farm my father owned, never produced much. But not once did I ever hear him complain. Like my father and the neighbors, I listened to talk of seedtime and rain, of harvest and drought.

Hope was planted with the seed and cultivated with no thought of failure. Growing up in that little world many great lessons awaited me, not least of which were love of earth and respect of nature.

The first years of childhood can usually be summed up in a sentence: "He was a good baby; he cried a lot; he walked early."

I remember hearing only two things of note from those early years. One, the sides of my playpen had to be built up—I was a climber. I think I ultimately had to be tied. Not with a collar around my neck, but with a belt around my waist and an attachment to the playpen. Much later when I had a degree of freedom I apparently got out of sight one day when my mother was visiting with Mr. Parker, our Presbyterian minister. When she found me I had got hold of a pound of butter and completely greased a cat. Probably the idea born of having heard my father use the expression "slick as a greased pig." For lack of a pig I had used a cat. I don't remember being punished—probably saved by the good minister.

It was decreed by my mother from the beginning that I should not be called Bill. I was never told but apparently my father had insisted on a name that my mother was only lukewarm about.

My father always called me "son." I can hear the softness of it in fond memory now. Even when he was speaking sternly about something I had done wrong,

The farmhouse where the author grew up in Collierstown, now Lexington, Virginia

there was never a change in that soft love-mellowed, hope-saturated sound of "son." Not until years later did I really understand the added softness that came into his voice when he had to explain why something I had asked for couldn't be had.

By the time I was five I had my own tablet and pencil and liked to write, especially on rainy days and Sundays. On Sundays we couldn't go anywhere, play in the creek, or do almost anything except go with whomever went for the cows. After Sunday school and church we changed our Sunday clothes to other clean clothes that we couldn't get dirty. So I wrote in my tablet. My mother or oldest sister (who wanted to become a teacher and later did) helped me spell places I had been: Morrison's Store, Wade's Mill, Lexington, Virginia, Church (Presbyterian came much later), Collierstown, Post Office.

Both Collierstown and the post office were mentioned often. There was talk that our village, named for the first settler, John Collier, and stretched along the creek named Collier's Creek, would lose its name and become Lexington, R.F.D.2.

To my five-year-old mind it meant losing a place to live. I had been told when we went to the county fair in Lexington: "Now if we get separated, don't cry. Just tell a policeman your father is Howard Armstrong and you live in Collierstown." So if they took away Collierstown where would I live? After years of debate we did lose our village, but only on envelopes. In our hearts and on our tongues it was forever Collierstown.

Sunday afternoons in summer were spent in the shade by the front porch or on the porch. Sometimes neighbors would stop and "set," as they called visiting. There was always "crop talk" and "growing-weather talk." Arrangements were made for borrowing and exchanging tools and machinery. No single farmer had all that was needed to operate. So borrowing, exchange, and barter welded the community together. The outsider was rare. Everyone knew who had the largest copper kettle for making apple-butter and the best Jersey duroc boar hog for breeding with a Poland China sow in order to get leaner bacon.

My father found many excuses for missing church. So my mother always found some suitable time to repeat what the preacher had said. Summer and winter she read the Bible to us every day. She read with great feeling and conviction. I doubt if she knew much about John Calvin but she was certain of the plan and "we had better be ready."

It worried her that my father would not leave the plough or haymower when the preacher was coming for a pastoral call. "He can say a prayer for me without seeing me," he would say. Sometimes my mother would ask the preacher to stay for supper and my father would be caught. He never questioned the preacher but he had doubts about whether or not everyone could possibly deserve the glory of heaven much less the torment of hell. "What about the spirit of the law?" he would ask.

Once on a winter evening my mother finished the nightly reading from the Book of Job (I must have been ten or twelve for I never forgot it): "For I know that my redeemer liveth, and that he shall stand at a latter day upon the earth. And though after my skin worms destroy this body, yet in my flesh shall I see God: Whom I shall see for myself, and mine eyes shall behold." My father opened the stove door and started to bank the fire for the night, saying as he worked: "Sometimes I think a man is like a horse. When he dies that's the end of it."

My mother said, "Don't bank the fire yet." And she began to leaf rapidly through the Bible. Then she began to read: "And he shall send his angels with a great sound of a trumpet, and they shall gather his elect from the four winds, from one end of heaven to the other. . . . But of that day and hour knoweth no man, no, not the angels in heaven, but my Father only. . . . Then shall two be in the field; the one shall be taken, and the other left. Two women shall be grinding at the mill; the one shall be taken, the other left. Watch therefore; for ye know not what hour your Lord cometh."

There was a long silence (at least long for me). Then my mother said, "Now you may bank the fire."

When I was a freshman at Hampden-Sydney

College I used this incident as the basis of a short story, names changed, of course, for English class. I gave it the title "Winterset." Several days after the paper was returned I met my professor, Dr. Asa Watkins, on the walk in front of the library. "Your 'Winterset' paper, Mr. Armstrong," he began, "interested me very much. It was so real I wondered if it had not been something you had experienced even though you marked it fiction."

"Yes," I said, "the background was from my own home."

"Very well written," he said, and added, "sometime I would like to talk further with you."

We never had a chance for that talk. Dr. Watkins died of a heart attack shoveling his walk in the first heavy wet snow that hit Virginia that winter. I think he was deeply concerned about my father's skepticism.

Only as a child did that skepticism frighten me. My father's early life had made him unsure of what tomorrow might offer. Both his parents had died when he was quite young. He had been brought up by his Alphin and Logan cousins—apparently shifted from one to another. His meager education at the Big Hill one-room school—because no one cared more for his schooling than getting an added pair of hands to pick up potatoes, shuck corn, and do all the other farm chores that a ten- or twelve-year-old can be yoked to—was a regret he carried silently.

When he was fourteen he walked over the mountain and entered the ore mines in Allegheny County. The pay was a dollar a day. Half of that he probably had to pay for board. Nevertheless, when he was twenty-two and about to marry, he paid cash for a fifty-eight-acre farm. And not once in his life was there ever a mortgage, even though he later acquired a second farm.

The farmhouse had belonged to a number of people named Clark. It was built in 1848 of logs, later covered with plank siding. Even when two younger sisters and a brother came after me, there was plenty of room. Upstairs there were four bedrooms plus a large, screened sleeping porch.

When architectural students from Washington and Lee University were making a study of regional architecture several years ago, they discovered that the pine logs with which the house had been built were no longer native to the region, suggesting that the land had been stripped to exhaustion of logs that kept their aromatic smell for ages. The same pine still grows in regions farther south.

There are the sounds of living within a house that reload the mind with memory. I always hated to sleep in the downstairs bedroom when I was sick. The front stairs were absolutely quiet during the day but they creaked at night. The creaking seemed to be timed as though someone took a step, then paused for a long time.

I would hold my breath waiting for that next step, all the while thinking of the story of old Jim Clark, a giant of a man who had died upstairs. There was a sharp turn at the top of the stairs past which the neighbors, who came to prepare the body for burial, could not get the body. So they rigged a blanket with ropes and let him down through a window (this being long before the addition of the double porch and backstairs). On the ground the old man's foxhounds surrounded the body and wouldn't let the neighbors near it. The story always ended there but I suppose the dogs were finally beaten off. As a child the sound of that creaking stairway meant only one thing—the ghost of old Jim Clark trying to get down the front stairs.

Could anyone ever forget the sound of rain on a metal roof? Day or night that peaceful, rhythmic certainty—I'm in out of the storm.

In what we called the back room upstairs there was a tall bureau. Three of the lower drawers were filled with rolled-up prints of beautiful paintings. On a rainy afternoon we could go up and look at those paintings and listen to the rain.

Never knew how they came to be there. I wish I knew. Now it is too late to ask. I do know my mother loved beautiful things—her flowers in summer . . . the quilts she and her neighbors sewed were lovely pictures. Scraps of many colors left over from sewing became shaded lanes, grainfields, and red-roofed barns.

I do not remember the titles or artists of the pictures, but twice in my life I have stopped short and said aloud: "There it is!" As a young stranger entering the administration building at Hampden-Sydney College there was a familiar picture: George Inness's *Peace and Plenty.* Years later when I took my three children—Christopher, David, and Mary—to the Peterson House, across from Ford's Theater, where Mr. Lincoln had been taken when he was shot, there in the room where they had laid him, hung Rosa Bonheur's *Horse Fair.* And, of the whole three drawers of pictures, this had been one of a farm boy's favorites.

Describing this pleasure for a child's rainy afternoon, or Sunday when we couldn't run out, has prompted a question from hearers: "Did three bureau drawers filled with rolled-up pictures have anything to do with two of your three children becoming successful artists?" David, a realist, and Mary, an impressionist—both able to establish themselves with New York City galleries before they were thirty years old.

While I went to Collierstown's six-room, white-washed public school I saw only one picture until the fourth grade. The one picture at the end of the hallway was Gilbert Stuart's *George Washington.*

Then one day our fourth-grade teacher explained that the state of Virginia would lend pictures to schools and also exchange them for different ones each year if the teachers paid the postage. The two pictures our teacher got were of a hillside apple orchard in bloom and a lone person standing on a high cliff looking at the ocean. One was called *Spring,* and the other *Dreams.*

For the rest of the day that the pictures were hung my arithmetic, spelling, and reading were totally neglected. I looked at the paintings. One could almost be our orchard that ran up the hill behind the house. But the other—so far away. The sea was far from Collierstown. How many miles had that person walked to get there? One day I would start with Collier's Creek, follow it to some river, and the river to the sea. The gray walls of the classroom were no longer a prison.

I hurried home at the end of school, found my father, and asked him if I could do something to make a nickel. (The rule was not to "ask for" but rather for a job to earn.) The next morning on the way to school I bought a box of crayons at Mr. Morrison's store. For weeks, or maybe months, whenever I had free time I colored those two classroom pictures.

The sound of winter's wind playing its wild symphony on the metal roof of a house is unforgettable. To me, buried deep in the feathertick under my mother's patterned quilts and comforters, the wind's wild rush became the sound of the sea, a sound I had never heard, but had colored into my picture.

Sometimes, but rarely, we were paid before the job was done. Always reminded, however, that "fore-pay is poor-pay." My big red wagon and my boy-size ax were two examples—the wagon, earned several years before the ax, was quite large for a five year old to pull up the orchard hill and glance off a tree or two and a gatepost racing down.

But that was not the purpose as seen by my father. At the woodshed he showed me how the stovewood should be packed. "And every day you will fill the woodbox for your mother; that's the way to earn a wagon." Later I earned a lightweight ax with a twenty-four-inch handle for splitting the wood I hauled. And if I remember correctly I was still earning both when I was carrying the wood in my arms and using a man's ax.

How many times I had to be called from playing in the creek to bring the wood I wouldn't dare try to estimate. Not always willingly then, for that and many other chores set for me. But looking back it all seems important; I was being taught the meaning of work.

Several years ago one of my former students, back for his thirtieth reunion, came to visit with me. He is now the president of a college.

"You know the most important thing you taught me," he said.

"No," I replied. I expected some profound lesson that had helped him become so successful.

"How to use an ax," he said. "And when I need to relax from the problems of student riots and faculty discontent I chop wood."

I too get great pleasure from having learned to use an ax. When the price of fuel oil became expensive in the 1970s I put a Vermont Vigilant stove in each end of my house. Kent School (where I have taught for nearly fifty years) allows me to cut dead trees on its thousand acres of woodland. Two friends are always trying to lend me their wood-splitting machine to rob me of the challenge of a gnarled log and the joy of warm sweat. When asked to list my greatest accomplishments, high on the list is the fact that one year I burned only six gallons of fuel oil.

Sometimes our most valuable lessons do not seem so at the time. Clearing the kitchen table after supper, doing the homework, and then my mother's reading the Bible stories were just a part of every day. Whatever the importance was yet far away, unseen, undreamed.

Once when my mother was reading about David, Jesse's youngest son, tending his father's sheep (a story which was a favorite and read often) I asked how old David was.

"Probably about your age. Tending the sheep means driving them to pasture and bringing them home, like you bringing the cows."

So I could be like David. I was ten years old, and with my slingshot in hand, up through the orchard and to the back pasture to bring the cows, I was ready for the lions and bears. And I could still be like David the next year and the next.

Thirty years later when I was preparing to write a book about devotion, love, self-respect, and the desire to learn I would use the importance of leaving out rather than putting in.

The importance of leaving out (reviewers of my book called it "the art of omission") by Old Testament writers had made me a part of the stories.

The author, having learned the "art of omission" from Old Testament writers

Nothing was written about how Joseph felt when he was mistreated by his brothers, but as a reader I became a part of the story—I was in Joseph's place. Joseph didn't utter a sound but I was crying out: "Please don't leave me here to die! Please, please don't sell me to be lost forever in a strange land!"

Thus it was that the book with the title of a dog named Sounder was written with wholesale omissions. If the boy's age was not given the reader could become a part of the story: "The boy must be about my age." Place and time kept vague, no name or description of the boy. The agony of the mother, like Joseph, expressed in silence—a heavy, thickly dark silence.

And no names for the family. With names they would have represented one family; without names they became universal—representing all people who suffer privation and injustice, but through love, self-respect, devotion, and desire for improvement, make it in the world. And, like the boy in *Sounder,* keep alive the precious memories of the best that life offered:

> Years later, walking the earth as a man, it would all sweep back over him, again and again, like an echo on the wind. The pine trees would look down forever on a lantern burning out of oil but not going out. A harvest moon would cast shadows forever of a man walking upright, his dog bouncing after him. And the quiet of the night would fill and echo again with the deep voice of Sounder, the great coon dog.

Not until I was an adult did I realize that from my mother's reading around that kitchen table I had kept a deeper impression than from all my early listening and reading in school. The only thing I vividly remember, having been read aloud in school by a teacher before the sixth grade, is a description from Washington's "Sketch Book" of a walleyed horse looking out of an open barn door on a rainy day.

I was, however, quite miserable during the early years of school. Suffering from chronic asthma I was never picked for a team on the playground at recess. I was a runt and the only boy in school who wore glasses—which the big boys broke several times. My loud breathing was a cause for laughter in the classroom. Many a morning I would try to convince my mother that I was too choked up for school. But she never gave in, and out the door and down the road I would go, crying half of the mile I had to walk.

All my problems with school seem to have been compounded early in the second grade. The horses trapped my beautiful spotted pony in a fence corner and kicked it to death. On the way for the cows after school I found the trampled body, a mixture of blood and mud. The silky mane and tail with no sign left of all my careful grooming. The grief left me with a jerking stammer. The doctor said it was the result of shock and would pass. My mother was sure that it would for when she heard my prayers at night every word was clearly spoken. At school the teacher was kind enough not to call on me, but everybody else kept mocking or forever asking questions to try to make me talk.

Then in the sixth grade my life changed in a single day. Coming in from recess the big boys had pushed me off the gravel walk into the mud. I was probably in tears, probably half choking from trying to breathe quietly. Then it happened. When Mrs. Parker collected the homework papers she held one up before the class and said, "William Armstrong has the neatest paper in the class."

She didn't hold up one of the big boys' papers who had pushed me out of line—not one of the girls who had snickered at my breathing. She held up *my* paper. She called me by name. For the first time in my life someone had called my name as a winner.

One girl across the aisle even gave me a faint smile. I was in love with her from that moment but she never knew it.

It was like being lifted up bodily. Now, suddenly, I knew where I could win. I could have the most nearly perfect written work—whether spelling, multiplication table, or sentence. I don't believe my mother ever again had to say after supper, "William, the girls have their books out. Get yours." Nor did she ever have to push me out the door in the morning. That day began a Depression-born country boy's determined journey toward "the gates of excellence."

From those other than our parents our lives are formed, directed, and the fruits of our labors the results of some teacher's (and if we are very lucky, teachers') influence. So it was with Mrs. Parker. I do not know how many lives she changed—of one I am certain.

Thirty years later her every move was as real to me as though yesterday. I wrote an article on her entitled "Something Lasting," for the *Independent School Bulletin.* The article was given the annual prize for the best essay written on a subject of general interest. Here is a sampler which will give a hint as to this remarkable person:

> Some of the things she did were so unusual as to start snickers up and down the rows of desks, but snickers quickly became unpopular. Her first day was typical of what all the days would be. She entered the room after the bell had rung, small and grey-haired, in her early fifties—perhaps. Halfway down the aisle she stopped, turned slowly and I believe looked straight into the eyes of every one of us. Then in a quiet, clear, gentle tone, said, "Gentlemen always stand when a lady enters a room." Everybody stood up, including the girls, and before we sat down again she had called our names from the class roster and seated us alphabetically, and she addressed each of us as Mr. or Miss. When a "wise lad" collided with one of the girls in the aisle as he stomped in resentment from a back seat to the front, for his name began with "A," Mrs. Parker quickly moved forward, reached up and took him by the shoulder for he was taller than she was, and moved him gently but surely to one side, speaking quietly as she did so, "A gentleman always stands aside for a lady to pass." I was not sure what the old-fashioned word "gentleman" really meant, but by the time we were seated alphabetically, I can remember to this day the queer feeling I had that I would like to be one.

I doubt if half the class could spell democracy or responsibility, but her explanations seemed so from the heart rather than from a book that we listened and remembered. It was all strange and new. Much that was said was doubtlessly lost, but she gave us a reason for everything.

> "Education in a democracy" does not mean the same thing as "education for democracy," she explained. Education in a democracy implies a privilege, but a privilege is like an apple—it has to grow on something, and the tree that privilege grows on is "responsibility." Education for democracy is our responsibility as it was the accepted responsibility of those who dared to dream, to think differently, to fight and to die for that responsibility down through the ages. And we have inherited a responsibility, not a privilege. How that responsibility (the tree) is nourished, pruned, and cared for will determine the size of the apple it will bear. Then, almost as though she were talking to someone behind us, someone looking through the door from the hallway, she said that the world had great need for us. She said that all the names of leaders in government, science, teaching, medicine, business, and religion will have disappeared in fifteen or twenty years and other names will have replaced them. The names that will replace them are the names of little people who sit in this classroom and thousands of classrooms like this throughout the country. But if we were contented to listen to a reason for our learning, the processes came quickly as a great shock to us.

Our Creator prepared us for two great adventures, she said. First, the glorious adventure of learning, and, secondly, the even greater and more glorious adventure of living.

> We were made rational (thinking) creatures and moral (knowing) creatures . . . We are able to think and reason, and God made us free that we may choose. We are also moral creatures in that we have within us a knowledge of what is right and what is wrong. Through the accumulated experiences that we have at home and at school and in the world (the ones at home being

> the far most important) we come to put value on right or wrong. If we choose the wrong we enslave ourselves against our nature. If we choose the right we are free to love justice, beauty, goodness, and truth, and to "do good and walk humbly" in the sight of our Creator.

Here was an academic maturity being offerec that was far beyond our years—or was it?

> We were never quite the same again. She wove into the hempish fibers of our hearts soft and golden threads of appreciation. Nothing she touched was ever quite the same again.

All that could be called a library in our school was a short shelf in each room, a place for not more than a dozen books.

The good stories that were there had been read so much that often the last pages were lost. How the stories ended we would never know.

On one of the shelves I found a book entitled *Pilgrim's Progress.* Thinking I would find an exciting story of the Pilgrims landing at Plymouth Rock, building houses, planting crops, making friends with the Indians, I took it home to read.

It was about a character named Christian and his journey through life, written by John Bunyan while in prison for not conforming to the Church of England. Even though I was hungry for reading and probably bored I couldn't manage it. Years later when I read somewhere that it had been translated into over a hundred languages and read more than any other book except the Bible, I did read it.

Visiting elementary schools today brings a lump to my throat. I remember the scarcity of books that surrounded my early years. I tell my audiences, usually sixth and seventh graders, that if I had by some magic been transported to such a library when I was their age, I wouldn't have gone home when school was out. I would have been reading until the last door was locked against me.

I try to picture for them the great thrill of owning my first book—other than regular schoolbooks. With two one-dollar bills I went to Mr. Henry Boley's bookstore in Lexington, Virginia, and paid $1.65 for Lord Charnwood's 468-page *Life of Abraham Lincoln.* Money I had earned digging sassafras sprouts from the pasture for five cents an hour began a study of that great man, collecting hundreds of books on his life and then writing my own book *The Education of Abraham,* which the *Wall Street Journal* called one of the most significant books written in the year 1974. The *Journal* statement: "Like his notable *Sounder* this is unbounded by categories—a book of simplicity, beauty, and wisdom for all readers."

Autographing the award-winning Sounder

So, you see, my young friends, buying one book can begin a whole lifetime of pleasure and satisfaction.

Following this conclusion to my talk, an important question-and-answer period brings more surprizes to the young people. One of the very first questions: "How did you feel when you won the Newbery Award for *Sounder?*"

A silence saturated by doubt settles over the whole audience when I answer: "I had never heard of it." Then I describe my school and the times of the Depression and a boy growing up. The students, even their teachers, a generation or two younger than I, with the special display of Newbery Award books ever present, shake their heads in doubt.

In remembering one's childhood it is usually customary to deal with one's contemporaries who were playmates and friends. Perhaps it is because I was treated so miserably at school that I remember only older people, my parents' contemporaries, as friends. They are the models for the adult characters in my books, the good and the bad.

The black man, Moses Waters; Enoch Morris, the storekeeper; and Anson Stone (my father) are the principal characters in *Sour Land.*

The fragment of memory (a dog named Sounder) from a story told me by a black man started the mystery of his childhood in my mind. How did he achieve such excellence? What, against all odds, in a world of neglect, hurt, oppression, and loneliness kept the desire to learn alive in him? That, long after he was dead, would be my story. I would create his boyhood with that desire to learn, supported by love and self-respect, which produced the remarkable man.

When I was moved to the men's Sunday-school class, after an argument with the teacher in the boys' class, my teacher was Enoch Morris. I had listened to the teacher read about Jesus sending the evil spirits into the Gadarene swine and drowning them in the sea. My question to the teacher was: "What about the poor man who owned the swine?" The next Sunday I was moved to the men's class.

Sitting among the men had a lasting effect I am sure. The minister, Rev. B. L. Wood, seemed to take an interest in me. He was a graduate of Washington and Lee, and even though there were yet years to go, he talked to me of college. My first visit to Lee's chapel on the Washington and Lee campus was with him. There I saw Valentine's famous recumbent statue of General Robert E. Lee, and the skeleton of his great horse Traveller.

Lexington and Rockbridge country were living history. George Washington had carved his initials high on Natural Bridge. Sam Houston had been born here. His father had helped start Liberty Academy, which became Washington College, and after the death of Lee, was renamed Washington and Lee. On the Virginia Military Institute campus was Ezekiel's statue of *Virginia Mourning Her Dead,* honoring the V.M.I. cadets who had marched the 120 miles and fought and died in the Battle of New Market. The stories of Sam Houston, governor of Tennessee, founder of Texas; and Big-Foot Wallace, Texas' most famous Texas Ranger—both sons of Rockbridge.

Our parents didn't have to make up stories to tell us. They only had to tell what had happened. Their parents were there. My grandfather had ridden with Jackson. For several years after the war, so used to being aroused at any moment to move by the secretive Jackson, he would sleepwalk to the barn and saddle his horse.

The old-timers who sunned themselves on the wall in front of the courthouse repeated a thousand times the order General Grant had given Sheridan: "Leave the Shenandoah Valley so barren that a crow flying over would have to carry provisions." And they remembered and reviewed the exact day, June 10, 1864, when "Sheridan's man, General David Hunter, bombarded Lexington, burned V.M.I. and Governor Letcher's house."

Little wonder that my favorite subject, after Mrs. Parker gave me a reason for learning, was history. Jackson had taught Sunday school in my church on occasion. When I was moved to the men's class I used to imagine how different his lessons would have been.

When the time came for me to go to Augusta Military Academy, forty miles up the valley at Fort Defiance, history was still all around me. Colonel Charles S. Roller, a veteran of the Confederate army, had founded the school to provide the returning soldiers a chance for an education. The Old Stone Church at the edge of the campus, where we went Sunday for service, had been built with stones carried by the women of the village on horseback from Middle River six miles away.

Mrs. Parker had started me on my first short steps toward the "gates of excellence." Now, at this splendid school, A.M.A., I would feel that longing to excel. An incident in English History class the second week of school probably added much fuel to the flame which Mrs. Parker had lighted.

Captain Hurt had seated us alphabetically. I was next to Charlie Bosserman. Right in the middle of class Major C. S. Roller, Jr., coprincipal with his brother, Colonel Thomas, came into the class.

"What'd you get on last week's test, Charlie?" he asked. (Weekly tests were required in all subjects.)

Bosserman was a second-year cadet so Major Roller knew his name.

"Fifty-five, Sir," replied Bosserman in a half whisper.

"Stand up and speak up, boy." And at the same time Major Roller had taken him by the shoulder and raised him from his seat.

Now it was my turn. Moving toward me, "What's your name, cadet?"

I was on my feet so scared that half my books hit the floor. "Armstrong, Sir."

"What was your grade?"

"Ninety-eight, Sir"

"And what did you miss?"

"I misspelled Norman—Normand."

"Your name is Armstrong, you say; I'll call you Army." And with that he shook my hand and gave me a pat on the shoulder.

For the next three years he knew me and he and the rest of the school called me Army. Wherever we met, and I was alone, he would ask, "How are things going, Army?"

Late in the summer of 1932, the year I graduated, I decided against going to the V.M.I. and wanted to go to Hampden-Sydney College. The recommendation he wrote to Hampden-Sydney ended with the sentence: "He is a glorious student."

This single incident, the second week of school,

As a cadet at the Augusta Military Academy, 1932

plus the fact that I was there with a scholarship and a job, made the desire and struggle for excellence a part of my breathing.

I experienced some great teachers, certainly more than one's share for a single school. After neglect and lack of interest in my early years plane geometry seemed a mystery never to be solved. My teacher, Captain Hodges, was aware of my struggle and made what appeared to be a rather strange assignment. I was to read the pages in the encyclopedia *The Book of Knowledge* on mathematics, and write him a theme on how geometry came to be—what the people who created it used it for, plus anything else I found of interest from the reading.

Even though I resented the added work the ultimate results were of lifelong importance. Beyond being able to understand what plane geometry was all about, I became excited about the Egyptians measuring out the thirteen-acre base for the Great Pyramid, getting all sides and angles exactly right. And the Babylonians' irrigation ditches—it all made sense. It was more than mathematical problems and homework; it was history, part of my favorite subject.

That assignment was really my first introduction to ancient history other than the Bible. Forty years later that beginning reached one of those unseen, undreamed of, goals in life; I became the coauthor of a successful history textbook, *Peoples of the Ancient World.*

I have also used Captain Hodges's method in my own teaching and made it an important chapter in my book *How to Study* (of which you will hear more later). I remember one case in particular worth noting.

A student came to me in tears. "Sir, in English class we are reading Homer's *Iliad,* and I'm failing every daily quiz. The characters are so many and so mixed-up I can't keep anything straight."

"I'll tell you how to pass all the daily quizzes, but it'll be an extra assignment."

"But I have more than I can get done now," he interrupted.

"Listen! Go to the library. Look up Homer in one of the junior encyclopedias, World Books, any of them, or a classical handbook from the reference shelf. If the *Iliad* is not under Homer you'll find it under *Iliad.* There the twenty-four books (or chapters) will be briefly explained—the characters and what they do. Take notes (who, what, why, where) on the assignment. Keep these in front of you as you read. I will guarantee a passing grade on the next quiz."

Three days later he came rushing into my classroom.

"Sir, look! Two quizzes—one, eighty—one, ninety. It worked."

"Learning is sorta like walking," I told him. "First we crawl, then some small steps. Not even a horse starts at a gallop."

That same important lesson of "the background" was so beautifully done for the study of the Latin language. There was a wonderful little book (in English) entitled *Roman Panorama.* It had chapters with titles like "The Setting," "Men and Women," "Children," "Houses," "The Daily Round," "The Day's Work," and ended with a short chapter describing ways in which we are like the ancient Romans. With such an introduction I don't remember ever having heard anyone say, "I hate Latin."

Surely one of my great experiences at A.M.A. (terrifying at the time—turned to pleasant later) came in Captain Joe Earnest's English class. We were studying *Brooks Composition Two* (was there ever a better book for teaching one the rules of writing?).

Our assignment was to write an original story. My story was about a crippled boy, who watched from his wheelchair as his pet cat climbed a tree outside his window and destroyed a nest of baby birds. The boy's mother was somewhere out of hearing, so all his yelling through the window availed nothing. He had watched the building of the nest, the comings and goings of the busy parents, the feeding of the young. Now all gone—but he loved his cat. To watch and be able to do nothing about it—that was the worst. And his beautiful pet—what was once love was now hate. Never again would he let "Roscoe," the name I gave the cat, climb up and sleep in his lap. And if his withered legs were real and strong like other boys' he would kick the daylights out of that killer.

The stories were read aloud in class. By the time my name was called I was ashamed of my offering. All the others seemed more right: Camping Trips, Baseball Games, Summer on Grandfather's Farm. All received much applause. Captain Earnest collected each story after the reading, he would write his comments when he graded them. There was a long silence when I finished reading my "Not Even with Wings." I was the last reader; Captain Earnest had started at the bottom of the alphabet.

When the next assignment was made, I was told to stay after class. "You didn't copy all; you read and copied because I see some mistakes," he said. "The assignment was for an original story. So where did you get it?"

"Sir, I didn't copy it."

"Then where did you read it?"

By this time I was scared, almost in tears, and my voice was being choked by a lump in my throat. I couldn't defend myself.

"All right," he said, "you may go now."

The next day after lunch the corporal of the Guard came and took me to Major Deane's office. Major Deane was head of the English department. Now the same questions were asked. It was evident that he too did not believe it was my work. I had never heard of Aristotle, but something he said I would remember and use years later: "Here is an example of Aristotle's two chief ingredients of tragedy—'pity and fear'. Were you ever sick? Did you ever have a pet cat? Do you know any crippled people? What kind—how many different birds do you know?"

I never had a chance to answer any of the questions. He hurried on, "Did you write this story?"

"Yes, Sir."

"You'll have a chance to write some more; you may go now."

I thought he meant they were going to make me write another story to test me. So for days I kept trying to figure out what I could have happen to the boy. But I was never asked to write the test story. My senior year Major Deane was my English teacher. Neither he nor Captain Earnest ever mentioned the story again. I'm sure Major Roller had his doubts, also. I was not given a grade, nor was the story returned.

Four years later, my junior year in college, I was editor of the literary magazine. I rewrote my story, correcting the kind of birds that were nesting. For the original they were bluebirds, and bluebirds never nest in the branches of a tree; they nest in holes in trees or houses put up for them. So in my change I gave the nest to robins—famous for sticking a foundation of a little mud morter almost anywhere and building upon it.

I sent copies to the three people involved. Beautiful letters came from each.

Several years later I was invited to come and teach in the English department, but deep roots sunk elsewhere made it unreasonable, not an easy decision. I owed so much to that school in my mythical, yet unknown, journey "toward the gates."

The school's system for examinations inspired one toward excellence. If your average in a subject was ninety you were exempt from taking the examination and free to leave early for vacation. We were too young to believe the axiom "Excellence has its own reward," so the practice had great meaning for us.

At Kent School, where I have spent about half a century teaching, there is a rule: No student is to be exempt from examination. Remembering that my father believed in the spirit of the law and not the letter and having, along the way, discovered the great Roman Cicero and his declaration ("To follow the exact letter of the law is the greatest crime of all") I very early began to break the rule of no exemption.

Have I changed some hardworking youngster's life by calling him in at the end of the term and saying, "You've worked hard, you've earned a reward, your grade is excellent, you don't have to take the exam," then asking him to keep it quiet because I'm breaking a rule? Nevertheless, the secret is whispered around, passed from year to year. The result, of course, is that more people dream of that point of excellence and some achieve it.

On occasion I have been beset by some faculty members with the complaint, "But it's not consistent, I think the rule should be followed." And my reply is, "Remember Ralph Waldo Emerson. Didn't he say 'consistency is the hobgoblin of little minds'?"

There has also been the grumble: "It takes away the practice that students need." This especially from a teacher who believes that exams should be three hours long, having the student rewrite as much as humanly possible of a stale textbook or even staler class notes.

From my wonderful years at A.M.A. I took much that added quality to life and influence as a teacher later. An incident in Major Deane's English class planted a seed—learning can be fun.

Below the classroom window, during one class, a carpenter was at work. One of my friends, Walton Stallings, was giving his total attention to the carpenter rather than to Major Deane's explanation of the tragedy of the character Iago in Skakespeare's play *Othello.*

"Mr. Stallings, tomorrow you will present to the class a paper on that carpenter. You may go now and gather your facts."

We all laughed. But what seemed a joke became important. The next day Stallings did the best he had ever done in front of the class. His nickname was "Puddin," and I think it came from the way he recited, but this day was different. No Puddin-head in front of the class this time. Reading with spirit and feeling he gave a brief life of the carpenter, why he became a carpenter, what he was repairing at the base of the building, the size nails, the kind of lumber, and why this particular kind of lumber.

I think he received the first applause ever for a recitation. He got the paper back with a better grade than he had ever got. And he got better grades from that day. Why? For the first time in his life learning had been fun.

After all the good years I was reluctant to graduate, hear taps at the last retreat, and leave A.M.A. I had taken exams, I had been exempt from some. I had studied hard and worked hard to stay in school. A child of the Depression, I had managed to stay when others had dropped out. I graduated *ad astra per ardua* (to the stars through difficulties) in 1932.

Among the many riches I carried away was how to plan my time—that most limited of all the blessings we have upon earth. Besides my classes I fed cattle for a lady, trapped rats in her corncrib for five cents apiece, met the mail train twice a day (6:00 A.M. and 4:00 P.M.), worked in the Fort (post exchange and post office), sold *Reader's Digest* subscriptions, and raked leaves on Sunday afternoons for a man who called his place Oak Grove—there were lots of leaves. What a glorious thing for my future that my father had taught me to work. One of the first things my students memorize is Marcus Aurelius's glorious axiom: "The present is the only thing of which a man can be deprived."

Hampden-Sydney College is an oasis set in the sand and clay of Prince Edward County, Virginia. Six months older than the Declaration of Independence, its giant trees bespeak its age. Scotch broom still decorates the roadsides; the seed, brought from England in sacks of horse feed, left from the British soldiers of the Revolution feeding their horses.

I walked under those giant trees for four years, supplementing what Mrs. Parker, Major Roller, Captain Hodges, Captain Earnest, and Major Deane had started.

The college, leaning heavily toward the Scotch Presbyterian classical education, required two years of Bible study and four of Latin or Greek. I chose Greek, and in so choosing, found another teacher who would become mentor, advisor, and friend, and determine to a large degree what I would do with my life.

In no other classroom, either at the college or later in graduate school at the University of Virginia, was there such action. He never sat down, but like one of his heroes, Aristotle, he was always moving.

Twenty-five hundred years of dust dissolved and Homer's "wine-dark sea" and "rosy-fingered dawn" were as real as yesterday. Antigone, with her "law above man's law," and Aeschylus, with Zeus's decree that "man must learn through suffering, and drop by drop upon his troubled brow comes wisdom," and a thousand other deathless lines—all poured forth from the mouth of Dr. David C. Wilson with no less grace and feeling than spoken in the ancient theater at Athens or Delphi.

"Wandering but not lost" (like William Cullen Bryant's migrating waterfowl) I still was not dreaming beyond the day when I would have money in the pocket of a new pair of pants and would never have to hitchhike again.

My first contact with Dr. Wilson outside the classroom came when I was digging a ditch for a waterline near his house. The W.P.A. (Works Progress Administration—providing work during the Depression) had established programs for college students.

One windy November afternoon as Bill Junkin (who would later become a missionary and be murdered in China) and I were finishing our two hours' digging (the pay was twenty-five cents an hour), Dr. Wilson motioned to us from his porch. Though besmeared with Prince Edward County red clay and minus shoes which we left on the porch, he took us into his kitchen and gave us hot chocolate and cookies.

Both he and his family, Mrs. Wilson and their son, David, about five years my junior, became close personal friends. They took me to a performance of Sophocles' *Antigone* at Randolph-Macon College in Lynchburg, Virginia, to Marc Connelly's *Green Pastures,* the first play I had ever seen onstage.

Mrs. Wilson had a small arch at the entrance to her flower garden with a blank board hanging at the top of it, waiting for the proper quotation. She was

"Outgrown by a student"

offering a reward for the proper inscription.

"'Let not a single spring flower pass you by' is in the Bible," I suggested. "It's one of the shortest verses in the Bible."

"Five dollars if you can find it, that's the reward."

"I'll find it," I said, never realizing the many, many references to Flower I would find in the *Student's Indexed Bible* in the library. But I found it: chapter 2, verse 7—The Wisdom of Solomon in the Apocrypha.

I looked for the garden and the neatly printed board forty years later when I returned to speak at the Phi Beta Kappa convocation. All was gone, the house had been moved and a road to a new row of faculty houses ran past where the garden had been.

I hoped someone had saved the neat entrance arcade and sign. I thought to ask but decided against it. Rather imagine some young man on the bulldozer, with sufficient aesthetic sense to put it in the back of his pickup truck, had taken it home at the day's end, and said to his wife, "Let's start a flower garden on part of the front lawn."

Mrs. Wilson taught Latin at the local high school. Latin was not my best subject, but for a reason then unknown to me, I was asked during my junior and senior years to substitute as teacher of her class when she had to be absent.

Dr. Wilson had listened as I mentioned from time to time my thoughts for the future. I wrote for the school newspaper; both poetry and prose for the literary magazine, and one summer a weekly column of contemporary affairs for the *Lexington Gazette.* All conversations seemed to somehow work around to his statement, "I've always enjoyed my teaching." Surely an understatement known by whoever had sat in his class.

Greek verbs and word accent on the penult or antepenult had to be learned. But Homer, Aeschylus, Pindar, and all the other Olympian artists, in their many fields of perfection, had to be made alive, and that Dr. Wilson, our own Olympian Zeus of excellence, did, with two thousand plus years of antiquity's dust swept away. He made their eternal newness a part of us, equally as lasting as Mrs. Parker's grace and empathy.

By graduation time the magic of Dr. Wilson had worked; I was going to be a teacher. So after some teaching with intervals of graduate study I landed at Kent School, Kent, Connecticut, in September 1944 (long before most of you readers were born).

There I have remained, teaching ninth-grade boys that listening to the teacher is the easy way to learn, that neatness is sacred, that courtesy makes what is ordinary noble, that time is the most limited blessing we have upon earth, that to do just the required is to be a slave, that to pursue excellence in whatever we do—farming, carpentry, teaching, writing (these I have done)—is to find a contentment and order in a world that seems to prefer discontentment and disorder.

I hear often: "How could you stand to stay in one school practically a lifetime, nearly fifty years, and not even retire when the time came?"

"Easy. I learned that teaching is more than the subject and the textbook; it's hopefully directing some young wanderer in a direction that will add quality, and, in rare cases, love of learning, to a life."

When asked by a stranger, "What do you do for a living?" my answer is, "I'm a teacher." I have never really thought of myself as a writer.

I enjoyed teaching so much, building my house with my own hands on a hill above the Housatonic River, reading to my children and helping my wife

"The house I built with my own hands on a rocky hill above the Housatonic River in Connecticut"

care for them that any thought of writing disappeared from my life.

One afternoon in 1950 the headmaster and Director of Studies came up to my house after school. I was then in my sixth year at Kent.

"We think you should write a book on how to study," the headmaster began.

"But I don't know anything about how to study," I quickly interrupted.

"You have the best organized, best disciplined, best prepared students in the school. Write what you do with them. It would be invaluable to both teachers and students. Think about it."

I thought about it and quickly decided something was missing in our approach to the whole business of learning. We expected results but offered no rules (methods) for achieving those results. The first thing the tennis coach, the football coach, the music teacher does is lay down rules for practice and improving. So why not for spelling, listening, writing correctly and neatly? And what about tests and examinations? Why not suggestions for, not only getting better answers, but taking away the fear of them?

Three years later the book was ready. From the first chapter ("Learning to Listen") to the last ("Motivation") the commonsense methods for practice (a study schedule, doing the hard subject first, trying interest and understanding by starting with a simple beginning—Captain Hodges saving me in geometry so many years ago) all were included.

The "Desire to Learn," chapter 2, the first step toward the "gates of excellence," set forth the yearning to know of men like Abraham Lincoln and Louis Pasteur. The book was published under the honest title *Study Is Hard Work.*

It has been successful. Spending the first two months on methods makes for more and better results and lifetime habits for better results are formed. One of my students recently said to me, "Sir, my father knows a lawyer in Rochester, New York, who makes out a study schedule for the week just the way you make us do. He told my father you taught him at Kent."

Other books have followed on various subjects but the method has remained about the same as the first. Early in the morning is my time to write—from 4:00 A.M. to 7:00 A.M. There is something very satisfactory about having one big job done before breakfast—like back on the farm with the milking before breakfast.

I write with a pencil on a lined tablet—just the way I wrote neat sentences for Mrs. Parker so many years ago. I'm afraid a typewriter or a word processor would somehow rob me of my own particular feeling. For most of my books begin with an idea that I take inside and keep there for a long time before I write a single word. It gets into my blood and is filtered through my heart until it is a part of me. *Sounder,* my most popular book, translated into twenty-eight foreign languages, was filtered through my heart about four years before any writing except a few notes on three-by-five cards.

The lady who types my penciled work once said to me, "You dot your *i*'s and cross your *t*'s."

"I had a teacher who once singled out my paper as the neatest in class. It made a lasting impression because I had never been singled out for anything. So, in speaking to young people who ask me how to start to become a writer, I say to them—dot your *i*'s and cross your *t*'s. Be proud of your schoolwork. To that advice I add a second and a third thing to do: two, read all the books you can, and three, listen to your teacher. These things you do now in order to get ready to write your book twenty, thirty, forty years from now."

"I wish I had had you for a teacher," she said.

Beautiful letters come to me from fourth graders and also from elderly people. So for what age group do I write? I write for anyone who can read. Perhaps that is why reviewers have written "from eight to eighty."

In the summer of 448 B.C. the great historian Herodotus read parts of his history in a contest in Athens. His audience was made up chiefly of Athenian statesmen and philosophers. Among them, however, there was a twelve-year-old boy named Thucydides, who had gone with his father. The boy was so taken by the writing that he informed his father that "one day I'm going to write a great history." And indeed he did. After twenty-five hundred years of his history it is said: "No statesman's education is complete without a study of Thucydides' history." And for more than two thousand years Herodotus has stayed in print probably because his readers range from children to philosophers.

I get many letters from children. I wonder if I would answer all of them if not for a notable experience with one of my own children. Catching snatches of conversation from my sons and half a dozen of their friends discussing their great disappointments in life, I heard my son Kip describe one of his. He was, I think, nearly twenty. One of his great disappointments was never getting an answer from the World War II pilot whose book was entitled *God Is My Co-Pilot.*

Until I heard that conversation I had not answered every letter. After that I answered even the

"Showing my children, Mary, Kip, and David, the field where I once dug sassafras sprouts for five cents an hour"

ones which begin: "My teacher made me write this." In each letter I include the following poem:

To You and Your Teacher

I have been watching
As you, so young, so bright
Puzzle and ponder today—
The human present—now—
You cannot fathom nor escape.

I have a thought for you—
So certain—changeless—law without excuse.
This present—now—is all there is
Which can make your future sure—
Make bright tomorrow's days and years.

For hopes decay and fortune's dreams
Move fitfully on airy wings;
They fly away—dissolve in time,
They'll leave you hurt and lost—
They will not bear you up.

So what will lift you then
To excellence greater than you dream?
Is not beyond your reach.
Just take your teacher by the hand.
—William H. Armstrong

So many things are needed to commemorate the journey: a flower that bloomed in a desert, a bird that sang to a brooding earth, a mother's hand on a fevered brow, a father's heart in a quietly spoken "son." Many books could not contain them.

One voice speaks loudly—it says, "Relax, you tried, that is sufficient. The time is short."

Another voice softly whispers, "It's toward the gates that perfumed the sweat, that gave grace and honor to the toil. Go now and read again Tennyson's 'Ulysses'. Pause on the lines: 'Tis not too late to seek a newer world. . . . To sail beyond the sunset . . . to strive, to seek, to find, and not to yield.'"

BIBLIOGRAPHY

For Young People

Fiction:

Sounder (illustrated by James Barkley). New York: Harper, 1969; London: Gollancz, 1971.

Sour Land. New York: Harper, 1971.

Hadassah: Esther the Orphan Queen. Garden City, N.Y.: Doubleday, 1972.

The MacLeod Place. New York: Coward, 1972.

The Mills of God (illustrated by son David Armstrong). Garden City, N.Y.: Doubleday, 1973.

My Animals (illustrated by Mirko Hanák). Garden City, N.Y.: Doubleday, 1974.

Joanna's Miracle. Nashville, Tenn.: Broadman, 1977.

The Tale of Tawny and Dingo (illustrated by Charles Mikolaycak). New York: Harper, 1979.

Nonfiction:

Study Is Hard Work. New York: Harper, 1956.

Through Troubled Waters. New York: Harper, 1957.

The Peoples of the Ancient World, with Joseph Ward Swain. New York: Harper, 1959.

Eighty-Seven Ways to Help Your Child in School. Woodbury, N.Y.: Barron's, 1961.

Word Power in Five Easy Lessons. Woodbury, N.Y.: Barron's, 1969.

Barefoot in the Grass: The Story of Grandma Moses (biography). Garden City, N.Y.: Doubleday, 1970.

The Education of Abraham Lincoln (biography). New York: Coward, 1974.

Study Tips. Woodbury, N.Y.: Barron's, 1975; second edition published as *Study Tactics,* with M. Willard Lampe II. Woodbury, N.Y.: Barron's, 1983.

Bill Brittain

1930-

Bill Brittain, 1988

"How," I'm often asked when speaking to groups of adults or children, "have you managed to combine your career as a full-time teacher with being a writer?"

Even now, having retired in 1986, after thirty-four years in the classroom, I still have trouble answering that one. On the one hand, writing can be delightful on those occasions when the ideas come easily and the words flow onto the page almost as if they had a will of their own. At other times, it can be aggravating, time-consuming, and totally frustrating. Still, I cannot imagine any other hobby that is so downright satisfying and fulfilling.

Make no mistake, to me, writing is, and will always remain, a hobby. Throughout my working life and right up until retirement it has always taken second place to my teaching. Since I don't depend on it for a living I'm in the enviable position of being able to write only when the spirit moves me, without having to worry about how I'm going to pay the water bill or my income tax. Fortunately, the spirit moves me quite often.

I was born in 1930, the second son of Dr. Knox Brittain—known to his friends as "Doc" or "Britt"—and Dorothy (Sunderlin) Brittain, called "Sunny." I was brought up in Spencerport, a small village just west of Rochester, New York. To give some idea of the flavor of the place, perhaps a short history lesson is in order.

In the early 1800s the Erie Canal was dug across New York State, connecting the Hudson River to the east with Lake Erie to the west and opening a water

Bill, at eight months, with brother Bob, 1931

route from the Atlantic Ocean to the Great Lakes. While it was considered the wonder of the age, "Clinton's Big Ditch" was only sixteen feet wide and a mere four feet deep. Since the barges and other boats were pulled by mules, it was necessary to build inns and hotels every twelve or fifteen miles along the route where crews, drivers, and animals could rest each evening.

Small farming villages soon grew around these inns. Being on the canal, many of them called themselves "ports." Such a place was Spencerport, New York. It had—and has to this day—one of the few lift bridges on the canal. When a boat comes through, the bridge is raised, stopping traffic—perhaps two or three cars in each direction.

Riding the lift bridge up and down was one of our few local amusements when I was young. There was no movie theater, no bowling alley, no large shopping mall. Two groceries, a feed store, drugstore, hardware store, Weber's Dry Goods Emporium, and Matthews' Ice Cream Shoppe constituted the business district. Friday was the big evening, with farm families coming in from the surrounding area to shop and gossip. Spencerport's population was perhaps three or four thousand at most.

When I began my series of books on the rural community of Coven Tree, I needed to look for a model no farther than the village where I grew up.

We lived in a Victorian house with a basement, two main stories, and an attic. My father was the local doctor—a general practitioner—and half of the ground floor was given over to his office, X-ray lab, and waiting room. In the depression years of the thirties, however, it was often impossible for his patients to come to him. Therefore he made regular house calls. I recall accompanying him on these calls and thought nothing of the fact that his two-dollar fee was often paid in vegetables or eggs rather than cash. One of his patients was a Mr. Stettner, a veteran of the Civil War. I've often regretted that those times I met the old man, I was too young to realize the historical significance of Mr. Stettner's musings.

The bane of my young life was my brother, Bob (Robert), who was a year and a half older than I. As a boy I felt Bob had been put on this earth with no other mission than to make me feel inferior. He was—and is—outstandingly handsome. His conversation was witty and urbane, and he made friends at the drop of a hat. He excelled in all sports. I sometimes wondered if he didn't have hidden away somewhere a costume with a large *S* on the chest and a great red cape. Indeed, his friends nicknamed him "Soop" to complete the Superman image.

I, on the other hand, was endowed with a pudgy baby face. "Hello" and "good-bye" constituted the major part of my discussions. I was a complete klutz at sports, I cried easily, and I was terrified at the idea of getting into a fight with anyone. This made for a somewhat lonely childhood.

There was, however, one place where I could turn into the hero I longed to be. That was in my imagination. Let the firemen hold their annual parade, and in my mind, I was the chief, driving the fire truck, unreeling the hoses, putting out the blaze, and rescuing mother and child from the fourteenth floor—all at the same time! Never mind that the highest building in town had but four stories. If I was going to be a hero, I was going to be *really* heroic.

Or, if my parents took us to the annual rodeo in Rochester, I became a cowboy for a week or two. Tex Brittain, the fastest gun and toughest bronc rider on the Texas-Montana border. What I lacked in knowledge of U.S. geography was more than compensated for by my vivid dreams of glory.

Aid in creating my imaginary worlds came from two sources. The first was our public library, a small, gloomy room above the firehouse. When I first went there—in about third grade—I was terrified by Mrs. Lapp, the librarian, who, with a pencil stuck in her bun of hair and glasses suspended around her neck on a silver chain, seemed more formidable than Darth Vader. As the years passed, however, she introduced me to the glorious characters in her small stock of books. King Arthur and his knights . . . Booth Tarkington's Penrod . . . Tom and Huck . . . and above all, Sherlock Holmes and Doctor Watson. Mrs.

Lapp had no truck with identifying books by their "age level" or whether something was too adult or too childish for a reader. If you could manage to read the first page—and liked it—you could take out any book in the place for two glorious weeks. Hooray!

A second influence on my fantasies was the movies. The first one I recall being taken to—as a reward for not howling my head off when given a vaccination—was *The Man in the Iron Mask* starring Louis Hayward. To actually see the Three Musketeers battling scores of enemies and rescuing the French king's twin brother from the awful mask into which he'd been locked was a wonder beyond belief. For the next month, not a yardstick or wooden lath around our house was safe as I used them to skewer the king's henchmen. All three musketeers rolled into one, I was invincible!

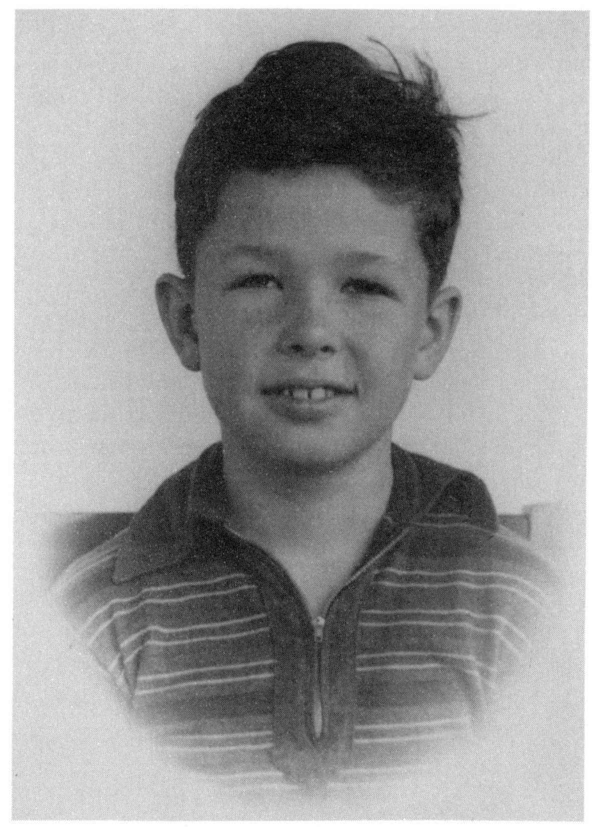

Age nine, in Yeadon, Pennsylvania, 1940

Spencerport High School was misnamed. It was not just a high school; it was *the* school of the village. A red brick building, it had two sets of double doors in front. On the granite slab above one were engraved the words: "Teachers guide; pupils educate themselves." Above the other: "Wisdom is to the soul what health is to the body." The building still stands, having recently been converted into an apartment house.

In my childhood, pupils entered the building as first graders and then, twelve years later and the State Board of Regents willing, graduated in the auditorium-gymnasium that was centrally located, like the hole in a donut. There was only one class for each grade level, with the average size being about twenty-five children.

On entering first grade I was terrified, just as anything new always terrified me. Then came an astounding discovery—I liked school! I already knew how to read, the work wasn't at all difficult, and if there was the slightest possibility of an altercation with another student, Miss Manter, the teacher, was there to protect me and put things right. I even found a friend.

Alfred Freestone, it soon became clear, was another boy who lived largely within his own head. As the weeks went by and I found I could talk to him about my imaginary worlds, I discovered he had fantasies I'd never thought of. We became playmates, and because our houses were both only a short walk from school, I made it a point to stop at his place, seldom arriving home until just before supper. As the elementary school years went by, we became first superheroes—from comic books—then daring policemen—from radio broadcasts—and finally sports champions. The imaginary adventures of the three young folks in my book *Who Knew There'd Be Ghosts?* owe a lot to the good times Al Freestone and I had together.

A couple of years passed, and I not only found myself entranced by school, but I made some other friends. Then . . . a year I thought would never end.

The summer before I was to enter fourth grade, my father rented our house to another doctor, packed up the family, and moved to Yeadon, Pennsylvania for a year to study proctology in Philadelphia. Yanked from my hard-won buddies and set down in unfamiliar surroundings, I was desperately unhappy and moped around for months in a manner designed to drive my parents up the wall—which it did.

The saving grace was the local movie theater. Now that I could walk to the movies, I could go every week. And I did just that. Admission was fifteen cents, which bought not only a ticket, but a candy bar, a comic book with the cover ripped off, a double feature with at least one western, a serial, and a newsreel. The fare ranged from Robert Montgomery in *The Earl of Chicago* (witty, sophisticated, and totally beyond my comprehension) to a young John Wayne in *Allegheny Uprising* (stupendous!). I was especially taken with the serials, although it was a disappointment that Victor Jory in *The Shadow* could not "cloud men's minds so that they could not see him."

Want me to take out the garbage, Mom and Dad? Want me to leap from the chimney top or do the backstroke through a pool of flaming oil? You bet! Just give me that fifteen cents each week so I can sit in the dark for a few hours and lose myself in those flickering images on the screen, and I'll do *anything*!

That horrible year—punctuated only by the glorious array of movies I got to see—finally came to an end. I went back to school in Spencerport, amazed to find my classmates there had been learning the same things I'd been taught in Yeadon.

In sixth grade I met the first of the many people who were later to appear as characters in my books. I sat next-to-the-last in the second row. Right behind me was a boy named Bill Souve. Bill appeared huge and fat and blubbery, and was subject to all kinds of teasing and abuse. Much of it, I regret to say, was mine. Yet Bill remained calm and placid through it all. The rest of us boys thought he was scared of us.

One day on the playground, I fell hard and hit my head against a swing support. It hurt, and for a moment the world pinwheeled around. When it stopped, I realized I was upright, being supported by hands under my armpits. My feet waved lazily a few inches off the ground. "You gonna be okay?" I heard somebody say.

It was Bill Souve. He was holding me at arm's length with no more effort than if I were a rag doll. As my head cleared, it dawned on me that Bill was not simply a fat boy as I had thought. He was incredibly strong and could probably have licked any three of his tormentors. He was just too good-natured to fight.

Harry the Blimp in *Who Knew There'd Be Ghosts?* is not only a character who meets the needs of the story, but also my belated tribute to Bill Souve. To be fair, I also included myself in the same book, in the person of Tommy Donahue, who has a habit of doing everything the wrong way.

My junior high school years brought a number of discoveries. Some of these were pleasant and others most disagreeable. First, I was old enough to go to work on my uncle Orville Sunderlin's farm, just south of town. This involved not only summers, but also weekends, and sometimes after school as well.

I soon learned that farming is not at all as charming an occupation as it's depicted in some books. Oh, there were some pleasures—particularly when I was allowed to drive the tractor or the ancient truck around my uncle's sixty-five acres. But for the most part, I found the work hard, monotonous, and unending, with no guarantee of a successful crop at its end.

On the hottest days of August, I'd be stowing hay in the loft, just beneath the barn's roof, with the temperature hovering around 120 degrees and my clothes soggy with sweat. In the cold of November, with rain or even snow falling, I'd be out in the fields, picking up cabbages in hands numb with cold and longing to get back to the barn where I could clasp a glowing light bulb to bring some feeling back into my fingers.

During those days I learned a great deal about farming life, methods, and tools. Along with a conviction such a life was not for me, I also developed a deep respect for those who earn their livelihood from the soil. While the magic in my "Coven Tree" stories comes from my imagination, the farming scenes are absolutely authentic. When one of my characters harnesses a horse, I know exactly what he's doing because I've harnessed horses, often getting my hand nipped while forcing the bit into the animal's mouth. I know how Adam Fiske of *The Wish Giver* felt, standing in a "crick" while bailing water into tubs, because I've stood in such a crick, my legs numbed by the icy water at the same time perspiration dripped from my chin.

To get away from farming, one year I took a job "in town" as a clerk at the Hart's Grocery. My duties were to stock shelves, bag produce, carry bags to customers' cars, and generally make myself useful.

The manager of the store was Harry Galup, a crusty old man who was a strict but fair employer. Not much escaped his notice. He knew how to spot a wholesaler's rotten eggs, exactly how much credit to extend to anyone in town, and when his newest clerk was stretching a fifteen-minute break into half an hour. And only a fool would try to get the best of him in a bargain. Though Mr. Galup has long since passed away, he still exists as "Stew Meat" in my "Coven Tree" stories.

In 1942, my father went to war. He accepted a commission as a lieutenant commander in the navy medical corps. I recall vividly seeing him off at the train station in Rochester. He stood there, brave and handsome, in his new uniform with the two and a half stripes on the sleeve. I was desolate, convinced that I'd never again see him alive. He was also afraid—afraid that some seaman would pass by and throw a salute which he'd then have to return.

For the next three years, while he was first assigned to Norfolk, Virginia and then to a medical

Graduation photo, Spencerport High School, 1948

base in the Philippines, I saw almost nothing of my father. He wrote constantly, however, often sending my brother and me bits of Japanese planes or other wartime mementos.

Meanwhile I entered high school, still in the same building. Suddenly some of those courses which had seemed so easy before got a lot more difficult. Math, science, and especially foreign languages presented problems which I found difficult and sometimes impossible to solve. English, however, was another story. Many of my classmates hated writing essays. I delighted in them. Given two weeks to write a paper, I'd knock it out the night before it was due and still get a good mark. And literature was just fuel for my overactive imagination.

I also discovered girls. Unfortunately they also discovered me and were quite bored with what they saw. I soon realized that the petite, pretty girls who showed any interest in me whatsoever were usually angling for a date with my brother, Bob, who, a year ahead of me, was a sports hero and, in general, a "big man on campus."

There was a bright spot, however. Students from Gates, a nearby area, went through junior high school in their own district. For the four high school years, however, they were bussed to Spencerport. They didn't know my brother, and, amazingly, they seemed to like me. I associated with this new "gang" almost exclusively, and often on Saturdays I'd pedal my bike the five miles to Gates just to be with them.

To my mother's everlasting credit, she tried to be fair to both my brother and me. "True, Bob does play baseball and basketball well," she'd say. "But Bill, you're by far the better student."

I didn't want to be a better student. I wanted to be a hero in fact, just as I was in my imagination. To make matters worse, in his junior year, Bob decided to go into medicine and knew he'd have to get his marks up. He became a studying machine, so even in the academic area, I was left in the dust.

The war ended, and my father came home. As if to make up for the years away, each summer he took the whole family on magnificent fishing trips to grand resorts in the forests of Canada. Alone together in a small boat, we often discussed my plans for the future.

He wanted me, like my brother, to become a doctor. Our family had been in medicine for five unbroken generations, and I guess I was expected to carry on the tradition.

I, on the other hand, had peeked into my father's small laboratory in the basement of our house where he kept tubs of calf organs in a preservative solution to aid his proctological studies. Having once experienced the sight—and smell—of these ghastly objects, I knew that being a doctor was not for me.

Staggering through history and civics classes with marks that were only minimally acceptable, I opted to study law. I also made another mistake.

Bob, who'd overshadowed me all through high school, decided to attend Colgate University. A year later, on graduating, I applied and was accepted there, too.

I don't know why I made this decision. Perhaps it was, again, fear of the unknown world of college life. At least at Colgate I'd have one familiar face around.

My two years at Colgate were a study in unhappiness. The instructors and professors there insisted that their students constantly discuss, debate, and challenge their remarks. I was used to simple acceptance of whatever the teacher said. I also had the feeling I was rejected socially and couldn't live up to what Bob, a year ahead, was achieving. I managed to maintain a *C* average and that was about it. Perhaps the only good thing to come out of that time was my realization that the law was not for me.

In 1950 I transferred to Brockport State Teacher's College—now part of the New York University system. I had no burning desire to be a teacher, but on the other hand, I had no great yearning to be anything else.

The process of discussion, debate, and challenge which had been required at Colgate simply didn't work at Brockport. For the most part, the instructors had material to cover, and they didn't want to be interrupted too much. It took me a while to learn this, and meanwhile I got a reputation as "that wise guy from Colgate who's always shooting his mouth off," among the gentler epithets.

Once back in the groove of listening, taking notes, and being tested, however, my marks improved tremendously. I found myself getting *A*'s and an occasional *B*. I was also among classmates who'd never heard of my brother. I took great pains to keep things that way.

I was also fortunate to take courses from, and get to know personally, two incredible teachers, Dr. James Edmunds and Dr. Eric Steele.

My first course with "Jim" Edmunds was something called "Fundamentals of English." Still full of hot air and my Colgate training, I had the temerity to challenge one of Dr. Edmunds's remarks. At that, he cast a baleful stare in my direction and then looked about the class. "How many of you agree with Brittain here?" he asked.

Not a hand was raised.

"And how many of you agree with me?"

Two tentative hands slowly crept upward. All the other members of the class busied themselves taking notes and peering into textbooks.

"Are you all a bunch of fence-sitting cowards!" Dr. Edmunds roared. "Is Brittain the only one in this room with the guts to hold an original opinion? Class is dismissed. Now see if the rest of you can develop a little backbone before the next session!"

I breathed a sigh of relief. Just then Dr. Edmunds turned to me. "Brittain, you stay. I want to talk to you."

I was going to die. I just knew it.

But no. Dr. Edmunds simply wanted to invite me to his house the following week, where a group of students and faculty members would be reading from the classics.

Throughout my two years at Brockport, Jim Edmunds was my mentor and unofficial advisor. He minced no words in telling me when I went wrong, but he also was ready with praise when I did something right. During my own years of teaching, I often found myself asking, "What would Jim Edmunds do in a case like this?"

Graduation photo, Brockport State Teacher's College, 1958

Years later, when I created the character of Mr. Strang, a high school teacher, for my mystery short stories, I gave him many of the characteristics of Dr. James Edmunds.

Dr. Eric Steele was a Scotsman, educated in France. Eccentric, opinionated, and brilliant, he taught survey courses in literature and seemed to know everything about every book ever written. He also played a mean game of golf, and he taught me the basics, perhaps so he'd have someone to discuss Chaucer with between drives that seemed to travel forever. He took a great interest in my writing and even had me appointed editor of the literary magazine. To this day, when the writing gets arduous and I want to quit, I can sense the spirit of Dr. Steele looking over my shoulder and whispering in his Scots burr, "Finish it, Bill. Finish up, now!"

At Brockport I was also introduced to the delights of acting in plays. Hey, this was even better than the movies! I could actually *be* some other person, and the more my imagination put me into the character, the better I'd be. My interest in amateur theater has never diminished, from those days until now.

Ten weeks of my practice teaching assignment were spent in the fifth grade of the campus school, an elementary school run by the college. The situation, as I saw it, was completely unrealistic. After a full day of teaching under the guidance of the master teacher, I was expected to go home and write some five or six lesson plans of two or three pages each. The plans were like scripts, in which I had to set down my opening remarks, how the lesson would be developed, expected questions and how I'd answer them, and finally, some kind of ending activity. If I arrived home at five and worked steadily until about midnight, I could usually finish what was expected. I quickly developed (*a*) the ability to type rapidly, and (*b*) the conviction that if teaching required such lengthy preparation, I wanted no part of it.

My second ten-weeks' assignment was as a junior high school math teacher in Le Roy, New York, a small town about fifteen miles from Brockport. At the end of the first five days, my supervisor, Helen Bernard, asked me to do the lesson plans for the following week. On Monday, after pounding out page after page all weekend, I set a pile of papers on her desk.

"What's all this?" she asked.

"My lesson plans. Now for today, this is my motivating remark, and . . . "

"Good heavens, Bill! All you needed to do was put down the number of the page where we'll start and where we'll end. I never expected all this!"

Whew! I was saved. Maybe I could be a teacher yet.

It was also at Brockport where I met my future wife, Virginia (Ginny) Connorton. On our first few dates I couldn't help looking furtively around to see if my brother were anywhere about. Incredibly enough, Ginny seemed to like me for myself, however. Shortly before graduation we became engaged. We planned to teach for a year or two—until we'd made our fortunes—and then make wedding plans.

After my student teaching at Le Roy, I was offered a teaching position there—fifth grade. I was to receive the princely sum of $2750 per year. I accepted, grateful to have a paying job of any kind.

I'd been teaching exactly one week when I got a phone call from my father.

The results of a physical I'd taken the previous summer had come back. I had hepatitis. I'd need total bed rest for at least two weeks, and perhaps three.

Most of my first month as a teacher was spent flat on my back.

After this inauspicious start, however, my fifth-grade class was delightful, my teaching colleagues were tremendously helpful, and it was a most happy year. There was, however, one problem.

I longed to teach junior high school.

At that time—1953—teachers were in great demand and jobs were plentiful. If I didn't teach in Le Roy, I could always go somewhere else. I therefore asked the superintendent either to place me in junior high school or, if there were no openings, to let me know so I could apply elsewhere.

My second year of teaching was spent with three classes of eighth graders. In the morning they would come to me for instruction in English grammar. This was my specialty, and I looked forward to those morning classes.

In the afternoons, I taught (?) science to the same three groups.

Science? Me? That I was put in such a position shows the awful extent of the teacher shortage in those long-ago days. I kept about two pages ahead of the students, said "I don't know" to most of their questions, and spent long hours at my rooming house after school trying to make sense of what I read in the textbook. Those wonderful students, although they had every right to do so, chose not to embarrass me in class, even knowing full well that most often their knowledge of science was greater than my own.

With the regular director on sabbatical, I was also assigned to direct the senior play. Loving mysteries, I chose Agatha Christie's *Ten Little Indians.* The play ends with a loud shot as the hero kills the villain, foiling his evil schemes. However . . .

The first night of the Le Roy High School production, the gun didn't go off. Somehow my stellar cast bailed themselves out of that one, and the following night several guns, loaded with blanks, were placed backstage. Fortunately the hero's pistol fired. Otherwise my backstage crew, fingers on triggers, would have sounded like the gunfight at the O.K. Corral.

During my second year of teaching, with the Korean War heating up, I was called up by my draft board. Blood tests showed that I had hepatitis in my system, and the military wanted no part of me. Ginny and I decided to get married.

We moved into an apartment in Rochester, and soon found that my teaching salary was nowhere near enough to support a couple. Whether we liked it or not, we realized that to make ends meet and raise a family, we had to move someplace where the salaries were higher.

With son Jim, 1969

In the summer of 1954, I took a position teaching eighth grade at P.S. #1 in Lawrence, Long Island, New York.

Moving into our new home—the second floor of a tiny summer cottage by the beach, which was almost completely deserted in the winter—Ginny and I got acquainted with our new surroundings. Lawrence, on Long Island's south shore, is a community of incredible wealth with a few small pockets of poverty. However giving up the "country" as we knew it for the wall-to-wall suburbs of Long Island took a bit of getting used to.

During our early years on Long Island, four major events took place in our lives.

Our son, James, was born in May 1955.

Liberally aided by a loan from my parents, we bought a house.

Almost exactly three years after her brother, our daughter, Susan, came into this world.

Having a special interest in mystery stories, I read one in *Ellery Queen's Mystery Magazine* and, imagining I could write a better one, I tried. I submitted my first story to *EQMM* in 1959.

It was promptly returned—rejected.

For five years I kept writing and submitting stories to *EQMM* and *Alfred Hitchcock's Mystery Magazine,* these being the only two periodicals on the market that specialized in mystery fiction. And for five years I received constant rejections. Those stories made quite a pile down in the basement.

Writing was, however, an enjoyable hobby, and quite inexpensive, requiring only paper and a typewriter. The game was to see if I could get anything—anything at all—accepted.

In early 1964, I saw an ad in *Popular Mechanics* for the Daniel Mead Literary Agency. They would take manuscripts from unpublished authors and try to sell them. After some correspondence with the Mead Agency to see if it was legitimate, I sent in a batch of the stories I'd written during the previous five years.

One of the stories was titled "Joshua." Years before, on one of our family fishing trips, we'd traveled to a Canadian lodge run by an Indian family. The youngest son spoke English quite well, but having been educated by nuns who came from Ireland, he had an Irish brogue thick enough to cut with a knife. I found the contrast between the Indian's sharp features and lilting speech fascinating. In my mystery story he became Joshua Red Wing.

A couple of months later, I got a message at school that I was to call my wife at home. Concerned that there had been some kind of accident, I picked up the phone.

"Guess what?" said Ginny with a giggle. "You just sold a story!"

"Joshua" would be appearing in the Hitchcock magazine. I would be paid more than two hundred dollars.

It's hard to say whether I was thrilled more by the fact that I'd made a sale, or by the money. My teaching salary allowed for few luxuries, and the payment went to purchase a clothes drier which was immediately dubbed Joshua.

The story appeared in the December 1964 *Alfred Hitchcock's Mystery Magazine.* It was my first fiction to appear in print.

Now, I believed, I had honed my technique to its sharpest and could dash off a short mystery whenever there was a bill to be paid. I sent a number of stories to *AHMM* and *EQMM.*

They were all rejected. I didn't make another sale for a year.

During this discouraging period I read everything I could lay my hands on about the writing of mystery stories. One article, by John Dickson Carr, concerned "locked room" mysteries, in which the reader's challenge is to discover how a murderer can escape from a securely sealed area. Mr. Carr, the undisputed master of this type of yarn, said that "under no circumstances is the chimney to be used as a means of escape. It's much too filthy."

This gave me an idea. That evening, while Ginny was out at a meeting, I sat down at the kitchen table and screwed a piece of paper into my typewriter. Four hours later I'd completed "The Man Who Read John Dickson Carr" which began with the villain scrubbing the inside of a huge chimney until it gleamed.

The following day, I mailed off the story to *EQMM.* In the weeks that followed, I received several postcards saying the story had been through first reading, second reading, etc. Then one day I arrived home from school, and my wife had a message for me.

"You're to call a Frederic Dannay up in Larchmont—collect."

I was speechless with astonishment. Frederic Dannay, true, was the editor of *EQMM.* More important, he, along with his cousin, Manfred B. Lee, had been writing mysteries since 1929 under the pseudonym "Ellery Queen." I had read many of the Queen books as well as seen him in the movies and on TV. Anthony Boucher, while mystery critic for the *New York Times,* had once written: "Ellery Queen *is* the modern detective story."

Now Fred Dannay—Ellery Queen himself—wanted *me* to call *him*!

On the phone, Fred introduced himself, and I engaged in a sickening display of hero worship. Finally he asked me to look at my carbon copy while he consulted the original. He made a number of suggestions for improvement.

"Are . . . are you going to print it?" I sputtered.

"Of course," he replied. "In addition to the other things, however, I do want you to cut it from fifteen pages to about nine."

I agreed to do it. I'd have agreed to cut it to a single sentence if that's what Ellery Queen desired.

"By the way," Fred concluded, "do you have any other material I could take a look at?"

Did I! There were boxes full in the basement.

After sorting out some of my better things for submission, I got to work shortening my story. It was not easy. Some of my cleverest lines had to go—a painful process indeed. However, the story that I had left was, I had to admit, far better than what I'd first submitted.

This was my first experience with the editing process. To this day I find it painful and tedious. It has, however, given me a great respect for editors, who have a unique ability to point out to the writer what's good in a story and what needs to be improved or eliminated.

"The Man Who Read John Dickson Carr" first appeared in the December 1965 issue of *EQMM.* It's since been reprinted throughout the world—often in languages I cannot read. To this day I still receive occasional small checks for its use.

Fred received my other submissions, called me frequently with editorial comments, and bought several of my previously written stories. I began a series in *EQMM,* called "The Man Who Read . . . " various famous detective-story writers.

A few years later, during a call, Fred asked me to consider a schoolteacher detective. The result was my "Mr. Strang" series, about a high school science teacher with many of the attributes of Jim Edmunds, whom I'd known at Brockport.

If ever anyone had expert guidance in his first attempts at writing, I was that person. To be tutored in the craft of mystery writing by Ellery Queen, one of the finest detective-story writers ever known, was far more than I could ever hope for. I wasn't, however, one of a small number of lucky souls. Frederic Dannay, in his lifetime, assisted more than five hundred beginning writers!

I first met Fred in person at the awards dinner of the Mystery Writers of America, which I joined shortly after my first story came out. He entered with a crowd of people surrounding him. I approached and shyly introduced myself. Fred waved a hand, and suddenly the crowd disappeared. He spent twenty minutes sitting at a table and chatting with Ginny and me about my work, his life, and mysteries in general. It was a generous gift of his time, and it was deeply appreciated.

Frederic Dannay died in 1982. But I'm convinced that if there is a writer's heaven, newcomers there will be met by a slight, spade-bearded man who'll approach with an encouraging smile, stick out a hand, and say, "Hello. I'm Fred Dannay. Can I *help* you?"

Nor is Fred the only one who helped. When I was doing the "Man Who Read . . . " series, it seemed only right to contact those whose characters and style I'd be copying to ask permission for such literary theft. Such writers as Rex Stout (who created Nero Wolfe) and Isaac Asimov (the Black Widowers) allowed me to borrow their creations without batting an eye. Edward D. Hoch gave one of his numerous series characters a "rest" because it might interfere with my plotting of Mr. Strang. The late Robert L. Fish was most encouraging, even including "The Man Who Read John Dickson Carr" in his anthology *Every Crime in the Book.* It's been my experience that most writers, in dealing with newcomers, are motivated by generosity, not jealousy.

By the mid-1970s, having had some fifty or sixty mystery short stories published, I began getting the itch to do a book. The first opportunity came from a rather unexpected source.

Leonard Cole, a friend, was a nature illustrator. He was involved in preparing a series of books for outdoor sportsmen and needed people to write the text while he did the pictures. He asked me to write one, called *Survival Outdoors.*

I told Leonard that I could scarcely find my way to the garbage can on a foggy day. He, however, made available a lot of source material from *The Boy Scout Handbook* to army and navy pamphlets.

Stealing time from my wife, my family, and my teaching duties, I wrote *Survival Outdoors* in a single month—January 1976—and it was published the following year. It was my first book to be published. I have a few copies at home, but whether it still exists elsewhere is hard to say.

Immediately afterward, I began what I hoped would be an adult mystery—"Bloody Instructions," featuring my teacher, Mr. Strang. It was rejected by every publisher I sent it to and exists today only as a pile of typed pages in a Campbell's Soup box. Two publishers were kind enough to comment on it, and both told me it fell between the adult and juvenile categories. Sorry—no sale.

All my writing was being done evenings, weekends, summers, and during whatever time I could spare. I still had my full-time teaching career to consider. By this time the Lawrence junior-high students had been moved from the elementary schools into a building of their own. After taking courses for certification, I had been assigned a program of remedial reading classes. My students had no aspirations to go on to college or even, in many cases, to finish high school. They needed to be taught the most elementary reading and writing skills necessary to get jobs, drive cars, and function as self-supporting members of society.

One day, I was seated on the floor next to a freestanding bookshelf in my room. On the other side of the shelf, two seventh-grade boys—who, I suspect, didn't know I was there—were engaged in whispered conversation. I heard one say, "I wish I had a new bike. Mine's got one pedal busted, and the wheel's bent, and I really need a new one."

His buddy took up the challenge. He had to make a better wish. "If I had a moped, I wouldn't even have to pedal. How about that?"

"Oh yeah? Well, with a motorcycle I could pass you like you were standing still."

"Not if I had a car. A real street rod, with dual carbs and . . . "

On and on the wishing went, from cars to airplanes to gold mines until finally I heard one boy murmur: "I wish I had all the money in the world!"

Over the next several days, I couldn't get that boy's last wish out of my mind. I couldn't help wondering what would happen if he got it.

Sitting down with a pad and paper, I began outlining all the problems that might arise if all the money in the world were concentrated in the hands of one boy. My scribbled notes slowly arranged themselves into chapters.

The author taking a bow for The Wish Giver, *a Newbery Honor book, at the Newbery Awards dinner, Texas, 1984*

During the summer of 1977, I wrote the first draft of my first book for kids. The title was a "natural": *All the Money in the World.* The setting was a farm, just outside the small village of Cedar Ferry. Similarities to my uncle's farm and the village where I grew up were purely intentional.

Having written the book, I went looking for a publisher. Five of 'em turned it down flat. Then I got a call from Elaine Edelman at Harper and Row. Would I be willing to come in to her office in New York City and talk with her about my book?

As it turned out, Elaine did most of the talking. She spent all of one day with me, pointing out places where the plotting was weak, where the motives of the characters were unclear, or where the action needed to be speeded up. At about four o'clock, I left for home with my manuscript under my arm, its pages covered with notes from Elaine's editorial pencil.

I rewrote the manuscript from start to finish. On its second submission, Elaine called on the phone.

"Bill, I like the changes you've made very much. But . . . "

She made her comments, and I noted them on my carbon copy. During the following six weeks, a third version of *All the Money in the World* came out of the typewriter. Only after she'd checked this over did Elaine assure me that Harper and Row would publish my book.

After some other minor corrections, *All the Money in the World* came onto the market in 1979. I reluctantly had to admit that the changes Elaine had suggested made for a far better story than I'd originally written.

It was chosen for the 1982 Charlie May Simon Award by the children of Arkansas, and the medal I received in Little Rock in June of that year is one of my proudest possessions. It was also made into an ABC-TV Saturday Special. My first knowledge of this triumph came when I read about it in a Long Island newspaper.

The family after Virginia's retirement party in 1985: wife Virginia, son Jim, daughter Sue

Shortly after the publication of *All the Money in the World,* I had quite a surprise in my classroom. There was an eighth-grade girl in one of my reading classes who simply would not read, no matter what motivation I used or what ruses I tried. To her, a book held all the charm of a rattlesnake.

One Monday, however, she met me at the door, bursting with enthusiasm. "Oh, Mr. Brittain," she cried, "I just read the greatest book this weekend. Lemme tell you all about it!"

The book she'd read—completely on her own, with no prompting by me—was *The Shaggy D.A.* It was the story of a detective who, on odd occasions, turned into an English sheepdog. Over the next several days, it occurred to me that if the story of a human who changes into an animal could create such interest, maybe I should try working with the idea myself.

Such was the beginning of *Devil's Donkey.* It was my second book for kids, as well as the first of what would become my series of "Coven Tree" stories.

The name Coven Tree, for my imaginary New England village where witchcraft and magic hold sway, came only after a lot of thought. I wanted the village's name to reflect its magical quality, and tried everything from Witch Bridge to Spellville. None of the names I played with, however, seemed to really "click." One day while driving to school, I began thinking about a trip Ginny and I had taken to England. One of the midland cities we'd visited was Coventry.

I said the word aloud, "Coventry . . . Coventry . . . Coven Tree . . . "

Of course! A coven, I knew, was a group of witches. The change from human to animal, then, would be by witchcraft. If somehow I could bring a tree into the story, I'd have the perfect name.

The manuscript, first titled "The Dang-Blast Donkey," originally had many of the characters changing from human to beast and back again, and was far more complicated and confusing than the final version. Elaine, however, was clever enough to see that somewhere in my outlandish plotting was the stuff of a good story.

"Simplify, Bill," she told me often during our many phone calls. "Keep it simple."

Once again, my writing went through a number of complete rewrites before I could even consider the lesser corrections. The title itself required six weeks of thought, with Elaine rejecting all my ideas and me doing the same with hers. It was finally Robert Warren, Elaine's assistant, who came up with *Devil's Donkey.* We all agreed it was the perfect title.

One Sunday, a couple months after the book was published, I was thumbing through the *New York Times.* There, on the children's page of the book section, was a review of my book. They liked it! It was, according to the reviewer, "a pleasing addition to children's folklore."

Knowing that some knowledgeable person had read my story and enjoyed it was one of the greatest thrills of my lifetime.

While *Devil's Donkey* required a tremendous amount of thought, work, and frustration, I was inordinately pleased with the end result. Of all my books, it's still my favorite. In it were characters similar to those I'd known as a boy and others I wished I'd known. The village itself was an idealized version of Spencerport, where I'd grown up. I was reluctant to give up my quaint New England village simply because the book was finished.

For this reason, I decided to return to Coven Tree as the setting for my next book, *The Wish Giver.*

I'd originally planned to use just one story (the section titled "The Tree-Man") for the whole book. It wasn't nearly long enough. The idea for "Jug-a-Rum" came next. The final section concerned a boy who longed to have his dead grandfather, whom he loved, come back to life.

While I was in the middle of writing *The Wish Giver,* I received a note from Elaine saying she was leaving Harper and Row to do some work on her own. I sent her a note wishing her well, at the same time feeling tremendously let down. How could she *do* this to me? Who else could turn my turgid prose into interesting stories?

Robert Warren, her assistant, took her place. In our first communication, Robert insisted that the "dead grandfather" section of my book had to be discarded. I was angry. Still, I had to show him I could come up with another idea . . . if I *had* to. Remembering a dowser who'd once showed my uncle where to dig a well on his farm, I wrote "Water, Water Everywhere," the final part of *The Wish Giver.*

The plotting of this book was the most difficult I've ever done. All three sections took part in the same four-day period, and since Coven Tree was a tiny farming village, the paths of the major characters had to cross from time to time. Making it all work out required a tremendous amount of guidance from Robert. Still, I was reluctant to admit that anyone could take Elaine's place as my editor.

In January 1984, I received a telephone call from Washington, D.C. The caller informed me that *The Wish Giver* had been selected as a Newbery Honor Book. I was astonished beyond words. Such an honor belonged to some real author, not to a teacher masquerading as a writer. Could I have been wrong about Robert's ability as an editor? Was it possible he knew more about what changes my work required than I gave him credit for?

Robert's editing ability has salvaged some of my poorer writing attempts and has made the good stuff even better. But for my own stubborn pride, I'd have realized it from the start.

For the next book, I decided on a good old haunted-house story, complete with ghosts. I decided, however, to make the ghosts the "good guys." *Who Knew There'd Be Ghosts?* (the working title was "Where the Parnells Lived") takes place in a modern small town—Spencerport again. The haunted Parnell house, however, is based on Rock Hall, a pre-Revolutionary home right beside Lawrence Junior High School where I was teaching. It was only necessary in imagination to turn the well-maintained Rock Hall into the moldering wreck of a building that was Parnell House in my story.

"In the classroom, shortly before retirement," 1986

For the book I had to do endless research on the Revolutionary era as well as the period just before the Civil War. The results of this research occupy perhaps three pages in the finished book but with an infinite ignorance of history, I had to get the facts straight.

Who Knew There'd Be Ghosts? came out to rather lukewarm reviews. Nevertheless, it has been on a dozen or so reading lists for state awards, a fact of which I'm most proud.

For *Dr. Dredd's Wagon of Wonders,* I returned to Coven Tree. The book began with a vision that seemed to pop into my head whenever I began plotting a new story.

A barnyard in the dead of night. Rain is pelting down, and flashes of lightning illuminate a gaunt, ghastly creature who is peering about, searching. A boy, the object of the search, crouches trembling with fear, beneath a bush in one corner of the yard. The creature spies him and approaches—closer . . . closer . . .

Suddenly a bolt of lightning blasts from the sky, striking the evil one to the ground!

That was the beginning. I had no idea where in my subconscious the scene was hatched. I didn't know how those two got to the barnyard or what happened afterward. From that start, I fashioned the book which, I hope, will send delightful shivers up the spines of my readers.

In 1986, after thirty-four years in the classroom, I retired. By then, both Jim and Sue were making their own ways in the world. Jim's in New Jersey where he's a drug and alcohol abuse counselor. Sue works for a trade-show firm in Buffalo, New York and, like her father, has developed a profitable avocation. She sings "The Star-Spangled Banner" before most of the professional sports events there.

My wife, Ginny, and I moved to Asheville, North Carolina, a mountainous, scenic area which we both enjoy. I continue to write. My latest book, *The Fantastic Freshman,* is based on the fears and apprehensions experienced by most students upon entering a new school. Another book, *My Buddy, the King,* is now undergoing the editorial process.

When asked for insights into the writing process, I can come up with few answers that would be of use to beginners. With so many different types and techniques of writing, perhaps the best method is to take any advice with a grain of salt and try to develop one's own style. What one writer may find extremely effective can be totally unworkable for another.

I can comment only on what works for me.

In my stories I don't try to teach any enduring lessons. If my audience considers what I've written to be "a good read," that's enough for me.

I like to start off my stories with a few sentences that will grab the reader at once and end each chapter with a "cliff-hanger" that will lead inevitably to the following chapter.

I don't like to present problems to which there is no real solution, which the main characters must simply learn to live with. By the time my last page is reached, I want all difficulties overcome, so that the book can conclude, either actually or by implication, with what I consider the most glorious words in all of

"Celebrating our parents' sixtieth wedding anniversary in 1986." The author (center left) with his parents, Dorothy and Knox Brittain, and brother, Bob.

children's literature: "And they lived happily ever after."

How did my students react to the fact that I was writing? They first expressed disbelief that I had actually written the books that suddenly appeared in the school library. The second phase was a kind of awe that their teacher could accomplish such a thing. But childish awe is an ephemeral thing. Among my students, it lasted perhaps twenty-four hours. Then they realized I was still the guy who assigned the homework and kept the class in order. So again, I was not the writer, but "the teacher."

What has my writing meant to me? Aside from the obvious financial gain, it has given me a chance to stretch my imagination in telling yarns that please me, and much to my amazement, seem to please others, as well. My various editors have provided me the opportunity to hone and improve my work until it's as perfect as I can make it. The process is often unpleasant, but the end result is well worth it. I've had the wonderful experience of exchanging ideas and methods with other writers—Johanna Hurwitz, Clyde Bulla, Lila Perl and Russell Freedman, to name just a few. Just recently I met Bruce Brooks, the author of the 1985 Newbery Honor Book *The Moves Make the Man.* Bruce and I write entirely different types of fiction. Mine involves magic and fantasy, while his is the young adult "problem" story. Yet we both are reaching for the same goal—to involve, to delight, and ultimately to satisfy our readers.

The future? Well, in retirement I'm sharpening up my golf game. We have a lawn which, when it needs mowing, seems to expand to the size of South America. We sometimes entertain guests, and I'm hoping for a visit from brother Bob, his red cape fluttering in the wind. There are plenty of excuses whenever I don't feel like pursuing my "hobby."

But at age fifty-seven, I have a lot of good years left in which to play with that magnificent toy which is the English language. I'll continue to write because I simply cannot imagine myself *not* writing.

BIBLIOGRAPHY

FOR CHILDREN

Fiction:

All the Money in the World (illustrated by Charles Robinson). New York: Harper, 1979.

Devil's Donkey (illustrated by Andrew Glass). New York: Harper, 1981.

The Wish Giver (illustrated by A. Glass). New York: Harper, 1983.

Who Knew There'd Be Ghosts? (illustrated by Michele Chessare). New York: Harper, 1985.

Dr. Dredd's Wagon of Wonders (illustrated by A. Glass). New York: Harper, 1987.

The Fantastic Freshman. New York: Harper, 1988.

FOR ADULTS

Nonfiction:

Survival Outdoors (illustrated by Leonard Cole). New York: Monarch, 1977.

Brittain has also written over seventy short mystery stories published in periodicals, including *Ellery Queen's Mystery Magazine, Alfred Hitchcock's Mystery Magazine,* and *Antaeus.* Many of these stories have been anthologized in books for children and adults.

Barbara Cohen

1932–

SOMETHING ABOUT ME

Barbara Cohen

In school, they tell kids, "Write from experience. Write about what you know." But most kids think their own lives are boring. If they are readers at all, they read to escape from the ordinariness of the everyday. If they are writers at all, they tend to write the kinds of things they like to read. They write about great adventures—visiting talking purple pods on Uranus, encountering a herd of runaway elephants on Main Street, falling in love with a rock star and then meeting him in the supermarket and having him fall in love with you.

Or at least that's how it was for me when I was a kid. Now that I'm grown up, and writing for a living, it's not so different. Of course I understand that everything I write does grow out of my own experience. It has nowhere else to come from. Sometimes I still write about talking purple pods and thundering herds of elephants. Now, however, I understand that they too in some way are connected to what has happened to me, and always were. But I also understand that in transmuting an experience into fiction, I am going beyond the experience. I write not so much to reflect what has occurred as to shape it, to give it meaning, to control it.

Turning experience into fiction happens largely unconsciously. Only after I've written about those Uranians can I look at the story and say, "Of course, that creature may look like a purple pod, but it feels like I felt when I didn't get the lead in the sixth-grade play." The idea for a book always comes from something very specific—an image, a character, a line of dialog, or an event. Later I finally understand what the book is really about.

I was born in Asbury Park, New Jersey, in 1932, the oldest of the three children of Florence Marshall and Leo Kauder. I started writing about the same time I started reading, which means I can scarcely remember not being able to do either. I loved reading right from the beginning, and wanted, also right from the beginning, to make things like those books I loved so much.

I also loved hearing stories. That started long before I could read, in those shadowy days before memory. Even after I learned to read, I still spent as much time as I could listening to stories.

I come from a family that admires a good story. I would sit on the front porch of my grandparents' house in Asbury Park on a summer night, while my grandfather, his brothers and sisters, and their children talked in a very funny and frequently malicious style about those family members who had made the mistake of not showing up. The other kids would be off playing somewhere, but I'd be sitting there, listening and listening.

And during the long, quiet summer days, on that porch, or on the beach, I'd be reading. And during winter days too. When I was eight, my parents moved from Asbury Park to Somerville, New Jersey, where they bought the Somerville Inn. My father had suffered a heart attack and the doctors decided his business selling eggs, dairy products, and poultry was too strenuous for him. I'm not sure why anyone

"My mother, Florence Marshall Kauder, with my brother, Louis, my sister, Susan, and me (far right)," 1943

thought running an inn which had gone bankrupt and been closed for a year would be any easier. But at least it was a business in which my mother could help.

A year and a half after our arrival in Somerville, my father died. He was forty-eight. My mother was thirty-three. I was nine, Louis was seven, Susan was not quite five. My mother was left with a pile of debts and a run-down hotel. But she stuck it out. She didn't want to return to Asbury Park and schoolteaching, which she had never liked. She knew that even if the Somerville Inn wasn't making money, it would always provide food for us to eat, and a roof over our heads. Above all, we would be together because where she worked and where we lived was the same place.

For many years, my mother had very little money, but we were never really aware of that. If I wanted a pair of Mary Janes my mother never said, "I can't afford to buy you school shoes and Mary Janes." She said, "Mary Janes are not good for your feet." She wasn't lying; she'd convinced herself that this was true. Such was the authority of her personality that I believed it too. Eventually she built the Inn into a wonderfully successful business. Soon after I married Gene Cohen in 1954, he joined her, and by the time our three daughters, Leah (1957), Sara (1962), and Rebecca (1963), came along, we could well afford Mary Janes. But I was never comfortable buying them. Some part of me remains sure to this day that they're bad for your feet.

Growing up at an inn was like most other childhoods—it had good parts and bad parts. It didn't seem exciting or different to me while it was happening. It was my life, and I thought it extremely ordinary at best and positively horrid some of the time. I hated giving up my room to a favored customer and sleeping with my sister when the Inn was full. I hated living across a wide highway that my classmates were not allowed to cross. We were Jewish in a town where anti-Semitism was still close to the surface. My mother worked at a time when most other mothers didn't. And she worked not in a school or office, but selling liquor and renting rooms to strangers. All these things served to make me feel isolated from other kids my age and forced me to depend on my brother, sister, and books.

But there were marvelous things about my childhood, too, and even then I knew it a little. Wonderful people worked or stayed at the Inn. They enriched my life in countless ways. We'd lie on our bellies at the top of the stairs and watch brides arrive for their wedding receptions or crazy celebrants in paper hats act silly on New Year's Eve. I was only eleven or twelve when I started checking coats and earning money of my own. And always there was my mother at the center, strong, stable, supportive, sane.

I read and wrote all the way through Somerville High School and Barnard College. When I was a college senior, my stepfather, Edward Nash, encouraged me to write a column of personal commentary for the three weekly newspapers he owned. He paid me five dollars a week, the first money I ever made from writing.

In 1954 I graduated from Barnard as an English major with a concentration in the area of creative writing. Then my life changed. For the next twenty years, I did almost no writing. I was too busy being Gene's wife, Leah, Sara, and Becky's mother, and a high-school English teacher to have time or energy left over for much writing. I managed the weekly newspaper column, one summer of reporting, plays for organizations to which I belonged, and a very occasional story. There were maybe half a dozen of these stories in twenty years. One was a romantic

"Somerville Inn, where I lived as a child. This building burned down in 1962 and was replaced."

novel; the others were all children's books. I didn't know why most of the fiction I turned out was clearly directed at kids; that's just the way it was. Though I sent these few things off to publishers, they were rejected. I was not surprised.

Then one spring evening in 1971 Gene and I were visiting friends. We were talking about the upcoming Jewish holiday of Passover. Another guest mentioned that when she was a little girl in Brooklyn, her mother kept a live carp in the bathtub in order to make sure she had a really fresh fish to turn into her family's favorite holiday delicacy, gefilte fish.

I'd eaten plenty of gefilte fish in my life, but I'd never heard of keeping a live fish in an apartment bathtub and bopping it on its head yourself for dinner. Though I've since learned that it was quite a common practice, it certainly was not in my own personal experience, or the personal experience of anyone in my family. But I couldn't get the image of that fish swimming around in the bathtub out of my head. I became obsessed with that creature. A few days later I sat down at my machine, rolled in a blank piece of paper, and typed *The Carp in the Bathtub* at the top of the page. The story poured out of me. I had the ambience from stories my own mother had told me about growing up in Brooklyn around the time of World War I. I had the basic idea from my friend.

But what my friend had told me was just an anecdote. An anecdote and an ambience don't make a story. For a story you need a plot. The action of a plot is motivated by conflict. No conflict, no story. So I made up a plot in which two children, Leah and Harry, fall in love with the carp their mother is storing in the bathtub. They name it Joe and try to save it from its inevitable fate at her hands. I explain this process now, in words. These words were not in my head before or while I was writing. The only things in my head that I was aware of then were the characters and the story.

When I was finished with it, I knew that I had written something better than anything I'd done before. A friend said, "Send it to my editor, Edna Barth, at Lothrop, Lee and Shepard. She's very nice." Indeed she was. She agreed to publish it with some revision. I learned more about writing from Edna Barth's notes on my manuscript than I had from all the writing courses I'd taken in college.

The Carp was a success from the beginning. It appeared in 1972 and has remained in print ever since. A universal idea cast in a particular ethnic mold, it is a story to which children (and grown-ups) of every background can relate. At the same time it provides insight into Jewish customs and ceremonies. To its advantage, it was published just as interest in ethnic stories for children was emerging. But of course I wasn't aware of that while I was writing it. You can't say, "It's the right year to write a popular Jewish story." You say, "I'm going to write this

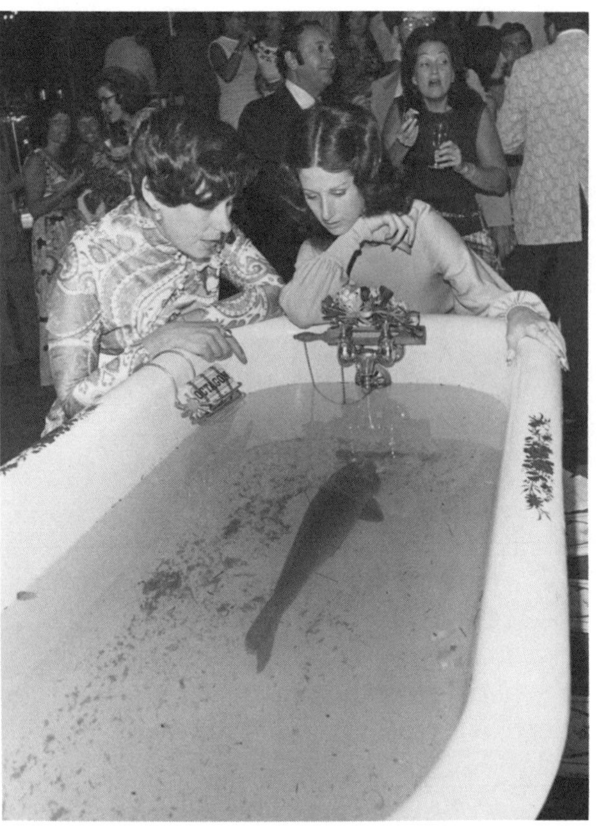

"At a party honoring the publication of The Carp in the Bathtub. *I'm with illustrator Joan Halpern (right), and the carp."*

particular story about these particular people at this particular time because that's what I want to write and need to write." Then you hope for the best, which sometimes happens and sometimes does not.

A successful book does not guarantee that editors will publish whatever else you write. It does guarantee that they'll read it with interest. Knowing that is a great spur to continue writing. No sooner was *The Carp* published than I started another book.

At about that time, Jackie Robinson, the first black baseball player in major-league history, died. As a boy, my brother had been an ardent fan of the Brooklyn Dodgers, the team for which Jackie Robinson had played. When I read Jackie Robinson's obituary in the paper, I wrote to my brother, by then a lawyer in Washington, D.C. It was really a letter of condolence, as if a personal friend or relative of his had died. He responded and we exchanged a few more letters, in which we reminisced about what I suddenly realized had been quite a remarkable childhood.

This brief correspondence released in me a flood of memory. Very quickly, perhaps in two weeks' time, over my 1973 spring vacation from teaching, I completed a rough draft of my first novel, *Thank You, Jackie Robinson.* The story of a fatherless white boy and his relationship with the black cook at his mother's hotel, it is based on the real friendship between my brother and Wesley Hoagland, for years the chef at the Somerville Inn. The two, in fiction, as in life, were connected by their love for the Brooklyn Dodgers in general and Jackie Robinson in particular. They went to many ball games together, and listened to many more on my brother's large battery-powered portable radio. I never saw a ball game until I was grown up, and I never thought I had listened to one either. But when it came time for me to describe the games attended by Sam and Davy in the novel, I discovered that a tape recorder had been running in my head when I was a kid, recording stuff I hadn't even known I was listening to. I could still hear the soft southern voice of Red Barber, the Dodgers' announcer, calling those games, and all I had to do was write down what he said.

But once again, though characters and background came from real life, the plot was something I made up. Davy gets sick and Sam conceives the notion that if only he can get his friend a ball autographed by Jackie Robinson, he can save his life. He gets the ball all right, with difficulty, and is very proud of himself. But there is no magic; Davy, like Sam's father, dies, leaving Sam, at his mother's urging, to take what comfort he can in memories and baseball.

After she read the manuscript, my daughter Leah, then about fifteen, said, "Mother, you're always writing about death." With a shock, I realized that what she was saying was true. Both *The Carp* and *Jackie,* in their very different ways, were about children coping with loss. And then I understood what I'd *really* written about—not my brother's feelings concerning my father's death, but my own. Of course, my brother and I must have felt some similar things. But the emotional truth of the book came out of my own experience. The impact remains. Like *The Carp, Jackie* is still in print.

My next book, *Where's Florrie?,* returned to the format of *The Carp,* and was illustrated by the same artist, Joan Halpern. It was based on two different stories my mother had often told us about her own Brooklyn childhood—the time she built a forbidden fire in a toy stove and the time she got lost following a horse-drawn carousel.

Florrie was followed by a novel, *Bitter Herbs and Honey,* chronicling a year in the life of a Jewish girl in a small New Jersey town in 1915–16. The summer I'd worked on our local newspaper I'd written a big feature article about the history of the Jews in Somerset County and it was that research I used for the background of my book. The heroine, Rebecca Levitsky, wants to go to college; her father thinks no man will marry a girl who's too smart. This aspect of the plot was again borrowed directly from my mother's life. She had had to overcome my grandfather's objections to educated women in order to attend college. The way she did this was another piece of the family mythology that shaped my consciousness.

But although *Bitter Herbs* takes place sixteen years before I was even born, once again the feelings it reflects are my own. The simultaneous constriction and comfort of small-town life, the pain caused by a community's subtle anti-Semitism, the excitement and guilt attendant upon a romance with a boy who isn't Jewish—these were all part of my own high-school experience. Once again, I didn't realize the degree to which the book was autobiographical until my brother pointed it out to me. "Becky is really you," he said. I had to admit he was right.

Soon after, I wrote what I thought was another picture storybook like *The Carp* or *Where's Florrie?,* about a boy who leaves his father's grocery store unattended in order to play in a baseball game. Both my agent and editor told me they needed to know more about the boy and his father. *Benny* was not a picture book, they said; it was part of a novel. And so I expanded it, using not the mythology of my own family this time, but the mythology of my husband's family insofar as I understood it.

While I was writing *Benny,* I was growing frustrated. The books that were lying at the top of my brain, crying out to be written, were done now. I was having to dig deeper to make a book, work harder and longer, depending more on technique, less on inspiration. And yet writing books had become the work I really wanted to do.

But I could only do it during school vacations. That was the only time I had energy for it. I get furious when I hear people talking about what an easy job teaching is, with all that time off. I'd like to see them spend the day with 120 kids between fifteen and seventeen years old, all of whom, if the English teacher is conscientious, are producing at least one essay a week which has to be read carefully and corrected. I loved the work, but to do it I used exactly the same creative power I put into my writing. I barely had strength at the end of the school day for my children, husband, and home, let alone writing.

Now that I was doing novels as well as picture books, I grew uncomfortable if I had to let a book hang untouched for months waiting for the next vacation to roll around. I realized I could no longer live so many lives. I couldn't be a wife, a mother, a housekeeper, a writer, and a teacher. One of those jobs was going to have to go. I wasn't going to leave the kids, divorce the husband, or sell the house. Much as I enjoyed it, teaching was the thing I had to dump. It was a scary thing to do. Though we didn't need the money I earned to put food on our table or keep the roof over our heads, we did count on it for vacations and our children's college educations. I knew that it would be years before my income from writing equalled my income from teaching. Maybe it never would. But I felt as if a train were in the station, and it was time for me to get on it. If I didn't, it would go away and leave me behind forever. In this decision I had Gene's unconditional support. "Don't worry," he said, "we'll manage. We always have."

I got through the summer without too much difficulty, but when autumn moved in and everyone went back to school except me, I felt as if I'd been left alone in a strange country. Except for the year Leah was born, it was the first September since I'd entered nursery school that I hadn't gone off to school! After forty years of living according to a calendar that ran from September to June, the readjustment required considerable effort.

It did for my kids too. Leah was in college by this time, but Sara and Becky were still in high school. They called one afternoon and said they'd missed the late bus, please come to pick them up. I did, and saw they had a friend with them. "Patty's mother works," they said. "Would you please take her home too?" Patty lived on the other side of our spread-out township, and the round trip took forty minutes. At that point I could hardly leave the kid stranded on the sidewalk. But after we got back home, I said to Sara and Becky, "Patty's mother is not the only mother who works. Your mother works too." My children were not the only ones who had trouble understanding that a parent at home could be as much a working parent as one who leaves every day at nine for an office or a school. Members of organizations I belong to called up and said things like, "You can chair the bake sale. You're not working any more."

Fortunately, my children soon grasped an essential fact which still eludes most of my friends. Writing is in part an art, in part a craft. So are painting, dancing, sculpting, composing, or playing a musical instrument. They all require a modicum of talent. But lots of people have talent. The ones who achieve a body of work are the ones who are disciplined, the ones who sit down every day and simply go to work, inspired or not inspired. I believe inspiration grows out of the work. The seed sprouts only in the

Leah, Sara, and Becky, 1964

prepared field.

As I continued working, I saw that what had been true of my earlier work was true as well of what came later. What I created emerged from the interplay of still-felt childhood emotions, and past and present experience, filtered through the shaping power of my imagination.

Three books came out of that Somerville Inn childhood which I'd hated and loved at the same time. I thought I'd write a novel about three kids growing up at an inn, but after I'd gotten quite far along with it, I realized I'd already written about the boy in the family. That book was *Thank You, Jackie Robinson.* There was no point in doing it again. I decided to write two more books, one about the younger sister and one about the older sister, although I'd have to change the names because of slight differences from the *Jackie Robinson* family. I examined the material I'd already written about the younger sister. Like my own sister, Susan, Rosie in my story longed desperately for a pet, although her mother kept saying, "An inn is no place for a dog." That problem was not enough to fill a whole book. What could I add?

Rosie was friendly with a bartender at the inn, and they spent long hours together telling each other stories. I realized that I would have to tell one of those stories too, alternating chapters between Rosie's real life and the fairy-tale world she and Tex were creating together. The resulting book was *R, My Name Is Rosie.* Several critics complained that Rosie's reality and her fantasy were not related. I asked a ten-year-old boy I knew if he thought there was any connection between the two. "Sure," he said. "Rosie thinks her mother doesn't love her, and Princess Rosalie thinks *her* mother doesn't love her. But both mothers really do." That was it exactly, of course. Grown-ups couldn't see it, but kids didn't seem to have any problem.

The Innkeeper's Daughter is the most directly autobiographical of all my books. It's not one of the most successful. Many of the passages coming directly from my own life are among the best I've written. The sixteen-year-old heroine, Rachel Gold, arrives at a classmate's Christmas party in a black dress. All the other girls are wearing sweaters and skirts. Everything else that happens in the course of the evening serves only to increase her sense of herself as an outsider. Her mother refuses to allow her to wallow in self-pity, but she can't erase Rachel's pain. I went to that party in that dress when I was sixteen, and the misery of that never-to-be-forgotten occasion was finally exorcised in writing about it. Teenagers often mention that chapter to me. It strikes them as the truth.

But the book as a whole does not work as well as *R, My Name Is Rosie* or *Thank You, Jackie Robinson.* The elaborate plot involving the identity of a mysterious painting is not a good metaphor for the book's meaning. It seems pasted on top of the book, not integral to it. Perhaps in this case I was too close to the experiences I recounted to transmute them successfully into fiction. I wish I could write *The Innkeeper's Daughter* over again. But maybe it still wouldn't work. Although every character I write about is in some sense partly me, maybe I simply can't handle a head-on confrontation with my own self.

None of my books is at first glance any further from my own experience than *Unicorns in the Rain.* This fantasy is the only one of my books which arrived virtually complete in a moment of inspiration. In college I had written a short story about a girl who boards a bus on a rainy day. She's picked up by a handsome, mysterious young man who convinces her to return with him to his family's farm. There she finds his father, his two brothers, and their wives collecting pairs of animals and constructing a huge ship. . . .

I got an A on the story and it was published in Barnard's literary magazine. But in the ensuing twenty-six years I never gave it another thought. I was on a train returning from New York after telling my editor I didn't have the vaguest idea of what to write next. I thought after seven books I was through as a writer. I gazed out the sooty window at a sodden landscape which perfectly reflected my own depression. Perhaps it was because of the rain, or because I felt, in that enclosed, overheated, dimly lit railway car, that the end of the world was indeed at hand—whatever the reason, the long-forgotten story simply popped into my head.

My depression lifted immediately. "I can make a novel out of that story," I thought. "But telling the Noah story as if it were happening to a teenager today isn't enough. I need another idea." By the time I got home, I'd decided to put in the unicorns and to set the story not in the present but in a time period which a reader might take for the future but which in my mind was actually the past. The Bible doesn't tell us what Noah's world was like. It tells us only that it was a wicked time. Why could Noah's time not have been much like our own, only just a little worse? One thing the Bible makes very clear—God promises never to destroy the world again by flood. Therefore Noah's story cannot happen twice. My version is my imagining of the way it happened the only time it could have happened. The events of the story are myth—not, this time, from my family's personal mythology, but rather from the shared mythology of the human family. However, the highway, the house, the railroad station, and the supermarket which figure in the novel can all be located in my neighborhood. So can the people. I believe such attention to realistic detail is almost more important in a fantasy than in any other kind of book. It helps make the whole thing convincing.

The author working at the beach, 1974

Though I considered *Unicorns in the Rain* the best book I'd ever written, I had a hard time selling it. It was so different from anything I'd published before that editors didn't know quite what to make of it. But once it found a home at Atheneum, it was well received by reviewers and quite popular with readers. I felt vindicated.

At first glance, *Seven Daughters and Seven Sons* would seem to have even less relevance to my own life than *Unicorns in the Rain.* An Iraqui friend, Bahija Lovejoy, showed me some tales she'd translated from an Arab folklore magazine. She wondered if they might form the basis of picture books. One of them was about a poor young woman who took a deeply satisfying revenge on the wealthy uncle and cousins who'd insulted her and her family, and found true love to boot. So charmed was I by this story that I wanted to sink down into it. A picture book would have been over too soon; I wanted to spend months on this material. With Bahija supplying the historical and geographical background, I turned the folktale into a novel.

What connection did I have with a Moslem girl living in Baghdad nearly a thousand years ago? I come from a long line of what I might call "practical feminists." My mother and my grandmother were not revolutionaries, but in their different ways they pushed hard against the limitations imposed on them by their time and place. They never said to their daughters, "You can't." They said, "You can." The woman Bahija and I named Buran is such a woman too; that's why I fell in love with her.

We love, we hate, we act. The events we thus cause or which simply happen to us are one kind of experience. But we have another kind of experience, the vicarious experience of books, movies, theatre, television. As I mentioned in the opening paragraph of this essay, enjoyment of that kind of experience is often the first impetus to writing. We want to make what we like so much. Vicarious experience has its own kind of validity. *Unicorns in the Rain* and *Seven Daughters and Seven Sons* owe as much to stories I loved reading as they do to events and feelings in my life, perhaps more.

Two other novels I wrote fall into the same class. One is *Lovers' Games,* a completely trivial book which I had an absolutely marvelous time writing. I adore eating tortilla chips and I adore reading Regency romances by Georgette Heyer—only by Georgette Heyer, no others. In *Lovers' Games* I transferred the conventions of a Heyer romance—the large, aristocratic family, the mismatched lovers, the duel, the ball—to a contemporary suburban high school. Writing *Roses* was great fun too, although it deals with somewhat more serious issues, like accepting one's own sexuality and putting away grief and guilt. After I grew out of *Cinderella,* my favorite fairy tale became *Beauty and the Beast.* When I read Bruno Bettelheim's *The Uses of Enchantment,* I understood why. *Roses* is an attempt to make Beauty's story convincing in a modern setting with a modern sixteen-year-old heroine and no recourse to magic.

Fat Jack reflects a complex combination of real-life and literary sources. Though I was not popular in high school (if I had been would I have become the writer I am today?), not every party I attended was the disaster I described in *The Innkeeper's Daughter.* Around the time of graduation a senior boy invited about a dozen of us to his house for a Sunday afternoon picnic. We'd been friendly in class, but that was all. His invitation came as a surprise, and the day spent messing around in the river that flowed through his backyard remains etched in my memory as one of the most pleasant of my life. I lost sight of him for years, but one day he called me to say he was passing through town, could he come to visit. I invited him for dinner. My husband was working, my kids were out. We spent a long, quiet evening reminiscing about our high-school days, the pain of which had been charmingly blurred by time's passage. This visit became the opening scene of *Fat Jack.* But Jack in the book is someone else, someone who really was named Jack, a talented and funny guy who attended Somerville High School for only about a year, and whom I could have loved, in spite of his size, if he'd given me half a chance.

In college I'd appeared as Mistress Quickly in a Columbia Players production of Shakespeare's *Henry IV, Part One.* From that time on I was hooked on the play. I managed to force its study into English classrooms where it had long been assumed that Shakespeare began and ended with *Julius Caesar.* I knew the play by heart. The fat Jack of my memory became Falstaff in the high school production of *Henry IV,* which is the main event in my novel. The wonderful drama coaches I'd worked with in high school, college, and in my own teaching days, as well as the joy that theatre gave and continues to give me, found their way into that book. Unlike *The Innkeeper's Daughter,* the plot of *Fat Jack* turns out to be the perfect metaphor for the book's meaning. Both Shakespeare's play and my novel are tales of friendship and betrayal. Countless strands of my own life went into *Fat Jack,* but so thoroughly were they reworked into fiction by my imagination and technique that I can no longer separate them from each other.

Though I attended high school in the late forties, I taught high school on and off from the late fifties to the mid-seventies. I set *Fat Jack* not in my own high-school days, but in the sixties, when I was teaching. Still, the sixties was not the present. I had not written one single contemporary book. I was afraid to. I didn't think I could deal with problems like drugs, divorce, pregnancy, and early sex. I didn't want to deal with them.

Yet I felt a pressing need to write a novel which was set in the present. Unless I could escape my own adolescence, I was scared that I'd run out of material, that I'd have to stop writing. And then what would I do?

One day I had lunch with a young friend who was studying to be a rabbi at the Jewish Theological Seminary in New York. Like many rabbinical students, he supported himself by teaching in an afternoon Hebrew school at a synagogue. He taught the seventh-grade boys and girls studying for the Jewish confirmation ritual, called bar mitzvah. Jonathan told me about one of his students who'd been an absolute terror, leading the other kids in the class to heights of deviltry Jonathan had never even imagined. But then one day the rabbi of that temple realized that the boy's mother wasn't Jewish. According to traditional Jewish law, there are only two ways to become a Jew. You have to be born to a Jewish mother, or you have to undergo a formal conversion. Since this boy was not Jewish, there was no point in his continuing to study for his bar mitzvah. His friends envied his good luck. He never had to come to boring old Hebrew school again. But he didn't see it that way. He elected to undergo conversion, continue with Hebrew school, and celebrate his bar mitzvah.

"Talking to schoolchildren in Los Angeles," 1979

As with the carp ten years before, I couldn't shake that boy out of my head. Why had he misbehaved in class to start with? And then, why, if he hated Hebrew school so much, did he convert? My answers to those questions became *King of the Seventh Grade.* It seemed logical to me that the hero of my novel, Vic Abraham, should be the son of divorced parents, neither of whom had a lot of time for him. It seemed equally logical that he be part of a gang involved in shoplifting. Scarcely even thinking about it, I'd written a novel set in the present, dealing with contemporary problems. I was able to do it because the central issues of the book, Jewish identity and survival, have always been of great concern to me.

I learned some important things in writing *King of the Seventh Grade.* I learned that no writer has to deal with every issue in order to remain both honest and relevant. If I don't want to write about abused children or sex among twelve-year-olds, I don't have to. Those things are part of modern life, but they are not part of *every* modern life. For every kid who is abused, there are a dozen who are not. For every twelve-year-old who has sex, there are a dozen who don't. They're contemporary kids too.

The other thing I learned is that feelings don't change. The surface of contemporary life may be different from the surface of life when I was a kid. Kids today may know more about sex, drugs, and violence than we did. But being young was never easy. Childhood as a time of joy and innocence was an invention of Victorian sentimentalists. That view never reflected reality. Children since the beginning of time have matured by learning to cope with life as it is. This is and always has been the great task of childhood and the great theme of children's literature. I knew about trying to figure out your place in the world. I knew about trying to establish who you were. I knew about needing your parents and at the same time wanting to be free of them. I knew about being on the outside and hungering to get in. I knew about longing for friendship and love and feeling utterly unworthy of such gifts. These are the very same things kids today know about. Although my childhood experiences might be different from the childhood experiences of modern kids, my feelings had been the same as theirs. Therefore I could write a contemporary book. After *King of the Seventh Grade* I never again doubted that.

I even began writing about my own children. I had never tried to do that when they were little. I need at least fifteen years' distance from events to turn them into fiction. Before that their reality is too overwhelming. I don't know what to leave out, what to include. I'm too aware of what actually occurred to have the nerve to change anything. In order to write about experiences, I need to have partially forgotten them.

When Sara and Becky were young, they belonged to a club called the Four Seasons. The other two members were my sister's younger children, Judy and Harry. The advisor was my aunt, Frances Marshall. They met monthly at Fran's house, where we knew they consumed quantities of delicious food. Whenever a family celebration occurred, they put on an original play. But we knew no more than that. The rites and rituals of the Four Seasons, like those of the Masons or the Mormons, were a secret to which only its members were privy.

I tried several times to write about the Four Seasons, but I could never come up with a plot. I'd been toying for a while with a book about the confusion and discomfort I as a Jewish child had always felt around Christmastime. When I remembered that my children had experienced a similar discomfort, I knew I had my Four Seasons book—*The Christmas Revolution.* It was followed by the Four Seasons at the beach in *The Orphan Game.* The beach in this case is Long Beach Island, off the southern New Jersey coast, where my family and I have spent summers for over thirty years. When I wrote directly about my own childhood in the three Somerville Inn books, I set the novels in the time the events actually occurred, the late forties. In writing about my own children, I did not set the books in the late sixties and early seventies. I set them in the present. The actual time didn't seem to matter so much any more.

In *Coasting* I used later events in my children's lives, even though I wrote it earlier than the Four Seasons novels. Like me, all three of my daughters attended Barnard College. Sara and Becky both had particular eating habits and wished to cook for themselves, so they spent two years in a coed dorm containing suites with four or five single bedrooms, a bathroom, and a kitchen. Living more or less on their own in New York led to some interesting and occasionally upsetting adventures—upsetting to their mother anyway. Some of these found their way into *Coasting.* But I think the heroine, Mattie, is as much me as she is any of my daughters. She's all four of us, I suppose.

People Like Us is a "what if" novel. What if a girl like me who during her high-school years went largely unnoticed by the opposite sex, should have, by an unlikely but not impossible chance, attracted the attention of the very biggest of the big men on campus? But then what if this marvel of intelligence, athletic prowess, good looks, and general niceness should be someone of whom her family totally disapproved because he happened to be of a different religion? What would happen then? The novel which grew out of that dilemma is again contemporary in its setting. The terms in which I couched the battle between Dinah Adler and her family over her non-Jewish boyfriend are contemporary too. But Dinah's agonies and Dinah's dreams are very clearly the ones I knew when I was in high school.

Tell Us Your Secret is another matter. I think it's my only book which comes quite clearly from what happened to me as an adult. During the summer of 1986 I taught a two-week writing conference at the Masters School in Dobbs Ferry, New York. Thirteen students between fifteen and eighteen years old lived and worked together with three teachers for two weeks. It was the best teaching experience of my life. I knew even as I lived it that someday I would try to capture its unique excitement and tension in a novel.

As a Jew who was alive, even though very young, during the years of the Holocaust, I of course have been scarred for life by that event. I have not been scarred in anything like the way survivors or their children have been, but I do feel that in some sense any Jew over forty is a survivor. I thought I could never write about the Holocaust. I didn't have either the authenticity or the courage to do it. Nevertheless, the notion began to take hold of me that I *had* to try. It was my duty to find a way to force an adolescent to acknowledge the Holocaust. That was something I, as a writer of popular fiction, might be able to do better than some others.

My editor at Bantam told me to put the daughter of Holocaust survivors in the writers' conference book. I resisted for a while, but then I realized that by doing as she suggested, I'd give myself a way of dealing with material I'd otherwise find unbearable. I don't know whether I accomplished what I hoped for in *Tell Us Your Secret,* and I found writing the book painful. But I'm very glad my editor made me do it.

During the years that I was writing these novels, I was also producing picture storybooks—*The Binding of Isaac, I Am Joseph, Lovely Vassilisa, The Demon Who Would Not Die, Gooseberries to Oranges, Here Come the Purim Players!, Yussel's Prayer, The Secret Grove, Even Higher, The Donkey's Story,* and *Canterbury Tales.* Every one of those books was based on some source outside of my own experience: a story from the Bible, a folktale, the work of a classic writer, or an event in someone else's life. And yet I feel that these stories are as much my own as the more obviously autobio-

Family portrait, 1987: from left, the author; daughter Leah; Leah's husband, Steven Chatinover, holding their son; Becky's husband, Andrew Stewart; husband Gene; daughter Sara; daughter Becky

graphical books. They are like *Unicorns in the Rain, Seven Daughters and Seven Sons, Lovers' Games,* and *Roses.* I did each one because something in a tale I heard or read and loved connected with something inside of me which made me need to retell that story in my own words. Why do I as a picture book writer select one story to retell out of the thousands and thousands of stories which are available? Because that story in some way reflects my concerns, my needs, my feelings. In that story I find particular delight. I want to play with it. I want to do things with it which will make other people connect with it as I do, and love it too.

But not all my picture books come from sources outside my own experience. *First Fast* is about the same children, Leah and Harry, and the same Brooklyn neighborhood which figure in *The Carp in the Bathtub.* I gave them another holiday to celebrate, Yom Kippur this time instead of Passover. I went from a holiday in which eating is the main thing to one in which not eating is the main thing. My Lothrop editor wanted a Yom Kippur story, but she didn't like *First Fast.* It was finally published eight years after I'd written it by the Union of American Hebrew Congregations.

I did do a Yom Kippur story for Lothrop, however—*Yussel's Prayer,* a retelling of a Hassidic tale illustrated by Michael Deraney. My editor liked this one so much that she asked me to find another story for Michael to illustrate. This was in 1981, when my mother and husband sold their business. The day the deal was closed, we invited a few relatives to the Inn for dinner to mark my mother's retirement after forty-one years as the owner of the Somerville Inn. The kind of family storytelling which I remembered so clearly from childhood was a main feature of the evening. One of the guests was a cousin, Bette, the granddaughter of my grandfather's sister, Molly Hyman. Bette recounted an incident involving her mother and her grandmother which I'd never heard before. As a child, Bette's mother was told by her teacher to dress a clothespin doll like a pilgrim. Aunt Molly offered to help, but as a Russian Jewish immigrant to the United States, she didn't know about Thanksgiving, and had never heard of the Pilgrims.

"A pilgrim," Bette's mother explained, "is someone who came from the other side looking for religious freedom."

"That's me!" my great-aunt exclaimed. "I'm a

pilgrim!"

I realized immediately I had the basis for a text for Michael to illustrate. Not that it was a story. As with *The Carp* so many years before, I'd been presented with an anecdote. I had to find the conflict which would turn it into a story. I made the little girl a recent immigrant herself, one of those outsiders who'd been the main character in so many of my books, teased by her classmates, and struggling to find her place. I called the book *Molly's Pilgrim.*

The book struck a responsive chord in countless hearts. From the beginning, it was the most popular book I'd written. About a year after it appeared, a young man named Jeff Brown approached me about making it into a movie. He couldn't offer much of an advance, but I liked him and trusted him. What's more, he said I could be in the movie. *Thank You, Jackie Robinson* was the only other book of mine which had ever been filmed. Martin Tahse made it into an *ABC Afterschool Special* he called "Home Run for Love" in 1979. Because it was filmed in California, I was not involved in the production in any way. I thought it would be fun to see how a movie was made, so I told my agent to let Jeff have the film rights. "They're not standing in line to make this book into a movie anyway," I said.

Molly's Pilgrim was shot in Montclair, New Jersey, in January 1985. I didn't see the finished picture until Thanksgiving Eve. It was a low-budget film, but it didn't *look* like a low-budget film. I was pleased with the job Jeff had done. Then I more or less forgot about the whole thing.

But in February 1986, Jeff called with amazing news. *Molly* was one of three films nominated for an Academy Award in the Best Live Action Short Subject category. We all traipsed out to Los Angeles for the Oscar presentations, and sat in the Dorothy Chandler Pavillion with fingernails digging into our palms until our category was announced. *Molly* won! It may have won in a category no one present besides the nominees cared very much about, but its Oscar is just the same as all the others.

The funny thing about being associated with an Oscar, even a minor Oscar, is that everyone gets excited about it. My books have been American Library Association Notables and Best Young Adults. They've won National Jewish Book Awards and Association of Jewish Library prizes. They've appeared on innumerable lists, and earned praise from reviewers and librarians. No one outside of the children's book world has paid any attention whatsoever to any of this. But every neighbor, every long-lost relative, every old college chum now living in West Nerdsville, heard about the Oscar and wrote or called.

Barbara and Gene, with Oscar for "Home Run for Love," based on the author's book Molly's Pilgrim, *Los Angeles, 1986*

Well, it was fun, but it was not important. I don't make movies, I write children's books; so I'd rather win a Newbery any day. But the Newbery doesn't matter much either. What matters is doing the work you want to do the best way that you know how. I can tell you which parts of a book came out of my own experience and which from my imagination. But I can only tell you that once the book is finished. Though I rewrite and rewrite, when a book is done, I have the sense that it was written by a stranger. The process remains mysterious.

My husband once said to me, "You were twelve years old when you were born. You'll be twelve years old when you die." That's as close as I can get to the source of what I do. I'm still there, at twelve. I was always there. That's OK. It's worked out.

BIBLIOGRAPHY

FOR YOUNG PEOPLE

Fiction:

The Carp in the Bathtub (illustrated by Joan Halpern). New York: Lothrop, 1972; (paperback edition) Rockville, Md.: Kar Ben Copies, 1987.

Thank You, Jackie Robinson (illustrated by Richard Cuffari). New York: Lothrop, 1974; (paperback edition) New York: Scholastic Press, 1989.

Bitter Herbs and Honey. New York: Lothrop, 1976.

Where's Florrie? (illustrated by J. Halpern). New York: Lothrop, 1976.

Benny. New York: Lothrop, 1977.

The Binding of Isaac (illustrated by Charles Mikolaycak). New York: Lothrop, 1978.

R, My Name Is Rosie. New York: Lothrop, 1978; (paperback edition) New York: Scholastic Press, 1979.

The Innkeeper's Daughter. New York: Lothrop, 1979.

Fat Jack. New York: Atheneum, 1980.

I Am Joseph (illustrated by C. Mikolaycak). New York: Lothrop, 1980.

Lovely Vassilisa (retelling; illustrated by Anatoly Ivanov). New York: Atheneum, 1980.

Unicorns in the Rain. New York: Atheneum, 1980; (paperback edition) New York: Macmillan Collier, 1988.

Queen for a Day. New York: Lothrop, 1981.

Yussel's Prayer (retelling; illustrated by Michael Deraney). New York: Lothrop, 1981.

The Demon Who Would Not Die (retelling; illustrated by A. Ivanov). New York: Atheneum, 1982.

Gooseberries to Oranges (illustrated by Beverly Brodsky). New York: Lothrop, 1982.

King of the Seventh Grade. New York: Lothrop, 1982.

Seven Daughters and Seven Sons (retelling, with Bahija Lovejoy). New York: Atheneum, 1982.

Lovers' Games. New York: Atheneum, 1983; (paperback edition) New York: Putnam, 1985.

Molly's Pilgrim (illustrated by M. Deraney). New York: Lothrop, 1983.

Here Come the Purim Players! (illustrated by B. Brodsky). New York: Lothrop, 1984.

Roses (illustrated by John Steptoe). New York: Lothrop, 1984; (paperback edition) New York: Scholastic Press, 1986.

Coasting. New York: Lothrop, 1985.

The Secret Grove (illustrated by M. Deraney). New York: Union of American Hebrew Congregations, 1985.

The Christmas Revolution (illustrated by Diane de Groat). New York: Lothrop, 1987; (paperback edition) New York: Bantam, 1988.

Even Higher (retelling; illustrated by A. Ivanov). New York: Lothrop, 1987.

First Fast. New York: Union of American Hebrew Congregations, 1987.

People Like Us. New York: Bantam, 1987; (paperback edition) New York: Bantam, 1989.

Canterbury Tales (illustrated by Trina Schart Hyman). New York: Lothrop, 1988.

The Donkey's Story (illustrated by Susan Jeanne Cohen). New York: Lothrop, 1988.

The Orphan Game (illustrated by Diane de Groat). New York: Lothrop, 1988.

Tell Us Your Secret. New York: Bantam, 1989.

Mary Francis Shura Craig

1923-

Mary Francis Shura Craig, at home with her Llasa Apso, "Miss Pooh," 1984

Nothing is more astonishing to me than to hear people recount the events of their lives in the manner of Scheherazade in *The Book of a Thousand Nights and Night.* I stand in awe to hear them link their years together into a seamless cord joined only by the words, "And then—"

My own life, my childhood included, is a collection of bright scenes vividly recalled. These are full pictures, rich with sound and smell and color. Many of these early brilliant flashes of memory would never have made any sense to me except that I come from a very verbal family.

Because everyone talked all the time, sooner or later every mysterious scene was explained in the context of a family conversation. My father was a wit and my mother a storyteller. Our family didn't so much "eat" meals as talk and laugh its way through them. Since I was the youngest of four daughters, I had the last and fewest turns to talk. That was all right because I didn't know all those wonderful stories anyway.

Could I have made up a story about a red-haired great-grandmother winning a horse race in competition with her own husband on her wedding day? (The scene is very real. She rode sidesaddle in a velvet riding habit of forest green. She raised such a cloud of dust on that sun-baked Missouri road that all you would see was the ostrich feathers on her hat waving frantically for deliverance.)

Although I was born in western Kansas, the family moved to the Pacific Northwest when I was still an infant. When I returned to visit that ranch as an adult, I recognized it, not from pictures but from stories. Everything was there. A golden eagle nests in the ravine where "Wild Bill" Cody bedded down his herd of cattle for the night. He must have been young and agile back in 1861 because it's a difficult climb up the rock bluff to where he carved his name above that date.

One of my favorite stories, as a child, was of my mother's constant war against the western Kansas pack rats. I could just *see* them scurrying on swift legs, always with a stick between their teeth, the stick they would trade for the next thing they saw that they liked better. What they liked best of all was silver salad forks. The discovery of a stick in her silverware drawer was enough to send my mother into what my father called "a conniption fit." Nothing would do but all the men available must stop their work and dig up the pack rat burrow until the missing fork was found.

In addition to family narratives, my mother and sisters told me other stories, read books aloud to me, and chanted nursery verses. Somehow poetry and nursery rhymes were always linked to real life. My mother, opening the door on a pewter gray morning with rain polishing the sidewalk and dripping like liquid icicles from the trees and bushes, would turn

"Our family's ranch in western Canada. It's been in the family almost a hundred years now."

with a smile and chant:

One misty, moisty morning,
When cloudy was the weather,
I chanced to meet an old man
Clothed all in leather;

Since everyone knew the rest, the sisters would join in.

He began to compliment,
And I began to grin—
"How do you do?" and, "How do you do?"
And, "How do you do?" again!

And for some reason this was funny to all of us, so that it ended in laughter.

To me the natural world was simply stiff with stories. I knew that the old woman with her broom was swinging out there in her basket beyond the moon. I wondered how Mistress Mary could possibly walk in a garden with all those heavy seashells sewed to her dress. The shoe box full of cockle shells I had gathered on the beach was almost too heavy to lift down. And at night I knew the only reason I couldn't hear Wee Willie Winkie racing down the street was because my window was closed.

I loved the stories from all countries, not knowing then how various their sources were: "Three Billy Goats Gruff," "Molly Whuppie," "The Brave Little Tailor," and, of course, "Aladdin and His Wonderful Lamp."

But, like most mothers, mine considered housekeeping duties more pressing than a child's desire to be read to all day. The older sisters went off to school, curiously nervous about their clothes and twitching at their hair one last time in front of the hall mirror. With everyone busy or gone, I was alone with my pets and the silence. This silence between stories seemed endless. I knew the stories were hidden in other people's heads and the books that always cluttered our houses. The problem was to get them out.

We lived in Portland, Oregon then. I couldn't find the house there now for my life but many scenes of it are very clear. I vividly recall pushing one of my sisters off the second-story porch because she took my little red chair just as a parade started by. I probably remember that because of the spanking Mother gave me. She used her silver-backed hair brush which had chubby bas-relief cupids on the side that didn't have bristles. Both sides hurt.

Yellow roses bloomed on a curved trellis above

the front gate. I was not allowed outside the gate because of dangers. These perils were variously described. My mother said I would be hit by a car. One of my sisters whispered that an ax murderer waited in the underpass by the corner. The woman across the street said the gypsies would kidnap me because of my white skin and sun-bleached hair.

The last danger was the only interesting one. Sometimes we passed gypsy camps on family rides. I used to look very hard and very fast to see as much as I could before our car rolled on by. How lucky gypsies were, I thought, to get to live out-of-doors all the time. Those quick glimpses never showed me enough. I saw hasty-looking tents and women in bright dresses and scarves. Sometimes smoke trailed upward from a cooking fire and lost itself in the trees where laundry had been hung to dry. Whatever else, I always saw a lot of horses and children about. I had this awful dread that, even if I ran away and got past the car and the ax murderer, the gypsies wouldn't want me since they already had so many children of their own.

"I'm the baby with the fist in its face, shown with my three sisters and cousin "

The front porch of that house was supported by fat, white pillars I couldn't get my arms around. I loved to sit on the top step and lean back against one of those sun-warmed posts. There, with one arm around Sweet William, I would study the pictures in my sisters' books, trying to make up the stories that went with them. Sweet William was a beautiful cream-colored goat with wonderful knobby horns, golden eyes, and a rakish cocoa-colored beard. He was a remarkably satisfying companion. He ate everything I fed him and followed me anywhere I wanted to go, bleating congenially as we went. It never occurred to me to wonder why we had Sweet William and his wife Daisy until years later when a friend reacted with astonishment when I described them.

"Then you lived in the country," he said.

"Of course not," I told him.

"You had to," he insisted. "Else why did you keep goats?"

I had to call Mother long-distance to discover that one of my sisters had been allergic to cow's milk and the only way to obtain goat's milk was to keep one.

Sometimes I think my childhood was like a foreign movie with the subtitles hidden until years later.

My first breakthrough toward getting all the stories I wanted came with the realization that every time anyone sat down, he or she made a lap. This was my signal to come running, book in hand, begging this hapless victim to "Read me a story."

"Read to that child," Mother usually said. "Poor little thing. She's had to play by herself all day."

This enforced sisterly service led to the second break-through when I was four. My sisters, sick to death of *Grimm's Fairy Tales,* Kipling's *Jungle Book,* and Hawthorne's *Twice Told Tales,* taught me to read.

To learn to read was to master magic. I have never lost a sense of wonder that the flat magic of ink on paper can create worlds more real and enduring than the one in which I have beds to make and teeth to brush. The books I practically memorized in the next few years still enrich my life. How many times have I seen a portly older man wheeling along a freeway in an open car and recognized Toad from *Wind in the Willows*? The White Queen from *Through the Looking Glass* is still alive and well (in modern dress) struggling with her fur stole and wisps of hair in the parking lots of shopping malls.

From that time on I balanced the two worlds precariously in my mind, the world of the stories and the brief and brilliant scenes of real life. My head was remarkably like a canning jar. I could only cram so

Mary, at a young age, with doll and buggy

many words into it before they started spilling out. At first I only made up verses (which my mother stoutly insisted were poems). Then, having drowned myself in fairy stories, I swam around in them as a character.

I became little Hans. His was the natural role for me, as a youngest child, to assume. In my own stories I always earned the classic offer of three magic wishes. (The hand of the princess always seemed a rather silly prize because everyone *I* knew, including myself, already had two hands.)

Since I certainly didn't want to waste those wishes when they came along as the characters in the stories always did, I thought a great deal about what I would ask for. Changing my mind about this list became a major distraction throughout my childhood. I like to think that is when I first learned the painful craft of revision.

During those years we moved to Spokane, Washington, a city I principally remember for the swift tumbling river that flows through its heart. Next to oceans I like rivers the best. They have as distinctly separate personalities as people to me.

I love the broad tranquil face of the American River as it flows through Sacramento, California. It is a Mona Lisa river, bland and smiling while it hides the gold that seduced a generation of Americans to leave their painted houses and plowed fields to seek gold in a hostile wilderness.

Not even the modern grocery store a few hundred yards from the Charles River in Concord, Massachusetts, can dissipate the sense of history that quivers my spine when I stand on its banks. I have more favorite rivers than I can list but the James River is special. There you can almost see America breathe, drawing the salt water of the ocean into its blood stream clear to the fall line, even as the continent drew those early immigrants into its mingled lifeline.

My father, whom I loved dearly, became very ill about the time I started school. My mother went to work and I became the responsibility of my older sisters and my invalid father.

There is no wind so ill that it doesn't blow kindly on a child. As the youngest, I was the first one home in the afternoon. I got to make tea and toast for my father and sit with him until the long-legged older people came home with their fresh supplies of stories and adventures.

I wasn't very good at school. It was boring and tedious and took place indoors. Since I already knew how to read and didn't like numbers, I spent that first year either in the cloakroom or in the principal's office for the crime of entertaining myself. The teacher variously defined my behavior as impudence or mischief. My father listened to my daily reports with a straight face and twinkling brown eyes so dark that you could hardly see the black of his pupils.

"You are a strange one, kitten," he would say, shaking his head over my future he could neither predict nor live to witness.

I thought I was strange, too. I knew I was naughtier than other children because everybody told me that. Since my head was always off in some strange other place, I was careless about my clothes. Only after I reached school was I really sorry that I had put a safety pin in my torn hem instead of asking a sister to sew it back up. The other children all looked very sure of themselves with their buttons on tight and their white cotton stockings fitting their legs as if they had grown there. My stockings were camel colored. In fact they were *like* camels in that they wrinkled around my knees and bagged at the ankles. Almost all the kids had blue eyes and mine were dark, "like two burned holes in a blanket," my ill-tempered great-aunt told me.

It took me a thousand years to realize that I had not invented self-consciousness, and that behind the smooth foreheads of my peers were hidden the same self-doubts and fears that cringed behind my own.

During these years I became a library hound. My library had rules about how many books a child could check out at a time. Only by checking out the maximum number and coming back the next day for a new set, did I finally break down that iron barrier. For the rest of my life I have managed to check out as many books as I could carry without staggering, which is the proper number of books one should always take home from a library.

My father died one dark Thanksgiving Day with the wind whipping sleet along our wintry street. I missed him with an anguish that no one would let me express because I was too young to understand. I have remained desolate at this loss forever except for the vivid scenes of those wonderful private afternoon tea parties that have never faded in all these years.

About that time I discovered another activity that was almost as much fun as making up stories. I realized that if you look at anything long enough, you see the shape hidden within it. Once you see that shape, you can draw anything you can look at. Since my sisters were all too happy not to have me tagging along or hanging on them, they left me to my wonderful private world of words and lines on paper.

Much later, when I was old enough to study history, I realized I had grown up during something called The Depression. I'm afraid I had to learn about it in books. I was never hungrier than any other growing kid and I thought every little girl waited impatiently for her sisters to outgrow things so she could wear them.

Two important adults entered my life about then, a wonderful couple known to me as Whitie and Uncle Walt. Since they lived between school and our house, Whitie often hailed me in from the storm on wintry afternoons. She warmed me with hot chocolate, wonderful tea muffins with tops like the hats of elves, and a friendship which was to endure for forty years. She was a gifted poet and the first writer I ever met. Uncle Walt taught me to play chess, one of the two games I really enjoy, and treated me with the same teasing gentleness that my father had.

The Whites offered Mother their lodge on Twin Lake in Idaho so that all four of us girls could be away from the city during the summer months. We left for the lodge on the last day of school and went back to the city on Labor Day.

The lake offered me paradise. Although my sister Jackie was always there for me with love and listening, my freedom was almost absolute. I watched tadpoles turn into frogs the size of my thumbnail, and held my breath to hang in under the wooden dock with my eyes open to watch the fish come near to examine me. I picked huckleberries in the woods, cracked pine nuts between stones, chewed sorrel leaves for the sour, hot, splendid taste I still love, and went fishing.

The only boat I was allowed to take out by myself was a flat boat which was lined with floral, waterproof cushions. It was difficult to row but I never used the oars very long. The splash of rowing scares away the wild things. Once the boat was a few yards out into the lake, the current picked it up and carried it along.

The best time to go was at dawn. I lay flat on the cushions on my belly watching with my chin on my arms. The boat followed the current into a green cove where turtles sunned on rotting logs and white-tailed deer brought their fawns to drink. There I saw my first and last cougar in the wild. His coat was the color of warm buttered toast and his eyes luminous. I was afraid and then insulted when he wriggled his nose as if I smelled bad and backed off to disappear into the woods. I told myself it was my fear that smelled bad, not me.

Small silvery perch were thick beneath the pads of the water lilies there. No matter how many I brought in, they were all exactly the same size. Back at the lodge, Jackie cooked them for our breakfast.

Time seems suspended during the summer in chaparral country, the halfway mark between the cessation of the spring rains and the slow pattering that refreshes the world with the coming of October. The needle carpet of the pine forest was layered with dust and the sky a formidable blue. Water spiders skated on the gleaming tension of the water below me and dark droplets of tadpoles swayed in the shallows.

The summer that I was eight years old, I lay along the prickly limb of a pine tree overhanging that wonderful glacial lake and knew what I was going to do for the rest of my life.

I would love to be able to say that I *decided* to be a writer. I might even be more comfortable if I could claim some mystical calling to the craft. It wasn't that way at all. I simply knew that since I was going to write, I needed to be aware of everything around me with a heightened intensity. I even knew *what* I wanted to write. I wanted to tell stories on paper. I have never deluded myself into thinking that I had any great message to impart, nor that fame, fortune, or eminence was involved. I wanted to quicken breath and touch hearts. I wanted to make the flat magic of ink on paper.

Finding out who you are changes you. That early recognition twisted a genial, indolent child into an abnormally contented but disciplined workaholic. But no matter how hard I work at it, I am always still learning to write. One is never through, you know.

Writing is not a craft but a lifelong apprenticeship.

Teaching myself to write was not easy. Poetry came more easily than fiction because I had good guidance early. Armed with the necessary self-confidence of a creator, I began to produce an endless stream of loosely rhythmic free verse.

One of my teachers who was not an admirer of juvenile hubris, pulled me up short. He had seen how carefully I designed the structures of my drawings, and cunningly used a simile I couldn't deny.

He showed me a book, filled with art of a kind I had never seen. The picture I remember I now recognize as Duchamp's *Nude Descending a Staircase.* He told me to study it until I could see the picture behind the picture.

Although I couldn't find it, I knew that what the artist had done was mysteriously successful. At that point the teacher posed his question. "Could the artist have done this painting without learning to draw first?"

When I admitted that he probably couldn't, he accused me of doing that very thing with poetry. He gave me a book in which every known form of poetry was explained and demonstrated. "Do one of each of these forms," he said. "Not just an exercise but a readable example. *Then* you may slop around in free verse all you want to."

For at least three years I didn't even try to write another story. I was too busy trying to wrestle the angel of poetry to the ground. The painted chest at the foot of my bed bulged with ballads and limericks, triolets and rondelets. By the time I had done both Shakespearian and Petrarchian sonnets that I would not have been ashamed to show him, my family had moved to a different part of the country and into a different world and I had forgotten his name. This saddens me because he had thrown a beam of light into one of the dark corners of my understanding. He had taught me that even as the human form is dictated by its bony skeleton, literary forms must have structure if their creatures are to rise and walk and dance with the semblance of life.

"On the Pacific, the ocean of my childhood," 1973

Both my parents had come from old, restless pioneering families who had made their way west from Virginia through Kentucky to Missouri. Mother's roots, in the form of her ailing mother, drew her back home, and I had my first, nearly terminal, case of culture shock.

Everything was wrong.

Summer smelled of mowed grass instead of dust on layers of pungent pine. The trees dropped their leaves in winter. It rained any old time it wanted to. There were chiggers in the grass and cicadas in the trees, and no ocean you could drive to. The people took forever to get their words out and absolute strangers stopped me on the street to say I had eyes like my grandfather's. I missed the Pacific Northwest as if a piece of myself had dropped off somewhere between *my* mountains, the Sierra Cascades, and *their* mountains, the Rockies.

I had always read too much, according to my mother who had stuffy ideas about little girls doing helpful domestic things around the house. I buried myself in reading in that new place. What I lacked in discrimination, I made up for in diligence. I read Thomas Hardy and Edgar Rice Burroughs, Sir Walter Scott and Rider Haggard, and an entire shelf of Oz books. I submerged myself in the British writers whose endless books were custom-designed for insatiable readers—Defoe, Dickens, Thackeray, Austen, the Brontës, and George Eliot. Without abandoning poetry, I retreated into trying to explain the world to myself through stories.

I still wasn't the greatest at school. Horrid scene! I *was* good at spelling and made it to the end of an important (for me) spelling bee. I went down on the spelling of the word "aeon" because that was the way it was spelled in my poetry books. No one ever had to explain the word injustice to me after that.

When I wrote my first "book," I really didn't think I was showing off. I was only trying to make an end run around boredom. When a seventh-grade teacher assigned a notebook report on nutrition, I did all twenty-odd pages of it in the metric form used by Longfellow in *Evangeline.* My startled teacher showed it to an aunt of hers who was a writer and artist. Rose O'Neill invited us to dinner in her home in the Ozark mountains.

A scene again, since all my life is made of scenes. I had brand-new patent leather shoes which wouldn't bend with my feet. We rode forever in a wooded darkness crushed down by stars. Only after crossing a wooden bridge did we reach the house. It was dimly lit and strangely built and decorated with massive paintings on all the walls. Rose O'Neill herself was a genial cherub topped by a cloud of white hair. She wore some long garment of rich dark red belted by a gold-colored rope with tassels. She talked to me of the responsibility of being gifted. Talent, she said, comes unsought and unearned, and therefore is no occasion for pride. On the contrary, it brings with it an obligation. You must nourish it, be generous with it, and be humble in the presence of others less generously endowed.

I was petrified. Since the age of eight I had listened to well-meaning adults deliver cautionary lectures to me about writing.

Didn't I know that writers lived alone (except for rats) in cold garrets and starved to death?

And what in the world did I have to say that anyone wanted to read?

Yet here was this remarkable woman fixing me with her glittering eyes and telling me that I not only *should* write but also *had to.*

This was the second writer I had met. Both the contacts had been enabling. Whitie had given me not only a peer variety of friendship, but had provided me with the freedom and solitude to discover myself. Rose O'Neill had placed on me the obligation of excellence.

Curiously enough, when writers gather as friends, you hear variations of this story over and over. Almost every writer I know had an early and deeply affective contact with another working writer.

My first work was published when I was fourteen. It was a poem. Its appearance on a printed page was so astonishing to me that I couldn't even tell anyone about it, and blushed and stammered when it was mentioned. I did the ordinary writer things in high school, news items for the school paper, serving as co-editor of the yearbook. Europe was going to pieces under the boots of tyrants and I won first prize in the state with a pacifist poem, probably the only political poem I have ever written.

Although this was a small high school in a small Missouri town, its faculty included two teachers I still remember as extraordinary human beings, my Latin teacher, Miss Titus, and my French teacher, Mr. Brown. To a child already in love with words, the study of other languages is exhilarating. Words which had been single bites in my mouth broke into delicious crumbs of combined separate meanings. A peninsula became "almost an island." Sabotage became "destruction by a wooden shoe." Instead of a lover of words, I became an addict. As a consequence, I am convinced that our wonderful English language has no true synonyms and that the resonance of effective writing rises from precision in word choice.

As a hedge against the disastrous lives of writers described by everyone except my mentors, I became an art major in college. By the time the war was over, I was married with a child. I applied for my first real job in the art department of a greeting card company. When they learned of my publishing record, I was hired instead as a writer and have never done a thing with my art training. I take that back. I'm a far more accomplished doodler than I would have been otherwise.

And all this time I wrote stories. I stopped once for a few years when my distraction with the make-believe world interfered with the happiness of the real people in my household. Once this problem passed, I flew back to my own reality.

It's difficult to describe the years of my middle life without invading the privacy of my family, which I consider unethical. Suffice it to say that I struggled very happily to balance a family that included a husband and three children. I ran a Girl Scout Troop, was a Boy Scout Den Mother, knitted sweaters, baked cakes, grew gardens, taught Sunday School, and wrote short stories.

Two important things relative to writing happened during this period. While everyone else complained of the postal service, my stories seemed to fly back to my desk as if they were homing pigeons with jet engines. A friend who was as wise as he was good gave me a lifeline to pull myself back from the despair of printed rejection slips.

"Never take a rejection personally," he said. "The editor is not rejecting *you,* just that particular story."

The other event was an illumination in my own understanding. I have always wished that my breakthroughs would come as they do in the comics, with a light bulb appearing over the head of the troubled character, shedding brilliance on the problem at hand. Instead, this understanding came as a slow dawning on what I realized was a very dim wit—my own.

My stories tended to be chains of linked events, one after another, as if I were saying, "And then. And then." My own life, however, had not left me with a narrative chain but a series of vivid scenes. Perhaps that was what life really was—glowing, textured settings in which people confronted and resolved, and moved on to new confrontations, new resolutions.

The scenes were, then, miniature stories in themselves with one important difference. Always, instead of a neat and tidy ending, one knew that the balance which had been restored was already threatened again. The concept was lively and somehow physical, rather like walking. In order to step forward, you must temporarily throw your body off balance. The step stabilizes you. You can only stop this process of unbalancing and balancing by standing absolutely still.

At that point I really stopped seeing a story as a continuum but saw it in terms of individual scenes with an ultimate destination. I experimented with writing the closing scene first, then going back and writing the scenes that led up to it. The stories began to sell in astonishing numbers.

For a long time I was embarrassed to talk about this curious approach to fiction, certain that, although my stockings no longer wrinkled at the knees, I still was passing strange. Yet the method had an incontestable logic to it. After all, I set out on other journeys the same way. How delighted I was to learn later that at least some other writers approached their work in the same perverse manner. Truman Capote also wrote his endings before his beginnings. Vladimir Nabokov simply wrote scenes in whatever order they came alive in his mind and shuffled them into the proper sequence to form a story.

During the summer before my husband's very premature death, I wrote my first book. I felt as if I had read a million children's books by then. I had sold about three hundred stories, and a generous fistful of poems. I decided that it would be fun to write a child's book that had everything *I* liked in it, a true exercise in self-indulgence.

The list was hard to limit because I like almost everything. I finally narrowed it down to animals, good things to eat, hidden treasure, games and songs, a tree house, and grownups who are hilariously funny and have no idea that they are. And, of course, the obligatory main character had to be the result of my final decision of what I would ask for when I was offered my magical three wishes. The book had to have an enchanted character in it whom adults couldn't see, but who could do anything I asked it to when there were only children around.

This book was *Simple Spigott,* published by Alfred A. Knopf in January of 1960, six months after my husband's death. The book was well reviewed and listed in World Book Encyclopedia's "One Hundred Best Children's books of 1960." All this was lovely but the book's success was meaningful for me for a very odd reason. What it said to me was, "Other people *do* like what you do. They *do* want to hear what you have to say." *Simple Spigott* was presented as a three-part TV mini-series on Japanese public television with puppets in 1986 and repeated in 1988. I was delighted and validated all over again.

A few years and a few books later, I remarried and had one more child. I am now divorced and live quite amicably (on my own part) with an aging Llasa Apso whom I call Miss Pooh. Her *real* name is "Winnie the Pooh" but she's not at all the kind of dog person who encourages first name familiarity. For any reader who is curious as to exactly how badly she behaves, she appears in *The Josie Gambit* as Miss Pod. I was using her first name in the writing of the book but she glared at me so crossly that I finally relented and gave her a pseudonym. I even halfway concealed her identity in the book's dedication by simply referring to her as "The White Queen." As I said, I live amicably. Miss Pooh can be, and usually is, quite contentious.

Which brings me to one of the five questions children most often ask me. "Do you use real people or your own children in books?" The answer, of course, is that I do not. When people ask, I always laugh and say that I don't use my children because they are almost all bigger than I am and know attorneys. The true reason is that I don't think it's fair to them. I always think of Christopher Robin Milne growing to great age and dignity and still having people ask him about his teddy bear. While that's not likely to happen to one of my children, I choose not to take the risk.

However, I have always loved animals and been happiest living with them about. I always use real animals in my stories because then I know their personalities will ring true. Also, if the book is lucky, the animal will get to live on in the minds of readers well past its natural life span.

"Tui (right), the goat who saves the day in Chester, Eleanor, *and* Jefferson, *with daughters"*

Ever since Sweet William, I have loved goats. Since I write about what I like, my books are rich in goats. I borrowed the antics of my cousin Jack's pets for the three goats Rick, Tick and Tawny in the book *Run Away Home.* The only problem I encountered in writing about goats is that few editors have had the good fortune to have had a goat friend. Therefore, they are occasionally hard to convince that goats are either as bright or as playful as they really are.

Tui, the big yellow goat who belongs to Chester's family in the companion books, *Chester, Eleanor,* and *Jefferson,* is also a real goat. She belongs to my son who lives on an old gold-mining ranch on the western slope of the Sierra Cascades. Tui is not a beautiful goat as Sweet William was, but she is far more interesting. Having grown up with dogs, she chases cars with some fairly dire consequences. It amazes me that no matter what crisis happens to the kids in the neighborhood of the Millard C. Fillmore School (the setting for *Chester, Eleanor,* and *Jefferson*), Tui manages to become the heroine of the book.

The piranha King, in the same set of books, is also a real fish who was fourteen years old when I put him in the first book. I could go on and on. The German Shepherd in *Mister Wolf and Me* was our own Guspodin Volkov III, a sable and silver German Shepherd who won the heart of everyone who knew him.

And even as I don't believe in made-up animals, I like precise and authentic settings. My books are always set in actual places and the people in them live in real homes. *Simple Spigott* is set on the tiny farm where we lived when the children were little. *The Barkley Street Six-Pack* takes place in our house on Palm Hill in Marin County, California. *Mister Wolf and Me* is set in Harvard, Massachusetts where Miles lives in our house on Partridge Hill Road on Bare Hill. The great Victorian house which appears in both *Don't Call Me Toad!* and as Aunt Harriett's home in *The Sunday Doll* has sat for almost a hundred years on a high hill overlooking the confluence of the Platt and Missouri Rivers in Nebraska.

When I don't *have* the right house for a book, I borrow one. Fortunately my friends are generous.

One friend, who has been my editor as well, has lent me her brownstone on Cobble Hill in Brooklyn for two books. She didn't mind my making it haunted in *Happles and Cinnamunger,* but I wore her patience a bit thin during the writing of *The Search for Grissi.* My passion for accuracy makes me thoughtless. When I called and asked her to go upstairs, lie on a bed in a certain bedroom, and tell me how many of the towers on the World Trade Building she could see, it was really too much. But she was a good sport and did it.

"Talking with kids," at one of many school presentations

The one question that both adults and children most often ask is, "Where do story ideas come from?" This is also the most difficult question to answer because each book begins with a separate and different recognition.

The beginning is not a story and often not even an idea. It can be something I see, or think, or feel, or hear. But at that special moment it is almost as if I hear a chiming in my head. I recognize what I have just experienced as belonging to me. I know it has a place in a story but I don't have any idea what the story is, or even what it is about. It is almost as if the chiming represented the sound of a seed falling into my mind.

I know from experience that if I let it alone and don't poke at it, it will grow. Like the sand grain inside an oyster's shell, it will be coated over and added to and changed until, every time I go back to look at it, it will be different.

Stories are about people. The people in a growing book come to me shadowy and secret. I watch them and wait for them to grow. One of them will step from the shadows first and I will know that I've met my main character. Again I have that thrill of recognition. I *know* that child. By the time I have seen the child's face in my mind and discovered its name, the scenes begin. I see the character living his own life in strong colorful scenes. The scenes begin to multiply at a great rate. Instead of one, there will be several people and each of them will have things they expect of themselves and each other.

In a lot of ways this is the most trying time of the whole book. Writing is really only thinking written down. But this is not the ordinary real-life kind of thinking. This thinking isn't the same as deciding whether you'll need a raincoat by the time you come home, or wishing that your friend would call and tell you how the party came out.

You simply watch the scenes and wait for the character to reveal himself to you. Since I have never won any prizes for patience, by this point I am bursting with curiosity. I want to know every single thing about this person. What does he like to eat? What does he love and what does he fear? Who are his friends and why did he choose them? Is he neat or messy, athletic or bookish, shy or confident? I have to know how he feels about subjects which will never arise in the book. I have to know all these things if I am to live inside this character's consciousness as the book is being written. All stories have problems. I have to know his problem and how he will solve it, because that will be the ending of the book. In short, I hand him the keys to the city and listen until his voice and those of his friends start echoing through its streets.

The voice is what I have waited for. By the time I first hear the voice of the book, the story has become too big for my head and I have to get it out and write down the ending.

The reader has a perfect right to say, "But that's ridiculous. Those characters have to come from *somewhere.* The story has to come from *somewhere.*"

True. The somewhere it comes from is where it grew, in the writer's mind. The brain is always described as being "gray matter." Maybe it begins gray but it picks up color with use. A good working brain is very like that wad of mixed and tangled yarn that you sometimes find in the bottom of a knitter's basket. Blue and green and black and white and the orange from Raggedy Ann's hair are all knotted in together like a whimsical bird nest.

In the process of the growing of the story, the character has pulled from that tangled heap of experience the little scraps of truth that the writer has claimed for his own. He dresses himself in them, gray for loneliness, a clear, transparent shivering for inadequacy, a little rose for laughter, and the dark tones of anger and resentment.

He is not the author. He is not anyone the author has ever known. He is a "possible" person by which the writer (to paraphrase James Stephens) clothes the naked and shivering thought in words to make it visible.

If you know the writer well and are patient, you can untangle those threads and follow them back to their sources. I have written too many books with too many of these dream children to labor anyone with a catalogue of them, but even I can see the strands and one isn't supposed to be able to see the mote in one's own eye.

My remembered childhood was happy. This combination of love and teasing and open communication is the kind of family background that appears over and over in my books without my planning it that way. Sometimes the mothers in my books work out of the home as my own mother did after my father's death. Sometimes they work inside the home as I almost always have. My character opens the door to the house I have chosen for him and an animal bounds out, something spicy is simmering on the stove, and somebody calls out a greeting. Or he turns a key in the lock and gets down his own peanut butter and jelly, then curls gratefully into the solitude I cherished as a child.

Some strands are as visible to me as they are important. Over and over, in such books as *The Seven Stone,* and the *Chester, Eleanor,* and *Jefferson* companion books, I have dealt with such warm, supportive relationships between older and younger siblings as I had with my sister Jackie.

During a lifetime of playing chess and tennis (which are both exercises in strategy) I have been aghast to see people use aggressive warlike strategies against each other in life. Freaky in *The Josie Gambit* came to me with the same shocked understanding but did something about it.

Peter Gregory, in *The Search for Grissi,* moving and disoriented as I had been so many times, also got the artist strand which has given me pleasure all my life. With a sister like his, bless her, he deserved an unearned gift.

I must mention one more strand. Starting clear back with Whitie and Uncle Walt, all my life I have been rich in older friends, and so have my children. The special rapport that springs up between the young and the old is not a well-kept secret. An automatic built-in compatibility comes with leap-frogging a generation. We human beings begin slowly, leaning against a porch pillar and hugging a goat. A single afternoon is a working definition of eternity. Life steadily picks up speed in the middle, "getting and spending" the poet called it. Finally, with greater age, comes the delicious slowing down when one has time to watch a spider spin a whole web without guilt.

The writing of dynamic fiction lays on the writer the obligation to test his protagonist with every impediment that can logically fall in his path. To do otherwise is to dilute the character's triumph in the story to a weak and pallid brew. But I know this possible child and love him or her for his imperfections as well as his commitments. Over and over I find myself giving a protagonist the sometimes crotchety companionship of an aging friend. When Emmy of *The Sunday Doll* first came out of the shadows, vibrating with resentment, and torn by confusion, Aunt Harriett was right behind her, not smiling, but watching and waiting.

I have never before dealt at such length or in such detail with my real life. Fiction writers are squids, inking the water about themselves to escape discovery. But mine has been a life of words, other people's and my own. When I am "in book," there is no other reality. Wallpaper can peel in fringed strips and the Loch Ness monster take up residence in the guest bathroom.

But books have last chapters, and when I have reached the last line of the last chapter of a book, its entire world collapses.

To paraphrase a cliche, a funny thing happens on the way to the publishing house.

A gray desolation overwhelms me. I know, by sad

repetitive experience, that this creature I have constructed and nurtured and suffered for will begin to fade when I mail away that manuscript and expose it to alien eyes.

He will fade, not all at once, but very like the Cheshire cat in *Through the Looking Glass,* he will become thinner and more translucent until the leaves show through his face. Restless, disoriented and lonely, I have to fly into another book to find comfort.

Sometimes, after a character is neatly entombed in a book, he will tweak at me and plunge me into tears at the sadness of my loss. These moments are rare and brief but I cherish them as one cherishes the memory of a lost "real" person.

The same early recognition that informed me that I was a writer bent my life in strange ways. I'm not very good company because I'm not always there for the companion. I'm not at all good at accepting the judgments of other people about anything. I can't afford to. If I am to be an honest writer I have to know, not what a society thinks about something, but what rings as truth to me.

Defining the world for yourself may sound like reinventing the wheel, but it is really the process of finding the wheel that will roll for you. Given time, the writer as human becomes the creature of his own definitions.

Mind you, one doesn't grope for these definitions in order to preach, or teach, or even to convince. They form the ground on which the writer stands to launch his words into unseen air.

Every once in a while, a child will ask me, "Do you start with a theme?"

I recoil in horror, feeling like Aesop without sandals.

The theme is the last to come. Every story is a love story. Unless your character loves something deeply enough to take uncharacteristic risks in its cause, you do not have a story. This can be anything—another human, a much loved animal, a country under threat. The point is not the object but the commitment. I believe that any time human beings stretch themselves to the fullness of their possible stature, meaning rises from their story as mist rises from the face of a river, naturally, gracefully, and silently.

When that meaning transcends the specific to embrace the universal, the work becomes art.

To be absolutely candid, I don't worry about that. I only keep trying to do what I have always wanted to do—quicken breath and touch hearts with the flat magic of ink on paper.

And listen for the faint chiming of recognition.

The author, taping a program for a cable network, Chicago, Illinois, 1987

BIBLIOGRAPHY

FOR CHILDREN

Fiction, under name Mary Francis Shura:

Simple Spigott. (Illustrated by Jacqueline Tomes) New York: Knopf, 1960; (illustrated by Sarah Garland) London: Hamilton, 1967.

The Garret of Greta McGraw (illustrated by Leslie Goldstein). New York: Knopf, 1961.

Mary's Marvelous Mouse (illustrated by Adrienne Adams). New York: Knopf, 1962.

The Nearsighted Knight (illustrated by A. Adams). New York: Knopf, 1964.

Run Away Home (illustrated by James Spanfeller). New York: Knopf, 1965.

Shoe Full of Shamrock (illustrated by N. M. Bodecker). New York: Atheneum, 1965.

A Tale of Middle Length (illustrated by Peter Parnall). New York: Atheneum, 1966.

Backwards for Luck (illustrated by Ted CoConis). New York: Knopf, 1967.

Pornada (illustrated by Erwin Schachmer). New York: Atheneum, 1968.

The Valley of the Frost Giants (illustrated by Charles Keeping). New York: Lothrop, 1971.

The Seven Stone (illustrated by Dale Payson). New York: Holiday House, 1972.

The Shop on Threnody Street. New York: Grosset & Dunlap, 1972.

Topcat of Tam (illustrated by Charles Robinson). New York: Holiday House, 1972.

The Riddle of Raven's Gulch (illustrated by Salem Tamer). New York: Dodd, 1975.

The Season of Silence (illustrated by Ruth Sanderson). New York: Atheneum, 1976.

The Gray Ghosts of Taylor Ridge (illustrated by Michael Hampshire). New York: Dodd, 1978.

The Barkley Street Six-Pack (illustrated by Gene Sparkman). New York: Dodd, 1979.

Mister Wolf and Me (illustrated by Konrad Hack). New York: Dodd, 1979.

Chester (illustrated by Susan Swan). New York: Dodd, 1980.

Happles and Cinnamunger (illustrated by Bertram M. Tormey). New York: Dodd, 1981.

My Friend Natalie. New York: Scholastic, 1982.

Eleanor (illustrated by S. Swan). New York: Dodd, 1983.

Jefferson (illustrated by S. Swan). New York: Dodd, 1984.

The Search for Grissi (illustrated by Ted Lewin). New York: Dodd, 1985.

Tales from Dickens. New York: Scholastic, 1985.

The Josie Gambit. New York: Dodd, 1986.

Don't Call Me Toad! (illustrated by Jacqueline Rogers). New York: Dodd, 1987.

The Sunday Doll. New York: Dodd, 1988.

FOR YOUNG ADULTS

Fiction, under name Mary Francis Shura:

The Silent Witness. 1983.

My Roommate Is Missing. 1983.

Jessica. New York: Scholastic, 1984.

Marilee. New York: Scholastic, 1985.

The Wrong Side of Love. 1985.

Gabrielle. New York: Scholastic, 1987.

FOR ADULTS

Fiction, under name Mary Craig:

A Candle for the Dragon. New York: Dell, 1973.

Ten Thousand Several Doors. New York: Hawthorn, 1973.

The Cranes of Ibycus. New York: Hawthorn, 1974.

Were He a Stranger: A Novel of Suspense. New York: Dodd, 1978; London: 1979.

Fiction, under name M. S. Craig:

The Chicagoans: Dust to Diamonds. New York: Jove, 1981.

To Play the Fox. New York: Dodd, 1982.

Gillian's Chain: A Novel of Suspense. New York: Dodd, 1983.

The Third Blonde: A Novel of Suspense. New York: Dodd, 1985.

Flashpoint. New York: Dodd, 1987.

Fiction, under name Mary S. Craig:

Dark Paradise. New York: Warner Books, 1986.

Fortune's Destiny. New York: Ace Books, 1986.

Shirley Glubok

Shirley, age three, "holding up a classical column"

It all seems so very long ago. Some people recall their childhood as if it were yesterday, but I could hardly remember anything about mine until I went back to St. Louis where it all began. After my family moved away I had returned to my birthplace only once, in 1969, to lecture at the library in the neighborhood where I grew up.

Then, last spring, I was invited to speak at a children's book conference at Southwest Missouri State University. Another St. Louis author, whom I met at the conference, drove me from Warrensburg to St. Louis. On the way we talked about growing up in our hometown. She writes stories that draw on her experience and could speak easily about her past, but I could think only of my present.

I had been warned that St. Louis has changed a great deal but I found that in many ways it is the same. When we zipped in from the highway onto the street where my new friend lives, I felt comforted. Even though the neighborhood I had grown up in was miles away, this was a street I knew well, and now it was just as I had remembered it. Appearing in a familiar area with a new friend was a welcome combination. Suddenly the trip I had dreaded for so long became a solace.

Once back at the "source" I was finally able to begin looking back on my childhood, and I realized that delving into my memory was an activity I had never allowed myself to enjoy, partly because I have always been too busy with the present to have a place in my mind for reliving the past. I have a tendency to block out memories, for if they are good memories I would regret their passing, and if bad, would be glad they are over. I once read a book by a famous actress that began with her admission that she never kept a diary because "once a day is gone it's gone." I more or less agree.

Now that I am finally looking backwards after all these years, it seems that everything I have become was predictable. My life must have been laid out for me from the beginning. Thinking about this makes me wonder if some of us determine at an early age who we are going to be and what we are going to do, then spend the rest of our lives acting it out. "Shirley was born wanting to be a writer," I heard my mother say to someone after I spoke at a luncheon. There was never any question in my mind. I inherited this ambition from Mother, who had a natural talent for writing but could not do much of it because she had a husband, three children, and two fashionable retail stores to look after. She expressed herself beautifully, wrote a few short stories as a young woman, and continued to send me exquisite letters all her life.

Mother had inherited the talent to write from her own mother, my maternal grandmother, who was never able to fulfill her own desire for a literary career because she had nine children to look after. Our ancestors in Europe had been scholars for

"With my brothers, Allan and Norman, and my favorite cousin, Maurice (far right)"

"My father and mother with me, Norman, and Maurice"

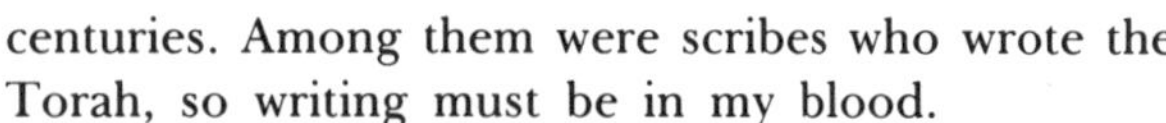

centuries. Among them were scribes who wrote the Torah, so writing must be in my blood.

Some people can express themselves well in speech but I find it easier to put my feelings down on paper. When I was in the fifth grade my teacher, Miss Mitchell, had chosen a few members of my class to read stories we had written. When she came to mine she said, "Now we'll hear Shirley's; hers are always good." I felt proud, and from then on I wanted not only to write but for my writing to be read. Later in grade school I wrote stories with my friends when we came home from school. I always thought I would write a novel; but they say first novels are autobiographical and it has become obvious that I have difficulty in thinking about my past.

Perhaps the earliest memory of my lifetime was of Quincy, Illinois, where I lived when I was three years old and where my younger brother, Allan, was born. I believe I remember going to a park with my father where we fed the pigeons and to the beach on Lake Michigan where I played in the sand with my favorite cousin, Maurice. I say "I believe I remember" because it is possible that I remember these events only because I grew up looking at snapshots that recorded them. In the same way, with the help of photographs, I remember my grandparents' backyard where I played with my two brothers and our cousins Maurice and Sheldon. I was the only girl.

Perhaps the earliest memory I actually have, without the help of photographs, is the birth of my brother Allan. He was a beautiful, chubby baby with big brown eyes and black hair. I was crazy about him and so was Hattie, our housekeeper. Hattie had been cook for a family whose friends included Colonel Charles Lindbergh, and they entertained him on frequent occasions after his nonstop flight across the Atlantic. Cooking for the aviator-hero made Hattie feel proud. When she wanted to do things her own way she reminded Mother she had cooked for Colonel Lindbergh. Sometimes she would get temperamental and threaten to quit, but then she would start to cry at the prospect of leaving Allan and she would decide to stay. When she finally did leave to be near her son in New York, she addressed her postcards to Allan.

Hattie would take us for a walk after our naps, freshly bathed and powdered. I remember the odor of the talcum and that of the freshly mown grass, which has always been my favorite smell. We had dinner early, before the grown-ups, and were tucked into bed soon afterwards. I remember the anguish of trying to fall asleep in the summertime when it was still light outside, and my mother coming into my bedroom to soothe me.

Friday night was special because it was our Sabbath. The children dined with the grown-ups on this sacred occasion. Everything was sparkling and so were we, and we had to be on our best behaviour. The tablecloth was smooth white linen, the candle sticks shiny Dutch silver, and the chinaware white with a narrow green trim and little pink roses. A crisp white napkin covered a "challah" (or twisted bread) and a knife, which my father used to slice the "challah" before he sprinkled salt on it and said a blessing in Hebrew. We also sipped red wine, ceremonially thanking God for the "fruit of the vine." Our dinner was traditional, always starting with clear golden chicken soup. Sometimes one of the children spilled dark red wine on the snowy white tablecloth, causing our father to rebuke us.

I remember little about kindergarten, only that I kept drawing the same picture over and over again: a house with a tree and a flower. It was a country cottage, not the kind of house we lived in; we lived in a three-storey apartment house. But I thought the cottage was the kind of house I was supposed to draw. All I recall about my kindergarten teacher was her thick ankles. When I grew up I taught school with that same teacher. By then she had a different name through marriage, but I knew who she was when I looked down at her legs. Alas! She denied having been my kindergarten teacher, thinking it made her seem old.

All I remember about first grade was that a boy named Don, whose sister Jane was in my class, liked me and he hit me over the head with a book. I learned early that love can be painful. And I can also recall winning races I ran against my classmates. I have always loved outdoor exercise and the thrill of competing in sports. Mother insisted that her children get plenty of fresh air every day. She and my father liked to be outdoors whenever possible and they took long walks on Sundays and summer evenings. They made it a point to be sure we never stayed inside on a fine day, and even now I would feel guilty if I went to a movie in the afternoon.

My parents were avid readers and encouraged us to read. Mother loved poetry, especially Longfellow, and I remember her reciting "Under the spreading chestnut tree / The village smithy stands," which she had learned as a schoolgirl. We had shelves full of books all around, especially the classics. I was surprised when friends who came over would remark about them. I thought everybody must have shelves full of books in their living room.

Having a library card, and using it, was a major requirement in our home. I still recall a particular Saturday morning when I walked through freshly fallen snow in my galoshes to the public library for story hour. When I got there the librarian gave me a dreary storybook about bears that talk. Except for the British teddy bear Winnie-the-Pooh, I never cared much for talking animals simply because they were not convincing, and I expected animals to act like animals, not people. It should not be surprising that I grew up to be a writer of nonfiction.

It seems that most of my grade-school years were uneventful. The mother of my classmate Jane sometimes invited me to dinner and admired my table

"My mother, Ann Astor Glubok, as a fashion model before her marriage"

manners. When she pointed this out I felt proud but slightly embarrassed. And I had a friend named Alice whose house I liked to visit after school, partly because her mother made fresh candy. Alice liked to visit mine because my mother made delicious pumpkin pie.

The two friends I played with the most were both named Betty. One lived across the street and the other next door. Both Bettys were far more sophisticated than I because their families talked about worldly things in front of them, whereas mine tried to shelter us from any conversation they considered inappropriate for children.

The mother of Betty across the street had been divorced. When she remarried, they moved to a hotel and sent Betty to a Catholic boarding school. On weekends I sometimes had dinner with her in the hotel dining room. It was the most glamourous thing I could imagine, ordering anything we wanted from the menu and signing a check for our dinner. We once saw Frank Sinatra at the hotel when he came through St. Louis to sing in a nightclub. Since we loved his records we were thrilled to get a glimpse of him. Even more thrilling was meeting the brilliant, gracious Eleanor Roosevelt when she spoke at a luncheon some years later. My friendship with Betty ended when I loaned her my entire savings to buy her boyfriend a Christmas gift and she never paid me back.

In seventh grade I secretly liked a boy named Bill and then found out that all of the other girls liked him, too. Bill went off to boarding school two years later but came back to spend his junior year in St. Louis and he was in my physics class. I was not very good at math or science and only took those courses because I thought I was supposed to. With Bill in my physics class I did even worse than I normally would have, but I had great fun with him. He sometimes walked me to the orthodontist and told me jokes he had picked up at boarding school.

When I was eleven years old I started to swim on the "Y" team. My older brother, Norman, showed some promise as a swimmer and Rudy Brand, the coach, said as much to my mother. I was very determined and made up my mind that I, myself, would make the team—and I did.

Swimming in competition was far and away the most important activity in my youth. Rudy was a dedicated leader and he instilled a feeling of good sportsmanship and team spirit in all of us. I wanted ever so much to be a champion athlete and put absolutely everything I had into my effort to reach that goal. I had to ask myself, "How can I win?" The first step was to have hope that it was possible, and then the only answer was to train. I knew I would have to concentrate and to work hard, consistently, and forgo activities that would distract me or tighten my muscles or do anything harmful to my body in any way. Concern with physical conditioning and the ability to "give it all I've got" to succeed in an endeavor are qualities that have continued to help me in life.

I trained to swim in freestyle races, which literally means "any stroke," but everybody swims "the crawl" in a freestyle race because it is the fastest. One summer night in an outdoor meet at the municipal pool in St. Louis, I was behind my opponents in a 100-yard sprint, and I turned over on my back and won. Moreover, I was high-point winner in this important swim meet and saw my name in headlines on the sports page of the morning paper. What a thrill!

Now I knew that the stroke that came naturally to me was the backstroke, and I changed my workout routine. My arms were stronger than my legs, so one summer Rudy instructed me to lie on my back in the water with my arms stretched over my head, tediously kicking the length of a fifty-yard pool for at least an hour every single day. It was torture but I was devoted to my coach and would have done anything he wanted me to do. It did improve my speed. For three years I reigned undefeated in the Ozark district of the Amateur Athletic Union in the 100-yard backstroke event, both indoors and outdoors, and held all of the local pool records.

The outdoor swim meets were fun because friends from other local teams were around, and swimmers came from as far away as Hawaii. The big indoor meet was on February 22, George Washington's birthday. One Valentine's Day, a week before the meet, a boy on the team named Johnny, who was three years older than I, gave me a silver necklace inscribed with the date and I wore it all the time. February has always been a special month for me.

When I was a senior in high school I went to the National A.A.U. indoor swim meet to enter the 100-yard backstroke. I lost but went on to win that event in the National Intercollegiates as a freshman in college. I enjoyed swimming on the team and it certainly broadened my world, but I knew I could not withstand forever the intense pressure of rigourous training and the tension that would grip me before and after a meet. I was relieved to give up competitive swimming and enjoy a full social life in college. After college I started playing tennis seriously; I still play tennis and swim, purely for pleasure.

It was my mother who inspired me to swim well

when I was quite young. She seemed to have had a "close call" in the water when she went on an outing with some friends, so it became important to her that her children learn the sport for safety reasons. Mother believed that everything should be done to the best of one's ability, so I not only learned the sport, but made sure that I did it well.

I loved and admired my mother and depended on her more than anyone in the world. She, in turn, had great affection and admiration for her own mother, a tiny woman who always seemed ancient to me even though she died when she was only in her early fifties. "Grandma Astor," as we called her, was wrinkled and wore a crisp cotton scarf over her hair and her dresses nearly covered shoes which laced over her ankles. I can recall seeing her and my grandfather sipping tea sweetened with strawberry preserves in their kitchen, which seemed ever so big, but I am certain that is because I was ever so small.

Grandma Astor was a wonderful person. Although tiny, she was very strong and extremely courageous. She came to America to join her young husband who had fled czarist Russia. She traveled by train and steamship with four tiny children; all of their luggage was stolen en route. It broke my heart to hear about those evil thieves. Altogether, my grandmother bore nine children, all of whom survived. My mother, Ann, was the eldest. Mother inherited my grandmother's courage as well as her keen intelligence and combined these qualities with a penetrating understanding of people, plus the ability to get to the heart of a problem in a flash.

Mother was a successful working woman at a time when few females were out in the world. She had been a fashion model in the finest women's store in St. Louis and she held onto her job for a time after she married. Then she left her work to become a housewife and mother of three. Alas! Because of economic difficulties her retirement was short-lived. When her third child was but an infant she suddenly found herself back in business with her own store, called, after her maiden name, the Ann Astor Shop. The clothes she chose were beautiful; I can still remember a black silk dress in the shop window that I wanted her to save for me until I grew up. That dress was sold to a wealthy customer, but I still wear one of Mother's very own silk beaded "flapper dresses" that all my friends admire.

My maternal grandfather was an imposing man, tall with a dark beard, and he wore a black suit and black hat with a brim. I have no memory of any communication with him; he died when I was eight. I shall never forget the night of his death. It was the evening of the Veiled Prophet Parade, an annual event that was a source of great excitement for St. Louis children. Prominent citizens of the city dressed in costume and masks and rode on imaginatively decorated floats. The Veiled Prophet himself, whose identity was kept secret, chose a young woman to be queen and reign over St. Louis society for a year. A friend's family took me to the parade and I never had such fun. We giggled all evening; we couldn't stop. When I got home my mother was crying because her father had died. The contrast between my own merriment and her grief devastated me.

"Grandma and Grandpa Astor in their backyard," St. Louis, 1924

My paternal grandfather was around to see me as a grown-up. "Grandpa Glubok" was a handsome, distinguished-looking man who seemed a fascinating character to my friends. He traveled most of the time and always returned with presents for us. I cannot remember the gifts as well as I remember struggling over thank-you letters to him. I always started them in the same way . . . "Dear Grandpa, How are you? I am fine." And I ended with . . . "Thank you for the gift."

Grandpa Glubok had a universal outlook and an intellectual interest in diverse philosophies. My paternal ancestors also had been scholars and they, too, were strong. I vaguely remember hearing that my great grandfather went swimming in the river every day until he was 102 years old. The story is surely exaggerated but there must be a degree of truth behind it.

Daddy took after his own father inasmuch as he was always interested in new ideas. Also, he loved to talk to all sorts of people and would pick up on a conversation with anyone, anywhere, and listen to that person's problems. My father would have been an excellent social worker, or perhaps a rabbi, as he had great faith in God. My friends liked to be around him because he was attentive to them when often their own fathers were not. Perhaps he was too attentive to me, as he always seemed to be fussing with me. At the same time, he had confidence in me and told me I could do anything I set my mind to. I grew up believing this and it has stood me in good stead.

"My father, Yale Glubok, with his grandfather, in Russia"

My father's mother, my paternal grandmother, was an eccentric woman. She lived in an old section of town but would not have considered moving away even when the neighborhood got run down. Her house was always cluttered, and the rooms were heated by individual coal stoves long after other people had central heating in their homes. My father dutifully went to see his mother every week to look after her. We rarely went to Grandma Glubok's house, but she often came to see us on Sunday nights. She brought us large juicy oranges and fresh walnuts, which we cracked with a silver nutcracker, using a little silver pick to dig out the stubborn bits from the shell. Going through this ordeal made the nuts all the tastier.

Grandpa Glubok first went to St. Louis to participate in the World's Fair of 1904. I grew up near Forest Park where the fair had been held and played on top of a hill by the pavilion that was constructed for the event. On hot summer evenings I had great fun rolling down the hill, cooling myself in the fresh dew on the grass. At the bottom of the hill was a fountain that shot forth tall spouts of colored water. It never occurred to me that the water itself was not colored, but that the effect was controlled by colored lights. Forest Park was wonderful. We had picnics in the summertime, and in freezing weather I skated on a lake that was amazingly quiet even though it was next to the main boulevard, just five minutes' walk from our house. I was usually the only person on the lake.

Ours was a solid neighborhood. One house we lived in for a time was just behind the home where the heroine of *Meet Me in St. Louis* supposedly lived. And the setting for Tennessee Williams's play *The Glass Menagerie* was also nearby. St. Louis is a wonderful city, well established and rich in history. My parents were always conscious of the cultural life all around us. We went often to the Municipal Opera, an outdoor theater for light opera in Forest Park, and to the symphony, theater, and, of course, the zoo, which is famous.

St. Louis is on the Mississippi River where it meets the Missouri. In fact, a fountain statue group designed by Carl Milles, a Swedish sculptor, stands in front of the city's railway station to commemorate the meeting of the waters. The nineteenth-century artist George Caleb Bingham, who lived in St. Louis, painted river scenes of fur traders in dugout canoes and of men who traveled the Mississippi on flat boats.

It was a joy to see Bingham's paintings in the art museum. And it was fun to walk along the Mississippi and dream about the past and to have lunch at an old-fashioned German restaurant near the river. Needless to say, I did this alone, as it would not have interested many, if any, of my friends.

St. Louis was a wonderful city, but I wanted to get away. I did not like the way people gossiped and their unwillingness to judge others on their own merit instead of money and family background. I cared about people if they were interesting and nice, no matter what their social standing; and I felt that I was a little "different" in a society where everyone was supposed to be "alike." As far as I could see, the people I admired the most were not "alike" and most of them were far away.

The Wabash Railway ran along a course near our house and at night I would lie in bed listening to the railway whistle, longing to be on a train. I always knew I would move away, perhaps to the Pacific, if not the Atlantic Coast, or maybe even to Paris. I did manage to get to Chicago now and then to visit my favorite aunt, named Tillie, and to see friends who attended the University of Chicago. I loved to be in that city; it seemed so sophisticated next to St. Louis. Chicago is built on Lake Michigan, which gives it a beautiful setting. I liked to stand alone and look at Lake Michigan, even in the wintertime when bitter winds blew off the water. One January day, while visiting Aunt Tillie, I stood gazing at the freezing waves happy to be on the lake again; I stood there for such a long time that two policemen who came by stayed to watch me, perhaps fearing I would jump.

Chicago is a great city. It has the Art Institute, with my favorite collection of French impressionist paintings, Michigan Avenue with its shops and restaurants, a long tradition of great jazz, and, in the summertime, international polo matches. Chicago seemed to have everything, but then I had not yet seen New York; and I was still in St. Louis.

High school is but a blur in my memory. The school I attended was big, the classes large, and somehow I never felt part of it. The only course that inspired me was English. My teacher Miss Koch read the works of her favorite authors with such energy and enthusiasm that in my mind I can still hear her reciting Chaucer and Shakespeare. Miss Koch instilled in me a love for English literature that will be with me always. I enjoyed my French class as well, probably because it nourished my dreams of going to Paris.

The first summer after high school I landed a job as lifeguard at an exclusive country club and got a glimpse of an atmosphere I had not known before. After witnessing the life-style of the wealthy members it took me awhile to put things in perspective. In time I began to be thankful that I was brought up in a family atmosphere where values were solid and people were not judged by the size of their purse.

Washington University, where I went to college, was only a couple of miles from my home but it was like a different world. The university campus is among the most beautiful in the country and the faculty is first rate. Freshman year I took Art and Archaeology 101 to fulfill a requirement, and my professors were so inspiring that I found myself involved in a study that I had never really been aware of. I decided to major in art and archaeology because I loved the subject, without any thought of making art history my career.

My interest in art came to me naturally. From the time I was two years old my parents had taken me to the St. Louis Art Museum in Forest Park (when I would get tired of walking my father would pick me up and carry me). Also, we had reproductions of famous paintings on our walls. Vincent van Gogh's *Starry Night,* an exciting painting of a swirling sky with yellow spots and a twisted cypress tree, hung in our hallway. Now I often admire the original in the Museum of Modern Art in New York. A print of van Gogh's bedroom in a boardinghouse where he stayed for a time hung in my room. His was a simple room (as was mine), with an orange bedstead, yellow chairs, and bright blue walls, on which hung a small mirror and some pictures. I often thought, "What a primitive room for such a great painter!" I did not realize that this artist, who is perhaps the most popular painter in the world today, was not appreciated during his lifetime.

Gainsborough's *Blue Boy* hung in our living room in a gold frame. What a thrill for me when I later saw it first hand at the Huntington Library in Pasadena, California! I was interested to learn that the youth in the painting was an ordinary neighborhood boy who posed for the portrait dressed in an antique costume. And when a Millet exhibition was held in Boston and I saw *The Sowers* and *The Reapers* in the flesh, I remembered the reproductions we had in our home and how sorry I had felt for those poor peasants in France who worked so desperately hard and yet were so very poor.

Not only did I go to the art museum with my family and have reproductions at home, but I looked at paintings with my friends, the two Bettys. The "Y" where I swam had a little gallery, where new works of local painters were shown. Also, a group of Midwestern painters exhibited at the Artists Guild, which occupied an attractive building around the corner from my house, and I often went there with my friends when we played together in the afternoon.

The study of art history and archaeology was so appealing to me that I enrolled in every course possible. At the same time I knew I wanted to be a writer and I took every composition course available and wrote articles for the campus magazine. And, at my parents' urging, I took two years of public speaking. This combination of courses eventually made sense in a practical way. As it turned out I earn my living by writing and lecturing on art.

Among my friends at college was a girl from Toronto named Joan who had taken a summer job as counselor at a coeducational camp on a lake in Northern Ontario. Through Joan I managed to land a position as waterfront director. It turned out to be an experience I would cherish for years to come. I traveled by train: first to Chicago where I made a quick visit to the Art Institute and then to Toronto to meet the camp director and his staff. For the first time I slept in a pullman berth. What fun! On the last leg of the journey I looked out at evergreen trees when I awoke in the morning.

I loved Northern Ontario: the quiet of the woods, the clean air, and the fresh clear lake, with water pure enough to drink. I loved the starry nights and the sound of the waves lapping on the shore as I fell asleep in my cabin. At the end of the summer I proceeded to New York to meet my mother who was buying costume jewelry for her stores. The big city seemed like the most glamourous place in the world to me. I began longing to live there, to be a writer and live in an apartment near Central Park. In time my dream would come true.

"Aboard ship on my first trip to Europe"

After college I took a job writing advertising copy. I thought it was fun to work in a downtown office building and meet friends for lunch. Writing an ad was a challenge; a strong message had to be spelled out in few words. It was an experience that would later prove valuable, but I longed for work with deeper meaning. Through the inspiration of a friend who was deeply religious, I had begun teaching Sunday school at a temple and found it fulfilling. Before long I left my job in the advertising business and went to Florida with my mother for a winter vacation. Back in St. Louis I fell into a temporary job teaching physical education in a public high school. I loved the work and enjoyed the students. Although it had never occurred to me before this, I now wanted to pursue teaching as a career and enrolled in summer courses taught by Miss Jenny Wahlert at Washington University.

Miss Wahlert was a superb person who had devoted her life to teaching St. Louis children. I loved to hear her stories about the Great Depression when she fed hot oatmeal to the little ones when they came to school. Miss Wahlert continued to live in the same house where she had been born even after the neighborhood became dangerous, so that she could best serve the people who lived there. She encouraged me to pursue a career in teaching and I have been grateful to her ever since.

At the suggestion of a tennis friend, I took a position teaching a second-grade class in the suburbs of St. Louis. The first thing I did was to fill the room with interesting books and pictures; next, I arranged for a school bus to take the class to the St. Louis Art Museum. Without consciously setting out to do so, I was developing a technique of introducing works of art to schoolchildren. I prepared my students in advance by showing them a catalogue of the museum's collection. When we arrived, our lecturer was amused. I had told her we wanted to see Indian art because that was what *my* class was shown when I was in the second grade. But the children said, "No! We want to see a knight, a mummy, and Jesus-on-a-cross!" These were the things they liked best in the museum catalogue.

On the next visit I took the children through the museum myself and I let each of them choose a favorite painting and talk about it. The child would tell the class why he liked it and then the others would voice their opinions before we went on to the next. I thought it was important for the children to know that they did not have to like a work of art just because they thought they were supposed to; they should form their own opinions. I also thought it was important for them to learn to express their ideas in spoken words as well as in writing, and to learn to listen to each other attentively. After each museum visit we would have recess in Forest Park. Back at school the children would write stories and draw pictures about the trip.

At Miss Wahlert's urging I went for a master's degree in early childhood education. She suggested that I go to Stanford University in California or Columbia in New York. By now I had taken two trips to the West Coast and I loved California, but I chose Columbia because I had friends in New York whom I had met in Florida and on a summer trip to Europe. My classes at Columbia were huge and most of them were dreadfully dreary. The professors droned on about things I had either worked out for myself in the classroom or I had learned from Miss Wahlert. Luckily I was required to write a lot of papers. These were admired by my professors who encouraged me to do more writing.

"Lecturing on knights in armor at the Metropolitan Museum of Art"

Meanwhile, the head of the education department at the Metropolitan Museum of Art expressed interest in my original approach for teaching children about art, and he hired me to give gallery talks to young people when my course work at Columbia was finished. My job at the Met involved lecturing on Saturdays. During the week I was a classroom teacher in a private school that was more "progressive" than I had bargained for. It was a difficult situation. I brought a wide-eyed naiveté with me from the Midwest. My third-grade students mistook gentleness for weakness and took advantage of me. In addition, I did not fit in with the other teachers. One of them, who was friendly to me, told me frankly that the others did not like me, and I was devastated. It was an excruciatingly painful year, but my courage and strength pulled me through, whereas another teacher, in the very same position as I, left before Halloween and went back to her hometown. My sensitivity has always made it hard for me to deal with difficult people, but in the long run that same quality has been an important element in my approach to young children and in introducing them to the wonderful world of art.

In contrast to the school, the museum was a kind of haven for me. The children who came to my lectures were appreciative and well mannered, as were their parents, and the quiet galleries filled with masterpieces of art offered a refuge from the outside world. The lectures I gave covered a wide range of topics from ancient Egyptian to contemporary American art. The children and I explored the galleries together. I urged them to look at a work and try to react to it personally before I gave them information about the materials, the artist who created it, when and how it was made, and what it stood for.

Through the museum I learned about a small furnished apartment that I could sublet for a year, only a block and a half from the Metropolitan. The apartment had real character; it was filled with eighteenth-century Dutch paintings and antique furniture. The disadvantage was that I had to walk up five flights to get there, but it was worth the effort. Everything was in one room, including the so-called kitchen, which was separated from the combination bedroom/living room/dining room by a mere screen.

I felt very much at home in the building because the tenants were either museum people or were related to the owner, so living there was like being in a college dormitory. By good fortune, just as my year's sublet was up, the man who lived across the hall told me he was getting married and his apartment would be available. It was even smaller than the first, but it was my own. I had the walls painted peach, dyed some plain white curtains the same color, and bought a bed that doubled as a sofa. Gradually, I furnished the place with things Mother sent me or the landlord gave me or that I bought from a secondhand furniture store. It was a cozy, cheerful little home.

I even had my own "penthouse" garden, which was actually a lower section of the roof. To get there I climbed through a window and across a wobbly steel "balcony," and there I was in the tops of trees, with ivy from the garden below spilling over the railing. Now for the first time I took up gardening. I acquired some window boxes, and I dug up earth when I went to the country and hauled it back to New York, dragging it up five flights of stairs. I raised mostly marigolds and geraniums and now and then a cherry tomato, which I was too proud of to eat.

"The entrance to my 'terrace'. I climbed through the window to get there."

The neighborhood was wonderful . . . a touch of old New York as it will never be again. All the buildings along my street, which was lined with trees, were attractive town houses, one quite different from the other. Many of them had been converted into apartments but some were still privately owned, and each had its own little garden in back. At one corner there was a shop where rich ladies could have their poodles clipped and manicured. On the street at that corner, Park Avenue, there were tall apartment houses with trees growing on the terraces of the penthouses. It amused me to bend my head back to look up and see trees in the sky.

After dark a private night watchman was on duty on the block so I always felt quite safe, even though he spent much of his time hanging out in a nearby delicatessen. The "deli" was on Madison Avenue, a commercial street at the other end of the block. My favorite shop on Madison was the French dry cleaner. The owner would hang beautiful clothes he had cleaned in the window. I often looked in and thought about what glamourous lives the people who wore those clothes must lead. One night, much to my surprise, I saw my own gold blouse with rhinestone buttons in the window. I was so excited that I asked a friend who earned extra money by painting portraits, to paint *me* wearing that blouse.

The neighborhood was inspiring. Every morning I would walk a block and a half to Central Park and take the Fifth Avenue bus to school. In the afternoons I headed straight for the Metropolitan Museum to prepare for my Saturday lectures. In the meantime I wanted in the worst way to get a book published. The last few years I was in St. Louis I had been trying to get a publisher interested in a picture book I had written. It was about a little boy who did not like to go to school. One morning he had a series of misadventures because he didn't know how to read or count. Well, he never did get to school and the book never was published, but my persistent efforts on that story, writing and rewriting it a hundred times, eventually paid off. A literary agent read the story and liked the way I wrote. She knew that Atheneum, a new publishing company, had started a children's book department and the editor was interested in art books. Atheneum invited me to submit a proposal. Since one of the most popular subjects, both with the children at the Metropolitan Museum and with my third-grade class, was ancient Egypt, and since there were no books on the subject, I decided to write one. I chose the obvious title, *The Art of Ancient Egypt.*

Everything seemed to fall into place. One of the fathers who brought his children to my lectures was an art director of a magazine, and he wanted to design the book. We worked out a format together . . . a large square book with clear photographs and the text describing them always on the same page as the pictures. When the publishers saw the layout and read a sample text they were thrilled and immediately offered me a contract. I was so excited to be having a book published that I threw a party, inviting all my friends.

Months of hard work followed. I was determined to write a book that would be beautiful and readable as well as thoroughly understandable and useful. It would be a visual book with emphasis on masterpieces of art and, at the same time, would reflect the culture in which the works were created. I made a thorough search through the Egyptian collection at the Metropolitan, looking for works of art that would photograph well, be appealing to children, and could illustrate the kind of information I thought would be interesting. I also went to museums in Brooklyn, Boston, Cleveland, Chicago, and St. Louis to choose works from each, so that children in other cities would know that they might find Egyptian art in their own hometown. At the same time I ordered photographs by mail from museums and private photographers in England, France, and Italy.

When I had gathered the photographs, I got together with the designer and we organized them into categories. Over the course of many, many meetings we chose those we wished to use and he made "doodles," tiny pencil sketches of page layouts on a huge sheet of paper. In that way we could view an overall plan for the entire book. Next the designer made a "dummy," a mock-up of the book in its actual size; he determined how big each picture should be and ordered a photostatic copy, to size, of each photograph. When these were pasted down he drew lines on the pages to indicate how much space I would have for the words.

In the meantime I read every book I could find on the subject of Egypt, spending day after day in the library. The research seemed never to end, but when the "dummy" was ready there was nothing left to do except begin writing . . . by far the hardest part. (I write in pencil on a lined pad, and make continuous corrections, and when I can no longer read what I have written I type, continuing to make corrections in pencil and retyping.) I must have written twenty or more drafts before the final manuscript went to the publisher to be edited. One of the most demanding aspects was cutting down the text to fit the page. I had to make every single word count.

While working on *The Art of Ancient Egypt* I met a very nice man named Alfred Tamarin at a party. He called himself "Al Tamarin" (as if it were all one word), and was very attractive, a good deal older than I, and worldly wise. For years he had been active in public relations work in theater and movies and he knew all the "stars," which I thought was glamourous. Alfred was a gifted writer and an excellent photographer as well, but took pictures only as a hobby. I was not satisfied with the Metropolitan Museum's own photograph of the pink granite sphinx of Queen Hatshepsut that stood in the main hall. Queen Hatshepsut was an ancient Egyptian queen who lived around 3500 years ago. She usurped the throne from her stepson and declared herself ruler, then had herself shown in all the poses of a male king. One of the standard poses for portraying a king was in the form of a recumbent lion with a human head to emphasize the combination of intelligence and

Ed Meyer

"A publicity photograph for the St. Louis Globe-Democrat, *which featured a story on my work,"* *1962*

"In Greece, working on Art and Archaeology*"*

strength. A friend tried photographing the sphinx on two different occassions, but her flash broke each time. Alfred came to the rescue and took the picture, partly with the idea of getting a date with me. Both the photography and the maneuver were successful.

The Art of Ancient Egypt was an instant success when it came out in September 1962. The *New York Times, New Yorker, Saturday Review of Literature,* and many other major magazines and newspapers throughout the country gave it rave reviews. This was the first serious art history book for young readers and was interesting and informative to grown-ups as well. As soon as my first book was finished I had started on the next, which covered the ancient Near East and was called *The Art of Lands in the Bible.* My agent and editor had argued that we should not have a "series," so my designer and I conceived a book in a different size and format; but when reviews on *The Art of Ancient Egypt* came out they changed their minds, and by 1980 thirty books in "The Art of" series had been published, on subjects that ranged from the ancient world to Far Eastern, American, and primitive art. These included two "mini-series," one on American art that began with colonial America and ended with contemporary American culture and another which had to do with our own native Americans. With the encouragement of the director of the Museum of the American Indian I had written *The Art of the North American Indian,* and for the first time I could see how very different the native peoples in various parts of our continent were from each other. In time I wrote six more volumes on these people, starting with the Eskimos and ending with the southwestern Indians. Perhaps the most interesting aspect of the differences in their art is the way each group adapts to its environment and uses the materials found around them to express themselves.

All the while I also wrote books in different formats, including *Art and Archaeology,* which covered important excavations throughout the world, and *Knights in Armor,* which was the most popular subject for children at the Metropolitan Museum.

My work took me all over the world. I went to Greece, Peru, and India with university or museum groups. My mother accompanied me to Italy, France, and England where the great museums are filled with treasures from every corner of the world, and to Mexico, which became the subject of a book on pre-Columbian art. Sometimes I got culture shock, moving from one continent to the next, and through different time periods. I can remember trying to finish my book on ancient Mexico while on my first trip to Asia, which took me to India and Nepal. Studying various cultures gave me a broader outlook and learning about the history of other people enriched my own life. By meeting people in other countries I learned that there are different ways of living and acting from those I had always known.

In the meantime Alfred Tamarin had become my most frequent escort and best friend. He was always helpful and supportive in every kind of problem dealing with my work. Alfred was my own private photographer as well, and referred to himself as "a photographer with one client." When he traveled for his work with Inflight Motion Pictures, which put the first movies in airplanes, he would take pictures for my books. Most important of these were the ones he took in the Etruscan tombs and in Mexico, both resulting in photographs that were used as covers for books.

In 1968 we were married in a simple ceremony in the rabbi's study with only a few friends and relatives attending. My seven-days-a-week work pace never ceased, and Alfred worked along with me. Our collaboration as a husband and wife team began the day after our wedding when we went to a country house in Connecticut and spent our days sitting in front of a blazing fireplace editing Alice Morse Earle's two 1890s volumes, *Home Life in Colonial Days* and *Child Life in Colonial Days,* consolidating them into one volume. Later that winter and spring we traveled around New York State and New England to take photographs for new illustrations for the project. For our official wedding trip we went to the Yucatan Peninsula to study Maya ruins and snorkel off Cozumel Island. In October of that year we flew to Japan and Taipei to gather material for three different books. Not only did Alfred photograph for my books, but he wrote his own and eventually we put out five books as coauthors.

Some of our most enjoyable and productive travels were in the American West. My parents moved to Colorado in 1968, where my brother Allan taught at a university, and we started going out West to visit them several times a year. I loved the state of Colorado and we enjoyed driving down to New Mexico and Arizona where we studied the art and archaeology of the Indian people, as well as the Spanish-American culture in the area. We also collected Navajo blankets and silver and turquoise jewelry, which I love to wear. In the course of our direct contact with the Navajo and Pueblo people, Alfred grew curious about the Indians who live on the eastern seaboard of the United States and he set out to write about them. To research the book we called on the leaders of Indian tribes from Maine and Quebec all the way down to the tip of Florida. Some of these people became our friends and came to see us in New York. Alfred's book *We Have Not Vanished* came as a revelation to those who thought there are no more Indians in the United States today.

The books that we coauthored required extensive travel. A trip to Greece in the spring of 1975 for *The Olympic Games in Ancient Greece* was especially memorable. I had wanted to write about the ancient games for a long time, because it combined my studies in Greek archaeology with my love for sports; so a dream was fulfilled. And then a trip to Egypt provided material for another book that had been in the back of my mind for years . . . *The Mummy of Ramose,* about ancient mummification and burial practices. We focused on an eighteenth dynasty nobleman who lived around the time of Tutankhamen and was buried in a tomb with beautiful carvings and paintings on the walls.

"With Alfred, in a rare moment of relaxation," Estes Park, Colorado, 1974

Alfred fell ill in 1976 but we were able to proceed with our lives without much change until the doctor diagnosed lung cancer in the winter of 1980. I could not believe it when our physician said he would be dead "within months." I thought this was one of those things that only happens to somebody else. Alfred died at home on a hot night in late August. It was a difficult adjustment for me. Our lives had been so closely intertwined emotionally, socially, and professionally. Two years later my mother, to whom I was deeply devoted, also died. I knew I would have to change my life drastically and I immediately began doing as many different things as I possibly could in order to change my routine and decide which direction to take with my life. I began traveling to Boston where I lectured to schoolchildren several weeks a year, and I also taught a graduate course on museum training at Boston University. Almost every summer I went abroad to gather material for magazine articles. I also managed to go to California to play tennis twice a year. Wherever I am, in this country or another, I wander through the museums. I always feel at home inside a museum, where I am surrounded by treasures created through the centuries by people who probably had some of the same problems as I.

Now that I have had time to sort things out in my head and rethink my life and make new friends, I am starting a new life. As I finish this first chapter of my autobiography I am sitting in the sun between tennis games in Palm Springs, California before returning to New York for another season of hard work. The next chapter of my life will be told in the second edition, to be read by children yet unborn.

BIBLIOGRAPHY

FOR CHILDREN

Nonfiction:

The Art of Ancient Egypt (designed by Gerard Nook). New York: Atheneum, 1962.

The Art of Ancient Greece (designed by Oscar Krauss). New York: Atheneum, 1963.

The Art of Lands in the Bible (designed by G. Nook). New York: Atheneum, 1963.

The Art of the Eskimo (designed by G. Nook; photographs by Alfred Tamarin). New York: Harper, 1964.

The Art of the North American Indian (designed by O. Krauss). New York: Harper, 1964.

The Art of Africa (designed by G. Nook; photographs by A. Tamarin). New York: Harper, 1965.

The Art of Ancient Rome (designed by O. Krauss). New York: Harper, 1965.

Art and Archaeology (designed by G. Nook). New York: Harper, 1966.

The Art of Ancient Peru (designed by G. Nook; photographs by A. Tamarin). New York: Harper, 1966.

The Art of the Etruscans (designed by G. Nook; photographs by A. Tamarin). New York: Harper, 1967.

The Art of Ancient Mexico (designed by G. Nook; photographs by A. Tamarin). New York: Harper, 1968.

Discovering Tut-ankh-Amen's Tomb (designed by G. Nook). New York: Macmillan, 1968.

The Art of India (designed by G. Nook; photographs by A. Tamarin and Carol Guyer). New York: Macmillan, 1969.

Knights in Armor (designed by G. Nook). New York: Harper, 1969.

The Art of Colonial America (designed by G. Nook). New York: Macmillan, 1970.

The Art of Japan (designed by G. Nook; photographs by A. Tamarin). New York: Macmillan, 1970; London: Collier-Macmillan, 1970.

The Art of the Old West (designed by G. Nook). New York: Macmillan, 1971; London: Collier-Macmillan, 1971.

The Art of the Southwest Indians (designed by G. Nook; photographs by A. Tamarin). New York: Macmillan, 1971.

The Art of the New American Nation (designed by G. Nook). New York: Macmillan, 1972.

The Art of the Spanish in the United States and Puerto Rico (designed by G. Nook; photographs by A. Tamarin). New York: Macmillan, 1972.

The Art of America from Jackson to Lincoln (designed by G. Nook). New York: Macmillan, 1973; London: Collier-Macmillan, 1973.

The Art of China (designed by G. Nook). New York: Macmillan, 1973; London: Collier-Macmillan, 1973.

The Art of America in the Early Twentieth Century (designed by G. Nook). New York: Macmillan, 1974; London: Collier-Macmillan, 1976.

The Art of America in the Gilded Age (designed by G. Nook). New York: Macmillan, 1974; London: Collier-Macmillan, 1974.

Ancient Indians of the Southwest, with A. Tamarin. Garden City, N.Y.: Doubleday, 1975.

The Art of the Northwest Coast Indians (designed by G. Nook). New York: Macmillan, 1975.

The Art of the Plains Indians (designed by G. Nook; photographs by A. Tamarin). New York: Macmillan, 1975.

Dolls, Dolls, Dolls (designed by G. Nook; photographs by A. Tamarin). Chicago: Follett, 1975.

The Art of America Since World War II (designed by G. Nook). New York: Macmillan, 1976.

The Art of the Woodland Indians (designed by G. Nook; photographs by A. Tamarin). New York: Macmillan, 1976.

Olympic Games in Ancient Greece, with A. Tamarin. New York and London: Harper, 1976.

Voyaging to Cathay: Americans in the China Trade, with A. Tamarin. New York: Viking, 1976.

The Art of Photography (designed by G. Nook). New York: Macmillan, 1977.

The Art of the Southeastern Indians (designed by G. Nook; photographs by A. Tamarin). New York: Macmillan, 1978.

The Art of the Vikings (designed by G. Nook). New York: Macmillan, 1978; London: Collier-Macmillan, 1978.

The Mummy of Ramose: The Life and Death of an Ancient Egyptian Nobleman, with A. Tamarin. New York and London: Harper, 1978.

The Art of the Comic Strip (designed by G. Nook). New York: Macmillan, 1979; London: Collier-Macmillan, 1979.

The Art of Egypt under the Pharaohs (designed by G. Nook). New York: Macmillan, 1980; London: Collier-Macmillan, 1980.

Dolls' Houses: Life in Miniature. New York: Harper, 1984.

Editor of:

The Fall of the Aztecs (designed by Leslie Tillett), by Bernal Diaz del Castillo. New York: St. Martin's, 1965.

Discovering the Royal Tombs at Ur (designed by Gerard Nook; photographs by Alfred Tamarin), by Leonard Woolley. New York: Macmillan, 1969.

Home and Child Life in Colonial Days (photographs by A. Tamarin), by Alice Morse Earle. New York: Macmillan, 1969.

Digging in Assyria (designed by G. Nook; photographs by A. Tamarin), by Austin Henry Layard. New York: Macmillan, 1970.

The author has also written articles on art for language-art textbooks, articles for teachers' magazines, and articles for adult magazines, including *Connoisseur* and *House and Garden.*

Rosemary Harris

1923-

It seems strange now that the Second World War lies like a black barrier between the modern world and days of my childhood—although really there must always have been these periods when change was gradual until some upheaval altered the whole pace and direction of life. Looking back, I see the years between 1939 and 1945 as a time which had that effect and must make the period just before it as inaccessible to the youth of today as the Great Rebellion must have done for late seventeenth-century people, or the War of Independence for inhabitants of the United States.

Because I was born into a family with a long history of service to the Crown, and to that—today outmoded and decried—symbol of Empire, the Raj, we were probably more aware of signs of coming violence than were some other people. On the surface, life seemed fairly placid. It was an age when the professional and upper classes in England employed many servants, even on the slenderest incomes. To be looked after by other people wasn't the prerogative of the rich. The ease with which this was generally accepted and the extent to which it upheld the whole structure of life, in the same way as muscles support bones, is probably unthinkable to people who only know the life and manners of today. Of course, the labour-saving devices by the hundred that exist now were unheard of, and if everyone had had to do everything for themselves, the whole tenor of life would have been impossibly slow. It was tough on the poor, just as hard for those who slaved on a pittance if the family they worked for were unpleasant—and most people didn't question it, or if they did they were looked on as eccentric.

So many of the things I can actually remember now seem to me positively Dickensian. The London I knew as a child was a darker, though in many ways more visually attractive place, than it is today. Some things about it, not only the pea-soup fogs caused by coal-burning fires, looked back not just to early years of the century, but to Victorian London.

Horses were as familiar a sight as buses or taxis: massive dray horses, Clydesdales or Suffolk Punches; little ponies that drew the milk carts; riding horses that were sold and paraded at Tattersall's ring in Knightsbridge close to Harrods, or carried their

Jerry Bauer

Rosemary Harris

immaculate riders through Hyde Park at Rotten Row. I can just remember lamplighters lighting the street lamps at night, and the winter muffin men ringing their bells while carrying on their heads trays of muffins neatly wrapped in white cloths. There were barrel organs too, endlessly churning out nostalgic tunes like Lehár's "You Are My Heart's Delight," which the great Viennese singer Richard Tauber had made his own. Tiny wistful monkeys in red flannel coats were chained to the organs, to draw money into the organ-grinders' caps. The last of the ancient lilting street cries, the lavender seller's, was still heard on summer and autumn evenings: "Won't you buy my—pretty lavender? Fifteen branches—for a penny. You buy it once—you buy it twice. It makes your clothes smell—very nice."

But for the poor it was not so pretty, beneath the surface it must have been a desperate grind. When we went on holiday to the seaside in summer the steam train passed through acres of appalling slums, black, unpainted, desolate deserts of misery. There were ragged children in the gutter, out-of-work Welsh miners sang in the streets, and soon there was the added horror of the Jarrow hunger march. Beneath the riches and glamour of Empire there was a poverty and fear you could almost smell. It's something that ought not to be forgotten in the fashionable race and struggle for easy money of today.

My father was a brilliant officer in the Royal Air Force, one of its first pilots who had joined in its infancy when it was the Royal Flying Corps. He had flown in Flanders, and trained the night-fighter pilots of the 1914–18 war. Because he was so rapidly promoted, my elder sister, Marigold, my brother, Anthony, and I were moved constantly from place to place, and we spent a good deal of time in between moves with our grandparents—my mother's parents—who lived in a small hotel at South Kensington with our unmarried great-aunt Ida, affectionately known to us as Auntie Nan. She was a swashbuckling character, with beautifully groomed white hair, who wore a monocle and was a fine photographer and gardener. In spite of the swash and monocle she was not at all mannish, only a very strong personality whose life had been partially blighted by some mysterious love for a difficult married man (now and then hinted at though never fully explained) but had then bloomed again into a passion for Christian Science; a mode of belief heartily scorned by my grandmother, who was vaguely though devoutly Anglican and who, in a charmingly tilted hat and with a fur coat weighing down her minute frame, would sometimes trot off to what she mystifyingly described as "Late Celebration, darlings." In her girlhood my grandmother, then Alexandra Gruinard Battye, known as Daisy, was said to have been as lovely as the Jersey Lily, Mrs. Langtry. I remember the charm of her room, with its scented geraniums and verbena, and its mixture of Coalport china with beige Woolworth vases, decorated with storks and bulrushes, that she had taken a surprising fancy to and defiantly bought for sixpence in that useful store.

She was a darling, though a naughty darling. Like the sun attracting planets she attracted members of the family to her, and like the sun she never let them go. "Aunt Daisy rules everyone from her bed," said one of my cousins, thoughtfully. Bed, in the sense of resting there frequently, she had taken to

Alfred Ellis

Maternal grandmother, Alexandra Gruinard Battye Money

early on, probably as a defence against the exuberant life-style of my naughtier grandfather—"Gaffer," we called him, to his amusement. Gaffer was incurably romantic and an incurable honey-pot to what Mr. Salteena would have called "the Ladies." He could not help himself, for from a strain of Stuart ancestry he had inherited all their charm and melancholy masculine beauty: each time I go to the National Portrait Gallery I can see his features looking down on me from Stuart portraits.

The last of "the Ladies," whom I remember well, was a tiny annoying creature, a distant relative and superb *raconteuse,* with alarmingly brittle bones which cracked on the slightest provocation. A lifelong devotee of Wagner's operas, my grandfather had cast her in the unlikely role of Isolde, and she was certainly as inclined to staginess as that overwhelming lady. "O poor pale face!" she would cry in a swooning voice, meeting some slightly sickly member of the family on the stairs. "She may think she looks

Maternal grandfather, E.W.K. Money ("Gaffer")

like a femme fatale," said my grandmother tartly, "but she really looks like a dead mouse."

Her presence on the outskirts of the family gave rise to one of the more dramatic incidents of our fairly dramatic childhood. For one Christmas her husband informed her that he was going to shoot my grandfather. The unwelcome news was conveyed to my grandparents at a dinner party to which they had taken my brother and sister, then just promoted to such outings. There was some discussion in the homebound cab as to who should get out first; in the end my brother was sent ahead to draw the fire (youth was not so highly prized then as it is today), followed by my sister, her skirts over her head as a curious form of defence against the flying bullet. But nothing happened. King Mark sulked at home; after a period of discretion Isolde continued to haunt our family, and my grandmother took again to the fastness of her bed.

Watching with a sharp beady eye from the neighbourhood of Nanny, I early absorbed an impression that men were attractive, mysterious, not always to be relied on. Nursery life in those days was in some ways a haven, but in others as open as the Garden of Eden, the in-between level of the "Upstairs, Downstairs" syndrome being greatly given to revealing chat. A child with pricked ears and a sleepy expression, deep in a book, was more aware of most things than its elders supposed, and mysterious nods and shakings of the head were interpreted with the accuracy of a trained code-breaker.

My family was mostly beautiful, impoverished, and rather wild. There was my naval uncle, Rupert Money, my mother's brother, a favourite in the nursery, turning out his pockets for half-crowns and joking with Nanny. He too had inherited the bold, black, havoc-wreaking Stuart eyes. He was almost a legend in the fleet, immensely popular with his fellow officers, and, though tipped for the top while still at Dartmouth, was given to the occasional punch-up with his commanding officers, which didn't favour his chances. He and his beautiful wife, my aunt May, spent too lavishly for their joint income, painting London red with the young Mountbattens. Predictably, they overspent. My uncle left the Navy for the stock exchange, for which he displayed no talent whatever, and then for the Secret Service. I cannot believe he was suited to this either, for he looked so mysterious in a black trilby, and behaved so like an oyster that "could an' if it would" that a child could have bowled him out. When war finally came he was given a ship, and after Germany collapsed he was offered a command in NATO. Sadly, he died of viral pneumonia before he could take up his appointment, a sudden blow that almost broke my grandmother's resilient heart.

She must have needed all her resilience. I remember her telling me that she had felt herself to be mainly a looker-on in life, and often quoted the saying that "lookers-on see most of the game." In spite of her looks she had a socially retiring nature, but she certainly had much to see. For my parents' marriage too had run into tempestuous disaster. They had met and married in 1916, one of those hasty romantic weddings of the First World War, when death loomed behind every young man's shoulder. There was extra glamour attached to the first pilots who flew without parachutes and in open cockpits above the mud and misery of the trenches.

No couple could have been more unsuited. My mother had been reared in a sheltered existence where cross words were seldom heard, and where she was the adored only daughter of a soldier who, though devoted to his family, spent a good deal of his time on country-house visits, where he was always welcome with his looks, his acting ability, and his guns. It was a world whose mould was to be broken forever by the Great War, one where birth was more important than money, and where cousins to the umpteenth degree were sprinkled across the land like a welcoming extended family. But with my grandfather away so often, and my uncle in the navy, my mother became the sole focus of my grandmother's loving attention, which gave her a shy uncertainty in her attitude to life, greatly at odds with her inheritance of charm and beauty. She had a well-trained singing voice, and was a graceful dancer, nursing a wistful desire to take up ballet or singing as a career—an idea quashed with horror by her father; though he himself at one time had risked being cashiered while on leave from his regiment, the King's Shropshire Light Infantry, by taking an assumed name and touring in Wilde's *Lady Windermere's Fan.* (Amongst his other charms he was a born actor; a well-known actor-manager had tried to lure him to the London stage, and we children were enthralled when he could be persuaded to recite "Kissing-Cup's Race," a dramatic and sentimental saga of the race course, at which he excelled.)

Unlike my mother's, my father's existence had been, from the first, one to toughen or break the most spirited. He was the third son of George Harris, a talented architect responsible for many fine buildings in India, who had left the Indian Civil Service to become architect to the Maharajah of Gwalior. By all accounts he was an extremely difficult man, in later years of a gloomy and morbidly sullen nature, who had felt himself somehow disappointed in life, and cut off by increasing stone-deafness. According to my paternal grandmother, Caroline, who was of Welsh stock, from Pembrokeshire, he had been quite unable to deal with my red-haired father's unruly nature, and before the small Arthur reached the age of three had resorted to merciless thrashings.

Like most children then of parents in India, my father and his two elder brothers were sent home to England, spending their holidays in a variety of welcoming or unwelcoming homes, and the rest of their time at school. Murray, the eldest son, precociously clever, was sent to Sherborne. Then came Uncle Fred, who seemed to have every gift. An Eton scholar, he gained an exhibition in Oriental languages to Cambridge. But my father was not at all academic, and by the time it was his turn to be sent home, his father—who had two daughters to provide for as well—was gloomily economising, convinced the money would run out, and so despatched him to a lesser-known public school.

From the first Arthur must have felt himself to be an isolated and rejected person. Unlike gorgeous Fred he was plain, and although usually able to charm when he set his mind to it, he suffered from a sense of inferiority towards this elder brother, which can hardly have been improved by total separation from family life: in his last years he told my brother, Anthony, that if, when he was eleven, he had met his parents walking down the street, he would not have recognised them. It may have been an exaggeration, but in the language of today, he was deprived.

Public school did nothing to break his turbulent spirit. His parents decided that the outdoor life was indicated, and sent him off to Rhodesia. But the Great War was looming, and in 1914 he joined the Rhodesian Rifles. Later, he told us that he became an expert bugler, and that a march right across Africa gave him a fixed and lifelong dislike of walking; so when the Rifles were disbanded he looked round for some service where, as he said, he could sit, lit on the idea of joining the newly-formed Royal Flying Corps and, in his own words, sat on the steps of the War Office until they let him join. The life was tough, glamorous, and exciting, with plenty of scope for initiative. In those days it also had an amateurish quality of adventure, the schoolboy's ideal, more Biggles than Bond. The night-fighter pilots in particular were an élite corps, comparable perhaps to the Few of Battle of Britain fame. My father found himself to be one of those fortunate men—considering the world in which we live—who find themselves totally at home in uniform.

This, then, was the unlikely couple who met and fell passionately in love in 1916, in the heightened atmosphere of war—a very gently bred girl who had seldom been outside her extended family circle, and a man who had consistently roughed it and seldom been inside his. They were respectively twenty-three and twenty-four and were so violently attracted to one another that Gaffer reportedly said he had never seen two people so much in love, and that if anything happened to break it he would never believe in love again. All the same, at first he opposed their marrying. Probably he saw, quite rightly, that they were deeply incompatible, and that the attraction was one of opposites. Grannie was completely won over by my father's charm, yet she told us later how Grandmother Caroline warned her frankly that he had a difficult temperament, and that if anything went wrong she would take my mother's side.

By the time I was born seven years later, the youngest of three children, tears and sulks were the stuff of our home life, for from the first my red-haired, energetic father was as attractive to other

The Harris children: (from left) Rosemary, Anthony, and Marigold

women as Gaffer had been in his more romantic, old-fashioned manner, and he simply couldn't see why anyone should mind. Anyway, for someone of his temperament he had married too young, and wild oats after marriage proved no recipe for success. Between producing children my mother wept, and then took to spirited though chaste romantic flirtation as a riposte. My grandmother, naturally, took her daughter's part, and came to stay rather often—yet this was a bonus to us children, for she loved children, had wanted more of her own, and was my first introduction to the born storyteller: she would enthrall my sister and myself with rambling serial sagas, in which we always starred.

Grannie helped me to read, too—"The cat sat on the mat / He saw the sun." Early in life words meant a lot to me. Perhaps they were a refuge from the gathering storms about us. Marigold and I were avid readers, animal lovers too. We wore anti-vivisectionist badges. But owning animals wasn't a constant factor in our lives, since we moved from place to place so often, and were so frequently in a hotel, that anything we acquired had to be given away, or came with the married quarters in the RAF station or rented house, and were passed on or back to another owner. Once, at Camberley, there was Jenny, a small white goat, who loved us so dearly that she would come into the house and be found upstairs on our beds, like a dog, to our family doctor's horror and amusement. At Camberley too there was beloved Spot, a black-and-white smooth-haired fox terrier. He was a roamer, a disobedient, brilliant baddie, who adored my father, and could learn anything he was taught, shutting doors and tossing sugar lumps at the word of command. Spot "went with" the house. Years later we went back to Camberley on a day visit. Outside the house my father gave his well-known whistle. After a pause Spot came running, threw himself at our feet, and in an ecstasy of excitement attempted all his best tricks at once.

At Camberley too there was a drag hunt, for which a seventeen-hand hunter named Waterford was retained, a beautiful bay creature which came to a sad end, breaking his back over a scarifying jump. Then there was a small borrowed pony of sly and evil habits, Merrylegs, too rightly named. My sister was ecstatic—she was horse-mad from the age of three, since the advent of a stuffed toy donkey—but I was less so. Merrylegs put me off riding for years, since the first time I was thrown up on him—I was five or six—he broke straight into a hustling trot, going sideways like a crab before I was properly in the saddle. I slipped, my left leg went down through the stirrup iron, and if my mother hadn't managed to run up and catch me I would have been dragged.

However, the idea of the Horse still ruled the nursery. My sister had inherited my father's fiery and dominant temperament, I, my mother's more retiring one. Generally I went along with the horse games. We put up race jumps in the woods at the back of the house, and hurdled them. We studied form in Nanny's daily paper before the Derby and Grand National, and were allowed, at second hand, to put one shilling on to win or sixpence each way on our chosen horses. We became so expert that one year we spotted first, second, *and* third in the National, though our combined shillings didn't get us far. Horse books, stuffed orange horses (why *orange?*),

Marigold and Rosemary playing with their dog, Spot, and their goat, Jenny, at Camberley, England

lead models of famous winners with detachable jockeys in correct colours on their backs (I wonder where they went to? They'd make a fortune at auction today) flooded the nursery. Occasionally I made halfhearted attempts to set up an opposing dog faction, but it didn't get far, not even when we wept over Kipling's "Thy Servant a Dog" and Ravager, the old hound, went blind. Also, my heart wasn't really in it. Secretly I preferred the Red, Green, and Blue Fairytale books, or *Swallows and Amazons,* or to be scared by George Macdonald's *The Princess and the Goblin.*

Why do most people like to be scared? The popularity of thrillers and horrific news stories proves the point. There was a children's magazine at that time which ran a spooky picture serial. I don't recall whether the apparition was a ghost or a member of the Ku Klux Klan, but anyway it wore a pointed white hood with black eyeholes, and pounced on its victims late at night. Weekly I begged to see this appalling serial, promising stoutly that it didn't worry me at all, no, I wouldn't need a night-light. Each week my promise failed and the serial would be banned, only to reappear later when my mother thawed under my renewed wheedling promises and falsely carefree face.

Our relations with our parents were complex ones. Childhood is seldom the idyllic time it's supposed to be, but I don't think the between-war years were specially good ones for children, for in that shifting quicksand world their parents were much at sea. The whole structure of Victorian and Edwardian England had gone, swept away by the Great War. Life was quickening to the rhythm of the Bright Young Things, though in some aspects it remained curiously static. It would be a long while before the permissiveness of life today, with its open questionings and knowledge of Freud and Jung would replace the authoritarian certainties that had foundered. The in-between state was an uneasy one, and nowhere more so than in the relationship between the nursery and the outer world.

My mother was a very loving person but, unlike my grandmother, not at that time a natural child lover, although she indulged me heavily because I was a delicate child, and I always had a very special relationship with her which remained constant throughout her life, with a few ups and downs in my teens and early twenties. I don't think, however, that she really understood us then—also, our parents' marriage was on the rocks and causing much misery, and the strain must have been depleting. Even in those not too distant days to divorce your husband was really quite a formidable step, still frowned on by society at large, to whom Noel Coward's plays seemed faintly daring and avant-garde.

Rosemary (far right) with her family at the beach: (from left) Aunt Ida, Marigold, Anthony, Cousin David Money, Father, and Mother

Towards us, my father's attitude varied between the instigation of periods of immense and hectic fun—he was quite marvellous at pillow fights—and gruff indifference, punctuated by rather deflating remarks. He was built on such a large scale, in every way, and had such an up-and-down temperament, that our life was a perpetual Tom Tiddler's ground: at their blackest his moods could permeate the house like the thickest London pea-soup fog—what Dickens called a London pertikler. (James Barrie's goddaughter has since told me that he could fog a whole house similarly when he was depressed.) In those days he was the closest thing to Nancy Mitford's "Uncle Matthew" that I've ever come across. When, years later, I wrote my first novel with the autobiographical overtones common to all such books, Hamish Hamilton gently accused me of poaching from *The Pursuit of Love.*

At the time of my parents' separation we were living in London at Pelham Street, while my father worked at the Air Ministry. Each evening, at about six o'clock, Marigold and I would peer from a downstairs window to assess the situation: if the bowler was jammed down on the forehead above a frown we would read the storm signals and speedily retreat to the top storey. I don't think he had any understanding of how or why he so affected us, and he would have been rather hurt to know that we felt as though a thundercloud, complete with flashes of forked lightning, had entered the house. He was desperately bored by city life, and was toying with the idea of resigning from the RAF and retiring to Rhodesia, to farm.

It was the time when Hitler had been returned to power, and the mood of the country, or rather of those who could foresee a gathering threat, was one of alarm, mingled with fear of another bloodbath—and it was distantly overshadowed by an equal threat: the policies of appeasement. Whenever I recall that time I'm reminded of the old Chinese saying that the effects of a mandarin's sneeze will be felt in Paris. In this case the sneeze was represented by a beauty called Daphne, whose advent in our family circle was too much for our long-suffering mother—she left Pelham Street, taking us with her. Faced with the disruption and expenses of a split in family living, and no doubt lonely and upset by our departure, my father threw himself with renewed zeal into his work at the Air Ministry, renouncing his plans for an open-air life in Rhodesia. His brilliance and grasp of air power strategy had always marked him out, and now the eventual policies that would be one of the main factors in Hitler's defeat (as Albert Speer himself asserted after the war) were ensured. Beautiful Daphne proved to be some sneeze.

At the time of the divorce I was eleven, my sister almost fourteen, Anthony at his public school, Oundle (where his housemaster was the engaging personality Arthur Marshall—who, on the sands of Dunkirk, was heard rebuking his soldiers for being butterfingers). The break-up of our home was traumatic, although in the past we had suffered separations from both parents, as well as continual moves. After Marigold's birth they had been at an RAF station in India for two years, leaving her behind with Nanny and our grandparents. Again, when I was six, they had departed to Egypt for another two years, although our mother had been recalled after six months when Anthony was threatened with a tonsils operation—often a lethal one in those days—and then my father's appointment had been changed to one in Mesopotamia, where neither wives nor children were permitted, the country being so unsettled. So we were used to comings and goings and upheavals: from RAF stations to London, from London to Sussex or Bedfordshire for summer holidays, although we did find it harder to adjust when both our parents later remarried.

However, there were soon larger issues than family life to worry about. Perhaps it's impossible for people born since that war to understand the insidious horror of Hitler's crab-crawl across mesmerized Europe, nor the sense of approaching doom that haunted us all, when leaders of European nations threw up their hands in dismay yet failed to arm. The present comprehensive nuclear threat has blinded people to what the world would be like now if the Nazi mob had won and set up their one-thousand-year Reich based on fear, torture, genocide, and Aryan supremacy. With hindsight we know that Hitler didn't win, which seems to diminish both him and the terror; and yet, till nearly the end of war in Europe, he so nearly did. No one seeing one country after another succumb would have bet heavily on a different outcome, and fifty-five million lives lost throughout the world was a heavy price paid for complacency during several years.

The atmosphere of that sad day in September 1939 when the ultimatum to Hitler ran out is unforgettable. So too is the old, tired voice of Chamberlain on the radio, at last admitting that gangsters don't listen to reason. I was in Scotland, for my stepfather, Gerald Boultbee, was Chief of Staff to the admiral commanding Clyde, whose offices were set up in a Glasgow hotel. They were lacking in trained personnel, so a few days beforehand the wives and daughters of naval officers were roped in, and sworn in, to serve instead, until more official help could be forthcoming from the Admiralty. Although I was only fifteen, I was roped in too. From some days before war actually broke out all messages into and out of the offices had to be coded, so we were hurriedly initiated—in some cases too hurriedly, for I remember presenting a perplexed commanding officer with a message describing an approaching convoy of German ships, an Italian destroyer, and a Japanese submarine.

On that first day of war everyone was nervy and also strangely exhilarated because all the uncertainty was over. At eleven someone said, "Zero hour," just as one of the paymaster-lieutenants was handing me a message to be dealt with; he was pale green, and his hand was shaking more than mine. Suddenly there was a tremendous crash, and we all jumped. "Adolf very quick off the mark," muttered somebody. But it was only a thunderclap—Jove, perhaps, setting his seal on war.

I must admit that I enjoyed those first weeks. A spirit of snug camaraderie reigned in our offices, and there was a pleasant sense of being at the hub of things; but the wife-and-daughter syndrome only lasted for some months, until the first lot of Women's Royal Naval Service officers arrived to oust us. Then the amateurs were invited to teach the professionals, before retiring sadly to the sidelines. For me it meant a temporary return to the schoolroom, rather a descent after having come under the Official Secrets Act at such a junior age.

Visually, those first days of war were enriched by

Harris (right) with Anthony and her grandmother on the terrace of the Elizabethan manor Bingham's Melcombe, 1941

some endearingly silly touches that will never be seen again. The dignified ascent of barrage balloons, rising like a herd of ponderous silver elephants to the full height of their cables, was often the first sign of approaching raiders. I'm still not sure what they were meant to do. If a Heinkel pilot had come face to face with a bloated gentle giant and tangled with its cable, his aircraft and its bomb load would have dropped plumb on the city beneath, surely a self-defeating outcome. When these balloons were very high up they turned from elephant to silver fish, and looked very pretty at sunrise or sunset, reflecting pink or golden light.

Glasgow's balloons, of which there were only fifteen or twenty, were shared by some ludicrous arrangement with Edinburgh. Probably we had pride of place because of the importance of Clyde shipyards, and we grew fond of them, as though they were a lot of grey sheepdogs guarding our homes. Now and then the crews who handled them would hurriedly haul them down onto lorries, and off they would trundle to the East Coast. We felt bereft until they came trundling home again, even though it meant we were suspected of being the next target for attack.

Much has been written about the raids on London and Coventry and the South Coast—of the British war casualties, one in every five or six was a civilian killed in the air raids—but I've seldom read anything about the terrible raids on Glasgow, which sometimes lasted all night, specially on nights of full moon. The German bombers came over in waves. The heavy double throb of their engines, ker-boom, ker-boom, was easily distinguishable. Our house was about a mile from the docks, their main objective, and lay in their path. Sometimes I thought the warning sirens were as bad as the raid itself: the first time we heard their banshee howl rising and falling like souls in torment—one tormented soul was mounted on the roof opposite—my stomach churned for twenty-four hours. Psychologically speaking, I always felt someone should invent a warning note less shredding to the nervous system.

At that time I owned a very beautiful dog, a gift from my cousin Margie Still—a long-haired dachshund called Hawka. He was chestnut-coloured, streaked with black, with tan kid-glove paws, and as heavily feathered about tail and legs and ears as a prize Pekinese. Hawka had a loving nature, a great sense of his own worth, a noble carriage, and two or three outstanding faults: he was obstinate—nothing would make him walk a way he didn't wish to; he had an unforgiving streak, and would coldly ignore for at least twenty-four hours anyone he felt had slighted or overlooked him; and he was cowardly about air raids.

He soon learned to associate the banshees with terror, and at the first howl would hustle to the semi-basement room where camp beds were installed, and stay there till the all clear sounded. If everyone else went back upstairs, he would stay where he was till one long banshee note declared the raid was over.

One day we missed him. There had been a slight raid in the morning, no one had bothered to take shelter, and soon the all clear sounded. We searched for him indoors and out, calling his name. At last we thought of the basement—and there he was, stretched out on a camp bed, waiting for the releasing howl he must have slept through. I've never seen an animal look more embarrassed. He came upstairs very slowly in a dignified manner, yawning, but all the feathered strut and air of liking basements for their own sakes could not hide the fact that he felt sorely put out, diminished in his own eyes, aware that we had *seen.*

Poor Hawka. Like all our animals he fell victim to the roving service life. My stepfather's term of duty in Scotland ended, and I went south, first to cousins in Herefordshire, then to a London hotel, where my mother was already staying with Grannie and Aunt Ida, Gaffer having died just before the war. For some while we managed to keep Hawka with one or other of us; for a spell he even joined the Wiltshires at their Devizes depôt, where my brother's batman fell victim to his charm; but eventually he was given away to a settled home with one of our former governesses where, in spite of wartime food shortages, he grew overfed and dull.

After the "phoney war," Dunkirk, the Battle of Britain, and the London Blitz, the war had entered a long-drawn grim phase, like a continual bleak mid-winter punctuated by the deaths of friends: Johnny Miller, Richard Swayne on a commando course, Victor Goss in the North African desert, and several of my brother's regimental buddies. I find it hard now to make a coherent pattern out of what was then the muddle of my own life. For several reasons, notably a meningitis-type virus when I was small, combined with frequent bronchitic attacks, my health had never been much good, and when, under universal conscription, I was summoned for a medical, the board turned me down for full-time national service. In the meantime my stepfather, Gerry, had been sent as second-in-command to the admiral in command at Trinidad, and the Admiralty made it known that wives and families of officers serving in the West Indies would be given permits to join them—always providing that passages on an Atlantic convoy could be found for them. Gerry approved the idea of us joining him, and suggested that I could try to join the WRNS out there. We applied for permits, and settled down to wait. In the meantime I enrolled with the Westminster Red Cross and became a part-time nurse at the first-aid post situated beneath the Ministry of Shipping in Berkeley Square, which also housed the heavy rescue and light rescue teams dealing with air-raid disasters—tough, ribald men, who made a joke of everything.

London was a strange place in those days, gaunt with ruins, unusually beautiful by night when the blackout was in force and a starry sky was swept by the pallid probing fingers of the searchlights. It was shabby, almost trafficless except for military vehicles—petrol was on coupon, heavily rationed because of the Atlantic losses—and there was a heartwarming camaraderie amongst its population, while restaurants and nightclubs flourished, in spite of all restrictions. The place to go was Quaglino's—Quag's—L'Ecu de France, or L'Aperitif in Jermyn Street. Poles and Free French were specially popular, since their countries had suffered so harshly under Hitler, and uniforms were everywhere, though the American one was yet to come. Of course there were stories of almost eighteenth-century type footpads (thieves), but in general it was a lot safer to walk down a dark street carrying a masked torch (a slit uncovered on its surface, to light the kerbs) than it is today. The danger then came from the sky, not from one's fellow countrymen.

Meanwhile, the idea of Trinidad had begun to fade; the convoys were suffering heavily from U-boat attacks, and though we haunted the Admiralty no passages were forthcoming on the threatened merchantmen. Service personnel like Gerry were transported through the danger zones on one of the two largest liners, the *Queens Mary* and *Elizabeth,* but there was no place on them for civilians. They were painted in battle colours as a stark contrast to their peacetime brilliance, and were judged swift enough without escort to beat the submarines.

I had been present at the launching of the *Elizabeth* on Clydebank, when her enormous hull-wave as she hit the water nearly upset the launch we stood in. Later, when she left the yard where she was built, the time of her departure a close-guarded secret in case bombers targeted her, I had watched her giant grey form, dwarfing riverside buildings and towering above that narrow stretch of the Clyde, gently coaxed into more open water where her final fitting out would be completed. It had seemed impossible that anything so large could negotiate such finicky bends, but a flurry of tugs managed it. She was the last of the great "personality" liners, and it was good that she came through the perils of the war unscathed.

Aside from the Red Cross, there were sometimes other part-time jobs—canteen work for the Free French forces in St. James's and at the Lycée. There was great rapport then between us and the French, and everything about them seemed immensely *sympathique.* Although rationing was severe, even their canteen food still had the national artistry—no good suggesting to a Frenchman that he should survive on beer and chips. The most nostalgic songs of that time were their popular ones filled with poignant yearning for civilised, cultured France prostrate under the barbaric jackboot. Someone at the British Broadcasting Corporation had had the bright idea of increasing Allied morale by a daily playing of the national anthems before the morning news, starting with the Marseillaise. It wasn't a glorification of war, but did give a sense that spiritual homelands were still intact, even the worst oppressions didn't last forever, one day we'd all go home again. At the war's worst stages the list grew ominously long. My favorite anthem was the Czech—flowing and beautiful with tragic overtones. It's sad to think that their people are still so oppressed, in a different way.

Music had been part of my upbringing, and in those war years it held a special place for most people. There were Myra Hess's famous lunchtime concerts at the National Gallery, where I went whenever possible, and orchestral concerts at the Albert Hall. All were packed out. When Hitler attacked Russia there was an immediate fashion for Tchaikovsky's symphonies and concertos. Once Yehudi Menuhin flew in to give three concerts—in aid of de Gaulle's forces if my memory's correct. People almost fought for tickets, and workers at the Lycée had a special allocation. Menuhin's personality had the astounding impact then that it still has today—always his extra dimension of insight; and his playing of the Elgar concerto and the Mozart D Major was like manna from heaven on the desertlands of war.

At times it was a relief to escape from London. There were short breaks at my father's house "Springfield" (he was then C-in-C Bomber Command with his headquarters at High Wycombe), or helping friends on their Berkshire farm—country occupations like haymaking and milking cows, and (at last) learning to ride properly on an ex-cavalry mare across the common near Bucklebury; all of them pleasant alternatives to the city on its wartime footing, and the air raids, which may have been more sporadic than the Blitz of 1940 as English air power increased and the German was spread over a wider front, but were still sharp, frequent, and indiscriminate. By that time the First-Aid Nursing Yeomanry had been mainly absorbed by the Auxiliary Territorial Service, and my sister had exchanged into the Fire Service, where she was a dispatch rider during the worst of those days.

I certainly don't wish to enter the bombing-of-Germany controversy, nor is this the place to do so, but those people who complain about it now from a safer position should perhaps remember that at no time did the Luftwaffe cease trying to destroy our cities by high explosive, firebomb, doodlebug, and those first pernicious rockets, the so-called V-2s, which fell from a clear sky at all hours of the day or night to kill and maim without warning: Hitler's scientists were on the verge of a breakthrough that would have made a London holocaust a certainty. During one of these last night-raids I was on fire-watch duty in South Kensington—there was a weekly rota for most adults. When the all clear sounded I went up on the rooftop. The silence, after the racket of the raid, was extreme, except for a gently sinister underlying hiss and crackle, like wireless interference. All around the London skyline blazed thirty fires, a strange and eerie sight.

After the long war, the grey era of lassitude. For ages the aftermath was with us, in the shape of really severe food rationing and other shortages. Everyone seemed very tired, aimless, and restless. My schooling had been thoroughly interrupted, and was anyway of the old style French and piano variety, and such talents as I had weren't exactly marketable. With no special training nor exams behind me I didn't want to become a secretary, which seemed a rather dead-end job, with no particular prospect in view. I had always enjoyed painting and writing, so with a vague sense that there might be a niche somewhere in the world of art, I enrolled in life classes at St. Martin's School, and at the Chelsea School of Art for a two-year course in painting and sculpture, after a searing interview with H. C. Williamson, then head of the faculty. Grey, lanky, and sardonic, he was quite as frightening in his own quiet way as the famously putting-down Professor Tonks of the Slade. I sat palpitating in a chair while he examined my portfolio of drawings with a scathing eye. As he closed it he gave a disillusioned sigh, saying, "Hm, I don't see why you shouldn't come here, you're no worse than anybody else."

The years at Chelsea were fun, and provided lifelong friendships, even if they didn't get me much further on. Ceri Richards taught the life class; he was a fine artist, a Welshman like Dylan Thomas, whose friend he was, and for whose work he had done some brilliant complementary paintings. Unless you were one of his pets, and luckily he liked my work, his gentle sigh of despair beside your easel could be as devastating as Williamson's, and many of his class were traumatised for life by the experience.

One of the things I found hardest to accustom myself to was the heat of the studio. The atmosphere was kept at boiling point, so that the naked models didn't freeze. There was one very famous model who was wholly *sans gêne.* At that time the Manresa Road buildings were still part-occupied by a sailor's canteen, heaven knows why, and the rooms were opposite the life class. This model was no beauty, just basic significant form. She was tiny, Spanish-looking, with lots of curly black hair, and was round all round and everywhere, like a pack of balloons blown up to their full extent. During breaks she would light a cigarette, drape a minute embroidered shawl over her shoulders, and, otherwise naked, toddle out into the corridor where she would ramble unconcernedly up and down, to the surprise and embarrassment of the young sailors who would dive pop-eyed and blushing into the haven of their canteen.

There were only eight or ten of us in the sculpture class. I enjoyed it immensely, more than painting, and though it didn't turn me into a sculptor it did introduce me to the grandeur of ancient Egyptian sculptures of the Old and Middle Kingdoms, which were a revelation—and a great influence later on when I was writing a fantasy Egyptian trilogy. Henry Moore was supposed to teach us for one whole day a week, though in practice he usually turned up for about ten minutes twice a term. He was as down-to-earth as a plumber, not tall, but with all the Yorkshire strength needed to hew away at enormous blocks of stone. We were in awe of his sudden appearances, and fame. I remember him as a very nice man who openly and rightly took none of us seriously. However, he was the most brilliant teacher I've ever come across, and after some words about our efforts which kindly and piercingly demolished his class, would turn to the model's pose, and in a few sentences reveal to our dazzled eyes exactly how weight and tension produced the form we were trying to copy in clay. Usually he ended the lesson by brief flirtation with the prettiest, silliest girl in the class—whose contribution to art was confined to slapping layers of clay onto a melon-shaped head—and then departed as suddenly as he had arrived.

Towards the end of the course I grew depressed by the knowledge that I was neither motivated nor quite good enough to make any substantial career in painting, despite the approval of Ceri Richards, who wrote me a charming letter of recommendation when I left. At that time the cousin of a friend was free-lancing as a picture restorer, so I joined him for a year to learn the techniques before talking myself into the Department of Technology at the Courtauld Institute of Art. Auntie Nan had just died, and had left me a small legacy of two hundred and fifty pounds, which paid my fees. It was a tiny class again, but this time an international one. The work was interesting, specially when the head of the department took us round a great auction house to point out the fakes. However, it wasn't long before I guessed that career-wise I had struck another dead end. Restoration then was an extremely competitive business with a limited number of opportunities, specially for women. I could have acted indefinitely as somebody's dogsbody, but the chances of making ends meet in more than the most basic way seemed as remote as ever, and a thoroughgoing drudge. Life is for living, after all.

The author, about 1950

In the end a change of direction came about through what seemed chance—although looking back I can see that the seeds had simply lain dormant since I was a child, and that the activities and experiences I'd been through, some funny, some painful, even horrific, had been ripening them all along. The catalyst was a real accident. We handled dangerous chemicals at the Courtauld, and somehow or other I managed to damage my right eye, making an enforced holiday imperative. My mother and stepfather were now living in Hampshire, for they had bought a tiny house with a large garden near Medstead for his retirement. I went down to stay, and bused in and out to Alton to receive treatment for my damaged sight, admiring Jane Austen's Chawton home on the way. There wasn't a great deal to do, except help Nanny in the kitchen (she had stayed with my mother through the years, and now cooked for the family), or laze in the garden. My thoughts turned to writing and I bought some notebooks and began to think about a play.

There was always a lot of interest in the theatre in my mother's family. Fine voices abounded in it; one of my great-aunts was even asked to sing at La Scala. There had been Gaffer's natural acting talent, and my brother too had taken part in all sorts of musical and acting entertainment during his army service. My first visits to the theatre and opera had securely hooked me—although I'd little acting talent, my only achievement having been a barrel organ-like rendering of "Come down to Kew in Lilac-time" at my Weymouth day school, which had earned me a surprising ten out of ten. Our Nanny, dear Lily Louisa Chappell, had been a wonderful reciter, keeping us enthralled with long, sentimental Victorian poems in which little boys (mostly) came to an evil or angelic end. Nanny had also been a storyteller like our beloved Gran; and from the earliest age, encouraged by over-praise and admiration of my worst efforts, I had dictated rambling stories to her, or written acutely embarrassing poems about nature's beauty. The other stimulator of my infant fancy had appeared later on the scene in the shape of Valerie Couch, the charming governess who had received Hawka as a gift, and whom I had shared with my sister for those thunderous years of the divorce.

Twice weekly Valerie had made us write essays. How we loved it. A change from the dreadful parsing of French, or the unfathomable, brutal equation. The only time I ever wept over an essay was when we were told to write one on Westminster Abbey. Gaffer had kindly driven us to see it the night before, in his cherished Armstrong Siddeley. The Abbey is big, but—enthralled by the drive and rather small on my grandfather's left—I hadn't seen it. "Where, Gaffer —*where*?" Too late. We'd passed it by.

Now I wrote an entire play in six weeks. It was called "The Burning Glass" (Charles Morgan used the same name, later) and had as subject a group of ill-assorted people summoned by a ruthless scientist friend to view the first fruits of his invention. Once I had finished it, I took it to London to show to writer friends. The verdicts were optimistic—though one said it really needed revision from end to end. I rewrote it. And again, several times. An agent accepted it. The team that put on the popular "Seagulls over Sorrento" voted on it, and it lost by one vote. In the end it was a bit of a heartbreak, that play—so nearly put on, so often. Meanwhile I wrote short stories and sent them to a famous journalist for an opinion, inconsiderately and cheekily, I think now. He sent me the kindest possible letter, in which he told me what I wanted to hear: You are a writer. (He also asked me—and how I agree with him now, as a fellow writer—not to write to him again!)

I had found what I was suited for at last, though the essential problem was to earn a living. My mother always helped me when she could from her small alimony, which she had agreed to have reduced after my father remarried before the war. Rooms in London at that time seem cheap by today's standards—though congenial ones were just as hard to find. By this time my sister had married and was living in Ireland, so for some while I moved from one dreary digs to another, until I could share with friends or relations, learning to cook from necessity and dire experience. I'm a reasonably good cook, but in those days it was hit or miss, mostly miss, and no one had warned me to seal the juices when cooking meat—sybaritic boyfriends were more inclined to take me out to meals than risk eating in.

Sometimes there were delicious meals at the Savoy or Claridge's when my father came home to England on flying visits; he and his second wife, Jill, and my half-sister Jacan were living partly in South Africa and partly in America. He was running a shipping line, Safmarine, which was later taken over. A service life doesn't necessarily fit you for commercial battling; although, as someone always interested in food and practical good living, he did take a keen interest in what sort of jam was served on board the ships.

Energy was always in short supply for me, as I struggled with various health problems. In order to write professionally, part-time work had to be found which would leave enough time and energy for my own work. I had talked my way into the restoring course at the Courtauld—now I went to see our dignified, exceptionally Germanic professor, to explain why I was talking myself out of it: he might have been furious, but couldn't have been more charming as he wished me luck. In finding work I had been lucky, though the pay was unremarkable. One of our greatest friends, Peter Watling, a wartime comrade-in-arms of my brother, was then covering the London stage for Metro-Goldwyn-Mayer, and got us onto their rota of readers: over not too long a period this sort of work can prove invaluable training.

Dear Peter himself was a fine writer, with a successful West End play already to his credit, and he expected high standards of craftsmanship. You wrote well for Peter, or you were out on your ear. Employees of MGM were expected to cover several new books a week. The essence of the job was to tear the heart out of them and put it down on paper: plot, style, and emotional content, if any, together with reasons for recommendation or none. A "no" meant merely three or four pages written work, but a "yes" entailed a fifteen-page detailed script. Peter was so adept that he could manage the whole thing in two hours, which included reading the book. It took me four, longer if I was recommending anything. Luckily, very little that comes off the presses is film material: there are few *Gone with the Winds* and *Day of the Jackals* around.

In the meantime, "The Burning Glass" was still with London managements, getting good reports, but never quite making it onto the stage. I wrote constantly—short stories, another play, books for musicals. Anthony, released after eight years' service in the Army, was writing music, and we hoped to pool our efforts; but the nearest we got to success was years later, when a joint musical with a Canterbury-pilgrim theme was nearly bought for the Canterbury Festival, only to be dashed at the last moment by the London stage success of another musical based on Chaucer's *Tales.*

After I had been with MGM for some while a bout of unusually bad 'flu left me feeling ill and depressed, for which I received rather ineffectual treatment. Perhaps it was set off by the fact that my personal life was going far from well, too, since I seemed fated to be drawn towards the same honey-pot syndrome that had so bedevilled the lives of my mother and grandmother in their different ways—shades of Freud! Also of Jung, whose writings have been of major importance to me. London then was not so frenetic a place as it is today, but it was never exactly a rest cure. I retreated to Hampshire, continued to work for MGM at long distance for a while, and also began work on a full-length novel, *The Summer-House*, which—to my happy amazement—was accepted by the first publishing house I sent it to, Hamish Hamilton.

It would be pleasant to record that from then on my career never looked back, but writing as a way of life is more like living on a Ferris wheel than anything else. I suspect that the reason it attracts too many people—what professional writer hasn't endured torments from the hundreds of friends and strangers who "always knew they could write if they only had the time," and worse still have a little manuscript with them to prove it?—is that they have not the least idea what it entails in the form of daily work and a capacity to endure repetitive, continual revision. Also, of course, there's the lure of a possible multi-sales success, a rare outcome, comparable to winning a Derby lottery. Even in the gaining of awards there's always this element of chance, or luck.

But to return from asides. Hamish Hamilton was delighted by that first novel's enthusiastic reception, yet disliked my second one so much that he returned it to me more in sorrow than in anger. It was accepted by the Bodley Head, whose editors in turn looked sadly on my third effort, *Venus with Sparrows.* I sent this last manuscript hopefully to Faber's—where I found a marvellous response, superb editing, and good friends, specially in Alan Pringle and Rosemary Goad, my editors for adult books, and in Phyllis Hunt, my editor for children's. And with Faber I've been ever since, with some agreed exceptions.

Writing as a career has brought ups and downs, pleasure and pain, and many fascinating contacts. Perhaps the most successful authors specialise—yet the variety of work is what stimulates me; from writing thrillers to texts of picture books, from TV stories for young children to TV plays for older ones. And from writing for teenagers to adult novels. I have worked as a critic for the *Times,* and my unassuaged desire for the stage has been partly met by the fun and privilege of working with teams of actors, some of whom are now household names. I am envious, though, of writers who really enjoy public speaking, and still more of those who do it well. I have suffered (so have my audiences) hilariously on occasions. One of the most scarifying moments was making a speech in the historic City of London Guildhall to seven hundred people. Why is it that all writers are expected to be natural talkers? It's so untrue. Or—come to that—ceaseless letter writers? One other lasting regret of mine is that I have not speeded up over the years, being by nature a plodder who rewrites every book at least three times, and avoids all unnecessary letter writing like the plague.

Of course I have many other interests besides writing, and in Northern Europe have travelled quite widely, though otherwise not extensively, which it would be good to remedy some day, specially as England has such a cold, rainy climate. For a long while now I have lived in Chelsea, which seems to have drawn me back to itself almost by accident

"With a picture by my illustrator Errol LeCain on the wall behind me. It was from The Lotus and the Grail."

rather than design. In fact, it seems to have quite a drawing effect on most of my family, as many of them live close by.

Chelsea today is no longer the painters' quiet village that it used to be: the King's Road has developed into a thriving attraction for tourists, come to view the punks on their home ground. The famous houses of Cheyne Walk must have raised their Georgian eyebrows to see Japanese monks building a Buddhist pagoda on the Battersea side of the river. The Royal Court Theatre in Sloane Square puts on some of the more controversial plays. Sadly, property developers and yuppies have moved into the district, company lets too, sending the price of flats and houses rocketing through the roof. In spite of everything Chelsea fights back, retaining its famous flower show, its Chelsea Pensioners' Royal Hospital inaugurated by Charles II at the request of Nell Gwynne,[1] and its air of absorbing the present into a historic past.

One in Chelsea, the other in Oxfordshire, my parents lived to a ripe old age, dying within three years of one another, all passion and all quarrels spent, and in the end sending each other courteous messages and remembrances. My mother died last year, and is greatly missed by my brother and myself. She was a sweetie—we had looked after her through various illnesses till the end of her long life, here in Chelsea. My father died two years before her. His memorial service was held in Westminster Abbey, attended by his two families. A great deal was written about him in the papers, and still is, for his wartime strategy will always make of him a controversial figure to be argued over by military historians. Much of the criticism was ill-informed and ill-directed, just as one or two of the eulogies were somewhat high-flown, and unrelated to him as the exceptionally human person that he was.

In his last years we had got on well together. He was really a grand old man, indomitable and opinionated to the last, with a sweetness of character in old age that had been rather lacking in youth, and a huge sense of fun and repertoire of jokes. Towards the end he showed me a letter that Albert Speer had just written him—it seemed to me then, and does now, a strange ending to that era of conflict: the exchange of polite correspondence between two old gentlemen, the one who had so energetically helped fashion Hitler's monstrous Reich, and the other who, with equal fervour, had helped demolish it.

As for myself, I suppose I shall continue to write, trying to resist the lure of too much diversifying—although I have just been sidetracked into selecting twentieth-century poems for a Hamish Hamilton illustrated edition; and my latest older children's (in fact, almost adults') book, *Summers of the Wild Rose,* a romance set in pre-war Austria, was published by Faber in February.

Perhaps the most complex side of things for a woman writer is to get some balance into your life: you must isolate yourself for periods to work properly, although paradoxically there is nothing more important to what you do than a good slice of extroverted living. The attempt to achieve both often produces a sense of mental squinting, not to mention exhaustion. The women writers I admire most are those like Susan Hill, Lisa St. Aubin de Teran, and Isabel Allende, who appear to have achieved a happy harmony—surely one of the most charming autobiographical books written in years is Susan Hill's *Magic*

[1]This actually—and I have only learned it since writing this article—is untrue: it was entirely the King's idea, and the "sweet Nell" side of it is pleasant romantic fiction.

Apple Tree, an account of her life in Oxfordshire with her husband and child.

There is more and more competition in the literary world these days, as in all sides of life, as younger people launch themselves on the scene; but luckily there are more outlets and chances too—for instance, in television. Also there is, at last, the saving grace of Public Lending Right, and the prospect of reform of the copyright laws. But it is a peculiar way of life, and for most people probably best combined with something else. As Alan used to say to me, at Faber's, shaking his head, "After all, you're a mad lot, you authors . . . ."

BIBLIOGRAPHY

FOR YOUNG PEOPLE

Fiction:

The Moon in the Cloud. London: Faber, 1968; New York: Macmillan, 1969.

The Shadow on the Sun. London: Faber, 1970; New York: Macmillan, 1970.

The Child in the Bamboo Grove (illustrated by Errol LeCain). London: Faber, 1971; New York: S.G. Phillips, 1971.

The Seal-Singing. London: Faber, 1971; New York: Macmillan, 1971.

The Bright and Morning Star. London: Faber, 1972; New York: Macmillan, 1972.

The King's White Elephant (illustrated by E. LeCain). London: Faber, 1973.

The Lotus and the Grail: Legends from East to West. London: Faber, 1974; abridged edition published as *Sea Magic and Other Stories of Enchantment.* New York: Macmillan, 1974.

The Flying Ship (illustrated by E. LeCain). London: Faber, 1975.

The Little Dog of Fo (illustrated by E. LeCain). London: Faber, 1976.

I Want to Be a Fish (illustrated by Jill Bennett). Harmondsworth, England: Kestrel, 1977.

A Quest for Orion. London and Boston: Faber, 1978.

Beauty and the Beast (reteller; illustrated by E. LeCain). Garden City, N.Y.: Doubleday, 1979; London: Faber, 1979.

Green Finger House (illustrated by Juan Wijngaard). Twickenham, England: Eel Pie, 1979; New York: Kampmann, 1982.

Tower of the Stars. London: Faber, 1980.

The Enchanted Horse (illustrated by Pauline Baynes). Harmondsworth, England: Kestrel, 1981.

Janni's Stork (illustrated by J. Wijngaard). Glasgow: Blackie, 1982; New York: Bedrick/Blackie, 1982.

Zed. London: Faber, 1982.

Heidi (reteller; illustrated by Tomi Ungerer). Tonbridge, England: E. Benn, 1983.

Summers of the Wild Rose. London: Faber, 1987.

FOR ADULTS

Fiction:

The Summer-House. London: Hamish Hamilton, 1956.

Voyage to Cythera. London: Bodley Head, 1958.

Venus with Sparrows. London: Faber, 1961.

All My Enemies. London: Faber, 1967; New York: Simon & Schuster, 1973.

The Nice Girl's Story. London: Faber, 1968; also published as *Nor Evil Dreams.* New York: Simon & Schuster, 1973.

A Wicked Pack of Cards. London: Faber, 1969; New York: Walker & Co., 1970.

The Double Snare. London: Faber, 1974; New York: Simon & Schuster, 1975.

Three Candles for the Dark. London: Faber, 1976.

Marguerite Henry

Tony Francis Photography

Marguerite Henry

If you happen to be the youngest in a family of five and were saddled during your growing years with hand-me-downs, you will share my loathing for an astrakhan coat that finally came to me after three previous owners had outgrown it.

I was seven and I hated my astrakhan coat. Astrakhan "sounds" grand, and maybe in the beginning my coat looked grand. It is really the tightly curled fleece of baby lamb with its lining of windproof hide. But as successive sisters wore it while sliding downhill without a sled, and making wingspread angels in the snow, the tight curls gave way to frays and tatters.

In my selfishness I gave no thought to the poor little lamb that had sacrificed his skin to keep me warm. All I thought about was a bright red coat that looked beautiful and didn't have to be grown *into* or *out of.* No amount of motherly logic could convince me of the superior warmth of lamb's fleece, nor how fortunate I was to own a good astrakhan coat while many children around the world had no coat at all.

In this "winter of my discontent" whenever I caught my reflection in a store mirror I wanted to die so I could be buried in something pretty, and wouldn't my mother be sorry she had made me wear the old astrakhan?

When I had been particularly obnoxious one morning at breakfast, I came home from school at noon wildly exuberant with the news that the vice-president elect of the United States in a motorcade had leaned over and, in my words, had "shooken hands" with me.

My mother shared my radiance. "Oh my dear child," she exclaimed, "you see, it wasn't your coat he noticed. It was your inner beauty that shone through."

The truth was that the vice-president elect had barely smiled in my direction. It was my rival, Dilla Blumquist, he had "shooken hands" with.

Shamefacedly I wanted to spill out the truth, but the words caught in my throat. There are some things you just can't say. Besides, who could be so cruel as to dim the sparkle in Mama's tired eyes? My self-imposed penance consisted of wearing that astrakhan coat another year, in abject silence.

It was in that seventh year of my life that I made up my mind to join the writer's trade. Then I could mix fact and imagination to make everything come out clear and believable. Quite unknowingly my father aided and abetted my plan by giving me a Christmas present to set the dreams of any seven-year-old afire.

On Christmas Eve while I lay awake hoping for, but not expecting, the rataplan of hoofs on the roof, a scenario was taking place in a corner of Mama's kitchen. My father was setting up a little red table with all the wondrous tools of writing.

At dawn the next morning I stood tongue-tied in wild delight at the magic world spread out before me. What caught my eye first was my own cream pitcher holding a bright bouquet of pencils—three reds, two greens, and a yellow. Brand new they were, with their erasers firm and unchewed, and all so freshly sharpened that to this day the memory of their cedarwood fragrance tickles my nose.

Beside the pitcher lay a gleaming pair of shears. They were tied to the table with a knitted string, just the way my mittens were fastened to my coat so they could never be lost. And there was an enormous jar of paste with the brush handle sticking straight up in the air, inviting me to grab it. And hanging on a hook by the side of the table was a punch for pressing holes in paper; it too was caught fast with a red knitted string. And there was my mother's hand-painted pin tray that used to sit on her dresser holding a pansy brooch. Now it was mounded with paper clips. There was even a pencil sharpener!

Best of all was the stack of fat pads of paper, in every hue of the rainbow. They were from my father's office. On the top sheet, in his no-frills script, he had written:

Dear Last of the Mohicans,
Not a penny for your thoughts,
but a tablet.
Merry Christmas!
Papa Louis XOX

Carefully I folded the sheet and opened the one little drawer of my table. In it I laid the paper, tucking it under a horseshoe paperweight. Papa's beautiful handwriting must never get mixed up with my scrawling.

All at once I was hearing my own portentous words. "I will join the writer's trade!" I picked up each tool—a pencil first, and sniffed the newly shaved wood. I worked the shears, and laughed in joy because they were not blunt-ended like a child's plaything. From the rainbow of paper I tore off a pink sheet and snipped it in two. My shears cut sharp and clean, the way professional shears should. With the good-smelling paste I swabbed the halves together.

Everything was right! I tried hard to hold back the tears. At last I had a world of my very own—a writing world—and soon it would be populated by all the creatures of my imagination.

While I scribbled and sketched at the little red table I was supremely happy. All about me were the most titillating smells and sounds—an egg whisk beating against its bowl, soups and sauces purring and boiling, the clink of clean knives and forks dropping into their trays, and Mama and the hired girl chatting away about things that didn't matter to me. But what *did* matter was that they were there, and they were working, too.

Some people think writing is a mysterious trade. Yet with paper and pencil, and a tabletop, anyone can write—as I discovered a year later. The *Delineator,* my mother's magazine, invited children to contribute stories based on spring, summer, autumn, or winter. I chose autumn because I had just come from an October birthday party. My friend, Beth, lived in the country, in a wilderness of trees. Red and yellow leaves were thick on the grass and the wind was swirling them into corners of house and barn. They made a nice crunching sound as I scuffed through them, and offered great cover-up for our game of hide-and-seek. When no one was looking I buried myself under a huge mound of maple leaves, and for the longest time I didn't think *anyone* was going to find me. Probably no one ever would have if Beth hadn't given her dog, Omar, one of my party gloves to smell. He found me just in the nick of time, for the hot chocolate was ready with marshmallows swimming on top, and the cake with frosting so thick you wished you had a long tongue like Omar's to lap it up.

Marguerite about one year old

So this is what I wrote about—"Hide-and-Seek in Autumn Leaves." Two months later when a twelve-dollar check came from the children's editor, with a letter suggesting I use the money for summer camp, I was overwhelmed to the point of dizziness. Writing was not only fun, it was such a pleasant way of earning a living. Already I was addicted!

Following "My Editor's" advice I did go to summer camp, at Lake Pistakee, in Illinois. The camp was sponsored by our church, one week set aside for boys and one for girls, aged eight to twelve. I just slithered under the wire, age-wise, and was delighted by my tallness so I could look eye-to-eye with several of the twelve-year-olds. Our leader, Miss Laura Bertelson, happened to be my Sunday-school teacher, and also happened to be beautiful beyond my words. I worshipped her, probably more than the lessons she taught.

On the first black night of lightning bugs and a glowing fire Miss Bertelson tried to develop a camaraderie between the younger and older girls. "Let's all tell our hobbies," she said, her eyes wide in expectancy.

The answers were spat out with pride and gusto. "I ski!" "I swim, forty laps!" "I like fancy skating." "Tennis is the best." Even cooking was mentioned, which elicited a "boo."

I noticed that all the hobbies, including cooking, spelled *action.* Suddenly it was my turn. My throat went dry. I felt as if I were on the high dive. How could these girls know? How *could* they know that my father had a printing plant, and often he let me read proof or watch blank paper feed through the presses and come out covered with exciting words? "My hobby," I stuttered, "is words."

The silence that followed was awesome. In the glare of firelight the red faces turned toward me were agape in disbelief, eyes popping as if I were some spooky creature, more ghost than real. I longed to throw myself on the fire and turn to ash dust.

Twelve years old

But God bless our leader. "What a coincidence!" she said. "I like to play with words, too. What kind do *you* like, Marguerite?"

It was too late now to become popular. I slid deeper into the quagmire of my misery as I confessed, "tin-tin-nabulation."

"Oh!" Laura Bertelson exclaimed. "You're thinking of Poe's *tintinnabulation of the bell, bells, bells,*" and her voice was so full of melody I could have died for joy.

The rest of that week I tried to hide my homesickness in athletic prowess. I played Ping-Pong with a vengeance. I swam fiercely my dog-paddle stroke, alongside the big girls' Australian crawl which was anything but a crawl. Often when I came out of the lake I hoped that my tears were camouflaged by Pistakee's clear water dripping down my face. My homesickness was ever present, for a father who yodeled like a Swiss Alpine climber and recited whole passages from Shakespeare, and for a big sister who explained the meaning of words more vividly than any old dictionary.

Back home again I slid back into my own world like a snail into its shell. Both my little red table and chair were wearing stilts, carefully whittled by my father. This gave my corner of the kitchen a business-like look, and made me feel tall, as a burgeoning author should. Only one thing was missing—a bulletin board like the one in my father's office. His was spattered with wise sayings, such as, " . . . that's a valiant flea that dares eat his breakfast on the lip of a lion"—Shakespeare.

I had garnered some wise sayings of my own, but where to put them? Mama's kitchen was newly painted and not to be desecrated with pockmarks of paper, even if they divulged nuggets of great wisdom. In desperation I invested half my week's allowance on colored pushpins and thumbed the precious gems to the margin of my table.

> Next to mother's milk books are the best nourishment.
> —Lawrence Clark Powell

> The more you read the better you write.
> —Anonymous

These encouraging words led to my habit of roller-skating every other day to Milwaukee's North Side Branch Library, a mile away, to take out a new book and return the old one in whose spell I continued to live and breathe. Often as I flew pell-mell to my destination, I was still climbing mountains with Heidi, or wrassling wildcats with Dan'l Boone, or plugging the hole in the dike with *my* thumb instead of Peter's.

One time I was Hans Brinker skimming across the ice so fast I was unaware of street crossings until I headed directly for a speeding motorcycle. The quick-thinking rider used his arm as a broom and sent me sprawling out of his way. When I came to, it was *Hans Brinker*'s bruises that concerned me more than my own. How was I ever going to explain to the librarian?

Many times I'd read the dire warning printed on the pocket inside the cover: "Books must not be defaced. Any injuries beyond ordinary wear shall be made good to the satisfaction of the librarian. The holder of any card having losses charged against him is debarred the privileges of the library. Failure to comply with this rule will forfeit *all* privileges of the library."

What greater punishment could there be than to forego a new book every other day? From the viewpoint of my scant years it would be far worse than a "no vacancy" sign on the gates of heaven.

With my head still bandaged I presented the torn copy of *Hans Brinker* at the library. Imagine the flood of relief that coursed through my skinny frame when Miss Delia G. Ovitz, for that was the librarian's name, tucked my hand under her wing and led me to a cubicle of a room behind the stacks. It was barely big enough for a table, but on it was a wondrous assortment of nostrums for battered and bruised books. There were rolls of buckram and cloth-tape in muted shades of green and brown and maroon. And there was an enormous jar of delicious-smelling paste with a paintbrush for swabbing it on. And there were shellac and labels and cockleboard papers. And a wilderness of lettering pens and bottles of white ink and india and even of gold. And gleaming shears hung from a chain fastened to the table, and a lone book, held in a vise, stood with its spine exposed for treatment from a long curved needle for stitching loose sections together. It was all like a doctor's office, but far more exciting.

In this new and magical world I learned my first lesson in book-mending, which I have not forgotten to this day. Every time I tape up a torn page I glow to my job as if I were a Mother Theresa saving the human race.

Is it any wonder that I worshipped Miss Ovitz passionately and considered her Queen of the Realm of Books? Miss Ovitz, I might add, had two loves, in this order: books and needlework. Above her check-out desk was a sampler with red and blue stitches that spelled out: "I come here to find myself, it is so easy to get lost in the world."—John Burroughs.

Each time I took out a book, I secretly hoped that Miss Ovitz's pencil point would break so I could linger longer and memorize the beautiful cross-stitched words.

Months later, after I had gobbled up Zane Grey's *The Spirit of the Border* and *Riders of the Purple Sage*, I needed money desperately to buy a ranch. I wanted a whole section of land, with a stallion for every mare, and they would be as prolific as rabbits so that fillies and colts would frisk about everywhere in wild abandon.

Where did I turn for a job? To the library, of course, to Miss Delia G. Ovitz of the shining dark eyes and hair like brown sunshine. Again she came to my rescue. After school and on Saturdays I was allowed to help her mend books. And more exciting still, to collate them and see that no pages were missing before the bill for them was paid. My diligence knew no bounds. Instead of riffling lightly through the pages, counting 1, 3, 5, 7, 9, 11, and so on, I read the books to make deadly sure that the last line on the left-hand page was fully and properly wedded to the

Marguerite at age sixteen

top line on the right-hand page. Not a phrase, not even a comma could be lost.

One Saturday morning when I had collated only two books in four hours, Miss Ovitz bore down upon me. I was so deeply absorbed in my reading that I didn't even hear her. It was her shadow across the page that made me look up into a face completely changed. The soft brown eyes were ablaze. As for the gentle voice, it was brittle and crisp. Each word pinged like hail, and was mouthed slowly with cold silences between. "You, Marguerite, will have to find other work. You may put on your coat and leave."

I slid down from my stool, my fingers still held in place. "I'll go," I said meekly. "But oh, Miss Ovitz, you've got to read this! Your sampler man, John Burroughs, wrote it."

"My sampler man?"

I pointed to the radiant lines and left the essay, "Summit of the Years," in her hands. Then slowly, with leaden feet, I walked to the book-mending room which also served as a cloakroom. I put on my astrakhan coat and cap, and battened down the cocker spaniel earflaps. I pulled on my overshoes and buckled all eight buckles, each one seeming to seal my doom. I had no handkerchief to cry into so I borrowed one of the soft cloths we used for wiping paste, and now the tears spilled over in a torrent. That delicious smell of library paste. It overpowered me. I would never smell it again!

Suddenly I heard heels clicking and Miss Ovitz was behind me, clasping my shoulders. Her voice was not brisk and brittle anymore. It was warm and breathy as she repeated the words I had found: "I go to books as a bee goes to the flower for a nectar that I can make into my own honey"—John Burroughs.

"Child, child," she comforted, "I shall stitch another sampler for the library. And you shall help me hang it when it is done. Now, off with your coat and get to work. Mind that you *count* this time, not read!"

Up till now I've bypassed writing about my baby years because, of course, I can't remember them, but I've been told and retold that I was born after a flash flood when whole nests of duck eggs were washed down our creek—all but one egg. The lone egg hatched out, and instead of the usual spring sight of the mother ducks, each with a trail of ducklings, there was only one yellow duckling with a whole parade of ducks and drakes waddling along behind him!

The lone duckling seemed especially favored; he had so many elders to teach him how to swim and dive and fish.

In many ways my childhood was similar to the lucky duckling's. I was born into a family of three sisters—two full grown—and a grown brother. Instead of having one mother to hover over me it seemed as if I had a whole flock of mothers and two fathers! If I called out the window to a playmate, "Mama says I can't go with you today," the answer usually was, "Ask one of your *other* mamas."

We lived in a modest but cozy home in Milwaukee, and no youngster had a jollier period of growing up. Marie, my oldest sister, made my dresses, embroidered and sashed in blue, and gave me music lessons. Elsie taught me the doorknob method of pulling teeth and provided an allowance from her nursing stipend, which was all the more exciting because of its irregularity. Fred, my big brother, used to take my hand and run with me, so that I flew through space in the most astounding manner, like a creature who could glide without wings. And Gertrude, who was nearest in age, became my unabridged dictionary. Winter evenings when we were both absorbed in our own reading I nagged my long-suffering mentor for definitions. "What does *gin ger ly* mean?" I asked, glancing up from a well-thumbed copy of *Little Women.*

Quick as a flash I had my answer. "Papa has a drippy head cold, and this morning when he accidentally dropped his handkerchief you picked it up very gingerly." How can one forget such sisterly specificity? The word became mine forever. She also taught me that contrary to Gertrude Stein a dog isn't a dog, a dog, a dog—he is a dalmatian or a dachshund or a collie or a droopy-eared basset hound or a mongrel. "You've got to make pictures in your reader's mind," she said, "quick pictures."

She was right! I still go to her with each story I write. Editors could be wrong, but not Gertrude.

I'm going to skip lightly over my years in grade school and high school because they were not much fun. I was skinny as an eel and awkward as well, and the boys referred to me as "that long drink of water." I wore two pairs of stockings at a time to "fatten" my pipe-stem legs. Luckily when I went to the University of Wisconsin–Milwaukee, I had to walk a long mile there and another back home. This sparked my appetite. A morning mug of rich cocoa rounded me out so I dared try out for plays, and I was even invited to my first prom!

I lived for two classes: Miss Schaeffer for English composition and Mrs. Anholt for drama. Playacting became so engrossing I seriously considered it as a second career to writing. I thought of being a Mrs. Anholt, who lived each role in a play so she seemed not to be teaching at all. I could hardly wait to try out for Molière's plays. How I wanted to acquire that elusive throaty elegance of the born-and-bred Parisienne. In my first play I had the startling stage business of waving a long cigarette between my forefinger and middle finger. I'm sure I never attained the proper élan or the sophistication for playing Angelique, but the attempt was enthralling. Our director suggested that Gertrude would understand my dangling a cigarette to fill the role, but my parents should perhaps wait until I played an ingenue.

At age twenty-one I suddenly grew up. My beloved father died and that same year I married Sidney Crocker Henry. We met—his family and mine—at Huber's Resort, a fishing camp in northern Wisconsin. Sidney came with his brother and sister-in-law, and all three were avid fishermen. I came with Elsie, my tooth-puller sister, and her husband; and Gertrude, my mentor, with her college fiancé. It was almost like a reunion . . . before we had even met! We fished by day and danced by moonlight to the music of a volunteer pianist on a piano that could have stood tuning.

At leave-taking our family was invited to stop off in Sheboygan to meet the Henrys' parents who lived in a rambling house with a thriving vegetable garden. We arrived at the peak of harvesting season, with delicious corn and plump red tomatoes. Over luncheon there was no lag in the conversation. Then we said good-by and hoped to meet again next year, same place, same time.

With Sidney Crocker Henry, shortly after they met, about 1920

But Sidney flew to Milwaukee a month later to meet my parents. Papa Louis was ill at the time, but Sidney saw the bond between us, and the two men were like Olympic runners. My father passed the torch to Sidney, who kept the flame of love for me burning all through our lifetime. Who needed encouragement to write, if Sidney Crocker Henry were in your corner?

Sid's sales managerial duties often had us spending a month or more in big cities across the country where I liked to try my hand at magazine articles. In Philadelphia I read Sid a list of local publishers.

"Why not call on the *Saturday Evening Post*?" he suggested.

"The *Post*!" I gasped.

"Why not?"

Why not indeed! To Sid's lack of surprise and my disbelief the *Post* bought a three-part series from me, "Turning Points in the Lives of Famous Men." My most memorable subject was Clarence Darrow, who seemed to do most of the interviewing himself. In a tone as if he were grilling a witness he asked, "Why are you more important than that mouse skittering across the floor?" He lit one question on the stub of the last, but never completely bypassed the turning point in his life.

The turning point in Sid's and my life came when we moved to the village of Wayne, Illinois. We discovered that we both had missed animals in our childhood and now we had room for a whole menagerie. How we met the first member was destiny.

One late evening Dr. Mary Alice Jones, my editor at Rand McNally, suggested there might be a story in the wild-pony roundup and the swim across the channel from Assateague to Chincoteague Island off the coast of Virginia. Sidney whooped at the idea. "Go!" he urged. "But take Blondie Coffin, the village equestrian, with you. With her experience she can help select the wildling I'm sure you'll bring home." The tiny filly that captured my dream turned out to be Misty, but I had to make peace first with a legendary character.

Sidney was right. There was not only a story in the wild ponies, but a people story as well in the Beebe family, especially Grandpa, who was known to all the island folk not as Clarence Beebe, but as Grandpa. Wiry, spry-legged as a grasshopper, Grandpa was also bigger than life. He "authenticated" my

"Grandpa Beebe, shaking the sand out of his boots"

childhood belief that writers had to interweave truth and imagination. When I asked him if it were fact or fable that the wild ponies on Assateague Island had been spewed out of a wrecked Spanish galleon, Grandpa jumped down from his horse and stamped his foot like a feisty stallion.

"Marg'ret!" he exploded. "Facts are fine, fer as they go, but they're like waterbugs skitterin' atop the water. Legends now, they go deep down and pull up the heart of a story."

I wanted to hug him on the spot.

I encountered Grandpa's wisdom a second time when I admitted having fallen in love with a tiny golden filly who wore a white mark on her withers in the shape of a map of the United States. "Couldn't Blondie and I please van her home so I could write a story about her? We've already named her Misty." Grandpa yanked his hat off his head and thwacked it against his leg.

"Marg'ret," he said with compassion in his voice this time, "I ain't a-goin' to let you do it. A nursin' young'un needs its mama. But when three–four months is up, I'll send her to you so's you can write yer story. Then when you're done you can send Misty back to Paul and Maureen, my grandkids."

Rand McNally later sent Grandpa a check for three hundred fifty dollars, but no money was exchanged at the time. None was needed. Only a handshake strong as a pump handle.

Back home, my husband and I had the fun of planning a stable with three stalls. We had no idea who Misty's stablemates might be, but meanwhile one stall could store hay and straw, and the other would make a splendid tack room. For now it held a tiny halter and saddle, and a guest book.

Misty arrived by train on a drizzling, bone-chilling November day. I caught my breath at sight of the homemade crate and the wee, still creature inside. Cautiously I slid my hand in between the slats, burying my fingers deep in . . . fuzz! Long, woolly fuzz! Where was that newborn silkiness I remembered?

The expressmen set down the crate just inside the stable and went off into the night. With hammer and wedge Sid broke open the front of the crate. Then we both stepped aside, expecting Misty to leap out like a wild thing crazy to be free. But she was so stiff-legged from her four-day journey that Sid had to lift her out.

I stared at an utterly strange pony. No golden coat, no golden eyelashes, no white map of the United States on her withers. She was all one color—the sooty gray of snow that has lain on the ground much too long.

Sid made a noise in the back of his throat that escaped in a gust of laughter. "So this is the beautiful filly with coat of gold! Humpf! She looks more like a Siberian goat."

Grandpa, I thought, had sent us the wrong pony. But that wasn't *her* fault. So we loved her anyway and called her Misty. How delighted I was the next morning when she showed enough wildness to kick me ever so slightly.

In the months that it took Misty to shed out, I groomed her story and Sid groomed her coat. He taught her to place her forefeet on a soapbox, and to shake hands like a politician running for the presidency. And when spring came her color returned in all its golden glory. Grandpa Beebe had sent the right pony after all!

Not until my semifinal draft of Misty's story did I give Sid so much as a peek. He took the pages out of my hand like a dog with a bone, and settled into his favorite chair. I hid just out of his peripheral vision so I could watch him read without being watched. When he brushed away a tear, I exulted. When his brow furrowed with puzzlement I knew from the diminishing pages almost the exact source of his displeasure.

Then back to the drawing board . . . to the challenge of rewriting the passage which I had bumbled. I think Sid had no inkling of my spying, nor of his editorial powers. I was loathe to tell him, for fear he would try to read stone-faced. As soon as Sid said, "Send the book away; now is the time to let go," I obeyed reluctantly, feeling like a mother bird pushing her fledgling out of the nest.

Sid was a born-in-the-blood traveler. In fact, my mother warned me, "Once a traveler, always a traveler." What a lovely left-handed compliment she

The author and her best critic: watching Sid read manuscript, 1981

paid him. In 1965 Sid had a great urge to visit the Middle East . . . Jordan, Israel, Lebanon, Syria.

"Would these faraway countries interest you, too?" he asked. I pounced on the idea. "Yes!" I said, "if we could go to London first, and then to Greece, and come home by way of Italy and the Spanish Riding School of Vienna."

Which is exactly what we did, and thus, between the two of us, we came home with the seed for *White Stallion of Lipizza* and *Gaudenzia, Pride of the Palio* (later to be titled *The Wildest Horse Race in the World*).

As time went on, Sid added lawyer and agent to his caring role. I remember the disturbing telephone call just before dinner one evening, when a publisher drummed on and on about the tremendous increase in the cost of paper, of offset printing, of full-color pages, and then suggested cutting, in reverse proportion, the royalties on a proposed book.

The voice over the phone carried so loud and clear that my husband, who was pouring our dinner wine, heard every word. I watched his hackles rise like the bony spikes on a dinosaur's back.

"You tell that penny-pinching Scrooge," he said in a dry-ice voice, "that your costs have risen too, and your husband insists that you not do the book at all."

It never ceases to amaze me how Sid wrought such wonders as increased royalties when the intentions of the publisher were quite the opposite.

It is doubtful too if Wesley Dennis and I would ever have become a team, if it had not been for Sid. I had just completed *Justin Morgan Had a Horse,* my first full-length book. This was a high landmark for me and, of course, I wanted the world's top-flight artist to do the illustrations. Off I went to the library to study horse artists. This was early on, before horse books had become as popular as they are today. Most of the great horse artists were dead, but I stumbled onto a little volume by a little-known artist and fell wildly in love with *Flip,* a first book with pictures and text by Wesley Dennis.

"Unfortunately," I told Sid, "Wesley Dennis lives in New York State and we live in Illinois."

"Why should that stop you? Just write Dennis a note that you'll be in New York City on such a date and could he meet you in the writing room of your hotel?"

"I'll do it! I'll mail the letter today!"

"Not so eager, beaver. Do you have an extra copy of your script . . . a good clean copy, without any of your snibblings and scratchings?"

"No."

"Well there's no point in going to meet Dennis

until he's had a full week to study your story and mark the places he wants to illustrate."

Exactly two weeks later at the dot of 2:30 I was in the writing room of a staid women's-only hotel. For one time in my life I was early. I watched the door like a cat waiting to snap up a mouse. But it was not a mouse of a man who suddenly entered; it was a big Saint Bernard sort of person wearing a Sherlock Holmes cap! His eyes skimmed over the room and by some strange instinct he loped directly in my direction.

"You Marguerite Henry?" he blurted.

I nodded in wonder.

"I'm dying to do the book and I don't care whether I get paid for it or not." With that bombshell beginning I knew at once that we would share royalties, share and share alike.

Soon we were sharing ideas for plots as well. While we were still down on the island of Chincoteague, still building the scenes for *Misty,* Wesley said, "I've got a plot for you, and it's as good as *Justin Morgan.*"

"Writing Misty, draft number two, on Sid's and my vacation at the Ferguson's summer home on the Saint Lawrence River"

My ears pricked. We were sitting on the front porch of Miss Molly's Inn with Wesley rocking back and forth in a wooden swing that creaked with each motion. We were still electrified with all the sights and sounds of our first Pony-Penning Day. We watched the town simmer down for the night, as one by one lights blinked out in the tidy white cottages along the shore. Suddenly the creaking of the swing stopped. Wesley extinguished his cigarette and flipped it into the darkness. Abruptly he got up and began pacing. I knew his mind was far away.

"For years," he said, "a relative of mine has been going to do a story of the great Godolphin Arabian, but she never will. We'll pay her for the idea . . . then we'll do it!"

A whole year of waiting went by while Wesley's relative made up her mind. And then, when the door was opened at last, I held in my hand a gem of history. An Arabian stallion, born in the stables of the Sultan of Morocco, was sent as a gift to Louis XV, the boy king of France. The king's courtiers laughed at the high crest and the delicacy of the stallion in comparison to their lusty horses. With a wave of their jeweled hands, they shunted the gift-horse into obscurity.

His lowly tasks were to draw a vegetable cart, a water cart, and a wood cart through the streets of Paris. Yet in spite of menial work and harsh treatment, the Arabian lived to become one of the three foundation sires of the Thoroughbred line.

Here were the seeds of a story, waiting for sun and rain. From the very start we had our title, *King of the Wind,* and were off and running.

At that pivotal point my concerned family, with the kindest intentions, set up the first hurdle: "*Must* you write about something that will take tons of research in faraway lands and long-ago times? Why not concentrate on our own country and an era you know?"

The publishers seemed in league with my family. They set up higher hurdles. I remember the exact dialogue.

"Are you sure you want to do this book?"

"Yes, of course. Why?"

"Because of your central characters."

"What about them?"

"You have a boy who can't talk."

I nodded in agreement. "But sometimes body language can speak louder than words."

"And your other characters—the horse and the cat—they can't talk either, except in indecipherable neighs and mews."

"Neighs and mews," I countered, "can say many things."

Allen, Gordon, Schroeppel, and Redlich, Inc.

An autographing party with illustrator Wesley Dennis, at Marshall Field and Company, Chicago

"But the settings . . . Morocco, France, England in the eighteenth century! They're so foreign to our good old U.S.A. readers."

There followed a long pause, and the crucial question repeated slowly, each word falling with a thud.

"Are you absolutely sure you want to go ahead with this book? As yet neither you nor Wesley has invested too much time; you could easily turn to a different story here at home."

"Too late!" I argued. "It's like being seven-months pregnant. I can't . . . I don't want to do anything but let the seed of the story grow."

And grow it did, at a breathtaking pace. Aware now of the warnings, we could make doubly sure that our characters, animal and human, showed their feelings in a universal language. Wesley, with his strong action paintings, jumped all the hurdles without fault, and I, with my reams of research, covered the course in tandem with him. When *King of the Wind* won the Newbery Medal we were both in shock.

The more we worked together the more I realized the soundness of Wesley's credo about Books and Life: IF IT ISN'T FUN, DON'T DO IT. This applied even to autographing parties, where he was at his hilarious best. He dressed for the part, wearing either a floppy clown's hat or his Sherlock Holmes cap, and he played both roles with gusto. While keeping up a monologue he made everyone ecstatically happy by drawing sketches of Misty or Brighty or Grandpa Beebe or a dancing Lipizzaner on the flyleaf of their books.

Eventually he tired of his double role. With a great stretching and yawning he came from behind the table, did a quick handstand, and walked upside down until his hat fell off. Then feeling greatly refreshed, he passed a whopper box of candy up and down the line of boys and girls, urging the shy ones: "Go ahead! Take a piece! It's good for your teeth!"

How everyone loved him! The more he said he didn't like children but loved animals, the more the children adored him.

Even parents (reluctant, at first, at parting with hard-earned dollars just for a child's book) were soon howling in laughter. And flustered floorwalkers hung onto their toupees when he suddenly burst out singing an old gospel song, "Oh, Je-sus, come and dry my tears away." That is the way it was when

Wesley Dennis came to a party.

Sid and Wes were good friends, each respecting the other for his very different role in the books we were creating. And Dorothy Dennis, Wesley's wife, soon joined the fun. She contributed the plot for *Cinnabar, The One O'Clock Fox,* which became a favorite of the fox-chase crowd, and was one of Sid's favorites.

Story ideas were by no means limited to the imaginings of the Dennises and Henrys. Ideas had a way of exploding like a barnful of hay in a burning sun. Mildred Lathrop, a librarian in Elgin, Illinois, touched off one of our best clues which gave Sid and me adventures in travel to last two lifetimes. She ran across an article in a *Sunset* magazine about a shaggy little burro named Bright Angel who ran wild in the Grand Canyon of Arizona. He lived a free and glorious life spending his winters in the warmth on the floor of the canyon. Then when summer came on, he high-tailed it up the wall to the north rim to hobnob with his two-legged friends in the coolth of the Kaibab National Forest. He avoided work as much as possible (though he did pack gear for Theodore Roosevelt and he did help solve a murder). But mostly his mind was concerned with mealtimes and he managed to show up just when his friends were ready to slather their flapjacks with molasses.

Here were all the elements of a lively story, and Mildred Lathrop kept adding fuel to the fire by finding vivid descriptions of Brighty's trail, that zigzagged precipitously up and down the walls of the canyon. "Tourists," she added in a footnote, "may walk or ride muleback to cover Brighty's vast territory: one day to go down the wall and one to come back up, with an overnight stay at Phantom Ranch."

Never would I have summoned the courage to travel the steep escarpment nor negotiate the thirty-inch-wide trail that Brighty's hoofs had pounded out, if Sid had not agreed to share the dangers and thrills.

On the February morning of our descent, Sid went into a small general store to buy some woolly underwear. There he overheard the shocked proprietor discussing the deaths of two guides who, trying to pass each other on the trail, had just crashed to their death.

In silence Sid came back to our room and in silence he pulled on his red woollies and was ready to go. He made no mention of the accident nor the fact that he suffered from acrophobia.

It was Valentine's Day. The temperature was six degrees above zero, and the trail packed with snow halfway down to the Colorado River. My own previous fears dissipated the moment our guide gave me a saddlebag of mail for delivery to Phantom Ranch. (The mail always gets through, doesn't it?)

Kolb Brothers' Studio

"Ready for the trip down to the Colorado River, with the guide in the lead," Grand Canyon, Arizona

Right from our takeoff I began enjoying the splendors of the ride on my stalwart mule—mainly because I felt snug and safe with the guide in the lead and Sid behind me. Sid, however, was filled with angst. Boob, his mule, kept lagging behind, then breaking into a rough trot to catch up. Along the switchbacks our guide would point to rare rock formations that resembled pipes of a church organ or to the brilliant slashes of color as the sun hit the rock strata. Sid made no comment at all. I figured he was just too awestruck for speech. I had no idea that he had this abnormal fear of high places. What a tremendous sacrifice he was making for the background of our story!

He didn't eat his bag-lunch halfway down, but neither did the guide nor I. The sandwich and the orange were both frozen, so we fed them to a pair of stunted deer.

Almost to Phantom Ranch we crossed the Colorado River on a swaying suspension bridge. And finally, with a heavy sigh of relief, we were shaking hands with the jolly proprietor of the ranch and his wife, who had prepared a feast of wild fowl and rice with heart-shaped cranberry gelatin and strawberry shortcake with cardboard angels dancing on the whipped cream. Of course our hosts hoped we would linger over our coffee for a nightlong visit after their winter months of isolation, but sleep overtook us both. We didn't bother to undress, or even take off our boots.

When, at sundown the next afternoon, we topped out on the south rim of the canyon, Sid threw his arms around Boob and kissed him right on his whiskery muzzle.

Before I could tackle the writing of Brighty's story I spent a week hunting down a real-life burro for my model. Then I found him only a few miles away on Blackberry Road in Sugar Grove Township. We promptly changed his name from Jiggs to Brighty and brought him home, where he fell madly in love with Misty, who barely tolerated him. She preferred the swarming of visitors who brought her treats of carrots and apples. By this time our stable also accommodated a shiny black Morgan, whom Misty bossed around as if she were twice his size. Although she was the youngest member of our equine clan she was definitely the matriarch.

Edwards Studio, Porterville, California

Sidney Crocker Henry

Often I felt a twinge of guilt about postponing Misty's return to Chincoteague, but I wore blinders to my selfishness and rationalized the delay. "Let her have a happy colthood," I told myself. "Let her grow to her full strength; she still has many good years ahead." Somehow she belonged to our meadow . . . like a tree that has taken root. She seemed so happy and was such a part of our family, bowing and shaking hands and nuzzling us and nipping our shirts in play, and allowing Alex, our dachshund, to jump up on her back for a free ride whenever he felt like it.

Then on a June morning when the world was a tumult of roses, Sid and I patted all the animals good-by, gave last-minute instructions to a neighbor, and off we went to a wedding in Wisconsin which had far-reaching effects not only on the couple being married, but on Misty's life as well.

For the wedding ceremony the minister intoned from the Book of Ecclesiastes:

To every thing there is a season,
 and a time to every purpose . . .
A time to be born, and a time to die . . .
A time to weep, and a time to laugh . . .
A time to keep silence, and a time to speak . . .

Better is it that thou shouldest not vow,
 than that thou shouldest vow and not pay . . .
Better is the end of a thing
 than the beginning thereof. . . .

Sid and I listened to the somber words of Solomon, and it was as though an electric current bridged the distance from where Sid sat in the congregation to where I stood at the side of the bride.

Driving home in the twilight, Sid's words, like Solomon's, were prophetic.

"Could now," he said, rather than asked, "be the time to send Misty back to Chincoteague. Could now be the time for her to have colts of her own?"

After a long silence I said, "Yes." I sensed the special proverb that Sid was turning over in his mind: "Better is it that thou shouldest not vow, than that thou shouldest vow and not pay."

With cars whirring past on both sides, we made up our minds. We'd do it. We'd send Misty back to Chincoteague to be a mother. Maybe the end of a thing *could* be better than the beginning . . . maybe life was just beginning for Misty.

A kind of peace and contentment entered our lives, but it didn't last. All too promptly Grandpa

Beebe sent a van for Misty, and with Roy Tolbert at the wheel, it barreled down Wayne Road, past our little wayside church on a Sunday morning when the congregation was just flocking out. Every eye caught the enormous sign painted on the side of Tolbert's truck that would soon be turning down our lane to load Misty: "MISTY goes home to Chincoteague *to have her colt.*"

Disbelief, anger, sorrow, outrage, indignation, sympathy ran through the parishioners in a welter of feelings. A catastrophe had hit Wayne! Upset and disturbed, the people hurried home to their telephones. Sunday dinners could wait. They called up the principal of Wayne School, and the teachers; they called up the nonchurchgoers—the bedridden, the truants.

Misty's little world was aroused. Yet no one could turn the tide now. The only calm being in the storm was Misty.

By seven o'clock next morning it was as though a dike had broken. Streams of children poured through the gate, each child wanting to touch Misty—her nose, her neck, her barrel, her rump.

Word spread locally and nationwide. Photographers from the Elgin *Courier* and Saint Charles *Chronicle,* from the *Chicago Tribune,* and UPI, and even *Life* magazine were all over the place, taking rolls of pictures and scattering little white wrappers in their wake.

One photographer gave Misty a respite from the excitement by suggesting a back view of her stepping daintily through the front door and into our quiet house for a snack of oats mixed with her favorite omaline.

The saddest shot of all was Misty's van traveling down the tree-lined road with everyone waving goodby.

When at last Sid and I were alone, except for Alex and Mom-cat, both of them curled up in Sid's favorite chair. Sid looked down at them and sighed. "Maybe," he opined, "Misty has so many friends she needs a whole island instead of a meadow."

Suddenly the air was shattered by a steam-whistle, "Yee-aw, yee-aw, yee-a-a-aw." Brighty was braying his heartbreak after Misty, as though his world were torn apart.

Gloom reigned until a letter arrived from Grandma Beebe:

> You should see Grandpa with Misty. He's hoof-shaking for all he's worth and showing visitors how easy it is to train up a Chincoteague pony. He tells folk—I sent a ugly duckling to Illinois and look what I got back. And he says the name Misty like it was made of stars.
>
> Wish you lived closer so we could chat.
>
> Love and prayers,
>
> Ida V. Beebe/Grandma

Weeks later came the news we'd been waiting for.

> You remember my son Ralph (he's Maureen's and Paul's uncle). Well he thinks he's found the mate that pleases Misty to a T. His name is Wings due to his markings like wings. We're nigh sure Misty is with foal. We are counting on her to bring forth a baby colt in the month of March.

On the 31st of March an airmail envelope from Chincoteague held nothing but a newspaper clipping from the Salisbury *Times.*

> Folks are getting uneasy, awaiting the arrival of Misty's foal.
>
> That is, all but Misty. She's as complacent as can be.
>
> Mrs. Beebe said this morning, "Misty's just fine. But we are all getting anxious. People keep calling to find out if it's happened, and I have a long list to inform when it finally comes."
>
> Rand McNally, publishers of her book, are anxious. The newspapers are anxious. They all want to do a story on the little foal.
>
> Misty's veterinarian, Doctor Finney, says, "Many times it requires more than eleven months, especially in the case of a firstborn."

March went roaring out like a mad lion and April breezed in. On the sixth day at 5:20 in the morning, I was jolted out of bed by the insistent ringing of the telephone. I picked up the receiver too excited even to say hello.

Ralph Beebe didn't bother with hellos either. He crowed the glad news. "It's a boy at Beebe's ranch!"

"Misty . . . ? Is she all right?"

"Seems a right proud mother."

"No trouble?"

"No trouble. She did it herself. But Doc Finney stayed the night. He was right there, case she needed help."

MISTY

Three months old

Showing off one of her tricks

Tolerating the antics of Brighty

Ready to return to Chincoteague
(Elgin Daily Courier-News)

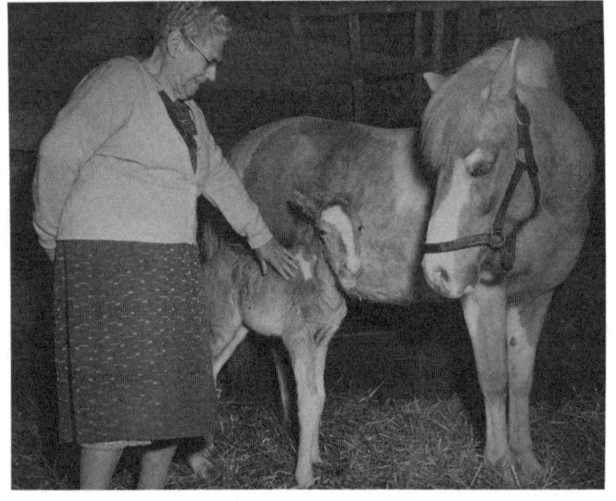

Admiring her first foal, Phantom Wings, with Grandma Beebe

With her second-born, Wisp O'Mist, still wet

"I'll be right there," I said, glancing at my traveling case, already packed.

It was as if *Life* had counted the months too. They arrived on Chincoteague the same day Wesley and I did to photograph the firstborn son of Misty. He was a gangling bay with white markings just like Misty's. He kept up with her every sortie . . . even to running away from the teasing antics of Skipper, a young collie.

Again school was let out and again the crowd of children swooped in on Misty bearing signs: "Misty! Misty! You're the star! You're the greatest yet by far!" and "Bravo! for Misty's colt."

How strange that these children living on an island of wild ponies should be so moved by the birth of yet another one.

I whispered to a girl standing beside me, "Why are you so thrilled about another colt?"

Indignantly the girl left no doubt: "He's *not* just another colt. He's special."

"Boy, is he special!" the girl next to her said.

"A Frisky Son for Misty," *Life*'s second story, scarcely hit the newsstands than the unbelievable happened. On a rainy Friday afternoon a busload of Brownies had come to visit with noisy questions and laughter. We were right in the midst of the refreshment hour of chocolate-chip cookies and cocoa when the telephone rang. It was a call from faraway California from Robert Radnitz (a producer for Twentieth Century-Fox) wanting to do a movie of Misty right on Chincoteague Island, using native actors and ponies. And of course he would call the film *Misty.*

In less time than it takes a mare to foal a colt, Robert Radnitz produced his film. *Life* called it "A Tiny Horse Opera for Youngsters." But there was nothing tiny about it except for little Emma. Did Misty play herself in the movie? No, she was too busy with her firstborn and too big with her second-to-be-born. Emma, her understudy, was a dark, dark bay. The makeup artist had constantly to daub on a fresh golden tint, especially to her muzzle hairs, which grew in very dark.

I first saw the film in a preview. I was in a state of suspended animation, too stunned to realize the fullness of the miracle. But when Sid and I watched a block-long lineup of children waiting to get into the theater where *Misty* was playing I realized again that Sid was the angel who had sparked her return to Chincoteague and the bright new chapters in her life.

My life on the other hand has run a totally upside-down course. In the 1930s most young women spent their early married years caring for their babies. Then as soon as the children qualified for school, the mothers dived into the careers of their yearning.

To Sid's and my surprise we had no chick or child of our own, even though we both came from large families. So I spent my young married years in the lively pursuit of word-chasing. And now, in my ungrandmotherly years . . . while three storybook characters from here to Greece are tugging at my sleeve, urging me to get on with their stories . . . I am instead taking care of the children I never had. These young readers identify with the people and animals in my stories so they think of me in a familial role—someone who *should* be able and willing to answer their questions about life. But this generation has such monstrous problems:

> . . . My little schnauzer died today. And today my parents got a divorce. I feel maybe I was to blame for both things.
>
> . . . My father takes drugs. He promises to stop but never does. Please suggest a place in my city where they can help me help him—for not too much money.
>
> . . . I think daily of suicide. Now that you

"My favorite picture of Sid, aka The Pied Piper. Wherever he went, dogs followed him. Baron had never met Sid before, but he must have sensed safety and protection in the arms of this stranger," Christmas Eve, 1980

"Sifting through children's letters for the book Dear Readers and Riders"

> know the details of my tragedy wouldn't that be the best way out for everyone?

Questions like these cry out for help. Sometimes a letter will serve, but thoughts of suicide require an immediate telephone call.

I feel exactly like the old woman in the shoe must have felt. I hope she got some funny letters too—like this one from Jennifer Kelly Knapp:

> . . . I don't really read your storys but from your movie I bet they're wonderful. I don't want to be a writer or have a horse because I'm thinking of being president.

Happily there are plenty of solid, stable, secure, staunch children who write of their travels to the islands of Chincoteague and Assateague, to Morgan horse country when the leaves turn red and gold; who tell of ribbons they've won, of diplomas, of fuzzy new puppies and spindle-legged colts. And some ask you a question you just can't wait to answer, such as Bobby Brock's from Texas: "If you have a husband, what is he like?"

> Yes! I have a husband. He is generous and openhearted, long-suffering and kind.
>
> Who else would suffer with me through the birth of many books?
>
> Who else would ride with me down the steep wall of the Grand Canyon so I could write the book about Brighty?
>
> Who else would tolerate as part of his household three fox cubs, a pony, a burro, a horse, a dachshund, and a mom-cat who never stopped having kittens? In fact, she had three in his lap. Who else would cherish kittens and all creatures in sickness and in health?
>
> And who else would invite a pony into the house to eat her Thanksgiving and Christmas dinners?
>
> Animal trainer, scrambled eggs-specialist, avid reader—that is my husband.

In 1987 Sidney Crocker Henry died. But no one has ever died less. He is still watching over Misty's world. What stronger proof than this? Cloudy (Misty's first grandson) and Stormy (Misty's last daughter) are getting along in years. They needed a new roof over their heads to shut out the burning sun and deflect the stinging botflies and mosquitoes. Sid must have sensed such problems might arise for he left in his will money to build that roof to shade Misty's children.

Life is nice and round, isn't it?

As Grandma Beebe, the comforter, said to me when Grandpa Beebe died, "No one ever dies, not a person or even a single pony. Nothing dies as long as there is the memory to enfold it and a heart to love it."

BIBLIOGRAPHY

FOR CHILDREN

Fiction:

Auno and Tauno: A Story of Finland (illustrated by Gladys Blackwood). Chicago: Albert Whitman, 1940.

Dilly Dally Sally (illustrated by G. Blackwood). Akron, Ohio: Saalfield, 1940.

Geraldine Belinda (illustrated by G. Blackwood). New York: Platt & Munk, 1942.

Their First Igloo on Baffin Island, with Barbara True (illustrated by G. Blackwood). Chicago: Albert Whitman, 1943; London: Gifford, 1945.

A Boy and a Dog (illustrated by Diana Thorne and Ottilie Foy). Chicago: Wilcox & Follett, 1944.

Justin Morgan Had a Horse (illustrated by Wesley Dennis). Chicago: Wilcox & Follett, 1945.

The Little Fellow. (Illustrated by D. Thorne) Philadelphia: Winston, 1945; (illustrated by Rich Rudish) Chicago: Rand McNally, 1975.

Robert Fulton, Boy Craftsman (illustrated by Lawrence Dresser). Indianapolis: Bobbs-Merrill, 1945.

Misty of Chincoteague (illustrated by W. Dennis). Chicago: Rand McNally, 1947; London: Collins, 1961.

Always Reddy (illustrated by W. Dennis). New York and London: McGraw Hill, 1947.

Benjamin West and His Cat Grimalkin (illustrated by W. Dennis). Indianapolis: Bobbs-Merrill, 1947.

King of the Wind (illustrated by W. Dennis). Chicago: Rand McNally, 1948; London: Constable, 1957.

Little-or-Nothing from Nottingham (illustrated by W. Dennis). New York: McGraw Hill, 1949.

Sea Star, Orphan of Chincoteague (illustrated by W. Dennis). Chicago: Rand McNally, 1949; London: Collins, 1968.

Born to Trot (illustrated by W. Dennis). Chicago: Rand McNally, 1950; excerpts published as *One Man's Horse.* Chicago: Rand McNally, 1977.

Brighty of the Grand Canyon (illustrated by W. Dennis). Chicago: Rand McNally, 1953; London: Collins, 1970.

Cinnabar, the One O'Clock Fox (illustrated by W. Dennis). Chicago: Rand McNally, 1956.

Misty, the Wonder Pony, by Misty, Herself (illustrated by Clare McKinley). Chicago: Rand McNally, 1956.

Black Gold (illustrated by W. Dennis). Chicago: Rand McNally, 1957.

Muley-Ears, Nobody's Dog (illustrated by W. Dennis). Chicago: Rand McNally, 1959.

Gaudenzia, Pride of the Palio (illustrated by Lynd Ward). Chicago: Rand McNally, 1960; London: Collins, 1971; also published as *The Wildest Horse Race in the World.* Chicago: Rand McNally, 1976; also published as *Palio: The Wildest Horse Race in the World.* London: Fontana, 1976.

Five O'Clock Charlie (illustrated by W. Dennis). Chicago: Rand McNally, 1962; London: Collins, 1963.

Stormy, Misty's Foal (illustrated by W. Dennis). Chicago: Rand McNally, 1963; London: Collins, 1965.

White Stallion of Lipizza (illustrated by W. Dennis). Chicago: Rand McNally, 1964; London: Blackie, 1976.

Mustang, Wild Spirit of the West (illustrated by Robert Lougheed). Chicago: Rand McNally, 1966; London: Collins, 1968.

Stories from around the World. Chicago: Hubbard Press, 1971.

San Domingo: The Medicine Hat Stallion (illustrated by R. Lougheed). Chicago: Rand McNally, 1972; London: Collins, 1975; also published as *Peter Lundy and the Medicine Hat Stallion.* Chicago: Rand McNally, 1976.

Marguerite Henry's Misty Treasury: The Complete Misty, Sea Star, and Stormy (illustrated by W. Dennis). Chicago: Rand McNally, 1982.

Our First Pony (illustrated by R. Rudish). Chicago: Rand McNally, 1984.

Nonfiction:

Birds at Home (illustrated by Jacob Abbott). Chicago: Donohue, 1942.

Album of Horses (illustrated by W. Dennis). Chicago: Rand McNally, 1951; shortened version published as *Portfolio of Horses.* Chicago: Rand McNally, 1952; also published as *Portfolio of Horse Paintings.* Chicago: Rand McNally, 1964.

Wagging Tails: An Album of Dogs (illustrated by W. Dennis). Chicago: Rand McNally, 1955; revised edition published as *Album of Dogs.* Chicago: Rand McNally, 1970.

All about Horses (illustrated by W. Dennis). New York: Random House, 1962; London: W. H. Allen, 1963; revised edition (photographs by Walter Osborne).

Chicago: Rand McNally, 1967.

Dear Readers and Riders. Chicago: Rand McNally, 1969.

A Pictorial Life Story of Misty (illustrated by W. Dennis). Chicago: Rand McNally, 1976.

The Illustrated Marguerite Henry, with W. Dennis, R. Lougheed, R. Rudish, and L. Ward. Chicago: Rand McNally, 1980.

"Pictured Geographies" series:

Alaska in Story and Pictures (illustrated by Kurt Wiese). Chicago: Albert Whitman, 1941.

Argentina in Story and Pictures (illustrated by K. Wiese). Chicago: Albert Whitman, 1941.

Brazil in Story and Pictures (illustrated by K. Wiese). Chicago: Albert Whitman, 1941.

Canada in Story and Pictures (illustrated by K. Wiese). Chicago: Albert Whitman, 1941.

Chile in Story and Pictures (illustrated by K. Wiese). Chicago: Albert Whitman, 1941.

Mexico in Story and Pictures (illustrated by K. Wiese). Chicago: Albert Whitman, 1941.

Panama in Story and Pictures (illustrated by K. Wiese). Chicago: Albert Whitman, 1941.

West Indies in Story and Pictures (illustrated by K. Wiese). Chicago: Albert Whitman, 1941.

Australia in Story and Pictures (illustrated by K. Wiese). Chicago: Albert Whitman, 1946.

The Bahamas in Story and Pictures (illustrated by K. Wiese). Chicago: Albert Whitman, 1946.

Bermuda in Story and Pictures (illustrated by K. Wiese). Chicago: Albert Whitman, 1946.

British Honduras in Story and Pictures (illustrated by K. Wiese). Chicago: Albert Whitman, 1946.

Dominican Republic in Story and Pictures (illustrated by K. Wiese). Chicago: Albert Whitman, 1946.

Hawaii in Story and Pictures (illustrated by K. Wiese). Chicago: Albert Whitman, 1946.

New Zealand in Story and Pictures (illustrated by K. Wiese). Chicago: Albert Whitman, 1946.

Virgin Islands in Story and Pictures (illustrated by K. Wiese). Chicago: Albert Whitman, 1946.

S. Carl Hirsch

1913-

S. Carl Hirsch, 1987

Aesop, that ancient teller of simple tales, has become for me my own complex, haunting enigma. I have traced his shadowy presence about the rim of the Mediterranean, only to remain in doubt whether he will ever emerge at the center of a book of mine.

My search for Aesop has led me to a ruin in Turkey that was once the slave market of historic Ephesus. But I am to this day baffled as to when and how he appeared there, and from where. Aesop was indeed a Greek slave, undoubtedly black. He was a non-Greek, according to the consensus among classic scholars that Greeks did not enslave Greeks, only captives. Even more compelling is the evidence that Aesop's fables had their origins in quite another culture, possibly a civilization that flourished along the coast of northeastern Africa. My halted research on Aesop is now gathering dust as an unfinished manuscript that may not ever appear in print.

And yet, my dilemma with Aesop is clearly characteristic of those twin elements that have informed my long career as a writer of nonfiction for young people—both ignorance and curiosity. From that coupling came a stream of books of which I am genuinely proud, but which appeared one after another out of the most astonishing circumstances. Such are the hazards of writing for children. One book may be the hare; the other, the tortoise. A third may never reach the goal line. Whenever I am coaxed into offering advice to would-be members of this fulfilling profession, I talk too much about the need for stubborn commitment. And the incentive of money is not enough.

I began life as a "city kid" in Chicago, and I remained that throughout my growing-up years. I was the oldest child in a family pursued by poverty, living on the edge of the ghetto, deprived of almost everything a boy wants except familial love. There was no bicycle, no treehouse and scarcely a tree. I had no "Flexible Flyer" sled, no baseball glove in my boyhood. I yearned for a pet dog, but one never appeared in our cramped city flat. The only horse I ever befriended dragged an ice wagon through our muddy alley in the sultry days of summer. I dreamed of going to the Boy Scout Jamboree, but never got there. My Boy Scout uniform was never anything but a neckerchief and a surplus army shirt, bedecked with merit badges. My parents were sympathetic but indigent.

Chicago was then a welter of recently arrived ethnic groups, enclaves of Germans and Italians, Blacks and Jews, the Poles and the Irish, each within their own fixed boundaries. For a young boy, it was hazardous to traverse these hostile territories. My daily mile-long trip to school took me from the Irish parish in which we lived as outsiders, across a Jewish strip, and deep into the domain of a people we called Bohemians. Trespassers like myself suffered the terrors of being set upon by gangs of ruffians, something far more often imagined than real.

Our child play in those years was spontaneous

At age four, in a World War I uniform

and self-run. The spring season began with several of us turning a littered empty lot into something approximating a baseball diamond in the rough. The game came out of whomever and whatever was available. We used a coverless core of an old baseball, re-covered with friction tape. A bat provided the well-known method of "choosing up sides." More often, there were street games, now long forgotten, such as "Run, Sheep, Run," "Kick the Can," and a bruising encounter called "Buck, Buck, How Many Fingers Up?" Winter sports were equally impromptu and makeshift.

I was part of a loosely formed band, forerunner of the highly organized juvenile gangs of today. The McInerny brothers were the leaders of the group with which I ran, though I was somewhat alienated by the fact that I was the only one who attended public school. I sat with the others around a small alley campfire where we baked stolen potatoes, and I listened amazed at their stories of the harsh treatment of kids in the nearby parish school.

My parents were both born in the same Lithuanian village and came to this country just after the turn of the century. They were Jews by heritage. But their socialist politics were to them more important than religion. Both were skilled in the needle trades, my mother being a milliner. However, she never worked at a job after her three children were born. The family in which I grew up was close and warmhearted.

Like countless city kids, I too yearned for the spaciousness of small-town and rural life, for natural settings and wilderness. My closest approach was in joining the Boy Scouts. I was still a year and a half too young when I wrote a letter to the national scout headquarters, pleading to be allowed in. (I like to think that letter had something to do with bringing the requirement down to age eleven, and, much later, the formation of the Cub Scouts.)

I had been even earlier an avid reader of juvenile novels that idealized scouting. One of my favorites was the tale of a "bee-line hike" by a group of boys who lived in the mountains of western Massachusetts, and who plotted a jaunt between two landmarks, making their way straight through the town, across streams and through quarries and even through a house where the family sat at dinner in order to reach their destination. My own ragtag scout troop never had such glorious adventures. We learned our knots, mastered the Morse code, passed the bandaging and compass tests, but never got lost in any wilderness and never even encountered a wild rabbit. I was later reminded of that era in my life by a *New Yorker* cartoon showing a group of city kids in the woods, studying the wildlife under rocks, one saying, "Yah, we have such a kind of cockroaches in our house."

These early years saw the beginnings of a pattern which I now see as "the double life." I was very much a part of the rough-and-tumble activities of the boys on our block. But I led a secret existence as well, being an avid reader, making clandestine trips to the public library a half a mile away. There were other ways too in which I was "different." I was fascinated with collecting stamps, especially with those from exotic places that are no longer on the map—Herzegovina and Persia, Abyssinia and Inhambane.

During World War II, that pattern of doubleness reappeared. As a squad leader in a combat engineer outfit, I had close ties with my eleven men. But during pass and furlough periods, I directed myself to cultured places and pursuits far different than those preferred by my army buddies. I was not a loner; instead, I could readily make friends in two totally different and separate social groups, moving back and forth comfortably between them. My "two lives" persisted into adulthood before I recognized the importance of being self-unified and authentic. In my middle years, I worked in the lithographic industry. The fact that I was then also writing and publishing

The author with his father, Barnett Hirsch, during World War II basic training

books remained sub rosa. I had learned by experience that merely my becoming known as a writer (of whatever) could erect a wall between my shopmates and me.

In my early years, I was dazzled by the prospect of a career as a newspaper reporter in the Chicago that then boasted such colorful notables as Carl Sandburg, Al Capone, Red Grange, and Mayor "Big Bill" Thompson. It was a Chicago neighbor, Sandburg, who was my idol and model—serially a newspaperman, poet, nonfiction writer. I even adopted his given name as my own, retaining the initial, "S.," from my original Hebrew name of Shimon.

As a high-school sophomore, I had a crush on my English teacher, Miss Henzel. She was tall and slender, with straight blond hair. In her very gentle voice, she read to us the poetry of Keats and Browning. This was the kind of enchantment I needed. It was she who first encouraged me to write. Editing and writing for the school paper, I went on to form links with a daily newspaper, the *Chicago Evening Post,* and wrote the book reviews for the children's page. At that time, I could envision my life ahead, stretched out for me like an open road. The hazards and the detours were still invisible.

Working after school, I was pressed for time to devote to my writing and print-shop duties as an editor of the weekly school paper. One year I worked in a Loop horse-betting parlor as a "flunkie." We were across the street from Chicago City Hall, serving that clientele. I was in luck with the job. I earned six dollars a day, the wage paid out at the end of each day, a practice common in such an uncertain occupation. The money was appreciated at home. From my own small portion, I saved carefully. By the end of the year, I had enough from tips to buy a gallery season ticket for the Chicago Symphony concerts. Each Thursday night I sped from the last wire report of the race at Santa Anita to my lofty seat, and munched my sandwich as I waited eagerly for the concert to begin.

There was a teenage year when I saw virtually every stage play that appeared in Chicago's twenty or more Loop theatres. The circumstance was a job with a firm that had the cloakroom and candy concessions in all of the city's professional theatres. Among us employees we arranged to rotate our workplaces each matinee and evening performance so that we could see every play between our checkroom and candy-selling chores. The theatre bills that year included everything from Sophocles to Shakespeare to Eugene O'Neill and Galsworthy. This was the heyday of the Barrymores, of the Abbey Players Theatre and D'Oyly Carte. Fascinated, I took it all in, and even tried my hand at playwrighting.

I remember 1930. I was the only "wage earner" in our household, with an after-school job that year as a delivery boy. My route ran between the wholesale district on the western edge of the Loop and the big department stores along State Street. With a box under my arm, I threaded my way on foot through the downtown traffic. I had come to know the Loop structures intimately, exploring them with all the fascination of an archaeologist unearthing Grecian temples. I was becoming streetwise. My pride lay in the fact that I could traverse my secret route in a downpour and remain bone-dry, simply by cutting through arcades, freight docks, corridors, subterranean passages.

I recall the day I passed through a huge protest demonstration outside the city and county government buildings. Public revenues had dried up in these depressed years. Schoolteachers were among those who went unpaid for many months. Among the teachers who formed the protest march that day, I spotted a familiar figure. Astonished, I saw my English teacher, the fair and fragile damsel of the Keats poetry, with a picket sign over her shoulder. I wept for her that day, too embarrassed to even say, "Hello."

Many Americans who are younger than I undoubtedly find it difficult to understand what my generation was all about. I was a World War I "war baby," who followed a much different path from most of the "baby boomers" of World War II. For my group, coming out of high school in the early 1930s, the way ahead suddenly lost all semblance of preplanning. The big Depression of the 1930s, seemingly endless, was on. My world had suffered a catastrophic breakdown. It would continue relentlessly for ten years, ended only by the beginnings of World War II.

As a small child I had felt secure in my close-knit and supportive home life. But I was in no way prepared for the psychic devastation of the Depression years. The sense of horror was felt not only by adults. Children were not mere bystanders. What abruptly appeared to me was a misshapen and terrifying world in which grown men (like my father) found themselves useless and helpless. For all their vaunted false fronts, banks were boarded up. For want of enjoyment, people came to dance to canned music in the city parks on concrete slabs laid down for that purpose. Jobless families survived as scavengers; our upstairs neighbors, the Mollenbergs, gathered discarded milk and pop bottles, worth two cents each. An elderly uncle, unemployed, moved in with us, sharing my bedroom. Some of the smallest delights of my life simply vanished.

"As a romantic adolescent"

It hit me hardest just after high school. I was barely able to complete two years of college. In our family, there was hardly enough money for food, let alone tuition. My sense of a future was unravelling like an old sweater.

In these years, music was my mainstay. I explored the arts, all of them. I was writing and reading poetry. I joined a free settlement-house class in modern dance, spent a year in a neighborhood "little theatre" group, tried my hand at charcoal sketching and watercolors. When I had the money, I was racing up the six flights to the unreserved seats of the Orchestra Hall gallery to hear a recital by Iturbi or Heifetz. With friends I haunted the tiny listening rooms of music stores, where I could hear classical music records without ever buying anything.

I was then a romantic youngster, moody and intense. But the cancerous economics of the times imposed on us a keen consciousness of politics. I enrolled in radical causes in the mid-thirties because I, like millions of other crisis-ridden Americans, felt that this country sorely needed some radical improvements. Always I offered my writing and newspaper skills, such as they were, and ended up with a widely increased range of news-reporting experiences.

My self-image was that of the "inquiring reporter," using my writing abilities to record the condition of everyday people whose stories needed to be told. What remained of that anxiety-filled decade of the thirties found me deeply involved in social and political struggles—but always as newsman and freelance writer. I moved cross-country to where the turmoil was most critical: the legislative battles in Washington for unemployment insurance, social security, low-cost housing; the "sit-downs" in Chicago and Detroit; embattled young people like myself gathered at the American Youth Congress in Cleveland; the so-called Memorial Day Massacre that broke the "little steel" strike; the organizing of migrant workers in the far West; a strike by sharecroppers in "swamp-east" Missouri.

Mine was just that kind of a younger generation which emerged from dislocated family life and from foreshortened education into a chaotic, futureless world. This was me in 1940, still somewhat amorphous, like half-formed clay. I needed order in my life. And I found it in a lovely marriage partner and in the family we created together. I married Stina Leander, a handsome woman of Swedish parentage who has given shape to my life for almost a half-century. She brought to our home a love for flowers and a fascination with water sports, the gifts of radiance and compassionate warmth. She became, and remains, the critical balance wheel in all of my

Hirsch as a newspaperman, 1946

writing, and an active participant.

We were duly married in Chicago's City Hall. Our honeymoon was spent in the village of Bronson, Michigan, where Stina's Finnish uncle, Elmer Johnson, had created for us a love nest in his barn loft, and he gave us the private use of his backyard sauna. Aunt Ketty treated us to her Girl Scout breakfast, pancakes cooked on the lids of upended large tin cans that were sitting in a campfire. The townsfolk treated us to a bang-up shivaree, and we were launched into an idyllic marriage, one that has never lost its magic.

My wife and I raised our two boys in our tiny flat in midtown Chicago. I became a systematic autodidact in those years, a self-directed reader and a constant journalistic writer, trying hard to make a living in that precarious profession.

My chief relaxation was in woodworking, somewhat frustrating in that I had no shop space except our small kitchen and only a limited number of hand tools. But my spare time was mainly spent with our two boys, touring the countless Chicago-area museums and zoos until we knew them by heart. Our family enjoyed a great many camping outings and auto journeys together.

Our two sons were to become the direct initiators of my writings for children. It all began with the stories I told them and the songs we sang together, the quiz and sight-seeing games we invented during hours spent on car trips. I was especially attentive to the queries that the boys directed to my wife and me. Long before they could read, they had the two of us running to the public library for answers of which we were ignorant. This was for me a time of valuable insight into the minds of two bright youngsters. At mealtimes we talked together a good deal about topics in which they were absorbed. And in the course of doing the dishes together, I discovered the extent to which many of their curiosities paralleled my own. I also learned how much of their questioning was left unresolved by school education. They knew a lot of science and math. What they wanted from me was something else: Who makes up the rules of our world? they needed to know. Why do people live in slums? What causes pimples? Why does God permit crime? Why do people smoke? Should we join a church, and why? Forever, Why?

The two of them were distinguished early in life by their contrasting traits. Peter, now deceased, had a keen, searching mind and a talent for symbolic thinking. Bruce is still (now in his forties) an engaging person, witty and outgoing. In their childhood years, we moved deliberately from urban to small-town living. Our family migrated fifty miles to Waukegan, Illinois, a lakefront community where we had familial roots. It was this town at which Stina's grandparents had arrived from Sweden with their eight children.

With his two sons, Bruce, age six, and Peter, age nine

Waukegan was then a town distinguished by its small lake-fishing industry, peopled by inner communities of Finns, Slovaks, and Armenians, and boasting a scattering of industrial plants.

Returning home after lengthy World War II service, I had new job skills to offer, and I entered into a field that had long intrigued me, namely, lithographic printing. I began an extended period with Rand McNally, working on maps and globes. But I was also drawn toward the children's-book department. I could see there a possible opportunity to return to my primary and lifelong interest in writing.

My first attempt at a book was inspired by an astronaut of my own age, John Glenn. He had just completed a historic space mission, three times circling the earth. What caught my particular attention was the fact that he had in his orbiting spaceship a kind of globe by which he secured his constant bearings relative to the earth's surface.

The manuscript I submitted to Rand McNally was an effort to explain to young readers some of the mysteries of space travel through the use of a terrestrial globe. Although the script seemed to me to be a "natural" for Rand McNally, they turned it down for reasons never clearly explained. It was then that I sought help from Ruth Gregory, the capable and peppery head librarian of the Waukegan Public Library, who read my script and liked it. It was at her urging that I sent it on to the Viking Press, where it drew speedy approval and publication.

Within a few months, I was informed that my book, *The Globe for the Space Age,* had won the prestigious Thomas Alva Edison Award as the best children's science book of the year, 1963.

The long-range effects of this award were somehow dreamlike. It all began with an elaborate ceremonial in a posh New York men's club, where I was properly celebrated and launched into my new career. The magical moment came as a kiss on the cheek from the last empress of ancient silent Hollywood, none other than the aged Mary Pickford. (I learned that she was then the doyenne of the Edison interests.)

From that beginning flowed wondrous and tributary events—television talk shows, tours that took me into the major book-publishing conventions, large and small book fairs, state and national librarian conclaves, literary doings in great variety, countless opportunities to be with children.

Somewhat bewildered and often embarrassed, I submitted readily to all these occasions. The more significant consequences appeared gradually. I realized that I now had the free opportunity to write for children according to my own deepest desires. For many productive years that followed I continued an excellent relationship with Viking Press and with a superb editor, Beatrice Rosenfeld.

Viking Press

"This is the photo used on the jacket of my first children's book—a true 'turning point' "

My own book-writing process may deserve some elaboration. I had by this time read enough published children's nonfiction to see what I understood to be major flaws in a good many of these books. Although well turned out and even widely sold (though not perhaps to children directly), they appeared to me to make little or no connection with young minds or needs. Most often, such books were written by experts, highly qualified in their chosen professional fields. I discovered that their relationship to young people was something else.

My best self-instructive example was a small, widely distributed volume written by a well-known astronomer. On page one, he had written (possibly with an editor's help) a series of clear and intriguing questions. By the middle of page two, he had begun answering them in the jargon of his profession, expounding theoretical formulas of unbelievable complexity. Too much for me, certainly.

The problem here was understandable. In the course of a lifelong devotion to study, research, teaching, the professor had developed certain language, rhetoric, assumptions, mind-sets, all familiar in the academic setting, using verbal shortcuts in the writings as well as in his discussions with colleagues and with advanced students. Such writing left the young reader confused. An experienced and intelligent editor might have intervened in such cases, but often did not.

My own reasoning took me in quite the opposite direction. For me, the book-writing process began with probing. I was looking for intriguing questions that represented the wide-ranging curiosities of young people, and I had my own as well. I had something more than conventional science writing in mind. How had the average human life span of Americans doubled in the brief space of two hundred years? What is a city, really, and why did it come into being? How did the map of America get put together from the discoveries by separate groups of explorers? That Plains Indian, whose likeness appeared on U.S. currency: who was he? and why had his life pattern become so flamboyant in the course of his struggle for survival and cultural identity? What goes on in the "communities" where animals and plants live together? (Or, as my son Peter posed the question: "They are always showing us pictures of animals killing each other," he said. "If that's the way it has always been in the wilderness, how come there are any live animals left?") Why does racism persist in a nation that has centuries of experience with its evil consequences? Do computers really think?

These are not merely possible book subjects. They are what I understand to be book ideas, central and cogent themes around which books may be built. And to the extent that they were questions perplexing the minds of young people, questions that often matched my own, they became the driving incentives for books I could and did write. There was little likelihood that I might resort to incomprehensible "shortcut" replies to such questions since I was myself in somewhat the same position as my eventual reader, a condition of both curiosity and ignorance. It was up to me to dig out the answers, beginning with the same unknowns that I shared with my intended readership.

The starting point was an itch that tickled the brain. "Why do I dream?" my eleven-year-old reader wanted to know. Similarly, who invented the metric system, and why? Is the night's chirping cricket a male or a female? How do we find our way across an uncharted sea, or reach an unmarked point in three-dimensional space?

The research was my own special delight. Whatever curiosity ever did to cats, it opened for me a purposeful way ahead. Enthusiastically, I went from public libraries to specialized libraries, and from there directly to the people and the places that held the answers I was looking for.

At work on a book on modern production technology, I spent months peering at assembly lines, conveyor systems, automatic processing and packaging equipment. At the same time, I investigated the development of the binary system, which led to the computer and in turn made robot-run factories possible. In the back of my mind lay the human and social equations as well, the possible threat of unemployment.

One wintry night, I lay asleep in one of the many tiny bedrooms in a sleep laboratory on a Chicago university campus. My head and my body were festooned with electrodes. My brain waves, and those of five others, were being simultaneously monitored. Through earphones clamped to my head, I was awakened periodically by a quiet voice that asked me whether I had been dreaming and, if so, what I was witnessing in my own "theatre of the night." This was dream research in action. Some weeks later, I entered actively into the advanced research being carried on in Lyon, France. Here a controversial theory was being tested; namely, that dreams are a natural process that appears in certain species and plays a part in the development of the prenatal nervous system. The theory was spelled out for me as I saw electrodes hooked to each egg in a basket of eggs, and I watched the recording equipment reveal the "dream" stages of unborn chicks.

Heavy scientific stuff? Yes. But I judged it to be well within the range of comprehension of the average junior higher. There was technical language involved. But the difficulties could be readily dispelled through careful unravelling of whatever unfamiliar words were essential in explaining the subject matter at hand. The more critical concerns were the concepts involved. Could they be grasped by the young mind I was trying to reach? Or were they too abstract?

The most serious challenge for me in this respect was my fourth book, which explored what was then (1966) a little-known concept for the lay public, namely, ecology. The title was *The Living Community.* The book opened the reader to such phenomena as symbiosis, the nitrogen cycle, predation and parasitism, speciation, ecological niche.

Mr. and Mrs. Jack Sprat are a comic example of symbiosis. But they are not the whole story. A serious danger for the writer of children's nonfiction is that of oversimplifying explanations. Such "talking down" in children's nonfiction is both misleading and demeaning as well. The danger is coupled with the equally serious one of writing that which is unsuited to the conceptual capabilities of the young reader. The writer's recourse is to offer only the most graphic explanations and where necessary to convey somehow to the reader that the subject matter does also contain further complexities and subtleties.

The Living Community won for me a second Edison Award, making me the only two-time winner. In addition, the book was honored with the Clara Ingram Judson Award, presented by the Society of Midland Authors. Hamish Hamilton issued a British edition; Italian and Japanese translations were published by Mondadori of Milan and by Gakken Limited, of Tokyo.

One of the most gratifying honors received by this book was its recognition by the *Arbuthnot Anthology of Children's Literature,* third edition. This authoritative collection not only reprinted an extended excerpt from *The Living Community,* but also listed the book as a "Milestone in Children's Literature" among those so designated for the period from the year 1600 until now.

My book-related curiosities carried me across the continents and the intervening seas. East African game reserves piqued my interest in animal habitats; the Middle East offered its antiquities; Europe provided some ultimates in human invention and discovery.

At the "chin" of Portugal, Sagres, I connected with the fifteenth century's Prince Henry the Navigator, who plotted the courses of sailing ships to unknown continents. This experience opened my book on "navigating in sea, air, and space."

Just outside of Paris is the "home of the meter," where I traced the historic events that gave rise to the metric system, the international measuring standard, from which the U.S. is still almost the lone official abstainer. My own interest and experience with lithographic printing led me to the city of Munich, the site of lithography's origin in a strange happening involving a laundry list. This story opened my account of "printing from a stone."

In 1976, I wandered, lost, in the Bavarian forests looking for the secret wilderness laboratory of the Nobel Prize winner, Konrad Lorenz. The honk of wild graylag geese overhead guided me at last to the woodland where these same geese had displayed for Lorenz their curious courting and mating patterns. From there, the quest took me to the Dutch haunts of Nobelist Niko Tinbergen, who studied the reproductive habits of several bird and insect species. Still another leg of that journey led me to the Austrian lakeside home of Nobel laureate Karl von Frisch. There, with the niece who assisted him, I visited the hives and meadows where the scientist had discovered the so-called communication "dance" of the bees. All this was only part of the research that went into a book on "how males and females behave." This volume, entitled *He and She,* received the Society of Midland Authors Award as "an absorbing, mind-expanding study of male and female behavior."

A good many of my book-related studies were conducted in the United States. My research on animal behavior benefited greatly from time spent in the Regional Primate Research Center at the University of Wisconsin. A book of mine on how the separate parts of the map of America were finally pieced together was itself the basis for several transcontinental tours. In Charleston, South Carolina, I was able to trace some of the shameful events which contributed to the spread of "scientific" racism in America. The town was once the center for a pseudoscientific group that "proved" the inferiority of the black race. The story of the overthrow of the false concepts of a few racists who called themselves anthropologists is dealt with in my book entitled *The Riddle of Racism.* The book received the Jane Addams Award "for its contribution to the dignity and equality of all mankind."

For a book on the Plains Indians, I was able to tap rich primary sources, some in urban Native American centers and others in the Indian communities of the Plains states. My interest was in the varieties of tribal lore. In this case, the publisher, Rand McNally, was enormously helpful, lacing the volume with a profusion of illustrations showing the skills and specialties of tribe after tribe.

In these books, I made no pretense of being an authority—only of being an author who had painstakingly gathered the most accurate and reliable data available. There appeared in each volume of mine a page or two of acknowledgements. These were the result of having written to a dozen or more of the most knowledgeable experts in each discipline I had chosen to explore. To my query as to whether they would do me and my readers the favor of examining my draft, the reply was affirmative, almost invariably. Their extensive and valuable criticisms and suggestions came to me gratis. These professionals were my safeguard against oversimplification and error. In some cases, their praise went so far as to acknowledge that I had written a text specifically for children of which they were not themselves capable.

This "vetting" process included extensive correspondence with the late anthropologist Margaret Mead, who helped me with parts of the book entitled *He and She.* Some of the top scientists in the NASA program guided me through a book on space exploration. Similarly, three scientists in the U.S. Bureau of Standards checked my facts on the history of the metric system. Lieutenant-Commander H. D. Howse at the National Maritime Museum in Greenwich, England, was one of those who assisted me with celestial navigation. One of the foremost inventors of the modern computer, J. Presper Eckert of Sperry Rand, was at my side in writing the book on automation. Every bit of such invaluable assistance was tendered to me simply for the asking.

My books were never intended as textbooks. But chapters and whole portions of a good many were reprinted with my permission in textbooks and "readers" adopted by school systems. Among these publishers were Macmillan; Scott, Foresman; Houghton Mifflin; Ginn and Company; Addison-Wesley. The textbook-publishing firm of McDougal, Littell reprinted the entire text of *The Riddle of Racism* as part of a social-studies curriculum. Many of the books were reissued as low-cost paperbacks.

During these years, I also wrote shorter pieces that appeared in such publications as *Boys' Life, Cricket, Highlights, Child Life.* I wrote also for a variety of media reaching out to children: a series of thirteen radio scripts for the Chicago Board of Education radio station, WBEZ, under the title "Peter and the Meter"; an educational program on anthropology, published by the Beacon Press; a teaching curriculum published by Science Research Associates; an audio-visual presentation on the metric system, prepared for the Chicago Museum of Science and Industry.

Sharing a book with two of his many readers

My own attachment to junior highers as a reading public began long ago. The experience of having been one myself was the source of my empathy for this group. Those few years of life, from ten to thirteen, are commonly the most hellish of all. One suffers the multiple tortures of change too rapid and too extensive for coping. The physical sprouting that takes place is like the sudden extension of Pinocchio's nose. But that is the least of it. The psychic transformation, the emergence of an anxious mind inquiring into areas undreamed is often unnerving. Alienation from adults and the shaky clinging to peers for support are common patterns. But should a rare adult show some compassion, accept a preadolescent as human, remember one's name—that earns a grateful response.

My wife and I were parents to two sons who lived through these metamorphic horrors. I entered into every available avenue for being with eleven-year olds—scouting, and all the sports interests and the fads of those years. I was a wide-eared listener, even an eavesdropper, as two sons, with two different sets of young friends, trooped through our home. These were book-writing years for me. And I was keenly eager to learn about their language, attitudes, interests. I tried more than once reading samples of my writings to small juvenile groups. They devoured my spaghetti, and mumbled compliments between mouthfuls, but rarely a useful, critical word.

These "middle age" children are a distinct breed, as every age group undoubtedly is. And I would never make the mistake of a blunderbuss, generic approach to children. One may disagree with the age-group spreads established by publishers or by libraries. But never doubt that developmental stages do exist and that your reader, if you are ever to reach him or her, unquestionably has a very specific identity. You had better know what it is, currently, and by personal experience.

A distinct advantage for those of us who write for children over those who write for adults is the wide opportunities that exist for meeting these young readers face to face. Throughout American cities and towns, in schools and libraries, there are numerous book fairs, Library Week assemblies, young-author recognition events, to which authors are invited. Organizations such as the Children's Reading Round Table of Chicago, with its chapters elsewhere, is a valuable resource for the writer, linking that writer with children and also with those who are close to children, teachers and librarians. I have found my years of such activity enormously beneficial. And if my writing for children has particular strengths, this undoubtedly has to do with my closeness to my chosen readership. No book critic has ever been more rigorous about my limitations in this field than I have myself. And I find that such shortcomings, when they occur, are invariably due to being momentarily "out of touch" with children.

I always hope that my books are the kind that readers would come upon by themselves, and read with personal enjoyment. That's the way they were intended and written. The heroism of creating the United States of America, the making and using of a pair of stilts, the planning of a great voyage of discovery, the invention of a unified standard of measurement—these can each be told as a "good story," and read with pleasure.

They are narratives that can come alive for the reader. There is drama in the conquest of smallpox, in the erection of the first skyscraper, in the first detection of Rapid Eye Movement (REM) in slumbering infants, in the plotting of longitude, in the perception of the "bee dance."

What I slowly came to understand is that, in a nonfiction book for young people, mere facts are far from enough. The information in such books may have been carefully checked for accuracy. But there is much more to consider than correct or incorrect. Facts beg for meanings. They can be interrelated so as to form mosaics that convey understanding, principles, significance, cause and effect.

Fact: The black slave in America was imported and marketed like any machine with a price tag on it and was turned into a working thing. But there is much more to be said about his or her dehumanization, about the expanded ways in which the continuing discrimination now persists, more than 125 years after legal emancipation. The plight of the slave will readily trigger a young person's sense of unfairness. A more developed understanding will move the child toward seeing the problem in its modern social context, thus enlarging his or her feelings of outrage. What the well-written text can also do is to help the young reader put those inchoate feelings into words.

In a self-chosen, self-reading nonfiction book, barren input falls short of the reader's needs. My own experiences found me turning away from simply listening for the child's questions, toward a closer insight as to what lay behind the questions.

In their middle years, children increasingly extend their grasp toward the more abstract ideas that constitute the social sciences. As they mature, their comprehension runs more deeply. They are seeking a set of their own values, a code of ethics. They are increasingly responsive to human relationships, more keenly aware of social problems, conscious of the feelings of others. They are trying out their own opinions and judgments, sometimes finding themselves mistaken, and trying again. They yearn for order in their world, but often seek to understand disorder as well.

As a writer, I have had to rid myself entirely of the notion that I was only a larger child. I came to understand that book writing necessarily edged me beyond a child's queries and toward suggesting the follow-ups and larger questions that needed to be asked. For example, it is clear that our society does despoil natural environments. But the middle schooler may be ready to ask about the consequences. In one book I tried to help the reader overcome a sense of frustration and helplessness over the problem of ecological havoc. This volume is a showcase of Americans who have courageously intervened to protect the environment, and with significant effect. These *Guardians of Tomorrow* help personalize some of the constructive action that can be carried on and enlarged.

As I read them, good books for children, whether fiction or nonfiction, are not impersonal. The writer invariably reveals his or her personality to the reader, as well as values, traditions, attitudes, and feelings toward children. Between reader and writer can occur an intuitive kinship.

For myself, the book text is the place where I invite the young reader onto my own turf, to a crossroads where the physical and social sciences and the humanities are joined. There we can share some of the big and small questions of life to our own satisfaction, and without condescension. One question leads to an answer, which calls forth a deeper question, and so on.

There came a startling moment when my relationship to that young reader seemed threatened. My own children had become adults. I had no grandchildren. I had not had the forethought to become a classroom teacher, or a children's librarian, thus securing close and daily links with successive generations in middle childhood. At that point I had to face the critical question of whether my career as a writer of children's books had come to an end.

I did know fellow writers who were necessarily leading childless lives, and were struggling vainly to avoid sterility in their work. They were relying, some of them, on a myth that, although the adult may change, the child does not. Perhaps they were trying to write for today's child on the basis of their own childhood, or of bygone memories of their grown-up offspring as youngsters. But I knew that wouldn't do for me.

Fortunately, an opportunity appeared. I was asked to join a government-supported educational program as "writer-in-residence," working with schoolchildren statewide on the learning of writing skills. So began a new phase of my life with children, and with my own writing for children as well. The program moved me into a wide range of classrooms for periods of from a few weeks to a few months. This was a live-in program, my being the houseguest of families that included some of my students. I taught no more than three or four small classes a day, staying close to my preferred junior-high or middle-school grade level.

I entered into this enterprise with zest and as much creativity as I could command. I was a new face in the classroom, but I was determined that I would not remain a stranger for more than a day or two. This was close personal contact with fifty or more junior-high kids each day, using a teaching method and style of my own design.

We had a fine time together, usually with the regular classroom teacher elsewhere. (I discovered that most of these teachers felt inadequate at teaching writing, but that is another story.) All kinds of writing-in-class were involved. But the focus was on producing something that approached bona fide fiction writing. Hazard Number One was the tendency for my students to do hack writing, picking up something they had previously read or seen on TV. More often than not it was a sentimental "my pet" tale, or a stereotypical "science fiction" fable, or a rehash story of talking animals or dolls.

My approach to original writing moved my students into personal experience, sensitively centered on some recent "turning point" in their own lives. From my side, the process involved winning their trust, assuring them that I would never betray or embarrass them. I also succeeded in persuading them that, since I was not a fiction writer, their highly personal stories would never appear in print as mine.

My success as "writer-in-residence" put me in demand. And I ranged widely in a variety of school settings over a good many years. I still hear from many of these young people. None has as yet become a published fiction writer to my knowledge. But the experience was apparently a valuable one for them, perhaps as part of their own growing-up processes. For myself, this was my way of keeping "in touch" with children in this fascinating age group.

I cling to this tie with the young as though it were a lifeline. And it is more. I had never believed much in immortality. But some years ago, writing a book on "the first man," I became a friend of the late anthropologist and superb writer Loren Eiseley. He was a man for whom time spread out in its longest perspectives. On an autumn walk together, I once caught myself looking at his wristwatch to see if it showed not the hours, but light-years instead. He managed to persuade me of an anthropological view that no person or living thing simply vanishes at the moment of death. As human beings, perhaps we cry out for some enduring echo of ourselves in the corridors of tomorrow, or we leave some mark or influence that in some way outlives us. And that hope perhaps underlies my own attachment to the young.

As for their influence on me, they constantly renew my curiosity and sustain me as a seeker throughout life. Eiseley spent his adult years looking, as he put it, for "a missing person." His searching eyes peered into a thousand likely caves and graves and sinkholes. He sought the ancient bones of one who had lived on this continent in the Ice Age, when the last great glacier capped the earth and overlay half of this hemisphere. My own life's quest was tied more narrowly to a better understanding of my contemporaries.

As my books for children evolved, I could perceive how my restless inquiries were changing me. I was becoming the sort of humanist who is absorbed in the perplexities of our species. As the music of Brahms probes the unanswered mysteries of sentient beings, and as Shakespeare's "problem plays" delve into the complexities of the human psyche, so I was prompted to beg the imponderable questions. And my methods were only lesser versions of what Copernicus and Darwin and Einstein sought through changing the point of view.

Someone said that "life can only be understood backwards; but it must be lived forward." For me, stultification is anathema. Of passionate significance is the scrimshaw art of Nantucket whalers; the communities of Serbia where, under Turkish rule five centuries ago, Turkish custom and religion were adopted, and persist to this day; the household inventions of Thomas Jefferson; the craftsmanship of workers in the Dutch village of 's Hertogenbosch, rendering in stained glass the color sketches of a California church architect; the vehement style of debate in the British Commons; the songs, symphonies, and chamber music that Dvořák wrote while a visitor in Spillville, Iowa; the palette of Pierre Bonnard.

Largely self-educated, I am no stranger to the classroom. As recently as June 1988, I received a second master's degree in literature at Northwestern University. At that institution, I helped a year ago to found a small peer-led subcollege which is called the Institute for Learning in Retirement. In my town of Evanston, my wife and I participate actively in neighborhood issues and in local as well as national politics. I have served terms on the Evanston Library Board and helped organize what is considered an exemplary local chapter of Friends of the Library.

I respond readily to the wonders of nature. Following the lead of the great and late naturalist Aldo Leopold, my wife and I have created our own natural reserve on a wooded hillside in what Leopold called the "sand counties" of Wisconsin. What I enjoy observing there is something that is called "ecological climax," meaning the optimum stage of natural development at which a variety of plant and animal species share a common environment.

I am much affected by the angle at which the sun strikes the side of my head, meaning that I am devoted to the equinoxes of spring and fall. I am there on our unkempt acreage with its small A-frame cabin as the spring season turns wet, wonderfully moody and evocative. The smells are peppery, arising from a mat of soggy leaves. Misty mornings and early evenings are pure impressionism, Debussy and Monet. Nothing viewed is hard-edged. It is to me a time for hearing long-forgotten music and remembering childhood scenes.

When Venus appears close to the horizon in late summer and the wild berries are ripe, I am up north with greater frequency. I remember what I call the Year of the Mushroom as living evidence that nothing quite repeats itself. That year, the fungi abounded on our hillside in more shapes, forms, styles, sizes, colors than I would have believed possible in any single habitat. As the days lengthened, I admired the flight and the sound of geese in the southbound flyway.

But nature aside, I am partial as well to the finest works of humankind. Back I go to the city and the magnificent sweep of Lake Michigan's shore, which the city fathers had the good sense to preserve for the public delight. The lakeside drive is unforgettable in some wintry dusk with the sky like welded steel overhead, the lake black, but really black, with white

Hirsch (center) with other founders of the Institute for Learning in Retirement, Northwestern University, 1987

The author and his wife, Stina, 1985

combers rolling in a long way—a drama without words and with soundless drums.

From boyhood, I have never stopped delighting in the city's great symphony orchestra. In recent years, a large number of new theatres have appeared here, more creative than the Broadway hand-me-downs that existed when I was working as a candy boy along the local rialto. There is stimulating activity around the two universities that are the double nucleus of the city's academia. And I can lose myself in wonder for an entire day in one of the truly outstanding art museums of the world.

In the early spring, I return as well to a favorite event, a day spent with some two hundred "young authors" at a public school nearby that has the good grace to honor them. Here, twenty or more adult authors of children's books sit with small groups of youngsters and discuss with them the stories into which they have poured their earnest writing talents. It is a flash point of my year, as I sit back and wonder idly what I might have become if I'd had the well-designed support these youngsters are getting.

Then I think of Aesop, with whom I am what Joseph Conrad called a "secret sharer." Yes, Aesop, who for millennia has delighted both the children and adults of the world with his thought-provoking tales. Aesop, who became renowned in every country in the world, and with a lot less guidance or encouragement than I ever had. Aesop, who looked up from abject slavery with never-failing humor and human compassion. Aesop, who finally bought his way out of bondage and became the wise advisor to ancient kings. Aesop, who remains for me a goading enigma, and an inspiration as well.

BIBLIOGRAPHY

FOR CHILDREN

Nonfiction:

The Globe for the Space Age (illustrated by Burt Silverman). New York: Viking, 1963.

This Is Automation (illustrated by Anthony Ravielli). New York: Viking, 1964.

Fourscore . . . and More: The Life Span of Man (illustrated by William Steinel). New York: Viking, 1965.

The Living Community: A Venture into Ecology (illustrated by W. Steinel). New York: Viking, 1966; London: Hamish Hamilton, 1967.

Printing from a Stone: The Story of Lithography. New York: Viking, 1967.

On Course!: Navigating in Sea, Air, and Space (illustrated by W. Steinel). New York: Viking, 1967.

Cities Are People. New York: Viking, 1968.

Mapmakers of America: From the Age of Discovery to the Space Era (illustrated by W. Steinel). New York: Viking, 1970.

Guardians of Tomorrow: Pioneers in Ecology (illustrated by W. Steinel). New York: Viking, 1971.

Stilts (illustrated by Betty Fraser). New York: Viking, 1972.

The Riddle of Racism. New York: Viking, 1972; also published as *Racism in America.* Evanston, Ill.: McDougal, Littell, 1974.

Meter Means Measure: The Story of the Metric System. New York: Viking, 1973.

Famous American Indians of the Plains (illustrated by Lorence Bjorklund). Chicago: Rand McNally, 1973.

Famous American Revolutionary War Heroes (illustrated by L. Bjorklund). Chicago: Rand McNally, 1974.

He and She: How Males and Females Behave (illustrated by W. Steinel). Philadelphia: Lippincott, 1975.

Theater of the Night: What We Do and Do Not Know about Dreams. Chicago: Rand McNally, 1976.

Anne Holm

1922-

I think I had better begin by saying that I have had a very happy life! Because while making a few notes on what have been important factors in forming my life and making me the person I have finally become, I have realised, clearer than ever before, that I had a fairly miserable childhood, shaped with the best intentions by my adoptive parents.

I know very little of the first three years of my life—only what I was told thirty to forty years later. It began in the best tradition of the classics . . . my father was a member of a large family of squires, civil servants, and merchants; my mother a trained nurse and daughter of a widower with grown children who remarried a woman thirty years younger.

Times were bad in Europe after the First World War, and when I was eight months old, my parents emigrated to the United States, hoping to make a future there for the three of us. I think my father did, eventually; but my mother stayed for little more than a year. As a nurse before their marriage at a hospital for patients with tuberculosis, she had caught the infection, and in the climate where they settled the old complaint broke out violently, and she sailed for home—no travelling by air in those days—bringing the baby girl back with her to the extremely primitive cottage in the smiling, mild climate of southern Zealand where my grandmother, already long since a widow, struggled to make both ends meet for herself and my mother's younger brother, handicapped already at the age of two by polio . . . hoping to be cured.

A local doctor and his wife were good friends of hers from her nursing days, and with their help my mother spent the winter in the nearby sanatorium, leaving me with my grandmother. She wasn't cured, but as my grandmother's cottage was in the middle of the countryside, on the edge of a lovely beach wood, she was allowed out of the hospital for the summer.

She spent it lying in a deck chair outside in the sun with me toddling around her chair, playing. Many years later my grandmother told me that my mother never dared to sleep when I was around, for fear of my climbing up on her lap. In those days tuberculosis was something you died of, more often than not, and, as a nurse, she knew how contagious it was. It is true that even today I have no remembrance of physical tenderness as a child, no memory of having my tears dried and being comforted with a kiss—probably I learned very early not to cry.

Anne Holm

Today the reader will ask, "But what about your grandmother?" But at that time, in the early twenties, the term welfare state was not even thought of; for a poor widow who couldn't support herself, there was only private charity or the poorhouse. In the country private charity was scarce—the farmers had enough to do supporting themselves and their old parents, and going to the poorhouse you lost your right to vote . . . anyway, my grandmother's fierce pride would never have permitted her any of those two "solutions."

She would have been highly qualified for a post

as housekeeper in a big house—had in fact as a young woman been head of the household for a Swedish prince—but with a small child on her hands most of the year, and an invalid boy of fifteen to be kept in a school for the handicapped, learning bookbinding—what could she do? So she toiled from early morning to bedtime at such jobs in the surrounding countryside as allowed her to bring me with her—cooking at weddings and funerals, helping with the harvest. She had no time for showing tenderness, even though she felt it.

My father wrote, of course; first he sent what money he could spare, then money for the tickets back to the States. My mother—by autumn back at the sanatorium—wrote back that she was too ill to travel, and that's where the mischief was done. My mother's young brother, an ambitious and intelligent boy, had been promised that he could go back to the States with us, and knowing no better, of course, wrote to his brother-in-law that "Elvira looks so well, her eyes shining and roses on her cheeks . . . ," both sure signs of an advanced stage of tuberculosis.

My father chose to believe the boy and was furious when the money he had sent for the voyage was used for food for us all.

By then my mother knew she was dying, and when next my father sent, not money, but the tickets, she had them sold, to stave off for a while longer the hunger in the small cottage by the woods. She wrote back, telling him that the doctors had said they couldn't prevent her from going, but that she would not reach America alive.

Evidently he didn't believe her. I don't know why—my grandmother never talked to me about him, except to tell me that he was bad through and through and had not cared that my young mother was dying and his child had not enough to eat.

I have a feeling that he thought my grandmother wanted to keep her daughter and grandchild in Denmark. From a few faded letters I found thirty years ago when my grandmother died, it is obvious that he had a quick temper, and my grandmother, certainly a formidable opponent, never knew that the boy, eager for the promised land, had contradicted my mother's messages.

On a cold February day, when I was three and a half years old, my mother died. She had made my grandmother promise that she would never hand me over to my father, and she didn't; the custody was his by law, of course, but having just got a very good job in the States, he wasn't able to ask for leave to come and fetch me. What he could do, he did—he refused to let me remain with my grandmother and gave the order that I was to be put in the care of some respectable people, until he could make other arrangements.

"My mother, Elvira Jensen Rahbek"

It so happened that the local doctor and his wife who had befriended my mother and grandmother knew of a childless couple in a smallish provincial town not too far away who wanted to adopt a child. At that time this sort of thing was managed privately; no public social workers meddled, in fact they had not been invented yet—and a child was the property of its parents.

Today Mama and Pappa would be denied even temporary rights because they were old enough to have been my grandparents; and next, their reasons for wanting to adopt would not be considered good enough: they wanted "a child to love and care for, in order not to be lonely in their old age."

At the time it was a nice and natural way of reasoning; they came down to look me over and to be approved of by my grandmother, and all was well. They really were nice, kind, respectable people. From the doctor Strodtman my grandmother knew they were well respected in the town where they lived and what quite naturally in the circumstances meant much to my grandmother: they were solidly well-off, Pappa

"My maternal grandparents"

Anne, with Martha and Bodil

at the time being the managing director of a factory, and they lived in a nice, white house with a garden. In short, I would lack for nothing. They were obviously pleased with me; I was a normal, nice-looking child, lively and trusting, and what made Mama feel "it was meant"—part of my name was Anne.

Grandmother told them that I must be brought up in the Christian faith, which they promised, and they promised, too, that they would bring me to visit her once a year. The fact that my father had refused to let me be adopted wasn't considered so very important; he was sure to change his mind in a not too distant future.

He didn't; they fought him for eight years before he relented.

I remember nothing from that time, not even that I wasn't very happy the first weeks. Many years later Mama told me that every day when the church bells rang the sun down, I sat in a small chair, telling them sadly that now the bells would be ringing over my little mother's grave.

"I burst into tears," Mama smiled, "and asked Pappa to drive you back to your grandmother."

I remember thinking, "How typical of you!"

But all in all I must have been happy enough for the first couple of years. Mama enjoyed dressing me nicely, played with me and my dolls, and Pappa was always ready to mend a broken toy. I was taught the names of the flowers in the garden, and how to greet people nicely, and always to remember to say thank you.

I was never taught to think; I suppose that's why I don't remember very much. I remember the highlights, of course. Christmas, and Easter when I put my shoes on the windowsill and in the morning they were filled with chocolate eggs. The small kindergarten where I played with other children, holidays at the beach a few miles away where friends of Mama and Pappa had a summerhouse. They had two daughters, a little older than me, Martha and Bodil. I admired them tremendously . . . because they were older, because they always were dressed alike in pretty clothes, and because they had very yellow hair. They liked me because I was like a big doll to them—I don't think they ever discovered that it was the doll who invented amusing things to play.

I liked it too when Mama played the piano for me and taught me a lot of songs. I was quick to learn the words, but for a long time it was Mama's despair that I didn't sing true; nobody had ever told her that all small children will sing off-key until they have learnt to control their voices.

When I was little more than four I was sent to dancing school, and I loved it; all through my childhood, dancing-school day was the happy day of the week. At five I went to have piano lessons because Mama loved music; she had been one of a penniless widow's six daughters, and was always, I realised many years later, ashamed of it.

I think her mother, who was dead when I came into Mama's life, must have been an amazing woman! Her youngest was only one and a half years old when she lost her husband, and she worked her fingers to the bone all day and nevertheless had songs and laughter left for her girls before they went to bed. And none of them were sent out as serving girls; she managed to keep them at home while they learned "a nice, clean trade," so that they could get nice, clean, respected jobs.

Mama ought to have been proud of her! But she only had a piano when Pappa had earned enough money to give it to her along with piano lessons.

I must say I found music lessons very boring; you had to play the same stupid little tune again and again and again, not proper songs. And my teacher, who was the organist at the town's church (a very beautiful one, by the way, built nearly a thousand years ago), had a big brown wart with three black hairs on it. I didn't like Miss Vimtrup much, and I cannot imagine that she liked me either—I always cheated with my practising. In a couple of years, though, it changed because she discovered I could sing. She loved music, had got together a big choir and trained it, and I was immediately put into the children's section. Long gone were the days when I sang off-key! Whenever we were practising a new polyphonic work, I was placed in the weaker group because I could be trusted to keep the note against all odds.

I cannot sing anymore, I have been smoking too much, but to this day I can still hum all four parts of a very difficult work called "Sunrise," written by our greatest Danish composer Carl Nielsen. I liked Miss Vimtrup's house, too; there was a dining room, the music room, and three drawing rooms, all of them with lots of paintings and beautiful furniture. I liked being invited in for tea with the family, the table daintily laid with thin cups and embroidered napkins. Miss Vimtrup sat at the head of the table, small, squat, always dressed in black with white collars in the winter, and in light-blue ones, cut the same way and with the eternal white collar in the summer, her brown hair short and straight like a man's—a funny contrast to the fragile porcelain and delicate table linen.

Every year she held a public concert with her pupils performing; I never shone on these occasions. Mama loved the old songs and was fond of popular music, waltzes, and tunes from operettas, but as no one made me listen to real classical music and explained little about it, I just found it boring and cheated about practising as much as I could. I remember one of these concerts where I was to play a small piece for four hands together with a girl called Aase; she was a painstaking, dutiful girl who wouldn't dream of skipping the difficult notes, with the result that I had finished the bass several seconds before she had worked her way through the treble. *I* didn't hesitate for one second—I took the beginning once more, played it softly in case the notes didn't quite fit, and stopped together with Aase.

This "jumping the fence where it's lowest," as we call it in Danish, is, I'm afraid, a habit I have developed into a fine art during a long life.

Otherwise I have never been good at jumping, or indeed any other sport; I think part of the reason has been that my imagination told me only too clearly the risks in climbing, skating, and the rest of it. Let's say that is one-third of it, the other two-thirds simply being that I'm lazy and a physical coward.

Strangely enough, my best playmates in those early years were two totally fearless girls living a couple of houses away. Their father was a doctor who was hardly ever at home as he was also a member of our Parliament. Ingeborg was my age, her sister Birthe two years younger. It was a very lively family; there were two teenage children, too, and a baby sister, and no one noticed much what Ingeborg and Birthe were up to—but it was always something which made them very dirty and their clothes look like rags long before lunchtime. Mama was scandalized at the way they looked and felt sure they probably didn't get enough to eat either—which they certainly did—but as their father was a doctor, they were, socially speaking, absolutely acceptable, and I think she was flattered, too, that their mother expressed the hope that they would learn a little from "their neat and well-behaved friend."

They didn't—although I stayed neat! They knew that I was afraid of doing anything that looked dangerous, so, being generous girls, they did all the neck-breaking things first, and then, when the way was paved, they helped me after them, being very careful that my clothes didn't suffer because I would be scolded, they knew—remarking cheerfully, "So will we, but *we* don't mind . . . *you* do."

It must have been about the time I was to start school that my happy childhood came to an end.

A year or so before, Pappa had left the factory. He was a very handsome man, a very honest man, and, as most not very intelligent people, stubborn, and quick-tempered to boot. He had begun in the office of the factory as a young man and worked his way up; Mama told me once that in his youth he had been charming, merry, and very popular, both with their friends and with the members of the company's board, who knew him as a pleasant and conscientious bookkeeper. Why they thought he was cut out to be a managing director I cannot imagine, but he was easily gotten rid of—they simply goaded him into losing his temper at a board meeting, which ended in his resigning on the spot after only four years as leader of the firm. Then he went home and told Mama. . . .

All this I didn't know at the time, of course, but I can well imagine that Mama must have first burst into tears, and next asked: "And what are we supposed to live on now?" Not an unreasonable question, but one to which I'm sure Pappa had not given a thought.

The board must have given him a certain sum in compensation—he had, after all, been a valuable man to the firm for many years—and Pappa, together with an old acquaintance, formed a firm with this money. I don't know what they were going to sell, but the later twenties cannot have been a good time for starting up something new, and the whole thing lasted one year . . . ending with Pappa having lost all his money *and* being left with the responsibility of all his companion's debts.

I do remember Mama crying and crying; I don't think she then, or ever after, reproached him or blamed him for the disaster, but it must have been then she realised that she had to insist on having some knowledge of money matters and a say in deciding how to spend what little there was. The house was split into two flats, and we moved upstairs, the ground flat being easier to let. Pappa got a job travelling for a big firm in Copenhagen. None of it can have been easy, but the real tragedy was that they were both ashamed; both felt that they had lost caste, and they were convinced that the town must despise them and that their friends were laughing behind their backs.

I have never known Pappa as anything but a morose, rather silent man; with me he was always gentle, but whenever Mama reproached him for having bought something not strictly necessary, while *she* struggled to put decent food on the table with next to no money, he would lose his temper, and I would escape to my own small room, frightened at their loud voices and angry words.

One thing they must have agreed on: as far as possible I should not feel the change in their circumstances. The money for my music lessons was there until I was about thirteen and it became too obvious that I didn't care much about them. I stayed in the choir because I liked singing . . . and my beloved dancing school was never in question, although it cannot have been easy, because I was by far the best dancer in my class and always picked as leading girl in formation dances at the big end-of-season balls and for solos with my dancing partner. Both meant fancy costumes, silk veils, and so on, which must have been difficult for Pappa and Mama to afford.

But essential things began to go wrong. We had been planning to go to school together, Ingeborg and I, and then, a month before the event, she and Birthe with their sisters and parents moved to another town, and I went alone to my first school day. It wasn't too bad, but I was not quite the happy, trusting child I *had* been; Mama discovered that a charming, cuddly, soft, little thing at a certain age turns into a creature with a mind of its own. She didn't understand mine, and what you do not understand, you do not like.

She liked *me,* of course; so she set to work changing me into the sort of nice, quiet, biddable little girl she wanted and would have been able to cope with. She never succeeded . . . but it did mean that all the years I should have spent in learning, asking questions, above all, feeling loved no matter what, were spent in rebelling, resisting—being made into something I knew I didn't want to be . . . and as a result being made aware that I was not there by right—I didn't belong—only when I was "good."

In those days it was quite an accepted thing when bringing up children that a box on the ear might do a naughty child some good. Mama and Pappa never once hit me—I don't think they would have found it decent to hit someone so much smaller—but poor Mama in her crass ignorance got a much better idea: whenever I was being especially difficult, pointing out, for instance, that something she insisted on didn't hang together logically, she would say, "Well, little Miss Rahbek!" My foster parents' surname was not Rahbek . . . but mine was, until my father finally gave his permission to the adoption, on certain conditions which my foster parents never kept. All through my childhood I was told what an evil, low man he was; I believed he had been in prison, or murdered my mother . . . I was twenty before I realised that he had done nothing of the sort, and that I was, in fact, much better born, to use an old-fashioned phrase, than my foster parents.

One day, towards the end of her life, Mama said: "Sometimes I am afraid I didn't always treat you rightly when you were a child."

I couldn't tell her what she had done, it would have been too cruel; but it made me into a secretive child. I still rebelled, I still resisted . . . but not openly, because the burden of that horrible, criminal name was too heavy. And I told her very little about what I thought, or what happened, because I never knew what might make her angry enough to remind me; I didn't understand the way her mind worked.

I was ten when I realised that my intelligence, such as it was, was greater than both Pappa's and Mama's. It was such a comic occasion . . . they had decided to celebrate Mama's birthday with a small party because it was her fiftieth; I cannot remember what I had offered to help with, but I was told I couldn't do it. Mama then found me in the drawing room playing with a lit candle, making the fluid wax drop on my hand, and she very reasonably told me not to—to which I smilingly answered, "There, you see! Idleness is the root of all evil. . . . " She was furious! She said that it was the usual thing with me, and now I had totally ruined her birthday.

It was yet another guilt on my shoulders. I remember that I crept around the rest of the day, unhappily aware of how seldom they spent money on a modest party, and now I had spoilt it all. But that night in bed I realised the truth: I had not *meant* to be impertinent . . . I had said it in fun, meant it as an amusing answer to laugh at . . . Mama was simply too stupid to understand anything.

In some ways my realisation helped. Pappa had never said anything, except "You must do as Mama says" and perhaps a mild question: "Couldn't you do a little better?" when I brought home a poor mark for mathematics. And now Mama had no power anymore to crush me with her anger, her tears and accusations. I simply disregarded them; it was no use talking to her. In other ways it wasn't a help at all. It has always exasperated me when people believe that a reasonably intelligent child also is more *mature* than the next one. I disregarded not only the silly things Mama said, but all of them, not knowing that experience teaches even the silliest person a lot of everyday common sense.

Which meant that in those difficult years there was no one at all to guide me, no one whose advice I respected. There were quite a few teachers I liked, and they rather liked me, too, I think. Away from Mama and Pappa my talent for feeling happy and gay revived; I was never a boisterous or unruly child, and a good teacher always found me a good pupil, interested, very willing to learn and ask pertinent questions. I was easily number one in class in Danish, English, German, history, and geography (sounds horribly like bragging, but it was a simple fact).

I was hopeless at mathematics, physics, and sports; to this day I cannot put three sums together twice without getting four different results.

But teachers at that time were supposed to teach their pupils the things they had to learn . . . not to see them as children. Class distinction was strong, and they must have known where their pupils' parents belonged in the small-town society, but as I remember it they didn't let it show. They didn't wonder, either, even when a seemingly quite bright boy was impossible in the classroom, as "word blindness" had not been discovered yet. And I'm sure they never noticed that around the age of eleven I had become a much-loved victim of mobbing by a large group of older children; it began with a nickname I disliked—don't know why, after all, the stork is quite a nice animal—but I hated it so much that I wanted to die every time I heard it. I said nothing at home. I knew very well that Mama would have telephoned their parents, gone to the headmaster, or done something equally disastrous.

The trouble was that I didn't cry either. Had I only cried at Mama's very first "Well, little Miss Rahbek," I'm sure she would never have used it again—to her it was just a desperate bid at what, in those days, was a parent's right: to get the upper hand over a child. But I only cried when nobody saw. So the mobbing increased and would probably have ended in violence if I had been disliked in my own class, but I wasn't.

I wasn't exactly popular; to be popular at school, as a girl, you had to be either good at sports, which I wasn't, or have yellow curls and blue eyes, and with my light-brown hair and dark-green eyes I fell sadly short of the ideal. But I wasn't a talebearer, and I was always willing to give a helping hand with an English paper or whisper answers if someone got stuck during a hearing in class, so my classmates took turns to stay with me at recess time.

And I very early discovered a wonderful way of escape for whenever life became too much to cope with: books!

By the time I was ten, I had read all the books in the school's library, but my teacher in Danish class, as an evening job twice a week, had to keep the town's library open, and on the condition that I didn't shout it from the treetops, he allowed me to come there and read some books.

I'm still an avid reader, but I think I read more from the time I was eight till I was eighteen than I have ever done later in life. There was no one to guide me—I think Mr. Lassen got his amusement out of watching my choice of books. I buried myself in stories about other people, lived with them, cried over them, and of course sometimes broke my neck

"Pappa"

"Mama"

over them. Hemingway and Steinbeck, for instance (we were not taught even about the bees and flowers in those days), and I remember an Icelander called Laxness. He was certainly tough work! And so gloomy that I gave him up after a couple of books. I loved romances with happy endings . . . stories which went on and on through four generations. . . . I read a lot of classics, without knowing that they *were* classics, and the authors' deeper intentions went clean over my head most of the time, naturally; I simply swallowed the plot.

It never harmed me, but that is the reason why I have tried for twenty-five years now to prevent teachers from giving a story to a class of nine year olds, when it is meant for children three years older. They do it, all over the world! And it does mean that the too young reader is cheated, as I was—something I only discovered when, as an adult, I reread books I remembered from my childhood and found the beauty of style, the thoughts, ideas, and wisdom to enrich my own life which had escaped the child I was.

Nevertheless, no matter how little I often understood them, books did become a lifebelt to me, and a much needed one, because life at home grew more and more joyless and grey, with Pappa always morose and silent, and Mama bitter and suspicious, imagining animosity and slights everywhere. The long walks with her—how I hated them! I liked a walk in our town, seeing people, looking at shop windows, but going for a walk with Mama meant being dragged along a lonely path to a little wood four kilometers away and back again, either in silence, or accompanied by lectures about never trusting anyone, people's malice, God's total lack of compassion . . . on and on.

I never believed any of it (well, I don't believe a young child wastes much time thinking about God—he's up there, somewhere, and that's that), but the rest of it I *knew* had to be nonsense, as I was a friendly child, and never met with unkindness in grown-up people.

There wasn't much talk at home, either, only remarks about neighbours and other persons who met with Mama's or Pappa's disapproval. There were never talks about interesting things or ideas, and the world outside our own small town didn't exist.

It sounds amazing, but I lived through the thirties without having the slightest idea of what was happening just south of the Danish frontier! At that time Pappa had bought a radio with a loudspeaker and would sometimes put it on to listen to Hitler speaking, but when I asked who that man was, screaming and shouting, Pappa would say, "Oh, just a German idiot. . . . "

Jews were people from the Bible—I hadn't realised that they also lived now, and my life went on without any changes.

Which isn't quite true because life at school had become less fraught with danger from menacing older girls. I had reached the age when boys and girls begin to discover each other, and as it turned out, I was not among the girls who were left out of things because they were "ugly" or "boring." I had quite forgotten what it was like not to be all wrong and "unbelonging," and it was an exhilarating feeling that at one point at least I was considered very much all right!

Youngsters fifty years ago were not as outspoken as they are today, and not so knowledgeable about "the facts of life." I believe it was all to the good that we were allowed time to dream and wonder, to have a secret crush on somebody without the slightest idea of what it was all about, to weave fairy tales to our best friends about the way "he stole a look" at us—so very far from what life is like today, where mere children feel obliged to vie with each other about having real, adult affairs to avoid being considered childish or prudish. I sometimes suspect that perhaps a lot of these affairs are invented simply to boast about, and feel relieved.

But, of course, there was the other side of the coin: nearly every idea which, then as now, came into the head of a normal girl of fifteen or sixteen was pronounced indecent. I remember my best friend and I had inherited, together, a half-used lipstick from her sister, older by ten years . . . the thrill of trying it on in secret! And the horrible scene when we were discovered by Mama! Obviously, we were well on our way to harlotry . . . not that we knew the word, or what it might have meant, but still.

All Mama's efforts to keep me on the narrow path from which I had no intention of straying didn't improve our relationship, and I would have been happy looking forward to the end of school and the beginning of grown-up life if she and Pappa hadn't had the idea of getting me a post in the local bank—such a nice, ladylike way of spending my time until I somehow caught a suitable husband. I had nothing against a husband, in the distant future—but a bank!

My teacher in Danish class became my saviour; when he heard about the plan, he forgot himself far enough to say that he had never heard anything more idiotic, and, unknown to me, he went to Pappa and told him: "That girl must be allowed to write, and I have already had a talk with the editor of the town's liberal newspaper, who is willing to take her on as an apprentice and even give her a small fee."

I don't think Pappa liked the idea—but he told me about it and asked me if I would like it. I don't know what I answered—I nearly fainted from sheer happiness.

And so, in the summer of 1939, I began a new life. The editor of the paper was a man in his fifties—well-read and interested in local, national, and international politics—a civilized man, and a cheerful and kind one. The editorial staff consisted of four people: the editor, the copy editor, a young journalist, and the apprentice. To have a girl as an apprentice was at the time a very newfangled idea, in a small town, even bordering on the daring. I didn't know; I simply adopted the rest of the staff as my family. The editor became the father figure, the kind, all-knowing, wise person whom I wanted to please, whose words of praise made sunshine out of a rainy day. The subeditor, an "old" man of about forty, became a nice and understanding elder brother, who advised me and helped me with the million things I was ignorant of and good-naturedly gave his opinion when asked about a new dress or another way of doing my hair. And the young journalist—later in life a famous globe-trotter—was a delightful playmate and confidante in my various affairs of the heart, he himself a merry chap with a never-ending row of rapidly changing girlfriends.

To the three of them, I suppose, a reasonably nice-looking seventeen-year-old girl was like a breath of fresh air in the old office. The two older men spoiled me and allowed me to charm my way out of jobs of which I was a little nervous or simply thought sounded boring; and the journalist, Jens Bjerre, and I shared jobs between us as we saw fit, covered up for and squired each other as occasion demanded.

Responsibility was a word I had never heard at home; a nice, good girl did what she was told, and I never realised that now I was given a chance of shouldering responsibility and forming my own opinions. I just loved my new "family," who approved of me. (At least most of the time! It was my job as the youngest member to fetch the mail from the post office at seven o'clock in the mornings, and it did happen, when I was more than fifteen minutes late, that the copy editor was a little cross.)

I took to the work like a duck to water. I did write fluently and well; I liked to form well-shaped sentences and tie them up with a small "bow" at the end of the column. I loved it when the editor trusted me with the description of a theatre performance, but I would happily write a report on the general assembly of the local rabbit farmers as well. Birthday articles, interviews . . . I was very good at interviews and was often sent out on errands like that. I was proud of my reporter's pass; it made me feel both safe and grown-up, once I realised that it was respected, and people never questioned my right to ask questions. I loved thinking out good questions and listened with respect to the answers I got—not a very common trait in journalists, I realised later in life! I would put in short comments on people's houses and try to paint a verbal picture of my "victims."

I still remember the day when my editor told me that an important man in our town had specially asked for "the little young lady in your office." The editor had planned to do the interview himself, but he said with that kind smile of his that he "had better bow to the star of my paper."

My reporter's pass had an added attraction: all doors were open to me. The two local cinemas, concerts, visiting theatres—in no time I didn't even have to show it.

But most of all I loved the office in the evenings when nobody was there. The newspaper has gone the way of all small local papers, the building gone too, I suppose, and my editor long since dead—but I only have to close my eyes to see the big, untidy room with the huge table, my chair at one side, the green-screened lamp making a circle of light in the middle. This was my home, my sanctuary, where I could read, write, and where no one would dream of opening my private drawer, slowly getting filled with the results of my secret vice: writing poems.

Sometimes one of the others would come in to write a report on a meeting or some such thing, but none of them even asked what I was doing. We just said hello, and minded our own business, unless something special had been going on in the town.

My foster parents didn't question my airy announcements of "I have a meeting tonight." It was work, and not to be interfered with, but in everything else Mama never stopped trying to change me and direct my life, my thoughts, my clothes, what I ought to do, and what I mustn't do. I disliked her most of the time; there were times when I hated her. I think I was thirty before it occurred to me that she had no rights over me anymore! It was when my husband once said, very gently: "*Must* you always do what your mama tells you to, or else hide from her that you don't?"

Then I rebelled! I told her firmly that this was *our* house, and she was welcome if she respected that *we* ruled here.

I think this is where I should make it clear that she was a soft-hearted, loving woman, who had simply got the wrong child. She was starved for tenderness, starved for companionship, her songs silenced a long time ago by lack of appreciation. I'm happy to say that the last few years of her life there was never an unkind word between us, and it was so easy to please her that it hurt. Asked to show me how to make a special dish or do some other household chore, she was not only delighted but grateful to be needed. When my husband called to show her some little thing which he thought might interest and please her, she came hurrying, eager as a child, humbly surprised that someone bothered to share anything with *her.*

I sat with her the last, long night. The nurse told me to go and get a little sleep, Mama didn't know I was there—but I couldn't, as I wasn't sure she was right, and I had failed Mama so often. I didn't feel guilty. Just as Mama got the wrong child, I had got the wrong mother; it was nobody's fault. I simply sat on, realising that Mama was a greater person than I could ever be; she had long ago forgotten all the bitter, unhappy years because in spite of everything *she* had never stopped loving *me.*

But all this was still in a far future. The present was a busy mixture of the work I enjoyed, the falling in and out of love the way young people do, *and* getting to know about the world around me with a vengeance.

Because the war broke out a month after I began my apprenticeship.

It seemed very far away and unreal, at first, with me struggling to cope with the typewriter which was put before me the first day. Given time, I could of course prick out the letters. (To this day I use only two fingers when writing! But I can do it as fast as people who have learnt to use all the ten we have.) But it was quite another thing to be told cheerfully that in a month or so I would be expected to take down the reports dictated by our bureau over the radio!

They were sent every hour and with all the war news the dictating speed got faster and faster, and more and more names appeared of foreign places I hadn't even heard about in school and of people who (most of them just as unknown to me) had names just as difficult to spell. I hardly noticed the text in my frenzied efforts to get the names right, because although the colleagues at the rival paper across the street were very patient and helpful when I telephoned an SOS, I didn't want to embarrass my own by doing it too often.

Outside the office, life went on in our sleepy provincial town as usual . . . until one early morning in April when on my way to fetch the mail another early riser passed me in the sunshine—a man in a uniform I had not seen before. Peaceful, neutral, little Denmark had been invaded by the Nazi-Germans at daybreak.

A few brave young soldiers died, valiantly trying to defend our frontier before the government surrendered and the King had to tell his people to accept the occupation and refrain from all hostile behaviour towards the German army.

Under the circumstances there was nothing else we *could* do, having spent the years up to the war believing that nothing very dreadful would happen after all—or at least that it would blow over. Very little had been spent on our defence; the Danes are not a warlike people, and we are slow to reach real, burning anger. So, quietly disliking the sight of those green uniforms, we trotted out to buy material for blackout curtains and, after that, a store of the things the older generation remembered from the First World War would soon become scarce. I remember Mama buying soap; all through the war I could wash myself in nice, fat, foaming, real soap.

My own life began to change though I don't think I realised it myself. I was still under Mama's rule, still incredibly immature, but not being really stupid, all the things I met with through the office made me more and more conscious of a world outside my own little limited one. The frontiers had closed, of course, but one evening on my way home from Copenhagen by train, I met a well-known critic from our biggest national newspaper. That is, I didn't know it was he, but I spotted his luggage, covered with worn labels from hotels abroad, and, scenting a possible "victim" for an interview, I showed my reporter's pass and opened a conversation, which ended in his suggesting that I send him the poetry I had written.

I did, and thought no more about it until he telephoned me that he had arranged a meeting for me with a publisher who might be interested in my poems.

And so, in one short year, I suddenly found myself with a debut as a poet, a husband, and a child!

A couple of hectic years followed, and my poetry not being too bad, coupled with my youth and my marrying the publisher, made me quite a figure in the literary life of wartime Copenhagen, a position to which I could bring nothing but my youthful ignorance, a quick tongue, and a pair of faultless legs. It all, inevitably, went to my head, and I suppose underlined in a way Mama's creed: The importance of pleasing people, conforming to pattern, being careful about "what would people say". . . .

It worked well enough; I moved among people twenty, thirty, forty years older than myself. They thought I had some talent, and for the rest, it was enough that I was young and lively, an amusing, light relief from all the cares at home and the killing and disasters abroad.

Now I think of all the brilliant minds I met those years, without learning anything but how to hide the fact that I understood very little of what they were talking about behind a quick comment!

Two things saved me from growing into a perennial butterfly: there was a war on, and the German occupation began to provoke the Danes. We could live with all the tiresome rationing of everything—it was even quite fun inventing dishes and things to replace disappearing goods—but all the clumsy German attempts to govern our minds riled us. We listened to the Danish Voice from London, and a resistance movement slowly grew—at first only a few courageous young people, but soon a lot of us were involved. Pamphlets were printed in secret, accidents began to happen to German transports and stores, and strange things were carried from one place to another at the bottom of a basket with vegetables. A red-haired person, with a well-known face, calling him- or herself Hansen, would appear on one's doorstep asking for a bed until Saturday, when a fishing boat would bring him/her to safety in neutral Sweden. A lot has been written abroad, since the war, about the heroism of those fishermen—they all risked their lives. It is also true that sometimes, if the refugees could pay for the trip, a poor fisherman would accept some money. I cannot see it detracted from their heroism that they thought of the family they would leave destitute if they didn't come back. After all, we all knew that the Nazi revenge for any resistance was invariably torture, concentration camp, or a bullet at dawn.

My dislike of smoked haddock was born during a week when we had five high-placed Danish officers sleeping all over the place in our flat, waiting for transport to Sweden. They had to be fed, and as their ration cards naturally were in the hands of their wives, smoked haddock with various vegetables was our mainstay. Thirty years later one of those officers, by then head of the Danish army, was escorting me in to dinner at a party; we hadn't met again in the meantime, and my surname was different, but the moment he saw me, he exclaimed, "HADDOCK!" and we spent a hilarious evening remembering.

I think that's the way the human mind works: once the fear, danger, and despair are in the past, we remember the fellowship and the comic things, and the rest exists only as indelible marks on our subconscious.

"My mentor, the Danish author Edith Rode"

The other thing which happened was that among all these talented, well-known people, I met an author, Edith Rode. It was towards the end of both the war and my short marriage, after my baby boy had gone with his father to Sweden for safety, and I didn't really know what to do with myself, now that the glorious, wonderful peace had saved us and normal, daily life knocked on the door.

I don't know why she did it—compassion, perhaps; or perhaps she sensed something in me which I didn't know was there. But I loved her till she died, as I shall always love the memory of her.

She took me under her wing. There was nothing sentimental about her—her wisdom was too profound—but she allowed me to do little things for her, and she would telephone me, telling me to come for lunch. I never knew if it would be a big party or just the two of us. I was simply as much in her house as in my own lonely little flat. She never tried to make me tell her things . . . she never criticized me. I think the only personal remark she ever made to me was said one day when I was feeling especially despondent and "non-belonging," because a friend whose loyalty I had trusted had let me down. I didn't doubt that the fault must lie with me—Mama had taught me too well—but I did ask in despair, "Edith, won't you tell me what's wrong with me, always? What *is* it that makes me somehow less worthy than other people?"

I had not asked for pity, and didn't get it, either; she looked at me in annoyance and told me not to talk such arrant nonsense. "There is nothing the least wrong with you! You're just very young." And then she laughed and said: "In fact, you remind me in so many ways of myself as a young girl . . ."

It was as if a much too heavy burden rolled off my mind for I knew Edith would never lie to me.

I could ask for her opinion or advice about everything, and be sure of a firm clear answer, devoid of disapproval. I followed her every suggestion implicitly. I knew she would always be right because all she said or did was right, and the manner in which she said and did it was always charming, tactful, and wise. I wanted passionately to be like her, and I noticed everything she said or did and imitated her as well as I could. A faint smile of confidence from her was worth more than the most elaborate compliments from others. A hardly perceptible shrug meant I had not come up to her expectations, but it was not mentioned.

When asked for her opinion, she would counter with another question: "What were you thinking of doing, yourself?" Then I would try and guess what I ought to do to be like her.

To this day, more than thirty years after her death, I sometimes ask myself: "What would Edith have done about this?"

And so, very slowly, the beginnings of the person I was meant to be emerged.

In the summer of 1948 I met a man. I had been sure I wasn't going to marry again . . . and he felt the same. Not that my marriage had been unhappy—only a stupid, boring mistake. I had not liked it, naturally, when my husband told me he wanted to marry another, because I have always felt that promises are there to be kept, but otherwise I didn't care very much, and we had parted decently, as friendly acquaintances.

The man I met had married very young, too—but unlike me he had had ten miserable years of it. We first saw each other in a friend's house. He did not at all look like the maiden's dream of Prince Charming on a white horse, just an ordinary, quite nice-looking, youngish man—until my eyes met his. Their colour was the light, clear blue of any Scandinavian's, but they held a serenity I had never encountered before, which made me wonder.

Not for long. The quiet serenity in his eyes and the gentle expression on his face simply reflected the person he was; he was unable to think a sordid thought, and his integrity was unshakable. We married a year after our first meeting, and nearly forty years of sheer happiness began.

We bought a house twelve kilometers north of Copenhagen, between the Royal Deerpark and the Sound, and I'm sitting in it now, writing this. From the upstairs bathroom you can see the blue of the Sound, and there is only a footpath between our small garden and the woods of the park . . . which makes weeding a hopeless task! Wild things *will* blow in across the hedge and mingle with our tulips and roses—but on the other hand we are protected by a private drive from the noise of the public road along the coast, and from our windows we can watch the deer and the stags grassing in the clearing just opposite.

There is nothing special about the house itself; it was built not quite a hundred years ago, and contains three bedrooms and a bathroom upstairs, a bathroom downstairs, and four rooms with no doors between them.

To this house I brought a fair amount of books and hardly anything else, having seen no reason why my former husband should be made to pay to get rid of me. This served us well; one would think that the house was big enough for two people, but my husband, having inherited beautiful things from both his father's and his mother's families, added to them like the collector he was, and the house was only just big enough for all the things which wanted room—not to mention books! There are books everywhere except in the bathrooms.

Europe was still licking her wounds after the war, but around 1950 it began to be possible to travel by car, and we toured all the free countries in the years to come, places my husband had known before the war, and new places alike.

It was often horrible to see what a war can do to a country and the poverty it brings to the people in them—but we were young, there was art and beauty enough left to drink in, and little by little we saw things getting better: repairs being made, people improving their living standard by cheerful, hard work. The tourist industry had not yet begun in earnest; there were no ugly skyscraper hotels, people were friendly and hospitable, but not yet spoiled and made mercenary by hordes of cheap, collected tours. We had our favorite small hotels where we were welcomed back and shown improvements year after year. Today they are very well-run places—typical of their various countries, but with all the modern conveniences fitted in.

Paris was Edith's favourite city, from even before the First World War, and every autumn we went there

"My husband, Johan Christian Holm"

for a week with her, until age stopped her travelling. Our own favourite country became Italy for the simple reason that it had always been my husband's, the classical world with its history, its buildings, and antiquities being his main interest. I always knew when we turned at a secondary road seemingly leading to nowhere that at the end of it would be the ruins of an Etruscan village, a Roman site, or a small museum where a few interesting things were kept.

We "did" the famous museums, too, of course. I have never listened to a guide, though—my own husband was always a much better one. His knowledge was vast, and he kept adding to it, looking, asking, and fitting it in with what he knew already . . . oh yes . . . he gave me a world.

He also gave me back my identity.

Once a year Mama and Pappa had always taken me down to visit my grandmother. I hated it as a child; she frightened me, and I sensed that Mama disliked her as she would start sighing several days before, and talk about duty and pity, at the same time deploring "some people" being "stuck-up" for no reason.

On our way home after the first time my husband had come with us, he suggested that he and I should drive down and visit her alone one day. It turned out to be quite a revelation! We had a delightful day, my grandmother being gay, wise, and charming, and obviously pleased, not the least with my husband. She must have been eighty-seven at the time, and was nearly blind, so we had to eat a very nice dinner alone, because, as she said: "I cannot see anymore where the plate ends and the tablecloth begins, and I won't have an audience for the mess I make!"

When we had left her, I asked my husband how on earth he had known, and he smiled and said, "I noticed when we were there last month that you were very much alike to look at, and thought that perhaps the likeness went deeper."

What I had seen all those years was simply an intelligent gentlewoman showing courtesy towards two people with whom she had nothing in common, knowing very well that they didn't like her, because they didn't feel at ease with her!

I loved her, and I was proud of her; we saw her as often as we could those last four years of her life, and she told me about my mother, about her own childhood. She had a firm faith and a quiet sense of humour; at ninety she couldn't see to read anymore, and thought it was time she died, but she came to the conclusion that God had probably forgotten she was still there. Knowing that old people die if left too long in bed, she went to bed and stayed there for a fortnight—but as she said when up and about again: "It didn't help . . . and it was too boring!"

She had had an incredibly hard life. At her funeral David's Psalm 103 was read . . . it was her choice.

I cannot think I'm really like her, although I wish I were; but I realise I have a a fair portion of her characteristics, none of them having helped to make my childhood easier . . .

I believe, though, that my granddaughter is like her.

I got my granddaughter in 1969. In 1964 a young man of twenty-two had looked me up—my son. After the war I had tried to find out what had happened—where he was. I didn't at the time know how to go about it, but I suppose I didn't try hard enough either: too much had happened in my life since then; his father had wanted him very much, and I knew the child had a kind stepmother. I was sensible enough to realise that it would be of little use to any of us, my breaking into his life as a total stranger.

But there he was, now; he had wrung the truth out of his parents, and curiosity had brought him to me. I introduced him to my husband and prepared to keep in contact in case he should need me sooner or later.

"My grandmother, Else Andersdatter, when she was ninety years old"

I do not think it would ever have been more than a polite, loose contact—he was obviously all his father's son—if he had not been engaged to a wonderful girl. She was intelligent and beautiful with a lovely sense of humor and a generous heart. We got on like a house on fire, and fortunately my husband fell for her, too, so in no time we had a ready-made young family, the granddaughter being followed by a grandson.

Not that we met more than a couple of times a year. They live in Sweden, and, like all young people nowadays, both have jobs—in their case, responsible ones, which don't leave them much time for holidays. But it was pleasant when a few days together was made possible, and we enjoyed watching the children grow up.

In 1965 we bought a modest house in a small Italian village by the sea . . . or perhaps I should say *in* the sea, because the village is at the very end of a peninsula sticking out in the Mediterranean between Genova and Pisa. It's about four hundred meters above sea level, and incredibly beautiful.

But it did mean that our touring days were over; we snatched a week in Greece now and then, a week in England . . . but what with our young family in Sweden and another house being *home* in Italy, there wasn't time for more.

In all those years I didn't *stop* writing, but I admit I was too busy being happy to be very industrious. During the fifties I wrote three light novels and then, around 1960, my Danish publisher asked me if I couldn't perhaps write him a story for older children. I like being asked—when people ask, it must mean that they think I can do it, and the confidence it gives me makes sleeping ideas wake up and begin to fly in and out of my head. It's like hunting in an anthill—but sooner or later one of them will catch hold of me and start growing, and all I have to do then is fight my own laziness.

There is no limit to all the good excuses for not working today, but wait until tomorrow! Once I have forced myself to the typewriter, it's fun and agony, of course, and enormously satisfying . . . after all, writing is the only thing I know how to do. I can run a house, I'm a fairly decent cook, I make my own shirts and skirts, but writing is what has always been my *metier.*

I wrote the story and felt that in a simple way it said something I thought—and still think—is important, for young and old alike. I suspected it might be good because my husband, who has always been interested in my work and encouraged me, kept asking once I got started if I had some more pages for him to read, and I knew that his sense of quality was unerring.

My publisher liked it too—but his reader did not! Those were the years when the left-wing movement was on its way in Europe, and he had chosen this consultant because he/she shared the taste governing the new generation of librarians ruling the public children's libraries.

I knew very well that no Danish publisher could afford to print a story the libraries wouldn't buy, so I admitted cheerfully that, as I had no intention of becoming a heathen and would remain an old-fashioned liberal to my dying day, I would put the thing in a drawer and we would stay excellent friends, which we did.

I forgot all about the story, until a couple of years later when my husband showed me an advertisement about a Scandinavian competition for a children's book. It was to be anonymous; you had to put your name in a closed envelope with just a code word on it. We struck a bargain: if he would pack and mail the story, I would let him have it. We then forgot all about it again, until a couple of months later we realised we had mislaid the advertisement, and couldn't remember which code word we had put on the envelope . . .

Well, one day late in September the then children's book editor arrived from the Danish publishing house with a huge bunch of flowers and a bottle of champagne. The story called "David" had won the first prize. We were having fried calf's liver for dinner—it's the only time we have had champagne with it.

It was all tremendous fun, of course—who wouldn't enjoy being praised and treated as a VIP for a few days at least, when the reason is a piece of work you have done?

It's been twenty-five years now. Since then *David* has been translated in some twenty countries—mostly under the title of *I Am David,* except in the United States where, for some mysterious reason, they called it *North to Freedom.* The story has been given awards in various countries. It's been reprinted and reprinted in England alone in more than a million copies, if I remember rightly. At least three film companies have given me contracts and paid option money; only they seem to go broke, one after the other, before the film is made.

The story has become what publishers call "a modern classic". I honestly don't understand why . . . perhaps because of its very simplicity?

But I sometimes wonder if the first consultant has followed its way in all five continents. It may be naughty of me, but I cannot help chuckling, just a little.

I have learned that success makes it difficult to be lazy. I get as many letters today as I did twenty years ago; it's sometimes fun, sometimes interesting, every once in a while moving—but as I have always been taught that when someone bothers to write you a letter, it should be answered, it costs me a lot of time and stamps! . . . and sometimes also worry. Why will some teachers hand out to a class of nine-year-olds a story which is written for older children? It's no way to teach a child the joy and richness of reading. The poor kids haven't got a chance to find out what the story really is about—they just swallow the plot, and then write a letter with sixteen questions to the author, nine of which would have been answered in the story had they only been old enough to think while they read. It's usually the same teachers who'll tell the class to pick out the parts of the story they "like best"—but what happens to the story then? To me, it's like picking a finished jigsaw puzzle to bits . . . choose those nice, pink pieces, and forget about the rest—but there's no picture left, then, is there?

After all these years I can spot an inspired

The author, at the home of friends in Scotland, 1987

teacher, just by leafing through a bunch of children's letters; you find them in a small village school, or in a famous college. Among twenty pupils there will then be five or six who have read "between the lines," so to speak, who have used both their imagination and their sense of logic while reading; they have formed their own opinion *and* are able to express it. And the rest of the twenty have made an effort to write neatly and think first.

In my mind I always sent those teachers a rose. Had it been possible to mail a real one, I could have kept at least two flower sellers in business for life.

Which is as it should be; only the best is good enough for the children who are to take over the world from us and try to make it better.

It may have been noticed that I began this by writing, "I have had a very happy life," and went on, I'm afraid, mixing my grammar in jumping from past to present. Sixteen months ago I would have said, "I *have* a very happy life" . . . but then my husband died . . . and the light has dimmed.

BIBLIOGRAPHY

FOR YOUNG PEOPLE

Fiction:

Dina fra Apotekergaarden. Copenhagen, Denmark: Jespersen and Pio, 1956.

Familien i Apotekergaarden. Copenhagen, Denmark: Jespersen and Pio, 1958.

Komtessen fra Baekkeholm. Copenhagen, Denmark: Jespersen and Pio, 1959.

David. Copenhagen, Denmark: Gyldendal, 1963. Translation by L. W. Kingsland published as *North to Freedom.* New York: Harcourt, 1965; also published as *I Am David.* London: Methuen, 1965.

Peter. Copenhagen, Denmark: Gyldendal, 1965. Translation by L. W. Kingsland. New York: Harcourt, 1968.

Adam og de voksne. Copenhagen, Denmark: Gyldendal, 1967.

The Hostage. Translation from the Danish by Patricia Crampton. London: Methuen, 1980.

Mollie Hunter

1922-

THE PORTRAIT

Almost an entire wall of this room is made up of windows. Light streams through them, the clear and cold light of winter days in my native Scotland. To the left and in front of where I sit, there is a large easel; and poised in front of this is the artist who is painting my portrait.

She is small. Her movements are as quick and neat as those of a bird. Her dark eyes are large and bright. She is also shy, and I know little about her except that she, too, is Scottish, and that her work has won her international recognition. In the stillness imposed on me by the sittings we have agreed on, I wonder how it has come about that this distinguished artist has been commissioned to paint *my* portrait. And by no less an institution, too, than the National Portrait Gallery of Scotland!

There is an official answer to my questions, of course, and I know what that is. The portrait is intended to recognise my work as a writer. Yet my work and my life are so closely interwoven that I have always thought of them as one; and so, if I am ever to find a personal answer to that question, I will have to disentangle each from the other, discover why and how these two threads have mingled to form this seemingly single strand. . . .

Mollie Hunter today

Childhood

One part of my life, at least, has trained me to think methodically; and so I begin with the fact that the wind, on the day that I was born, was set in the wrong direction. Was that symbolic? Of course not! It was simply a nuisance, this being the direction of wind that always caused the smoke from our kitchen/livingroom fire to blow back down the chimney. But still it did give me something of a dramatic entry into life!

That was on the 30th of June, 1922. The house where it happened was a small one in a village in southeast Scotland. Like the two sisters who had been born before me, like the sister and the brother who were to be born afterwards, I was a little blondie—although the smoke billowing into the room at the time made it hard to tell *what* I was. Soot from the smoke drifted down to settle on me; and in my mother's words as she afterwards told of the event:

"On the day Mollie was born, you couldn't *see* her for soot!"

She was exaggerating, of course. My mother always did have a strong sense of drama. But even so, it must have been a dreadful enough experience for her, especially since her life before marriage to a penniless veteran of World War I had been the comfortable one still being led by her family in nearby Edinburgh. Still, she was happy with her ex-soldier, which made her quite able to brush aside their criticisms of the life she had chosen; and we children took our cue from her.

Let the various aunts and uncles patronise us as

"Like my two elder sisters, a little blondie"

they would on the occasions we were all gathered at the grandparents' Edinburgh home. We still recognised them for the snobs they were. And just let the cousins of our own generation try to lord it over us! They soon learned that pampered little "townies" like them were no match for the sturdy country children that *we* were! Besides which, we knew very well that our father had no time, either, for pretentious people like them.

He was, indeed, a man of strong social conscience, always on the side of the underdog. He could be a charmer, too, whenever he chose to be; despite which, he was still a stern disciplinarian—which made him just the kind of father needed to control four girls and a boy, all close to one another in age and yet all diverse from one another in character. I was never afraid of him, however, as the others sometimes were. When he glowered at me, I glowered straight back at him—something that always made him laugh and tell my mother:

"She's got a touch of the old rebel in her, that one."

And indeed, I had. But I was just as much aware as he was that I had inherited my rebel touch from him, and so my father and I understood one another very well. As for our mother, she was so kind, so gentle, such a genuinely good woman, in fact, that it never took more than a word from her to shame me out of my wilder moods. Not, mind you, that there was anything at all wishy washy about her! On the contrary, she was a woman of the most lively humour—and with such a gift of storytelling, too, that it must surely have been from her I have inherited such abilities as *I* have in that direction!

But all of us, it seemed, the whole of our family gang of five, had inherited something of her dramatic flair. We proved that nightly, too, long after we were supposed to be safely asleep and our part of the house raged instead with shouts and movement as we improvised theatre out of the stories our mother had told us, the songs she had sung, the long poems she had recited from memory.

We were all voracious readers, too, with certain favourite books that gave us further splendid material for our acting games. And of course, there were also the dramatised tales of our own weaving, all of these as wildly inventive as our combined imaginations could make them. But such diversions, naturally, were still only for the housebound dark of winter evenings. Out of doors, we had for our enjoyment a part of the countryside so beautiful and so fertile that, for centuries past, it has been known as "the garden of Scotland", and every free waking moment of other seasons saw us either there or in the village of Longniddry itself.

That too, is an ancient place, and was then so small that the heart of it was only a single street of little cottages built of stone and roofed with the red pantiles traditional in that area. There was a school too, of course, a Post Office, a garage that could more than cope with the small amount of motor traffic of those days, the blacksmith's workshop that we called "the smiddy", and a church. And so, with manmade entertainment therefore limited to the occasional show of photograph slides in the church hall, we grew up there as truly country children who quite cheerfully made their own diversions.

At the farm that gave most of the village folk their living, we begged rides on the backs of the Clydesdale plough horses that were as gentle as they were huge. When the blacksmith had blown up the fire of his open forge into a titanic flare of red and gold flames, we stood watching in fascination as the metal he heated in it grew whitehot, and listened in equal fascination to the musical tap tap of his hammer working the metal. The village street was our playground, especially in the long twilight that ends each summer day in our northern clime—"the gloaming", as we call it—when we would play the kind of games that involved much running and chasing and hiding, along with ritual calling back and forth.

From end to end of the village the cries would echo, sounding thin and eerie in that mysterious half light which has always seemed to me to be the ghost of the day that has passed. And listening from whatever hiding place I had chosen for myself, I would sometimes have the strangest feeling that I was hearing the voices of ghost children calling, calling . . . It was a feeling that could often send me into what we call a "dwam", a state of mind so much like a trance that the outside world seems barely to exist. Or even to matter, supposing one did recall it!

There was never anything of this feeling, however, on the summer evenings when we made fire-cans, whirling these around our heads while the potato placed on top of each one roasted in the fire and the wild shouts we gave then cheered on the process! Or when we stoked up equally dangerous fires of driftwood to cook the shellfish we collected beside the arm of sea that bounds one aspect of the village.

We spent long, long summer days on this and other seaside activities—hunting for shells, swimming, angling for small fish, or netting the even smaller minnows that thronged the stream running down to the sea. But summer was also the time for expeditions inland over meadows thickly-golden with buttercups, past fields where poppies wove a brilliance of scarlet through the barley's ripening gold, and so on to the old limestone quarry where we could gather our fill of the wild strawberries that dappled with red the gray rock of the quarry's floor.

In Spring, we sought the first of the wood violets—deep purple in colour and always well hidden under their heart-shaped leaves, but with a scent so intoxicatingly sweet that discovering them was—to me, at least—like suddenly coming on the secret source of all perfume. Our activities in the Autumn woods, on the other hand, were of a strictly practical nature. Autumn was the time for gathering berries and nuts and anything else that was even remotely edible. There were no keener gatherers, in fact, than our gang of five, and no greater explorers either, of every aspect of our village and its environs.

As for time spent in school, this was something I found worth while only for the English language periods when I had the chance to write essays that indulged my passionate pleasure in the music and meaning of words. On the way to school, also, we had to pass the smiddy; and this, for me, was a fatal

"My father, William McVeigh—war veteran, disciplinarian, and charmer," 1918

McGeachie Dunoon

"My mother, Helen Waitt McVeigh—so kind, so gentle," 1942

attraction since I almost always lingered long enough to make me once again the bad girl who had to be punished for lateness as well as inattention to lessons.

The village has a new school now, the large and modern one needed to cope with a school roll vastly increased by the children of incomers commuting back and forward to the city of Edinburgh. But the minnows we fished for are all dead from pesticides. And even if those children on the new roll were forced to rely, as we were, on making their own amusements, I doubt very much if their citified habits would allow them to know where to search for violets or wild strawberries. But maybe these too, in any case, are now all dead, wiped out by weedkillers. Certainly, that is what has happened to the poppies blazing scarlet among the gold of the barley.

The buttercup meadows are gone too, covered by a rash of modern housing. There are tractors drawing the ploughs now, instead of the big and patient Clydesdales. And as for the heart of Longniddry itself, this has suffered a living death, with all the small red-roofed cottages tarted up and run together to form the trendy "Longniddry Inn", and even the smiddy converted now into the equally trendy "Forge Bar."

And so what has it meant for me, as a writer, to have been brought up in that place at a time before all this happened to it? There was a comment my mother used to make of me in those childhood years, one that was usually voiced in tones of amused pride.

"Mollie was only nine months old when she started to walk and talk."

To this boast, however, there was a rejoinder that could come from any of the family who happened to be present.

"And hasn't sat down or shut up since!"

They were right in this, too, but not entirely so. It's true that I have always been a great talker; true also that, from the very start of my life—sooty birth notwithstanding—I have had a very high degree of physical vitality. What none of the family ever realised, however, is that there is another aspect of my nature—one that relates to the part of my mind which is always silently recording, always soaking in all the impressions made on all my senses, the part that loves the feeling of falling into a dwam. But this, even although I was aware from very early days of the way in which it set me apart from the rest of the family, was something I never mentioned to any of them.

To these others, indeed, I was simply the most talkative, the liveliest of our lively gang. But even so, I was still the one who would habitually wander off by herself to sit staring in silent delight at the shape and colour of a flower, the texture of a leaf, the curl of a breaking wave—at anything, in fact, which fulfilled what I later came to realise as my deeply sensuous appreciation of the natural world around me.

I had an instinctive sense of past generations, too, in my constantly-wondering gaze at the various ancient buildings dotting our rural landscape. At the farm, I was always aware of something in myself responding to the evidence of old beliefs still held, old customs still practised. And it was not only the red and gold flare of the blacksmith's forge that would make me linger overlong at the open door of the smiddy.

I was absorbing also every detail of the atmosphere of the place; and it was simply because I had done so that I was later able to write the scene of the forging of the iron wheel rim that forwards the magical element in my fantasy, *Thomas and the Warlock.* As for the blacksmith himself, sweat gleaming on the face that reflected red from the flames, I was always keenly aware of sensing in him a force that spoke of the efforts and skills of countless generations of men bending metal to their will. And even later than the writing of that fantasy, it was this awareness which bred the character of Archie Meikle, the blacksmith who has such an influence on the plot of my novel *The Third Eye.*

Without my having the least awareness of what was happening, in fact, that childhood environment of mine was nurturing a whole range of feelings so essentially part of my nature that they were quite inevitably destined to become also an integral part of my writing. But even so, what I did realise in those childhood years, was that I revelled, literally revelled, in being what I was then—partly a little country savage, but partly also an exalted dreamer finding total fulfillment in a world where (metaphorically speaking, at least) the sun always shone.

For all of us, however, there was to come a day when the sun went in. That was the day my father died.

He and my mother had been the great and only love of one another's lives. For her, thereafter, there was to be not only intense grief, but also a struggle against poverty that shortened her own life.

I had been the favourite one of his children, the one who delighted him with her high spirits and what he called her "gift of the gab." To me, he was God. And it was when I was nine years old that God died.

I have written about all this in a book I called *A Sound of Chariots,* a book that has been referred to as being my "emotional biography." I admit the justice of this, too, since it was certainly my attempt to come to terms with my long-continuing grief for my father. Equally so, however, it was a tribute to my mother, battling so courageously to make a living for us—and with never so much as a gesture of help, either, from that uncaring family of hers!

I wish she could have lived to read that book. She had recovered all her old humour, all her old storytelling spirit long before I wrote the first word of it. But she was still only just a memory for me by the time it was published. She never lived to see any of my published writing, in fact, never even knew it was the impact of my father's death that had given me the first glimmerings of insight on the shape my own life was destined to take.

In all that I thought and did from then on, I realised, there was an even keener awareness of both myself and the world around me—so keen, sometimes, that I could hardly bear the experience. I began to take with me on my lonely expeditions a pencil and notebook—the notebook that held my previous attempts to express myself in some original form of words. And gradually, out of all this came one further realisation that embraced all the others.

I was going to be a writer. And for preference, my writing would take the form of poetry.

Teens

There was a problem waiting ahead for me in all this, the problem of education. How could I be a poet, I argued to myself—how, indeed, could I be any kind of writer—without having had what I called in my own mind, "a proper education"?

It was about the middle of my thirteenth year that this first occurred to me, and from then on I began to work so hard at school that my teachers saw in me what they thought of as "good University material." But much good that did me in those Depression years of the nineteen thirties when higher education was only for the well-to-do, and even the scholarship I might have won would not feed and clothe me till I had reached University entry age!

Unwilling as I was to fact the fact, my fate was still that of the rest of the family. I had to leave school at fourteen—the earliest age at which one could legally do so. As my two elder sisters had already done, also, I had to find some kind of a job. But, it seemed, there was nothing on the market for me, and so my mother did the only thing she could do then—put her pride in her pocket and ask those uncaring Edinburgh relatives to take me into their family business.

"Because you really could go far in it," she tried to reason with me when I persisted in begging to be allowed to stay on at school; and did her best to close her ears to the howl of rebellion that was my only response to this.

"And maybe become a wee bit more civilized in the process," added my grandfather when it came to

A cottage traditional in the area of southeast Scotland

handing me the meagre paypacket that rewarded my first week's work in one of his Edinburgh flower shops.

He was quite jovial about this. Joviality, indeed, was part of his nature in anything that did not concern money; and in his terms, at least, I was lucky not only to have a job but also to be now in a situation where I could acquire some of the genteel ways of those city cousins we had always so detested.

But I wouldn't, I wouldn't let myself be sat on in this way, I decided furiously. There was nightschool, wasn't there? And libraries. I would use them both, and educate myself. Stubbornly then, I followed up my decision with a routine that had me travelling back and forward between home and Edinburgh to work a six-day week in the shop, with nightschool study to follow on four evenings of each week, and the other two evenings spent in research reading at The National Library of Scotland.

"The *National* Library!" exclaimed the uncle who ran the shop for my grandfather. "You're daft, Mollie!" But he, too, was good-natured enough in the way he spoke. And maybe I should not have felt so humiliated by his remark, because there *was* something daft, I suppose, about an ignorant fourteen year old haunting the greatest library in the whole country. But not in my terms. And the good nature, I noticed, did not extend to any offer of shortening my ten hour day in the shop.

But still, I had some achievements to show for my efforts, the first of these being that my nightschool studies enabled me to pass an exam that gave entry to a job in the Civil Service. It was clerical work, dull stuff, among people who were themselves incredibly dull; but it did at least mean a shorter working day for me, and even more importantly, a salary that was of much greater help to my mother than my previous miserable earnings.

As for my library studies—"God," I had stated when I was asked just what I wanted to study. "I want to find out about God."

I was not thinking of my childish feelings about my father when I said this, but simply of all I had absorbed at that time from the fundamentalist Christianity that was my mother's faith. God, in this, was responsible for everything. God was the great I AM. And thus, I had reasoned to myself, if I studied God, I would be truly educated; because then, in effect, I would be studying to find out all the secrets of the universe.

The librarian did not blink. Nor was there even a hint of a smile on his face. Politely, instead, he guided me to the stacks on Comparative Religion—and so to my first discovery of primitive belief in the power of magic and the part this had played in shaping religious practice. With a feeling of intense excitement, then, I recognised some of the very superstitions that had survived into the time of my own childhood—such things, for example, as creating the shape called "the corn dolly" out of the last sheaf to be cut at harvest, and perching this on top of the highest stack as a guardian figure throughout the coming winter.

So often as a child I had watched and wondered at such things, and now I knew them at last for what they were! All of them, they were simply vestiges of that same belief in the power of magic, vestiges that had survived in folk memory right up to the time of my own childhood. And so now I knew, too, why I had always felt that instinctive response to them. The folk who had carried out such practices were *my* folk. I had their blood and bone. Somewhere deep in my brain moved the same fears and longings that had moved for untold generations in theirs.

In effect, I had a share in that folk memory! And now was my chance to find out more about it, to explore the origins of all those superstitions I had witnessed, the stories I had heard, the sayings that had been part of my childhood's conversation; to move, in fact, from the point where my mind was just one more link in the chain of folklore, to a situation where I was making a proper academic study of the subject.

With gusto, and a tremendous sense of fulfilment, I forged ahead with that study; but very soon found I had to parallel it with another one—that of the history of my own country. There were many points, after all, where the two subjects crossed—particularly where it was a case of some practitioner of magical arts falling foul of the law of the land. My nightly walk to the library, also, took me through street after street of ancient buildings that spoke most powerfully to my sense of the past; and so it was all the more inevitable that I would become as much intrigued by my country's history as by its folklore.

It was impossible for the library staff to guess, of course, that these two interests would remain with me lifelong. And I've no doubt that they found it peculiar to see me sitting there night after night—myself so young and all the books I drew from the stacks concerned with matters so ancient! Yet even so, I was still always treated with the same grave courtesy that had greeted my first entrance into the library; and my gratitude for this was something else that was to last lifelong.

Absorbed as I was in all this study, however, it was still poetry that remained my writing love—something that suited me very well, as it happened, since this was also the time when love in another sense had begun to hit hard at my emotions. I fell in and out of love very easily, in fact. Until, that is, I reached the beginning of my eighteenth year and met again someone I had known earlier—the young man who was to become, as my father had been for my mother, the great and only true love of my life.

The village, by that time, had become a place of the past for me. All the other members of the family had left home, my grandparents were in failing health, and they had persuaded my mother it was her duty to look after them. Noble as always, she had given up her home in the village in order to do so, which meant that she and I were now living in the grandparents' house. So, with no travelling to eat into my free time, I said a temporary goodbye also to my studies, and gave all that free time instead to this new love.

Love and War

We were two people of widely differing temperaments, but we had many tastes in common. And we were both romantics! Our courtship was a time of sheerest bliss; but we were living, of course, under the threat of World War II, and when war was declared, we knew that our self-contained little world of happiness had, quite literally, been blown apart.

He was approaching his twentieth birthday, when he would be drafted into the Armed Forces. And we were so well aware that this would happen! Yet still, when he showed me his draft papers, I could feel that my face was as white and taut with shock as his was. He opted for the Navy, and by the end of that year he had written me from his training depot:

"I've got ten days leave before we sail. It's a woman's privilege to name the date. You've got a choice of ten days."

And so we got married. So also, we had to part again at the end of our ten days with only one vague comfort to keep in mind. As the wife of a Serviceman, I was not now subject to the draft applying to women; and so there was no longer the danger of my being sent far away to some Service post where he could not reach me on the occasional leaves he hoped to get when his ship was in port.

My mother had not approved of that hasty marriage; and so now, too, I was on my own in a rented room. The grandparents died. Their house was sold. My mother's years of service finished up with her also in a rented room, but with wartime shortage of accommodation meaning that this had to be in a different part of the city from mine. But at least by then, we were reconciled and she had accepted that my insistence on going my own way had not meant I loved her any the less.

Edinburgh, just like the rest of the country, had all its lights blacked out for fear of air raids. Everything was on ration or else, quite simply, unobtainable. My young brother went off to war. Other shifts and changes meant that our gang of five was finally broken up beyond all hope of ever coming together again in the tightly knit form it had once had. As for my young husband out there on the ocean where German submarines were daily taking such a heavy toll of Allied shipping. . . .

Bite my nails as I would over visions of ships in flames, ships sinking, the death agonies of men in seas alight with flaming oil spilled from torpedoed oil tankers, there was still nothing else I could do in the end but to follow everyone else's example of getting on as best I could with life in wartime.

I took up my library studies again. On other evenings, I did voluntary work in a Servicemen's canteen. And I danced! I always had, after all, from the moment my infant legs had allowed me to maintain my balance. Besides which, this was the era of the "big band sound", and everybody in our generation was mad about dancing to it. Somehow also, to be one moment in a street that blackout regulations had made dark as the darkest pit, and the next moment in a brightly lit hall full of young people like oneself, was to have such a sudden and positive joy in the mere fact of being alive that war and death seemed just as suddenly to be something unreal—a nightmare dreamed up in the collective unconscious.

Every now and then, too, my husband had those brief leaves he had anticipated—as short as twenty-four hours, sometimes, and never more than a few days. Separated again, we wrote constantly to one another. Most of my writing during those years, in fact, was in my letters to him, most of the thoughts that would otherwise have been expressed in poetry went into those letters instead—although in the kind he wrote to me in return, I sometimes had the feeling that he was a better poet than I was! Hard as this separation was on us both, however, there was still one supremely important way in which I was the gainer from those war years.

The mere fact that they meant a great shifting of young people from country to country and town to town, meant also a multifarious contact of minds that were naturally at their liveliest and most questing. Our generation, also, was one that acknowledged itself to be, as it were, under suspended sentence of death; and this, of course, was an added stimulus to the exchange of ideas so freely flowing then.

"And so we got married." Hunter with husband, Thomas McIlwraith, about 1940

So we read, and talked, swopped books, and read and talked again. And again, and again . . . Lord, how my generation talked! And how many types of book we read! We listened to music, too, we argued about politics—especially when it came to the root cause of the events involving us in a war that we all recognised *had* to be fought if the evils of Fascism were ever to be defeated, but which we still resented as being the fault of the elderly politicians who had for so long tolerated those evils.

The atmosphere created by all this, in fact, was such as to make me feel at times that the whole country had become a sort of open University; and that I, at last, was receiving the "proper education" of which I had once felt so bereft. My poetry took on a sharper edge, and sharper yet. I began making occasional attempts to break into print, but the wartime scarcity of paper and other factors had reduced publishing almost to nothing. And with the end of the war in Europe, also, I suddenly found I had other fish to fry.

A General Election had been called; and, like the vast majority of my generation, I was determined that the old men of the pre-war regime would not hold power again in peacetime. Like my father, also, I had an active social conscience that had put me determinedly always on the side of the poor and deprived; and so I was immediately in the thick of the election fight. And "fight" was definitely the operative word in those days of speaking at street corners instead of broadcasting on TV!

I loved it. I loved the whole theatrical business of holding a crowd. I loved the flashes of inspiration that came to me as I spoke, loved the feeling of using the power of words—most especially because I was doing so for a cause I believed in. But I loved it most of all, of course, when our side won!

For once, it seemed to me then, I could feel that generations who came after me would have a better deal than I had had. And for a little while, too, I was tempted by the offers from those who had both noticed my fiery speeches and had the power to start me off in a career in politics. But the final end of the war, by then, was in sight. The men were beginning to come home; and soon, I knew, my husband would be among them.

So there I was one sunny summer morning, walking through the heart of Edinburgh to meet the train that was due shortly to arrive in the railway station at the east end of Princes Street. The gardens that lined one side of the street were all in bloom—the same gardens where my husband and I had walked on that long ago ten days leave when we got married.

"You're too young for marriage," everyone had told us then. "You'll be separated," they had said, "and you don't know the strain that can put on a marriage." And frequently throughout the war years there had been Jeremiahs who cried, "It won't last, you know, it won't last." But it *had* lasted. The strains of a wartime marriage had been real enough, certainly; but I knew, and he knew, that the love of our courting days had still always remained as strong as it had been then.

A column of young sailors came marching towards me. The officer at its head drew level with me, raised his hand to the salute and gave the order, "Eyes left!" Smartly the column obeyed, and from out of its ranks came a voice raised high in a tone of mock surprise:

"Oh! What a pretty girl!"

As one man, then, the column chorussed, "Oh! *What* a pretty girl!"

The war had taught me a lot about the brand of humour enjoyed by the men of the Navy—"skylarking", as they called it—and so I knew very well, that

"The girl who blew kisses to sailors," about 1943

these sailors would have made the same joke supposing I had been the age I am now instead of the age I was then. Yet still, the sheer lightheartedness of it was so much a reflection of my own high spirits then, that I could not resist playing up to the skylark. And so, with a great grin on my own face, I stood blowing kisses to every laughing face in that column before I finally went on to meet my own sailor coming home to me—not for a short leave this time, but for good!

Children and Books

Children! They had always been part of our plan; and now we were eager to start a family—myself desperately so. Very soon, too, it looked as if we would have our wish. And then, and then . . . The child, a boy, was born prematurely; and forty-eight hours later, he was dead.

"What are you crying for?" demanded the doctor making ward rounds. "It was only a miscarriage that lived."

The child had kicked in my womb and we had laughed over that. We had given him a name. Lying together in bed at night, we had sung silly little songs about him. But that was all he was—"a miscarriage that lived."

"It doesn't look as if you'll have another," said the doctor who gave me a brief and brutal examination before I was discharged from hospital.

And I had never held my first child in my arms. I had never even seen him, in fact. The hospital rules did not allow of that.

I was to prove that second doctor wrong, as it happened, but not before some time had passed. It took quite a few years, indeed, before we were finally established with our family of two sons; and, simply because we had to live during that time, my main preoccupation had to be the effort to help my husband climb the career ladder in his own line of work.

He was so much in sympathy with my writing urge, however, that he took the first chance he could to buy me a typewriter—a battered old thing, but still the only one he could lay hands on during those post-war years of machine scarcity. And it was his encouragement, too, that was responsible for my writing my first book.

We had moved a bit around the country by then, and had come to rest finally in the north of Scotland, in the mountainous region of the Highlands. By then also, I had resumed my historical research—this time by means of an excellent inter-library loan service. I was appearing frequently in print, too, in the fiercely-competitive world of the newspaper feature article. Additionally, I had succeeded in publishing my work on some original discoveries made in the course of my research. I was also experimenting with the short story form; and it was while I was busily engaged in fitting all this in with looking after two very young children, that my husband said to me one evening:

"All this study you've done—it's given you such a massive body of knowledge. Why don't you try to write a novel out of it?"

Write a novel? I gaped at first, and then laughed a little. It was true that my study of folklore had given me the background for several of my short stories; but I had not yet considered using my historical research in that way. As for writing a novel—no, that wasn't my line. On the other hand—a thought that struck me suddenly began to make me ask myself, "Well, why *not* have a try at it?"

There had been so many marvellous stories in

the stuff I had read! The one that had always intrigued me most, also, was one that centred around a mystery of identity—and it was the possible solution of this mystery that had been the subject of the research findings I had published! I had been a great fool, I thought, not to have realised that I had already given myself the bones of a book by doing so; and straight away I sat down to my typewriter.

Every spare minute I had for the next two years, I sat there, sometimes—and quite bitterly, too—telling myself that I was the fool of all the world to be spending my leisure time thus, while all the rest of humanity was engaged in sensible pastimes—such as going to parties and dancing its feet off! But even so, the more I laboured over that story, the more I became intrigued by it. The harder I worked, too, the more my husband encouraged me. And besides all that, giving up is something that is simply not in my nature.

At the end of that two years of patient thumping on the old machine, I had a novel, a very long one. I spent another year revising it, made a couple of futile attempts to publish it, and then put it away in my bureau where, to this day, it still lies. And so what, then, becomes of that boast of never giving up? And one other question—was that a wasted three years? I had answers eventually to both these questions, and it was through my children that the answers came.

I had given these two boys an upbringing that reflected as much as possible the one that had been my own; always allowing them total freedom to roam the woods, the fields, the hills that were our surroundings. On every possible occasion, also, I was out there with them—housework, in my view, being something that could always wait to be done. Housework would always be there, but life was passing, life had to be caught on the wing; and that, I reckoned, applied to me as an adult as much as it had done to me as a child.

Both out of doors and indoors, too, I entertained the boys as my mother had entertained me—with songs, poems, and stories, but especially with stories. And, of course, they had favourites among the stories I made up for them, particularly those I wove around a boastful Irishman I had invented, and whom I called Patrick Kentigern Keenan. He had flashed complete into my head, this Patrick, on a day when my elder son was only a tiny baby; and now, here was that same boy at ten years old, saying rather peevishly to me:

"Why don't you make a book out of the Patrick stories, and then we could read them for ourselves instead of having to wait for you to tell them."

And again, I thought, *Well, why not?* If there is one style of storytelling that fascinates me more than any other, it is that of the Celtic folktale, so bone-smooth in its form of language, so gloriously lit with moments of high poetic imagery. "*And they would be at drinking and singing and telling of tales till the white day should come . . .* "[1] To try to write like that, I thought, would be once again to try to use language as a poet should—"at its two extremes of exactitude and subtlety."[2] And that, indeed, had been the motivation behind the short stories I had already written out of my knowledge of folklore—with two of these efforts having been among those that the children called "Patrick stories."

But could I sustain a whole book around that character? Would it really be possible for me, moreover, to recreate through such a book the authentic

"Our sons, Brian and Quentin, given total freedom to roam," 1956

[1] *Popular Tales of the West Highlands*, collected and translated by John Francis Campbell. Edinburgh, Scotland: Edmunston & Douglas, 1860–62.

[2] From "The Last Lord of Redhouse Castle," by Mollie Hunter, in *The Thorny Paradise*, edited by Edward Blishen. Harmondsworth: Kestrel Books, 1975, p.134.

ring of the *told* tale? And supposing I could do so, who would be interested in the result? Nobody, I decided; nobody except the boy and his brother. But even so, what difference would that make? To write what I wanted to write—that, after all, was the only thing of real importance!

I made a bargain with the children. I would write a part of the book every day if they, in return, would observe a few rules that helped to keep the household peace. The bargain was honoured on both sides. I called the finished book by the name of its hero *Patrick Kentigern Keenan;* and for no other reason except that it *was* a finished book, I sent it off to a publisher.

An editor in the firm had read the two original "Patrick" tales and had enjoyed them. He enjoyed even more this full length "fantasy", as the book was classed; and against the opposition of the entire sales force insisting that there was "no market for fantasy", he had it published. The book succeeded beyond even his expectations—so much so, indeed, that it is still in print today under the much easier to remember title of *The Smartest Man in Ireland.*

"More! More!" clamoured the delighted editor; and I was certainly willing to oblige him in this. But not with another fantasy—or not as yet, at least. I was well away, by then, into the work of writing another kind of book for my children. And by then also, I was fully realising that *nothing* of either the study or the writing I had done up till that time, had been in any way a waste of effort.

My early attempts at poetry had taught me to express myself very concisely; and it was to this, in large part, that I owed my success as a journalist. To say much in little, also, is the true craft of descriptive writing; and without having mastered that craft I could neither have written that long unpublished novel, nor have learned from it, in turn, the technique of structuring a book.

My feeling for poetry, finally, had been the spur to writing that first fantasy; and so what I had been doing, in effect, was to serve a long and thorough apprenticeship in two forms of writing—that of fantasy, and the historical novel. For both forms, my research work had laid down a fertile seedbed of ideas. But even so, it had still needed my children themselves to make me realise that all this could be combined with my love of story to show that I had what could at least be called some kind of gift for writing for children!

So it was, then, that I entered the most productive period of my writing life! The publication of that next book—my first historical novel for children—was quickly followed by *The Kelpie's Pearls,* another fantasy. Another historical followed that, then another fantasy, with myself continuing happily to alternate between the two forms, and getting an entirely different kind of pleasure from each.

The first fantasy had been set in Ireland, but this was due to no more than the fortuitous circumstance of finding a character suddenly springing from an Irish name that had been running for some time in my mind. The Celtic branch of folklore, however, bears much the same kind of flower in Scotland as it does in Ireland. Throughout most of my life, also, I had been determinedly a country person; and, with evidences of that folklore thus naturally continuing to be part of my existence, it was equally natural for me thereafter to give all my fantasies a Scottish setting.

There is a peculiarly lilting way of speech in Scotland, too, which admirably lends itself to the form of language I had evolved for the fantasies. To become absorbed in the rhythms of this language form, I found, was to work at a level of creativeness that indulged the dreamy, visionary part of my nature—the part that loves to fall into a dwam! But here, of course, in that capacity to reach a state transcending reason, is the underlying aspect of all Celtic culture; and so it was in these books that I could identify most closely with my personal share in the Celtic heritage.

In the historical novels, I found also, there was a further and more direct form of identification. I had walked where my characters had walked, seen with their eyes, breathed the very air that they had breathed; and so, with each story evolved from them, my sense of the past became ever stronger, the deep-rooted love of the country that had bred me grew ever deeper.

Always before me too, as I wrote, was the knowledge of the great tradition set by earlier Scottish exponents of historical fiction. Always I was well aware of the literary excellence, the sheer power of storytelling that, by general consent, had combined to make them pre-eminent in this field. And now, here was I striving my utmost to follow in that tradition, and finding in this yet another form of professional fulfilment.

I could not have been happier in my work, in fact, and so it was small wonder that my publications grew very rapidly in number. Included among them, too, was a book I called *The Thirteenth Member,* a historical novel set in sixteenth-century Scotland. I had spent many years of research on the source material for that book, but it was still not one that ever received any of the awards that other books earned for me. Yet even so, that story from the sixteenth century remains in print to this day; and the significance this holds for me is two-fold.

First, the book was a complete rewrite of that long novel lying, unpublished yet, in a drawer of my bureau. So much therefore, not only for wasted effort, but also for "giving up." Yet it was still not only persistence that gained the day eventually for me; still not because this version was for a youth audience instead of for adult readers. That second version, rather, not only told a story, it also contained an element the first one had lacked—something important to me in terms of my attitude to what I saw as the perpetual struggle between good and evil.

I had long held, in effect, that one would be better off dead than tamely accepting that evil would eventually triumph. Thus, in all the books I had written since that unpublished one, I had in some way portrayed the struggle and had also maintained my own conviction that good *had* to be the eventual victor.

In the fantasies, this had been achieved through conflict in which the human characters overthrew the soul-less power of the supernaturals. In the historicals, the struggle sprang from situations in which the story's characters were confronted by personal decisions, with the balance always hanging on the outcome of these decisions. In both, it is the conflict that creates tension. Tension is always the key to the reader's interest. And so, as the published history of that rewritten book confirmed for me, it was quite simply by injecting the story with that underlying theme of the good/evil struggle, that I had finally managed to give it the drive it had needed.

Family life, meanwhile, had been going on as busily as ever for me—beginning with the fact that, like myself, my husband was always happiest in the open air. He fished, and he also shot—an activity that demanded a good gundog. So I bought for him a Golden Labrador pup which was the first of a long succession of gundogs I bred from her and exercised daily for five miles over the hills. I bred German Shepherds too, until I had the particular dog from this breed that I wanted for myself—all of which also ensured joy for the children as the various litters of puppies made their appearance.

Other family interests lay with Inverness Cathedral, where husband and sons were all choristers and where my love of theatre led to my involvement with a drama group known as The Cathedral Players. I wrote and directed plays for the group, and when the sons' primary school needed a musical play, I wrote and directed this too. My husband also sang with a local opera company, which led to more stage direct-

Family life: Hunter with husband, Thomas, and their children, Brian and Quentin, about 1959

ing for me; and then again, when our sons progressed to senior school, to directing operetta for their contemporaries.

The time I needed for writing was respected, nevertheless, by all of the family; and so, as well as all the other books produced during that period, I still managed to diverge into writing *A Sound of Chariots,* the autobiographical novel of my childhood loss. It had become essential, indeed, that I should write this as the form of therapy a writer inevitably uses for exorcising ghosts, for finally healing the deepest of wounds. But there was no market in those days for such a book. That did not come until the passage of another eight years had made considerable changes in publishing for young readers and a series of chances brought it to the attention of an editor who was determined that it *would* be published.

There had been changes in my own life by that time, too, of course. Our sons had left home to take up their chosen careers—a fact that drew my husband and myself even closer together than we had been before. I began to receive the invitations that eventually sent me travelling world-wide to speak about my work. I joined other writers in campaigning against the danger of atomic annihilation. I started the teaching sessions that have since helped to set a number of young writers on their road. The recognition my work had received was confirmed when my historical novel, *The Stronghold,* was awarded Britain's equivalent of the Newbery—the Carnegie Medal. But the most significant event of all for me was still the one that occurred right at the beginning of this period of change.

Ray Mantell

The author holding a Carnegie Medal awarded for The Stronghold *in 1974*

That was when the Chief Archivist of the National Library wrote to ask if I would consider donating my working papers to his institution. *Would* I! I had previously refused similar requests from other libraries, principally because I disliked the idea of my papers leaving Scotland. But to have my own country's National Library ask for them—there was nothing I could have wanted more than that!

I visited the Archivist to tell him so. But as I sat there face to face with him, my mind's eye was going beyond his figure to that of another man—that of the librarian who had not smiled at the hunger for knowledge in the eyes of a shabbily-dressed fourteen year old, the grave and courteous man who had led me to the stacks of books on Comparative Religion.

Gently I cut short the Archivist's thanks for my donation. I was not doing the National any favour in this. I was simply repaying a debt, the old, old debt I owed to that one librarian; and through him, perhaps, to all those other librarians who had helped me on my way. I told the Archivist so, and finished my visit feeling full of the relief that always comes with the sense of having discharged a long-standing obligation.

Home again, I settled down to my next book—and also to the interest of knowing that, as my life had changed, so too had my work changed in some ways. I was still writing the historicals and the fantasies, of course, but I was also beginning to find an altered perspective for my imagination in terms of realising that there were other and different types of book to be gleaned out of the experiences of my own life rather than from the material of my study.

It was this later period of my writing, then, that saw the publication of young adult novels such as *The Third Eye, Hold On to Love,* and *Cat, Herself,* all of these being books that allowed me to express myself in a way that had happened only once before in my writing. Previously, and largely because the type of story demanded that this should be so, I had projected through male protagonists—the exception to this having been *A Sound of Chariots,* where I had projected through a girl I called Bridie McShane.

All of the female characters I had created both before and after her time had been as strongly drawn as I could make them; yet still, none of them had been the protagonist of a book. But now, in these young adult novels, I *was* speaking through female protagonists. And by doing so, it seemed to me, I was finding a furtherance of the release that Bridie had given me—and so also confirming in myself a specific *kind* of voice through which to tell each of these stories.

It was when I wrote the present-day story of *Cat, Herself,* however, that I found this voice speaking out on the loudest and clearest note I could summon for it; and speaking, too, in a way that enabled me to use aspects of my own life more fully than had ever before been the case with me.

Catriona McPhie ("Cat" to her friends) is the daughter of one of Scotland's travelling families—"tinkers", as they are often called. They are a distinctive and traditional feature of the Scottish countryside, these people, and their wandering way of life meant that Cat was necessarily a child of the open air. So, through this girl, I could recreate all the halcyon days of my own childhood, making her as physically hardy as myself, giving to her all my own love of freedom, all my own sensuous pleasure in the colours, the shapes, the smells, the very *feel* of the countryside I have always so passionately loved.

Despite their footloose life, however, travellers have very conservative work patterns. There is "men's work", which a woman must never do; and "women's work", which a man *would* never do. To my girl Cat, however, I gave the independence of mind that enabled her to cross the barrier of set work roles. Cat refused to be dictated to in this, just as I had refused to be dictated to in the use I would make of *my* life.

Additionally, through the circumstances of Cat's mother, I brought the girl herself face to face with the fact of a child dying as my own first baby had died, and with the pain of the cruel treatment I had received then. But later, when she acts as midwife at the birth of her own young brother, I enabled her to come happily face to face also, with the joy of bringing into the world a child that undoubtedly *would* live.

By that time too, Cat had to make up her mind about marriage—and travellers are as conservative in their attitudes to this as they are to work patterns. Always, in traveller marriages, the man is the dominant partner, even reserving to himself the right to beat his woman. But on this too, Cat had made up her own mind. She would have the kind of marriage in which she would always be just Cat, herself—a person, not subject to *anyone's* dominance.

And so finally, to let that voice of mine be heard in a way that young women readers, at least, would hear as coming from my deepest heart, I gave Cat a young husband who loved her enough to understand that she *had* to be herself, just as mine had always loved me and understood that I had to be *my* self.

So also, the wheel on which my life had been turning came full circle at last. Or in a manner of speaking, at least, that was so; because there have been other books since that girl's story was written, other books that have taken me back to the medium of fantasy that started it all. And why? Because now I have grandchildren, along with whom has come a renewal of the childhood demand for the story. And that, it seems to me, is the most delightful of all renewals for one who, at heart, has never really been other than just a storyteller!

The artist's work on the portrait is finished now. We stand before it, she and I, and I wonder what had been going through her mind as she painted it—just as, possibly, she may have wondered what had been going through mine. We discuss the details of what will happen to it.

There are so many paintings in the National Portrait Gallery, all of them portraits of people noted in their time for one thing or another; and this newly finished one will be hung in the series the Gallery has named "Eminent Scots of the 20th Century". I am still finding it difficult to relate that fact to my knowledge of myself as someone who has done no more than work hard at conveying, in story terms, all those aspects of life that have always meant so much to her. Unless—

Is it because I have written so consistently from within my native heritage and yet still always tried to touch some chord that vibrates universally? Have I brought Scotland a little nearer to my readers by doing so, linked it in some way with their own humanity? And if I *have* somehow touched that chord, created that link, then surely that must be the answer to my own wondering on why the portrait should have been commissioned—just as now, it seems to me, it is also the answer to my question on why and how the strands of my life and work have so completely merged into one thread.

The artist asks me what I think of her finished effort. The portrait shows me seated at my desk. Behind me are the shelves holding the books that are still my source of reference and still my constant joy. The pose in which she has caught me is that of looking up from my work, with my gaze fixed on some point in the far distance.

"Now I have grandchildren," 1978

There has been no attempt to prettify me. The network of laughter lines is there around my eyes; but so also are the wrinkles of age and the deep lines that now run from nose to mouth on either side of my face. I look, in fact, exactly what I am—an elderly woman who has always extracted enormous enjoyment from life, but who has still always taken life seriously. Yet still too, I can trace in that face the touch of the old rebel, the enthralled library student, the girl who blew kisses to sailors. . . . And that lost-in-the-distance gaze is so characteristic of me when I go into a dwam!

"Listen," I say. "I'm going to tell you a story!"

I link arms with the artist and we go downstairs together with me telling her as we go the tale of a Scottish grandmother who had sat for long hours of winter days dreaming back through the story of her own life—right back to the time when she was a carefree wee lass whirling a firecan around her head, picking wild strawberries, playing hide-and-seek in the gloaming . . . And then had wakened up to find the essential *feeling* of that, and everything that had followed from it, right there before her on an artist's canvas!

The artist laughs; but her bright, dark eyes grow brighter yet. And why not? It's not only children, after all, who love a story. Everyone does—always and at any time, a story.

BIBLIOGRAPHY

FOR YOUNG PEOPLE

Fiction:

Hi Johnny. (Illustrated by Drake Brookshaw) London: Evans, 1963; (illustrated by M. Christopherson) Hawick, Scotland: Byway Books, 1986.

Patrick Kentigern Keenan (illustrated by Charles Keeping). London: Blackie, 1963; also published as *The Smartest Man in Ireland* (illustrated by C. Keeping). New York: Funk, 1965; London: Methuen, 1986.

The Kelpie's Pearls. (Illustrated by C. Keeping) London: Blackie, 1964; (illustrated by Joseph Cellini) New York: Funk, 1966; (illustrated by Stephen Gammell) New York: Harper, 1976.

The Spanish Letters (illustrated by Elizabeth Grant). London: Evans, 1964; New York: Funk, 1967.

A Pistol in Greenyards (illustrated by E. Grant). London: Evans, 1965; New York: Funk, 1968.

The Ghosts of Glencoe. London: Evans, 1966; New York: Funk, 1968.

Thomas and the Warlock. (Illustrated by C. Keeping) London: Blackie, 1967; (illustrated by J. Cellini) New York: Funk, 1967.

The Ferlie. (Illustrated by Michal Morse) London: Blackie, 1968; (illustrated by J. Cellini) New York: Funk, 1968; also published as *The Enchanted Whistle* (illustrated by M. Morse). London: Methuen, 1985.

The Bodach (illustrated by Gareth Floyd). London: Blackie, 1970; also published as *The Walking Stones* (illustrated by Trina Schart Hyman). New York: Harper, 1970; London: Methuen, 1986.

The Lothian Run. New York: Funk, 1970; London: Hamish Hamilton, 1971.

The Thirteenth Member. London: Hamish Hamilton, 1971; New York: Harper, 1971.

The Haunted Mountain. (Illustrated by Trevor Ridley) London: Hamish Hamilton, 1972; (illustrated by Laszlo Kuhinyi) New York: Harper, 1972.

A Sound of Chariots. New York: Harper, 1972; London: Hamish Hamilton, 1973.

The Stronghold. London: Hamish Hamilton, 1974; New York: Harper, 1974.

A Stranger Came Ashore. London: Hamish Hamilton, 1975; New York: Harper, 1975.

A Furl of Fairy Wind. (Illustrated by S. Gammell; includes "Hi Johnny", "The Brownie", "The Enchanted Boy", and "A Furl of Fairy Wind") New York: Harper, 1977.

The Wicked One. London: Hamish Hamilton, 1977; New York: Harper, 1977.

The Third Eye. London: Hamish Hamilton, 1979; New York: Harper, 1979.

You Never Knew Her As I Did! London: Hamish Hamilton, 1981; New York: Harper, 1981; also published as *Escape from Loch Leven.* Edinburgh, Scotland: Canongate, 1987.

The Knight of the Golden Plain (illustrated by Marc Simont). London: Hamish Hamilton, 1983; New York: Harper, 1983.

The Dragonfly Years. London: Hamish Hamilton, 1983; also published as *Hold On to Love.* New York: Harper, 1984.

I'll Go My Own Way. London: Hamish Hamilton, 1985; also published as *Cat, Herself.* New York: Harper, 1985.

The Three-Day Enchantment (illustrated by M. Simont). New York: Harper, 1985.

The Brownie (illustrated by M. Christopherson). Hawick, Scotland: Byway Books, 1986.

The Enchanted Boy (illustrated by M. Christopherson). Hawick, Scotland: Byway Books, 1986.

A Furl of Fairy Wind (illustrated by M. Christopherson). Hawick, Scotland: Byway Books, 1986.

FOR ADULTS

Nonfiction:

Talent Is Not Enough: Mollie Hunter on Writing for Children. New York: Harper, 1976.

Plays:

A Love-Song for My Lady, produced in Inverness, Scotland, 1961. London: Evans, 1961.

Stay for an Answer, produced in Inverness, Scotland, 1962. London: Samuel French, 1962.

Diana Wynne Jones

1934-

I think I write the kind of books I do because the world suddenly went mad when I was five years old. In late August 1939, on a blistering hot day, my father loaded me and my three-year-old sister, Isobel, into a friend's car and drove to my grandparents' manse in Wales. "There's going to be a war," he explained. He went straight back to London, where my mother was expecting her third baby any day. We were left in the austere company of Mam and Dad (as we were told to call them). Dad, who was a moderator of the Welsh Nonconformist Chapels, was a stately patriarch; Mam was a small browbeaten lady who seemed to us to have no character at all. We were told that she was famous in her youth for her copper hair, her wit, and her beauty, but we saw no sign of any of this.

Wales could not have been more different from our new house in Hadley Wood on the outskirts of London. It was all grey or very green and the houses were close together and dun-coloured. The river ran black with coal—and probably always had, long before the mines: they told me the name of the place meant "bridge over the river with the black voice." Above all, everybody spoke a foreign language. Sometimes we were taken up the hill into suddenly primitive country to meet wild-looking raw-faced old people who spoke no English, for whom our shy remarks had to be translated. Everyone spoke English to us, and would switch abruptly to Welsh when they wanted to say important things to one another. They were kind to us, but not loving. We were Aneurin's English daughters and not quite part of their culture.

Life in the manse revolved around Chapel next door. My aunt Muriel rushed in from her house down the road and energetically took us to a dressmaker to be fitted with Sunday clothes. On the way, she suggested, as a way to stop us feeling strange, that we should call her *Mummy*. Isobel obligingly did so, but I refused on the grounds that she was not our mother—besides, I was preoccupied with a confusion between dressmakers and hairdressers which even an hour of measuring and pinning did not resolve.

The clothes duly arrived: purple dresses with white polka dots and neat meat-coloured coats. Isobel and I had never been dressed the same before and we rather liked it. We wore them to Chapel thereafter,

Diana Wynne Jones, 1938. "This photograph is one my husband particularly values. Its battered condition is because he always carries it in his wallet."

sitting sedately with our aunt and almost grown-up cousin Gwyn, through hours of solid Welsh and full-throated singing. Isobel sang too, the only Welsh she knew, which happened to be the name of the maid at the manse, Gwyneth. My mother had told me sternly that I was bad at singing and, not knowing the words, I couldn't join in anyway. Instead, I gazed wistfully at the shiny cherries on the hat of the lady in front, and one Sunday got into terrible trouble for daring to reach out and touch them.

Then my grandfather went into the pulpit. At home he was majestic enough: preaching, he was like the prophet Isaiah. He spread his arms and language rolled from him, sonorous, magnificent, and rhythmic. I had no idea then that he was a famous preacher, nor that people came from forty miles away to hear him because he had an almost bardic tendency to speak a kind of blank verse—*hwyl*, it is called, much valued in a preacher—but the splendour and the rigour of it nevertheless went into the core of my being. Though I never understood one word, I grasped the essence of a dour, exacting, and curiously

"My grandfather, T. F. Jones, holding me aged about six months," London, 1935

magnificent religion. His voice shot me full of terrors. For years after that, I used to dream regularly that a piece of my bedroom wall slid aside revealing my grandfather declaiming in Welsh, and I knew he was declaiming about my sins. I still sometimes dream in Welsh, without understanding a word. And at the bottom of my mind there is always a flow of spoken language that is not English, rolling in majestic paragraphs and resounding with splendid polysyllables. I listen to it like music when I write.

Weekdays I was sent to the local school, where everyone was taught in Welsh except me. I was the only one in the class who could read. When the school inspector paid a surprise visit, the teacher thrust a Welsh book at me and told me in a panicky whisper to read it aloud. I did so—Welsh, luckily, is spelt phonetically—and I still understood not a word. When girls came to play, they spoke English too, initiating me into mysterious rhymes: *Whistle while you work, Hitler made a shirt*. War had been declared, but I had never heard of Hitler till then. We usually played in the chapel graveyard, where I thought of the graves as like magnificent double beds for dead people. I fell off the manse wall into such a grave as I declaimed, "Goebbels wore it, Goering tore it," and tore a ligament in one ankle.

After what seemed a long time, my mother arrived with our new sister, Ursula. She was outraged to find Isobel calling Aunt Muriel *Mummy*. I remember trying to soothe her by explaining that Isobel was in no way deceived: she was just obliging our aunt. Unfortunately the voice I explained in had acquired a strong Welsh accent, which angered my mother further. We felt the strain of the resulting hidden rows as an added bleakness in the bleak manse. We were back in Hadley Wood by Christmas.

Looking back, I see that my relationship with my mother never recovered from this. When she arrived in Wales, she had seen me as something other, which she rather disliked. She said I would grow up just like my aunt and accused me of taking my aunt's side. It did not help that, at that time, my hair was just passing from blond to a colour my mother called *mouse* and I looked very little like either side of the family. My parents were both short, black-haired, and handsome, where I was tall and blue-eyed. When we got back to London, my mother resisted all my attempts to hug her on the grounds that I was too big.

Meanwhile, the threat of bombing and invasion grew. London was not safe. The small school Isobel and I were attending rented a house called Lane Head beside Coniston Water in distant Westmorland and offered room in it to my mother and her three children. We went there in the early summer of 1940. Here were real mountains, lakes, brooks racing through indescribable greenness. I was amazed—intoxicated—with the beauty of it.

We were told that Lane Head had belonged to John Ruskin's secretary and that this man's descendants (now safely in America) had been the John, Susan, Titty, and Roger of Arthur Ransome's books. Ruskin's own house, Brantwood, was just up the road. There was a lady in a cottage near it who could call red squirrels from the trees. This meant more to me at the time—this, and the wonder of living in a rambling old house smelling of lamp oil, with no electricity, where the lounge (where we were forbidden to play) was full of Oriental trophies, silk couches, and Pre-Raphaelite pictures. There was a loft (also forbidden) packed with Titty and Roger's old toys. The entry to it was above our room and I used to sneak up into it. By this time, war shortages had made themselves felt. There were no new toys and no paper to draw on and I loved drawing. One rainy afternoon, poking about the loft, I came upon a stack of high-quality thick drawing paper. To my irritation, someone had drawn flowers on every sheet, very fine and black and accurate, and signed them with a monogram, JR. I took the monogram for a bad drawing of a mosquito and assumed the fine black pencil was ink. I carried a wad of them down to our room and knelt at the window seat industriously erasing the drawings with an ink rubber. Halfway through I was caught and punished. The loft was padlocked. Oddly enough, it was only many years later that I realised that I must have innocently rubbed out a good fifty of Ruskin's famous flower drawings.

The school and its pupils left the place towards the end of summer, but we stayed and were rapidly joined by numbers of mothers with small children. The world was madder than ever. I was told about the small boats going to Dunkirk and exasperated everyone by failing to understand why the Coniston steamer had not gone to France from the landlocked lake. (I was always asking questions.) Bombs were dropping and the Battle of Britain was escalating. My husband, who had, oddly enough, been sent to his grandparents barely fifteen miles from us, remembers the docks at Barrow-in-Furness being bombed. He saw the blaze across the bay. During that raid a German plane was shot down and its pilot was at large in the mountains for nearly two weeks. It is hard now to imagine the horror he inspired in all the mothers. When he broke into the Lane Head pantry one night and stole a large cheese, there was sheer panic next morning. I suppose it was because that night the war had briefly climbed in through our window.

Being too young to understand this, I had trouble distinguishing Germans from germs, which seemed to inspire the mothers with equal horror. We were not allowed to drink water from the washbasin because it came from the lake and contained typhoid germs. The maker's name on the washbasin was Twyford. For years I thought that was how you spelled typhoid. I had a terrifying recurring dream of these typhoid Germans—always dressed in cream-coloured Anglo-Saxon tunics—running across the surface of the lake to get me. When a large Quaker family arrived to cram into the house too, bringing with them an eleven-year-old German-Jewish boy who told horrendous stories of what the police did—they took you away in the night, he said, to torture you—I had no idea he was talking about the Gestapo. I have been nervous of policemen ever since.

The Quaker family, all six of them, had a cold bath every morning. We were regularly woken at 6:06 A.M. by the screams of the youngest, who was only two. In their no-nonsense Quaker way, this family got out the old boat in the boat house and went sailing. I can truthfully say that I sailed in both the *Swallow* and the *Amazon,* for though this boat was a dire old tub called *Mavis,* she was the original of both. I didn't like her. On a trip to Wild Cat Island I caught my finger in her centreboard, and my father nearly drowned us in her trying to sail in a storm on one of his rare visits from teaching and fire-watching in London.

"My husband, J. A. Burrow, seated in Ruskin's stone seat with a bottle labeled 'Ruskin Sherry.' Ruskin's parents were wine merchants." Lake District, 1985

The mothers gave the older children lessons. Girls were taught womanly accomplishments. Being left-handed, I had great trouble learning to knit until a transient Icelandic lady arrived with a baby and a large dog and began teaching me the continental method. She left before teaching me purl or even to cast on stitches. I had to make those up. Another mother taught sewing. I remember wrestling for a whole morning to sew on a button, which became inexplicably enmeshed in my entire supply of thread. Finally I explained to this mother that I wasn't going to grow up to be a woman and asked if I could do drawing with the boys. She told me not to be rude and became so angry that—with a queer feeling that it was in self-defence—I put my tongue out at her. She gave me a good shaking and ordered me to stand in the hall all the next morning.

The same day, other mothers had taken the younger children to the lakeshore to play beyond the cottage of the lady who called squirrels. The noise they made disturbed the occupant of the houseboat out in the bay. He came rowing angrily across and ordered them off, and, on finding where they lived, said that he wasn't going to be disturbed by a parcel

"A view across the Lake to Coniston Village and the mountain, taken from just below Lane Head"

of evacuees and announced that he would come next morning to complain. He hated children. There was huge dismay among the mothers. Next morning I stood in the hall, watching them rush about trying to find coffee and biscuits (which were nearly unobtainable by then) with which to soothe the great Arthur Ransome, and gathered I was about to set eyes on a real writer. I watched with great interest as a tubby man with a beard stamped past, obviously in a great fury, and almost immediately stormed away again on finding there was nobody exactly in charge to complain to. I was very impressed to find he was real. Up to then I had thought books were made by machines in the back room of Woolworth's.

My brush with the other writer in the area was even less direct but no more pleasant. We were up near Sawrey, which was a long way for children to walk; but, if the mothers were to go anywhere, they had to walk and the children had to walk with them. No one had a car. Isobel and another four-year-old girl were so tired that, when they found a nice gate, they hooked their feet on it and had a restful swing. An old woman with a sack over her shoulders stormed out of the house and hit both of them for swinging on her gate. This was Beatrix Potter. She hated children, too. I remember the two of them running back to us, bawling with shock. Fate, I always think, seemed determined to thrust a very odd view of authorship on me.

The boy who kept talking of the Gestapo was only one of several disturbed children among us. The madness of those times got into the daughter of the sewing lady too. She began systematically pushing the younger children off high places. She told me and swore me to secrecy. I knew this was wrong. My grandfather haunted me in dreams and I kept telling myself that I was feeble not to tell someone—but I had sworn. Even so, when the girl pushed Isobel down a deep cellar I summoned my courage and told my mother. This caused a terrible row, as bad as the row in Wales, and I think that as a result of it my mother decided to leave Lane Head. She went to York to find a teaching job, leaving us in the charge of the other mothers. That night, the daughter of the sewing lady suggested it might be fun if I sneaked into her bedroom to eat aspirins with her. Feeling like an adventure, and also feeling bad at having betrayed this girl's trust, I did so. Aspirins were horrible. I swallowed mine with huge difficulty and asked her what she saw in them. Nothing, she said. It was just that you were forbidden to eat them. And she spat hers out on the carpet.

Here her mother irrupted into the room.

I remember that a Court of Justice was hastily convened. Three mothers. I stood accused of leaving my bed in order to spit aspirins all over another's carpet. I remember I was bemused to find that the other girl was not accused of anything. Sentence was that I and my bed were taken downstairs to a lumber room and I was to sleep there. I rebelled. I got up again and went into the forbidden lounge, where I did what I had always wanted to do and took down one of the heavy, slightly rusty Indian Army swords. I wondered whether to fall on it like a Roman. But since it was clear to me that this would hurt very much, I put it back and went out of the open window. It was near sunset. The grass was thick with dew, but still quite warm to my bare feet. The sky was a miraculous clear auburn. I tried to summon courage to run away in my nightclothes. I wanted to. I also had a dim sense that it would be an effective move. But I could not make myself take another step. I went back to the lumber room knowing I was a coward.

In fact, when my mother came back late the next night she thought I *had* run away—or been taken ill. Since nobody had told her, I suspect that the punishment was aimed at her too. There were further rows before we left for York in September 1941.

Despite this, that time in the Lake District is still magical to me. The shape of the mountain across the lake has, like my grandfather, become part of my dreams. Since the mountain is called the Old Man of Coniston, they sometimes seem to be the same thing.

In York, we boarded in a nunnery. The blitz was on and the war was moving into its grimmest phase, which may have been why we never got enough to eat there. Granny—my Yorkshire grandmother—used to send us hoarded tins of baked beans which my mother heated in an old tin box over a gas ring in our bedroom.

My sister Ursula was now old enough to be a power. She was a white waifchild with black, black hair and a commanding personality. While my mother was teaching, Ursula had various nannies, whom she ordered mercilessly about and did imitations of in the evenings. I had long known that Isobel was the best and most interesting of companions. It was marvellous to discover that Ursula, at two-and-a-half, could make us fall about laughing. I knew I was lucky to have sisters.

My mother decided that Ursula was going to be an actress. Isobel, she told us, was beautiful but not otherwise gifted. As for me, she said, I was ugly, semi-

The author in Troutbeck Valley, Lake District, 1985

delinquent, but bright. She had the nuns put me in a class with nine-year-olds. This was the first I knew that I was supposed to be clever. I did my best, but everything the class did was two years beyond me.

Religion was beyond me, too. The nuns, being an Anglican order, worshipped in York Minster and took us with them. This huge and beautiful cathedral must have been ten times the size of the chapel in Wales. I could not make head or tail of the mysterious, reverent intonings in the far distance. I fidgeted and shamed my mother until one of the nuns took me instead to a smaller church from then on. There I sat, wrestling with the notion that Heaven Is Within You (not in me, I thought, or I'd know) and of Christ dying for our sins. I stared at the crucifix, thinking how *very* much being crucified must hurt, and was perturbed that, even with this special treatment, religion was not, somehow, taking on me. (I put it this way to myself because I had baptism and vaccination muddled, like germs and Germans.)

Weekdays, I joined a playground game run by the naughty son of another teacher. It was called the Soft Shoe Brigade, in which we all marched in step and pretended we were Nazis. I could not understand why the nuns put a stop to it.

My pleas to be put into a class of younger children were granted near the end of the time we spent there. After a few weeks' bliss, doing work I understood, we went back to Hadley Wood in 1942. By then, the bombing was beginning to seem like the weather, only more frightening. When the siren sounded at night, we went to the ground floor where we sat and listened to the blunt bang and sharp yammer of gunfire and the bombs whistle as they fell, or watched searchlights rhythmically ruling lines in the sky. Recently I was talking to a woman my own age: we both confessed that any noise that resembles these, or the sound of a low-flying plane, still makes us expect to be dead next moment.

The world was mad in daytime, too, not only with rationing, blackout, brown paper stuck to bus windows, and notices saying "Careless Talk Costs Lives." The radio talked daily of bridgeheads, pincer movements, and sorties, which one knew were terms for people killing people. My father was away most nights fire-watching and at weekends he exercised with the Home Guard.

One Sunday I almost fell over one of our neighbours who was crawling about in the field behind our house with—inexplicably—a great bunch of greenery on his head.

"Oh, Mr. Cowey!" shouted I, in much surprise. "What are you doing crawling about with a bush on your head?"

He arose wrathfully, causing the greenery to fall into two horns. "Get out of it, you stupid child!" he snapped, the image of an angry nature god. "You've spoilt the whole bloody exercise!"

Considering this madness, it is not surprising that, at the latest of many private schools we went to that year, when the forbidding teacher announced, "All those children for elocution stand up and go into the hall," I mistook and thought the word was *execution*. I trembled, and was astonished when they all came back unharmed. At that same school, Isobel's teacher used to punish her for writing left-handed. She was shut in a bedroom, being punished, one day when the air-raid siren went. The rest of us were marched into the moderate safety of the hall, but Isobel was forgotten. I wrestled with my cowardice and managed to make myself call out that Isobel was still in the bedroom. The teachers were, I suppose, scared to go up there during a raid. They told me fiercely to hold my tongue and made me sit for the rest of the week behind the blackboard as a lesson for impudence. There was more disgrace than hardship to this. I used that time for reading.

I read avidly that year, things like *The Arabian Nights* and the whole of Malory's *Morte d'Arthur*. Soon after I was eight, I sat up from reading in the middle of one afternoon and knew that I was going to be a writer one day. It was not a decision, or even a revelation. It was more as if my future self had leaned back from the years ahead and quietly informed me what she was. In calm certainty, I went and told my parents.

"My mother with my son Colin, at his Cambridge graduation," 1984

"You haven't got it in you," my mother said. My father bellowed with laughter. He had a patriarch's view of girls: they were not really meant to *do* anything. Though he never said so, I think it was a disappointment to him to have three daughters. My mother, as always, was more outspoken. She said if it were not for the war, she would have more children—boys.

I think my mother was very discontented that year. She was, after all, an Oxford graduate who had dragged herself up from a humble background in industrial Yorkshire by winning scholarships—and all she had for it was the life of a suburban mother. I know she encouraged my father to apply for the husband-and-wife job they took in 1943.

The job was in a village called Thaxted in rural Essex. My parents were to run what would nowadays be called a conference centre for young adults, a place where teenagers who worked in factories in urban Essex could come for a week or weekend to experience a little culture. It was one of many schemes at that time which looked forward to the widening of horizons at the end of the war, and it had considerable propaganda value, since it was by no means clear then that the Allies were going to win the war. My father believed in it utterly, and it became his life for the next ten years.

I was already wrestling to make sense of the experience of the previous four years—particularly the religion. Now I had a whole new set, three or four new sets, in fact, all going on at once. Thaxted, to take that first, was straight out of a picture postcard, with houses that were either thatched and half-timbered or decoratively plastered, and a medieval guildhall straddled the main street. The church, at once stately and ethereal beside a majestic copper beech, stood at the top of the hill opposite Clarance House (the house my parents ran). Industry was represented by a little sweet-factory at one end of the village and a man who made life-sized mechanical elephants at the other. The place was connected to the outside world by sporadic buses and by a branch railway that terminated a mile outside the village (but the train driver would grudgingly wait for anyone he saw panting up the hill to the station). On holidays, people did folk-dancing in the streets. There was also much handweaving, pottery-making, and madrigal singing.

This idyllic place had the highest illegitimate birthrate in the county. In numerous families, the younger apparent brothers or sisters turned out to be the offspring of the unmarried elder daughters—though there was one young woman who pretended her daughter was her sister without grandparents to help—and there was a fair deal of incest, too. Improbable characters abounded there, including two acknowledged witches and a man who went mad in the church porch at full moon. There was a prostitute not much older than me who was a most refined person, with a face like alabaster, a slight foreign accent, and tweeds. There was another who looked like an artist's impression of Neanderthal woman; she had a string of pale thin children, each with huge famine-poster eyes.

I had assumed you had to be married before you had children, so all this was quite a shock. I began to suspect the world had always been mad. In self-defence, my sisters and I assumed our home life was normal, which it certainly was not.

Clarance House was as beautiful as the rest, built in the days of Queen Anne, with graceful wall panels indoors, although the interior was somewhat bare because the Essex Education Committee which financed the place could seldom spare much money. Here my father threw himself into life as an educator and entertainer, for he was as gifted in his way as my grandfather and could hold an audience like an actor, whether he was making intellectual conversation at table with my mother, introducing a lecture, or telling ghost stories to rapt teenagers. His main story was about Clarance House. There was the remains of an old stair in a cupboard where, my father claimed, you could hear disembodied feet, climbing, climbing. . . . We knew he was right to call the house haunted, but the really haunted part was the main entrance hall, which I always felt compelled to run through if I had to cross it, shaking with fear. Eventually one of the cleaners saw the ghost. She had been chatting to it while she polished the hall for some minutes, thinking it was the girl she worked with. Then she looked properly and found she could see through it. She had hysterics and left at once for a job in the bacon factory in Great Dunmow.

My mother organised the cleaners, the cooks, and the domestic side, and in her spare time went feverishly into local history and madrigal singing. Not a day passed without some fearful crisis, in which my mother raced about inveighing against the Committee, the war, or my father, while my father stormed through the house in a fury, forgetting to speak English in his rage. His life was wholly public: my mother's three-quarters so. Neither had time for us. For a short while the three of us children shared a room at the top of the house; but my parents were so dedicated to making a success of the centre that they decided that room was needed for additional guests. We were put out into The Cottage. This was a lean-to, two-room shack across the yard from the main house. The mud floor of the lower room was hastily covered with concrete and our beds were crammed into the upper floor. And we were left to our own devices. Looking back on this, we all find it extraordinary; for damp climbed the walls and, almost as soon as we had arrived in Thaxted, I had contracted juvenile rheumatism, which seriously affected my heart; and Ursula also contracted it soon after.

The only heating was a paraffin stove—and how we failed to set The Cottage on fire I shall never know. The stove was often knocked over during games or fights, or encased in paper when we dried paintings. There was nowhere to wash in The Cottage, so we seldom bothered. Nor did we comb our hair. Ursula, whose hair was long, wild, and curly, tied it in two knots on her forehead to keep it out of her eyes. My mother did not notice for six months. Then I got into trouble for allowing it. But Ursula always did what she wanted. The following year she refused to eat anything but three slices of bread and yeast-extract a day, whatever Isobel or I said, and my mother never knew about that at all.

I was supposed to be in charge of my sisters and

it weighed on me. I did my best, but at nine and ten I was not very good at it. The worst thing happened just after Isobel had been to a pantomime with a school friend, where she had been entranced to find the fairies swooping over the stage in flying-harness. She wanted to do it too. So Ursula and I obligingly tied skipping ropes together, slung them across a beam above The Cottage stairs, and hauled Isobel up there by a noose under her armpits. She dangled, rotating gently, looking worried. "Look more graceful," we advised her. She stuck out her arms—and her legs, too, like a starfish—and went on hanging. Absorbed in her experience and knowing that one had to suffer for art's sake, she failed to say she was suffocating. Luckily, Ursula and I became worried and cut her down with blunt nail scissors just in time.

Around this time, my mother decreed that Isobel should become a ballerina, because of her looks. My mother's main substitute for attending to us was to assert periodically that Isobel was beautiful and a born dancer, Ursula a potential actress, and me an ugly semi-delinquent with a high IQ. Her other substitute for attention was to make our school uniforms herself. She would buy half the required garments, angrily protesting at their cost and the number of clothing coupons they took, and make the rest. Other children jeered, because our uniforms were always the wrong style and material, and it always mystified us that *their* parents could afford enough coupons for a complete uniform. Other clothing my mother got from the local orphanage. The matron, who was a friend of my parents', used to give us all the clothes donated which she did not think suitable for the orphans. We often looked very peculiar. When I protested, my mother would angrily describe her own childhood with a widowed mother in World War I. "You're all extremely lucky," she would conclude. "You have advantages I never dreamed of." At which I felt acutely guilty.

Even so, I might protest that my mother had had proper clothes. I was prone to spot flaws in any argument and I had an odd theory that you ought to be truthful about your feelings. This usually sent my mother into a vituperative fury. This was part of the reason why she called me semi-delinquent. Another reason was that I had inherited my father's tendency to fly into towering rages. I also used to shout at my sisters because they seldom listened to mere speech. But I think the main reason was that I was always at some more or less mad project: some of which were harmless—like dressing as a ghost and pretending to haunt the graveyard, inventing a loom, or directing a play; some of which were liable to cause trouble—like the time I tried to organise a Garden Fête without asking anyone; some of which were outright dangerous—like walking on the roof, or the time I could have attracted enemy aeroplanes by signalling Morse code by flashlight to friends outside the village. For some reason I believed it my duty to live a life of adventure and I used to worry that, for a would-be writer, I had too little imagination.

Clarance House had two gardens, one ordinary one and a second, much bigger, across a lane at the back. This other garden was kept locked. I was always begging for the key. It was like paradise, or the extension of life into the imagination. Here were espalier applies, roses, lilies, vegetables, and a green path running under an arcade of creepers to an old octagonal summer house in the distance. Near the summer house my father kept bees. These were a notoriously fierce strain, and the gardener could often be seen racing down the green path pursued by an angry black cloud of them. But the bees never attacked *us*. I used to go and talk to them, because I had read that bees were part of your family and you should tell them all your news—although I never spoke to them when the gardener was by. He hated superstition. He was very religious. As a young man, he told people quite frankly, he had attended both church and chapel to be quite sure of heaven; but one day on the Sampford road he had had a vision in which an angel descended and told him always to go to chapel. And he was only one of a crowd of remarkable people who swarmed through the house. There were ham actors, gays, politicians, hirsute artists, hysterical sopranos, a musician who looked like Dr. Dolittle, another who believed in the transmigration of souls, an agriculturalist who looked like Hitler, a teddy girl, local vicars, one long thin and gloomy who grew tobacco, another stout and an expert on wine. . . .

The vicar of Thaxted was a communist and people used to come from Great Dunmow in hobnailed boots specially to walk out noisily during his sermons. Actually his politics derived more from William Morris than Marx. The church was hung with light drapery to enhance its considerable elegance and he taught any child who wished to learn a musical instrument. "Not you," said my mother. "You're tone deaf." Or maybe just deaf, I used to think, on Thursdays when the bell ringers practiced. The Cottage was almost opposite the bell tower and the sound was deafening. In fact I had little to do with the church otherwise because I settled my religious muddles by deciding that I had better be an atheist.

School brought more strange experiences—with an uncomfortable tendency to pick up motifs from the past. Isobel and I were sent to the village school, where we came up against the English class system for the first time. As children of intellectuals, we ranked above village kids and below farmers or anybody rich, but sort of sideways. This meant we were fair game for all. The headmaster had only contempt for us. He said I was never likely to pass the exam to enter grammar school ("the Scholarship," everyone called it) and almost refused to enter me. My mother had one of her rows over that (by this time I was dimly aware that my mother truly *enjoyed* a row). In school, we spent all but one afternoon a week knitting endless scarves and balaclavas for the forces, while one of the teachers told us about tortures, shivering with strange excitement while she spoke. I once nearly fainted at her account of the rack. The other afternoon, the boys were allowed to do drawing and the girls sewing. I protested about this. The headmaster threatened to cane me for impertinence. At which a berserker rage came over me. I seized a shoddy metal ruler and tied it in a knot. I was sent home, but not caned, to my surprise.

Being fair game for all meant that the school bullies chased you home. One winter day, in snow, a bully chased me, pelting me with ice. It cut. Terrified, I raced away down the alley between the blacksmith and the barber and shot into the glassy white road ahead. Too late, I saw a car driving past. I think I hurtled clean over its bonnet, getting knocked out on the way. I came to, face down, looking back the way I had come. "Help!" I shouted to the blacksmith in his forge. "I've been run over!" Not accurate, but I *was* upset. The blacksmith's wife improved on this by racing into the barber's, where she knew my father was having a haircut, yelling, "Mr. Jones! Come quickly! Your daughter's under a car!" Even less accurate, because the car was down the hill, slewing about as it braked. My father dived out of the barber's with his hair short one side and long the other. The driver got there about the same time and his face was truly a light green, poor man. I was quite impressed at the effect I had had.

I passed "the Scholarship" later that year. My parents' connection with the Essex Education Committee enabled them to discover that my marks were spectacularly good. I continued to get spectacular marks most of my school career. This is not a thing I can take much credit for. I just happened to have a near photographic memory and an inborn instinct about how to do exams—which always struck me as cheating, because whenever I was in doubt about a fact, all I had to do was close my eyes and read the remembered page. But it was the one thing my parents cared about. My mother decided that I was to go to her old Oxford college, and added that to the ugly, semi-delinquent, brainy list.

As a semi-delinquent I was sent as a boarder to a school in Brentwood; but there was no room in the boarding house and I had to live for one endless term with the family I later put in *Eight Days of Luke*. Then a girl left the boarding house and I had her bed. This was an old overused hospital bed and it broke under me; and the matron made public discovery that my ears were unwashed. As a punishment—and I am still not clear whether it was for the bed or the ears or

Diana, aged twenty (at left), her sisters Ursula (center) and Isobel

both—I had to sleep on my own in an old lumber room. Just as before, in Coniston, I could not muster courage to run away. Nor could I muster courage to tell my parents: I was too ashamed. But I did tell them, because I enjoyed it so, how the matron marched us in line every Saturday to the cinema to see every film that happened to be showing. This philistine practice horrified them. I was removed and sent by bus to a Quaker school in Saffron Walden as day pupil instead. I was there from 1946 to 1952. It was mainly a boarding school, which meant that I, and later my sisters, were as usual part of an oddball minority. Quakers do not believe in eccentricity or in academic success. They found me highly eccentric for getting good marks and for most other things too.

As time went on, my parents had less and less time for us. We never went on holiday with them. When they took their yearly holiday, we were left with the gardener, the minister of the chapel, or the matron of the orphanage—or simply dumped on Granny. Granny was truly marvellous, five feet of Yorkshire common sense, love, and superstition. She was always saying wise things. I remember, among many sayings, when one time she had given me a particularly good present, she said, "No, it's not generous. Being generous is giving something that's hard to give." She was so superstitious that she kept a set of worthless china to break when she happened to break something good, on the grounds that breakages always came in threes and it was as well to get it over. I would have been lost without Granny, that I know.

That was a grim time in the world. The war, which had receded when we left London, came close again as rockets and pilotless planes. They were terrifying. Then there was the anxiety of D Day, followed by the discovery of the concentration camps, which made me realise just how mad the world had been. This was followed by great shortages and the cold war. Hiroshima horrified me: the cold war made me expect a Hiroshima bomb in England any day.

Things were grim at home too. When a course was running at Clarance House—which was continuously during summer and two-thirds of the time during winter—we quite often came home from school to find that nobody had remembered to save us anything to eat. If we went into the kitchen to forage, the cook shrieked at us to get out. When no course was running, my father would sit slumped and silent in the only family room, which was also his office. He rarely spoke to any of us unless he was angry, and then he could not remember which one of us he was talking to and had to go through all our names before he got the right one. Almost every night during winter, my mother would shout at him—with some justice—that he kept all his charm for his job and none for her in private; whereupon he would fly into a towering Welsh rage and they would bawl at one another all evening. When it was over, my mother would rush into the kitchen, where we had retreated to do homework, and recount angrily all that had been said, while we waited with pens politely poised, knowing that any comment only made things worse. This routine was occasionally lightened by ludicrous incidents, such as the time the cat locked us all into that office by playing with the bolt on the outside of its door; or when our aged corgi suddenly upped and bit my father in the butt while he was chasing Isobel to hit her.

My parents *did* remember birthdays and Christmas, but only at the last minute. That is how I remember that day peace was declared with Japan. It was the day before my eleventh birthday and all the shops were shut in celebration, so I got no presents that year. This left a void, for birthdays were the one occasion when my father could be persuaded to buy books. By begging very hard, I got *Puck of Pook's Hill* when I was ten and *Greenmantle* when I was twelve. But my father was inordinately mean about money. He solved the Christmas book-giving by buying an entire set of Arthur Ransome books, which he kept locked in a high cupboard and dispensed one between the three of us each year. Clarance House had books, he said. True: it had been stocked mostly from auctions and, from this stock, before I was fourteen, I had read all of Conrad, Freud's *Interpretation of Dreams*, Bertrand Russell on relativity, besides a job lot of history and historic novels—and all thirty books from the public library in the guildhall. Isobel and I suffered from perpetual book starvation. We begged, saved, and cycled for miles to borrow books, but there were still never enough. When I was thirteen, I began writing narratives in old exercise books to fill this gap, and read them aloud to my sisters at night. I finished two, both of epic length and quite terrible. But in case someone is tempted to say my father did me a favour, I must say this is not the case at all. I always would have been a writer. I still had this calm certainty. All these epics did for me was to prove that I could finish a story. My mother was always telling me that I was much too incompetent to finish anything. During her ugly, semi-delinquent litanies she frequently said, "When you do the Oxford exams, you'll get a place, but you won't do better than that. You haven't got what it takes."

In his stinginess, my father allowed us one penny a week pocket money. Money for anything else you had to ask him for. Looking back, I see I accepted this, partly because I thought it was normal and knew I wasn't worth more, but also because asking for money at least meant he spoke to me while he was enquiring suspiciously into the use of every penny. He also allowed me to darn his socks for sixpence a pair (by this stage I was sewing clothes for myself and my sisters and doing the family wash in spare moments). My sisters, however, rebelled at their poverty and bearded my father in his office. Groaning with dismay, my father upped our allowance to a shilling a week when I was fifteen, on condition that we bought our own soap and toothpaste. A tube of toothpaste cost most of two weeks' allowance. Isobel and I were by then civilised enough to save for it. Ursula squandered her money.

Ursula always took the eccentric way, particularly over illness. The cardinal sin we could commit was to be ill. It meant that someone had grudgingly to cross the yard with meals for us. My mother usually made a special trip to our bedsides to point out what a nuisance we were being. Her immediate response to any symptom of sickness was to deny it. "It's only psychological," she would say. On these grounds I was sent to school with chicken pox, scarlet fever, German measles and, for half a year, with appendicitis. Luckily the appendix never quite became acute. The local doctor, somewhat puzzled by my mother's assertion that there was nothing wrong with me, eventually took it out. He was an old military character and, in keeping with the rest of life, he had only three fingers in his right hand. I still have a monster scar. I had the appendix in a bottle for years, partly to show my mother the boils on it and partly to live up to the title of semi-delinquent. But Ursula, having concluded that "only psychological" meant the same as "purely imaginary," deduced that it was therefore no more wrong to pretend to be ill than to be really ill. She drew on her strong acting talent, contrived to seem at death's door whenever she was tired of school, and spent many happy hours in bed.

I put some of the foregoing facts in *The Time of the Ghost*, but what I think I failed to get over in that book was how close we three sisters were. We spent many hours delightedly discussing one another's ideas and looked after one another strenuously. For example, when I was fourteen, Isobel was told by the Royal Ballet School that she could never, ever make it as a ballet dancer. Her life fell to pieces. She had been told so firmly that she was a ballerina born that she did not know what she was any longer. She cried one entire night. After five hours, when we still could not calm her, I crossed the yard in my pyjamas—it was raining—to get parental help. A mistake. My mother jumped violently and clutched her heart when I appeared. My father ordered me back to bed, despite my explanation and despite the fact that we had been ringing our recently installed emergency bell before I went over. I trudged back through the rain, belatedly remembering that my mother hated giving sympathy. "It damages me," she had explained over my appendix. Ursula and I sat up the rest of the night convincing Isobel that she had a brain as well as a body. We were close because we had to be.

"My husband, looking much as he did when I first met him," 1951

This solidarity did not hold so well when our parents laughed at us. I became very clumsy in my teens and they laughed at anything I did that was not academic. Perhaps they needed the amusement, because, for the next year, my father sickened mysteriously. When I was fifteen, he was diagnosed as having intestinal cancer. To my misfortune, something painful went wrong with my left hip at the same time, so that I could only walk with a sailor-like roll, causing much mirth. It was the beginning of multiple back trouble which has plagued me the rest of my life, but no one knew about such things then. The natural assumption was that I was trying to be interesting because my father was ill. It is hard to express the guilt I felt.

My father, full of puritanical distaste, weathered that operation. He developed secondary cancer almost at once, but that was not apparent for the next three years or so. Once he had recovered, it occurred to him that I would need special tuition if I were to go to Oxford as planned. The Friends' School was not geared to university entrance. Academic ambition vied in him with stinginess. Eventually, he approached a professor of philosophy who had just come to live in Thaxted with his wife and small children and asked him to teach me Greek. In exchange, my father offered the philosopher a handmade dollhouse that someone had given my sisters. My sisters loved the thing and had kept it in beautiful condition. But the philosopher accepted the deal, so no matter what their feelings, the dollhouse was given away. In return, the philosopher gave me three lessons in Greek. Then he ran off with someone else's wife. I must surely be the only person in the world to have had three Greek lessons for a dollhouse.

After that, pressure mounted on me to succeed academically. In my anxiety to oblige, I overworked. I did nothing like as well as was expected. I did scrape an interview at my mother's old college. There a majestic lady don said, "Miss Jones," shuddering at my plebeian name, "you are the candidate who uses a lot of slang." She so demoralised me that, when she went on to ask me what I usually read, I looked wildly round her shelves and answered, "Books." I failed. At the eleventh hour, I applied for and got a place at St. Anne's College, Oxford, where I went in 1953.

It was not a happy time. When I got there, I found that John Ruskin had taken belated revenge for the rubbed-out drawings: I had to share his vast, cold studio with a girl who required me to wait on her hand and foot. And my father died after my first term there. I had to stay at home to see to his funeral, and spent the rest of my time at Oxford in nagging anxiety for my sisters, who were not finding my mother easy to live with. However, C. S. Lewis and J. R. R. Tolkien were both lecturing then, Lewis booming to crowded halls and Tolkien mumbling to me and three others. Looking back, I see both of them had enormous influence on me, but it is hard to say how, except that they must have been equally influential to others too. I later discovered that almost everyone who went on to write children's books—Penelope Lively, Jill Paton Walsh, to name only two—was at Oxford at the same time as me; but I barely met them and we never at any time discussed fantasy. Oxford was very scornful of fantasy then. Everyone raised eyebrows at Lewis and Tolkien and said hastily, "But they're excellent scholars as well."

Michael Shepherd

"My three sons: Richard, Colin, Michael," 1964

Let's go back now to the empty swatch of time before I went up to Oxford, when my father was periodically at home between times of being guinea pig at an early and unsuccessful form of chemotherapy. I have not said much about the young people who came to Thaxted on courses, because most of them were mere transients; but there were some who came often, some my own age, with whom we became firm friends. One was in love with Isobel (many people were) and he was coming to the house with ten friends to relax after doing finals at Oxford. Now this is an occasion comparable to the time when I was eight and knew that I would be a writer. As soon as I heard they were coming, I was seized with unaccountable excitement. I raced round helping get ready for them and made the tea far too early. They arrived while I made it. In the small hall outside my father's office I ran into a cluster of them talking with my father. One of them said, "Diana, you know John Burrow, do you?"

I sort of looked. Not properly. All I got was a long beige streak of a man standing with them in front of the old Arthur Ransome cupboard. And instantly I knew I was going to marry this man. It was the same calm and absolute certainty that I had had when I was eight. And it rather irked me, because I hadn't even looked at him properly and I didn't know whether I *liked* him, let alone *loved* him.

Luckily both proved to be the case. The relationship survived two years at Oxford when John was a graduate student, and a third year when he was a lecturer at King's College, London. It also survived my mother's impulsive purchase, after my father died, of a private school in Beeston outside Nottingham, in a *very* haunted house. We moved there in the summer of 1956. I had been ill all that year, but after four months of listening to invisible footsteps pacing the end of my bedroom, I went to Granny, who was living in Sampford (near where the angel appeared to the gardener) in order to be married to John in Saffron Walden, in a thick fog, three days before Christmas 1956. There are no photographs of the wedding because, as my mother explained, her own wedding was more important. She married Arthur Hughes, a Cambridge scientist, the following summer.

John and I lived in London until September 1957, where I seemed unemployable. I used the time to read Dante, Gibbon, and Norse sagas. Then we moved back to Oxford to a flat in a large house in the Iffley Road, with another family downstairs who became our lifelong friends. Meanwhile, Ursula failed all her exams in protest against academic pressure and made it to drama school. She is now an actress. Isobel was at university in Leicester, working grimly for a good degree, when my stepfather turned her out of his house. She arrived on our doorstep, shattered,

"On the eve of Richard's wedding. Left to right: Colin, Michael, Dawn (bridesmaid), Harriet (the bride), Richard, myself."

around the time I discovered I was pregnant, and was living with us when my son Richard was born in 1958. She stayed with us until my next son, Michael, was born in 1961, and was married from our flat. Her husband is an identical twin. John, who gave Isobel away, was mightily afraid of handing her to the wrong twin. She is now one of the few women professors in England. Ursula and I always think we did a good job of persuading her she had a brain.

My third son, Colin, was born in 1963. My aim, from this time forward, was to live a quiet life—not an easy ambition in a house full of small children, dogs, and puppies. During this time, to my undying gratitude, John and my children taught me more about ordinary human nature than I had learned up to then. I still had no idea what was normal, you see. After that I found the experiences of my childhood easier to assimilate and could start trying to write. To my dismay, I had to learn *how*—so I taught myself, doggedly. At first I assumed I would be writing for adults, but my children took a hand there. First Michael threatened to miscarry. I had to stay in bed and, while I did, I read *Lord of the Rings*. It was suddenly clear to me after that that it was *possible* to write a long book that was fantasy. Then as the children grew older, they gave me the opportunity to read all the children's books which I had never had as a child and, what was more, I could watch their reactions while we read them. Very vigorous those were too. They liked exactly the kind of books—full of humour and fantasy, but firmly referred to real life—which I had craved for in Thaxted. Somewhere here it dawned on me that I was going to have to write fantasy anyway, because I was not able to believe in most people's version of normal life. I started trying. What I wrote was rejected by publishers and agents with shock and puzzlement.

In 1966 we moved briefly to a cold, cold farmhouse in Eynsham while we waited for my husband's college, Jesus College, to have a house built that we could rent. There Colin started having febrile convulsions and almost everything else went wrong too. I wrote *Changeover*, my only published adult novel, to counteract the general awfulness.

In 1967, the new house was ready. It had a roof soluble in water, toilets that boiled periodically, rising damp, a south-facing window in the food cupboard, and any number of other peculiarities. So much for my wish for a quiet life. We lived there, contending with electric fountains in the living room, cardboard doors, and so forth, until 1976, except for 1968–9, which year we spent in America, at Yale. Yale, like Oxford, was full of people who thought far too well of themselves, lived very formally, and regarded the

The author, January 1988

wives of academics as second class citizens; but America, round the edges of it, I loved. I try to go back as often as I can. We went for a glorious time to Maine, and also visited the West Indian island of Nevis, where, to my astonishment, a number of people greeted me warmly, saying, "I'm so glad you've come back!" I still don't know who they thought I was. But an old man on a donkey thought John was a ghost.

On our return, now all the children were at school, I started writing in earnest. A former pupil of John's introduced me to Laura Cecil, who was just starting as a literary agent for children's books. She became an instant firm friend. With her encouragement, I wrote *Wilkins' Tooth* in 1972, *Eight Days of Luke* in 1973, and *The Ogre Downstairs* the same year. I laughed so much writing that one that the boys kept putting their heads round the door to ask if I was all right. *Power of Three* came after that, then *Cart and Cwidder*, followed by *Dogsbody*, though they were not published in that order. *Charmed Life* and *Drowned Ammet* were both written in 1975.

Also on our return, we acquired a cottage in West Ilsley, Berkshire, as a refuge from the defects of the Oxford house. The chalk hills there, full of racehorses, filled my head with new things to write. It was at this cottage that John was formally asked to apply for the English professorship at Bristol University. He did so, and got the job. We moved here in 1976 and were involved in a nightmare car crash the following month. Despite this, I love Bristol. I love its hills, its gorge and harbours, its mad mixture of old and new, its friendly people, and even its constant rain. We have lived here ever since. All my other books have been written here; for although the car crash, followed by my astonishment at winning the 1977 Guardian Award for Children's Books, almost stopped me dead between them, I get unhappy if I don't write. Each book is an experiment, an attempt to write the ideal book, the book my children would like, the book I *didn't* have as a child myself.

I have still not, after twenty-odd books, written that book. But I keep trying. Nor do I manage to live a quiet life. I keep undertaking things, like visiting schools and teaching courses as a writer, or learning the cello, or doing amateur theatricals, or rashly agreeing to do all the cooking for Richard's wedding in 1984. Every one of those things has led to comic disasters—except the wedding: that was perfect. My aunt Muriel came to it just before she died, wearing a mink headdress like a Cardinal's hat, and gave the couple her blessing. My mother also came. She was widowed again in 1975 and keeps on cordial terms with the rest of her family. She thinks John is marvellous.

Another thing that stops me living a quiet life is my travel jinx. This is hereditary: my mother has it and so does my son Colin. Mine works mostly on trains. Usually the engine breaks, but once an old man jumped off a moving train I was on and sent every train schedule in the country haywire for that day. And my books have developed an uncanny way of coming true. The most startling example of this was last year, when I was writing the end of *A Tale of Time City*. At the very moment when I was writing about all the buildings in Time City falling down, the roof of my study fell in, leaving most of it open to the sky.

Perhaps I don't need a quiet life as much as I think I do.

BIBLIOGRAPHY

FOR YOUNG PEOPLE

Fiction:

Wilkins' Tooth (illustrated by Julia Rodber). London: Macmillan, 1973; also published as *Witch's Business.* New York: Dutton, 1974.

The Ogre Downstairs. London: Macmillan, 1974; New York: Dutton, 1975.

Cart and Cwidder. London: Macmillan, 1975; New York: Atheneum, 1977.

Dogsbody. London: Macmillan, 1975; New York: Greenwillow, 1977.

Eight Days of Luke. London: Macmillan, 1975; New York: Greenwillow, 1988.

Power of Three. London: Macmillan, 1976; New York: Greenwillow, 1977.

Charmed Life. London: Macmillan, 1977; New York: Greenwillow, 1977.

Drowned Ammet. London: Macmillan, 1977; New York: Atheneum, 1978.

Who Got Rid of Angus Flint? (illustrated by John Sewell). London: Evans, 1978.

The Spellcoats. London: Macmillan, 1979; New York: Atheneum, 1979.

The Four Grannies (illustrated by Thelma Lambert). London: Hamish Hamilton, 1980.

The Magicians of Caprona. London: Macmillan, 1980; New York: Greenwillow, 1980.

The Homeward Bounders. London: Macmillan, 1981; New York: Greenwillow, 1981.

The Time of the Ghost. London: Macmillan, 1981.

Witch Week. London: Macmillan, 1982; New York: Greenwillow, 1982.

Archer's Goon. London: Methuen, 1984; New York: Greenwillow, 1984.

The Skiver's Guide. London: Knight, 1984.

Warlock at the Wheel and Other Stories. London: Macmillan, 1984; New York: Greenwillow, 1984.

Fire and Hemlock. London: Methuen, 1985; New York: Greenwillow, 1985.

Howl's Moving Castle. London: Methuen, 1986; New York: Greenwillow, 1986.

A Tale of the Time City. London: Methuen, 1987; New York: Greenwillow, 1987.

The Lives of Christopher Chant. London: Methuen, 1988; New York: Greenwillow, 1988.

Chair Person. Forthcoming.

Plays:

The Batterpool Business. First produced at Arts Theatre, London, 1968.

The King's Things. First produced at Arts Theatre, London, 1970.

The Terrible Fisk Machine. First produced at Arts Theatre,

London, 1971.

Editor of:

Hidden Turnings (a collection of stories for teenagers). Forthcoming.

FOR ADULTS

Fiction:

Changeover. London: Macmillan, 1970.

Carol Kendall

1917-

I can't be sure why or how I became a writer, but I strongly suspect that having six older brothers had a great deal to do with it. No matter how much the baby of a family is treasured, one small girlish voice is no contest in a houseful of enthusiastic masculine voices. By all accounts, I was a baby content to observe and be amused by anybody and anything that passed into my view. There were no outcries, no clamorings for attention—and no recounted anecdotes having to do with my early days, the sole example being one dry comment on the event of a clattering entrance and exit of my nearest brother, Arden. "Thank goodness," I said with a three-year-old's resignation as the door slammed shut on Arden's heels, "that noisy thing is gone."

Clearly, the only way to be heard in my family was to write out what I wanted to say. That made school the first major event in my life. Learning to read words was a revelation; writing them was magic, the secret of life. Before that beginning year was out, I had launched my career as a writer. My premier work took the form of a journal, the first sentence of which was, "I saw my first robin today." That was also the last sentence, as, clearly, my inspiration ran out concurrently with the words I could spell.

By the time I'd reached fourth grade and been duly inducted into the pure joys of grammar, however, I was armed with enough words and ideas to start my second work—a novel. I knew all about novels from having read the Attic Books, those yellowing volumes that were relegated to the top floor as my older brothers left home to seek their fortunes. There was a lot of reading in the crammed bookshelves and the spillover stacks, including an enormous volume of riddles and conundrums and a thick account of the Civil War's Andersonville prison with fascinating drawings of prisoners scooping cockroaches out of their soup. Tom Swift and the Rover Boys and other heroes now forgotten were piled next to a cache of dime novels by Horatio Alger, but all of these paled beside the three red-jacketed volumes about Joe Strong the Boy Fish. Joe Strong overcame all obstacles by his own skill and determination. I loved the Boy Fish with a passion—and I didn't even like to swim.

Carol Kendall, 1982

So I started my novel, a sort of poor man's *Oliver Twist* out of Bucyrus, Ohio, by way of the slums of Chicago. I had never been in Chicago, but my half-brother Jerry (the hero of my own life) and his family lived there and that gave me certain rights to the territory. Instead of a boy-hero, my hero was a girl, a unique departure from the Attic Books, and perhaps the first indication of my feminist leanings. Betty Judd, hero, valiantly resisted her father's efforts to "l'arn" her the art of pickpocketing. (My villains were as full of sloppy speech as they were of vice.) When sent out to steal, she maintained her honesty by running errands for nickels and dimes, which she duly turned over to her watery-eyed, ungrammatical parent as "loot" from innocent victims. Her mother was "a regular stepmother," but one day Betty discovered in an old trunk in the attic a picture of a mysterious and beautiful lady, clearly no relation to the Judd family. . . .

By the time I reached page nineteen of this harrowing tale, written large in pencil in a speckly brown composition book, I could no longer keep the thrill of writing to myself. I had to share my glorious work with somebody—and who more worthy of the honor than my fourth-grade teacher? I gave the composition book into Miss Heinlen's hands on a Monday morning after a weekend of serious revision. She proved to be a slow reader. Tuesday passed, Wednesday, Thursday. On Friday I knew I could never wait out the weekend, so at the end of school, rather like Oliver Twist humbly asking Mr. Bumble for more, I approached the dais that held both Miss Heinlen and her desk well above the common herd, and asked if she had had time to read my novel. Miss Heinlen, lip curling into a smile of scorn, reached two disdainful fingers into a drawer, plucked out my beloved composition book, and dropped it into my hands with a withering, "Don't be so silly, Carol."

I was stricken, but not struck down. Miss Heinlen was wrong. I wasn't silly. My book had as good a plot as a lot of the Attic Books and *they* were written by grown-ups. She surely didn't think that I could write like the two *real* books I'd read at the top of my house? A fourth-grader wasn't up to the likes of *The Secret Garden* or *The Queen's Page,* or the books I got from the public library.

Smarting under the enormous injustice of that "silly," I put the speckly composition book to rest and over the next twelve years confined my writing to what I knew firsthand. I wrote feature stories and columns, both chatty and serious, for school and college newspapers; a trial poem or two; several stories that were more like sketches or scenes drawn from life; and thought of Miss Heinlen as little as possible. Even so, she had taught me a thing or two: (1) beware of flaunting fast-fried manuscripts, as they probably need more thought; (2) choose a critic who knows something about reading and writing; and (3) (with apologies to all those sterling people who share the name) don't show your manuscript to anybody called Heinlen.

Those lesser Attic Books haunted me long after I learned to scorn them as models for writing. The girls that occasionally showed up in their pages were gigglers and squealers who were afraid of everything, especially the toads and snakes that boys incomprehensibly carried in their pockets. The little cowards led stupid and boring lives playing with dolls and whining a lot—when they weren't shrieking at the sight of a mouse. There were enough of these among my own acquaintances to make me agree with the boys in the boys' books. The female person in general was clearly inferior to the male—all except *me,* of course, and those few friends who passed the test. I had no wish to be a boy, but I was fiercely determined never to take an inferior place to one, and with no trouble at all I became the tomboy of the school. I had a boy's haircut at six, played football and baseball and tennis, and once volunteered in assembly to have

First grade, Norton Elementary School, Bucyrus, Ohio, 1923. "I'm the one with the boy's haircut, standing far left with the boys, of course."

a seven-foot cobra draped round my neck. It didn't occur to me then that boys who read boys' books were victims too of this belittlement of girls, to say nothing of the frog-in-pocket roles mapped out for themselves.

The family I grew up in was an odd mix of relationships. Because both my mother and father had been married before, I inherited five half-brothers and one half-sister. Two half-brothers were Seegers, three were Millers, and the Miller half-sister, married, already had a daughter two years old when I was born. My "whole brother," Arden, and I were the final complication to the mixture. I loved all my brothers, but I worshiped Jerry, the younger Seeger "half"—mostly from afar, as he was in college before I reached first grade. He had chosen my names when I was born: Carol, for the smartest girl in his class; and Louise, for the prettiest. As though that wasn't enough to earn my devotion, I was frequently compared to him. "Her nose is always in a book, just like Jerry." "She sticks her tongue out when she's writing something, just like Jerry." To be "just like Jerry" was all I could wish for.

My father was a cabinetmaker and could turn his hand to any crafting job, from the classic "readers' desk" in our church to an enormous casing built on the bed of a local furniture van. I must have seen the last horse carriage in Bucyrus, Ohio, in my father's shop, where it had come for renovation. My clearest memory of the big, echoing shop is of the enormous spools of heavy thread that were lined up on a rack. When they were empty, they became tanks for Arden and me. Pop, as we always called him, notched wheels in the rims for us, and threaded a stout rubber band through the bore, held at one end by a bit of matchstick, and on the other by a full-length matchstick, the "arm." A big spool, wound up, could clicket along the entire length of our dining room table. Arden and I made our own tanks out of the smaller spools donated by our mother, so that we sometimes had regiments of tanks traveling together. But I never associated them with war. They were just—locomotion. Violence, aggression, arguments, even destructive words, were not a part of my life.

Christmas was a great occasion in our house. My first real memory of it started just after dark one Christmas Eve, when up from the cellar, directly from the furnace (we had no fireplace), came Santa Claus with a pack on his back and lots of *ho-ho-hos*. Arden and I were shooed away, but somehow we were allowed to sneak back and peep through the sliding doors into the living room where Santa was putting gifts under the tree. Then he brushed past us on his way back to the furnace, and we were overcome with joy, or at least I was. Arden, three years older, must have known who was in the Santa Claus suit, but he wasn't one to disillusion a baby sister.

Carol and brother, Arden, about 1922

After supper, it was time to light the four-inch candles that we'd clipped onto the branches when we decorated the tree. We let the candles burn for a magical five minutes before snuffing them out—and then we opened the presents. Christmas Eve has always seemed to me to be the true Christmastime, full of warmth and soft light, with the darkness closed out beyond the windows, the family all together and loving. Although I later acceded to the morning tradition to please my husband, a "stocking" man, I still feel that morning is a cold time of day for opening presents and being jolly. My "new custom" of opening one present each on Christmas Eve at least preserved a remnant of the real thing.

Being a girl, naturally I was given dolls, but I took little joy in those bisque-headed, blinkety creatures that bore no relation to anything living. Of course I never confessed to this so-called abnormal response. It wouldn't have been polite to complain that I really wanted books, books, books. When I was six, my mother sewed an elaborate wardrobe for my two main dolls. I was overcome by the elegance of the clothes—velvet cloaks and capes and hats trimmed with fur, organdy ruffled dresses with velvet bows, lacy underclothes, tiny socks and shoes—but once this finery was on the dolls, there it stayed. It seemed pointless to take the clothes off again, only to put them on again. The dolls would never know or care, nor would they ever be smart enough to dress themselves.

That was the last Christmas of Santa Claus for me, although Martha up the street had been working on my education for months. The real proof was in the scraps of velvet and organdy I came across in the sewing machine drawer and, still later, in the Santa Claus suit I found in an attic trunk. That last Christmas brought the biggest, grandest doll carriage I had ever seen. Pop, still excited over having a girl in the family at last, had chosen it himself. Although roller-skating, skipping rope, marbles, and mumble-ty-peg were more my style, I walked my elegantly dressed dolls in the awesome carriage to show my appreciation, and probably to show off before the other children in the neighborhood. It was the first really big present in my life—a solid representation of my position in the family: last but not least.

Pop died two years later, in November of 1925. The principal sent Arden to fetch me from the third grade and take me home because our father "wasn't feeling well." I thought this was a great lark, until Arden, who was seldom solemn, curbed my jumps and skips with the sober suggestion that this could be *serious.* I'll remember forever the exact spot we were passing—a neighbor's garden border of four-o'clocks—when I stopped skipping. Arden was right. Pop had died of a heart attack. The next few days were a jumble of extraneous visitors invading our house along with more familiar but strangely hushed relatives. A cousin, David, strummed on a banjo and to my surprise was severely reprimanded by Alice, my two-years-older niece. *I* didn't see anything wrong with cheering up the crowd with a little music. I tried not to look at Pop in the casket, but curiosity overcame me. People kept saying how natural he looked, but he didn't look any more natural than the bisque heads on my dolls. The whole affair was unreal, and I an outsider to the event. I was neither sad nor glad, not happy or unhappy. I just seemed to be wandering through.

Not long ago, listening to a teen-aged girl complaining that her father was too strict, I suddenly realized that my own father's early death had rendered him perfect in my eyes. He would always be the tank-maker, the one who carried me up to bed when I fell asleep in the family circle at night, the one who made fluffy milk for me on Tuesday nights when he got home from council meeting. He had no faults, never spoke an angry word. When I was born at four in the morning, he was so beside himself with happiness at having a daughter that he woke up the neighbors to tell them. With his own hands he had picked out the most magnificent, the most expensive doll carriage in all of Bucyrus. He even had a special Santa Claus suit. What more could one want of a father?

My mother was splendid in a more realistic way. After Pop died so unexpectedly, funds were low, and the onslaught of the depression in 1929 pretty well wiped out our few remaining stocks and bonds. Laura, as I preferred to call her because it brought her closer, had to get a job. But she was trained for nothing beyond housewifery. By this time only Arden and I took up space at home, so she followed the obvious course open to her: roomers. Their comings and goings were an excitement in our lives—until we fell heir to a distantly connected spinster. She had a secretarial job in town, endlessly complained of her lumbago, and wanted the biggest bedroom for her precious belongings, of which the principal item was an enormous hope chest. I'm afraid Arden and I later enjoyed many a mean joke about the hopelessness of *that,* perhaps in revenge for Laura's having to move into a lesser room to make way for it. Nothing about this lodger raised my opinion of women in general, including the fact that her dresser was a fright of cosmetics and appliances, the lace runner thick with spilled face powder, and *I* was supposed to clean up *her* mess. Such ignominy led to bitter reflections that boys' chores were outside in the fresh air and sunlight while girls were penned inside the house with dust and dirty dishes—and somebody else's spilled powder.

Meantime, my mother undertook various enterprises in an effort to keep the mortgage paid and the three of us fed and clothed. The oldest brother sent a check home every month, and other brothers helped out as they were able, but the depression took its toll. Laura sold "better frocks" out of a catalogue, worked part time at Woolworth's, and eventually became the bookkeeper for a coal company—six days a week, six to six. Arden and I, in high school and junior high then, made our own lunches, shopping for them on our way home from school. We had bananas and cereal on Arden-days, soup on mine. Neither of us was crazy about the other's choice, but we rubbed along.

I did very well in school, but Arden didn't take kindly to organized learning. He had a great bubbling sense of humor that endeared him to family and

Carol with her mother, 1928

friends, but interfered with any seriousness of purpose. He scorned clubs and organizations, including organized sports, while I joined every high school activity in sight—from French club to band and orchestra, from cheerleader and Boosters Club to columnist for the school newspaper and editor of the 1935 yearbook.

My club years didn't end until I had gone through four years of college, and after that I never joined another organization. Instead, I got married and began my real writing career. That's all the club I ever needed.

People talk about having had a happy childhood. Mine was neither happy nor unhappy: it just happened. My mother, forty-two when I was born, had little time to probe my psyche and was wise enough to love me, let me grow, and never insist that I be "ladylike" in place of being just honest and true and kind and thoughtful. When I think "happy," I see myself hunched over a book in the attic, hot in summer, icy in winter. "Happiest" is the day I found the little book of French stories when I was ten, and discovered I could translate them from the vocabulary in the back. The first story was about the French *drapeau,* which, I learned with mounting excitement, was colored *"rouge et blanc et bleu."* "Happiest," too, were the hours I spent committing to memory pieces like "Mrs. Caudle's Lecture" from the old McGuffey Readers that were stashed in the attic bookshelves along with Joe Strong the Boy Fish. "Happiest" was the day I bought my first book: *Robin Hood.* I was eleven. "Happiest" was playing backyard baseball with Arden and his friends, or sitting on the garage roof eating cherries off the tree which I had climbed to get there.

But I was one to be plagued by memories of inadequacies, which assumed outsized proportions in my mind and stayed with me for years. There were embarrassments as minor as being crushed-with-a-glance in fifth grade for immoderate laughter when somebody pronounced a word "pedesteranian." When my married Seeger half-brothers treated me to a month's visit divided between Milwaukee and Chicago, I felt so socially awkward—I was just twelve and had never been out of my private cabbage patch—that I remember only the gaucheries I uttered, like calling Jerry's smart apartment house in Chicago a tenement. I was said to be sensitive, but nobody ever suspected that as I was busily trying to stamp out bad memories, I managed to erase a lot of ordinary good ones.

There were obviously good memories to be had. I remember the joy of walking to Saturday afternoon matinees in the charge of my brother, even though he made me walk ahead of him when we met his friends and once made fun of me for crying during a sad movie. The serials, especially "The Perils of Pauline", were tremendously exciting, the suspense almost unendurable when we had to leave Pearl White tied to the railroad tracks at the end of an episode, with no rescue possible until the following Saturday.

I remember the winter of the incredible snow, when I helped my older brothers build a marvelous igloo and snow fort in the front yard.

I remember our big Jackson touring car, with side curtains. It made a dandy place to play school, but I didn't like poky Sunday drives in it.

I remember the thrill of winning spelling bees.

I remember the exact shelves in the public library that held *East o' the Sun and West o' the Moon, At the Back of the North Wind,* and *The Trumpeter of Krakow.* Only the first of these has kept its magic over the years.

I remember Saturday nights in summer when we drove downtown to park on Main Street and watch the passing crowd. We bought popcorn from Foxy's stand on the square, smoked salmon from Wagner's grocery, and the Sunday roast from Smith & Son on a side street. Like any proper butchers, fat father Smith and skinny son Smith wore straw hats and walked on sawdust; at closing time the skinny son used a great wire brush to scrape even more humps and valleys into the worn butcher tables.

I remember learning the latest dance craze, the Charleston, from a big-city sister-in-law and teaching it to the other fourth-grade girls at school. The restroom was our practice hall.

I remember surprise visits from out-of-town relatives. Nobody ever telephoned in advance because we were always at home, anyway. Telephoning would have spoiled that delicious sensation of astoundment, that moment of thrill and delight and love all mixed together. It was like the old prairie days in books, when visitors were welcomed and treasured for the tidings they brought from the outside world.

And I remember, best of all, the very first time I felt the inexpressible joy—of bliss absolute—that all was right with the world. It happened in one brief moment of a summer's day as I glanced up through whispering sunspecked leaves to the sky beyond. It was warm, there were bees humming, the tree was a white birch: it was perfection.

We were not demoralized by our instant poverty after Pop died, but it was always *there.* Grocery bills got out of hand, and once our telephone was embarrassingly "out of order" for a month. Our wardrobes, never shabby, were certainly skimpier, and I, for one, was delighted to be spared our former dressmaker's scoldings for wiggling while she pinned my hems. I early decided not to accept favors I couldn't repay, so that even now I say an automatic "No, thanks" oftener than "Yes, please." We didn't complain, perhaps because I, at least, never doubted that I could and would do whatever I set out to do—like Joe Strong the Boy Fish. "Today" and "tomorrow" were looking-ahead words; "yesterday," like "yesteryear," was tinged with regret.

I didn't realize that my future was already taking shape. Having no money for fads was surely the reason I was so struck by a story in *Child Life* that I tucked it away in a deep recess of my mind. I was nine or ten when I read the story, but I didn't consciously think of it again until just five years ago. Someone had asked me where I first got the idea of conformity for *The Gammage Cup,* and I found that story—fifty-five years later—still lurking in my head. It was about a child who insisted that her birthday party be in costume because *everybody* had costume parties that year, with the usual prizes for pretty or ugly or funny. Her mother, probably as weary of making costumes as she was of all the fads her daughter slavishly copied from her school friends, invited the other mothers to tea and some serious talk. Together they decided to end copycatism for once and all, and went home to sew up their children's costumes for the party. Of course, the costumes were a deep secret until the great day came and the children began to arrive at the birthday house.

And lo—every last one of them was a child in sheep's clothing.

Further events kept me thinking about conformity. All my friends in high school had shiny new girls' bikes, but I hadn't even a hope of one. There was only Arden's derelict Silver Ring. It had two flat tires, no fenders, and no brakes; and of course it had a proper crossbar—proper, that is, if you were a *boy.* Little by little I put the Silver Ring in running order, although the brakes were always feeble and new fenders were beyond my means. I loved that nonconformist bike with a passion, and, just in case somebody might look down upon it, I never failed to point out that it didn't wobble like girls' bikes, had less wind resistance with no fenders, and furthermore, I could—and did—give rides on the crossbar to any friend who lacked wheels.

I was even a nonconformist in religion, quite unintentionally, being the only Christian Scientist in Norton Elementary School once Arden had moved on to junior high. We were Christian Scientists of a moderate variety, and I was not a devoutly religious child, but I was shocked when I ran into the Lord's Prayer outside of my Sunday school to find that other children and even grown-ups got it all wrong, saying things like Our Father *who,* instead of *which,* and *trespasses* and *trespassers* in place of the correct and pronounceable *debts* and *debtors.* Furthermore, they stuck an *Amen* at the end of the prayer. That was a real affront. "The power and the glory forever" shouldn't be cut short like that, but ring on and on—forever-ever-everrrrr. . . .

I shared these thoughts with no one, but I went on thinking them. Of my two lives, the one with books and thoughts seemed more real than the one with people. I liked other people and was gregarious, like the rest of my family, but I seldom felt that I was actually "onstage" with them. I was in the wings, and like any understudy for a part yet to come, I listened and I watched and I noted well.

It seems to me, looking a long way back, that it was between the ages of nine and twelve that I learned the really important, the basic, noes and yeses of my life. I learned, mostly from books, the pitfalls to avoid: stealing, snooping, reading other people's letters, nagging like Mrs. Caudle in the

McGuffey Reader, telling lies, and name-calling. I learned from experience that a girl was paid twenty-five cents for mowing a neighbor's lawn, while her brother got fifty cents for the same job, which may be the reason for my deep-seated abhorrence of injustice. I learned the differences between ignorance, stupidity, insensitivity, and plain nastiness, between honor and dishonor, and to trust my own judgment as to which was which. I learned that housekeeping and cooking could never harness my imagination, and that reading a book was more exciting than "The Perils of Pauline" on Saturday afternoons.

In junior high and high school I happily went through all the motions of a student, including boyfriends and cokes and covertly reading *Cap'n Billy's Whiz Bang* at Bill Nedele's Place—and I lived every minute with enthusiasm. But after the valedictory address and the passing out of diplomas, I was astounded to see tears flooding the eyes of my classmates. One of them sobbed on my shoulder, "The best years of our lives!" Startled, filled with guilt for my lack of feeling, I got rid of my happy face and hugged my friends back. But didn't they realize that far from being the best years of our lives, life had scarcely begun?

Of course there was no money for college, but I went anyway. We had moved out of our house the year before, my mother to live with a Miller half-brother in another town, and I to stay in Bucyrus with a neighbor friend for my senior year in high school. Arden was working on an assembly line in Columbus, putting off college for yet another year. I had wanted to go to Ohio State like the two Seeger half-brothers, but Ohio University offered me a scholarship and a National Youth Administration job at thirty cents an hour, and after looking up Athens, Ohio on the map, I cashed in my small insurance policy for seventy dollars, and was on my way. My mother said she didn't see how I could make it, but she was for me all the way, in spite of two sisters-in-law who thought I should get a job in a dime store and support her. I thought this was downright prejudice against the youngest, and so, obviously, did Laura. There was no way that I could be kept from my rights to an education, especially after President Roosevelt provided the NYA job. As the quotation attributed to me in my high school annual read, "I'm in a hurry right now. . . . "

The college years were crammed with study and dates and activities, my job at the Service Bureau on campus, and the after-hours of typing theses and dissertations for graduate students. One way or another—with the aid of scholarships, a small loan or two, and three summers of full-time work at the

1939, the year the author received her A.B. degree and was married

Service Bureau—I finished college with honors and a Phi Beta Kappa key.

And now, I thought, it was time to come out of the wings onto the stage. All the years that had gone before, I had been marking time . . . waiting for the writing to begin.

In an odd sort of way, the writing had already been at work shaping my life. It found my husband, or rather, through it, my husband found me. Paul Murray Kendall came to Ohio University in 1937 with three shirts, two threadbare suits, a pair of well-worn shoes, and five mismatched socks. Before running out of money at the University of Virginia, he had finished all his work on a doctorate except for the dissertation. Never short of words, either written or spoken, he wrote some nine hundred pages in the next two years, but found time to read *The Green and White,* where he saw my column. He claimed that he looked at my picture, read my words, and said, "I'm going to marry that girl." There were a few hitches to his plans, one of them being that I was "pinned" to somebody else. Wearing a fraternity pin was a collegiate romantic symbol for the "going steady" of high school days, or, as my cynical roommate Gwen called it, "a sure date for Saturday nights." Beyond that snag to Paul's intentions, moreover, *I* had no slightest intention of marrying and turning into cook and dust-chaser, neither occupation holding any charm for me. I was a writer born, and I would work in a publishing house for starters. Paul Murray Kendall might be the fabulous, dynamic teacher that everyone claimed, and the wittiest mortal walking, but I felt no inclination to date a faculty member, let alone set myself up for the role of faculty wife. However, curiosity being one of my strongest traits, and not wanting to miss the instructor everybody was raving about, in my final semester I signed up for Paul's course in English literature.

It was love at first lecture. The students who praised this instructor had forgotten to mention his voice. A month later, driven by curiosity as much as by perennial poverty, I signed on to type the final draft of his dissertation. Along about page 630 I became unpinned from "the other." By page 810, I decided that Paul's views of marriage were not just idle talk. His was no offering of carpet sweepers and soapsuds, but of a lifetime of writing. "I *want* you to write," he said. "If I wanted a housekeeper, I'd hire one."

I finished typing the dissertation the day before I got my A.B. degree at Ohio University. Two weeks later, Paul was draped in his Ph.D. hood at the University of Virginia in Charlottesville and we were married in the university chapel. It was June of 1939. Never mind the letter I had written to myself at fifteen, to be opened at twenty-one, declaring that I wouldn't get married until I was thirty, life being over by then, anyway.

Our wedding present to each other was the collected short stories of Saki, which we took turns reading aloud that summer in Charlottesville. This cozy habit carried us through a good many years' worth of books that eventually included the 1146 pages of *War and Peace,* and therein lay the reason I took up the study of Russian. I couldn't bear not knowing how to pronounce the characters' names.

In September, just before we headed back to Athens in the Iron Horse (a sturdy Ford coupe), we spent our expiring resources on our first piece of furniture. It was a rebuilt Royal standard typewriter, for which we paid five dollars down and five dollars a month for the next eleven months.

We were poor and we were busy and we were happy. Our first apartment was a big joke with its dismal brown plush furniture and walls of a horrid color that was known as goose-turd green in the Middle Ages and still applies. Paul taught and I wrote. My study was a sunroom tacked on to the bedroom like an afterthought, and before very long one wall was papered with rejection slips. There was a problem I hadn't fully faced before. I was a writer, yes, but of what? Perhaps humbled by Miss Heinlen's pronouncement, I felt that I had nothing to say that hadn't been said many times by many people, and much better, at that. But write I must and would. Still sounding in my ears was the advice of a novelist I'd met in Charlottesville. Start low, she said, and work up. Try the pulps. Pulps? Magazines on cheap pulp paper, she said. Love stories. Girl meets Boy, Girl loses Boy, Girl gets Boy. Study the formula, she said. So I went to the local news shop and brought home a pile of pulp-paper magazines that had "Love" or "Sweetheart" in the titles, and began my research.

Alas, although my Virginia friend had warned me against writing down to my readers, I couldn't *not* write down to them. It's true that I began to get personal notes from editors, spurring me on. But I also began to have sinking spells each time I sat down to a new story. So I tried writing for the slick paper magazines—*Collier's, Ladies' Home Journal, Saturday Evening Post*—with no better luck. I had slipped down the crack between pulp and slick, and neither way up was the direction I wanted to go.

Then, "*Curley Green*!" said Paul one day as I was posting yet another rejection slip above my Royal. "Did I ever tell you about Curley Green?" He hadn't. Curley Green was an elfin creature that his mother had conjured up for bedtime stories. Paul couldn't remember any of the stories, but the name had never left him, and maybe I would like to use it? Excited by the idea, I wrote the first story over a weekend; then, to form a book, I wrote, but with less enthusiasm, two more. These eventually came to the hand of a major art book publisher, who wanted to start a series of children's books with illustrations by well-known American artists. A sample contract came in the mail, naming an artist of some renown, and I quickly said I would be glad to sign the real thing when it came along. All that came along, however, was word that the project had to be canceled. World War II had just erupted and there was an acute paper shortage. The publisher's idea died aborning. Eventually, *Jack and Jill* magazine published the first story. The other two lurk somewhere in my files. I had said all there was to say about Curley Green as an elf in that first story. The second and third let me know that I wasn't agog to continue with elfin creatures.

Besides these trial stories, my Royal typed out theses and dissertations for graduate students, and with the proceeds I bought a small record player, our second piece of furniture. We began to haunt the local music store, and there we met another avid collector, John Rood, who was a wood sculptor. Before long we were meeting nightly in his studio to play our latest buys, Mozart mixed with Mahler, Gregorian chants with Prokofiev. John sculpted and there was lots of talk about art and music and books and writing, but I was often a half-listener. As a child I could read a book and hearken to family talk at the same time; now I kept track of the conversation while I thought about my own writing affairs.

The war touched our lives in more ways than the missed chance of the Curley Green stories. Paul, at thirty-two and with a bad back from tennis days notwithstanding, was drafted into the infantry. I took a job in Cleveland with the Red Cross, but when Paul was transferred to Special Services and posted to Ft. Slocum, New York, I posted myself there to take a job as general factotum to the secretary of the YMCA. The soldier who met my train was of a frightening thinness, scarcely recognizable. Paul had lost fifty pounds in the infantry and was just now out of the army hospital where he had languished fever-ridden for the past month. But he was laughing, the same old hearty laugh. I had wired the date and time of arrival, adding "K466," our private symbol of love and constancy, and signing it "Siggy." This was too much for military intelligence. They descended on the hospital in force. Who was this "Siggy?" Short for Siegfried? What did the obvious code "K466" signify? What was the meaning of the dates and times in the telegram? They accepted Paul's explanation that Siggy was short for Seeger, his wife's surname, but the "K466" they found hard to swallow. A *piano concerto* as a theme song? And written by a German, too, no matter how dead Mozart might be!

We were back in Athens by the summer of 1945, and I settled to my next writing project. Both Paul and I had become addicts of mystery novels, lately come into popularity. Inevitably, I ran across novels about which I could say, "I can do better than *that,* '" and I set out to prove it with *The Black Seven.* My detective was a twelve-year-old boy called "Drawers" by his friends. He was an intelligent, somewhat brash kid, and I loved writing about him and his raffish friends. In spirit he was not unlike my brother Arden. The adult characters were not so real as the children to my mind, nor were they as interesting to write about.

The Black Seven, "The Adventures of Curley Green," and our first daughter all made their appearance in 1946. Paul and I were bemused by the resemblance of this new Carol to the Curley Green of the stories, and the name stuck to her. Neither of us Carols makes use of our shared name except as a formality. Paul had bestowed the name Siggy on me the day we met, and we were Siggy and Paul to our children. Curley Green remained Curley Green or Curley until college days, when she became Corky for a period, and finally turned into a Callie.

I wrote another mystery with Drawers in charge, *The Baby-Snatcher,* at which point I felt that I had said all there was to say about *him.* Clearly, I had not yet discovered my rightful place in the writing world.

I pondered mightily over my problem while we got ready to go to England for a year—Paul had a Ford Foundation grant to do research on a biography of Richard III—and it finally came to me that if my greatest enjoyment was writing about children, wouldn't it be logical to write about children *for* children? I was egged on by Dick Hough, the British editor who had published my two mysteries and whom I now met for the first time on the platform of Waterloo Station as our boat train drew into London. His family and ours formed a friendship that lasted through the succeeding years of our stays in England, and far beyond. We met Judy Taylor that first year, too, a dear young friend who later became my editor at Bodley Head, and even later married Dick.

It was a very good year for Kendalls. We lived in the village of Chiddingfold, in Surrey, and entered Curley Green/Callie in St. Hilary's School in Godalming, up the road. Paul went into London to the British Museum two or three times a week by train, and I started to write *The Other Side of the Tunnel.* It was a cautious passageway into children's books. I still leaned on the mystery format as a prop, and was mildly pleased with the result, though I ached to write a book with meaning, a book that readers would take to their hearts and remember always, the way I remembered the books from my childhood.

Most people at that time, I found, considered children's books a lower form of writing for a bona fide author; some would even ask if I had thought of writing a real book? Anything written for adults was a "real" book, no matter that plot, characters, title, and author's name would be forgotten in six months. Writers of children's books were even suspect. I once heard an English woman say, "There has to be something *very* peculiar, don't you know, about people who write for children. Unless, of course," she added, seeing my eyebrows climb, "unless they're writing just for pin money or for the housekeeping." I believe this is what is called a double whammy.

My own version of a real book was actually already on its way, jolted into being by the people of England. The country itself looked exactly the way I had expected, from chimney pots to village commons. But the people . . . ! No ordinary present-day mortals like Americans, they were characters straight off the pages of a Dickens novel. The woman who sold sweets in our village was a dead ringer for Mr. F.'s aunt in *Little Dorrit,* the Pecksniff sisters from *Martin Chuzzlewit* lived at the bottom of our hill, and there was always a Pickwickian character to be seen crossing the village common. Think of it: a land full of people out of another time, but living in a quite ordinary, albeit quaint, manner. Like a sponge, I soaked up the sights and sounds of this strange, yet familiar, country. From our house in Chiddingfold, on a clear day we could see Chanctonbury Ring, an ancient circle of trees on a distant hill. Many, many years later, I planted a poplar circle in my back garden in Lawrence, Kansas, not realizing at the time that my fancy was a distant echo of Chanctonbury. I am still amazed that people ask me what the poplar circle is *for.* It seems obvious to me. It isn't *for* anything. It is simply being a poplar circle.

Of course we didn't just sit amongst the Brussels sprouts those fifteen months in Chiddingfold, or in England, for that matter. The first summer we bought a minute Morris Minor with a convertible top and traveled England in pursuit of Richard III's historical trail. Bosworth field, where Richard perished in battle, was full of stinging nettles. In Yorkshire we prowled the ruins of Middleham Castle, where Richard was born, and heard our first Yorkshire accent. Heard, but understood scarcely a word.

At Callie's spring break, we crisscrossed France and Italy and Belgium. In southwestern France, I claimed Les Baux for my own—a mountaintop of ruins from the Middle Ages, with traces of cave people before that, the stuff of storybooks, my sort of storybook. I was enchanted by the cave dwellings along the Loire River and by gargoyles on cathedrals. I ate my first snails. We all burst untunefully into "Sur le pont" at sight of the famous bridge at Avignon. I could feel books taking hold in my mind, a lot of books, a host of stories.

In the summer, before returning to the States, we went to Greece and Troy and Istanbul. I filled a bottle with water from the Kastalian spring for inspiration's sake, but the Oracle at Delphi I put away in the same place that had the *Child Life* sheep story on hold.

Once back in the States, with Callie in the second grade, I found the differences between American and British education even greater than I'd thought. I had forgotten how bright and shiny and *warm* American schools were, how new and clean the books, how fashionably turned out the teachers, and—how plasticized and unreal it all seemed! English schools were grubby by comparison, furnished with dingy desks and antiquated equipment, staffed by teachers in sensible dark clothes and no lipstick, and exuding a chill that went to the bone. The windows were thrown open at regular intervals to keep the air, and the children's brains, from growing mold. Callie's American school, actually, was stifling hot in winter because opening windows would interfere with the automatic heating system. In England I had resisted the idea of children's being pushed willy-nilly into school uniforms, but when one of Callie's American schoolmates began to show up in extravagantly ruffled frocks, I saw a point I'd missed. English uniforms, scruffy and stained by the end of term, often ill-fitting hand-me-downs, made everybody alike on the outside, leaving only the mind free to break out of the common format. Clearly there was a lot more to uniformity than I'd hitherto imagined.

We contrived to save enough money to go back to England in 1955, this time on the Kendall Foundation, which was a shaky edifice at best and good for only a modest six months, during which time I did the index for Paul's *Richard the Third* while he got on with the research for his next book. The indexing was a good background—like other people's conversation—for thinking about my own next book, the subject of which was obviously going to be conformity. It was a stern and heavy-handed word, conformity, and I didn't fancy a moralistic here-and-now framework. My best side was clearly lightness and humor. Fantasy, then? My mind slid over elfin fantasies with a slight shudder. My story was too real for elves. Then, strangely, all at a jump, I had the feel of the whole book inside my head, or in my stomach, as the Chinese would put it. Mine would be a fantasy of people, very real people, made of the stuff of folktales. Fantasy with a touch of magic, but only a touch—the amount of magic that exists in all our lives. There would be no fairies at the bottom of *my* garden.

My very real fantasy people would be little folk, to set them apart from our own realism. Little folk, like children, would be fun to play with, just as soon as I had gathered my cast together.

The first character, oddly, came from a single word. "I'm always in such a *muddle,*" our next-door neighbor in London liked to say. And she was. The Scarletts, like many English people after World War II, had come down in the world. But as they fully expected to go back up in the world, they had moved their enormous pieces of furniture from the enormous house they had had to give up, into the tall skinny house next to the attached tall skinny house that held our apartment. Their dining table (for twelve) all but filled the dining room and when the splendid chairs were hoisted into place, it took a serious effort to edge past. This room and the kitchen were the center of the household. The sitting room on the next floor was a gathering place for the chairs and end tables and cabinets retrieved from the former house, leaving little space for people.

Frances and her family were full of jokes and good humor and of endless help to us, once outfitting Paul with evening dress (and numerous safety pins) from York's closet, another time getting an emergency dental appointment for Paul when a cap dropped off his front tooth one hour before a luncheon engagement to meet his British publisher, the temperamental Sir Stanley Unwin. Frances always had Ribena currant juice and rock buns or cake as after-school treats for her Caroline and our Callie; and for herself and me, some ghastly retsina that she dug out of her defunct wine cellar. We sipped that retsina drop by drop over the months, determined to finish it—for our sins, we said.

But the best present from Frances was her "muddle" word. A whole character sprang into being just from the sound of it. As names of characters are extremely important to me, I spent three days getting this one right and was finally reduced to combining "muddlish" syllables until I stumbled onto the sound I wanted. Muggles would be her name, and muddly would be her house. Some time after *The Gammage Cup* was published, my friend Ming Lin pointed out that my own kitchen back home looked like Muggles'. True. I didn't keep things in heaps, but I had Peg-Board lining the walls. Like Muggles, if I stowed things in cupboards, out of sight, how would I know where they were?

When I put Callie, as Curley Green, into the script as a painter, I had no inkling that she would in fact study painting twenty years later. Walter the Earl was another matter. He was named after Callie's blue stuffed toy rabbit, but he inherited Paulish characteristics. Paul's outside was invariably dressed in white shirt, black tie, and dark suit, but his inside. . . . Ah, inside he was an Ideal Knight in a cloak, an embroidered cloak that swept and swirled and could be flung over one shoulder with a flourish. He never disputed this.

The Gammage Cup and our daughter Gillian were born in a dead heat in the spring of 1956. I proofread the manuscript with pencil in one hand, bottle of milk in the other, and Gillian crooked in my left elbow.

A year later we were on our way back to England, this time on a Guggenheim scholarship. In the hold of the ship we had a Rambler Six station wagon as well as eleven pieces of luggage composed of paper diapers by the gross, collapsible baby bed, potty chair, portable typewriter, tape recorder, reference books, manuscripts, and even a few clothes. We debarked at Le Havre, Rambler and baggage, and started on the trail of Louis XI for Paul's third biography.

"Back to work after Gillian's birth," summer, 1956

It was a rough-edged trail and a rough-edged year, but like everything that ever happened to us, it was never, never boring. Gillian, having joyously learned to walk on shipboard, protested every hour she had to spend in her car seat. Her collapsible baby bed was not the home-away-from-home that the ads had proclaimed. It was, in fact, an affront to her dignity. Eating in restaurants was an exercise in keeping Gillian amused until food arrived, and picnicking at lunchtime lost its joys when Gillian started indiscriminately tasting roadside berries and plants. Our troubles multiplied when we got to England. The dazzling turquoise-and-cream Rambler developed a dying hiccup that would overtake it without warning. Mechanics scratched their heads and muttered, "American cars. . . . " The first nanny we found for Gillian was extremely deaf, played the "telly" at top volume, refused to take Gillian for a walk if an east wind was blowing, and endlessly compared Gillian's toilet training to that of a baby "Lordship" she had tended in the long-ago. His Lordship inevitably won. The electric heaters we bought to heat the flat warmed the twelve-foot ceilings, leaving us to shiver far below. Electric bills were astronomical.

The Aladdin paraffin heater we finally bought had a sullen look, but it became our close friend. Paul and I angled our work tables in one corner of the sitting room and set the Aladdin in all its ungainliness at our backs. When our hands turned blue and brittle, we stretched them behind us for defrosting. Occasionally we stretched at the same moment and our hands ran into each other and we laughed at Fact and Fancy warming at the same fire. It was companionable, that Aladdin, and we came to love its squat homeliness. It warded off chilblains while I wrote *The Big Splash,* an adventure-mystery for children that was quite different from *The Other Side of the Tunnel.* In a more realistic vein, it was about children entering a float contest to raise money for the hospital and discovering the chicanery of the hired fund-raiser. As in all good endings, they won the first prize. Their float was a ducking pond, in action.

The good news that arrived in the spring of 1958 erased all the bad. Margaret McElderry, then at Harcourt, Brace, saw a way to cut *The Gammage Cup,* which four other editors had declared "too long, but too perfectly constructed to be cut." It took me thirty days to cut, paste, revise, and rewrite chapters two through eight, and before the year was out, I had signed a contract for the book. It became a Newbery Honor Book, an Ohioana prizewinner, and, twenty-eight years later, a Hanna-Barbera animation for "CBS Storybreak." I didn't meet the magical Margaret McElderry until 1961, when we happened to be in London at the same time, and our paths have not crossed since then. No matter. Her letters through the years have drawn us closer than many people manage with friends next door.

One other memory clings from that bad-to-good year in England. In the dreary, sunless days of November 1957, a bare five months out of the seventeen we planned to stay in Europe, we ran dreadfully short of money. Six moves in search of a suitable flat, troubles with the balky car, the expense of changing schools for Callie from one end of London to another, the electric heaters, our commitment of work to our much-loved charwoman, Mrs. McAdam, from our last stay—all this added up to more funds than we had, or even had immediate prospects of having. Yet there we were in our bright Rambler, sliding past bus queues of grey-faced people slumped over their shopping bags as night silted down. Just seeing them made my own feet ache. We must have looked very rich and carefree in our turquoise-and-cream, but inside the cozy warm car I was mentally totting up our bills and chewing my lip.

The family on board the Queen Elizabeth, *en route to England in July 1961: from left, daughter Gillian; the author; husband, Paul Kendall; daughter Callie.*

I still remember the sooty air, the leaden sky, the lowering Craven A building we were passing when I came upon an ultimate truth. My mental reckoning had just shown that one thousand dollars would put us in the clear. I might as well have wished for ten thousand, but it was not my nature to be greedy. One thousand was all we needed to keep our typewriters tapping. And then, like a shiver of silver light through the gloom, "it"—the Ultimate Truth, the U.T.—came to me. No matter how much money we might win in a sweepstakes, one thousand or a thousand thousand, it would not, could not, produce on the page one better sentence, one better paragraph, one better book. I put arithmetic aside.

In the end, Paul borrowed the thousand from our friendly Athens bank, and Mr. Palmer sent the draft immediately, along with the latest scores of the Ohio University football games.

When we returned to Athens, Ohio in the fall of 1958, we bought for a song a peculiar house on a hill. It was long on charm and short on convenience, and we loved it. Just across the street we found the Lin family: Ming (Julia) and Henry Lin and their son, Tan, who was a year younger than Gillian and as tidy as she was raggle-taggle. The next year Maya Lin was born, and we discovered that both she and Paul were under the Chinese sign of the pig. Paul always said that Maya was going to be our first lady president, and while she hasn't yet reached that position, she is already responsible for one great architectural design. Tan, like Ming, became a poet and a teacher; Ming's Ph.D. later led to a professorship at Ohio University; and Henry was a potter, a teacher, and eventually a dean. Over the next twelve years, until we left Athens, our two families celebrated Thanksgiving and Christmas together. Ming was to become very important to my writing life.

Various people urged me to write a sequel to *The Gammage Cup,* but I was reluctant. As in the early Curley Green stories, I had said all I had to say about the Minnipins of Slipper-on-the-Water. Anything more would simply be further action with no growth of character. I groaned a good deal, until my friend Laura Summers jolted me into a new plan of attack. "Well, Siggy," she said one day, interrupting my self-pity, "why don't you make it a hundred years later?" I had no intention of going forward a hundred years, but I was jostled into doing *something* besides dithering. I moved two villages down the Watercress river, set the clock at five years past *The Gammage Cup,* and wrote my tale of how heroes happen, *The Whisper of Glocken.* I put Gillian into it as Silky, a name she fancied. With this book I became an annoyance to my family and friends, for I got so immersed in my little people's simplicity that I automatically transposed what people said into Minnipin speech. "Inadequate shelving facilities plague university library," Paul would read from a newspaper headline. "Mmmm," I would say, at once translating into Minnipin, "the real trouble is there's not enough room for the books."

Anglia Television in England produced *The Whisper of Glocken* in a thirteen-week series, which appeared on BBC in 1980. The narrative was read by a well-known storyteller in conjunction with camera work on the 350 illustrations painted by artist John Worsley—a presentation unfortunately not compatible with the American idea that children will look only at cartoons.

By this time we had fallen into a pattern of living abroad every third year or so. The plan of action was for Paul to apply for a fellowship to carry on his research for further biographies in England while we madly saved money towards the following year in case he got the grant. He always did, and off we went. We always had to borrow money to get home again, which meant that the following year we had to pay back the borrowing. The second year we patched the roof and bought shoes for the whole family so that in the third year we could start saving towards the next departure in case the grant came through.

We weren't the only people waiting out a grant. In 1960 our close friends Jeanne and Arvin Wells and their daughter Leslie (Douglas appeared later), applied for a Fulbright fellowship to Germany. Jeanne and I gathered up textbooks and began to study German, Jeanne for practical use in case Arvin's grant came through, I for the pleasure of tackling another language. I was still studying Russian on my own, but my tongue didn't take easily to the exasperating coming-and-going verbs, and it wasn't a very jolly language. German was jolly. Jeanne became fluent, especially after a year in Germany, and I read a lot of good German novels and plays while she was gone. It has always been easier for me to read or write a language than to speak it, probably because, as in writing, I prefer to correct my mistakes before making my words public.

Paul's next grant started in 1961, just as the Wellses were to return home from Germany, so we met them in Cherbourg and the two families spent an idyllic month traveling round northern France and southern England until the Wellses took ship at Southampton and the Kendalls settled into an apartment in Highgate village. Gillian was accepted at Byron House, Callie's former school, and Callie went on to Camden School for Girls and soon forgave us this trade-off for her sophomore year at Athens High

School. Paul and I settled down to work on our current books, meet friends at "The Flask" on Sundays, and play tennis with the Houghs whenever the weather was good. Besides Mrs. McAdam as our char, we had acquired a Mr. Sullivan, who "only did floors." We began to feel like real Londoners. At the children's spring break we cruised the Greek Islands, walked the ruins of Troy and Ephesus, and, between mosques, got lost in the Great Bazaar of Istanbul. We ended the school year in July with a glorious beach holiday in Italy, and soon after sailed for home.

When I finished *The Whisper of Glocken* in 1964, the essence of the next book was already more than a shadowy shape in my mind. That summer in Yellowstone National Park *The Firelings* had come bubbling and swirling out of the pink paint pots. I stood so long over the plopping mud that the family thought I must be overcome by the sulphur fumes, but I was seeing a frail, bent-over, none-too-clean speaker of oracles—rather like the priestess at Delphi, only male. A seth-sayer, he would be called. He would read messages in the mud, and his name would then be MudLar, because he learned from the mud. All this I read in the blup-blup-and-plop of the pink mudpots.

Old Faithful, nearby, eased its way into the plot, and it took little stretch of the imagination to resurrect Mt. Etna's fiery glow from our 1962 travels. Everywhere I went from then until the book was finished produced more parts of *The Firelings.* There were stone memorial tablets by the River Dog in Lebanon and rune stones in Sweden. There was an earthquake in Japan and hissing steam vents along the floor of Kilauea's caldera; lava tubes in Hawaii and lava flows in Kenya. Superstition was its framework, escape and the following of dreams its theme. *The Firelings* was a book that grew and grew, until it got so out of hand and so cumbersome and so long that I had to cut one-third of it before it was finally published in 1982 A.M.P.—eighteen years After MudPots!

Those were eighteen years of disruptions, most of them pleasant, one of them not. Paul's books flourished; honors descended on both of us; we began to prosper. Callie entered Stanford University in the fall of 1964 and married Kerry Ahearn upon graduation, but between those two events we had a last fling together as a family in the summer of 1964, when we traveled by Eurailpasses over the face of Europe. We spent a lot of time laughing together on those trains, and off them. There were the seven hours we spent in Port Bou on the French-Spanish border, waiting for the Madrid train. The remote railway station was without merit, without anything to read except out-of-date timetables, without butter or mayonnaise on yesterday's gangrenous-shaded ham sandwiches, but with a plethora of flies and heat and overflowing toilets. Our four punched Port Bou tickets are still magnetized to my refrigerator door as a philosophical reminder that even the darkest hours must come to an end.

There was Lisbon, where the hotels were full of delegations and the only rooms available were in the flat belonging to our taxi driver's brother-in-law, whose wife served an all-white dinner: fish in bland white sauce, boiled white potatoes, cauliflower in more white sauce, and a white blancmange for dessert. Flies circled above the table, come to visit from the bathroom that was just across the hall from the dining room. The cats that had been turfed out of our bedrooms yowled and scratched at our doors all night. We left Lisbon the next day on the first train that had four seats.

There was another train, another time, that had been booked twice over out of Florence. It was like a moveable refugee camp outside our compartment; bodies slumped against bodies in the aisles, in the other compartments, in the restrooms. The latter were reluctantly vacated as needed.

Through setbacks and advances alike that summer, I happily studied Chinese from the textbook I'd bought at Foyle's in London just before we set off, for I had vowed to surprise my friend Ming with a Christmas card written in Chinese characters.

This was the beginning of a long and happy relationship with the Chinese language. In London that fall, BBC radio obliged with weekly short lessons in spoken Mandarin, and I haunted London bookstores in search of mostly nonexistent character texts. Writing Chinese characters satisfied an interior artistic desire that pedestrian sketching and painting couldn't touch. The Christmas card went off to surprise Ming in December, but I continued to get up at six every morning, when the world was quiet, to work Chinese into my day.

Callie flew to London to spend her Christmas holidays with us, but the following spring we had to leave her out of our Nile River cruise from Luxor to Aswan Dam, and felt very guilty about this, our first trip without her. In the Cairo airport, as our flight to Luxor was delayed, we followed a crowd to the visitor's balcony, where small paper flags were passed out to everybody. We waved ours enthusiastically with the rest as a yellow-and-white plane landed and an important-looking official debarked. We had just helped to welcome President Nyerere of Tanzania. Flying back to Cairo from Aswan, one of the two propellers of our plane stopped going round, and we

Easter Island, 1978. "It was even more than I had dreamed."

had to land at Luxor and wait for another plane to come from Cairo to get us. Almost twenty years later the same thing happened to the small plane I was on in southern China, although we made it, edging uneasily past clouds, to our destination in Kunming. A son of President Nyerere was one of the other passengers. It's the sort of coincidence I try to avoid in writing.

When Callie and Kerry were married in 1968, friends asked me what advice I meant to bestow on my daughter. Advice?! Me? Never having been one to dispense maxims except through Muggles' mouth, I spluttered a bit and finally dredged up the only thing I could think of: "When cooking with tomatoes, always add sugar." This bit of wisdom, now oft repeated by the family, went with Callie and Kerry to Kenya, where they spent the next two years in the Peace Corps, teaching school. The remaining Kendalls joined them for a month in the second year to make the rounds of the game parks and lodges. Our rented Land Rover was prone to flat tires. During one of the five valiant tire changes by Kerry the expert, I found a pawprint of a lion in the sandy road, and scooped it up. This bag of dust, clearly labeled "Lion's Pawprint," sits next to my sealed bottle of Kastalian springwater. I find it hard to throw anything away, even jokes. Especially jokes.

In 1970 we said good-bye to our friends in Athens and moved to Lawrence, Kansas, where Paul taught at the University of Kansas, collaborated with Kadi (Charlton) Hinman on a Shakespeare text, put the finishing touches on *Louis XI,* and started writing a novel about sixth-century Gaul. We bought a house that was abuilding and had it carpeted in grey and white shag, which matched our old English sheepdogs so well that we couldn't see where Heather and Daffodil ended and the rug began. Callie and Kerry came home from the Peace Corps and stayed awhile with us before going to live in our peculiar-charm house in Athens, Ohio, in pursuit of further education. We didn't realize then how serious was Callie's determination to return to Kenya. As for us, we loved Kansas with its big blue sky, its fresh air, and its friendliness. As Gillian put it, "Even the boys at school say 'Excuse me' if they bump into you." It was a glorious time, all too short a span.

We had meant to return to Europe in the summer of 1973, but after shipping Gillian off to her favorite horse-and-music camp in Colorado, Paul and I went instead to Maine and settled into a quiet motel on Mt. Desert Island. Paul wrote the bulk of his novel on sixth-century Gaul there, while I climbed all over Cadillac Mountain, for I found it impossible to concentrate on my own book. By August's end, with all of us back home in Lawrence, Paul could no longer ignore his increasingly ill health, and was soon undergoing weekly chemotherapy treatment for lung cancer. In November I was on my way to see him in the medical center in Kansas City when a drunk driver smashed up my car; I paid my visit after a detour through the emergency room, arriving on a gurney at Paul's door with one arm in a cast, a battered face, and a head full of stitches. I had scarcely been settled in my own room for overnight observation when Paul's doctors arrived to tell me they had done everything they could for Paul; there was nothing more. Then Gillian came walking in. She had eluded the kind friend who was looking after her in this emergency and driven posthaste from Lawrence to cheer up both parents.

Malcolm Barnes, Paul's British publisher and our good friend, made the final revisions that Paul didn't have time to do on *My Brother Chilperic,* for he died just ten days later, in the same bleak month of

November.

The following year Callie gave up her cataloguing job at the Ohio University library, Tick (Christopher Kendall) Ahearn was born, Kerry got his Ph.D. at Ohio University and a teaching job at Kansas State, Gillian went off to Stanford, and for the first time since I was born I was fully in charge of my own life and no other.

It was a time in which a decision was called a statement, and everybody was making one. My statement was to pick up Gillian in the summer following her second year of college and take her round the world with me. Another summer we went to Russia and East Berlin and Poland, rather like fitting the last pieces into our jigsaw puzzle of Europe. My taste in countries, however, ran to the strange, the exotic, the stuff of fantasy. When Gillian developed her own private life with her college friend Rob Dorit, I went off on *my* own. Easter Island had been beckoning me since 1952, when I first saw the stone *moai* standing in brooding loneliness halfway up the stairs in the British Museum. When I finally touched down on the island itself in 1978, it was even more than I had dreamed. Machu Picchu had been splendid, the Galápagos Islands a paradise, but Easter Island was *mine.* I adopted its fantasy, all forty-five square miles of it. Since then I have found other territories that I feel akin to, whose fantasy is my fantasy. These spaces, large and small, range from the Tibetan sky to Samarkand, from Timbuktu in Mali to Japanese neighborhood Shinto shrines. . . .

Another statement was made for me by Ming Lin, who declared that I was ready to translate Chinese into English, and sent me a book of Chinese folktales as a lure. In the meantime I had found a friend in Lawrence, Yao-wen Li, who was working on translations from the Chinese, but felt dissatisfied with her retellings in English. We agreed to put together a volume of translated folktales. This became *Sweet and Sour: Tales from China* and was published in 1978. We have gone on working pleasantly together, with stories appearing in *Cricket* magazine from time to time.

As usual, one more thing led to one more thing. On the strength of *Sweet and Sour,* Sally Hoffman, the program coordinator of the Spencer Museum of Art at the University of Kansas, asked me to retell some Japanese stories for a book to be issued in connection with their exhibition "Japanese Ghosts and Demons." My six tales were published as *Haunting Tales from Japan* in 1985.

Then, astonishingly, I was back in the storybook business, this time with a Chinese folktale that I

"On safari in Kenya with Callie," 1980

couldn't resist, nor could Margaret McElderry, now publisher of Margaret K. McElderry Books with Macmillan. *The Wedding of the Rat Family* is illustrated by James Watts, who clearly understands Chinese rats.

The Firelings had continued to be a seemingly unending part of my life until with one gigantic effort and expert critical readings by both Gillian and Callie, I finished the final revisions on Christmas Eve in 1980. I was in Kenya, with Callie—and Dr. Jim Crees.

Callie and Kerry's marriage had come apart. In late 1979 Callie married Jim, a British veterinary surgeon, who, like Callie, felt that Kenya was home. The wedding was on the "second knuckle" of the Ngong hills just south of Nairobi; the wedding party a mixture of five nationalities and four tribes. We arrived at a lower point by Land Rovers and walked the rest of the way to the top. Two assistants carried the officiating district commissioner's table and chairs for the signing of documents, and Rob Dorit escorted Callie up the final steep slope. Gillian and Rob had arrived one hour before the wedding, flying in from Greece, where they were taking a break between their five years at Stanford and the six to come at Harvard. Those two were married two years later in the garden of a California synagogue, and this time *I* got to give the bride away.

After the Ngong wedding we three stayed on with Callie and Jim, and over Christmas we packed up the Land Rover and went on safari to the game parks. Christmas night we were camped in the Samburu Game Reserve, sorry that we'd seen no lions at all that day, when out of the night the lions came to see *us,* five of them. They arrived shortly after eleven o'clock, just as we had gone to sleep, and they came with a cacophony of roars that shook our tent. We had outrageously camped on the "prowl" perimeter they had marked out for that night. After twenty minutes of heart-stopping roaring behind our tent their bellows diminished; they were moving away. Not for long. Jim had scarcely replenished the campfire when back they came to continue their protest. Again and again until four in the morning, they made our tent their stop between their twenty-minute patrols, venting their rage for an equal twenty minutes. Gillian and I shook with dread the whole night through, but the other three slept. I decided that, in case I lived through the night, as a writer I must remember just how it felt to be afraid of being eaten. I had been in an earthquake in Japan, walked on a volcano floor full of steam vents in Hawaii, flown twice in airplanes with one engine missing, been attacked by bats, and even mugged in Dakar, Senegal—but none of these came close to the horror of imagining that first crunch of a lion's jaws on flesh and bone, *my* flesh and bone. I now wear a lion's pawprint etched on a gold charm to protect me from further frights. Like all good magic, the charm is infallible. Not a single lion has disturbed my sleep since that night.

"Wearing the lion's paw charm in Somalia," 1984

Actually, I wasn't free of *The Firelings* just yet. The Bodley Head edition was published in 1981, but Margaret McElderry wanted further revisions for the Margaret K. McElderry Books edition, with which of course I willingly complied. The book won a Parents' Choice award and the Mythopoeic Fantasy award.

With *The Firelings* at last off my mind, I could get on with the plotting and planning of the next book, which at present has no title beyond its call-up name on my word processor: "fantasy.4." "Fantasy.4" acquired a history before it was three chapters old. I was in Somalia spending my usual Christmas with Callie and Jim and Tick when a BBC team arrived from London to help set up the Mogadishu radio station. Would I consent to be interviewed to give the Somali team some practice? All went reasonably well until I was asked to describe the book plot I was working on at present. At best, I never talk about a book I'm working on, but I was caught. Stumbling quite a lot, I described how big, powerful people were pretending to be helpful to the Minnipins but were in reality interested only in what they could gain from their aid to the little people. At this point I began to sweat. When I got to the part of how the Minnipins forced the Grafs out of their land, I was in something of a panic. Here was proud little Somalia, overflowing with aid groups from big powerful countries and surely resentful of having to accept their charity, and here I sat, fomenting rebellion of the little against the big. Each sentence I uttered was worse than the last. When I finally tottered out of the room, I wondered how long I had before the British Embassy would put me on the first plane out. My fears were set to rest several days later when I ran into the BBC man at a party and he apologized because, alas, something had gone wrong with the taping machine, making the interview one long buzzing sound. I was relieved, but by no means certain that something quite else had not happened to that tape.

There are other things inside the computer begging to be let out as time permits—rough sketches of future fantasies, a bookful of Chinese folktales awaiting final revision, and three African stories that reflect Christmases spent with Callie in Ghana, Kenya, and Somalia. With all that, I trust that "fantasy.4" won't take eighteen years to write!

I still live alone, if one could call having a houseful of books and music, color and sunlight, being alone, but I see my daughters and sons-in-law often, and talk to them on the telephone oftener. Gillian teaches Shakespeare at Smith College; Rob commutes from Northampton to Harvard for his post-doctoral work in evolutionary biology. Callie is now a picture editor at the Cambridge University Press in England; Jim is called to places like Uganda, Nepal, or Lesotho as a short-term consultant; and Tick at thirteen has won a seat with his trumpet in the Junior Symphony of Corvallis, Oregon, where he lives the school year with his father, Kerry, a professor of English.

I drive a Triumph Spitfire because I like the wind in my hair, but I like even more hiking and hobnobbing with my photographer friend Carol Shankel. As the managing editor of the Spencer Museum of Art she has a keen eye for flaws in manuscripts, my own included. Ofttimes, when the world wants putting in order, I meet other friends Gunda Hiebert (business woman) and Ann Cobb (artist) for breakfast at the Paradise. I talk to Ming Lin, still in Athens, every two weeks. Chinese is so much a part of my life that I use chopsticks at meals, though I don't cook Chinese. My favorite dress is jeans and handcrafted tops from far places, and, like Mingy in *The Gammage Cup,* I prefer them well broken-in and lovingly faded. Mowing my lawn—in a maze—is a summer pleasure, as is my fancy of cutting paths through my miniature bamboo grove. I don't have pets or plants to hamper my going to China to climb a sacred mountain or to Outer Mongolia to sleep in a yurt, and I do have a fabulous friend and travel consultant, Faye Watson, who knows just how to get me there.

I have a burning desire to see everything there is to see, but three months of travel a year is almost all I can manage, because I also have a burning desire to write down all the fancies I've brought home in notebooks or in my head. Fantasy, for me, is a different view of life, another way of thinking, a world slightly askew from everyday in Kansas or Ohio, or even California. I find fantasy in Torii gates and ancient Mayan temples, in Vietnamese graveyards and Burmese "lifting stones"; and once in a Cambodian monastery I met a monk with Curley Green's pointed elfin ears.

My life and my writing have always been inextricably entangled. When people who don't know me well ask if I'm still writing, I say, "Am I still breathing?"

"In my Triumph Spitfire," Kansas, 1982

BIBLIOGRAPHY

FOR YOUNG PEOPLE

Fiction:

The Other Side of the Tunnel (illustrated by Lilian Buchanan). London: Bodley Head, 1956; New York: Abelard-Schuman, 1957.

The Gammage Cup (illustrated by Erik Blegvad). New York: Harcourt, 1959; also published as *The Minnipins.* London: Dent, 1960.

The Big Splash (illustrated by Lilian Obligado). New York: Viking, 1960.

The Whisper of Glocken (illustrated by Imero Gobbato). New York: Harcourt, 1965; London: Bodley Head, 1967.

Sweet and Sour: Tales from China (reteller, with Yao-wen Li; illustrated by Shirley Felts). London: Bodley Head, 1978; New York: Seabury, 1979.

The Firelings. London: Bodley Head, 1981; New York: Atheneum, 1982.

Haunting Tales from Japan (reteller). Lawrence, Kan.: Spencer Museum of Art, University of Kansas, 1985.

The Wedding of the Rat Family (illustrated by James Watts). Forthcoming.

FOR ADULTS

Fiction:

The Black Seven. New York: Harper, 1946; London: J. Lane, 1950.

The Baby-Snatcher. London: J. Lane, 1952.

Steven Kroll

1941-

Steven Kroll

To my great surprise last year—had it really been that long?—I found myself invited to my Harvard twenty-fifth reunion. Before these festivities were to take place—and I ended up enjoying them tremendously—a form was sent out to all the old grads. We were asked to provide the relevant details of our lives—occupation, marital status, children, etc.—but we were also asked to write a one-page account of what had happened to us since graduation and, if we wished, include how we felt about the world. Each of these accounts was to appear in a fat red book, to be published and distributed among the classmates before we returned to Cambridge in June.

Summing up twenty-five years in a page seemed, at best, a perilous task. (Commenting on the state of the world was clearly out of the question.) But as I wondered what to do, Holiday House, my principal publisher, and I were asked permission to have three of my books for younger children appear as part of a new Holt reading series. The "unit" devoted to my work was to be called "Surprises," and at first I couldn't understand why. Many of my books are about things going wrong and getting put right, but the element of surprise didn't seem particularly strong in them. Then I had a revelation. Not only was most of my work preoccupied with surprise. My entire life since college had been *nothing but* surprises!

So that's what I wrote my page about. I included the important details of becoming an editor and getting married and divorced and struggling to become a writer, but surprise—how little of my life had gone according to plan—is what I emphasized. And now, as I begin this essay, I am preoccupied with it once again, because even the most conservative among us are continually surprised by life, and no one ever teaches us how to cope. We grow up thinking we are in control, and what a shock it can be when we learn we are not.

Then again, there was nothing at all surprising about my arrival in the world on August 11, 1941, in the Harkness Pavilion of Columbia Presbyterian Hospital in New York City. My father, Julius Kroll, and some friends of my parents were already waiting, and when the baby had successfully made his appearance and they had gone to see him, they adjourned to the hospital cafeteria for a champagne party. For years afterward, my mother would occasionally mention how much she missed being at that party.

There was nothing atypical in that response. My mother, Anita Berger Kroll, was always a genuine enthusiast. Throughout my childhood, it was she who became den mother of the Cub Scout troop, supported me in everything I did, and gave me the confidence to do well.

Even after my father died, when I was thirteen, the enthusiasm never dimmed. Instead, it found new paths to follow. My father had been a diamond importer, with offices at 580 Fifth Avenue in Manhattan. For a year after his death, my mother ran the business. Then, having decided not to continue, she realized she would have to get a job. Enthusiastically, she decided to attend the Speedwriting Institute and

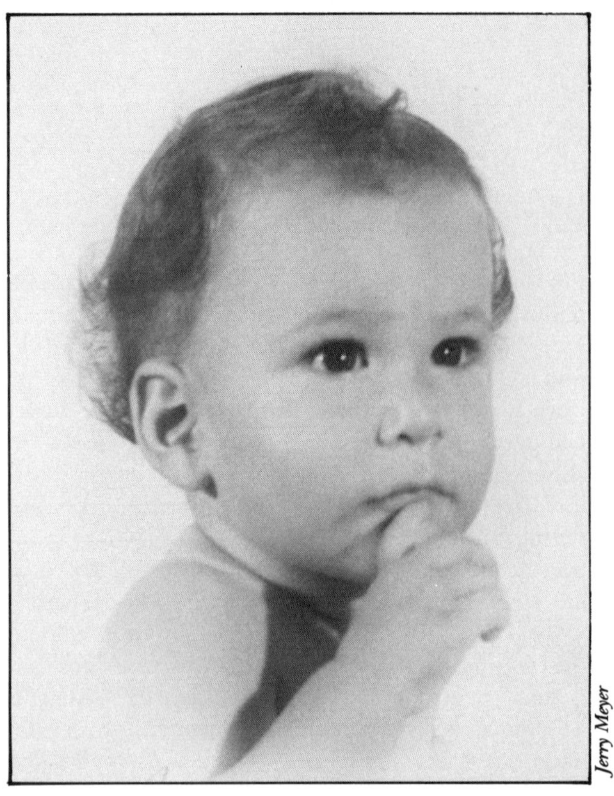

Steven, 1941

learn their ABC shorthand.

The school liked her so much that when she finished the course, they offered her a job as a registrar. For the next twenty years, as registrar, director of the Brooklyn school, and eventually regional director of the New York office, my mother was the force behind Speedwriting's success. When she finally retired—because ITT had bought the company and they discovered she was over sixty-five—the place went into an instant decline.

But even in retirement, my mother continued her enthusiasms. Always a liberal Reform Jew, she became active in the Community Church, a nonsectarian Unitarian/Universalist church in New York City. For several years, she was chairperson of the Church Council, and up until she died, at eighty in 1984, she continued to do all the publicity for a little Off-Off-Broadway theater, attached to and sponsored by the church, called the Theater Off Park.

I'd be at home relaxing, and the phone would ring. "Steven," I would hear, "there's an opening next week and a party afterwards. You have to come."

The play would sound a little questionable, not quite my sort of thing. "Well, Mother . . ." I would say.

"Come on," she'd say, "you'll love it. We'll go out for coffee afterwards, or maybe some dinner."

And I would go, of course, and sometimes it would be great and sometimes it would be terrible, but what it actually was never mattered a bit. My mother's affection for the cast, the play, the occasion, the young people doing something creative, would transform the evening and make it terrific.

Of course this kind of enthusiasm spilled over into everything. Mother was always finding the latest, interesting, out-of-the-way restaurant, the most exciting, undiscovered Off-Broadway play, the fabulous movie that just happened to be showing around the corner. And of course she wanted to tell you about it because part of the fun was in letting the people she cared about know.

An extension of that excitement involved her love of family. To her, the family came first. She was always close to my grandmother. She maintained a lifelong friendship with her older sister, Beryl. My sister, June, and I were more important than anyone else. And every year at Thanksgiving, the gala family dinner was held at her apartment.

Because my mother felt so strongly about family, the coolness of my father's family toward her was a frequent source of pain. Both my paternal grandparents, Lazar and Bertha Kroll, died before I was born, but pictures of them reveal a stern, unbending couple. He was Prussian, she Viennese, and they had come to this country with their eldest son, Charles, several years before my father's birth in 1895. The best-known story about Lazar was that my father had been forced to drop out of City College after his second year and join the family diamond business, then located on Maiden Lane right off Wall Street, because he refused to become a doctor. (Supposedly, my father had been interested in that most precarious of professions, writing. I often feel I have, in some way, turned that blighted dream into reality.)

But if Lazar and Bertha Kroll had a somewhat sinister quality hovering just beyond my reach, Uncle Charles, Aunt Janet, and Aunt Eve, in all their humorlessness, were very real. I almost never saw them—they were certainly not included at what I thought of as family gatherings—but Charles and Janet shared an apartment in—of all places—our apartment building! This was 277 West End Avenue, a large, gracious, pre–World War II building on Manhattan's Upper West Side. There were two lines of apartments, one off an elevator in the front, one off an elevator in the rear, with a long lobby corridor dividing them. We lived in the front. Charles and Janet lived in the back. During my entire childhood, we never moved. Unfortunately, Charles and Janet

The Kroll family in New York City, about 1925: from left, Gilbert and Eve Kroll Kellner; Julius; Lazar and Bertha; Charles; Janet Kroll Wolff and her husband

never moved either.

Charles was a dogmatic, well-to-do stockbroker. Janet, who seemed not to do anything, was best known for stocking up on horrid little items in Europe, then packaging them up in special department-store boxes and passing them off as gifts from Saks or Lord and Taylor. Occasionally I would be told I had to visit them.

Not at all happy, I would slouch the distance between the two apartments. Upon arrival, the door would open and Aunt Janet would usher me into what felt like total darkness.

Beyond the entrance foyer was a long, dark hallway flanked, on either side, by mahogany bookshelves with glass doors. All the bookshelves were filled with leather-bound books. All the glass doors were locked. Midway along was a small marble table. On the table was a replica of a Greek bronze called *The Discus Thrower.*

Reaching the end of the hallway, I would be sat down in the dark and formal living room and offered "smelly" cheese, usually Port du Salut. This was the one thing Janet knew I liked, and in her only gesture of affection toward me, she always offered it. There was a highly polished piano, but it was never played. Charles would appear, and he and Janet would quiz me about my schoolwork, my parents, and how things were at home. Then I would be allowed to leave.

All of this would seem to indicate that not even the Queen of England would have met with a very warm reception in the Kroll family. Given my mother's history, she never had a chance.

Born in 1903, she had been a beauty in her youth and danced at more than one elegant New York party. She married a wealthy young man, gave birth to my sister, June, and was divorced early. For several years after that, she and June lived on West Eighty-sixth Street in Manhattan with my aunt Beryl, my uncle, Manny Kaufman, their son, Jay, and my grandmother, Libby Silman Berger.

When she eventually married my father, my mother was already thirty-four and June eight. My father was forty-two, a bachelor and man-about-town who had always lived with his parents. It was time my father got out of his parents' house, and my mother was very charming. But attitudes were different then, and my father's family didn't see things that way. Not even his formal adoption of my sister or my arrival four years later made any difference. All the family saw was that my father had married a divorced woman with a child.

Just how much the Kroll family's attitude bothered my mother, it was never possible to say. The subject was never discussed at home, everyone remained cordial, and the Krolls were not very likeable anyway, but my mother's generosity of spirit and love of being liked were obviously wounded.

How could she have Kroll-family stories to tell if none were forthcoming? The question would have been on her mind, because more than anything, I realized long after childhood, my mother was a storyteller.

I did my first piece of real writing when I was in the sixth grade. It was an autobiography (complete with pictures), and my teacher, Mrs. Carey, told me afterwards that if I wanted to be a journalist when I grew up, she knew some people I should contact. I wrote my first fiction when I was thirteen and went for a walk in the rain along the outer edge of Central Park. The glistening streets looked as if they were made of glass, and I rushed home and without removing my raincoat pulled out the old Remington portable and wrote a story that began, "The world is made of glass, layer upon layer of glass, like the glass in the doors of the West End Plaza Hotel."

Even though I went for years believing I couldn't be a writer because writers were like gods and I wasn't at all like a god, I always felt that those two moments were the ones that put me in touch with what it meant to be a writer. They made me understand how delicious it was to put words on paper and how much I enjoyed telling stories. Only much later did I realize I was wrong, that although those two moments had been important, it was really my mother's storytelling that had piqued my interest in language and stories and begun my lifelong fascination with the written and spoken word.

Around the dinner table, at holiday gatherings and on lazy winter afternoons, my mother told stories. Needless to say, the stories she enjoyed telling most were about her family.

Her mother, my grandmother, had grown up in St. Mary's, Pennsylvania. She was one of nine children, and her father, my great-grandfather, had founded the first department store in town. The only Jewish family in Catholic St. Mary's, all the girls were educated at the local convent. Years later, when I went to visit my great-uncle, Jack Silman, I found him living alone in the big old Silman-family house on Main Street. In his seventies and with five or six choices available, he still slept in the smallest bedroom. He had been the youngest in the family, and that had always been his room.

My mother's father, my grandfather Simon Berger, had come to work in the store. Mother had been born in St. Mary's, but Simon moved his family to New York—and an apartment in the Bronx—when she was three. By then there were three daughters: Beryl, Anita, and the eldest, Reva, who would die of diptheria at eleven. Simon had a men's clothing store in the Bronx and was beloved by everyone. I always wished I'd been able to meet him.

Stories galore came out of all this, but the one my mother liked telling most was about her grandfather, Hyman Silman.

It began with his arrival in New York from a village in Russia called Romshashock. He hated New York—the crowds, the dirt, the noise—and decided to leave. But he had only twenty dollars in his pocket. Where could he possibly go?

He went down to Grand Central Station, strode up to the ticket counter, and asked the clerk: "Where can I go for twenty dollars?"

"Where would you like to go?" the clerk replied.

"Where can I go for twenty dollars?" Grandfather Silman asked again.

"Sir," said the clerk, "you must tell me where you'd like to go. Then I will sell you a ticket."

Grandfather Silman drew himself up. "Where can I go for twenty dollars?" he asked once more.

At this point the clerk was totally exasperated. He looked at his chart. "St. Mary's, Pennsylvania," he declared.

"Fine," said Grandfather Silman. "That's where I'll go."

I'd like to think that the spirit that allowed me to

Miller Art Photo Shop

"My grandmother Libby Silman Berger, with my mother, Anita, before she became a Kroll," Atlantic City, about 1925

"My parents, Julius and Anita Kroll, on their honeymoon," April 1937

struggle through years of rejection to my particular success as a writer was based, at least in part, on the kind of peculiar determination revealed in this story. But then, my mother showed her own kind of determination when she was widowed in her fifties, and my father had his special strengths as well.

My father was a man who knew what he wanted. Thwarted in his choice of career, he wanted to do well for his family. At the same time, he wanted his family to do well for him.

Sometimes this fierce desire to succeed became too much. In his insistence that my sister and I do well, he could make us feel that nothing we did was ever good enough. Even though I followed through and was always a top student, there were times when my mother had to take my father aside and say, "Go easier."

There was a special kind of love between my parents, but my father's principles were so strong, his determination and integrity so great, that there were moments when he would get terribly frustrated. There were arguments, seldom in front of me but often within hearing distance of my room. It is a legacy I have managed to overcome, though that fierce devotion to principle and that desire to continue doing well, I will carry with me always.

My father was a tall man, and quite robust in his later years. He had a mustache and wore three-piece suits, a homburg, a watch chain, and a Patek-Philippe watch with an alligator band that is now my own. Always handsome and elegant in a way I don't mind emulating, he spent a lot of time traveling, mostly to Antwerp and Amsterdam, to buy diamonds. Toward the end, he sometimes went by plane, but mostly he traveled by ocean liner. The romantic names of ships—the *Rotterdam,* the *Statendam,* the *Mauretania*—floated through my consciousness. Frequently my mother went along on these journeys, and there were always champagne parties in the staterooms before sailing. Of course I was too young to attend these parties. I stayed home and was looked after by my sister, who at twelve years older than I was more like a second mother than a sister, or by our housekeeper, Ayrie Smith.

My sister, June, was never very happy about these absences of our parents. When she went to the shipboard parties, she was often uncomfortable. I remember the ship names and the visits of glamorous European friends. I remember my father being away and my mother sometimes going, too, but for some reason it doesn't seem as if anyone was ever away for very long. I never had any of that sense of deprivation or abandonment that comes with having parents not at home. Perhaps it's because my sister, by being there, did such a good job.

And when my parents were around, my mother was always attentive—and sometimes there were terrific things to do with my father.

The best was baking. For some reason, my dapper, world-traveling father was an avid baker. He loved nothing more on a Sunday afternoon than to put on his apron and get down to the delectable business of baking his famous sand torte or orange chocolate-chip cake or brown edge cookies. Mother was always called on to assist—she continued baking these specialties herself after my father's death—and I, though also given the title of assistant, was really there to lick the mixing bowl. My father's favorite expression was "When there's a boy in the house, have a cake in the house," and there almost always was.

Second best was going to the office. Because my father imported diamonds, his office at 580 Fifth Avenue had a bulletproof door. You rang the bell, opened a normal, clouded glass, office door, and stepped into a little vestibule. My father's secretary slid up a panel that revealed a bulletproof window. She scrutinized you to be sure you were okay and then painstakingly unlocked the heavy inner door.

Inside was the view of Fifth Avenue and my father's mahogany desk with the black-enamel and gold pen set and the pictures of the family and the cream-colored clay mouse I had made and glazed in sculpture class. There was the Deer Park watercooler with the spigot that turned and the dome filled with water that gurgled as you turned the spigot. And then there were the scales.

They were jeweler's scales. They were small and delicate, and my father weighed diamonds on them. I would watch him weigh the stones, never quite understanding the meaning of carats, and I would be enthralled.

As marvelous as these moments were, there never seemed enough of them. As much as I felt my mother's involvement in my life, I felt my father's remoteness. He seemed always to be there urging me to succeed but seldom there just for fun. I remember a special walk along the Hudson River one cold and sunlit winter afternoon. I remember a night game at the old Polo Grounds, the first night baseball game I had ever been to. But there isn't too much more.

Part of this was due to the fact that as I grew older and more interested in being with my father, my father grew less and less well. He developed a heart condition, had several heart attacks, and eventually died of one in 1955, at the age of fifty-nine. I always felt that his inability to control his temper had played a part in his condition, but for many years, I also felt, quite mistakenly, that I had been indirectly responsible for his death.

This was how I remembered my father's last day. The two of us spent a quiet Sunday afternoon at home alone. For some reason, we decided to have soft-boiled eggs and toast for dinner. After eating, we sat in the living room—a comfortable, warm room with bookshelves, a red couch, and two blue easy chairs—and talked. I said something—I don't know what—that angered my father. He got so angry he began having a heart attack. My mother rushed in and helped him to bed. She called the doctor. The doctor came. There was some commotion and muffled conversation. When I woke up the next morning, I was told my father was dead.

Years later, when I was almost thirty, I wrote the second of three wildly experimental, unpublished, adult novels. In the book was a character called The General, who might or might not have been dead. The General was based on my father, and the way in which he might or might not have died was more or less the description I have given.

I showed the manuscript to my mother, to whom I showed everything I wrote. When she had finished her reading and we sat down in her apartment to talk, she immediately brought up The General and his death.

For the first time, we actually discussed what had happened the day my father died. I had never discussed my fears or feelings of guilt with anyone, and although I hadn't intended the subject to come up in this way, I was both pleased and relieved that it had.

My mother said that I was entirely wrong, that my father's last day had been totally different from what I had imagined. It had rained, she said, and we'd spent time looking out the window. The three of us had baked a cake together and had felt very close. The heart attack had been completely unexpected, and my father had died peacefully in his sleep.

Of course I realized that my mother might have been saying these things to make me feel better, but once I'd gone over them in my mind, I knew she had not. If my fears had had any foundation, she would have wanted me to deal with them.

This conversation eliminated any feelings of blame I might have had with regard to my father's death, but it wasn't until 1983 and the publication of *Take It Easy!*, my first novel for young adults, that I really came to terms with that death.

I came to writing for young adults by a route both circuitous and—incredibly—connected to my childhood. Alice Miller Bregman, a longtime children's book editor now turned children's book reviewer, had grown up at 277 West End Avenue at the same time I had. Our parents had known each other, and we were about the same age. Somewhere there was even a photograph of the two of us side by side in our baby carriages. Alice and I had known each other only slightly during those growing up years. Mostly we had run into each other visiting with Tony, the night doorman in the building, on our way home from weekend dates in high school. It was completely by coincidence that we both found ourselves in children's books.

In the late 1970s, I was back in New York from four years in Maine and starting to make a reputation as a writer of picture books. I was living on West Eleventh Street in Greenwich Village, in the same cozy apartment I'm living in now. One morning the telephone rang. It was Alice, then an editor at Delacorte Press. Would I like to have lunch?

I hadn't seen her in a long time and wondered what this might be about. But a struggling writer is not too likely to refuse a nice lunch with a friendly editor. Besides, I was flattered. Of course I said yes.

Alice took me to lunch at Le Bistro, one of the classier New York restaurants. We had a marvelous talk, and in the midst of it, she began asking me about those adolescent years when we kept running into each other visiting Tony. She'd never really known what was going on with me then, she said. She wanted me to tell her now.

So I told her, and when I was through, she said, "You know, a lot of that would make a wonderful novel."

I was struck dumb, remembering my earlier failed experiments. "But I'm not writing novels," I said. "I'm writing picture books."

"You should think about doing a novel," said Alice.

I went home, thought about it, and got distracted by picture-book projects. A year later the telephone rang. It was Alice. Would I like to have lunch?

We had another marvelous lunch. Again Alice asked if I would write the novel. Again I said I would think about it.

And once again I thought about it and did nothing.

Another year passed, and the phone rang a third time. By now I was starting to get embarrassed. When, over lunch, Alice said she thought she might be able to get me some option money from Delacorte if I would send her a proposal letter for a novel, what could I do but agree?

I wrote the proposal letter, but it was too late for the option money. Alice was just leaving Delacorte and could do nothing about the project. But at this point I was hooked. I wrote the book anyway, and it caught up with Alice at Scholastic/Four Winds Press. She bought it for them, and after a lot of rewriting and careful editing, it was eventually published.

Take It Easy! is a fiction. Only a few of the incidents have any basis in reality. But on a gut level, the novel is about the horrible time I had in high school and the boy who made my life miserable during those years. Thrown into the middle is the question of how, as a teenager, you cope with your father's death.

Nick Warner, the central character in the book, is fifteen when his father dies. I was thirteen, but thirteen going on twenty-one. Nick's father is a hard-driving, perfectionist New York lawyer in his forties. My father was fifty-nine but fit all those other characteristics except lawyer. Nick's father seems as remote as mine always did, and when he dies, Nick is forced to deal with the same feelings of loss and humiliation I had to deal with. Like me, Nick refuses to go to the cemetery after attending his father's funeral. Like me, he runs off and—without thinking—goes back to school.

Take It Easy! went through a number of rewrites. New material was written for the beginning. Other parts of the book were moved around. The whole last section, set in a summer camp, was dropped—and eventually became the basis for my second young-adult novel, *Breaking Camp.* Through all the rewriting, the portion of the book that deals with Nick's father's death never changed. It got moved around a bit, but I had finally come so fully to terms with my father's death and the feelings surrounding it that my expression of those feelings came out whole, all of a piece, immutable.

With so much of my emotional life as a teenager coming into focus in *Take It Easy!,* the one thing that was missing was a relationship with a sister. The book had no need of a sister and no room for one, but my own relationship with my sister was very important to my growing up.

By the time I was old enough to be aware of her, June was herself a teenager. A few years after that, she was a college student, playing Titania in *A Midsummer Night's Dream* at Hollins College and then returning home, for her final two years, at the Columbia School of Painting and Sculpture.

My sister was going to be a painter (though she eventually became and remains a highly successful fabric designer). She was a red-haired free spirit who wore bizarre costumes to costume balls, had strange, intriguing boyfriends, and took me everywhere, sometimes even on her dates.

But best of all were the times we spent in her room. I was allowed to sit in a plaid chair and read or

Steven, with his sister, June, on Riverside Drive, New York City, 1942

strum my guitar (which I was never very good at practicing) while June painted and talked to me about art and adventure. To prove the point, there is even a June Kroll portrait of Steven Kroll in chair with guitar. I think it was there and then that I got my earliest introduction to art and culture and first saw the possibility of becoming an artist. And even though it took me years to make that choice, it was in my sister's room that I think I realized I had one.

Early on, however, the whole question of our rooms involved a different kind of choice.

The apartment at 277 West End Avenue was large and spacious, with seven rooms. Through the front door, you entered an ample foyer, with the kitchen, pantry, dining room, and maid's room on the right and the living room on the left. On the other side of the foyer was a long hallway, with two bedrooms (the first with its own bathroom) on the left and another bedroom at the end on the right. All the rooms on the left faced West End Avenue. All the rooms on the right faced a back courtyard, though if you looked out the window of the back bedroom on the right, you could glimpse, through a crack between buildings, Riverside Drive and the Hudson River. The two back bedrooms, left and right, shared a bathroom between them.

I dwell on the details of the apartment because it occupies an important place in my imagination. Whenever an urban apartment or child's room appears in a story of mine, more often than not it resembles where I grew up. In two illustrated books—*Is Milton Missing?* (my first published picture book) and *T.J. Folger, Thief* (an easy-to-read mystery)—the apartment was consciously in my mind as I wrote, though inevitably the artists involved represented it differently in the pictures. In *Take It Easy!,* the apartment is more or less there, but it's located not at Seventy-third street and West End Avenue but in a building at Seventy-ninth and Broadway.

When I was little, my bedroom was the one in the front on the left, the one with its own bathroom. I really loved this room. It had lots of light, a dark-blue linoleum floor, and two closets. I would set up a row of chairs, install myself in a blue leather one at the end, and imagine I was in a boat sailing on a deep blue sea. When I got a few years older, I would climb up the shelves along the side of one of the closets, reach the top shelf that ran all the way across, stretch out around the light bulb, and daydream for hours. Sometimes my mother would come into the room and wonder where I was.

In those years, my sister's room was the back bedroom on the right. It was a bit smaller and a lot darker. It had that weird, almost nonexistent view of the Drive and the Hudson and a bathroom to share with our parents. When I was about five, my sister decided she wanted my room.

Somehow she convinced me that this was a good idea. Her reason, as I recall, was that she needed more light for her painting, but I was so devoted to her, the reason wouldn't have mattered.

And I took immediately to my new room. It was more out of the way, more private, and it became my sanctuary. Once I had permission, it was where I listened Friday nights to "The Lone Ranger" and "The Fat Man" on the radio and later—under the covers, with the volume turned low so no one could hear—to Johnny Addy announcing "The Friday Night Fights." It was where, on Sunday afternoons, I listened to "The Shadow" and "True Detective Mysteries" and imagined that the escaped criminal announced as "somewhere in your vicinity" at the beginning of "True Detective Mysteries" was climbing through my window. It was where I hung my horse-show ribbons (won at summer camp) and kept my rows of plastic antique cars (made out of Revel model kits) and my model airplanes. It was also where I kept my green-and-white bike and did my studying and had my bookcase full of books.

In retrospect, my childhood reading was a little unorthodox. The first book I can remember loving was Dr. Seuss's first picture book, *And to Think That I Saw It on Mulberry Street.* I never owned a copy, but I spent hours, at the age of six, poring over the text and the pictures at a large oak table in the children's section of the public library at Amsterdam Avenue and Eighty-first Street.

It was the fantasy I loved, and even though I

have written as many realistic stories as I have those that are not, fantasy remains especially close to my heart.

After *Mulberry Street,* my favorite book became an odd little story by Al Graham called *Timothy Turtle.* (I'd always thought this book was about a turtle who triumphed over adversity and climbed a mountain. When I looked at it again last year, it turned out to be about a turtle who didn't quite climb the mountain but believed the publicity that said he had!) And then there were the Grimm and Andersen fairy tales and *Millions of Cats* and *The Little Engine That Could* and *Ferdinand the Bull* and *Tubby the Tuba* (which was also on a record) and *Little Toot* and of course *Winnie-the-Pooh* and eventually *Bambi* and *Alice in Wonderland.*

But before I graduated to *The Adventures of Huckleberry Finn, The Catcher in the Rye,* and *The Great Gatsby,* books I first read around the age of twelve and still count among my favorites and most important influences, I took a detour into dog and horse stories.

I had two dogs growing up. The first, a delightful, fuzzy, little mutt called Suzette, was given away when I was at summer camp and my father had one of his heart attacks. The second, a cocker spaniel puppy called Spike, was given away after he nipped my father's ankle. Those reasons provided the official explanations for the dogs' departures, but it always seemed to me that the real reasons were that my mother didn't especially like animals and was probably afraid of them. It was perhaps out of this knowledge that I became absorbed in the novels of Albert Payson Terhune.

There were many of them, and I had over a dozen. Terhune had a collie breeding farm in New Jersey, and almost all the books were about collies who did heroic things. All these collies—precursors of Lassie that they were—seemed pretty much the same dog, but that didn't bother me. As I recall, the most famous of the books was the first: *Lad: A Dog.*

Then there were the horse stories. I'd become very involved with horses at summer camp, so it seemed natural for me to want to weep through *Black Beauty.* From there, it was an easy leap to Walter Farley and the "Black Stallion" books.

I had all of them. *The Black Stallion, The Black Stallion Returns,* and *The Island Stallion* were magical to me. I loved the adventures of these spectacular horses, loved the dignity and glamour of their personalities. I wished, over and over again, that I could be part of their world. Just like other kids, I had a whole cabinet full of *Superman, Batman,* and *Archie* comic books (though I hated horror comics and still hate them and horror films even now). But Walter Farley and Albert Payson Terhune were my literary heroes.

Though I never found either one of them at the Corner Book Store, which was on Seventy-second Street between West End and Broadway. It was just down the street and around the corner from my building and across from Manbro's Drug Store, where I drank the best ice-cream sodas in the world.

Mr. and Mrs. Kramer owned the Corner Book Store. They sold books, comic books, magazines, and candy. In what was actually a terribly small space, they also had a lending library. They would let me sit on the floor near the shelves of comic books and look at anything I liked for as long as I liked. Their kindness and the coziness of their store were just the right kind of introduction to the world of books I would eventually want to join.

But even as I enjoyed my reading, I was also an athletic, outdoor kid. West End Avenue in the 1940s and 1950s was a sedate, mostly residential avenue. Except for the tearing down of the Schwab mansion across the street from 277, a sad event that took place when I was about three, zoning regulations have kept it pretty much as it was. But zoning regulations haven't kept the traffic from becoming impossible or, ironically, the increasingly upscale neighborhood from becoming less safe. When I was growing up, you could play, almost unsupervised, on West End Avenue until dark.

The boys and girls from 277 seemed to do exactly that, at least during the months when it wasn't too cold and no one was away at summer camp. Everyone gathered in front of the building after school and on weekends. There were kids from about seven to about twelve. They all more or less knew one another, and many of them played together.

The girls played hopscotch around the corner. The boys played stickball in the side street. There were games of catch and a lot of hanging out on the fenders of parked cars under the occasionally watchful eye of Gordon, the day doorman. But for some reason, what captured the most attention was a narrow ledge that ran along the front of the building.

At its highest point, the ledge was about five feet above the pavement; at its lowest—because the building was on a slight hill—it practically met the ground. It was set at about a forty-five-degree angle to the building, and the idea was to throw a pink rubber ball, called a Spaldeen, in the direction of the angle. If you hit it, the ball would pop up in the air. There were records for who had hit the most pop-ups, who had hit the most in a row, and so on. This endlessly boring activity occupied us for hours.

But I wasn't always hanging out in front of the

"With my green-and-white bike," West End Avenue and Seventy-third Street, 1952

building. Sometimes I was up in the penthouse with my friend Arthur Gordon, dropping water bombs on unsuspecting passersby. (Fortunately we never hit anyone. The penthouse was sixteen floors up!) Sometimes I was learning how to play gin rummy with my friend Paul Funt and his little brother, Butch. And sometimes I was in Riverside Park, just a block away.

I went there to play baseball and to ride my bike along the river, where lots of elderly ladies and gentlemen sat on benches, nodding in the sun. There was a spectacular view of New Jersey and what was then still Palisades Park, an amusement park I loved going to with my Saturday day camp. Sometimes I rode up past the softball diamonds to the boat basin, where fancy yachts and cabin cruisers were always tied up at the dock.

But mostly, in the years before I was twelve, I went to the park to climb my favorite tree and to play cops and robbers. The tree was always wonderfully difficult to climb. Near the top, it had a horizontal branch, almost totally covered in leaves, where I could sit and dream. (I had a similar spot in Central Park, a little nest near the transverse at Eighty-first Street and Central Park West, but I wasn't there so often and it wasn't as special as the tree.) When I was through dreaming, it was always fun to jump from the branch to the ground, though the distance seemed fairly great and I had to be careful how I landed.

Years later, as an adult, I went back to look at my favorite tree. It was very small, but my memories of that special branch and summoning the courage to jump down were in no way diminished by the discovery.

When we played cops and robbers, I was always the robber. When we played cowboys and Indians, I was always the Indian. Cops and cowboys had to chase robbers and Indians. Robbers and Indians got to figure out where to run and where to hide. Cops and cowboys seemed dull and unimaginative. Robbers and Indians were the artists of Riverside Park.

When I got to be older than twelve, and especially when I reached high-school age, the park took on a different dimension. By then a playground had been built and in the midst of the playground a group of basketball courts. Basketball was the one sport I was never good at, but the kids in the neighborhood all seemed to hang out at the courts and that was where the girls were. So frequently on weekend afternoons, I would be found trying to get into a game and talking to the girls, most of whom were much more interested in the big-time jocks scoring the baskets.

The world of the courts was never my world. I was always too much of a loner. Except for my position as center halfback on my high-school soccer team, the sports I liked best were individual sports: tennis and horseback riding. Though I loved the illusion of being part of the gang and loved going to the Optimo candy store on Seventy-eighth and Broadway to talk about the games, the moments I loved best at the courts were when someone suggested going to play stickball—one-on-one—at the baseball diamond down by the railroad yards.

The cement diamond was so old and full of cracks, it was almost never used for baseball anymore. Behind it was a fence concealing abandoned New York Central railroad cars. Above them, mounted on huge pillars, soared an expanse of the West Side Highway. You would stand at home plate with your broomstick bat. Your opponent would stand at the pitcher's mound and hurl a Spaldeen across the plate. There were various rules for hits, but the only way you could hit a home run was to loft that Spaldeen onto the highway.

There were several of us who played, and the only statistic we ever kept was for home runs. I never hit the most in a season, but I was second once, with fifty-two. Even now, my mind reels as I imagine all those Spaldeens bouncing onto cars on the West Side Highway.

When I wasn't in the park or in front of my building, there were all the stores on Broadway, there was tennis in Central Park, and then, of course, there were the movies.

The neighborhood had two fabulous movie theaters within walking distance of my apartment building. They were cavernous and old and filled with the elaborate ornament and detailing of a bygone era. They were the Loew's Eighty-third Street (now torn down and rebuilt as an antiseptic six-plex) and the Beacon at Seventy-fourth and Broadway (defunct as a movie house for years and now constantly in danger of passing into history). As a teenager and before, these were the places I spent rainy Saturday afternoons.

I saw *Kismet* and *The Red Badge of Courage.* I saw *Gentlemen Prefer Blondes, Three Coins in the Fountain, The Day the Earth Stood Still, The Boy with Green Hair* (which terrified me), *The Red Shoes* (which terrified me even more), *High Noon, Shane,* and a million other westerns (all of which I loved). I found movies wonderfully entertaining, but I could never take them seriously the way I could books. Of course, once I was a teenager, the movie was no longer the point anyway.

The trouble with the movie theaters was they both had children's sections. Until you were sixteen, you were not allowed to sit anywhere else, and if you did, there was a stout, muscular matron in a white uniform and carrying a flashlight whose specific job it was to track you down. Everyone tried to sneak into the balcony to make out. At one time or another, everyone got caught and endured the humiliation of being summarily dispatched downstairs to you know where.

By the early 1950s, of course, TV was beginning to compete with the movies. At the age of ten or eleven, I remember watching early children's shows like "The Magic Cottage," "Captain Video and His Video Rangers," and "Kukla, Fran, and Ollie" on my friend Arthur's small set with its round screen. But for me and my family, TV in those years seemed curiously irrelevant. It was a kind of reverse snobbery, but I remember being very proud to be the last one in my seventh-grade class to get a TV. And then we only got one because my sister, with money from one of her first jobs, gave it to our parents as a present.

After the TV arrived, we all watched a little. We watched "Playhouse 90" and "Robert Montgomery Presents" and the "Hallmark Hall of Fame." We watched and were appalled by the Army-McCarthy hearings, and then there were the ritual, Sunday-night "TV suppers" when we would all gather round for "Lassie" and Ed Sullivan.

But TV never really became important to us. Even toward the end of her life, my mother hardly watched. My sister and I don't watch very much now. We have always been too busy, and in those years, for reasons unknown, I would much prefer to come home from school, spread some Arnold Brick Oven white toast with butter, pour myself a Coke, stretch out on the green chaise lounge in my mother's bedroom, and listen to those late-afternoon radio programs—"Sky King," "Stella Dallas," and "Lorenzo Jones and His Wife Belle."

But I was seldom home from school early enough for such indulgences. I spent nursery school and kindergarten at the Walden School, still a progressive private school here in New York City. After that, I went to P.S. 87, still on Seventy-seventh Street and Amsterdam Avenue (though in a new building), for first and second grades. By the time I had skipped third grade and reached Hunter College Elementary School, a school for so-called "gifted children," I was already committed to extracurricular activities.

At Hunter, I played punchball and kickball after school. I helped put together a school paper and joined a radio workshop, where we taped our own radio programs and at one point I got to play the part of Oscar, the talking seal. I was the captain of the monitors, class president several times, and Santa Claus in the sixth-grade play, though I was absolutely mortified when my sleigh carrying the presents got caught in the curtain and no amount of tugging would jar it loose.

In school and out, these years were quite idyllic for me. I was surrounded mostly by smart kids. I did my famous autobiography and got praised for it. My principal at P.S. 87 had liked some clay ducks I had made and told my parents I should go to sculpture class at the Museum of Modern Art; I did that, too, every Tuesday afternoon, and even had a piece on display in the museum. One day my mother and I were walking on Fifth Avenue when a man came running up and insisted I be in a movie short on cameras. We both ended up in the short, I was given my first camera (a Brownie), and a few months later, we were on view at our local newsreel theater! I had many friends and even—from fourth through sixth grade—a girlfriend whom I accompanied to school

"With my mother, appearing in a movie short on cameras," 1947

every day. (The boys I knew were not happy about this. They told me I would have to stop seeing Linda Berman or they would no longer be my friends. I stood my ground and prevailed.)

My one bad memory of this time concerns the flooding of the boys' bathroom when I was in sixth grade. No one knew who had done it, but for reasons that were never made clear, I was accused and marched up to the principal's office. The principal, Florence Brumbaugh, was a haughty woman who loved cats and drew a picture of one whenever she signed her name. When it became obvious I knew nothing, she sent me back to class.

Because the culprit was never caught, the stigma of suspicion never quite left me the rest of the year. Since then, except for my closest friends, I have never quite trusted human nature.

But I still loved Hunter. It was with great sadness that at the end of the sixth grade, I prepared myself for McBurney School.

At that time, Hunter didn't allow boys to continue past sixth grade. My parents didn't like the local public junior high school. They didn't have the money for one of the fancy private schools in the city or in Riverdale. McBurney was considered good academically. It was at Sixty-third Street off Central Park West, just a little more than ten blocks from my home. It was under the auspices of the YMCA and eager to have me from seventh grade through high school.

The school was dark and dreary. It was all boys, and half of them were thugs. The atmosphere was relentlessly repressive, and the teachers all seemed incredibly unimaginative or, at best, eccentric.

During my seventh-grade year, the principal of the lower school, who was also the math teacher, decided we would do nothing but math. Most of our other subjects were canceled. We spent endless hours on drills and speed tests in arithmetic. When this fellow was finally fired at the end of the year, he threw open the classroom window and threatened to jump out in front of us.

And so it went. There was the history teacher who rapped you on the knuckles with his pointer if you misbehaved. There was the headmaster who wore white gloves because he had "athlete's foot of the hands," and the martinet of a gym teacher who had no respect for personal privacy, and the English teacher who asked me to grade his papers because he couldn't be bothered. There was the history teacher who always stood with his hands clasped as if in prayer, and briefly, and for me endearingly, another English teacher who loved to talk about how he'd once met Dylan Thomas in a men's room at Princeton.

With rare exceptions, my impression of these teachers was that they didn't much care about what they were doing, that they were just going through the motions. What seems amazing to me is that having such a feeling, I continued to excel.

But I was a very motivated student. I'd been pushed by my father and been told that if I wanted to get into a good college, I would have to do well. I'd decided I wanted to go to Harvard. I set out to do everything I could to get there.

I was valedictorian of my class. I was editor of the school literary magazine, business manager of the newspaper, chairman of the social committee, the leading actor in the drama group, and, as I've mentioned, center halfback on the soccer team. I was a member of every club and honor society. I was also arrogant, self-assured, and not very well liked.

The arrogance, however, concealed a feeling that there was no one in that place whose intelligence

I could trust, no one on whose word I could rely. On examinations, I could never be sure what a teacher might mark me down for. So when I answered an essay question, I included not just the material that was requested but everything I knew about the subject as well. Sometimes I'd be told I didn't need to do this, but it took me a long time to stop.

I also began to notice that the stories I was starting to write at home came out sounding very different from the papers I wrote for school. The writing in the stories was relaxed and economical. The writing in the papers was stiff, contorted, filled with clumsy locutions and subordinate clauses. Without being able to do anything about it at the time, I recognized that a point was being made here, that my way of being in the world was different from the way I was at school.

And outside of school, I seemed to fare better. In my early teens, I was the well-liked recording secretary of a neighborhood boys' group called the Stags. I was bar mitzvahed and confirmed at Temple Rodeph Sholom and made some friends there. Later on, I had other neighborhood friends and girlfriends and went to dances and parties, but what made the biggest impression on me was *Venture* magazine.

Venture was a small, "bohemian," literary magazine published in Greenwich Village. Their editorial board met every other Friday night to read manuscripts out loud and consider them. In my senior year of high school, through a friend of a friend, I was invited to one of their meetings, got invited back, and became an unofficial member of the board.

It was the time of the Beats and smoky coffeehouses and proliferating jazz clubs. After the meetings, most of us would end up at a dive called Emilio's for pizza and beer or at Paul and Dorothy Ryan's on Grove Street. The Ryans were members of the board. They had a tiny apartment, a tiny baby, and Briscoe, a Dalmatian named after the Jewish Lord Mayor of Dublin (because Paul was Irish and Dorothy was Jewish). Paul would make his famous Dagwood sandwiches for all of us, and of course he would have beer, too.

Wherever the group ended up, the talk was of literature and philosophy and went on till dawn. As the sun rose, usually around 6:00 A.M., Paul and I, still talking of Sartre or Kerouac or Mailer, would take Briscoe for a walk in Washington Square Park.

There was no need and no place for arrogance here. These writers were serious professionals, and I was delighted and honored to be accepted by them. There were some big egos and some poor talents to go with the good, but this was my first real exposure to the world of writing, and despite having convinced myself I was going to be a lawyer, I was right at home. My mother didn't even complain about my coming in so late on those special Friday nights.

How splendid it would have been to have been able to transfer those feelings of belonging back to school. But even had that been possible, it would have been made doubly difficult by one boy.

This boy was in my class. Everyone admired him and thought he was terribly smart. He was the ringleader of a clique of smarter, more sophisticated boys called, affectionately, the "Tweed Ring," because they all wore tweedy Brooks Brothers clothes. He had a lot of power in the school, but he was below me in the class standings. He hated me for this and for my arrogance and did everything he could to make my life miserable.

When I first wrote *Take It Easy!,* Kurt Barnes defeated Nick Warner the way this boy always defeated me. By the time I had finished rewriting the book, the novelist's art had taken over from real life. Sticking it to Kurt provided a much more satisfying ending, and as I wrote the words, I felt like cheering.

How I hated McBurney School! But what's extraordinary to me is that I never told my parents. Had I said something, another school would have been found. Instead I—perhaps afraid of risking my number-one ranking—kept on slogging away.

But if there might have been a reason for my saying nothing about how I felt about school, there was really no excuse for my refusal to object to what went on at summer camp. I had gone off to my first sleep-away camp, Alderkill, in Rhinebeck, New York, just before my sixth birthday. I was never homesick, and I loved learning how to ride and play tennis at such an early age. During my third summer at Alderkill, one of the other campers told me about a special riding camp in New Milford, Pennsylvania, called Susquehanna.

Immediately I wanted to go! My parents were impressed that I'd found my own camp. The director came over with interesting slides, and for the next six summers, four as a "horseman" with my own horse to look after and one as a counselor in training, I went.

At first I wasn't popular there either. Eventually I won a best camper award. But even as my fortunes fell and rose, the riding program and the camp's facilities remained terrific. There was just a whole lot else that wasn't so terrific.

On Saturdays, there was a forced dip in a freezing cold lake at 6:00 A.M. There were late-night ritual visits to "haunted houses," where kids were purposely scared and mistreated. There was an annual, late-night walk down the Old Harmony Road,

The author, second from left, as third-place winner in the Camp Susquehanna Horse Show, 1955

where you were shocked by dangling electric wires and, if you were unlucky, thrown naked into a stockade filled with horse manure.

When I came to write about these things in *Breaking Camp,* I pushed them one step further into evil and invented a villain to take the blame. But even now it's hard for me to make sense out of my willingness to accept what went on, summer after summer, for six years. I mentioned it in letters home, but I was never alarmed and never critical enough to make anyone take action.

After the vicissitudes of school and camp, it was a pleasure for me to get to Harvard in the fall of 1958. Cambridge was beautiful, and I was on my own. Just about everyone I met was smart. I had two odd freshman roommates, but I didn't have to spend much time with them. There were fascinating courses, interesting Radcliffe girls, and Widener Library. There were professors whose very names held me in awe, scholars like Perry Miller, Howard Mumford Jones, and Arthur Schlesinger, Jr.

Having begun to realize that I might want in some way to be involved with writing, I decided I needed a firm grounding in things American and took as my major American history and literature. But that was as close as I got to any sort of commitment. When I went to an open meeting of the *Advocate,* Harvard's distinguished literary magazine, the whole staff seemed incredibly effete and I decided not to try out. I became active in the Young Democratic Club and the drama society instead. And when it came to writing courses, I wouldn't go near one.

The writing courses were led by important people. There was even the special English S, led by Archibald MacLeish. I dismissed them all with the excuse that no one could teach you how to write.

Of course there was some truth in that notion, but the real reason why I wouldn't take a writing course at Harvard was my fear that someone would tell me I wasn't any good. Instead, on a fluke, I went to work part-time at Harvard University Press.

All through college, I held a part-time job to help pay my way. At the end of sophomore year, weary of linen delivery and dining-hall cleanup, I stopped by the university employment office. They told me the Press was looking for a "faculty aide."

It meant assisting in every department, and for the next year, that's what I did. Senior year, I did nothing but read manuscripts part-time, but the whole experience, coupled with two weeks' reading manuscripts at the *Atlantic Monthly* at the end of my junior-year summer, convinced me that what I wanted to be was an editor and critic!

My tutor/advisor junior and senior year was Walker Cowen, who later became director of the University Press of Virginia. We had become great friends and even written a paper together one Easter

Harvard graduation, June 1962

vacation. He was the first to really encourage me in my writing and the most important teacher I ever had. When I told Walker about my decision, he said, "Don't be an editor, my boy! Do the writing yourself!"

I wasn't ready to listen. I'd been a dean's-list student but never felt I had a handle on psyching out the professors, the way friends of mine intent on becoming academics seemed able to do. Excluding my friendship with Walker, I seemed in much the same position I'd been in in high school. What I learned outside the classroom seemed much more profitable than what I learned within it. So when graduation rolled around in June of 1962, I was eager to leave for London on the nearest plane and in the spirit of adventure begin a career in publishing!

My contacts at the Harvard Press and the *Atlantic* had given me a list of people to see in New York. Those people had given me a list for London. George Plimpton had offered me an assistant's job in the Paris office of *Paris Review,* but they weren't going to pay me and I wanted to be in London anyway. It took me three weeks of interviewing to turn up several book-reviewing assignments, an associate editorship of *Transatlantic Review,* a full-time manuscript-reader's position at Chatto and Windus Limited (publishers of Aldous Huxley, Iris Murdoch, and Henry Green), and a bed/sitting room in Chelsea (though I later moved to South Kensington and then Hampstead).

I stayed three years. C. Day-Lewis, soon to be poet laureate, was a director of Chatto. He and I became friends. Chatto had bought Leonard and Virginia Woolf's Hogarth Press after World War II. Leonard, in his eighties, was still running it, and I got to know him, too. I got invited to T. S. Eliot's memorial service at Westminster Abbey and saw Ezra Pound, wizened and alone, step out of a Bentley. I was invited to the Society of Bookmen dinner in honor of the American publisher Alfred Knopf's seventy-fifth birthday and heard Knopf thank his hosts while confessing it was only his seventieth birthday. I went to dinner and cocktail parties at the home of Joe McCrindle, editor of *Transatlantic Review,* and met Muriel Spark, William Trevor, and L. P. Hartley. I did book reviews for the *Listener,* the *Times Literary Supplement,* the *Spectator,* and the *London Magazine.* I got promoted to reader/editor at Chatto and traveled around Europe on vacations. I got married.

Her name was Edite Niedringhaus. She was German but had become a British citizen. She was director of foreign and subsidiary rights at Chatto, but before very long and with no background in the field, she was appointed editor of children's books.

Edite and I had been a couple for a year and a half when I got drafted. It was the beginning of the Vietnam buildup, but there was still a Kennedy ruling that said no married men. Neither one of us believed in the war. The recurring growth in my right eye that we thought might get me a medical deferment failed. We made the decision to get married.

A year later, I decided to return to the States. I'd become very comfortable in England, but I'd been reviewing a lot of American books and realized I was getting out of touch. If I was ever going to do any writing, I knew it would have something to do with America. It seemed time to return to New York or Boston.

Edite, of course, came with me. The best job offer I got was as an editor at Holt, Rinehart, and Winston in New York. She became a children's book editor at Pantheon/Knopf and later at Holt. The moment we started work, the Kennedy ruling was rescinded. I got called up by the army once again, but this time the growth in my eye (now long since disappeared) got me off.

With me when I arrived in New York was the manuscript of my first adult novel. I had finished it that summer at Edite's parents' home in Germany.

The author in Paley Park, New York City, 1978

Walker Cowen had written to me frequently in London, saying I must write fiction. I had followed his lead. With high hopes, I got myself an agent and the book went nowhere.

During the three-and-a-half years I spent at Holt, I wrote another novel, over a series of Sundays. It, too, failed to find a publisher. Finally I found myself in a crisis of conscience and had to decide what to do with my life.

We had a new editor in chief at Holt. Shortly after his appointment, I received a manuscript of poems everyone in the department loved. But the editor in chief didn't want management to think he was going to publish books that wouldn't sell a lot of copies. He refused to let me publish (though Random House eventually did and the book was named one of the twenty best of the year by the *New York Times*).

I was furious, but I had to understand that until I became the boss, decisions like this would be made against me regularly. I had a long talk with my agent at the time. He said he believed in me, that I should get out of the business and go away and write while I was still young and unencumbered. Edite and I talked things over. At my suggestion and completely on a whim, we decided to move to Maine the following spring.

Coincidentally, we fell into a big house in North Yarmouth for eighty dollars a month. And for four years I wrote my experimental novels and did book reviews for the *New York Times Book Review* and *Book World.* One year I taught writing at the University of Maine in Augusta, and one summer I taught riding at the local inn, where there was also a stable. Edite did translations from the German, free-lance editing, even worked in a private library in Portland. We kept on struggling and I knew I wouldn't give up, but in all that time, nothing happened with my books.

It became clear we would have to return to New York. Because Edite and other people we knew in children's books had encouraged me, I was now writing for children as well as adults. I needed to be closer to editors. Edite wanted to be back in children's book publishing. I found us an apartment, and she began looking for a job (which she found first at M. Evans and later at Harper before going out on her own as an agent).

One of the people Edite saw on her job hunt was Margery Cuyler, then children's editor at Walker and Company, soon to move to Holiday House. Edite was sure Margery would like my work.

I went to see her. After years of crossed signals, here was instant rapport. Margery took away several of my stories, came back and said she liked my imagination and what I was trying to do in *Is Milton Missing?* and *The Tyrannosaurus Game.* If I would strip those stories back to their original ideas and rewrite them according to her suggestions, she would be interested in publication.

I was overwhelmed. I also went back and did the work. *Is Milton Missing?* (1975) and *The Tyrannosaurus Game* (1976) became my first published books and my first books at Holiday House. Holiday House itself, with John and Kate Briggs at the helm, became like family. Since 1976, I have published books with several other houses, but only at Holiday House have I gone on regularly publishing two books a year. It is also wonderful to be able to count Margery, John, and Kate among my closest personal friends.

In other respects, however, my personal life was not going so wonderfully. Edite and I were divorced in 1978, and the years that followed were not easy. Now, to my delight, everything has turned around again.

In recent years, artists have been coming to me with illustrations and asking if I might write stories to go with them. *Woof, Woof!* began with a picture of a Victorian little girl and a barking bullterrier by Nicole Rubel. *Don't Get Me in Trouble!* began with a dog-food ad Marvin Glass did for the *New York Times.* And the just-published *Looking for Daniela* began with a sketchbook full of drawings by Anita Lobel.

Steven Kroll and Abigail Aldridge, 1988

This past Valentine's Day, I was moping in my apartment. I was sick, and I was alone. The telephone rang. It was Anita. She had just that minute finished the artwork for *Daniela!* Could she bring it over?

I wasn't about to say no. Anita arrived in half an hour, and of course the artwork was beautiful. When I had finished marveling, as we sat and talked about our lives, she said out of the blue, "I think you should meet my friend, Abby."

Abby was Abigail Aldridge, a Broadway costumer and milliner. Anita was having dinner with her that night. Why didn't I bring out a copy of one of my books with my picture on it? Anita would show the book to Abby and ask if it was okay for me to call.

It was okay. I called. We met and are now planning for the future. Could anything be a better surprise than that?

BIBLIOGRAPHY

FOR CHILDREN

Fiction

Is Milton Missing? (illustrated by Dick Gackenbach). New York: Holiday House, 1975; London: Warne, 1978.

That Makes Me Mad! (illustrated by Hilary Knight). New York: Pantheon, 1976.

The Tyrannosaurus Game (illustrated by Tomie de Paola). New York: Holiday House, 1976.

Gobbledygook. (Illustrated by Kelly Oeschli) New York: Holiday House, 1977; (illustrated by Jared Lee) New York: Avon, 1985.

If I Could Be My Grandmother (illustrated by Lady McCrady). New York: Pantheon, 1977.

Santa's Crash-Bang Christmas (illustrated by T. de Paola). New York: Holiday House, 1977; London: Methuen, 1984; Paris: Gallimard, 1984; Madrid: Altea, 1984.

Sleepy Ida and Other Nonsense Poems (poetry; illustrated by Seymour Chwast). New York: Pantheon, 1977.

Fat Magic (illustrated by T. de Paola). New York: Holiday House, 1978.

T. J. Folger, Thief (illustrated by Bill Morrison). New York: Holiday House, 1978.

The Candy Witch (illustrated by Marylin Hafner). New York: Holiday House, 1979.

Space Cats (illustrated by Frisco Henstra). New York: Holiday House, 1979.

Amanda and the Giggling Ghost (illustrated by D. Gackenbach). New York: Holiday House, 1980.

Dirty Feet (illustrated by Toni Hormann). New York: Parents Magazine Press, 1980.

Monster Birthday (illustrated by Dennis Kendrick). New

York: Holiday House, 1980.

Friday the Thirteenth (illustrated by D. Gackenbach). New York: Holiday House, 1981.

Giant Journey (illustrated by Kay Chorao). New York: Holiday House, 1981.

Are You Pirates? (illustrated by M. Hafner). New York: Pantheon, 1982; Paris: Gallimard, 1983; London: Moonlight Publishing, 1986; Madrid: Altea, 1986.

Banana Bits (illustrated by Maxie Chambliss). New York: Avon, 1982.

Bathrooms (illustrated by M. Chambliss). New York: Avon, 1982.

The Big Bunny and the Easter Eggs (illustrated by Janet Stevens). New York: Holiday House, 1982.

The Goat Parade (illustrated by Tim Kirk). New York: Parents Magazine Press, 1982.

One Tough Turkey: A Thanksgiving Story (illustrated by John Wallner). New York: Holiday House, 1982.

Woof, Woof! (illustrated by Nicole Rubel). New York: Dial, 1982.

The Hand-Me-Down Doll (illustrated by Evaline Ness). New York: Holiday House, 1983.

Otto (illustrated by Ned Delaney). New York: Parents Magazine Press, 1983.

Pigs in the House (illustrated by T. Kirk). New York: Parents Magazine Press, 1983.

Toot! Toot! (illustrated by Anne Rockwell). New York: Holiday House, 1983.

The Biggest Pumpkin Ever (illustrated by Jeni Bassett). New York: Holiday House, 1984; London: Deutsch, 1986.

Loose Tooth (illustrated by Tricia Tusa). New York: Holiday House, 1984.

Happy Mother's Day (illustrated by M. Hafner). New York: Holiday House, 1985.

Mrs. Claus's Crazy Christmas (illustrated by J. Wallner). New York: Holiday House, 1985.

Annie's Four Grannies (illustrated by Eileen Christelow). New York: Holiday House, 1986.

The Big Bunny and the Magic Show (illustrated by Janet Stevens). New York: Holiday House, 1986.

Don't Get Me in Trouble! (illustrated by Marvin Glass). New York: Crown, 1987.

I'd Like to Be (illustrated by Ellen Appleby). New York: Parents Magazine Press, 1987.

I Love Spring (illustrated by Kathryn Shoemaker). New York: Holiday House, 1987.

It's Groundhog Day! (illustrated by J. Bassett). New York: Holiday House, 1987.

Happy Father's Day (illustrated by M. Hafner). New York: Holiday House, 1988.

Looking for Daniela (illustrated by Anita Lobel). New York: Holiday House, 1988.

Newsman Ned Meets the New Family (illustrated by Denise Brunkus). New York: Scholastic Inc., 1988.

Oh, What a Thanksgiving! (illustrated by S. D. Schindler). New York: Scholastic Inc., 1988.

FOR YOUNG ADULTS

Fiction:

Take It Easy! New York: Four Winds, 1983.

Breaking Camp. New York: Macmillan, 1985.

Multiple Choice. New York: Macmillan, 1987.

Emily Arnold McCully

1939-

Emily Arnold McCully, 1988

I was born left-handed. This won me a surprising amount of special attention, perhaps because so many adults of that period had been forced to use their right hands in school. It meant that my mother, seeing me arch my fist over my paper, smudging all in its path, stood by like a drill sergeant until I learned to hold my pencil like everyone else—but in my south paw. It meant that I was seated at the end of the table at meals, was a switch-hitter, could not use a scissors or an iron properly, and still have trouble paring a potato. Being "gauche" was the first of many ways I relished being set apart, a maverick, and, I hoped, exempted from a few of life's onerous rules and regulations. Sometimes I got away with that notion, but not nearly as often as I tried.

My hometown was Galesburg, Illinois, a humming, medium-sized, perfectly American, prairie town—railroad center, home of Knox College, site of a Lincoln-Douglas debate and underground-railway stop, and the birthplace, also, of Carl Sandburg, who had been a friend and mentor to my father and was the subject of many of my first portrait drawings.

My parents had met at Knox, playing leads in school plays. My father went on to New York, to act and write for some of the very first network radio shows, in 1928. My mother joined him, after a year as a scholarship student in Paris. She was gifted, too, as an actress and singer, but some failure of nerve apparently kept her from pursuing a career.

They were loyal alumni, and when, in 1937, he was asked to write and produce the Knox Centennial celebration, they moved back to Galesburg. I don't know why they decided to stay. I was born there in July 1939, and we lived in a rambling frame house on North Cherry Street. My sister, Becky, arrived in 1940. My father left for Washington soon afterward,

"My parents, Wade and Kathryn Arnold, the year I was born"

sought out an environment then coming to full flower: the suburb. Garden City, on Long Island, had impressive homes, broad streets, and an excellent school system. There we settled, in a modest and bizarre little house on a tiny plot. It had steep roofs, dormers, window seats, a cypress-panelled basement, and the fleur-de-lis stamped in the plaster of the living room wall. And my Francophile mother was already teaching us French.

It was a time of prosperity, conformity, convenient foods and convenient appliances, and the town was just the place to take advantage of them. I was never happy there. I imagined that I had been uprooted, and habitually described myself as "from Illinois," even years later. We did go back nearly every summer, intimate with the country because there weren't super interstates, to visit my grandmother's little town. Surrounded by breathtakingly flat farmland and enraptured by the Saturday night concert at the bandstand, I was confirmed in my refusal to belong in Garden City.

Nevertheless, there was plenty of fun to be had. We played at cowboys and Indians, storming up and down the stairs of the two-storey garage, overturning a "saloon" table made out of a barrel. My sister and I fought so much that the older neighbor children tied

to work for the Office of War Information. I don't remember seeing him during the war, but we made a record of our voices to send to him.

Becky and I played in a huge yard with swings, a "teeter-totter," slide, and sandbox. Judging from photographs, we liked to dress up in funny clothes. My mother's summary of those years emphasized that I was a difficult baby. We certainly got off to a rocky start and the showdowns continued over clothes. I refused to wear dresses, even to birthday parties.

Mother tended an enormous victory garden and was, I think, fairly contented in the society of a college town. Becky and I had everything little children could wish for, except a father on the scene. We didn't know, of course, that with the end of the war, our lives would change radically and a certain innocence in American life would vanish forever.

In 1945, my father resumed his post at NBC. My mother held an auction, packed up what was left afterward, and took Becky and me to New York City. I remember leaping through a fountain in Central Park, riding the double-decker bus on Fifth Avenue, and once, in a downpour, walking barefoot on the sidewalk to save our shoes. My mother didn't want us to grow up in New York, to my lasting regret, and

At age two

boxing gloves onto us, charged admission to a crowd, and turned us loose. There was lots of playacting. A favorite drama was the smothering of the little Princes in the Tower. I also admired the mischief of Tom Sawyer, Huck Finn, Penrod, Tom Brown, and others, so that many games had an antique quality. We roamed the town after dark, pulling pranks—dressing up someone's iron deer, sending out snipe hunters, and playing hide-and-seek.

And we were forever practicing, riding our bikes for hours on end, throwing a ball back and forth or against the garage door until we could unfailingly hit the strike zone. I practiced everything except the piano and the violin like a demon. The conventions of the suburb, an enclave protected from the depredations of city life, may have been stifling, but in reality, we had enormous freedom. I could go on my bike from the north to south shore of the island. Becky and I pedaled for more than an hour to get to a place where we could rent horses and ride them around a ring. Further east lay villages little changed since the eighteenth century and to the north was an abandoned motor parkway that dated from before Gatsby's time. It was hidden away in the woods and weeds sprouted through rents in the pavement. After I was sixteen and had a license, I ran solitary, high-speed races along it in our baby-blue Studebaker.

My sister and I climbed trees like monkeys, but we didn't stop at that. We scaled buildings, going hand over hand up the cornerstones of our school. Once, we popped up over the third-storey gutter of our house, surprising a workman, who cursed us for our foolhardiness. All of this was an expression of wanderlust and rebelliousness. Becky paid for it more dearly that I did. Once, on a dare, she leapt from a porch roof and broke both wrists and sprained both ankles. It was quite in character for her to accept an invitation to water-ski with her casts wrapped in plastic. My only memorable fall was much earlier, from a dogwood tree. I landed flat on my back and lost consciousness long enough for Becky to be sorry I was dead and anticipate being held responsible.

One of my first ambitions was architectural, or even imperial: I constructed a village out of twigs in a dirt patch by the garage. It became an attraction; even my first-grade teacher came to see it. Next, I decided to be a naturalist, like my heroes John Muir and John Burroughs. A naturalist was an independent person, a wanderer full of interesting information, and that appealed to my instincts. I decked myself out with nature notebook, binoculars, penknife, compass, magnifying glass, and sack for specimens, and spent hours in a "hide" in a mock orange bush, or on the "trail" behind peoples' backyards.

Emily (left) with her sister, Becky, in Galesburg, Illinois

There were many cats who appeared and lingered for varying periods, but they attached themselves more to our mother. The most beloved pet was a stray miniature English sheepdog we named Moppet, just a puppy and completely resistant to training or discipline. He was forever running off and we forever looking for him. After he was killed by a car, we never recovered enough to get another.

Parakeets were all the rage in the fifties and we bought one we called Blynken. In time, he learned to talk. In time, too, he exited through an open window and was lost for days. We despaired, until someone telephoned from thirty miles out on the eastern end of the island. "A bird flew into our kitchen window," the woman said. "He sat on a chairback and said, 'Hello, my name is Blynken Arnold and I live at 115 Roxbury Road, Garden City, New York. . . . This is ridiculous, birds can't talk!'" We fetched back our hero bird, who lived to a ripe old age.

As much as my sister and I played, we labored at chores, too. My mother was a compulsive and angry homemaker. One thing that made her angry was our father's irregular comings and goings. He wanted little to do with suburban do-it-yourself improvements and my mother always found something that needed fixing. When he was home, he slept in a little back bedroom, rising before dawn to sit in the kitchen, drink coffee, and write or work crossword puzzles. I know now that the pall cast over our lives was due to his alcoholism, but it was never mentioned in our childhood. Rather, my mother raged against his unreliability, his glad-handing ways, and insufficient salary. To us, he was an amusing, supremely clever man, who loved puns and other jokes, whittled on a scrap of wood when he walked home from the train station, didn't care for physical exercise, and never drove a car. I longed for him and had fantasies of running away with him. My mother reminded me bitterly that I was "just like him" and I had to draw my own conclusions as to what that meant.

Mother poured energies and talents that might have taken her out into the world back instead into her unhappy domestic life. Becky and I helped buy groceries with a toy wagon before we had a car. We transplanted shrubs and sod and dug crabgrass with paring knives, mowed, raked, edged, and weeded. Every weekend, we cleaned, waxed, puttied, scraped, painted, and polished. Although I was the first child in my class to read, and therefore to have a library card, and always performed at the top of my grade, I almost never read a book in the daytime because in the back of my mind lurked knowledge of something more useful to do.

An idle activity that was exempt from this stricture was drawing. Drawing was my talent and therefore to be developed. My mother noticed when I was three or so that I drew from observation, and so she had me practice until I mastered ears, hands, feet, and so on. Soon I was making up little stories and binding them in books, complete with copyright pages. Some featured Tony the Fruit Man, others a boy who ran away to work at a harness-racing track. Girls didn't interest me at all. Their traditional occupations were too passive and confining. I didn't even like to draw girls because they were delicate and I was attracted by ruggedness and the picturesque. My mother urged me to draw things people would enjoy looking at, but I stuck to men and boys in action, interestingly ugly, grimacing faces, gnarled

From The Show Must Go On, *written and illustrated by Emily Arnold McCully. (Copyright © 1987 by Emily Arnold McCully. Reprinted by permission of Western Publishing Co., Inc.)*

From Picnic, *written and illustrated by Emily Arnold McCully. (Copyright © 1985 by Emily Arnold McCully. Reprinted by permission of Harper & Row, Publishers, Inc.)*

stumps, barns, and so on.

Mother conveyed to Becky and me in various ways the sense that the world is pitiless; selfish and crass people usually triumph in it, and we'd better be prepared to take care of ourselves. This meant: be self-supporting, using our abilities. Applauded for our talents at school and often awarded special privileges because we were intelligent, Becky and I assumed we could do anything boys could. Until the onset of puberty, that is. The first rude sign that my life was going to take a new direction came when the mother of one of the boys I played with every day called my mother to tell her I could no longer be permitted to participate in tackle football games. I was aggrieved and humiliated. All through the years, Becky and I and one other girl had been the only ones always invited to play ball with the boys. We were every bit as good at throwing, passing, running, batting, and catching as most boys. Now, other sorts of girls—pretty, helpless, silly ones—excited my former companions in a way I did not and would not. To make it worse, Becky herself seemed better equipped to succeed in this new arena. "Popularity" took on a narrow and subversive meaning. The crowd called "popular" was simply that group of individuals attracted only to each other, exchanging steady partners and paying attention to themselves. How they became "popular," while so self-absorbed and boring, was beyond my understanding and sympathy.

But there is one more element to recall about preadolescent days. Radio was my father's business and it was my great companion. We all listened to Sunday-night comedy—Jack Benny, Fred Allen, and the rest. It was the only occasion for much family laughter. At other times I listened alone in my room, drawing pictures that were illustrations of the action. It is often said that TV deprives the imagination and radio was a boon to it. That was certainly the case for me. The styles of my favorite illustrators, N. C. Wyeth, Howard Pyle, the artist who drew Prince Valiant in the comics, were well suited to "The Lone Ranger," and "The Shadow." I was interested in dramatic points of view and telling characterisations.

A more elevated radio figure was the maestro

Toscanini, who conducted the NBC Radio Symphony. I was taken to his broadcasts, sketched him at the podium, and presented him with my efforts afterward. As our father's little girls, Becky and I also got to sit in the control room during many shows. It was a heady experience to be insiders there and planted a determination to grow up to be in the center of things.

An exhibit of Leonardo da Vinci's notebooks and models of his inventions toured the country. I was fascinated by it all and particularly pleased to see his grotesques. It meant that my drawings of faces were in the tradition of genius. I also loved to copy paintings from books in our large home library. (That library was the great treasury of my childhood. Books, *those books,* defined a personal world that was both broad in its references and secure.) The heroic, muscular, sentimental works of the American twentieth-century school seemed part of my particular heritage. The rubric "Ashcan School" certainly spoke to me. Instead of a lemonade stand, I set up a "newsstand" at the foot of the driveway and peddled old magazines and my copies of the masters.

As class artist, I was always recruited to make posters, backdrops for plays and concerts and programs. I usually decorated research papers thoroughly too, and doodled on any blank paper in reach. Repetition produced a personal style and a growing ability to solve pictorial problems. Practice helped give me the confidence later to embark on a professional career without formal training.

My childhood encouraged a penchant for improvisation, for making do with whatever lay at hand, for "found art," and the potential in limited ingredients. We were poorer than most families in town, and my mother had to manage without my father's help. She was a nervous, erratic, self-taught repairer and rearranger of never quite satisfactory furniture, gardens, and wardrobe. (Although we lived with antiques, principally from my father's family, and my mother had great flair, so the house was always impressive.) She made most of our clothes, either from scratch or hand-me-downs and I still have a few things she'd bought in Paris or New York and later altered for me. She saved everything. There were always tools and odd materials to put to use. I made a fly-casting rod out of a bamboo stake, window crank, and bandage cylinder. I made surveying instruments, stilts, boats, magic tricks, puppets, bows and arrows, carts, and sewed extra pockets in my clothes, using stuff in the attic or the basement or the garage. Becky and I built lean-tos in vacant lots and houses in trees. I still have a hard time throwing anything away—and a hard time acquiring anything new.

The fifties are remembered as a gray, complacent decade, but for me they were intensely political and scary. There were atom bomb shelters and drills, the Rosenbergs' executions, Alger Hiss, and the McCarthy hearings, which we watched on TV after school, our mother disconcertingly watching too, in broad daylight. Adlai Stevenson brought his gentlemanly finesse to the scene and I campaigned for him at school, but everyone else supported Ike. (Similarly, my passion was for the Brooklyn Dodgers, amidst the fatuity of Yankee rooters.) My parents knew plenty of people in the entertainment business who had been blacklisted by the anti-Communist witch-hunters. Alone among my friends, I could spot some of the credits on the TV screen as aliases.

Adolescence, then, brought awareness that the world was not benign. My parents' marriage hardly resembled one at all, but I knew little of anything different. I did see that other parents weren't nearly as clever as mine, nor as full of pain and anger. I didn't know anyone who shared my yearnings for a poignant, enviable, successful future. I never ran with the crowd and chose boyfriends who were loners, too. I lost myself in self-glorifying daydreams and affected an ironic, capable personality to mask the other, seething self.

My sister and I held office every year in the student government. For me, it was a chance to make funny campaign speeches, design posters, and, once elected, enjoy certain privileges, such as hall passes and a council office to hide out in. Leadership shored up my self-importance in teen society. I also performed stand-up comedy routines when the opportunity arose and made announcements over the PA system in preposterous foreign accents. I supposed that I was grooming myself for fame, but how would it happen? I was a hash of insecurities and bravado.

My parents finally divorced when I was a senior. My father had found a new wife, a colleague at NBC—"no young thing," he assured us—who truly admired him and had been present when he'd created his award-winning documentary radio shows. At last, he would live with praise instead of invective. But his professional life was all but over; my mother's accusations of failure seemed borne out. I never wanted to be on her side, but in his last years, when I finally saw him on his own turf but ill and with nothing much to do, I was more than a little frightened for myself.

My mother guided my selection of a college. Becky and I had learned to get along at home by being selectively passive. Art school was considered, but the liberal arts won out. In those days, girls at the top of a class applied to a clutch of women's colleges

William L. Rooney

McCully (standing) with fellow Brown University-Pembroke College coeds, collaborators on a musical comedy, 1960. At center is playwright Elizabeth Diggs, with whom the author now shares a house in New York.

on the East Coast and I followed suit. Pembroke College, now absorbed by Brown University, offered a scholarship and the option of courses at the Rhode Island School of Design. During the summer, I took a job as "dramatics counselor" at a little camp in Connecticut. I assumed the persona of an eccentric thespian and had a grand time, directing my own adaptation of *As You Like It* and, off duty, inciting the misgivings of the senior staff.

It was a good transition. In college, I was to abandon most of the activities that had absorbed me in high school—student government, the literary magazine, and the role of "class artist." I threw myself instead into theatre.

College life had three great themes: friendship, drama, and intellectual excitement. At the end, there was also love. I felt far more confident away from home, able to appreciate other people and to discover happiness. I made friendships that are vital still. Most of us acted and three of us collaborated on a musical comedy, set in Empire France, because we liked the dresses of the period and the idea of women running salons. On opening night of its production, during a number called "Gentlemen On the Make," all three of the Pembroke deans rose from their seats, lips pursed and brows knit, and marched up the aisle and out of the theatre. Scandalising them tickled us pink.

I began my acting career as a French maid in *The Boyfriend.* I didn't think I could sing or dance, but I adored being part of a lively cast who could. A part that required only a broad French accent was perfect. Eventually, after playing another maid, Dunyasha, in *The Cherry Orchard,* I landed a major singing role, that of the mother who flees with her baby in *The Caucasian Chalk Circle.* The epic production had original music, which I belted out in the manner of Lotte Lenya.

The rehearsing of Brecht and Chekhov, in particular, were significant components of my literary education. Analysis there could be immediately applied, unlike lecture notes. And acting involved testing, disciplining, and extending myself, good preparation for the work I've done since.

Brown was experimenting with a new curriculum emphasizing independent study. Even as a freshman, I was able to work with eminent faculty, sometimes on projects we designed together. I often roamed the stacks of the library in a fever, plucking volumes that struck me. I'm afraid that, devoted as I was to learning, my approach was still the scattershot one, as it always had been.

I enrolled in the Foundation Course at RISD, but after two semesters I withdrew. Social and academic life on the Brown campus had all my interest and I felt at a disadvantage among the art students who could devote all their time to work on projects. Except for a few pastel portraits of friends, done to earn extra spending money, I drew very little in college. A single incident at RISD, which made no impression on me at the time, has considerable significance now: the introductory illustration course consisted of a series of problems, including the rendering of a sample picture for a children's book. That was the part of the assignment that engaged me least, and I dashed it off. But when the class gathered for a crit, everyone agreed that my picture showed a real flair for children's book illustration, while my other pieces were merely ordinary. But I was on my way out of art school and forgot the episode.

I wrote several short stories and some poetry, kept journals, especially during love affairs, and wrote many letters. With friends, I wrote book and lyrics for two more musicals. I had hardly been aware of learning, by osmosis, about the form, or formulas, in this case, of plays and shows, but my mother's abiding interest and my father's dormant playwrighting had been a great influence. I kept them at a distance, in person, and did not invite them to see me perform, although my mother saw our notorious French musical. I still thought about becoming a writer. Two of my professors, in English and comparative literature, encouraged me to go to graduate school. I was a good student, elected to Phi Beta Kappa, and in those days, a large number of graduates did continue with liberal education. I never heard anyone admit to wanting to go out and earn a lot of money. But I couldn't make up my mind. I think that I was too happy in my protected environment.

In junior year, I played a Tennessee Williams heroine, a garrulous, neurasthenic drifter clad in her slip in a furnished room, soliloquising vaporously to her lover, also in his underwear. Afterward, a young man I knew as the president of Brown's student government came backstage to congratulate me on my performance. He said it was so authentic that I must "be like" the woman in real life. I didn't correct his impression. Instead, we entered upon a mutual deception: that I was fragile and fey and he had to take care of me.

After the play ended its run, my father's wife arranged for us to audition for someone at NBC. Nothing resulted from this brief flirtation with trying for an acting career, but the young man who played the lover did wind up a professional, on TV.

My admirer and I fell in love and insisted on getting married the day before my graduation. My mother strenuously opposed us, then resignedly cooperated. This was her worst fear come true, and she knew my need for a husband was an evasion of my destiny. But I wasn't sure what my destiny *was* and couldn't deal directly with the anxiety that arose when I imagined facing life in the world.

Still, I wasn't the only Pembroker to marry hastily. A great many of us did, whether we were shrinking violets or self-professed amazons in the dorm. It's hard to remember how different society was for young women in 1961 and how differently society perceived us. We were not allowed to wear pants to class. Most girls dressed according to a formula; there was little variation and despite the fact that this made fashion totally predictable, people passed judgement on others according to the correctness of their attire. Professors could ridicule women in class and get away with it. Brown students married Pembrokers, but not until after they had heaped scorn on them with the contempt bred of familiarity, not to mention availability. We could entertain them in our rooms one hour a week, with the door open. We had to be inside the front door at midnight; the terrace was crowded with madly kissing couples, like a convention of storks, for ten minutes before the deadline every night.

Young women did not necessarily contemplate careers and an education by no means led to one. We were years away, in 1961, from "The Sixties." It was a becalmed period, neither one decade nor the other. Ours was a class that fell between. And most of all, of course, we married because, whatever our practice had been in reality, we were not expected to have sexual relations until we did.

There *were* intimations of change, most notably Kennedy's cliff-hanger election, which seemed to promise a government of youth and daring. My husband-to-be was involved in the campaign to desegregate the Woolworth lunch counters and he received letters from the South containing death threats. On our "honeymoon," visiting his parents in Chicago in 1961, we spent time with his old friends who'd just come back from Mississippi, and I sang "We Shall Overcome" for the first time. Music was going to power the decade ahead, that song more than any other.

But I was more concerned with myself then and true enough to my dreams to insist that we live in New York City. My husband altered his plans and entered Columbia's graduate school in history. For several weeks, I answered want ads, unnerved by the kinds of jobs available. The resumé I had prepared made me sound qualified for a senior editorship, or a CEO, but the only place that would have me was a dingy three-man paste-up studio on West Forty-sixth Street, where they wanted me to send out bills. Its only recommendation was that it was a block from the Gotham Bookmart. The boss worried constantly that I would become pregnant and quit because I was a newlywed and he wouldn't let me try paste-up, but I picked up some techniques by observing. Wildly frustrated, I outlined a screenplay of Kafka's *Castle,* studied an Italian book, and began a novel about a motherly ticket seller at a Times Square movie house. I worked inconsistently on these schemes in free moments, of which there were many.

There was no improvement when I became a mat cutter at a big advertising agency, this an entry-level job for someone who wouldn't type. But I could teach myself typography design, raid the supply closet, and get advice from art directors. At home at night I began a portfolio of sample illustrations and design.

I quit the job after three male sidekicks were all promoted and I was still in the mat room. I made appointments to show my portfolio to as many art directors at publishing houses, ad agencies, magazines, and newspapers as would see me. When I ran through the lot, I started over and over again. A few jobs designing paperback book covers trickled in, then a few pharmaceutical advertisements, which tended to be evasive, pictorially, and therefore "arty." Despite the exhaustion of presenting myself repeatedly for review and rejection, life was much improved. I wasn't cooped up any longer in an office and could savor the romance of Gotham. I learned every arcane trick of getting around, admired art-deco lobbies and elevators, views from on high, gargoyles, pediments, towers, and canyon avenues.

Still, I was beginning to envy my husband's intellectual pursuits and to worry that my mind would atrophy as I followed a routine not much different than a messenger's. I took out a loan from the state and entered the graduate school at Columbia in art history, which had been my formal major at Brown.

Although it was clear that more degrees were just a detour for me, I loved to study. Among the faculty were some of the great masters of iconography. I thought that decoding the messages hidden in Renaissance images was rarefied detective work and a superb way to understand European history. I treasured my hours in the library, where the books I was using were reserved on my own private shelf. I couldn't overtax my powers there, because I had also landed a free-lance job with a textbook publisher. The position paid all of six dollars per hour. I was to design book covers, do paste-up, and re-color the skins of children in the pictures if they were all white. The pay was handsome (my previous jobs paid sixty dollars a week for forty hours) and I could earn exactly as much as I had time for! So far, life in the world had been a struggle under dreary limitations, but the work-school combination was more fun.

The next year, my husband was awarded a Belgian American Fellowship for a year's study abroad, in Belgium, where he could research his doctoral thesis. I tailored my master's essay to make use of this good fortune. My topic was Rubens's title pages, which had never been collected into a critical catalogue. The material lay in libraries in Brussels, Paris, London, Rome, Madrid, and, principally, the Museum Plantin-Moretus in Antwerp. We rented dank rooms at the top of an ancient building off the Grand' Place in Brussels. Our view of roof and chimney tops was just like those recorded by so many garret dwellers in nineteenth-century Paris. A shop two flights below us sold fusty sheet music, which we could see in great untidy piles on every surface as we climbed the cramped stair. What if one of the decrepit smokers (the shopkeepers were very old) dropped a lighted cigarette onto the cantatas? We decided to buy a great length of canvas rope and kept it tied to a rafter by a window, ready for us to shinny to the courtyard five flights down if we smelled a fire. (We would have landed next to Horta's magnificent worker's hall, since torn down.)

Quaint as it was to live there, neither of us liked Brussels very much. I was happiest in Europe when pretending to be one of the natives, and I had no desire to do that in bourgeois Brussels. Antwerp, less modern, with so many houses and churches and paintings I already loved, a climate that made it a struggle to be comfortable, and faces everywhere that matched those in the paintings, was more endearing. But the best part of the year was spent travelling, on trains, third class, in hostels and pensions and with consistent joy, even in adversity. My husband and I had been Europe-oriented since childhood and in all of our schooling. At that age, we'd never have thought to go anywhere else.

Our first visit to Paris was a true pilgrimmage. We arrived at 6:00 A.M. and walked all day and into the night, laying claim to the city of our dreams. We also spent time in Holland, Spain, London, and journeyed the length of Italy. Everywhere, we paid homage to the monuments of the Renaissance, to churches and museums, libraries, and universities. It is a great thing to be young and worshipful and abroad.

Early in the year, in November 1963, a chance glimpse of a newspaper headline informed us that President Kennedy had been shot. We were thrown into turmoil, our shock and sense of loss intensified by our estrangement. We followed succeeding developments—more deaths, theories of conspiracy, the nation apparently thrown off course after so much optimism and stylishness—in a foreign language, at a distance. This experience probably groomed us, as the general questioning and probing did many others, for the sometimes paranoic protests against the government during the Vietnam War. Even the McCarthy years had not made it seem that an entire administration could be blighted. We saw the sinister machinations of men driven to wrongheaded goals.

That year, too, in our absence, the Beatles conquered America and Bob Dylan made his indelible impression. We missed it all and returned oddly aged by Europe, so that for the rest of the sixties, I often felt a bit more earnest than many of my contemporaries.

My husband was hired for his first full-time teaching job by Swarthmore College. By now, I was designing book jackets and illustrating stories for magazines. Although I could lay claim to a full-time career, I became, first of all, a faculty wife. This was demeaning, but the small society was intense, intellectually stimulating, and I made friends with a painter. The oldest students were close enough in age for us to enjoy each other's company. Little attention was paid to women's issues, however, and I remember driving back roads to consciousness-raising sessions so remote it felt like an act of conspiracy to attend.

I also tried to find out as much as I could about Southeast Asian history in order to understand how our misguided national policy had been shaped. Swarthmore is a Quaker center, and people had long worked for peace. We attended countless meetings and joined busloads of protestors in Washington and New York. We found out what tear gas was. The war and the social climate pitted generations against each other. Younger faculty were preparing "holistic" courses which they taught in teams, extracurricularly. New values were rising, we felt, to replace the old. At Swarthmore, the issues were not precisely of relevance, but of a unified approach to knowledge as a way of preserving the planet. We were much concerned with ecology and I fancied myself to be an anarchist, that position being most consistent with respect for nature and humans alike.

With son Nat, Swarthmore, Pennsylvania, 1969

Meanwhile, in 1966, my career took a new turn. I had made a series of posters, featuring children at play, to advertise a radio station. They were hung in the New York subway cars. Even though subway workers went on strike soon after they were put up, a new editor at Harper and Row saw them and got in touch with me. Was I interested in illustrating a children's book? I was!

She sent me the manuscript for George Panetta's *Sea Beach Express* and then Emily Neville's *Seventeenth Street Gang,* both set in New York City. I went up and made on-the-spot sketches. This activity, formerly just an exercise, was now part of my work! I was going to be one of those supremely lucky people whose work is fun and vice versa. Furthermore, I felt that contributing to books for children was far more worthy than illustrating advertisements.

The next story I worked on was *Rex,* which I could set anywhere. I chose a house in Swarthmore, because I liked it. This was another of the arbitrary pleasures of children's books. The challenge lay in pacing the story and maintaining consistency of characterisation. I used my theatre experience, imagining scenes being played, blocking them, directing the action, gestures, and expressions. I am told that while I draw, my face reflects whatever the character is feeling.

I had to honor the texts of the books. I couldn't usually draw what I felt like drawing, or what was easy. My job was to extend the story, not just decorate it. A picture book is more than words with pictures, and a good illustrator will enlarge a story. I learned to enjoy creating within the limitations of a strict form, remaining faithful to someone else's initial concept—but I also wanted to come up with ideas of my own. Alas, for many years, my manuscripts were all turned down.

In 1967, a powerful and unexpected emotion took hold of me. I wanted to have a baby! When I did become pregnant, I felt blessedly happy, worthy, and purposeful. So expansive was this sensate conviction that I don't recall any apprehension, although I knew nothing of babies and had never even liked to play with dolls.

Nathaniel was born on April 4, 1968—the night the Reverend Martin Luther King was assassinated. I had been drawing pictures for *Journey from Peppermint Street,* which later won the first National Book Award for a children's book. I noted the intervals between contractions, when they began, on the margins of the pictures. In the room with me, in a former dormitory given over to housing for younger faculty, was a screen I had made out of cardboard egg cartons (dozens and dozens of them, a project truly worthy of my improvisational childhood). This was to be a divider between the nursery and my studio. I had also painted a giant mural of brightly colored jungle beasts on one wall. We planned to suspend the baby in a basket from our bedroom ceiling most of the time, this said to promote a serene temperament. As the contractions increased, I realised that the time was come! My husband and I had practiced the LaMaze Method together and were ready with our little bag of necessities and guidebook. By 8:30, after hours of alternating impatience and forced calm, we were about to leave when the telephone rang. Someone thought we ought to have the horrific news of Dr. King. We departed, then, in a state of shock. The birth became a mix of exertion, ecstasy and gloom. The hospital, in Media, Pennsylvania, was small and nearly deserted. The next day, crowds of blacks rioted in the streets outside. Of course, our joy dominated our sadness and outrage, but I will always remember that night, and the long hours I lay, a brand-new little son by my side, for its apprehensions of uncertainty ahead and no protection from violence.

My mother died that year and the painful end of that long, fraught relationship haunted me for many months. In time, we learned, to our astonishment, that she had left an inheritance. My share was enough, in those days, to make a down payment on a house. The one we fell in love with was out in the country, away from the campus. It dated from 1710, was built of amber stone, with walls eighteen inches thick, the plaster mixed with horsehair. To my endless delight, every room had a door to the outside. I felt very much at home. The alienation of my "from Illinois" years seemed over.

We discovered a mutual enthusiasm for gardens, and laid a brickwork walk, in the colonial style, along the front of the house. We planted herbs, wild strawberries, and flowers there. Inside, I unpacked my half of my mother's furniture, thus weirdly reconstituting my childhood memories in a kind of museum. I loved living in that house. It was set deep on its plot, in a world apart, despite the encroaching suburb. Much of the time I worked in my attic studio, with baby Nat at my feet, amusing himself for long stretches, his temperament sunny and placid after all. I worked on *Hurray for Captain Jane* and *Maxie,* among many other books. We grew vegetables and shopped at a Pennsylvania Dutch farmer's market. In a way, we had managed to fashion a "safe," traditional, and sensuous existence.

But it was not to last. In 1971, Thaddeus, called Tad, was born. This time, I whisked in and out of the hospital in twenty-four hours. Tad went into the hanging basket, but without the calming effect. This baby was different! Having two children was very different—more than twice as many as one! Tad

"The old stone house," Pennsylvania, 1971

was restless and adorable and a shock to Nat, who loved him even as he was bumped from his throne. But we were all dealing, consciously or unconsciously, with a crisis. My husband had lost his job. Apparently the junior faculty's radical teaching had not been well received and most were denied tenure. We were stunned. In a sense, our lives together never recovered. A temporary solution presented itself in the form of a year's post at Princeton. We sold the house, put our furniture in a warehouse, and moved to rented quarters, where we lived rather miserably, plotting our next step.

We spent many weekends house hunting, in Pennsylvania, and, with greater conviction, New England. We felt an emotional and spiritual kinship with that region and an affection for the architecture and landscape. We thought that if we found a house in an area with schools, he would be sure to find a new position. Our relocation paralleled a national impulse. Lots of people were taking up the rural life for its purity, if not its simplicity, and its hands-on directness, fleeing the society that had betrayed its ideals. It was popular to restore an old house or join a commune and grow one's food.

What we didn't know about our new life was that it was fated to fail. By 1971 I had entered the acute stage of alcoholism. In those days, the awareness we now have of the disease didn't exist and even doctors often didn't recognize it or were ignorant of any treatment. In Princeton, I did consult one who told me I couldn't be alcoholic because I didn't fit the stereotype. This reassurance was sufficient to allow me to deny the illness a few years longer.

Sons Nat and Tad, New Ipswich, New Hampshire, 1973

We finally settled on an already restored eighteenth-century house set dramatically against a vista of mountains on the outskirts of New Ipswich, New Hampshire. The town was unspoiled, with many beautiful houses, a small library, store, school, and people with like interests. Our house had a great long panelled living room where travellers had once taken their rest and a Shaker meeting was briefly ensconced before the believers were run out of the area. The hearth took six-foot logs. Outside, there were ideal situations for flower and vegetable gardens, orchards and groves. There was a huge, beautiful barn and a gemlike swimming pond, enclosed by poplars, and our own little mountain, covered with blueberries and fitted out with a homemade rope tow and ski runs. We began to dig, plant, explore, cultivate, and harvest. The boys roamed the yard and the barn (although Tad had usually to be confined to an expanding fence, causing him much indignation). We swam and skated and skiied cross-country and downhill, went on picnics, joined a tennis club, and worked. Nat and his friends posed for the pictures in such books as *How to Eat Fried Worms.* I threw myself into working, gardening, and maintaining shaky control of my life.

I worked as I do now with pen and ink and watercolor. I have a pan of dry paints just like the one I used as a child and supplement it with tubes and bottled dyes. When I receive a manuscript, with specifications (size, number of pages, color limitations, if any), I divide the story up with an eye to pacing it for meaning and graphic possibilities. I decide what should be illustrated and in what style, for my style varies with the nature of the story. Most important, I decide what the characters should look like and where they are. Sometimes I look at photographs, sometimes I think of friends, sometimes I make it all up without knowing what my buried sources may be. If I have trouble with a pose, I ask someone to assume it for me, or, in a pinch, go to a mirror. My first sketches are very messy—I want lots of movement and energy. I put tracing paper over them and make refinements. After the black line is set I make a loose color "dummy" of the book, cutting up the typed manuscript and pasting it in with the pictures. Now I know for sure that the story reads well. I send the dummy to the editor, who may make suggestions for changes. Finally, I paint the finishes.

First I make the line drawings on tracing paper. This is put onto a light table, with watercolor paper on top. The light allows me to see the outlines

The author/illustrator, 1974

through the heavy paper. I draw again, using them as a guide. This saves time and prevents some mistakes. But if even a tiny line is wrong, especially on someone's face, I redo the whole picture. The psychological truth is what interests me most, and that comes across through expression and gesture. I want readers to be able to grasp and identify with feelings in the stories.

The pictures are sent to a copy editor, who examines them carefully for inconsistencies or omissions. I rely a great deal on these hawkeyes because children are offended by careless errors in books.

I have been lucky and worked with some fine editors. I might never have turned to children's books at all had not that first Harper editor, Ellen Rudin, taken a chance on me. We worked on several books over the years, including *MA nDA LA,* by Arnold Adoff. It stands as a fine example of the latitude allowed an illustrator in interpreting a manuscript. This one consisted simply of monosyllables derived from the word *mandala.* I made up a story to go with them and the book received a citation for graphic excellence from the Brooklyn Museum and the Brooklyn Public Library in 1975. Ellen also assigned me Sylvia Plath's *Bed Book,* flattering me, but raising some anxiety. I admired Plath's writing for its dark energy and unflinching disclosures. I also felt that her life was almost a paradigm of the worst that could befall a gifted, ambitious, young woman caught between feminine impulses toward helplessness and control while fifties sexism made mature choices almost impossible. But *The Bed Book* should reflect her interestingly skewed sensibility, be antic fun, and also comforting, the last thing a child would see before drifting off to sleep.

By the time Nat and Tad were in school—Tad in a Montessori class—I had resumed writing fiction with a new determination. I felt a need to "explain" myself and what I observed of life as alcohol relentlessly isolated me. I worked on a single long short story, rewriting it many times over several months. I enrolled in an adult-education class in Cambridge when my husband took a consulting job there and we became weekenders in New Ipswich and in a graduate writing program at Brown when our alma mater hired him as an assistant dean. Each time, I presented the instructor with my story, honed a little further during its last exposure. It turned out to be a good way to work at my craft. Eventually, I sent it to *The Massachusetts Review,* which accepted it. The following year it was chosen for *The O.Henry Collection: Best Short Stories of the Year.*

The story struck farcical notes, but was basically a harrowing picture of marriage, motherhood, and rural life. I was blind to it at the time, but it was also a portrait of an alcoholic. By the time it was published, our family had been split asunder, my children were living with their father, and I had been hospitalised.

I emerged a few weeks later with none of my former life intact. But I had been rescued, in a profound sense; I now knew what was the matter with me and that recovery was possible. The next years were terribly difficult, but not without hope. My work sustained me more than ever.

I attended my fifteenth college reunion and spent time there with my musical-comedy collaborator. Her life had also reached a turning point and we decided to share a house in New York. I sold the tavern in New Hampshire, packed up, and arrived in Brooklyn, much bemused by the twists and turns of fortune. Who could ever have predicted that I would end up in Brooklyn? (Of course, that was far from the "end.") My friend, who had been a teacher, switched to playwriting and has had a great success at it. We became two writers in one house.

McCully with son Tad during a summer in Vermont

She also owned a farmhouse in Vermont and some horses, so in the summer the boys and I recovered country pleasures together. Her daughter was a teenager and gracefully assumed the role of big sister.

I began a novel. With some reluctance, I found myself telling of the long slide into alcoholism that I, and now many people I had come to know, had experienced. Gradually, I developed a sense of mission. Most people didn't understand the disease. What better way to present it than with a character readers could care for, in a story naturally suspenseful? I was fortunate to discover a writing workshop led by Paula Fox, whose novels I had devoured. She generously steered me past many writing reefs and shallows. When I'd finished, I had more good luck and became the client of a great agent, Harriet Wasserman, who has been unfailingly encouraging and has negotiated on my behalf with publishers ever since. *A Craving,* as the book was called, was published first by Avon, then by Dell, and was nominated for an American Book Award.

One summer we discovered an artists' colony in the Berkshires that ran a program for the offspring of the artists. This was perfect, we thought. It did prove to be a productive time. Nat and Tad were exposed to a range of bohemian observances. The next year, my friend had a play produced at a theatre in the Catskills. The boys and I became backstage helpers, painting scenery and doing odd jobs. Nat memorised large sections of *A Midsummer Night's Dream* just by hanging around rehearsals and Tad was confirmed in his determination to become a drummer. I put together a little story about a family of acting bears who inherit a farm, try farming, fail, and then turn their barn into a theatre—much like the one we were visiting. Eventually, this became *The Show Must Go On* and has been followed by *You Lucky Duck!, Zaza's Big Break,* and *The Evil Spell.* These were my first texts for children's books, but the real breakthrough as an author had come earlier, without words.

The summer after we left the Catskills, we rented a house in the Hudson Valley, with wonderful views of the Berkshire Hills. I was attracted by an adorable red pickup truck. That image was the beginning of *Picnic.* More doodles produced a plot consisting of pictures alone and I realised that words would be superfluous. That summer, too, I took Paula Fox's suggestion and made pictures to go with Christopher Smart's eighteenth-century poem *For I Will Consider My Cat Jeoffry.* Creating my own books was like being let out of school!

In the following months, I began another novel. My idea was to explore, for my sake, and, if I succeeded, for the entertainment of readers, the insights and revelations, accidents and choices, that

Nat and Tad at summer camp, Cummington, Massachusetts, 1980

would allow a talented young woman to become a painter. I wanted to find out what it was like to embark upon works of art with no reference to text and no preconceptions of how they turn out. I was moved, too, to write something about my childhood. This novel became *Life Drawing,* published by Delacorte Press and Dell/Laurel and edited by the same superb editor who had first acquired *A Craving.*

Whenever possible, I try to be present when one of my picture books is printed. The paintings for *Picnic* had a great range of greens and blues, with deep shadows and bright, sunny patches. The printed version was paler. I mused that a winter book might produce sharper contrast, since the background would be white. By the time I had finished the sequel, *First Snow,* I realised that the seasons were characters along with the mice and the pickup truck. As basic as summer and winter were the themes of each book—early experiences all children share, such as being lost, or afraid, resourceful, brave, jealous, left out, and so on. Finally, in *Christmas Gift,* that holiday is celebrated for its mayhem and innocent greed, as well as for generosity and gratitude. All of these books have given me great pleasure to create and I marvel that it took me so long to rediscover the methods of my childhood, when I often made stories with pictures alone.

From For I Will Consider My Cat Jeoffry, *by Christopher Smart. Illustrated by Emily Arnold McCully. (Illustrations copyright © 1984 by Emily Arnold McCully. Reprinted by permission of Atheneum Publishers, an imprint of Macmillan Publishing Co.)*

Lately, I have been writing much longer texts for the Harper "I Can Read" series. They feature a pair of idiosyncratic grandmas who share the supervision of a hapless child. The first two are called *The Grandma Mixup* and *Grandmas at the Lake.*

We have owned three Abyssinian cats over the years. The current one is named Sido and I am mad about her. Lately I have illustrated Lucy Diggs's *Selene Goes Home,* about a cat just like Sido. In observing my cat intently as I drew, I came to know and love her even more. This is the effect of drawing from life: it sharpens the eyes and the reflexes that guide the hand and it sharpens the affections, as well.

Since *Life Drawing* was published, I have spent nearly all of my time writing and illustrating children's books. I am eager, however, to begin another novel. In the past, I was fortunate to receive fiction-writing grants from the National Endowment for the Arts and the New York State Arts Council. Writing a novel is a very long undertaking and involves periods of passionate commitment when one may be loathe to put the work aside in order to earn the rent and the groceries, not to mention the tuitions. But while writing less, I have been drawing and painting more. *Picnic*—which won a Christopher Award and was exhibited at the Biennale at Bratislava—and its sequels are like tiny novels, in a way, and call forth feelings that may not be as complex as those in adult stories, but are as elemental.

Now, quite unexpectedly, I am about to take up acting again after all these years. My friend Elizabeth Diggs, author of *St. Florence,* a play about Florence Nightingale that has won awards even before its premiere, asked me to fill in for an absent actor at one of its readings. I was good enough to prompt the artistic director of the theatre and the playwright to campaign for me to audition for the full-fledged production. To my amazement, I won the part over a field of a dozen professionals in New York! Now I will join the cast, as well as Actors' Equity, for my debut/return in Albany in October 1988. Performing is a powerful concentrating of ability and energy. All else in the world falls away when you assume another identity before an alert audience. It is the most

Left, "Tad drumming at summer camp," 1985.
Right, "Nat headed for college, in front of the Austerlitz house."

focussed and yet fleeting mode of expression I know. Since this will be my first professional experience of theatre, I am in the odd position of not knowing just what the next couple of months of my life will hold in regard to work.

Both my boys are grown up and both are, incidentally, left-handed. Tad has one more year of high school and, as a gifted and dedicated drummer, he will probably go to a music school. He has lived with me in New York for the past four years and I have rejoiced in his growth and the growth of his talent. He also draws well enough to be an illustrator, but that isn't his passion. Nat, who became a star Russian-language student in high school, went twice to the Soviet Union, and was invited along when a group of American doctors collected their Nobel Peace Prize, is now an even greater star in the Japanese department at the University of Chicago. He has just been awarded a prestigious fellowship by the government of Japan to study for a year at a university in Tokyo. Nat's interest in Japanese began when he washed dishes at a sushi bar here in the Berkshires one summer. In an odd way, the older the boys become, the more they inspire stories about young children. Distance always lends perspective, and I was a nervous, conscientious parent. Now that I am more relaxed, I see the humor in growing up, see how things change and yet retain constants that touch everyone alike. Wonderfully, it is always possible to retell an old tale in a new, personal way.

I still love athletics and play tennis and squash, swim and ride a bicycle. I attend the theatre often, read, write, and follow politics closely. I have homes in two places, each of which satisfies a different inclination: one is a loft on the edge of Soho, in Manhattan, with Greenwich Village right around the corner. The other is an eighteenth-century house in the New York Berkshires, where I garden and cook and swim in the most exquisite of ponds! In short, I still do the things I began to do when I was a child, or dreamed of doing. I didn't become the person I thought I would, but I was probably the only one who couldn't predict my future when I was young. Anyone observing me at seven or eight, sprawled on the floor or bent over my desk, the radio bearing me into one imaginary world and some little storybook I was creating into another, might have known that my life's work would be exactly what it is.

BIBLIOGRAPHY

FOR CHILDREN

Books written and illustrated:

First Snow. New York: Harper, 1985.

Picnic. New York: Harper, 1985.

School. New York: Harper, 1985.

The Show Must Go On. Racine, Wis.: Western Publishing, 1987.

Christmas Gift. New York: Harper, 1988.

The Grandma Mixup. New York: Harper, 1988.

New Baby. New York: Harper, 1988.

You Lucky Duck! Racine, Wis.: Western Publishing, 1988.

The Evil Spell. New York: Harper, 1989.

Grandma's at the Lake. New York: Harper, 1989.

Zaza's Big Break. New York: Harper, 1989.

Books illustrated:

Sea Beach Express, by George Panetta. New York: Harper, 1966.

The Seventeenth Street Gang, by Emily Cheney Neville. New York: Harper, 1966.

Luigi of the Streets, by Natalie Savage Carlson. New York: Harper, 1967.

Rex, by Marjorie W. Sharmat. New York: Harper, 1967.

Animals in Field and Laboratory: Science Projects in Animal Behavior, by Seymour Simon. New York: McGraw, 1968; Maidenhead, England: McGraw, 1969.

Gooney, by Barbara Borack. New York: Harper, 1968.

Journey from Peppermint Street, by Meindert De Jong. New York: Harper, 1968; London: Lutterworth, 1969.

That Mean Man, by Liesel Moak Skorpen. New York: Harper, 1968.

A Year to Grow, by Felice Holman. New York: Norton, 1968.

The Fishermen, by Jan Wahl. New York: Norton, 1969.

Here I Am: An Anthology of Poems Written by Young People in Some of America's Minority Groups, compiled by Virginia Olsen Baron. New York: Dutton, 1969.

The Mouse and the Elephant, by Barbara K. Walker and Naki Tezel. New York: Parents Magazine Press, 1969.

Tales of the Rue Broca, by Pierre Gripari; translated by Doriane Grutman. Indianapolis, Ind.: Bobbs-Merrill, 1969.

Twin Spell, by Janet Louise Swoboda Lunn. New York: Harper, 1969.

The Cat and the Parrot, by Jeanne B. Hardendorff. Philadelphia: Lippincott, 1970.

Friday Night Is Papa Night, by Ruth A Sonneborn. New York: Viking, 1970.

Gertrude's Pocket, by Miska Miles. Boston: Little, Brown, 1970.

Hobo Toad and the Motorcycle Gang, by Jane H. Yolen. New York: World Publishing, 1970.

Maxie, by Mildred Kantrowitz. New York: Parents Magazine Press, 1970; London: Bodley Head, 1972.

Slip! Slop! Gobble!, by J. B. Hardendorff. Philadelphia: Lippincott, 1970.

Steffie and Me, by Phyllis Hoffman. New York: Harper, 1970.

The Extraordinary Adventures of Che Che McNerney, by Evelyn C. Nevin. New York: Scholastic Books Services, 1971.

Finders Keepers, by Alix Kates Shulman. Scarsdale, N.Y.: Bradbury, 1971.

Finding Out with Your Senses, by S. Simon. New York: McGraw, 1971.

Go and Hush the Baby, by Betsy Byars. New York: Viking, 1971; London: Bodley Head, 1980.

Hurray for Captain Jane!, by Sam Reavin. New York: Parents Magazine Press, 1971.

MA nDA LA, by Arnold Adoff. New York: Harper, 1971.

Michael Is Brave by Helen E. Buckley. New York: Lothrop, 1971.

The Boyhood of Grace Jones, by Jane Langton. New York: Harper, 1972.

Girls Can, Too! A Book of Poems, compiled by Lee Bennett Hopkins. New York: F. Watts, 1972.

Grandpa's Long Red Underwear, by Lynn Schoettle. New York: Lothrop, 1972.

Henry's Pennies, by Louise McNamara. New York: F. Watts, 1972.

Jane's Blanket, by Arthur Miller. New York: Viking, 1972.

Black Is Brown Is Tan, by A. Adoff. New York: Harper, 1972.

How to Eat Fried Worms, by Thomas Rockwell. New York: F. Watts, 1973.

Isabelle the Itch, by Constance C. Greene. New York: Viking, 1972.

That New Boy, by Mary H. Lystad. New York: Crown, 1973.

When Violet Died, by M. Kantrowitz. New York: Parents Magazine Press, 1973; London: Bodley Head, 1974.

Her Majesty, Grace Jones, by J. Langton. New York: Harper, 1974.

I Want Mama, by M. W. Sharmat. New York: Harper, 1974; London: Harper, 1974.

Jenny's Revenge, by Anne Norris Baldwin. New York: Four Winds, 1974.

Tree House Town, by M. Miles. Boston: Little, Brown, 1974.

Amanda, the Panda, and the Redhead, by Susan Terris. Garden City, N.Y.: Doubleday, 1975.

Stand in the Wind, by Jean Little. New York: Harcourt, 1975.

The Bed Book, by Sylvia Plath. New York: Harper, 1976.

My Street's a Morning Cool Street, by Ianthe Thomas. New York: Harper, 1976.

Martha's Mad Day, by Miranda Hopgood. New York: Crown, 1977.

Professor Coconut and the Thief, by Rita Golden Gelman and Joan Richter. New York: Holt, 1977.

That's Mine, by Elizabeth Winthrop. New York: Holiday House, 1977.

Edward Troy and the Witch Cat, by Sarah Sargent. Chicago: Follett, 1978.

The Highest Hit, by Nancy Willard. New York: Harcourt, 1978.

I and Sproggy, by C. C. Greene. New York: Viking, 1978.

No Help at All, by Betty Baker. New York: Greenwillow, 1978.

Partners, by B. Baker. New York: Greenwillow, 1978.

The Twenty-Elephant Restaurant, by Russell Hoban. New York: Atheneum, 1978.

What I Did Last Summer, by Glory St. John. New York: Atheneum, 1978.

Where Wild Willie, by A. Adoff. New York: Harper, 1978.

Last Look, by Clyde Robert Bulla. New York: Crowell, 1979.

My Island Grandma, by Kathryn Lasky. New York: Warne, 1979.

Ookie-Spooky, by Mirra Ginsburg. New York: Crown, 1979.

Whatever Happened to Beverly Bigler's Birthday?, by Barbara Williams. New York: Harcourt, 1979; London: Harcourt, 1979.

The Black Dog Who Went into the Woods, by Edith Thacher Hurd. New York: Harper, 1980.

How I Found Myself at the Fair, by Pat Rhoads Mauser. New York: Atheneum, 1980.

How We Got Our First Cat, by Tobi Tobias. New York: F. Watts, 1980.

Oliver and Alison's Week, by Jane Breskin Zalben. New York: Farrar, Straus, 1980.

Play and Sing—It's Christmas! by Brooke Minarik Varnum. New York: Macmillan, 1980; London: Collier Macmillan, 1980.

The April Fool, by Alice Schertle. New York: Lothrop, 1981.

Joseph on the Subway Trains, by Kathleen Benson. Reading, Mass.: Addison-Wesley, 1981.

Mail-Order Wings, by Beatrice Gormley. New York: Dutton, 1981.

The New Friend, by Charlotte Zolotow. New York: Crowell, 1981.

Pajama Walking, by Vicki Kimmel Artis. Boston: Houghton, 1981.

The Seeing Summer, by Jeanette Eyerly. New York: Lippincott, 1981.

Fifth Grade Magic, by B. Gormley. New York: Dutton, 1982.

The Halloween Candy Mystery, by Marion M. Markham. Boston: Houghton, 1982.

I Dance in My Red Pajamas, by E. T. Hurd. New York: Harper, 1982.

Mitzi and the Terrible Tyrannosaurus Rex, by B. Williams. New York: Dutton, 1982.

Alice and the Boa Constrictor, by Laurie Adams and Allison Courdet. Boston: Houghton, 1983.

Best Friend Insurance, by B. Gormley. New York: Dutton, 1983.

Good Dog, Bad Dog, by Corinne Gerson. New York: Atheneum, 1983.

Mitzi's Honeymoon with Nana Potts, by B. Williams. New York: Dutton, 1983.

The Christmas Present Mystery, by M. M. Markham. Boston: Houghton, 1984.

For I Will Consider My Cat Jeoffry, by Christopher Smart. New York: Atheneum, 1984.

Mitzi and Frederick the Great, by B. Williams. New York: Dutton, 1984.

The Thing in Kat's Attic, by Charlotte Towner Graeber. New York: Dutton, 1984.

The Explorer of Barkham Street, by Mary Stolz. New York: Harper, 1985.

Fourth of July, by Barbara Joosse. New York: Knopf Books for Young Readers, 1985.

The Ghastly Glasses, by B. Gormley. New York: Dutton, 1985.

Mitzi and the Elephants, by B. Williams. New York: Dutton, 1985.

Lulu and the Witch Baby, by Jane O'Conner. New York: Harper, 1986.

Wheels, by Jane Resh Thomas. New York: Clarion Books, 1986.

Jam Day, by B. Joosse. New York: Harper, 1987.

Lulu Goes to Witch School, by J. O'Conner. New York: Harper, 1987.

Molly, by Ruth Shaw Radlauer. New York: Simon &

Schuster, 1987.

Molly Goes Hiking, by R. S. Radlauer. New York: Simon & Schuster, 1987.

Richard and the Vratch, by B. Gormley. New York: Avon, 1987.

The Boston Coffee Party, by Doreen Rappaport. New York: Harper, 1988.

Breakfast by Molly, by R. S. Radlauer. New York: Simon & Schuster, 1988.

Molly at the Library, by R. S. Radlauer. New York: Simon & Schuster, 1988.

The Takealong Dog, by LaPorte. New York: Greenwillow, 1988.

Winning by Magic, by B. Gormley. New York: Avon, 1988.

Dinah's Mad Wishes, by B. Joosse. New York: Harper, 1989.

More Fifth Grade Magic, by B. Gormley. New York: Dutton, 1989.

Selene Goes Home, by Lucy Diggs. New York: Atheneum, 1989.

FOR ADULTS

Books written:

A Craving. New York: Avon, 1982.

Life Drawing. New York: Delacorte, 1986.

George Mendoza

1934-

My heart has followed all my days
Something I cannot name . . .
—Don Marquis

I do not believe in the words of Jean Cocteau: "An artist cannot speak about his art any more than a plant can discuss horticulture." An artist must speak about his art and how it synthesizes with his life. If an artist remains pure to his art then his life becomes his art. I do believe in George Santayana's wisdom: "An artist is a dreamer consenting to dream of the actual world."

When I was about nine years old my father rented a summer cottage by a brook in Jamaica, Vermont. The brook was wide and shallow, and downstream there was an iron bridge crossing where the water suddenly became mysterious and deep.

The brook was like a wild child tumbling spring-cold from the Green Mountains, its banks filtered with fern and birch and alder leaves. I remember the finger-deep coves near the edge of the bank that sheltered minnows and little trouts. Here, as a boy from the city, I came to dream, to drift, to get lost in a world I had never known before.

I did not know it then but that brook was to shape my life forever. It was to make poetry of my manhood, turn all my being onto the course of natural things—stars in the eyes of fish, pebbles in the grass, and the sound of wind in dreams. It made me a romantic, a lover, a gypsy.

All that summer it seemed I spent my time wandering from one rock to the next along that brook. Upstream I went and downstream, discovering, listening, sometimes falling asleep with the song of the brook playing in my head.

A trout would splash and I would feel a wild sensation come over me. What was the fish seeking? The mystery of this underwater creature suddenly blooming in air like a bird, then gone into the pebbly depths. How can I catch you? I wondered, *bring you to my hands?*

My first trout rod was a wobbly metal contraption with a reel wound with black string that looked more like a toy for Central Park goldfishing. But I took that rod and reel seriously; indeed I did, as I had

George Mendoza

assured myself that this was the rod and reel that would take my first trout.

I went back to the place where I had seen that glorious trout appear, and, sticking a sweet worm on my hook, I cast for the fish. It was a sloppy cast and my worm went everywhere but into the water. Again a worm, again a cast.

Nothing happened. Where was that fish hiding? I tried again and again, hoping my fish would reward me for my efforts. I had about given up hope, thinking that this brook held no fish, at least no fish for me, when suddenly a tug, a great shock came into my hand—a fish! I had hooked into my fish!

That trout leaped and thrashed, how he leaped

and thrashed, a brook trout of about twelve gleaming inches, a garden of flowers growing out of its silvery sides. I couldn't believe my eyes. Then I felt my knees and legs begin to tremble, my hand and arm quivered down into my heart and it seemed as though I could hear the trout talk to me: *You'll not hold me, wandering boy, but this day I'll give you a memory that will haunt you for all your days.*

I've got you now, I had thought. He had flopped upon a nest of rocks in a shallow of the brook. I remember I had just begun to reach for him when he wiggled free of the hook. For a stunned moment I could only watch him slip slowly back into the water.

Frantically I fell upon the fish with my whole body. I wanted that trout. More than anything in the world I wanted that trout to be mine forever.

I don't know how my fish got away but he did, and I've been looking for him in brooks and rivers and ponds and along banks ever since that time.

I know he's somewhere, big and strong and beautiful. I tell myself he will never be caught. And if he has been hooked, he got away as he did when he was young and a daring fighter.

Something else too, a secret thought: I don't think I'll ever find my trout, and in my heart I hope I never will. If I did, maybe the haunting road of river calling would be gone, and a brook would come to be only the bones of a long-ago time. I would never want that to happen, so I keep searching.

I hear splashing
under a tree.
Trout rolls over
like a crescent moon
in the water dark.
If you see my eyes
by a river bank
I have come a-searching
like a gypsy boy.

Sailor Searching for a Brook

After that summer I never wanted to leave Vermont. I begged my father to buy a farmhouse, to give up the city and dig into the wild country. I'd do anything to live where there were meadows and flowers and streams to follow, and my fish still to catch.

We even looked at a few houses as I remember, but my father explained how unrealistic I was being.

"We're not of the Vermont marrow," my father had said. "You're the son of a Spaniard born and we'd be foreigners here until the prophets wrote the next Bible."

I didn't understand my father's words. What did my being Spanish and Irish have to do with living among the gentlefolk of Vermont?

"You'll learn the American way when you return to this country someday," my father had warned me, and that was the end of Vermont for many long summers.

You were born in Chicago,
were you stranger?
You were born in Ohio,
were you stranger?
You were born in Texas,
were you stranger?
If you didn't know where you
were born,
you wouldn't be a stranger.
You'd be a flute player
looking for the back of a tree.
You'd be a poet spinner
flying with a yellow finch.
You'd be a lean and handsome
lover
loving every loving thing.

A few years later we moved from New York and settled in Stony Brook, Long Island, a reconstructed Revolutionary village surrounded by seawater tides, endless grass flats, screaming gulls, and intoxicating smells from the ocean beyond.

Schooners and square-riggers had put into this port around the turn of the century; this romantic reality made the little village authentic and not really anything else.

Here I learned the ways of the sea and I became a sailor and a swimmer and built my own sailboat.

Out on my boat wearing my black turtleneck, I felt like Jack London; I had the look of an adventurer and thought that as long as the world was wild and full of nature then I would be free.

When I went sailing I always took my rusty old Vermont trout rod, for I loved to troll for mackerel and weakfish while my little sloop ran before a good breeze. Summer days and nights on into the fall I was a boy sail-bent and fishing out the ocean. I believe I must have caught and eaten every kind of fish, clam, crab, or eel there was, but something was missing in this basketful of happiness.

I was still yearning for my trout and for my brook. I was a sailor on an ocean as deep as God's voice, but all the while I was looking for a mountain slide of stream, a run of freshwater rocks, the spongy bank full of shadow drift and whispers.

I was seeking the magical, wandering trout born

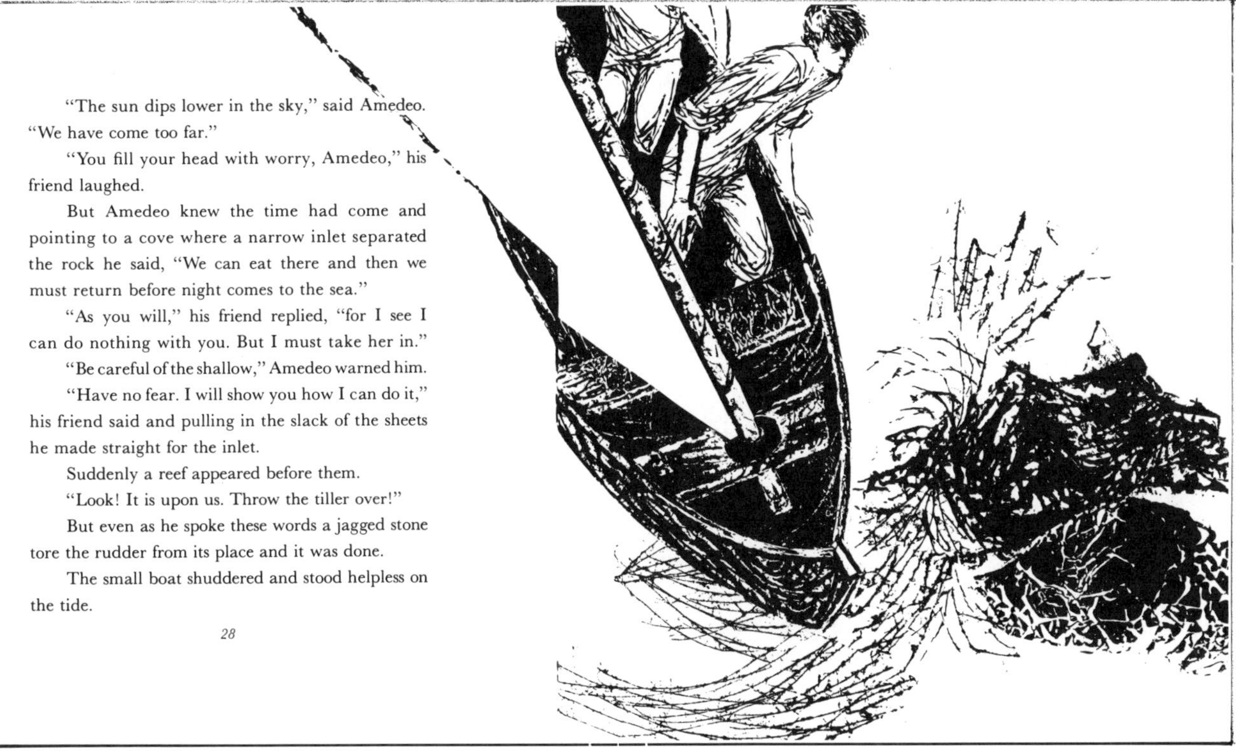

"The sun dips lower in the sky," said Amedeo. "We have come too far."

"You fill your head with worry, Amedeo," his friend laughed.

But Amedeo knew the time had come and pointing to a cove where a narrow inlet separated the rock he said, "We can eat there and then we must return before night comes to the sea."

"As you will," his friend replied, "for I see I can do nothing with you. But I must take her in."

"Be careful of the shallow," Amedeo warned him.

"Have no fear. I will show you how I can do it," his friend said and pulling in the slack of the sheets he made straight for the inlet.

Suddenly a reef appeared before them.

"Look! It is upon us. Throw the tiller over!"

But even as he spoke these words a jagged stone tore the rudder from its place and it was done.

The small boat shuddered and stood helpless on the tide.

28

From And Amedeo Asked, How Does One Become a Man? *by George Mendoza. Illustrated by Ati Forberg. (Copyright © 1959 by George Braziller, Inc. Reprinted by permission of the author.)*

out of a poet's noonday dream, fiercely colored by a meadow painter and let to fly in the sky called stream, called brook, called river, where men become boys again.

I remember how sweet were those days of my youth and how romantically inclined I was to the sea. I thought the oceans of the world were out there just waiting for me to touch them. "Where does the sea go?" I had asked an old fisherman who lived in a shack by the sea in our village. He looked at me with his deep-lined, sun-darkened face and then, looking out toward the soft curve of the horizon, he answered simply: "As far as you can dream."

I went back home that night and wondered about what the old man had said. Surely he knew something I didn't know, I thought, and he knew you just couldn't answer a question like that because, if you really want to know where the sea goes, you have to find out for yourself.

Then I knew that the dream is the challenge, the challenge of facing the sea and conquering it.

That's what I thought I would do when I was fourteen. I stowed food and water aboard my 13½-foot sloop, raised anchor, and sailed out of my hometown port of Stony Brook for Block Island.

September had just started, and the red storm flags were flapping wildly from the poles and there was not a boat to be seen on the water anywhere. I was alone with my little boat and we made good time the whole part of that day. The wind was full in the sails and my sloop surged along with the sea. The sky was clear and the sun was bright, and if you dug your toes into the floorboards, you could feel the current throbbing under the keel.

We rose and dipped and rose again in the singing sea and life was keenly good and we flew down the north shore past Montauk into the Atlantic Ocean.

But when night came, the rudder came loose and the centerboard broke and the jib sail blew to ribbons. It was terribly dark; the stars were glassy and there was no moon. The winds were no longer warm but cold now, and I remember shivering in the darkness. We began to flounder helplessly. Finally I took down the mainsail, put the sea anchor over the side to keep the boat from getting hit broadside by the waves, and stayed with the tiller.

That was a long night. In the morning I raised my red McGregor shirt to the top of the mast and hoped a passing boat would spot me. It did. A twin-propellered yacht towed me back to Port Jefferson.

And what an indignity that was. I was angry. But I learned something about the sea that night. I learned it can be your friend one moment then turn against you and slap you down. But if you love the sea, you try again because you react with a sense of challenge; you see it as a dare to survive some awesome anger or danger.

Years later I crossed the Atlantic in a 38-foot sloop—alone—and again in 1962 in a 33-foot sloop. What makes you do it? Why? I guess because you have to find out how far the sea goes.

Indubitably, those extraordinary experiences helped forge many ideas for children's books and novels. My first book, *And Amedeo Asked, How Does One Become a Man?*, begins:

> Once in a small village near the sea there lived a boy who more than anything else in the world wanted to become a man. And his name was Amedeo.
>
> "How does one become a man?" Amedeo asked his father who was the carpenter of the village.
>
> His father looked down into the black luminous eyes and tried to answer.
>
> "When you can see the tallest tree and smell the earth and roots of it and hold a piece of wood of it and know your hands can shape from it whatever form you will—then, my son, you will be a man."
>
> Amedeo looked at him and nodded.
>
> But when he walked away his father lit his pipe and thought about what he had told him and wanted to call him back and make him understand.
>
> And then, feeling the teeth of his saw he set himself to work.

And then my first novel, *The Hawk Is Humming*:

> He was a man who drifted alone on the sea in a sloop. He had been on the sea for many days now and his boat carried him across the Bay of Fundy and he hoped to reach one of the small fishing villages along the northern coast of Maine before the storm came.
>
> He pulled in the sheets to catch the wind but the boat was old and would not respond readily and he knew it. He had to haul down hard on the lines and he cursed the storm.
>
> It was a gaff-rigged sloop with a clipper bow and it lugged full bilges beneath the waterline. It was old and worn and exceptionally wide across the beam. It had once been used to carry lumber up and down the New England coast. Now the boat belonged to him and he spent his days on it.
>
> He lived like this on the sea out of reach of land. When he needed fresh water or food he put into a small village. He took any work he could find. He worked as a laborer with the nets, with his back and with his hands. He worked until he earned enough money to buy provisions and then he returned to the sea. It was many years since any person or place had held him.

And so many other children's books were born because of my sailing days: *A Poem for Putting to Sea; And I Must Hurry for the Sea Is Coming In; Alphabet Boat; The Scribbler.*

Unfortunately, during my growing up years, my years of discovery of the world of nature which was to become my poet's beacon forever, I cannot recall many good moments between my father and me. It was as though we were on two entirely different paths without one ever crossing the other. While it's true that we used to talk about Milton, Blake, Hemingway, Faulkner, Plato, and Aristotle, sometimes for hours at a sitting, we never really ever talked to each other from the deep, exposed corners of the heart where you could get to know somebody inside out. Looking back I guess I can say we were never really friends. I never remember my father throwing his arms around me and saying: "I love you, Son."

But that's all right. He was responsible for introducing me to Vermont rivers and meadows and pine-smelling woods. He was responsible for taking me down to the sea and he made me aware that within the world of nature lay my true calling. And so for that I will always feel a profound sense of fragmented love for that strange European who happened to be my father.

> Who cannot remember his father?
> Are you not the son?
> All his son?
> Is he not the father of your tidal desires?
> Are you not the son of his dark spun songs?
> O speak the son, where is the son,

Nicole Sekora-Mendoza

On a stream in New York State: "The natural world is where I'm able to feel the poetry in me again...the innocence...the return to the time when I was a boy on the streams of Vermont."

who would crush a feather of his father's
soarings?

Another poem that recalls the mystery of my father:

I had a calling
to wander like a drifter man
from town to town . . .
to look into dusty windows
that never looked back at me . . .
I've sailed across many roads
hitched-up to things behind
I didn't understand.

I've slept in the orchards of a flower
along the lonely tracks
of beggar trains
that clinked upon the rails of mournful dreams.

I've walked the shores of sea
when the seasons were tunes of solitude . . .
I've larked in the nests of sun-falls
pooled in clearings carved from wood . . .
I'll say on a penny's toss,
I've gone ahead of you, Sir . . .

I've floated in the knots of moon-drifts
when the hills were waves of golden flows . . .
I've let the stars fall upon me
until I could taste the light-year wine . . .
my soul,
I've given to the silken rain . . .
I've followed the river of meadow days
when the little plum fish
were waxing their pebbly beds . . .
I've made love in Heaven
to a creature of rare petal dust . . .
I've gone ahead of you, Sir . . .
and beyond myself—
because I was hitched-up
to things behind
I didn't understand.

The last time I saw my father was late one night. I was about seventeen years old then. I remember he and my mother had a terrible argument and I asked him to leave the house. I pressed him a shirt and walked him to the train station. I never saw him again although years later, when I was living in Paris, I was walking through a park and at that moment I knew he had died. Heartless as this may seem to you, I never wanted to know where he was buried. On that day I bought some flowers near the Parc Monceau and gave them to the first beautiful girl I could find. "These are from my father," I said. She took them and I walked away without saying another word.

The artist is the lover of Nature; therefore he is her slave and her master.
—Sir Rabindranath Tagore

After college and adventuring all over the world, I began to think of writing in a very serious way. I felt that writing was more than just a visitor but within me to stay. I had read all the great poets, novelists, philosophers, essayists; and I could never feel satisfied that I had ever read enough. How I admired writers like Jack London, Ernest Hemingway, Camus, Dostoevsky, Cervantes, and the one that fired my imagination most—James Joyce.

Could I ever be like one of these truly great writers, I wondered? I knew I didn't want to be just another slick, Hollywood, money-hungry character who sloshes out junk in the name of writing or in the name of the unholy buck. I abhorred creatures of this

"In Madrid I had a pair of hunting boots made for me by Tenorio, the same famous zapateria who fitted Ernest Hemingway in 1956"

ilk. For me writing was a pure thing and you wrote to experience what was honest and good within your heart. When you look at the best-seller lists and see what publishers are pushing out these days you have to cringe with a frisson of disgust at what companies publish and what people read.

One bit of wisdom that came from Hemingway always sticks to my creative rhizomes: "Always start with one true sentence," he said. "Write out of what you feel, write with your heart full of passion and pain of what you are feeling; and don't be afraid to make a fool of yourself. Others will try soon enough."

What wonderful, sagacious advice.

All my books, novels, children's books, poetry, more than one hundred now, published in countries all over the world, came directly from some kind of deep personal experience. Not only from my sea-adventuring but mostly from my trout-fishing journeys that continue to this day. I've been now all over the world touching the streams and wild places of trout and salmon. I've walked the cliffs and banks of the dreamlike Boulder River in Montana, and I've picked purple loosestrife along the Loue River in Franche-Comté. By wintertime I will be flying to the Malleo, Quilquihue, and Chimehuin in Argentina.

When will the madness be gone? Glorious in visions, all my rivers are like my fingers, a part of me forever, and I am possessed by them. I've never broken a blind date with a river. And I keep going back as though haunted by the primal forest that shelters the eternal stream. Is there music over the river? Is there humor and contentment? Is there a reawakening of love? Yes, and if you gaze deep into the face reflected in the water you might see yourself as you were once, young and wandering free.

One of the stories I like to tell is about the time I went to fish in New Zealand during our icy month of February.

I was fishing the Hunter, one of Prince Charles's favorite rivers, when I found myself snagged up on the river bottom. Another good muddler, I thought, gone! But then my line began to move, slowly at first, and then suddenly it was moving deep and hard and I knew I had hooked a tremendous fish.

For more than a half hour the fish fought; with all his strength he tried to make his break to freedom. He sounded, he charged, he jumped, he tore line from my reel, he made me slip and fall into the river. But I held him and took him in until he lay, all twelve pounds, on the sandy bank, his huge toothy jaws held fiercely open.

"Forgive me, trout, " I said aloud and struck him all at once stone dead.

Wet and cold, arm aching, trembling with my unexpected victory, I sat beside my beautiful scarlet-streaked rainbow trout talking to myself like an idiot, shouting my joy to the snowy peaks of the southern Alps, for surely I was reeling with my conquest.

I told myself that all a fisherman had to do was make a catch like that, one rare catch, and the day belonged to him, for God had smiled upon him.

When I opened the trout, I discovered an eight-inch freshly swallowed river rat entombed in its pearly belly. I had never seen a rat in a trout's stomach before, only beetles and grasshoppers and minnows. The sight of the rat disturbed me and I heaved it back into the river, feeling almost sorry I had killed this fish because he must have been a savage and brave hunter.

Later that evening, when I returned to my lakeside hotel with my trophy trout in hand, there were two elderly and very refined American ladies from Greenwich, Connecticut, who, greatly admiring my fish, asked if I might share him for dinner.

"Don't you want a picture of your fish?" one of the silver-haired ladies asked.

"Never cared for pictures of dead fish," I said.

"You should have had him mounted," ventured the other. "Why, he's as big as the ones mounted in the bar."

After dinner, I thought, Mendoza, why don't you go over to the Connecticut ladies and inform them that they have just eaten a trout that had an eight-inch river rat in its stomach. Go on, tell them, and watch their faces turn all red and confused. Dare you, Mendoza, do it, tell them.

But I didn't. I don't know why I didn't tell them because it's something that I would have done, perverse being that I sometimes am.

Now the trout was part of me forever and, I suppose, so was the river rat. As for the ladies from Connecticut, they departed early the following morning, leaving behind a gift for me—a rare and very expensive bottle of New Zealand's best Pino Chardonnay.

If I had told them about the river rat, I might have been drinking beer.

It's stories like the "River Rat" that come out of adventures *lived,* and I feel that's the best way to write: you've got to go out and experience life so that you can taste and feel your words.

I know that when I wade into a river fishing for trouts I feel as though I am entering another part of my soul. And as I watch the early lights flower in the shadows, I know I have come to the river seeking more, much more, than the catching of the trouts.

Mendoza fishing for trout: "Fishing is my church. I go to it the way some people go to Sunday mass."

How can I describe this to you—you who have fished the morning lonely and you who were never there?

I must relate an experience I had while fishing a river called Gacka in Yugoslavia, which holds trout as large as your imagination. These native monsters are called white wolves and they are rarely seen anymore . . .

For several years, and more I hope will come, I've been returning to this one particular limestone river in the flowerswept valley of Croatia. Why this most difficult, certainly most unpredictable, river attracts me more than any other river I've fished in the world is no mystery to this incurable nympholept.

Simply, in my mind's river-searching eye, the Gacka represents the quintessential river—it has in it a little bit of all the rivers I've ever touched: the slow and wide Batten Kill in Vermont; the fast-running Boulder in Montana; the mint-flowing Test in England; the wild, moon-haunted rivers of Chile and Argentina.

By the end of the first week in June, I was suddenly there with my river Gacka. It had taken me nearly fourteen hours from my door in New York City to reach the Hotel Gacka, Licko Lesce, Yugoslavia. Fourteen hours waiting to cast a fly for brown and rainbow trout that you knew from past trips ranged from two pounds to fourteen pounds and larger! A man who has his heart pumping wildly to get to his river could die in that time just from the sheer overwhelming yearning of wanting to be bankside before he physically reached his destination.

When I finally arrived at the Hotel Gacka, situated about fifty feet from the gurgling river, I had a strong espresso to try to stay awake. How I wanted to fish that very evening after so many hours of bumping around in the air and on the ground. But my second cafe could not keep me awake; I staggered to my room with its wraparound balcony overlooking the lovely, meadow-winding river and, opening the doors of the balcony wide to let in the sweet, mountain-valley breezes, I was soon falling into a deep, swoonlike sleep.

I woke at about an hour before dawn the next morning, and after a quick, hot shower and shave, I was soon dressed and stepping gingerly into my new Ranger hip boots. Gathering up my old Garrison eight-footer and a few fly books containing some of my favorite patterns for Gacka trout, I was out of the hotel like a furtive, hunting cat.

As I made my way upstream along the yellow and plum flowering bankside to the place I loved where the river took a sharp bend and channeled suddenly very deep, I thought to myself: Here I am, I'm really here, I'm back again with you, old river, don't you recognize your faithful, wandering friend?

If a river could speak, I suppose it would answer a man, but a river talks in other ways deeper than words, and what you hear lasts forever and doesn't easily expire the way inconsequential conversation does between people; a river sounds a man if he's got any sounding room at all and then it goes deep and stays, and that's a fact, not poetry.

I don't know what fly or streamer I knotted on first; it's really not important. What was more important than anything else in the world to me was that very moment standing before my beloved river and knowing that somewhere very deep in her secret, undulating vaults there were great trout lurking in snakeweed and shadow.

One good, working cast and my line was across the river, sinking down across the hole of eternity, and though I could not see my fly darting through the darkness with its brilliant feathers opening and closing as it flashed over and under both weed and stone, I could see it as though it were the only star in the night. A trout fly sunken deep is like a star, when you think about it; it dazzles, it sparkles, it shoots out lambent messages to preglacial creatures, and it is as alive as you want it to be. It is a star, for it is being looked up to, and if you play your line right, it will take that native Gacka trout, rarely caught anymore, the brown trout the Croatian fishermen call the white wolf.

As the saturnine clouds began to filter through the first rays of summer light, I felt an electrical jolt at the end of my line that sped like a rocket to my heart and capsized all my romantic thoughts of being with my Gacka once again. What was this fury that had my treasured bamboo rod bent to the breaking and all my line running off my reel down into the hole of eternity? Had I struck, finally struck after all these years, the elusive white wolf trout? Had my star-fly aroused in him some instinctive urge to strike from his paradisiacal cave, to take down the twitching, breathing, feathery intruder? Was it hunger or anger that made this unseen missile rake the barb of the hook and nail my heart against the bank with fear?

For more time than I can remember the great force that came from the hole of eternity held me fast as though, indeed, I were the prey; it held me until my arm ached and my fingers felt they would never open again. Once the rod shook with such violence that I nearly fell from the slippery ledge of the bank into the river.

I tried desperately to take in line, but the trout was unrelenting and would not be budged from its snakeweed crater. Truly, I thought, this must be the rare white wolf trout that I have heard fishermen talk about and search for, a native holdover from years past, a survivor from the time before the glaciers to the present age of our doomsday world.

"I can't fight you much longer," I said to the trout. "My hands are numb. My arm feels dead. Won't you give a little?"

My rod shuddered with the shock of an even greater force trying to wrench it from my grip.

"You are the white wolf trout, aren't you?" I shouted, hoping some other fisherman might hear.

Suddenly an explosion shook the center of the hole of eternity and millions of sun-filled droplets showered up into the sky, filling with the earth colors of flowers and grasses and sky. It was a towering, bursting, rainbow fountain erupting all at once with tremendous force and beauty, and concealed within its dazzling plumes was the thrashing, rare white wolf trout.

For a flash of time, the great trout slashed across my eyes, and then it was gone like a dying storm into the whirl of the hole of eternity. Shaking, wet all over, I sat down on the bank and tried to recapture in my mind what I had just seen and experienced.

"No need to try to measure it," I kept saying to myself over and over again. "No need to know it was the largest trout you've ever seen in all the world. It's gone and maybe you're finished too, because losing such a battle makes a man feel like he can never get up again."

Then I shouted into the hole of eternity: "You killed me, white wolf trout! How many men have you killed like this?"

Now the river throbbed in the deep, calm channels where the blue, inky currents came together, folding over and under each other, and I listened a long time to the river. Closing my eyes, I let it heal my wound, my defeat.

"But it's gone," I said to the river, talking out loud. "How many chances has a man to come so close . . . to taking such a great and rare trout that all fishermen seek?"

The river kept moving through me and soon I heard the sounds of birds singing as they sailed back and forth over the hole of eternity. I opened my eyes and got to my feet. The sun was warm and sparkling off the river and the flowers seemed to be dancing in the sunlight. All I wanted to do now was to go back to the hotel and have a double espresso and perhaps talk to another fisherman who might find my morning interlude with the white wolf trout more than an apocryphal tale told by a river dreamer.

That adventure on my river Gacka became an almost mystical, transcendental experience for me.

And I believe it to be the most powerful of all my fishing memories.

I remember my mother used to tell me, "If you don't think there's anything out there in the world, then go find a leaf and look at it closely, at all its veins (I believe she called them rivers) and colors and even in the smallest corner of a leaf there is a story . . . "

But you've got to open your eyes, you've got to look, you've got to be aware, and, I guess, sometimes you've got to push off in your small, unproven boat and face the sea, undaunted by your fear of the unknown.

My point is that you just can't sit on your thumbs and expect to come up with creative and original ideas: you've got to go out and seize them. *Carpe diem!* They're not going to drop off the trees and say, "Hello, here I am, write me."

Sure you can say, well, that's easy for you, you've done it, but where am I going to find ideas?

My answer: everywhere. You get ideas by looking, listening, reading, and by being acutely aware of what is happening around you.

On the lighter side of experience, I recall one evening when my wife and I were having dinner at a friend's sumptuous home in the country. Just about the time dinner was to begin, our hostess informed her beleaguered-looking husband that there was a dead skunk floating faceup in their lovely, olympic-sized swimming pool.

I looked at my wife, she looked at me, and we both instinctively knew that there was a children's book in the wake of that bizarre request. Back at my desk later that evening, I stuck a piece of paper in the typewriter and typed *The Skunk in the Pond,* which began something like this:

> There was a simple woodcutter who lived with his wife, a nagging goat of a woman, and his thirteen children, all fat and always very hungry.
>
> Every night when the woodcutter came home to eat his supper, his wife would start nagging him the moment he walked into the house.
>
> This night, as he dipped his spoon into his bowl of stew, his wife bleated, "There's a dead skunk floating in the pond outside. I can't eat until you get rid of it."
>
> "Now?" cried the woodcutter. "Must I do it now?"

Once again a children's book drawn from personal experience. And for me this was always the best way to capture a story, to feel deeply and sincerely about what it was I was writing.

Looking back over the past thirty years of writing children's books, poetry, and novels, I can't think of one book I ever got involved with for which I wasn't touched in the first place by some kind of real-life experience, whether it was humorous or life-threatening or, in many cases, just born out of plain whimsical nonsense.

When my beloved Batten Kill River in Vermont was being threatened by pollution, I wrote *Goodbye, River, Goodbye,* with stunning photographs by George Tice; when a New York vacuous socialite remarked that she had just bought a set of rare dinner plates for ten thousand dollars, I wrote *The World from My Window,* a book that at once revealed the plight of our nation's poor and suffering children; when my children wanted to learn guitar, along came *My Book of the Guitar* with Andrés Segovia; and when my son, Ryan, wanted to become a tennis star, I wrote *Hitting Hot* with the world's number one tennis ace, Ivan Lendl.

Back in those early days when I first started to cut a reputation as an up-and-coming children's book author, I was asked by Hofstra University to conduct an experimental workshop for anyone on or off campus interested in the art of writing, illustrating, and selling a children's book.

Held twice a week in the evening hours, those classes proved to be more than interesting indeed. For most of my pupils were very beautiful young women, especially the ones who sat in the front-row seats.

All I can remember from that whole session is that I had to be very serious and if I allowed myself to flirt just once—I knew I was finished as a teacher.

But what temptations I had to overcome. On more than one occasion, I told myself I had to be like a doctor, a priest; I was determined not to let one of those seductive sirens get to me. After all, this was my first teaching assignment and I wanted to be regarded as a good teacher, a teacher with his mind on his subject.

To get my class thinking very seriously about the subject of children's books, I immediately challenged each student's intellect with the question: "What does the baobab tree symbolize in *The Little Prince* by Antoine de Saint-Exupéry?"

Of course, everyone knew or had read *The Little Prince* but no one could readily answer the puzzle of the baobab tree.

"Now!" cried his wife. "Get rid of that dead skunk now!"

Meekly the woodcutter got up from the table, went outside to the pond, fished out the dead skunk with a pole, and heaved it by the tail into the bushes.

But when he returned to the house his bowl of stew was gone, and his nagging wife and thirteen children were all asleep in bed.

The next night as the woodcutter sat down to eat his fish his wife bleated, "There's a dead skunk floating in the pond outside. I can't eat until you get rid of it."

The woodcutter looked at his wife with despair in his eyes and then he looked around the large wooden table at his thirteen children, all twenty-six eyes wide and gleaming on his fish.

48

From The Crack in the Wall and Other Terribly Weird Tales *by George Mendoza. Illustrated by Mercer Mayer. (Text copyright © 1968 by George Mendoza. Illustrations copyright © 1968 by Mercer Mayer. Reprinted by permission of the author.)*

When you think about it, it's amazing how much we think we know and yet we really know nothing at all.

So off my students went and back they came with hundreds of different answers: some said it was just an odd tree with a fat trunk that grew in Africa; some said it depicted ugliness; one person said it represented the good and evil forces that exist in the world, and on and on . . .

Of course, there was no real answer to the significance of the baobab tree although I will always think of the baobab as being symbolic of one of Saint-Exupéry's characters in *The Little Prince* who are always running around looking for labels and symbols just so that we all remain confused. But I was able to accomplish—in one devilish stroke—an intellectual basis for my classes, and once that was established we got down to some very serious business that proved helpful to all my students.

For instance, the art of putting a picture book together became their favorite topic and we discussed many books and why and how they worked.

Specifically, we analyzed alphabet books, counting books, all kinds of picture book formats. In most cases, I pointed out that each picture book originated with a simple concept and built around it. But I stressed that a good picture book had to have a strong theme to begin with and then you could build upon that theme naturally and humorously. I always advised my students to try to create out of their own original ideas and to avoid treacly themes.

During the course, one of my own books was used called *The Beastly Alphabet Book.* This book showed how repetition works and in this particular case not only repetition but there is also a chase taking place. We worked sedulously on many different forms of repetition and chase concepts and many picture books were created, written, illustrated, and blocked out using the thirty-two page and forty-eight page formats.

One of my most successful picture books—*The Gillygoofang*—regarded as being a classic even today, tells the story of a fish called the gillygoofang which swims backward to keep the water out of its eyes. You must see how this enduring picture book weaves its graphic, repetitive spell.

Some of the Famous People I've Worked With

I honestly believed I had Woody Allen convinced that he should work with me on a new concept I had in mind called *The Sesame Street Book of Opposites.* Imagine Woody Allen in a clown costume acting up/down, happy/sad, light/heavy, in/out. After several meetings with Woody at the Russian Tea Room and also with his agent at ICM, Woody finally said no. I remember I was in an awful jam, for I had promised Children's Television Workshop that Woody Allen would do my book, and now what was I going to do? Who could I possibly get who would be as funny as Woody Allen?

Fortunately, luck fell out of the sky and hit me on the head, for I was able to convince Zero Mostel that he should do my book. But once he said yes I had no idea what madness lurked around the corner.

I suppose I should have known from the very beginning. When I first met Zero it was at his art studio located on the dingy west side of Twenty-eighth Street. I'll remember that day for the rest of my life.

I knocked at Zero's door and in a moment I saw a huge eyeball appear at the peephole.

"Who's there?" boomed a ferocious voice coming from the other side of the door.

"George Mendoza," I answered firmly.

Suddenly the door flew open and a gigantic hairy arm grabbed me and pulled me inside. "Get in here so I can sue you."

Those were Zero Mostel's first words to me. After that he showed me his art studio, his paintings, his sculpture, and then we sat down at an enormous round oak table where we talked for hours about the concepts of *The Sesame Street Book of Opposites.* I must say that Zero Mostel brought much wisdom and humor and depth of understanding to a project that I thought was fairly basic.

For instance, Zero was totally captivated by the concept of On and Off. We talked about it for hours. As far as I was concerned it was so simple but Zero's curiosity about *how* to show it was overwhelming.

"The simplest things are the most difficult," he said as he drew several ideas on paper for On and Off.

I was beginning to think that perhaps he was stretching a point too far when, all of a sudden, he looked up at me, smiled, and said, "I've got it."

Then he put on his old battered top hat and from that moment on I knew we were going to have a classic.

"What should I wear for the book?" Zero asked, looking at me with his eyes bulging owl-like behind his thick lenses.

Sheldon Secunda

With Zero Mostel, while working on The Sesame Street Book of Opposites *and its film adaptation*

I hadn't thought of that aspect of the book.

"What about baby-dentons and a diaper?" he said, opening his eyes still wider.

I looked at Zero and wondered where in the world I was going to find his size.

"Don't worry," said Zero, precognitive of my thoughts, "there's a shop for whales downtown that will have my size."

Around that time I recall that the phone rang and Zero picked it up, burped into the receiver, and hung up.

"Who was that?" I couldn't help blurting out.

"That's my agent, Sam Cohn," Zero answered.

Sam Cohn, I thought, the most powerful agent in the world and Zero burps into the phone and hangs up. I couldn't believe it especially since Sam Cohn was known as the man who never returns phone calls, even if they are from God himself.

"He'll call back," said Zero looking down at the

phone.

Once again the phone rang. Zero picked it up. "Now what do you want? Don't you know I'm working on a very important new script?" Once again he burped into the receiver and slammed the phone down.

Not much later I discovered that Zero always played out these kind of puerile games with Sam Cohn and Sam loved every bit of Zero's bizarre humor.

When I finally left Zero's studio late that evening, I was extremely elated. I couldn't wait to get home and tell my wife about all my good luck.

I remember jumping out of the taxi in front of our house on Sixty-fourth Street, tripping in the gutter, twisting my ankle so badly I thought it was broken. Slightly crippled, I told my wife all the good news, and even though I had a swollen foot for a week we were extremely happy to be working on a new children's book with a comic genius like Zero Mostel.

But it was a totally insane experience: for instance, there was the time I was having lunch with Zero at the Russian Tea Room and he asked the waiter for some more butter. The waiter brought back more cubes but Zero looked down at them with disdain.

"May I please have some butter?" he pleaded unctuously.

Once again the waiter returned, this time with a quarter pound of hotel bar butter on a silver dish.

Zero was not pleased. "May I have *some* butter, p-l-e-a-s-e?" he implored with growing impatience.

I just sat there looking at Zero in stunned silence, not knowing if he was actually serious or if this was just one more of his crazy games.

Finally the waiter brought him a whole pound of butter on a huge platter.

"Thank you," said Zero with a great warm smile spreading across his face, and he started, at once, to butter his bread, butter his arm, butter his chest, and, if I were not seated safely opposite him, I believe to this day, he would have buttered me too.

While everyone in the Russian Tea Room stared at Zero (I think Woody Allen was there scowling at me) he very nonchalantly took a bite out of his buttered bread and proceeded to eat as though nothing at all had happened.

The book was finally published (along with a worldwide "Sesame Street" film) and Zero and I were sent to the American Book Association in Washington, where we signed thousands of books like we were movie stars.

Needless to say, *The Sesame Street Book of Opposites* was a huge success and sold nearly two hundred thousand copies. A hard act to follow.

After my first book with Marcel Marceau, *The Marcel Marceau Alphabet Book*, I wanted to follow up with the *Marcel Marceau Counting Book*; after all, what would be a more natural companion for the first book? But, for some arcane reason, I couldn't come up with the second concept as easily as I had created the first.

Then one day while we were summering in Vermont, my wife asked me to join in while she and my young daughter, Ashley, were watching their favorite TV show, "I Love Lucy." Picture this frustrated children's book author trying to come up with ideas for a new book and being asked to watch "I Love Lucy."

Reluctantly, I watched the show, munching cookies with Ashley and my wife, Nicole, while Lucy and her family were checking into a country inn. Then something caught my attention: everytime Lucy asked the innkeeper where the town officials kept themselves, the innkeeper suddenly disappeared behind the check-in counter only to reappear wearing the hat of a policeman, fire-chief, town mayor, etc.

That was it! Marcel Marceau would be photographed wearing twenty different kinds of hats. How very simple, and I would have missed the idea completely had I avoided "I Love Lucy." When I called Marceau in Paris and explained my concept to him, he was overjoyed. "Let's do it," he said. "Let's strike while the iron is hot!"

This book, conceived from such a simple idea, worked for several important reasons: 1) the hats themselves were colorful; 2) Marceau acted out each profession in a wonderfully authentic and amusing way; 3) the young reader could keep going back over the hats as they continued to accumulate on each page; 4) children love hats in the first place.

That book, photographed by Milton Greene (Marilyn Monroe's photographer), was a truly unique experience for Marceau and me. At the end of our "shoot" Marceau practically begged to keep the Indian chief's headdress. But we had to keep explaining to him that it was a rented prop that did not belong to us. Marceau could not understand why he could not have it and in that respect he is very much like a child. But when I look back at those lambent days when I worked with Marcel Marceau, I regret that I did not find some way to buy the Indian chief's headdress and give it to him as a token of my love for him.

Marceau and I have remained friends over the years since our books. I would love to work with him again but ever since "I Love Lucy" no further ideas

1 is a cowboy

is an artist

is an Indian

is Mr. Bip!

Selected from The Marcel Marceau Counting Book *by George Mendoza. Photographs by Milton H. Greene. (Copyright © 1971 by Doubleday & Co., Inc. Reprinted by permission of the author.)*

have struck to keep the "iron hot."

I've worked with other celebrities, including: Michel Legrand (*Michel's Mixed-up Musical Bird,* the book and "ABC Afterschool Special"); Andrés Segovia (*My Book of the Guitar*); Norman Rockwell (*Norman Rockwell's Americana ABC, Norman Rockwell's Boys and Girls at Play, Norman Rockwell's Diary for a Young Girl, Norman Rockwell's Scrapbook for a Young Boy*); Pope John Paul II ("Pope John Paul II—His World of Children"); Marc Chagall ("Lovebird"); Shirley MacLaine ("Overcoming," a TV series showing great people overcoming great obstacles); Muhammad Ali ("Roddy Dancer Is Waiting for Muhammad Ali," a one-hour TV special); Ivan Lendl (*Hitting Hot*); Milton Glaser (*Fish in the Sky*); Maurice Sendak (an interview for *Look*); Alexander Calder (*Masks,* a book and film project); Carol Burnett (*What I Want to Be When I Grow Up*); Prasanna Rao (*Shadowplay,* a "Sesame Street" book and film); and Hoagy Carmichael, Jr. (producer for "Mister Rodgers' Neighborhood").

What was my most interesting celebrity-book experience? I think the book with Andrés Segovia in which the maestro taught our children, Ashley and Ryan, the technique for guitar. A seemingly endless labor of love, it took nearly three years of countless trips to Spain, letters, and long-distance phone conversations to convince Maestro Segovia that he should work with me to produce such a work. But most of all, it required patience, for it must be understood that I was asking a genius to divert himself from the set course of his work and life, to spare time to give guidance to the beginner of the classical guitar.

Looking back over those years of working with some of the world's stellar personalities, I feel I was so fortunate to be able to produce books and films with these extraordinary human beings. I don't think any other children's book author has ever equaled my record there.

One Great Book

My son, Ryan, is going to be seventeen years old by the time this autobiographical sketch is published. The other evening he looked at me after dinner and said: "Wouldn't you like to have *one* great book that you would be remembered by for all time?" I looked at him very thoughtfully and silently. "You know what I mean, Dad, like James Joyce had his *Ulysses* and Dostoevsky his *Crime and Punishment* and Dante Alighieri *The Divine Comedy* and Goethe his *Faust* and Voltaire *Candide.*" He could have gone on and on, for he is such an avid reader and reminds me of the time when I was his age pouring through my mother's voluminous library. I guess I looked at him for a long time brooding over his question.

Working with wife, Nicole, and Andrés Segovia on My Book of the Guitar, *Madrid, 1978*

Yes, I thought to myself, I'd love to have written that one book like Hemingway wrote *The Old Man and the Sea* and Don Marquis created *the lives and times of archy and mehitabel,* and look at what Jack London had done with *The Call of the Wild.* That's forever, that's the world, that's being remembered not just for a time but for all time. Or was my life one long struggle of passing through the pages of many books trying to arrive at the one that is the culmination of an entire life's creative passage?

I answered my son with these words that finally wanted to be said:

"I wrote a book once, a long time ago, called *A Piece of String,* that became a classic of its kind for awhile. But that wasn't important. What was important is the fact that one day I received a letter from a young woman studying literature at a university who told me that she was seriously thinking of ending her life until she read *A Piece of String.* At first I couldn't believe the contents of this letter. But then I realized that my book had actually brought about a change in another person's struggle to be loving and kind and sensitive. My book had made a dent on one single human heart."

Nicole Sekora-Mendoza

Mendoza with son, Ryan, about 1976

Ryan gazed into my heart, with his dark, luminous eyes searching the very depths of my soul. "You know," he said, "it is so amazing what you have done with your life; you have survived as a writer doing basically what you wanted to do. We all want that in this world. We all want to be pure and true to ourselves. That's what that girl saw in you and you touched that chord in her."

"But I'm still in search of the 'one great book,'" I told my son. "I'm still climbing my mountain."

My son smiled that very warm and loving smile I have come to know so well. "You're still very innocent," he said, "like the children you love to write for. I'm very proud of you, Dad, for everything you have already done; I just want you to keep thinking of that one great book that I know is inside you and will come out someday. You see, Dad, I want to read that book. I know it will be as great as any book I have on my bookshelves. In fact, I have a space reserved for you next to Herman Melville."

I would like to close this sharing time with you by coming back to the beginning again. To where dreams are.

In front of me the mountain grows up, a lion's head of fossil stone faces away from the sun. The mountain is like a huge rock pillow against the sky. If the mountain had a voice it would say:

> rest against me stranger,
> wait with me till night falls
> and stars come beaming
> and Venus mound of light
> pours us a glass of wild
> dandelion wine.

I'm looking at the mountain and thinking many things; my head is a net for memories and thoughts and dreams, all coming and going like fish in the sea. I don't wish to hold anything long. I never did, except for the rare moments of life—like morning of this day that began cool, and the noon of this day filled with a Montana river-song and rainbows dancing down the falls of the canyon, and this evening, honey-glow evening, that will be coming by soon now, looking for a fishing friend.

Call me butterfly under mountain. That is my name. I am under the river and under the sea and there is the mountain and I am under the mountain, a butterfly lighting the flowers, flaming the fields.

I have no path and no stars guide me home. I am a blade of grass taller than a mountain. I am at my best when I'm in my boots on the brook and both ways upstream and downstream are empty of people and the traffic of sounds from the cities. I am the fallen leaf of October yellow and the wildness of weeds and grasses growing together out of the same earth.

Call me butterfly under mountain. I am a poet. I am a notebook of dreams that opens without words and goes on without words, for the word has come to be a vacant husk, and I would rather we could speak without the use of words, for they are meaningless and full of false weights.

Oh, let us put our dreams into the air and let them go like the time before when we were children and not so mixed into the ways of the world.

Walk with me into the night high up into the mountain wind. The trail is dark, no street lamps to secure our feet. The stars are distant. I've never felt they were friendly, only far away like where you began and where you think home is and the voice of someone you tried to love.

Darkness is in the wind and it comes down upon the world filling it like a tide and we become fish

Nicole Sekora-Mendoza

The author at the Ritz Hotel in Madrid

once more, and so we sleep under our ledges while dreams move into us creeping with fog.

And now, after all this, what have we understood? Who can answer? A grasshopper rattles and flies. There is something to learn from an inconsequential creature. Perhaps that it lives, keeps coming back, tunes the fields, lights the flowers, flames the fields.

> And so the boy still walks in me
> as he wandered long ago
> on a Vermont brook
> when the boy discovered
> the world had a beginning . . .
> and in the trees
> the wind made songs
> and the leaves were like
> the lips of a child . . .
> And in the boy
> there is no ending
> as the man watches him
> and tries to catch up.

SELECTED BIBLIOGRAPHY

FOR CHILDREN

And Amedeo Asked, How Does One Become a Man? (illustrated by Ati Forberg). New York: Braziller, 1959.

The Puma and the Pearl, with Wendy Sanford (illustrated by A. Forberg). New York: Walker, 1962.

Gwot! Horribly Funny Hairticklers (illustrated by Steven Kellogg). New York: Harper, 1967.

The Crack in the Wall and Other Terribly Weird Tales (illustrated by Mercer Mayer). New York: Dial, 1968.

Flowers and Grasses and Weeds (illustrated by Joseph Low). New York: Funk, 1968.

The Gillygoofang (illustrated by M. Mayer). New York: Dial, 1968.

The Hunter I Might Have Been: A Tale of Anguish and Love (illustrated with photographs by De Wayne Dalrymple). New York: Astor-Honor, 1968.

The Practical Man (illustrated by Imero Gobbato). New York: Lothrop, 1968.

A Wart Snake in a Fig Tree (illustrated by Etienne Delessert). New York: Dial, 1968.

And I Must Hurry for the Sea Is Coming In . . . (illustrated with photographs by D. Dalrymple). Englewood Cliffs, N. J.: Prentice-Hall, 1969.

A Beastly Alphabet (illustrated by J. Low). New York: Grosset & Dunlap, 1969.

The Digger Wasp (illustrated by Jean Zallinger). New York: Dial, 1969.

Herman's Hat (illustrated by Frank Bozzo). Garden City, N. Y.: Doubleday, 1969.

The Starfish Trilogy (illustrated by A. Forberg). New York: Funk, 1969.

Are You My Friend? (illustrated by F. Bozzo). Englewood Cliffs, N. J.: Prentice-Hall, 1970.

The Good Luck Spider and Other Bad Luck Stories (illustrated by Gahan Wilson). Garden City, N. Y.: Doubleday, 1970.

The Inspector (illustrated by Peter Parnall). Garden City, N. Y.: Doubleday, 1970.

The Marcel Marceau Alphabet Book (illustrated with photographs by Milton H. Greene). Garden City, N. Y.: Doubleday, 1970.

Big Frog, Little Pond (illustrated by P. Parnall). New York: McCall, 1971.

The Christmas Tree Alphabet Book (illustrated by Bernadette Watts). New York: World Publishing, 1971.

The Fearsome Brat (illustrated by F. Bozzo). New York: Lothrop, 1971.

Fish in the Sky (illustrated by Milton Glaser). New York: Doubleday, 1971.

Goodbye, River, Goodbye (illustrated with photographs by George A. Tice). Garden City, N. Y.: Doubleday, 1971.

The Hunter, the Tick, and the Gumberoo (illustrated by Philip Wende). New York: Cowles, 1971.

The Marcel Marceau Counting Book (illustrated with photographs by M. H. Greene). Garden City, N. Y.: Doubleday, 1971.

Moonfish and Owl Scratchings (illustrated by P. Parnall). New York: Grosset & Dunlap, 1971.

Moonstring (illustrated by Charles Jakubowski). New York: World Publishing, 1971.

The Scarecrow Clock (illustrated by Eric Carle). New York: Holt, 1971.

The Scribbler (illustrated by Robert Quackenbush). New York: Holt, 1971.

The Thumbtown Toad (illustrated by Monika Beisner). Englewood Cliffs, N. J.: Prentice-Hall, 1971.

The Alphabet Book: A Seagoing Alphabet Book (illustrated by Lawrence Di Fiori). New York: American Heritage Press, 1972.

Poem for Putting to Sea (illustrated by A. Forberg). New York: Hawthorn, 1972.

Sesame Street Book of Opposites with Zero Mostel (illustrated with photographs by Sheldon Secunda). New York: Platt & Munk, 1974.

Shadowplay, with Prasanna Rao (illustrated with photographs by Marc Mainguy). New York: Holt, 1974.

Doug Henning's Magic Book, with Howard Minsky. New York: Ballantine, 1975.

What I Want to Be When I Grow Up, with Carol Burnett (illustrated with photographs by S. Secunda). New York: Simon & Schuster, 1975.

Lost Pony (illustrated with photographs by Rene Burri). San Francisco: San Francisco Book, 1976.

Magic Tricks (illustrated by Jean-Paul Colbus). Glasgow: Collins, 1978.

Michel's Mixed-Up Musical Bird, with Michel Legrand (illustrated by De Patie Frelang Enterprises). Indianapolis: Bobbs-Merrill, 1978; London: Robson, 1978.

Segovia, My Book of the Guitar: Guidance for the Beginner, with Andrés Segovia (illustrated with photographs by Gerhard Gscheidle). Cleveland, Ohio: Philomel; Glasgow: Collins, 1979.

Need a House? Call Ms. Mouse! (illustrated by Doris Susan Smith). New York: Grosset & Dunlap, 1981; as *House by Mouse,* London: Deutsch, 1981.

Alphabet Sheep (illustrated by Kathleen Reidy). New York: Grosset & Dunlap, 1982.

Counting Sheep (illustrated by K. Reidy). New York: Grosset & Dunlap, 1982.

The Sheepish Book of Opposites (illustrated by K. Reidy). New York: Grosset & Dunlap, 1982.

Silly Sheep and Other Sheepish Rhymes (illustrated by K. Reidy). New York: Grosset & Dunlap, 1982.

Henri Mouse (illustrated by Joelle Boucher). New York: Viking, 1985.

Henri Mouse, the Juggler (illustrated by J. Boucher). New York: Viking, 1986.

"Norman Rockwell" Series:

Norman Rockwell's Americana ABC. New York: Dell, 1975.

Norman Rockwell's Boys and Girls at Play. New York: Abrams, 1976.

Norman Rockwell's Diary for a Young Girl. New York: Abbeville Press, 1978.

Norman Rockwell's Scrapbook for a Young Boy. New York: Abbeville Press, 1979.

Norman Rockwell's Four Seasons. New York: Grosset & Dunlap, 1982.

Norman Rockwell's Happy Holidays. New York: Putnam, 1983.

Norman Rockwell's Love and Remembrance. New York: Dodd, 1985.

Norman Rockwell's Patriotic Times (with foreword by Ronald Reagan). New York: Viking, 1985.

The Norman Rockwell Illustrated Cookbook: Classic American Recipes. New York: McGraw Hill, 1987.

Compiler of:

The World from My Window: Poems and Drawings. New York: Hawthorn, 1969.

FOR ADULTS

The Hawk Is Humming. Indianapolis: Bobbs-Merrill, 1964.

A Piece of String (illustrated by Norma Jean Koplin). New York: Obolensky, 1966.

Hunting Sketches (illustrated by Ronald Stein). New York: Astor-Honor, 1968.

The Mist Men, and Other Poems (designed by Paul Bacon). Garden City, N. Y.: Doubleday, 1970.

Fishing the Morning Lonely (illustrated with photographs by D. Dalrymple). Rockville Centre, N. Y.: Freshet Press, 1974.

Lord, Suffer Me to Catch a Fish. Quadrangle, 1974.

Secret Places of Trout Fishermen. New York: Macmillan, 1977.

Hitting Hot: Ivan Lendl's Fourteen-Day Tennis Clinic, with Ivan Lendl (illustrated with photographs by Walter Iooss, Jr.). New York: Random House, 1986.

Slammin' Sam: An Autobiography, with Sam Snead. New York: Donald I. Fine, 1986.

Many of Mendoza's more than one hundred books for children and adults are included in the George Mendoza Collection at Boston University.

Robert Quackenbush

1929-

Robert Quackenbush

Every book I have written and illustrated has been like a diary to me. There are nearly one hundred and fifty of these "diaries" so far. Each book reveals some aspect of my life and many of the books published after 1974 tell the story of my son's growth and development.

I am involved in a book for a long time. As I work on a book, many things are going on in my life at the same time. Very often the things that are happening around me find their way into the story and/or illustrations. The characters may take on the personalities and characters of people I've met and am involved with at the moment. Or an idea for a story may be sparked by the recollection of something or someone from my past which also becomes integrated into the book.

Writers and artists are like that, I am told. They repeat moments in their lives—either consciously or unconsciously—in their creation. I have also heard that writers and artists master their conflicts with their talents and that they replicate themselves, at their deepest and most significant level, in whatever they create. True or not, I am sure of one thing: I enjoy being a writer and illustrator of books for young readers.

I was born in Hollywood, California. My father was a graduate of Oregon State at Corvallis and a mechanical engineer by profession. My mother was from Virginia and attended Sweet Briar College. My mother and father met through relatives my mother was visiting in California. They were married soon afterwards. I have an older brother, Emory, and a younger sister, Annie Laurie.

Six weeks after I was born my family moved to Phoenix, Arizona where I grew up. My father and mother had two plans. The first plan was for my father to introduce air-conditioning to Arizona. The second plan was to build and sell houses in the fast-growing community of Phoenix. My father's first air-conditioning installation was in the Goldwater Department Store in downtown Phoenix. He designed and built a house at 309 West Cypress Street. But it was the only house he was ever able to build. The depression that followed the Wall Street crash, a few months after the house was nearly completed, put a sudden halt to progress in Phoenix, as it did everywhere. We moved into the house and my grandmother—my mother's mother—came to live with us following the sudden death of my grandfather that same year.

I have always loved the house we had in Phoenix. It was Spanish style and built of stucco-on-brick in a U-shape around a patio. The house had ten rooms and a large backyard with an ash tree that I climbed and in which I built a tree house. My mother and father kept both the front yard and the backyard planted with pretty flowers.

My parents entertained frequently. The parties must have been fun. I remember seeing pink, green, and white candy mints in silver dishes and a log cake covered with candy violets. I recall a red cloth-covered guest book in which guests—blindfolded—were invited to draw a pig, and how after each party I would run to see the latest funny drawings.

My grandmother, a Virginia belle, planned and prepared most of the meals. It was all southern-style cooking. I was brought up on corn bread and black-eyed peas. She also cared for us children with the help of servants we hired to come in some days—more often after my sister was born, in 1935. More than that, my grandmother helped us to survive the Great Depression. Whenever my father had trouble finding work, my grandmother would provide for the household expenses with what money she had left from grandfather's estate. My grandfather, a former sheriff in the town of Monterey, Virginia, was a wealthy land investor with property in West Virginia and orange groves in Florida. He was a self-made man who, when orphaned at age twelve, supported himself and seven younger brothers and sisters. When he died, the bulk of the estate, including the orange groves in Florida, was lost during the crash on Wall Street. However, there was enough money remaining for my grandmother to live comfortably.

Robert, about age six, with his parents, Virginia and Roy Quackenbush

As a child I loved to draw, paint, and listen to stories. I grew up in a family of storytellers who brought history to life. My father told of ancestors on the transcontinental railroad, of spectacular train wrecks and daring rescues. My mother told of a gracious and grand style of living in turn-of-the-century Virginia and Florida. My grandmother told of ancestors chased on horseback by thieving Bluecoats. We were also a family of readers. My mother would read fairy stories to me, and my favorite book when I was three or four years old was about the adventures in a community of tiny undersea creatures called *The Kelpies.* Then, when I learned to read, I looked for more fairy stories. By age nine I had read every classic fairy tale in our home library. I particularly liked the tales in *East of the Sun and West of the Moon,* and Kay Nielsen's exquisite illustrations. I was deeply moved by Oscar Wilde's stories for children, especially *The Selfish Giant.*

Robert, at age three

In 1938, when I was nine, my father died. The family was hard-pressed for funds after that. While my father left money from an insurance policy, it was not enough to cover more than two years of expenses. In addition, my grandmother's money was running out. My mother was forced to go to work. She attended secretarial school to learn typing and dictation and took odd jobs. When Pearl Harbor was bombed by the Japanese and America was thrust into the Second World War, my mother worked for G2 (United States military intelligence) for a while. After that, she worked as an assistant to a lawyer. Finally,

Robert (far left), standing on the porch of his childhood home, with his father, mother, brother, and two grandmothers, Phoenix, Arizona, 1932

she settled with the Phoenix Title and Trust Company (now called TransAmerica West) as a trust clerk and eventually became a vice president in the company. She supported three children, her invalid mother (who fell and broke her hip), and herself with her wages and money from bank loans.

I was in my early teens during the war. I saw Phoenix become a center of activity. It grew from a sleepy town of twenty-six thousand to a place crowded with soldiers, sailors, and air-force pilots, as one military and air-force training base after another was erected on the desert outside Phoenix, as well as a German prisoner-of-war camp, and a Japanese internment camp. My brother joined the navy and my mother rented a back bedroom my brother and I had shared to tenants for additional income because it had a separate entrance. I moved into the den at the front of the house that my father had used as an office.

I loved my room. It kept me in touch with the memories of my father. Many times I had drawn alongside him while he was working on his air-conditioning plans. He taught me methods of drawing, such as the use of scale drawings. The year *Snow White and the Seven Dwarfs* was released, we took small magazine reproductions of the characters from the Disney movie and penciled a grid over them. Then we copied each square of the grid onto the matching square of a larger grid that was penciled on large pieces of cardboard. Finally, we painted the scaled-up drawings and cut them out. The finished product was life-size renderings of the Disney characters.

All through high school, I painted, decorated, and built furniture for my room. I even painted see-through Spanish folk-art designs on the windowpanes that cast interesting shadow patterns about the room when the sun shone through the windows. Even then my main interests were drawing, painting, and reading. I copied the paintings of Diego Rivera and the war art that was reproduced in *Life* magazine. I read the novels of F. Scott Fitzgerald and J. P. Marquand.

When I graduated from North Phoenix High School, in 1947, I went to New York to study art for a summer at the Parson's School of Design. My high school art teacher convinced my mother to let me go. I was able to do this with money I had saved my senior year at high school from working after school in the stockroom of a department store and by staying with an aunt and uncle, who lived in nearby Newark. I went there by bus.

At the end of the summer, I stopped off in Omaha, Nebraska on my way back home to visit some

"Sketching on the beach at Rockaway, Oregon, with a pal," 1948

cousins. I decided to stay. I found work as a mail clerk in an advertising agency and moved into a basement room of a boarding house. My plan included enrolling in the local art school. But when the first snow fell, I came down with pneumonia. As soon as I was well, I headed back to Phoenix and enrolled at Phoenix College. While I did well in my grades at the college, I was not happy. I wanted to pursue an art career. So I went to Oregon the following summer and worked in plywood mills to earn enough money to enroll in the fall '48 program at the Art Center College of Design in Los Angeles.

At nineteen years of age, I was the youngest student at the time to be accepted at Art Center. A great majority of the students were war veterans and I had to work very hard to keep up with them. When the first year was completed, I went back to work another summer in the mills in Oregon in order to enroll for a second year at the school. But at the end of the second year I was drafted into the army during the Korean conflict. Fortunately, I did not go to Korea.

During my two years in the service I was stationed in infantry camps in South Carolina and Indiana. I kept up with my art by painting signs for my company and by painting watercolor portraits of the enlisted men and officers at ten dollars each. In addition I was given a post as a T.I. and E. (Troop Information and Education) lecturer.

While I was away from home, many changes were happening in the family. My grandmother passed away in a nursing home. My brother married and left home. The house on Cypress Street was sold and my mother and sister moved to a two-bedroom apartment. Then my sister went away to college.

In 1953, I received an honorable discharge from the army, a letter of commendation from the commanding officer of the company I was with, and two citations from the commanding general of the post—the Thirty-first Infantry Division—for my T.I. and E. lectures on defense. After my discharge, I went back to Phoenix and worked as art director for a year at a small agency that serviced the Phoenix Chamber of Commerce account. Then I returned to Los Angeles to complete my studies at Art Center on the G.I. Bill. I graduated with a bachelor of professional arts degree, in 1956, and went directly to New York to pursue my chosen career in art.

My first four years in New York I worked as an art director designing posters and brochures for the Scandinavian Airlines Systems account at an advertising agency. One summer I was sent to work in the main offices of SAS in Stockholm, Sweden. In Stockholm I was introduced to the graphic art mediums of woodcuts, etchings, and lithography. When I returned to New York I enrolled in a woodcut printmaking course at the New School. Within a few months I had created enough woodcuts for a portfolio and my woodcuts were exhibited in national shows, including New York's Whitney Museum and the Philadelphia Academy of Fine Arts. Galleries took on my prints to sell and soon I quit my work as an art director to devote full time to printmaking. I was kept very busy making prints for shows. I also received fine art commissions: the New York Hilton at Fifty-third Street and the Avenue of the Americas commissioned me to print an edition of one hundred woodcuts for the rooms of the new hotel; the National Parks Division of the Department of the Interior commissioned me to do a series of woodcuts of the Blue Ridge Parkway in Virginia and North Carolina on location for their art collection at the Smithsonian Institution; the United States Air Force commissioned me to do woodcuts of the astronaut training base at Brooks Air Force Base, in San Antonio, Texas for the Air and Space Museum at the Smithsonian. All the while, I kept looking for new outlets for my prints. I took a collection to show the art director at *Sports Illustrated,* Richard Gangel. He commissioned me to illustrate several nature articles

Drawing by Quackenbush at age nineteen

on camping and outdoor life. Then I went to see Robert Craven, art director in Holt, Rinehart, and Winston's elementary school division, in 1962, and he gave me that first book illustration assignment.

The assignment was to illustrate, in woodcuts, Hans Christian Andersen's *The Steadfast Tin Soldier.* I was asked to do one sketch over a weekend for the editors to see if I was the right artist to do the illustrations. Instead, what I brought back was the whole book laid out in colored ink sketches. My eagerness to illustrate a book paid off, because I got the assignment.

The finished illustrations required carving 144 woodblock surfaces and took several months to do. The project was a deep, emotional experience for me, and put me in touch with images and memories of my childhood that were buried in my unconscious. I recalled the first time I read Andersen's tale about the brave tin soldier with only one leg, who—after surviving a treacherous journey—was picked up, at the end of the story, by a little boy and thrown into the fireplace for no reason at all.

I read *The Steadfast Tin Soldier* when I was nine, just after my father was killed in a tragic automobile accident. The story distressed me at the time I read it, and as I set to work on the illustrations, I was able to understand why.

The accident occurred at 1:45 A.M. on December 13, 1938, when my father was returning from inspecting the installation of some of his air-conditioning designs upstate. He was travelling alone on a highway into Phoenix when his car crashed. Afterwards, it was said that he might have been temporarily blinded by the sudden appearance of bright headlights from an approaching car and went off the road. The trunk of his demolished car was discovered to be filled with Christmas presents for us children.

What I was able to understand when I was at work on the illustrations for *The Steadfast Tin Soldier* was why the story upset me so when I read it as a child. It was because I identified with the boy who threw the tin soldier in the fireplace. I believed, as many children do when a tragedy happens in a family, that somehow I had something to do with my father's death. When these early feelings surfaced, as I worked on the illustrations, I became a father to the child in me and came to terms with those feelings and a number of other feelings connected with my childhood. It was truly a liberating experience working on that first book. When the illustrations were completed, I wanted to get started on another book right away.

Robert Craven gave me three more books to do. The first was called *Poems for Galloping,* which was a collection of poems about various childhood activities like running, hopping, and skipping. This book was also illustrated in woodcuts and included in an American Institute of Graphic Arts Fifty Best Books Show in 1964. The second book was called *Poems for Counting* and the illustrations were rendered in watercolors because I designed the book to take place on a farm and wanted the illustrations to have the look of Pennsylvania Dutch folk art. The third book was a story of my own selection. After the insightful experience I had working on *The Steadfast Tin Soldier,* I was eager to illustrate another favorite story from my childhood, which was Oscar Wilde's *The Selfish Giant.*

I was given a book of Oscar Wilde's stories for children on my tenth Christmas by my mother. "The Selfish Giant" was one of the stories in the collection. I read it over and over. The story couldn't have been more appropriate for a boy of ten to read who had lost his father and was out of touch with the feelings of despair, hopelessness, and anger that come with the awful rejection by death of a parent. Needless to say, working on the illustrations for a picture-book version of Wilde's classic story was a very meaningful experience for me. I rendered them in pen and ink

Woodcut from The Open Boat and Three Other Stories *by Stephen Crane. Illustrated by Robert Quackenbush. Originally published by Franklin Watts, 1968. (Reprinted by permission of the illustrator.)*

and watercolors. They were a departure from anything I had ever done before. The scene of the giant's garden where the children played every afternoon after school, before the giant chased them away, received a citation from the Society of Illustrators' annual exhibition, in July 1966. It was the first of many citations I have received from the Society.

After those four books I was hooked. I went out seeking more book publishers to show what I could do. Many more books came my way to be illustrated. The prestigious Limited Editions Club for book collectors commissioned me to illustrate editions of James Fenimore Cooper's *Pilot* and Weems's *Life of Washington,* in which the illustrations in the finished books were printed from my actual woodblocks. In the years to follow I received similar commissions from Franklin Mint to illustrate a collection of Stephen Crane short stories and the *Reader's Digest* Book Division to illustrate Nathaniel Hawthorne's *Scarlet Letter.* I was also sought in the 1960s and early 1970s by children's book editors to illustrate works by contemporary authors of books for young readers. For Macmillan's elementary school division, I illustrated Charlotte Zolotow's *You and Me,* a 128-page book telling the different ways children live around the world. For Jean Karl, editor of junior books at Atheneum, I illustrated Eleanor Clymer's "Horatio" series, in which I used my tabby cat, Hansy, as the model for the rather fat, middle-aged cat of the popular stories. For Edna Barth, editor at Lothrop, Lee, and Shepard Books, I illustrated Miriam Young's "If I Drove" series, including *If I Drove a Truck,* about a little boy who imagines the many different kinds of trucks he could drive when he grows up.

After illustrating sixty books by well-known authors, I wanted to write my own stories and illustrate them. I began by adapting the classic folk song "Old MacDonald Had a Farm" (1972) into a picture book for J. B. Lippincott. While I was working on the book, in 1971, I met Margery Clouser. She was a graduate of Pratt Institute and working in New York as a fashion designer. She came into my gallery/studio that I established in a storefront on East Seventy-eighth Street in 1968 to display my paintings and books and to offer classes in art instruction for children and adults. The day Margery came in, I was struggling over one of my illustrations for *Old MacDonald.* She offered me some helpful suggestions because she had lived on a farm in Pennsylvania. A romance grew out of that first meeting and our mutual interest in art. In six months we were married, and an ending was provided for my picture-book version of the classic song: I have the famous farmer and his bride elope and get married at the end, just as Margery and I did, on July 3, 1971.

The book was an immediate success and my Lippincott editors, Barbara Seuling and Dorothy Briley, decided to have me do a series of picture-song books based on classic folk songs. *Go Tell Aunt Rhody* (1973) was the next book, in which I told about two little boys goosenapping Aunt Rhody's prize goose and sending everyone who comes along, from a bicyclist to a crew of firemen, to go tell Aunt Rhody her old gray goose is dead. I based the story on two naughty little boys I knew when I was a child, who were hiding in a tree. They called down to a neighbor's house the alarming news that her dog had just died, when indeed it hadn't. The neighbor came running from the house screaming and then saw her dog very much alive and wandering about her back-yard. (You might have guessed the identify of one of the boys who were hiding in the tree.) For the ending of the book, I asked some of the schoolchildren, who came into my studio to watch me work, how the little boys in the story should be punished for what they did. I was relieved that the vote was not for too harsh a punishment; simply to send them to bed early with just a little bit of supper. That's the ending I used for the book.

Then came *She'll be Comin' 'Round the Mountain* and *Clementine* (1974). I also reached back into my childhood experience to write and illustrate these picture books for young readers. When I was a child I always wondered who "she" was and what "she" was doing coming round the mountain in the classic folk song "She'll Be Comin' 'Round the Mountain." And I was quite disturbed by the fact that Clementine, in the song "Clementine," drowns while taking her ducklings to the water. I set about clearing up these issues in my picture-book versions of the songs. In *She'll Be Comin' 'Round the Mountain* I tell about Little Annie, costume mender and horse tender of a travelling Wild West Show, who saves the train from robbers and becomes the star of the show. Memories of rodeo performances I saw as a child at the Phoenix fairgrounds sparked the fireworks illustration at the end of the book.

Clementine led to exciting library research of old mining records in Santa Monica, California where Margery and I were vacationing the summer of 1973. I have a fondness for Santa Monica. My grandmother took us there in the summer of 1935, the year my sister was born, to spend the summer. I was six years old at the time. It was the first time I had been away from the desert and I was overwhelmed by the sight

Quackenbush, with wife, Margery, inside their studio/gallery, 1972

of the Pacific Ocean. After that I always dreamed of living near the water someday. During that summer I was also fascinated by the Van De Kamp bakeries in Santa Monica that looked like Dutch windmills and where the salesgirls wore Dutch costumes. I drew windmills and Dutch girls for the next seven years. Those pleasant memories and the happiness with Margery, my bride, were reflected in *Clementine.* I had Clementine saved by a handsome hero and the splinter that she tripped on when she fell into the water became a lump of gold to pay off her father's overdue mortgage payments.

In April of the following year our son, Piet, was born. Piet (rhymes with "neat") was named after the Dutch painter Piet Mondrian and the first Quackenbush ancestor, Pieter Quackenbosch, who arrived in America from Holland in 1660. That same year, 1974, a little girl wrote me a fan letter:

"Dear Mr. Quackenbush. I like the books you make. Where did you get the name you put on your books? Are you really a duck?"

I thought of Piet when I read the letter, and wondered if he would get the same ribbing I got through the years about the Quackenbush name. The thought urged me to write and illustrate a book that I wanted, for Piet's sake (pun intended), to be the last word in silliness connected with the Quackenbush name. (No, Groucho Marx did not have a friend

A young Piet, inspiration for many of Quackenbush's works

named Dr. Quackenbush—that was Dr. Hackenbush.) So I wrote the book, titled *Too Many Lollipops,* about a disaster-prone duck, named Henry, who lives in a bush. Henry gets involved in one mishap after another: he bumps his head; he smashes his wing; he twists his leg; he mangles his tail; he gets a sore throat; he hurts his foot. For each ailment Henry calls his doctor who recommends rest for Henry and that he eat a lot of lollipops. In the end, poor Henry nearly meets his doom from eating too many lollipops.

Parents Magazine Press published the book in 1975. Then a surprising thing happened: children took to Henry at once. Many children would send me their own "Henry" stories they had written and illustrated about Henry-like disasters. They wanted me to write and illustrate more books about Henry. There have been eleven "Henry" adventures published so far. The most popular is *Henry's Awful Mistake* about Henry trying to get rid of an ant in his kitchen and literally demolishing his house in the process.

I got the idea for *Henry's Awful Mistake* when I called my mother out in Arizona one Saturday afternoon. I commented that she sounded depressed. She said she was "feeling low" because she had planned to have friends over for dinner that evening and discovered a roach in her kitchen. She called the exterminator and he literally demolished her kitchen going after that roach, and she had to cancel her dinner party. "I'm very sorry to hear about that, Mother," I said, "but thank you for the story."

I believe this book is in every doctor's and dentist's office in the country (there are 3,500,000 copies in print). As a result I am often introduced, at school and library visits from Alaska to Argentina, as the father of Henry the Duck. It seems that my response to the little girl who wrote to ask me if I was a duck has merely drawn more hilarity to the Quackenbush name than I intended. Just like a "Henry" story.

Henry's adventures are about my character and the character of the Quackenbush family, in general. This is because I was raised in disastrous times. Consider the year I was born: 1929, the year of a stock market crash that led to a ten-year world-wide economic depression! Then came a second world war. There was much to be frightened and confused about back then, just like today. Humor became a key to survival in my family when I was growing up. Thus, humor became the keynote of all the books I wrote and illustrated for Piet (I've dedicated every book to him since his birth) and young readers everywhere. I wanted them to know, just as I found out when I was growing up, that as long as we keep our humor, our spirits cannot be crushed.

Piet's arrival inspired material for many new books. Not only did I complete eight picture-song books by 1976 for Lippincott (now with the Harper and Row Junior Books Group), but I also began a twelve-book easy-to-read series for Lothrop, Lee and Shepard, called "Fun-to-Read-Books," and a biography series that started with Parents Magazine Press and then moved to Prentice-Hall for a total of eighteen books at this writing.

Skip to My Lou (1974) was the next book in the picture-song book series and tells about a disastrous engagement party ("Cat's in the cream jar, ooh, ooh, ooh," and "Hair in the butter dish, six feet long," for example). After that I did *There'll Be a Hot Time in the Old Town Tonight* (1974), in which I used historical research and letters of the period to tell in new, original lyrics, written to the music of the old song, the story of the great Chicago fire of 1871. Then I did *The Man on the Flying Trapeze* (1975), in which I told about the life of circus clown Emmett Kelly, Sr. to the tune of the famous old song. And for the last book in the series I did *Pop! Goes the Weasel and Yankee Doodle,* in which I combined the two revolutionary war songs to tell how New York survived the war under seven long years of British siege.

The first "Fun-to-Read Book" for Lothrop was called *Animal Cracks* (1975). The idea came to me about two weeks after Piet was born. Forgotten childhood memories began to surface and I recalled my grandmother saying things to me like, "Don't put all your eggs in one basket," or, "You can lead a horse to water, but you can't make him drink." As a child, these sayings would make my head spin; they made absolutely no sense to me. With Piet in mind, I decided to make something out of the sayings and put them into a book. I wrote a series of fables about a community of animals. At the end of each fable, I put one of my grandmother's tag lines. In the fable "Mrs. Duck," Mrs. Duck's ducklings are afraid to swim until it rains suddenly and they see that the water is repelled by the oil in their feathers. After that they swim easily "and they didn't even get wet." The tag line for this story is: "Is that why people say: Easy as water off a duck's back?"

As soon as this book was published, I knew, and the publisher knew, that this community of animals begged for more stories about them. I wrote about animal characters because animals in literature can say and do so much more than their human counterparts and they come across funnier. I gave them names like Ed Cat (named after a friend), Elmo Elephant (named after an uncle), Lola Fieldmouse (named after Lola Montez, who danced during the days of the Wild West), to name a few. Right away I thought this community needed a detective. So the natural follow-up was a book about a detective. *Detective Mole* (1976) was the result. I gave the good detective my father's middle name, Maynard, and even patterned his quiet, unassuming manner after my father. The book included a pack-rat character from Arizona who also begged for more stories about him. The result was the book *Pete Pack Rat* (1976), about Pete's showdown in the town of Pebble Junction with a wanted outlaw named Gizzard Coyote. In that book Pete has a girl named Sally, whom I modeled after all the high-spirited and assertive women I have known in my life, including my mother, my sister, some of my editors, my wife, and many, many others. Sally becomes the Sheriff of Pebble Junction, and she goes on to her own book called *Sheriff Sally Gopher and the Haunted Dance Hall* (1977). Then Pete and Sally work together to catch the robbers of the Pebble Junction Bank in *Pete Pack Rat and the Gila Monster Gang* (1978).

In addition to these books, four more "Detective Mole" books were published. The first book was *Detective Mole and the Secret Clues* (1977), in which a garden pea is the main clue to solving the mystery of a hidden key to the front door of a mansion. The second book was *Detective Mole and the Tip-Top Mystery* (1978), which I based on a hilarious family outing to an upstate mountain resort that Margery, Piet, and I took one weekend. While we were at the hotel, the lights went out, there was sugar in the saltshakers and salt in the sugar bowls, we stuck our feet through holes in the sheets on our beds, the water in the shower kept changing from hot to cold, and so on. The third book was *Detective Mole and the Seashore Mystery* (1979), in which I portrayed some of my favorite beaches on the East Coast and the West Coast in the illustrations. The fourth book was *Detective Mole and the Circus Mystery* (1980), in which I incorporated scenes from my favorite amusement park in Santa Monica, California in the illustrations.

Other books in the "Fun-to-Read" series included: *Calling Doctor Quack* (1978), based on the gentle character of our family doctor; *Mr. Snow Bunting's Secret* (1978), which was inspired from the days when I was a child and would be secretly wrapping Christmas presents with my grandmother using a special bowmaker she devised because of problems with arthritis in her fingers; *Moose's Store* (1979), which was inspired by my seeing two surviving old-time general stores, one at a family reunion in Monterey, Virginia, and the other during a visit to my sister in Arcata, California.

Detective Mole, Pete Pack Rat, and Sheriff Sally Gopher went on to be published in large-size picture-book format because of their popularity with young readers. First came *Detective Mole and the Halloween Mystery* (1981), which won an Edgar Allan Poe Special Award in 1981 for the best juvenile mystery of that year. In the second book, *Pete Pack Rat and the Christmas Eve Surprise* (1981), I told about the traditions of Christmas in Arizona. In the third book, *Sheriff Sally Gopher and the Thanksgiving Caper* (1982), I told about how the pilgrims might have celebrated Thanksgiving from a tradition they picked up in Holland on their way to America—a fact I discovered while researching my family genealogy for Piet. Finally *Detective Mole and the Haunted Castle Mystery* (1985) was created. The idea for this story came about when I recalled an incident that happened when I was a teenager and involved my brother. My mother asked him to dig a trench in our backyard and to have it ready for her when she came home from work so she could plant a bed of sweet peas. When she got home from work, she saw—to her horror—a trench six feet deep along the wall of the garage and the wall about to collapse. What she had meant by a "trench" was an impression in the ground that was six *inches* deep. Unfortunately, my brother, just back home from serving in the navy, had taken my mother literally regarding her use of the word "trench." Borrowing from that recollection, my book begins, "One morning, when the Rabbit family was digging a hole in their garden to plant sweet peas, they struck oil and became rich overnight."

My biographies had different roots. They coincided with different stages of our son's growth. My first biography, *Take Me Out to the Airfield!* subtitled *How the Wright Brothers Invented the Airplane,* was published by Parents Magazine Press in 1976. Selma Lanes, the author of several critiques on children's literature, was my editor at that time at Parents.

Airfield was created the year before the book was published, when Piet took his first steps. Piet was so excited about being able to walk that he must have thought he could fly, too. He climbed up on a couch and started flapping his arms and before Margery and I could catch him, he fell to the floor and landed on his nose. I figured it was time to tell him about the Wright Brothers. But I didn't want the book to be another dry approach I remembered reading as a child about famous people and how they suffered, starved, and did without before they achieved success. Who wants any part of that?, I remember thinking at the time. The missing ingredient in the biographies I read was humor. I wanted to change that and entice children to want to read about the lives of great men and women by offering humorous asides to the factual material. In *Take Me Out to the Airfield,* the asides are made by two pigeons who offer their comments on flying from their personal experience.

At age three, Piet liked to collect toy cars and play with them. I thought a biography about Henry Ford would be appropriate and wrote and illustrated *Along Came the Model T!,* subtitled *How Henry Ford Put the World on Wheels,* which was published by Parents in 1978. This time the humorous asides were provided by two children who pedal into a gas station in their toy car to ask a mechanic to tell them about the first cars.

When Piet became interested in space flight I wrote and illustrated, also for Parents, *The Boy Who Dreamed of Rockets,* subtitled *How Robert H. Goddard Became the Father of the Space Age* (1978), with the humor being provided by two children talking with an astronaut.

A great deal of time and research went into creating the biographies and I sought out the opinions of many authorities on the various subjects. When each book was completed I had great feelings of accomplishment and satisfaction that I had learned a subject well and had enjoyed all aspects of the process of seeing the project through to publication. When Parents changed their book line to focus on their book club and a beginning reader program, I continued my biography series with a new publisher, Prentice-Hall, and my editor there was Barbara Francis. Piet's ever-changing interests kept me busy writing and illustrating: *Oh, What an Awful Mess! A Story of Charles Goodyear* (1980); *Ahoy! Ahoy! Are You There? A Story of Alexander Graham Bell* (1981); *What Has Wild Tom Done Now? A Story of Thomas Alva Edison* (1981); *Watt Got You Started, Mr. Fulton? A Story of James Watt and Robert Fulton* (1982); *Here a Plant, There a Plant, Everywhere a Plant, Plant! A Story of Luther Burbank* (1982); *The Beagle and Mr. Flycatcher: A Story of Charles Darwin* (1983); *Quick, Annie, Give Me a Catchy Line! A Story of Samuel F. B. Morse* (1983); *Don't You Dare Shoot That Bear! A Story of Theodore Roosevelt* (1984); *Mark Twain? What Kind of Name Is That? A Story of Samuel Langhorne Clemens* (1984); *Once Upon a Time! A Story of the Brothers Grimm* (1985); *Who Said There's No Man on the Moon? A Story of Jules Verne* (1985); *Who Let Muddy Boots into the White House? A Story of Andrew Jackson*

"Reunion 1988"—an original drawing by Quackenbush of a few of his characters

(1986); *Old Silver Leg Takes Over! A Story of Peter Stuyvesant* (1986); *Quit Pulling My Leg! A Story of Davy Crockett* (1987); *Who's That Girl With the Gun? A Story of Annie Oakley* (1988).

In the meantime, the success of Detective Mole prompted editors at various publishers to want me to develop mystery series for them. For Eleanor Nichols at McGraw-Hill, a series about Piet was created when children wrote and wanted to know about Piet and what he did in New York. Piet became a detective called Piet Potter and our apartment building and the places the real Piet went for amusement became the focus of the action for each mystery. The books in the series are: *Piet Potter's First Case* (1980), *Piet Potter Returns* (1980), *Piet Potter Strikes Again* (1981), *Piet Potter to the Rescue* (1981), *Piet Potter's Hot Clue* (1982), and *Piet Potter on the Run.*

Then a series of mysteries was created for Barbara Francis at Prentice-Hall about a "ducktective" named Miss Mallard—a Miss Marple type—who solves her mysteries in different countries around the world. I usually pick places I have visited for the settings of the stories, the most recent being an invitation to visit schools in Alaska. The experience led to *Dogsled to Dread* (1987). Others in the series are: *Express Train to Trouble* (1981), which takes place on the Nile Express; *Cable Car to Catastrophe* (1982), which takes place in the Swiss Alps; *Dig to Disaster* (1982), which takes place in Central America; *Gondola to Danger* (1983), which takes place in Venice; *Stairway to Doom* (1983), which takes place in Scotland; *Rickshaw to Horror* (1984), which takes place in Hong Kong; *Taxi to Intrigue* (1984), which takes place in London; *Stage Door to Terror* (1985), which takes place in Paris; *Bicycle to Treachery* (1985), which takes place in Holland; *Texas Trail to Calamity* (1986), which takes place in San Antonio; and *Surfboard to Peril* (1986), which takes place in Hawaii.

The titles of these books all sound quite ominous, but befit the hilarity of the characters which are all types of ducks with names such as George Ruddy Duck, Sir Reginald Baldpate, and Count Kisscula. Count Kisscula is a vampirelike duck, called a kisspire, who seeks other ducks to kiss when the moon is full—and if there is anything ducks hate it is being kissed because their beaks get in the way and it hurts. Have you ever seen a duck kiss another duck?

Jack Lee and Chris Medina at Parents Magazine Press wanted me to develop a mystery character for Parents beginning reader series. Sherlock Chick is the detective character this time. In the first book in the series, called *Sherlock Chick's First Case* (1986), Sherlock Chick is introduced when he pops out of his shell wearing a detective's hat and asks his parents, Emma Hen and Harvey Rooster, if they are in need of a detective. It so happens that they are and they provide him with his first case, which is to solve the mystery of who has been stealing the feed from the bin in the chicken yard. The second book in the series is called *Sherlock Chick and the Peekaboo Mystery* (1987), in which Sherlock Chick is asked to find Mother Mouse's lost child, Squeakins Mouse. I got the idea for this book when I was author/artist in residence during Halloween week, 1986, in an elementary school in Kentucky. I asked the children to draw the scariest picture they could think of. One child drew an old hollow tree with a dark hole and two eyes peeking out from the hole. The drawing appealed to me because it was so mysterious-looking and fun. It sparked the idea of having Sherlock Chick go around the farmyard looking for dark holes where a mouse might hide and asking at each one, "Peek-a-boo! I see you! Are you a little mouse hiding in there?" The third book in the series is called *Sherlock Chick and the Giant Egg Mystery* (1988), in which Sherlock Chick solves the mystery of what is inside a giant egg that arrives at the farm from Africa. The latest book in the series is called *Sherlock Chick and the Noisy Shed Mystery* (1989). Our cat Putty gave me the idea for this book. We are often awakened in the night by Putty crashing and banging objects to get our attention because he hopes we will get up and feed him. That became the basis for this Sherlock Chick mystery.

Not all the books I have done have been for a series. Quite a few have had to do with Piet when he was growing up. His experiences were so much a part of life that I felt children everywhere could identify with them. One book, *First Grade Jitters* (1982), for J. B. Lippincott, reveals Piet's trauma one summer when he was about to enter first grade and thought he had to know everything the first day, just like many of us adults do when we begin a new job which, for me, is starting a new book. Another special book about Piet is *I Don't Want to Go, I Don't Know How to Act* (1983), also for J. B. Lippincott. The book tells about Piet before he was five years old and how he didn't want to go out with Margery and me to parties or to restaurants. When we encouraged him to talk he was able to reveal the reason and let us help him to resolve the problem. A third book, called *The Boy Who Waited for Santa Claus* (1981), for Franklin Watts, tells how Piet wrote his letter to Santa Claus one September and then refused to go anywhere but kindergarten (which he loved) for fear he would miss Santa. Finally, there is a book for a story that Piet told himself, which was also published by Franklin Watts. It is called *No Mouse for Me* (1981). Piet said to me one morning at breakfast that we shouldn't get a pet mouse in our house because our cat Hansy might chase the mouse and then the dog next door would come and chase Hansy and then the dogcatcher would come, the police, reporters, the army, the navy, and on and on until: "TERRIBLE THINGS WOULD HAPPEN!" Piet ended the story by saying, "So please don't ever get a pet mouse in our house." I said, "Don't worry, I won't, Piet. And thanks for the story." I sketched it out at once, presented it to the editor, Frank Sloan, at a luncheon meeting that day, and it was taken for publication right away.

Worked into all these books were two histories of film that I felt compelled to do since I grew up with movies. Once in Sunday school, when I was five, the minister asked the class what we wanted to be when we grew up. "Fireman!" "Nurse!" came the answers. I kept waving my hand and at last I was called upon. "I'm going to be a movie star," I said proudly to everyone's amusement. One book is a history of movie comedy called *Who Threw That Pie?* (1979) and the other is a history of the horror film called *Movie Monsters and Their Masters* (1980). Both books were published by Albert Whitman and Company.

In addition, I was creating new books for the "Henry the Duck" series for Parents Magazine Press. The idea for *Henry's Important Date* (1981), about Henry racing with the clock to deliver a birthday cake to his friend Clara, came to me when Piet was learning to tell time. The idea for *Henry Goes West* (1982) was the result of a Henry-the-Duck-vacation to Arizona to take Piet to see his grandma and there were flight delays, it rained every day, and other disasters. The idea for *Henry Babysits* (1983) came when Margery and I would leave Piet in the morning with a babysitter and return in the evening to find there were many more children in the apartment because neighbors had dropped off their children when they learned there was a !!!!BABYSITTER!!!! in the building.

Golden Books has also come out with a line of "Henry the Duck" adventures in response to children writing and asking what Henry was like as a baby, what he was like when he went to school, how he met his friend Clara, and how he celebrates his birthday. Marc Gave was my editor for this series of "Henry" adventures. He was also my editor for *Henry's Awful Mistake,* when he was at Parents. The first Golden Book was a reissue of *Too Many Lollipops* (1987), followed by Henry as a duckling in *Too Many Ducklings* (1987), then *Too Many School Days* (1988), and finally, *Too Many Pizzas* (1988), with the latter book being about Henry's favorite birthday treat.

Son Piet today, at age fourteen

As Piet keeps growing (he is a teenager now) and my life becomes increasingly more accelerated with my writing, illustrating, painting, teaching, lecturing, etc., the pace is reflected in a new series that was developed for Jim Giblin, editor in chief and publisher of Clarion Books. The humor is broad in these books in the manner of classic comedy from the days of vaudeville, the silent films, and films of the early thirties. *Funny Bunnies* (1984) has set the tone for this series. It is about bunnies being crowded one after another into a tiny hotel room to do some specific thing like changing a light bulb or dusting and sweeping the room, until they are all hilariously released at the end by a little bunny named Lucy. In *Chuck Lends a Paw* (1986), children learn through the hilarious antics of Chuck to check out all details when offering to lend a hand to a friend. The idea for this book came to me when I realized that I was constantly being interrupted in my studio by delivery persons who would ring my bell or knock on my window and ask me to take a package—anything from a mattress to an air conditioner—for someone else in the building who was not at home. In *Mouse Feathers* (1988) the humor was inspired by the limits we go to sometimes to keep things from going out of control. And in the end it is the smallest thing—something we completely overlooked—that undoes the best laid plans of mice and men: like planning a marvelous garden party and then suddenly it rains. Poor Maxine, in the book, is undone by pillow feathers! When I was writing this book, I was also thinking of the story of the boy who found the leak in the dike that I remember my father reading to me as a child. Parents and teachers who work with small children know about this kind of tension. In *Funny Bunnies on the Run* (1989), Lucy Bunny and her mother and father are back to make a slapstick comment on a world controlled by machines, which came to mind upon hearing too frequently from all types of services, "We regret that we cannot serve you because we have had a computer failure."

Presently, I am at work on new books, including a biography on the life of George Washington called *I Did It With My Hatchet!,* a treasury of humor, and a new "Miss Mallard" mystery titled *Danger in Tibet;* scheduling school and library visits cross-country for the coming year; setting up author/artist in residence programs; teaching classes for adults and children at my studio; completing the filming for a television series for public service channels—titled "Dear Mr. Quackenbush"—in which I answer letters from children on writing and illustrating their own books. And—for sheer relaxation—Margery, Piet, Putty, and I plan vacations together.

Teaching and traveling on author visits have become integral parts of my career. Two days a week are devoted to teaching adults and children, and I make about ten out-of-town author visits a year—the most recent being to American schools in Buenos Aires, elementary schools in Anchorage, Alaska, and schools, libraries, and colleges in California, Mississippi, Virginia, Iowa, Ohio, Indiana, Michigan, Upstate New York, Long Island, and North Carolina. Forthcoming trips will include visits to American schools in Thailand, Brazil, and Germany. It is truly exciting for me to meet people from so many interesting places and gain new ideas and new information. I especially like meeting children and

Meeting with schoolchildren at Woodside School, Sacramento, California

finding out their likes, their thoughts, their current slang that I can include in new books, for their interests change rapidly from month to month—even day to day. Nine-year olds, for example, very much want to express their views about ecology and an unjust social and political world, which can include their world of home and school. It is important to me to listen to children of all ages and think of them and where they are at the moment when I am writing and illustrating my books.

My career has been very satisfying to me. I am married to a beautiful woman. We are blessed with a marvelous son who exhibits the best of both ourselves and our ancestors. My brother, Emory, continues to work in the field of mechanical engineering in Phoenix, where he lives with his wife, Doris, and their three boys, Eric, Marc, and John. My sister, Annie Laurie, and her husband, Bruce, both have their doctorates in political science and are professors at Humbolt State College in Eureka, California. They are the parents of two children, Laura and Roger, who are presently earning their doctorates, too. Our mother, who retired from TransAmerica West, in 1969, passed away in 1985 at the age of eighty-one.

Often I am asked when I meet with teachers and students if I have any advice for someone who is starting out in art or writing. My reply (in the words of Winston Churchill) is: "Never give up! Never give up! Never give up!" Then I add: "And don't forget to keep your sense of humor." This is what has worked for me.

BIBLIOGRAPHY

FOR CHILDREN

Books written and illustrated:

Old MacDonald Had a Farm. Philadelphia: Lippincott, 1972.

Go Tell Aunt Rhody. Philadelphia: Lippincott, 1973.

She'll be Comin' 'Round the Mountain. Philadelphia: Lippincott, 1973.

Clementine. Philadelphia: Lippincott, 1974.

There'll Be a Hot Time in the Old Town Tonight. Philadelphia: Lippincott, 1974.

Animal Cracks. New York: Lothrop, 1975.

The Man on the Flying Trapeze. Philadelphia: Lippincott, 1975.

Skip to My Lou. Philadelphia: Lippincott, 1975.

Too Many Lollipops. New York: Parents Magazine Press, 1975.

Detective Mole. New York: Lothrop, 1976.

Pete Pack Rat. New York: Lothrop, 1976.

Pop! Goes the Weasel and Yankee Doodle. Philadelphia: Lippincott, 1976.

Take Me Out to the Airfield! How the Wright Brothers Invented the Airplane. New York: Parents Magazine Press, 1976.

Detective Mole and the Secret Clues. New York: Lothrop, 1977.

The Holiday Song Book. New York: Lothrop, 1977.

Sheriff Sally Gopher and the Haunted Dance Hall. New York: Lothrop, 1977.

Along Came the Model T! How Henry Ford Put the World on Wheels. New York: Parents Magazine Press, 1978.

The Boy Who Dreamed of Rockets: How Robert H. Goddard Became the Father of the Space Age. New York: Parents Magazine Press, 1978.

Calling Doctor Quack. New York: Lothrop, 1978.

Detective Mole and the Tip-Top Mystery. New York: Lothrop, 1978.

Mr. Snow Bunting's Secret. New York: Lothrop, 1978.

The Most Welcome Visitor. New York: Windmill Books, 1978.

Pete Pack Rat and the Gila Monster Gang. New York: Lothrop, 1978.

Detective Mole and the Seashore Mystery. New York: Lothrop, 1979.

Moose's Store. New York: Lothrop, 1979.

Who Threw That Pie? The Birth of Movie Comedy. Chicago: Albert Whitman, 1979.

Detective Mole and the Circus Mystery. New York: Lothrop, 1980.

Henry's Awful Mistake. New York: Parents Magazine Press, 1980.

Movie Monsters and Their Masters: The Birth of the Horror Film. Chicago: Albert Whitman, 1980.

Piet Potter Returns. New York: McGraw, 1980.

Piet Potter's First Case. New York: McGraw, 1980.

The Boy Who Waited for Santa Claus. New York: F. Watts, 1981.

City Trucks. Chicago: Albert Whitman, 1981.

Detective Mole and the Halloween Mystery. New York: Lothrop, 1978.

Henry's Important Date. New York: Parents Magazine Press, 1981.

No Mouse for Me. New York: F. Watts, 1981.

Pete Pack Rat's Christmas Eve Surprise. New York: Lothrop, 1981.

Piet Potter Strikes Again. New York: McGraw, 1981.

Piet Potter to the Rescue. New York: McGraw, 1981.

First Grade Jitters. New York: Lippincott, 1982.

Henry Goes West. New York: Parents Magazine Press, 1982.

Piet Potter on the Run. New York: McGraw, 1982.

Piet Potter's Hot Clue. New York: McGraw, 1982.

Sheriff Sally Gopher and the Thanksgiving Caper. New York: Lothrop, 1982.

Henry Babysits. New York: Parents Magazine Press, 1983.

I Don't Want to Go, I Don't Know How to Act. New York: Lippincott, 1983.

Funny Bunnies. New York: Clarion, 1984.

Investigator Ketchem's Crime Book. New York: Avon, 1984.

Detective Mole and the Haunted Castle Mystery. New York: Lothrop, 1985.

Chuck Lends a Paw. New York: Clarion, 1986.

Too Many Ducklings. New York: Western Publishing, 1987.

Mouse Feathers. New York: Clarion, 1988.

Sherlock Chick and the Giant Egg Mystery. New York: Parents Magazine Press, 1988.

Too Many Pizzas. New York: Western Publishing, 1988.

Too Many School Days. New York: Western Publishing, 1988.

Funny Bunnies on the Run. Forthcoming.

Sherlock Chick and the Noisy Shed Mystery. Forthcoming.

"Humorous Biography" Series

Oh, What an Awful Mess! A Story of Charles Goodyear. Englewood Cliffs, N. J.: Prentice-Hall, 1980.

Ahoy! Ahoy! Are You There? A Story of Alexander Graham Bell. Englewood Cliffs, N.J.: Prentice-Hall, 1981.

What Has Wild Tom Done Now? A Story of Thomas Alva Edison. Englewood Cliffs, N. J.: Prentice-Hall, 1981.

Here a Plant, There a Plant, Everywhere a Plant, Plant! A Story of Luther Burbank. Englewood Cliffs, N.J.: Prentice-Hall, 1982.

Watt Got You Started, Mr. Fulton? A Story of James Watt and

Robert Fulton. Englewood Cliffs, N.J.: Prentice-Hall, 1982.

The Beagle and Mr. Flycatcher: A Story of Charles Darwin. Englewood Cliffs, N.J.: Prentice-Hall, 1983.

Quick, Annie, Give Me a Catchy Line! A Story of Samuel F. B. Morse. Englewood Cliffs, N.J.: Prentice-Hall, 1983.

Don't You Dare Shoot That Bear! A Story of Theodore Roosevelt. Englewood Cliffs, N.J.: Prentice-Hall, 1984.

Mark Twain? What Kind of Name Is That? A Story of Samuel Langhorne Clemens. Englewood Cliffs, N.J.: Prentice-Hall, 1984.

Once Upon a Time! A Story of the Brothers Grimm. Englewood Cliffs, N. J.: Prentice-Hall, 1985.

Who Said There's No Man on the Moon? A Story of Jules Verne. Englewood Cliffs, N.J.: Prentice-Hall, 1985.

Who Let Muddy Boots into the White House? A Story of Andrew Jackson. Englewood Cliffs, N.J.: Prentice-Hall, 1986.

Quit Pulling My Leg! A Story of Davy Crockett. Englewood Cliffs, N.J.: Prentice-Hall, 1987.

Who's That Girl with the Gun? A Story of Annie Oakley. Englewood Cliffs, N.J.: Prentice-Hall, 1988.

I Did It with My Hatchet: A Story of George Washington. Forthcoming.

"Miss Mallard Mystery" Series

Express Train to Trouble. Englewood Cliffs, N.J.: Prentice-Hall, 1981.

Cable Car to Catastrophe. Englewood Cliffs, N.J.: Prentice-Hall, 1982.

Dig to Disaster. Englewood Cliffs, N.J.: Prentice-Hall, 1982.

Gondola to Danger. Englewood Cliffs, N.J.: Prentice-Hall, 1983.

Stairway to Doom. Englewood Cliffs, N.J.: Prentice-Hall, 1983.

Rickshaw to Horror. Englewood Cliffs, N.J.: Prentice-Hall, 1984.

Taxi to Intrigue. Englewood Cliffs, N.J.: Prentice-Hall, 1984.

Bicycle to Treachery. Englewood Cliffs, N.J.: Prentice-Hall, 1985.

Stage Door to Terror. Englewood Cliffs, N.J.: Prentice-Hall, 1985.

Surfboard to Peril. Englewood Cliffs, N.J.: Prentice-Hall, 1986.

Texas Trail to Calamity. Englewood Cliffs, N.J.: Prentice-Hall, 1986.

Dog Sled to Dread. Englewood Cliffs, N.J.: Prentice-Hall, 1987.

Danger in Tibet. Forthcoming.

Books illustrated:

Adventures for Americans, edited by W. L. Schramm, et. al. New York: Harcourt, 1962.

A Long, Long Time, by Inez Rice. New York: Lothrop, 1964.

The Steadfast Tin Soldier, by Hans Christian Andersen. New York: Holt 1964.

My City. New York: Macmillan, 1965.

The Selfish Giant, by Oscar Wilde. New York: Holt, 1965.

The Boy Who Woke Up in Madagascar, by Robin McKown. New York: Putnam, 1966.

Rakoto and the Drongo Bird, by R. McKown. New York: Lothrop, 1966.

The Two Worlds of Damyan, by Marie Halun Bloch. New York: Atheneum, 1966.

The Diamond Necklace, and Four Other Stories, by Guy de Maupassant. New York: F. Watts, 1967.

Election Day, by Mary Kay Phelan. New York: Crowell, 1967.

I Feel the Same Way, by Lilian Moore. New York: Atheneum, 1967.

If I Drove a Truck, by Miriam B. Young. New York: Lothrop, 1967.

Mrs. Herring, by Margaretha Shemin. New York: Lothrop, 1967.

A Sunday in Autumn, by Anthony Rowley. Syracuse, N.Y.: L. W. Singer, 1967.

Billy and Milly, by M. B. Young. New York: Lothrop, 1968.

Billy Budd, Foretopsman, by Herman Melville. New York: F. Watts, 1968.

Busy Winds, by Irma Black. New York: Holiday House, 1968.

Horatio, by Eleanor Clymer. New York: Atheneum, 1968.

The Open Boat, and Three Other Stories, by Stephen Crane. New York: F. Watts, 1968.

Befana's Gift, by Natalie S. Carlson. New York: Harper, 1969.

The Dirt Book: An Introduction to Earth Science, by Eva Evans. Boston: Little, Brown, 1969.

Little Hans, the Devoted Friend, by O. Wilde. Indianapolis, Ind.: Bobbs-Merrill, 1969.

To Smoke or Not to Smoke, by Luther L. Terry and Daniel Horn. New York: Lothrop, 1969.

When the Monkeys Wore Sombreros, by Mariana Prieto. Irvington-on-Hudson, N.Y.: Harvey House, 1969.

The Baker and the Basilisk, by Georgess McHargue. Indianapolis, Ind.: Bobbs-Merrill, 1970.

Beware the Polar Bear! Safety on the Ice, by M. B. Young. New York: Lothrop, 1970.

Busy Seeds, by I. Black. New York: Holiday House, 1970.

"D" Is for Rover, by Leonore Klein. Irvington-on-Hudson, N.Y.: Harvey House, 1970.

If I Flew a Plane, by M. B. Young. New York: Lothrop, 1970.

The Key to the Kitchen, by John Stewart. New York: Lothrop, 1970.

You and Me, by Charlotte Zolotow. New York: Macmillan, 1970.

The Bellfounder's Sons, by Lini R. Grol. Indianapolis, Ind.: Bobbs-Merrill, 1971.

Blue River, by Julian May. New York: Holiday House, 1971.

Demo of 70th Street, by Harry S. George. New York: H. Z. Walck, 1971.

A Home for Hopper, by Rosemary Pendery. New York: Morrow, 1971.

If I Drove a Car, by M. B. Young. New York: Lothrop, 1971.

If I Sailed a Boat, by M. B. Young. New York: Lothrop, 1971.

The Peasant's Pea Patch, translated by Guy Daniels. New York: Delacorte, 1971.

The Scribbler, by George Mendoza. New York: Holt, 1971.

Six Silver Spoons, by Janette Lowrey. New York: Harper, 1971.

Giraffes at Home, by Ann Cooke. New York: Crowell, 1972.

If I Drove a Train, by M. B. Young. New York: Lothrop, 1972.

Lines, Segments, and Polygons, by Harry and Mindel Sitomer. New York: Crowell, 1972.

A Gift for Lonny, by Anne Eve Bunting. Lexington, Mass.: Ginn Custom, 1973.

If I Drove a Bus, by M. B. Young. New York: Lothrop, 1973.

If I Drove a Tractor, by M. B. Young. New York: Lothrop, 1973.

If I Rode a Horse, by M. B. Young. New York: Lothrop, 1973.

Red Rock Over the River, by Patricia Beatty. New York: Morrow, 1973.

Pronghorn on the Power River, by Berniece Freschet. New York: Crowell, 1973.

Seal Harbor: The Life Story of the Harbor Seal, by John Frederick Waters. New York: F. Warne, 1973.

The Wizard Islands, by Jane Yolen. New York: Crowell, 1973.

If I Rode a Dinosaur, by M. B. Young. New York: Lothrop, 1974.

If I Rode an Elephant, by M. B. Young. New York: Lothrop, 1974.

Leave Horatio Alone, by E. Clymer. New York: Atheneum, 1974.

Engine Number Seven, by E. Clymer. New York: Holt, 1975.

Horatio's Birthday, by E. Clymer. New York: Atheneum, 1976.

The Peanut Cookbook, by Natalie Donna. New York: Lothrop, 1976.

The House on Stink Alley: A Story about the Pilgrims in Holland, by F. N. Monjo. New York: Holt, 1977.

Horatio Goes to the Country, by E. Clymer. New York: Atheneum, 1978.

The Black Pearl and the Ghost, by Walter Dean Myers. New York: Viking, 1980.

Horatio Solves a Mystery, by E. Clymer. New York: Atheneum, 1980.

Compiler of:

Poems for Counting. New York: Holt, 1963.

Poems for Galloping. New York: Holt, 1963.

FOR ADULTS

Books illustrated:

The Pilot, by James Fenimore Cooper. New York: Limited Editions Club, 1968.

Torregreca, by Ann Cornelisen. Pleasantville, N.Y.: Reader's Digest Condensed Books, 1969.

Life of Washington, by Mason Locke Weems. New York: Limited Editions Club, 1974.

An Iceland Fisherman, by Pierre Loti. Pleasantville, N.Y.: Reader's Digest Condensed Books, 1978.

Stories, by Stephen Crane. Franklin Center, Pa.: Franklin Library, 1982.

The Possession of Sister Jeanne, by Norah Lofts. Pleasantville, N.Y.: Reader's Digest Condensed Books, 1983.

The Scarlet Letter, by Nathaniel Hawthorne. Pleasantville, N.Y.: Reader's Digest Association, 1984.

Nicole St. John

THE KEEPING DAYS OF MY LIFE

Nicole St. John

Once upon a time there was an insufferable brat. That's how I began my first college writing assignment. "Write me your autobiography," the professor said. "Make it short because none of you insufferable brats have lived long enough to have any experiences worth writing about . . . !" He didn't know me . . .

Who am I? I'm Nicole St. John, and also (in the order in which readers know me best) Norma Johnston, Lavinia Harris, Kate Chambers, Pamela Dryden, Catherine E. Chambers, Elizabeth Bolton, and Adrian Robert. I'm an author, editor, ghostwriter, entrepreneur, actress, director, designer, stylist, retailer, teacher, counselor, and (as some critics have said about me, and I'm proud of it) preacher. Those aren't merely job labels; they're who I am, how I live out the covenant to use the talents I've been given—because that we all *do* have talents of one kind or another, and that we all have a responsibility to use them for the common good, is one of the things in which I most surely believe.

That English professor didn't know any of this, and I didn't want him to. I was almost twice my classmates' age, intimidated by the teacher ("I eat freshmen for breakfast!" he said), and had already published several books—all of which could make me fair game for his celebrated put-downs. So in that writing assignment I hid behind a mask—and ended, as always, in finding that when we put on the mask of a character, we drop our own.

In that autobiography, I included everything *important*—things that had happened to me, and things I'd done; how they'd made me feel, and how they'd made me grow. I *showed* all of what I believed, what I lived for, what made me *me*—without ever *telling* any actual facts. Try it sometime, when you have to write. It's what every good fiction writer does, consciously or not.

I can't write a chronological resume, because my life has not been chronological. Everything overlaps; everything comes round, not full circle, but in spirals. Everything hooks back onto the center, then spins out again.

The circle of rocks on which the house of my life is built are these: my grandmother, and the family heritage I was born into. Books I've read and written; plays I've seen or been in or directed. My faith, and the church I became deeply involved in as a teenager—and my theatre training, for in a weird and wonderful way these two interpreted and illumined each other and all the rest. My travels. And one other thing—but I'll get to that later.

Have you ever tried memorizing history just as a succession of dates? None of us remembers our life just as a one-after-the-other series of events. What we remember are *moments,* some enormous, some small, in which everything comes together—moments which (in our conscious or unconscious) remain with us forever. Like fleeting images in a music video, or the way sight and sound and taste and touch and smell suddenly stand out sharp and clear, for a brief

"My paternal grandmother, Catherine Dryden Chambers Johnston, with my father, Charles Eugene Chambers Johnston"

instant, when we have a high fever, or are very very tired, or spaced out on medications. Those come-together, make-a-memory moments are our Keeping Days.

> There are moments when everything's so sharp and bright it almost seems I cannot bear the pain and beauty of the world. But whenever I find myself thinking that way, I cross my fingers quick and take the wish back. Because if I wasn't sensitive, I would never have stumbled onto being a writer. . . .
>
> I found the first Keeping Day the summer I was ten. It was an August evening, and the dishes were done, and all the kids were playing Kick the Can in the street. When it started getting dark, we drifted down to Lathams' side lawn, the way everyone did that summer. [Somebody] had found a nest of baby rabbits, and my sister had the rabbits in her lap and was trying to feed them milk from a medicine dropper. When I looked up the sky behind the maple tree was purple. Lights were going on in windows, and from houses all down the street our mothers started calling. . . . From far, far down the street came the sound of Mama's bell. All at once I could feel it all inside of me, the purple and silver, the shimmer of fireflies and flowers, the tender look in my sister's eyes, and the familiar silver tinkle of the bell. And I knew I had found a Keeping Day.[1]

That's from *The Keeping Days,* the first book in my best-loved series, and (with its sequel, *Glory in the Flower*—they were originally written to be one volume) my own favorite of the books I've written. I didn't have a sister, the girl with the rabbits was someone else. But otherwise the scene came straight out of my own memories, as has the major part of everything I've written.

The family in the "Keeping Days" series is definitely my family—that is, my maternal grandparents' family as I imagine them to have been from the stories my great-uncles told. The roots of my family tree stretch on my mother's side back to colonists from the Netherlands, the Messlers (originally *Metselaar*) and Van Zandts, who settled New Amsterdam in 1632 (and during the next hundred years settled New Jersey, too, making me "Jersey Dutch"), and the Pierces from Dorsetshire, England, who colonized Dorchester, Massachusetts, in 1630. On my father's side (see the "Carlisle Chronicles") I come from English and Scottish families who settled in the Middle Atlantic colonies prior to the American Revolution. All these strong-willed, Calvinist, fiercely independent (my grandmother called it *pigheaded*) men and women have been a major influence on me, and on my writing, through the anecdotes, values, and customs that were passed down from one generation to another.

The earliest Keeping Days that I can remember were when we lived at the school (that's the way I always thought of it) in Ridgewood, New Jersey, where I was born. (Ridgewood in 1920–21, the year my mother and grandparents moved there, is the setting for *If You Love Me, Let Me Go.*) The school was a beautiful Greek Revival mansion built sometime

[1]From *The Keeping Days,* copyright © 1973 by Norma Johnston. New York: Atheneum, 1973. Reprinted by permission of Atheneum, the Macmillan Publishing Co.

Pen-and-ink drawing of Ridgewood Secretarial School, where the author was born

around the Civil War, and many years later I used that house as the mansion in both *Ready or Not* (I "moved" it to the Wyckoff, New Jersey, location where I actually lived while in high school) and *Shadow of a Unicorn*:

> Whenever I remembered Unicorn Farm, I remembered sunlight. I could close my eyes and see it all again. . . . White-pillared, gracious, with its spreading porches, three stories of tall windows, and a red mansard roof. And white wicker furniture. . . . The carved front door, with its leaded glass fanlights and sidelights. . . . carved paneling and old Oriental rugs, the double parlors, the library [that] was an office now. Ledgers were piled on the big double desk. . . . [2]

That's the way I can still see the school. My grandparents' Ridgewood Secretarial School was on the ground floor, their apartment was on the second floor, and my parents' on the third, up under the mansard roof. My main Keeping Days memories from Ridgewood are of my mother teaching me to read and write when I was four (I've never stopped doing either of those things since!) . . . of memorizing "The Night before Christmas" to recite to Aunt Emma and Uncle Elmer on Christmas Day . . . of having the chicken pox while we were staying at a summer hotel in Asbury Park . . . of Fourth of July picnics on the spreading lawns, attended by aunts and uncles from both sides of the family, Pierce and Messler.

My grandmother, Margaret Messler Pierce, was a remarkable woman who was totally liberated because the idea that she wasn't never crossed her mind. In her opinion, if a thing mattered enough, you made it happen, and that was all there was to it. If you had brains and common sense and gumption and health, then you could do it.

What mattered to Nonnie was family, a high code of ethics, being a good businesswoman, and living well. She found no problems or conflicts in running a house and a business, being a great hostess, and raising a daughter, all at the same time. She was a very feminine woman, sharp as a tack, who believed you catch more flies with honey than with vinegar—but she kept the vinegar handy, just in case! It's always amused me that most people found her not only fascinating but also totally intimidating,

[2]From *The Shadow of a Unicorn*, copyright © 1987 by Dryden Harris St. John, Inc. New York: Bantam, 1987. Reprinted by permission of Bantam/Doubleday/Dell.

Harris Pierce

"Grandmother Margaret Messler Pierce (Bronwyn in The Keeping Days) *in her wedding gown"*

which I never did. (My cousin Bolton, who as a career military and foreign-service officer was pretty intimidating himself, told me in a letter written for Nonnie's eightieth birthday, "Margie always scared the hell out of me!")

Nonnie was born in West Farms, Bronx, New York; she had two older brothers and two younger ones; and when she was twenty-one she married a widower thirty years older than she with a teenage son. The house she moved into when she married was her "dream house," one she'd walked past as a girl and longed to live in someday. That was long before she started "walking out" with Harris Pierce (my grandfather)—and *that* came about because her Kings' Daughters group at the Episcopal Church was having a girls-invite-the-gentlemen "basket party" and her girlfriends dared her to invite Harris. (He may have been pushing fifty, but according to photographs he had a dashing mustache and a devilish twinkle in his eye!) Having been brought up with four brothers, Nonnie wouldn't chicken out on a dare—and the rest is history. According to Nonnie, no one in either family (other than Aunt Emma Pierce, who became Aunt Kate in "Keeping Days") had any negative reaction when she and Harris announced they were getting married. I don't believe it.

What I do know is that the family agrees "Margie" was the only family member that *everyone* in both families got along with. (Got along with? They were crazy about her!) My grandparents' romance and marriage became the love story of Bronwyn Sterling and Mr. Albright in the "Keeping Days" books. But I gave my grandparents' secretarial school, and how and why it was founded, to Ma and Pa Sterling. The rest of Pa and Ma is the way I imagine them to have been from family stories. And Bronwyn (and Tish) lived in Nonnie's dream house before, not after, the marriage.

Having been born into a large and close-knit extended family, I was frequently dragged to family reunions. Fourth of July picnics were fun, but long car trips to visit Uncle Joe in Basking Ridge, New Jersey, and Uncle John in Katonah, New York, were *boring.* I liked my aunts and uncles, but there was nobody else in my particular age bracket, so from my perspective things got pretty dull. They livened up considerably after I discovered I could get my great-uncles to tell tales about each other; Uncle Elmer (Ben in "Keeping Days") and Uncle Joe were both newspapermen, and they and Uncle John knew how to tell good stories. My school compositions livened up after that, too. My grandmother had ten fits when I wrote about how John and Elmer once got their father drunk on year-old cider as a sort of scientific experiment, but my eighth-grade classmates liked it fine. That story got recycled, of course, in "Keeping Days," and then my mother had the ten fits.

By the time I was collecting family skeletons, my grandmother had sold the school, which she'd run during Harris's old age and then her widowhood, and we'd moved (when I was a seven-year-old fourth grader) to a split-level three-generation house in the Ramsey Country Club Estates. *That* house became the home of Sidney Scott Webster in the "Computer Detectives" series, except that the "apartment" Sidney's lucky enough to have to herself in it was my grandmother's apartment. And "the club," transformed into a condominium community, is the setting—clubhouse, swamp, swans, and all—for *Dreams and Memories*:

> A stone mansion stood upon rolling emerald lawns. The stones were those of the New Jersey fields, but the shape of the mansion

> was the style of Old England. A tower rose against the darkling sky. . . . Angled steps led to verandas framed with arches. And on the lawns . . . My throat constricted and I could scarcely breathe. The white forms were so relaxed, so still, the swans' heads tucked beneath their wings. Why did I feel, so surely, that they were watching us?
>
> The clubhouse steps led to a carved oak door that opened onto a great hall, L-shaped, covered with linen-fold paneling that looked hand-carved. You could roast a whole steer in the fireplace. Above its copper hood hung round bronze plaques—bas-relief portraits of a king and queen. . . . I was dazzled by the building . . . the sunken dining room with its hand-painted mural of an English garden on the walls; the rose garden beyond it, framed by arbors. . . . the scent of climbing roses was everywhere.
>
> We walked across the road and down twin flights of steps into a sunken garden. *There* were the roses, and a pair of fountains, and matching peeled-wood gazebos at each end. Beyond a stone ledge the landscape dropped again to a maze, the golf course, and a large lake where swans were sailing. They [had] a nest at the far end. . . . We saw tennis courts, the golf shop, the small low building that housed the bowling alley. . . . [3]

"The club" was a wonderful place for children and dogs to grow up in (both could wander at will, singly or in groups, all over the place, to everybody's houses, because all the families who lived there were friends). My elementary-school boyfriend, who used to love to go to Saturday-afternoon horror movies and then scare me to death telling me the stories as gospel truth, was the one who originally paralyzed me into horrified belief that there was a body hidden somewhere beneath the falls!

Elementary school was a mixed blessing. I was two years younger than everyone else in class; I was the littlest (obviously); I think they thought of me as a cross between a pet and a pest; *I* thought of myself as an adult, because I was used to hanging around with

"My parents, Marjorie and Gene, with me on the boardwalk," Ocean Grove, New Jersey

adults. As a result I showed off a lot (hiding behind the mask of the character I wished I were) and spent a lot of time indulging myself in feeling Misunderstood (with a capital M), just like Tish Sterling. Except that as the only child of an almost-only child (Mother's adored half-brother, my Uncle Bolton, was a teenager when she was born and so seemed like part of a different generation), I didn't have as good a sense of humor as Tish with her six brothers and sisters!

I've been told by people who know me well that it's because I was an only child that I've been writing ever since about the big family I never had. I do know my definition of "family" (ideal version) came from *Little Women* and Nonnie's stories (everything was *always* sweetness and light in them!); my experience of "family" (reality version) came from my uncles' unexpurgated versions of the stories (see "Keeping Days," except that Grandma and Grandpa Messler, Nonnie's parents, never to my knowledge had the marital problems Ma and Pa Sterling had), and from my "kin of the spirit" families of church and theatre.

My main Keeping Days memories from Ramsey are the one quoted earlier about the baby rabbits . . . holidays . . . going to movies and the theatre with my grandmother and her best friend (and my "other mother"), Gus (Augusta)

[3]From *Dreams and Memories,* copyright © 1982 by Lavinia Harris. New York: Scholastic, Inc., 1982. Reprinted by permission of Scholastic, Inc.

Lamm . . . rainy afternoons when my mother made tea or hot chocolate and the neighborhood kids and/or she and I put puzzles together in our living room . . . nights when the same kids would start card games on our dining-room table, and eventually parents would come in search of them and stay to join the game . . . all the times Billy would scare the wits out of me with his horror stories and then gleefully pedal away, leaving me to walk home (in the twilight, past the swamp with its supposed slimy monsters) *alone.* And dance recitals. Those were the highlights of the year.

I "took ballet" from the time I was three, and my mother could make the most gorgeous costumes (so gorgeous that neighborhood kids would con her into making their costumes when we put on plays). I got to wear *rouge and lipstick.* The aunts and uncles came to stay all night, watch the performance, and *applaud.* I'd get *flowers,* handed up across the footlights—baskets of flowers from the aunts and uncles and my grandmother; an old-fashioned bouquet in a paper-lace collar from my father. Heaven on earth to an introverted, younger-than-the-others loner!

All through elementary school I wrote poetry, having started (according to my mother) when I was four. I was tone-deaf, and not allowed to sing in music class, so the music teacher took pity on me and let me read my poems aloud to the class (I danced in school assemblies, too, considerably more dramatically than my dancing teacher had intended). And the winter I was eleven, in eighth grade, I wrote my first book.

The whole of my eighth-grade year was a kind of extended Keeping Day, in the sense of how it was to affect my life. It was definitely a turning point, and most of my books revolve around turning points in the heroines' lives.

That eighth-grade winter I was sick, really sick, for a whole marking period. I'd always had coughs and colds and "sinus trouble" from the time I was very small; Mother's always said the reason I missed most childhood diseases was because I was always home from school when they went through the classroom. I'd had to be carted down to the Jersey shore in the winter to "breathe the salt air." I was "allergic to everything" (I'll admit sometimes it made a great excuse). But all during eighth grade I kept coming down with cold/coughs/fever; I'd get enough better to go back to school, but in another week I'd be worse and home in bed again. Finally the doctor told my parents to keep me home the whole January/February marking period, in the hope I could lick whatever ailed me once and for all. My teachers gave me my tests over the phone; Billy used to bring my books and assignments over. And when I could breathe, when I wasn't coughing too hard, I read. And wrote.

That was the winter I read *Gone with the Wind* in one sitting, all eight-hundred-plus pages of it, finishing by flashlight under the covers during the night and ending up with the worst headache of my life. *My* book, a full-length book, was about an Abolitionist girl in the 1850s, living on a Maryland plantation that was a station on the Underground Railroad, who fell in love with a gorgeous young man who turned out to be the son of a slave-catcher!

I never showed the book to anyone, unless maybe Mrs. Cadman, my English teacher, but I still have it. I may do something with it yet someday. Eventually, I went back to school, but the cough still lingered, and after that I started getting pains in my chest.

At the end of my first year of high school my grandmother, my parents, and I moved to a big old brown-shingled house in Wyckoff, built in 1923 and perfect for parties. After that life was like the young-adult novels I'd been reading, my favorite of which was Maud Hart Lovelace's "Betsy-Tacy" series.

The first thing that changed was that (like Betsy) I started going to a different church and joined its Youth Fellowship. The Messlers had been Dutch Reformed back to the seventeenth century, except that Wyant Van Zandt turned Episcopal, the "English religion," and is buried in Trinity churchyard in New York (see *The Legacy of Lucian Van Zandt*). When my grandmother was a girl her family started "going Episcopal" in West Farms, and that's how I'd been raised. My mother was married, and I was baptized, in Christ Church, Ridgewood, New Jersey, the church the heroine goes to in *If You Love Me, Let Me Go.* By the time I was twelve I was very rational and skeptical and didn't believe in God. (See Ben Sterling, in *The Keeping Days,* for my thoughts on the subject then and what changed my mind.) In Wyckoff, *everybody* went to the Reformed Church. The really great kids in school went to the Youth Fellowship on Sunday nights (it was a direct model for the fellowship, and The Crowd, in *The Wishing Star*). So, of course, I went too, once I'd gotten somebody to "drag me there against my will"! And that made everything change.

What the minister at the Wyckoff Reformed Church said made sense to me. The church wasn't dark like churches I was used to; it was full of light. When a young seminarian came to be youth minister, membership in Fellowship shot up to more than fifty. Pretty soon our big house was the only house large enough to hold the meetings. Being an only child, with no cousins near my age and most of the aunts and uncles a good deal older, I'd never experienced "family" as my mother and grandmother knew it; now that youth group became my extended family. All this later went into my first book, *The Wishing Star.*

I had another crowd, too, the "art-class crowd." My graduating class at Ramsey High School (where Wyckoff sent its students in those days) was unique; we had a lot of highly creative students, and regardless of whether our field of creativity was art, we hung out in the art room. The art teacher was young, and had been second-grade teacher and Presbyterian Sunday-school teacher to most of the Ramsey kids, so they regarded her as more friend than teacher, an attitude the rest of us picked up on. We spent study-hall time in the art room, we spent lunchtime (when we could get away with it) in the art room, we did other homework, and daydreamed, and worked on *The Ram* (the school newspaper) in the art room. We were one of those rare classes in which the "creative crowd" was as respected as the "jocks."

A lot of that class have gone on to success in creative fields, though I'd like to bet that most of them, like me, were told it couldn't be done. But here we are today, living, breathing proof that, just as my grandmother told us, *yes, it can!* That's one of the major things I want to pass on through my books: It *is* possible to make things happen. It *is* possible to make it. Especially with the encouragement and faith of friends and family, of blood or of spirit.

I'm an author. I think one of my classmates is a newspaper writer somewhere. One's a packaging designer and corporate executive. Another, Stephen Bruce, is a nationally known restaurateur/entrepreneur who when he was twenty-one founded (with two friends) the "restaurant and general store" Serendipity III in New York City. It now has branches in other major cities, and many famous people go there. Connie Bond Ftera used to doodle horses in class; now she's a graphics artist who designed my Macmillan "international intrigue" book, *Return to Morocco.* Barbara Stegen Shear is an artist and designer. Her husband, David Shear, was the iconoclast of our class, clear back to elementary school; he's specialized in Third World development, working for the U.S. government and later for nongovernmental agencies, in both Africa and Washington, D.C. David's work in famine prevention won him a Rockefeller Foundation award.

I lost track of Barbara and Dave for several years, but one day after my first four books had been published she telephoned; the Shears were home from Africa on stateside leave, and she wanted to tell me that her daughters Liz and Jessica had brought my books home from their English-language school *in Africa.* "My stock went up considerably when they found out *I knew Norma Johnston!!!*" she told me, laughing. Which tickled me, because in elementary school Barbara had been one of the "in kids" I'd have given my eyeteeth to have hung around with!

The major Keeping Day of my junior year was when I was costumes chairman for our class play, *Our Hearts Were Young and Gay.* It was set in 1923, and Mother (who was and is a pack rat) had lots of beautiful Twenties clothes and accessories (many of which she'd made) in which I'd been dressing up for years. Practically everyone on stage was wearing things that belonged to her (not all of them borrowed with her permission) and what I hadn't been able to beg, borrow, or filch, I made. The cast party was held at my house afterwards. Everybody loved to come there for parties because (1) we had a huge sun porch where they could dance, play shuffleboard and games (cutthroat Chinese checkers was the rage one year); (2) my father would put red light bulbs in the ceiling fixture to make the sun porch look like a real ballroom (meaning dark; meaning kids could make out in relative privacy); (3) my mother always made her famous "party sandwiches" (girls could usually find the most desirable boys sitting in a circle around the kitchen table, eating the sandwich crusts as fast as Mother trimmed them off!) and Nonnie made her famous Pierce family punch; (4) Mother felt a party that ended before 1:00 A.M. was some kind of failure, and a party that lasted till 3:00 (many of ours did) was

"My favorite high-school photograph: from left, Lois Gaeta, my Canadian boyfriend, and myself"

even better. Parents liked having the kids hang out at our house, because they knew where to find them, and knew they were chaperoned.

It was with that junior play, and then through my senior year in high school, when I was fifteen, that I began to believe I finally belonged. I was an officer in Fellowship and several other clubs, and Feature Editor of *The Ram.* I had a Canadian boyfriend who used to go with his family to the same summer hotel in Ocean Grove that Nonnie and I always went to (see *The Swallow's Song*). His mother was everything I wanted to be someday—except that she made a career of being a "company wife" and hostess in Montreal, and I knew by then I wanted to be a famous dress designer and author!

His mother and *my* grandmother took the two of us on a cruise to Bermuda as graduation presents (me from high school, he from university). That fall his mother "presented" me at the St. Mary's Hospital debutante ball in Montreal. (She didn't have a daughter, so I was her "honorary niece.") It was my first taste of being a celebrity, and I felt as if I'd stepped into the pages of one of my favorite books.

I'd never wanted to go to college, I wanted to study design at art school, but my parents felt sixteen was too young to commute to New York City. So I was staying home for a year—I made and sold hand-painted writing paper and other art items, as I'd been doing since I was twelve; I read a lot and went to lots of movies and plays; I did a lot of community service work through Fellowship and other organizations. I was invited to join the Village Players, the area's adult Little Theatre group. I made my debut. And I began writing my first "real" book. It was patterned on the format of Maud Hart Lovelace's "Betsy" books, and drew on a lot of things that had happened in my Crowd.

In late winter, most of us were in a charity revue that a local young man staged annually for the Lions Club. I threw a party after the last performance of that, too. And early the next morning we left for a trip to see the azalea gardens in Charleston, South Carolina—my parents, my grandmother, Stephen Bruce, and I.

And on the third morning, in Fayetteville, North Carolina, my father died.

We were sitting in a hotel coffee shop having breakfast, and laughing at my father taking his first taste of hominy grits, and he just fell over out of his chair onto the floor. He'd never had any heart trouble that anybody knew of, but he had a heart attack, and he died. If you want to know more details, hunt up a copy of *The Wider Heart,* because the death of the heroine's father in it is my father's death.

After that, the plan for me to go to art school was never mentioned again—to my relief, because I'd already decided I didn't want that anymore. I wanted to be a writer.

Everybody told me there was no future in it, but I wrote anyway. I finished my book, and entered it in a contest, and it came back. I gave it to one of my best friends to read, and she returned it (liking it but guessing wrong about which character was based on her!) while the Crowd was in our favorite hangout after Fellowship. The boys got ahold of the manuscript, and laughed themselves silly reading choice bits of a love scene out loud!

When I reread my journal for those first two years out of school, it seems I was always either sick, or writing, or working on plays, or all of those together. The chest pains and leg pains and cough and breathing problems were getting much, much worse. I taught art at the local Y's summer day camp, and then opened a Saturday School of Arts and Crafts on the sun porch during the school year. My mother opened a lingerie shop, and I did buying and displays and advertising for her. I went to the summer writers' conference at the University of Connecticut, and got really valuable advice, and rewrote my book. It was again rejected. Ann Freeman, the mother of one of my Saturday School students, was instrumental in my being hired to run the whole art program at her town's summer recreation program. Being me, I managed to write, produce, direct, and do most of the costumes for a historical pageant there as well. The following winter, through too much enthusiasm coupled with too little practical experience, I tried to teach drama and produce *A Christmas Carol* with the same junior highers. It was a disaster.

That experience taught me a lot. My grandmother always said if you want a job doing something, go out and *create* the job; start your own business. Now I knew (what she'd also told me but I hadn't heard) that first you had to know *how* to do what you wanted to do. You had to pay your dues. I started paying mine.

If I wanted to sell what I wrote so people other than just my friends could read it, I had to learn how to write professionally. If I wanted to do theatre, I had to learn how to act and direct professionally. I was accepted as a member of Tufts University Theatre summer theatre company, and signed up for a writing course at Tufts as well.

That was another disaster. The professor was an educator, not a writer, and the class's goals were not my goals. I wanted to write for and about young people, and work with them through drama, to help them understand themselves, just as I'd learned through identifying with the characters in good books and plays. I wanted to write the kind of books Mrs. Lovelace wrote. I'd been corresponding with Mrs. Lovelace for a year or so, and she'd encouraged me, insisting I should always write about what I really knew. The opening night of the first play, I was told by the professor that I'd *never* be a writer. After the performance I sat up the rest of the night writing to Mrs. Lovelace, asking her advice.

Her publisher forwarded the letter to Mankato, Minnesota (Deep Valley in her books), where she was guest of honor at a townwide celebration. She wrote back by return mail, for which I'll be forever grateful; she said I should *quit the class!!!* pleading bad health or something (which was no lie); never take lessons or advice from anyone who isn't a professional in the same field or isn't on the same wavelength with me; start another book right away! I've been passing that good advice on to others ever since.

My grandmother was my role model as a businesswoman, Maud Hart Lovelace was my mentor as a writer. Ann Freeman, who has a special gift for nurturing, was my mentor in learning how to use sensitivity constructively (as a bridge to understanding and helping others) and my role model of a woman with real soul. In the summer theatre company, I tried to do as she did: hold the circle together; help people defuse and believe in themselves again. At the end of summer, I was told I was wonderful at nurturing but would *never* be an actress or director.

In spite of that, I'd become so involved in theatre and with people that I moved back to Boston that fall. Because of my retailing experience, I was hired as a buyer's assistant in a Boston specialty store. I lived in a one-room apartment on Marlborough Street, and worked days at the store and nights and weekends at the theatre. It was rotten for my health but wonderful otherwise. I was so poor that the soles of my shoes had holes in them, and I went barelegged in snowstorms when I had no money to buy stockings, but I wouldn't give up. I was very lucky in discovering the real theatre of toil and tears and sweat and glory which lies beneath the surface glamour. Every day I walked to work past a house with lavender windowpanes that later became the setting for my first gothic novel, *The Medici Ring.*

When I did move back to New Jersey, I was asked to become "book" director (and eventually costume designer) for fund-raising charity musicals. I wasn't getting much further with my writing (I was too afraid of rejection slips to send things out) but I had plenty of opportunities with regional theatre, and I knew enough now to know I needed to learn much more. So I auditioned and was accepted into the American Theatre Wing's Professional Training Program in New York.

I was lucky enough to have teachers who'd trained with each of the major acting "schools": Actors' Studio, Berghof Studio, Group Theatre, Moscow Art Theatre. *That* was how I really learned to write—when first Ellen Andrews and then Mme. Barbara Bulgakov taught us step by step how to break down scripts, find the main "spine" of the plot and of the character, understand (and *show,* not *tell*) the character's background and motives and objectives. How to include everything that was necessary, and nothing that was not. How to "hold something back," so that what the audience saw was only the tip of an iceberg, with the other eight-ninths merely sensed. How to make the audience "walk in the character's moccasins" and experience empathy. Above all, in Tennessee Williams's words from *The Glass Menagerie,* how to "give truth in the pleasant disguise of illusion."

All this was a revelation, because I could see instantly how the same method could be applied to writing books, and also how it linked with everything I had been taught in church and Fellowship about "not judging one's brother until one has walked for a moon in his moccasins" and about how doing so could help us gain better understanding of ourselves, of others, and of the love of God.

That's something else I try to do in my writing—give readers the chance to walk in the footsteps of characters like and unlike themselves, and have the same kind of suddenly-seeing-in-a-mirror experience I've always had from books and theatre.

While I was at the Theatre Wing, I moved to New York, first to a walk-up studio apartment in a Murray Hill brownstone (that was haunted), and then to an apartment in Gramercy Park. Both of these settings, and other New York experiences as well, I used in my "Diana Winthrop" detective series. In addition to studying acting full-time at night, I also worked full-time days as an editorial assistant on a fashion trade publication put out by the legendary "Miss Tobe," who had literally created the occupation of fashion consultant. Miss Tobe and Mme. Bulgakov were two more inspiring role models for me.

During the first summer at Theatre Wing I was producer's assistant, costumes and props person, and sometimes actress at a summer theatre in Pennsylvania operated by the man who'd produced those high-school-years reviews and the charity musicals. That was probably the most significant summer of my life. Everything I'd learned everywhere came together; I was no longer hiding behind masks or trying to be what others wanted me to be, or protecting myself from feeling or from being hurt. I was deeply emotionally involved with someone, and feeling responsibility for a few others, too, and those experiences are hidden between the lines in *The Crucible Year* and *Myself and I,* and in many other books as well.

The turning point of that crucible summer came (as it often does in any creative project) about two-thirds of the way through. I was doing too many jobs for which I had too little time and experience (we did a different play every week) and like everyone was having very little sleep. I was being a mother hen, crying towel, and advisor, often at the expense of my job responsibilities, and was trying to protect cast from crew and crew from cast, person from person, *everyone* from the director (he, too, ate novices for breakfast), and the company and producer from one another. With the best intentions in the world, I was building walls that separated people, instead of bridges that could have led to understanding.

Everything came to a head the day I had to drive into an Allentown torn up with road repairs, in the stage manager's old stick-shift car (I didn't know how to drive anything not automatic), to look for props instead of being at rehearsal. I was exhausted, in over my head, worried sick about the very lives of two people I cared for deeply but couldn't seem to help, and in a lot of pain, physically, emotionally, and spiritually. Suddenly I longed to be back home, on Ann's screened porch being comforted with tea and sympathy, or in the security of my Fellowship circle. But I wasn't a schoolgirl anymore. I couldn't run backwards in time, and I wouldn't have even if I could. I had taken on responsibilities; I cared about people and projects and my work; if I backed out I'd let people down, but nothing about how I felt would change.

I could not go home. I wasn't even sure where "home" was anymore. I felt like Tom Wingfield in *The Glass Menagerie,* a wanderer, and like Laura Wingfield too. What I did do was go into a church and sit in a pew in the empty silence, just as I used to go sit in St. Patrick's when I got too swamped with psychic overload at Theatre Wing.

I kept a journal, as recommended by both Mrs. Lovelace and my acting teachers, almost constantly all that summer. But, astonishingly, I never wrote an account of that afternoon. It was too intense; it was too personal; I think I was afraid someone might see it and, what would be ever more awful, laugh. What I do remember was how still everything was, and how peaceful, and how the place was filled with pale gray light. I remember starting to cry, and starting to shake, because I was so tired and so worried. And so angry, because nothing I tried to do seemed to be getting anywhere, not really. My book still wasn't selling. People I cared about were still hurting. *I* was hurting. I remember screaming to God inside my head: *Okay! I know everything's supposed to have a reason! I know our gifts and talents come from You! But what's the use of having them if they're not doing anybody one darn bit of good? What's the use of being one of the creative ones. . . . having our nerves on the outside of our skins. . . . if it's never going to accomplish anything?!?* Something like that.

I remembered how late one night another cast member had stormed that being sensitive was supposed to be an advantage in our art, but that really it was like being born with two heads; "One's fine, but who needs two!!!" I'd been so shocked when she'd said she almost hated being "creative," and I'd tried passionately to convince her there was some good reason for it. Now I found myself crying out silently, *God, if You want me to be like this, sensitive, feeling things so deeply, torn up with talents, tell me why! If there's a use for me going through all this, USE it. Otherwise take it away! If there is a purpose for it, I promise I'll always write, and do theatre, as a means of communication and of "passing on" the gifts and truths that I've been given—no matter how much it hurts. If there isn't, promise I'll give up writing and theatre, and accept being one of the contented cows! Just tell me which I should do, go on or quit!*

I wasn't shaking anymore. I just felt drained. I got up and went back to the theatre. I didn't tell anybody. I didn't "get told" anything. But I think I did get shown. For one thing, I wasn't so torn up anymore—on the outside, yes, but not inside. For another, there's a long entry in my journal, written what I think was a few nights later, halfway through the run of *I Am a Camera,* the play on which the musical *Cabaret* is based. I was cast as Mrs. Watson-Courtneidge, the heroine's mother, and I was awful.

> *It was the strangest thing. I was sitting in the dressing room last night about halfway through the performance, when suddenly I closed my eyes and SAW her—Mrs. Watson-Courtneidge—there in front of me. . . . I saw her sitting on the train coming to Berlin, with her hands on her purse and her umbrella and valise beside her. And then I saw her earlier, in England, with her husband; in their country home outside of London. It was a very still quiet afternoon, about four o'clock. They were in a very airy high-ceilinged room with parquet floors and Georgian furniture, standing beside a high bowed window with small rectangular panes and crimson satin drapes looped back with dull gold*

knobs. The window ran from floor to ceiling sending a shaft of light into the quiet dimness and making golden patterns on the parquet floor. And outside the window there was a formal border that curved to follow the contours of the house—there were rhododendron bushes with very pale pink flowers, very neat outside the window, and beyond that rolling English lawn of pale green grass as far as eye could see; only low box hedges and tall thin poplars between it and a very bright blue sky that was strung with wispy clouds.

There was a sense of stillness and serenity, and of peace, that hung over it like a veil—that feeling that comes from a family's having known for centuries its place in life. . . . an island lost in time. . . .

I saw the Watson-Courtneidges standing in the window talking and I could even hear what they were saying. She was wearing a blue crepe dress that matched her eyes, and pearls, and her hands were clasped and her little heels planted firmly on the floor, and she was saying, "Now you know very well that I can handle it. I shall be kind, but firm. You know perfectly well that if you should go you would doubtless do something quite violent." And I heard him sputtering, "Now, Cecily . . ." and somehow knew that was her name. And then I saw her pack her bag—including her hot water bottle, for she never goes anywhere without her hot water bottle. And I saw her crossing the Channel, and arriving in Berlin, and going into Fraulein Schneider's house. I even know what she was thinking as she went upstairs, and what the landing looked like, and where the plaster was cracked along the wall—

And then I opened my eyes and she was still with me—I looked in the mirror and it was not my face but Cecily's—I looked at my hands and knew how she would fold them, and knew how she would sit which was different from the way I sat—I went to hook my arm around the back of the chair the way I do, and could not, because Cecily could not—I looked around the room and saw everyone the way Cecily would see them: the tear in Schneider's dress, the cobwebs, the dust—suddenly I was reacting to it the way Cecily would. . . .

I went onstage and saw the set not as it was but as it ought to be, and when I picked up Sally's red slip, which I always knew I had been doing wrong, I picked it up and dropped it without even thinking and suddenly knew that it was right . . . . After the show everyone was laughing and talking and somehow I could not, somehow it was wrong because I was still Cecily. I wanted to be alone. . . .

This was my first experience of what's called "the artist's duality"; of being in what scientists call "alpha state," in which the creative unconscious takes over, and yet at the same time having our conscious mind fully aware and "standing off observing." It's rather like an out-of-the-body experience. That's also the state in which I do most of my writing; certainly my best writing—the book I'm working on never comes alive until I "psyche in." (If you want to read the best definition of the creative process—and of the creative person's responsibility—I've ever seen, read the last page of choreographer Agnes de Mille's first autobiography, *Dance to the Piper.*)

That, for me, was the proof that "to everything there is a season" (which was the theme of *Of Time and of Seasons*), or perhaps more accurately, "to everything there is a reason." The "season" for being full-time professional author and theatre person didn't come till later. But I knew that I'd made a covenant about my gifts and talents. What other people knew was that something in me had changed and that now the magic started happening when I was onstage. And when I wrote. As an ex-GI classmate demanded bluntly when I got back to Theatre Wing, "What the ——— happened to you this summer? You aren't the same person."

That fall I began to really understand Stanislavski Method acting, and how the actor's emotions (and everything of self and study the actor brings to a character) are not an end in themselves (any more than happiness, or being loved, etc., etc., can be achievable objectives, as many of my book heroines ultimately learn) but are means of making the audience (or the readers) "walk in the moccasins" of the character and wind up with a "wider heart." (The title of *The Wider Heart* comes from an Edna St. Vincent Millay poem.)

That winter at Theatre Wing, all the pieces began falling into place. The next summer, I couldn't bear to not do summer theatre, but neither I nor many of the others could afford to give up our jobs. Being the granddaughter of an entrepreneur I started my own summer theatre. I rented a red barn in Wyckoff that was used the rest of the year as a dance studio, and my mother made a sign saying *Bandbox Theatre.* I persuaded our speech teacher, Raymond Edward Johnson (who'd created the role of Thomas Jefferson in *The Patriots* on Broadway, and was famous for many years on radio), to take the job of director. Most of the cast members were Theatre Wing class-

"Holding Theodore Bear at Rockport, Massachussetts, which became the setting for Watcher in the Mist"

mates, and a recent local high-school graduate phoned to ask if she could apprentice as stage manager; she is now an internationally known producer.

We rehearsed in apartments all over New York during the week, and performed in Wyckoff on the weekends. The cast, crew, and director lived at our house those weekends; the sun porch became the men's dorm and was wall-to-wall mattresses on the floor. My mother, while running a store six-plus days a week, rounded up props, delivered publicity to newspapers, and paid the grocery bills; my grandmother, who was in her late seventies, cooked the meals and ran the box office. We must have all been crazy! Because I was known locally from school days, and I was afraid I wouldn't be taken seriously, I produced under the name of my father's grandmother, Pamela Dryden.

After I completed studies at the Theatre Wing, I opened a dress shop in an old Victorian house in Wyckoff, and my mother moved her store into half the space. I had three months between when I resigned from Miss Tobe's and when the store would open, and during that time, in addition to vacationing at Rockport, Massachusetts, which much later became the setting for *Watcher in the Mist,* I reread and rewrote the book I'd written when I was sixteen. Only now the theme changed from "be like everybody else and you'll be liked" to "be true to yourself, your best self, even if it's hard and lonely." The title of the book was *The Wishing Star.*

I was so busy once my dress shop opened that I didn't finish rewriting the manuscript, particularly since I was staging a lot of fashion shows and directing a few plays locally. Once I did finish the rewrite, I wasn't sure what to do next. I knew the manuscript was too long. I knew I should "send it out" to publishers. But it's much easier to believe you'll be a successful author when you aren't risking receiving rejection slips!

Ever since sophomore year in high school, Lois Gaeta (my first friend in Wyckoff) and I had been critiquing each other's writing. I gave her the manuscript and asked her what to cut. She read it, said, "It's too long, but I don't know what you should take out. Send it out!" I protested. She said, "Get an agent!" I pointed out that was easier said than done. She said, "I know of an agency who handles stuff for somebody I know. [Lois was in advertising then; she's now an executive, writing and coproducing TV programs for continuing medical education.] Call them!" I said I couldn't. "*I* can," Lois said firmly, and marched into a phone booth in Rockefeller Center, with me protesting frantically that it wasn't protocol!

The agent sent *The Wishing Star* to Funk and Wagnalls, where the editor said she'd publish it if I cut a hundred pages. I had to reduce the book to an outline before I saw where to cut; since that experience I *always* work from outlines. I wrote *The Wider Heart* (based on an incident in our stores) and *Ready or*

The author, leaning against the post, sailing for Europe on the Riviera, *the summer her first book was published*

"At my Bicentennial party," July 3, 1976

Not for Funk and Wagnalls, and consulted with Phyllis Whitney at a Syracuse University writers' conference, between when *The Wishing Star* was bought and when it came out. *The Wishing Star* was chosen as a Junior Literary Guild book club selection, and I closed my shop and sailed on my first of many trips to Europe.

Now all the different spirals of my different careers began to come together. Because of my school-newspaper and art-class training, I'd gotten the jobs I'd had already and working in my mother's store had also helped with the Tobe job. Now, because of those, plus my own published books, I became assistant to an editor in a religious publishing house. Because of *all* my various experiences I was asked to be a youth counselor at church, and one of the ministers and I founded Geneva Players, producing major Broadway plays and classics (like *The Miracle Worker, The Diary of Anne Frank, Romeo and Juliet*) as a platform on which teens could speak out (through the characters they played) on the issues and conflicts of contemporary life. Our aims were to comfort the troubled and trouble the comforted, and to get people to "walk in other people's moccasins" and broaden and deepen their angles of vision—not bad objectives for a writer, either.

The first Geneva Players production was Arthur Miller's *Crucible,* and it opened on the night of President John F. Kennedy's assassination.

> For the rest of my life, I thought, I'll remember sitting here *[in the auditorium]* this afternoon, alone yet not alone, sewing on Danforth's cloak. I looked at the clock at that moment; I did not know why. The hands stood at exactly twenty to three. And all at once I realized that I was no more alone.
>
> Gramps had come in . . . an odd cracked look on his old face. . . .
>
> "I just heard it on the car radio, driving over. The President's been shot."
>
> . . . At twenty to three, on the afternoon John Fitzgerald Kennedy died, I sat in the auditorium, sewing a costume for *The Crucible,* and the red fabric, fallen from my lap, lay on the floor like a pool of blood.[4]

Those lines in *The Crucible Year,* and much else in that book, came straight from my own journals.

Everything was coming full circle . . . everything in the Keeping Days of my life found its way into counseling, and teaching, and books, and plays. Because I was spending so much time teaching theatre, communication, how to find what's between the lines in books and plays, and how to write ("Miss J. *help!!!* I have a term paper due tomorrow! Yes, I *know* I should have started it sooner, but. . . . !!!") I decided to go to Montclair College and get my teaching certificate. I was still giving at least twenty hours a week to youth work and Geneva Players; I became a research assistant to my psychology professor; I edited a newsletter on a free-lance basis. I was no longer working at the publishing house but I did free-lance editing and also ghostwriting for that house and others. I finished *The Bridge Between* (set in the Revolutionary War farmhouse across the street from the split-level house in which I now lived) and began working on *The Keeping Days* while I was in college. After graduation, I taught eighth-grade English for two years. At that time the cofounder of Geneva moved away, and the members voted to dissolve the group rather than risk its being changed. Many of them joined Geneva Players, Inc., which I formed as an interfaith (the original Geneva had

[4]From *The Crucible Year,* copyright © 1979 by Norma Johnston. New York: Atheneum, 1979. Reprinted by permission of Atheneum, the Macmillan Publishing Co.

been, too, but unofficially) and intergenerational drama company.

Up till now I had only written one book a year. *The Keeping Days* and *Glory in the Flower* began as one book but became too long, and Jean Karl, the famous editor at Atheneum, could see how it could be divided into two. Much of the "Keeping Days" books came from my grandparents' youth; much came also from my own teaching experiences.

Suddenly the publishing market changed as paperback publishers discovered young-adult books. My life changed, too. I said earlier that there was one other major factor that has shaped my life. This was my health—or I should say, my lack of it! I'd had "breathing problems" from childhood; I'd had aches and pains ever since that bout of illness in eighth grade. While I was in college the aches and pains were identified as several forms (one offbeat) of arthritis. ("Is there anything about you that isn't offbeat?" my friends inquired.) It got much worse; the breathing problems got much worse.

At this same time, I began writing for several publishers at once, both hardcover and softcover, becoming one of the small percentage of authors who support themselves totally from their book writing. I write under eight different names, for different writing genres and different publishers; names all taken (in whole or in mixed combinations) from ancestors on both sides of the family. My father was an orphan when he met my mother, but there's a story and a half in the lives of *his* mother, Catherine Dryden Chambers Johnston, and her two husbands. (Read *Carlisle's Hope* and *To Jess, with Love and Memories.*)

"Mother, holding Oliver Twist, and Annie (Anatasia), the dog-rescued-from-the-river in The Case of the Dog-Lover's Legacy," 1973

I also give speeches and have taught writing and drama courses, and travel for personal appearances and for research. And I do free-lance editing and ghostwriting. With all those "different identities" being juggled, something had to give, and what did was my health. I found myself "working horizontal" (but with my head propped up so I could breathe) much of the time. I had to take high-school or college students with me on trips to help me. All of them are now themselves in creative fields. Karen Louise Hansen, my "almost daughter," is an editor. Susan Wilder is an art director. Elizabeth Lund is an actress and producer/director of a New York showcase theatre she founded; the old Bandbox Theatre sign is now repainted to say *Stepping Stone Theatre.* My cousin Kimberley Pierce, who is my "horse books expert," is still in high school but a gifted writer. But even with a wonderful support network, I found it hard to keep up.

Two years ago my doctor shocked me. "Do you know that for the past two years you've been seriously ill and gasping for breath two months out of every three?" she demanded. "How do you get any books written? You're going to get much worse unless you stop pushing yourself so hard and find a breathing specialist who can pinpoint what's doing this to you." The antibiotics and cortisone were no longer working.

She was right. I almost collapsed during a public appearance that June and spent the summer struggling for breath. In the intervals when I could get off a respirator, Karen and Liz helped me move from my townhouse and office back into the split-level with my mother. Being allergic to the household pets—German shepherd Susie, mostly-sheltie Missy, and rooster Red—didn't help. I'd already given up acting and directing; now I had to cut down on other things as well and save my "functioning time" for writing.

But I've written half a dozen books since then. I'm able to work, part of most days, at least half the time. Just as I finally found a doctor who diagnosed and treated the arthritis, I've recently found one who diagnosed my lifelong respiratory troubles as severe chronic asthma-and-then-some, meaning that my respiratory system "dramatically overreacts" to *everything,* not just things to which I'm genuinely allergic. *Dramatically overreacts*; there's poetic irony there somewhere, considering my background! More important than putting a name to the condition, we've apparently put a stop to its getting worse.

I'm writing again. I'm still giving speeches and making personal appearances and teaching workshops. I belong to the Authors League and Mystery Writers of America and Sisters in Crime, and serve on the Rutgers University Council on Children's Literature. I'm still traveling, even if with cane and sometimes respirator and wheelchair. In fact I'm working on a book now for my Macmillan editor, Cindy Kane, which has a "handicapped" heroine and starts with a traumatic Keeping Day I had last summer.

If you've got brains and gumption, nothing can stop you, Nonnie used to say. *Don't fight it, use it!* Mme. Bulgakov would say, eyes snapping, when we came to class at Theatre Wing with excuses for why scenes did not go well. *Twist your troubles round and make them bless you,* Mrs. Lovelace wrote in *Betsy's Wedding,* making Betsy remember the story of Jacob wrestling with the angel. If I hadn't been out of school so much when I was little, I wouldn't have read so much, I wouldn't have hung around so much with adults and had my horizons widened. I know I wouldn't have had as much empathy for others. Perhaps I wouldn't even have been a writer. Being sidelined for *time-out* often gave me *time.* Even if I'm not well enough to write, I can lie around and read—and watch television; I watch about eleven hours a day (yes, even when I'm writing!) and get all kinds of plot ideas from news and science programs. So this is something else I want to pass on through my characters—you can't control what life dishes out to you, but you can control how you react to it and what you do with it. You can use your gifts—if not one way, then another.

Getting back to that college professor and his assignment:

> *Who am I? A Victorian. A cat curled by the fire (but I'm allergic to cats). An herb-and-flower garden. The color red. Old houses with low-ceilinged rooms, a teakettle on the hearth, and a fire burning bright. Caftans, antique rings and earrings, crosses on silver chains. Big-brimmed hats. Candlelight. Shakespeare, mythology, John Donne's poems, mysticism. Somebody in Geneva once described me as a total environment.*
>
> *Why do I write? Because I have things that I must say, and I can no more hold them back than I can cease to breathe and still be alive. Because I believe, with Tennessee Williams, that writers of fiction can share real truths through the pleasant disguise of illusion.*

As my grandmother said, "You catch more flies with honey than with vinegar." I write in a romantic, often gothic, style, because I know from my own reading and from theatre that when you draw people into the circle of a rosy glow, they become more open to the thrust of truth. I write about young people facing today's realities without flinching. I write mysteries and detective and suspense stories because deep down they're the age-old story of the struggle between good and evil—and besides, they're fun! I write about love—all the different meanings of the word—and about family, and all that word's different meanings.

Today I write a great deal about broken and blended and nonrelated families, because I see so much of that around me, and besides I've had them in my family and know they aren't the end of the world. My father was abandoned by his birth-father, and raised by a stepfather he was very fond of. My grandmother was a much-loved stepmother, and she married a man who'd had a stepmother himself. So adoption, divorce, death, remarriage—even desertion—appear in my books, from *The Keeping Days* to the "Carlisle Chronicles" and *The Potter's Wheel*:

> I was thinking about that word *home.* When Mother took off, I'd felt as if I no longer had one. That wasn't true. Not in the literal sense. It wasn't that I didn't *have* one, I didn't have *one.* Not just one. Home, I thought with satisfaction, was inside me. Home was wherever my heart was, wherever I had friends and kin. I had many homes. I was rich indeed.[5]

Like Laura in that quotation from *The Potter's Wheel,* I have several people in my family circle who have no blood or legal ties to me. And as a result, my life has been enriched.

And so I write of the Keeping Days that remain in our memories forever; of the turning points in which we go from innocence to knowledge; of the abstract truths I believe to be unchanging in a changing world. And of facing change without feeling threatened by it. My grandmother used to say, "The world's going to keep turning whether you want it to or not, and you'd better go forward with it or you'll find yourself going backward!"

That essay that started out, "Once there was an insufferable brat," ended like this: "Call her a roman-

[5]From *The Potter's Wheel,* copyright © 1988 by Dryden Harris St. John, Inc. New York: Morrow, 1988. Reprinted by permission of William Morrow & Co., Inc.

Tender Visions

The author, 1988

ticist, but she still believes, in spite of everything, that man has at heart the potential for good as well as evil; that life is no mere accident or dirty joke but has meaning and purpose. To her, that's realism. Perhaps commitment's out of style these days. This artist is past the point of no return—and she's very glad she is!"

The Keeping Days of my life have been *wonderful!*

BIBLIOGRAPHY

FOR YOUNG ADULTS

As Norma Johnston:

The Wishing Star. New York: Funk & Wagnalls, 1963.

The Wider Heart. New York: Funk & Wagnalls, 1964.

Ready or Not. New York: Funk & Wagnalls, 1965.

The Bridge Between, New York: Funk & Wagnalls, 1966.

Of Time and Seasons. New York: Atheneum, 1975.

Strangers Dark and Gold. New York: Atheneum, 1976.

A Striving after Wind. New York: Atheneum, 1976.

If You Love Me, Let Me Go. New York: Atheneum, 1978.

The Swallow's Song. New York: Atheneum, 1978.

The Crucible Year. New York: Atheneum, 1979.

Pride of Lions: The Story of the House of Atreus. New York: Atheneum, 1979.

The Days of the Dragon's Seed. New York: Atheneum, 1982.

Gabriel's Girl. New York: Atheneum, 1983.

Timewarp Summer. New York: Atheneum, 1983.

The Watcher in the Mist. New York: Bantam, 1986.

Shadow of a Unicorn. New York: Bantam, 1987.

The Potter's Wheel. New York: Morrow, 1988.

Return to Morocco. New York: Macmillan, 1988.

Whisper of the Cat. New York: Bantam, Morrow, 1988.

The Delphic Choice. New York: Macmillan, 1989.

The Five Magpies. New York: Macmillan, 1989.

Such Stuff as Dreams Are Made Of. New York: Morrow, 1989.

Summer of the Citadel. New York: Bantam, 1989.

A Small Rain. New York: Macmillan, 1990.

"Keeping Days" Series

The Keeping Days. New York: Atheneum, 1973.

Glory in the Flower. New York: Atheneum, 1974.

A Mustard Seed of Magic. New York: Atheneum, 1977.

The Sanctuary Tree. New York: Atheneum, 1977.

A Nice Girl Like You. New York: Atheneum, 1980.

Myself and I. New York: Atheneum, 1981.

"Carlisle Chronicles" Series

Carlisles All. New York: Bantam, 1986.

The Carlisle's Hope. New York: Bantam, 1986.

To Jess, with Love and Memories. New York: Bantam, 1986.

As Pamela Dryden:

Mask for My Heart. New York: New American Library, 1982.

As Lavinia Harris:

Dreams and Memories. New York: Scholastic Inc., 1982.

"Computer Detectives" Series

The Great Rip-Off. New York: Scholastic Inc., 1984.

Soaps in the Afternoon. New York: Scholastic Inc., 1985.

A Touch of Madness. New York: Scholastic Inc., 1985.

Cover Up! New York: Scholastic Inc., 1986.

As Kate Chambers:

"Diana Winthrop" Series

The Case of the Dog Lover's Legacy. New York: New American Library, 1983.

The Secret of the Singing Strings. New York: New American Library, 1983.

The Legacy of Lucian Van Zandt. New York: New American Library, 1984.

The Secrets of Beacon Hill. New York: New American Library, 1984.

The Threat of the Pirate Ship. New York: New American Library, 1984.

FOR YOUNGER READERS

As Catherine E. Chambers:

"Adventures in Frontier America" Series

California Gold Rush: Search for Treasure (illustrated by Alan Eitzen). Mahwah, New Jersey: Troll, 1984.

Daniel Boone and the Wilderness Road (illustrated by George Guzzi). Mahwah, New Jersey: Troll, 1984.

Flatboats on the Ohio: Westward Bound (illustrated by John Lawn). Mahwah, New Jersey: Troll, 1984.

Frontier Dream: Life on the Great Plains (illustrated by Dick Smolinski). Mahwah, New Jersey: Troll, 1984.

Frontier Farmer: Kansas Adventure (illustrated by Len Epstein). Mahwah, New Jersey: Troll, 1984.

Frontier Village: A Town Is Born (illustrated by D. Smolinski). Mahwah, New Jersey: Troll, 1984.

Indiana Days: Life in a Frontier Town (illustrated by J. Lawn). Mahwah, New Jersey: Troll, 1984.

Log Cabin Home: Pioneers in the Wilderness (illustrated by A. Eitzen). New Jersey: Troll, 1984.

Texas Roundup: Life on the Range (illustrated by J. Lawn). Mahwah, New Jersey: Troll, 1984.

Wagons West: Off to Oregon (illustrated by D. Smolinski). Mahwah, New Jersey: Troll, 1984.

As Elizabeth Bolton:

The Case of the Wacky Cat. Mahwah, New Jersey: Troll, 1985.

Ghost in the House. Mahwah, New Jersey: Troll, 1985.

The Secret of the Ghost Piano. Mahwah, New Jersey: Troll, 1985.

The Secret of the Magic Potion. Mahwah, New Jersey: Troll, 1985.

The Tree House Detective Club. Mahwah, New Jersey: Troll, 1985.

As Adrian Robert:

The Awful Mess Mystery. Mahwah, New Jersey: Troll, 1985.

Ellen Ross, Private Detective. Mahwah, New Jersey: Troll, 1985.

My Grandma, the Witch. Mahwah, New Jersey: Troll, 1985.

The Secret of the Haunted Chimney. Mahwah, New Jersey: Troll, 1985.

The Secret of the Old Barn. Mahwah, New Jersey: Troll, 1985.

As Pamela Dryden:

Riding Home. New York: Bantam, 1988.

FOR ADULTS

As Nicole St. John:

The Medici Ring. New York: Random House, 1975; London: Collins, 1976.

Wychwood. New York: Random House, 1976; London: Heinemann, 1978.

Guinever's Gift. New York: Random House, 1977; London: Heinemann, 1979.

Also author of several books ghostwritten for publication under other persons' names (fiction, mystery, biography, cookbook, reference, religion, popular culture); seven manuscripts not released for publication (poetry and prayers, drama, young adult, suspense, cookbook); columns on writing for writers' newsletters; cooking/entertaining column, "Keeping Days Cooking."

Paul Showers

1910-

Paul Showers

As a newspaperman, I never set out to write children's books, but then, I never intended to be a newspaperman. It began as a joke. One night in an idle moment on the copydesk of the *New York Herald-Tribune,* I scribbled some doggerel verse, rhyming in the manner of Ogden Nash: "Commodius II was the King of the Persians / And he rode on an elephant led by four sturgeons." A few more couplets and then came: "Ataxia was Queen of the Cantharides / A virago who doted on pythons and bees." A couple of nights later, further doodling had produced a little story, ending: "And the Queen gave a feast in the great palace hall / And they dined on roast peacocks, tail feathers and all."

Christmas was approaching, and I decided to turn my story into a picture book for Tom, the young son of a college classmate. I bought some watercolors and india ink (for outlining the figures) and laboriously produced a series of illustrations on the blank loose-leaf pages of a large photo album I had bought at Woolworth.

I suspect that Tom was more mystified than entertained by "The Royal Visit," but it amused his parents, so the next year I made another picture book for his younger brother, Bill. This one was about an octopus named Olga. "She loved little fishes and she hated Wilbur Whale / Who was much too big for comfort and was careless with his tail." An octopus and fish were easier to draw than an elephant and human figures, and I had fun painting with yellow and blue, the two colors my partial color blindness allows me to appreciate fully.

Once I had made books for Tom and Bill, I considered a book for Mary, their little sister. This time it would be something to show what a map was all about. I worked out a variation of one of my favorite stories when I was little—"The House That Jack Built," which librarians classify as a cumulative text. My text began with a bird's egg, then the nest holding the egg, then the branch holding the nest, the vine from which the branch sprouted, the house on which the vine grew, and so on, right up through the solar system to the infinity beyond. This needed more perspective drawing than the two previous books, but before I got around to attempting some sketches, the Japanese bombed Pearl Harbor and I was in uniform, first in the Air Corps in Texas, later on the staff of *Yank,* the army weekly magazine. I never got around to making pictures for the map book, but at the urging of the children's parents, I did locate an agent, who circulated Olga among half a dozen publishers, all of whom turned it down. One female editor commented primly that an octopus was "unsuitable" as a subject for a child's book. The year was 1943.

That would have put an end to my career as a children's author, but some years after the war, I happened to tell my idea for the map book to an old friend who was working at the American Museum of Natural History. She had learned that Franklyn Branley, then coordinator of educational services at the American Museum-Hayden Planetarium, was developing a series of nonfiction primers to be used as supplementary reading material in the early grades. Working with him on this project was Roma Gans, professor emeritus of Columbia University's Teachers College, and Elizabeth Riley, children's books editor of the Thomas Y. Crowell Company. The idea was to create some books that might be a little more interesting than the "See, Sally, see. Run, Spot, run" epics then dominating the reading classes for beginners.

Dr. Branley's team was looking for ideas and writers, and my friend offered to show the old map-book text to Dr. Branley and introduce me to him. The map book, however, wasn't the sort of thing he was looking for, and over lunch he suggested that I try a book about the sense of touch. It would describe a little game the readers could play, giving them something to do while introducing them to a large vocabulary of common nouns and adjectives. That was *Find Out by Touching,* my first title in Crowell's "Let's Read and Find Out" series. I had to make several revisions of the very simple text before my editors were satisfied. Miss Riley never let a manuscript go to an artist until she felt it was in final shape. "In the beginning was the word," she liked to say. In this case, the artist she sent my words to was Robert Galster.

Find Out by Touching was one of the first titles in the "Let's Read and Find Out" series. The copyright date is 1961. I was then a copy editor in what was known as the Sunday Department of the *New York Times,* and the requests for rewrites of my little book didn't come as a surprise. The *Times' Sunday Magazine* routinely demanded at least two major revisions of its articles, which ran anywhere from 2,500 to 3,500 words or more. It also routinely paid $200 for the final product. My final text for *Find Out by Touching* totaled 644 words and the advance on the royalties was $300. Obviously children's nonfiction held greater promise than adult nonfiction, and I tried a second book.

This one was *In the Night.* Originally I called it "In the Dark" because the object was to reassure children who were afraid of the dark, but my editors insisted that "dark" implied a total absence of light—zero visibility—and since this was about night vision, "night" made a more accurate title. Being an editor myself, I knew better than to argue.

After a book about touch and another about night vision, it was logical to look for other subjects in the five senses, and from there to move on to physiology in general. I wrote primers about smell, taste, the eyes, teeth, skin, and the speech process. Eventually, the map book that started it all found a publisher and an artist and was given the title *The Bird and the Stars.*

As I worked on these little books, memories of things long forgotten came to mind, memories from the days when I first began to read and of my early attempts to get sensible explanations about the world and its mysteries. As a small boy, I very soon learned never to expect intelligent answers from the grown-ups. According to a story my mother liked to tell more often than I liked to hear, I was about four when I first heard the word "hydrophobia." Rabies was not then a term in common usage.

It was a hot summer. There was a mad-dog scare in our small town. People said somebody had been bitten. Children were warned not to approach strange dogs, which might attack them. What was the matter with the dogs? They were mad. Why were they mad? They had hydrophobia. What was hydrophobia? Something inside the dogs that made them foam at the mouth and bite people. Never pet strange dogs.

One day my mother took me with her to visit some friends. I was given paper and pencil to play with but was soon bored. My mother pointed to one of the ladies in the chattering group, who was an art teacher. "Take your paper over to her," my mother told me. "She'll draw a picture of anything you like." I presented my paper to the art teacher. "Draw me a dog and put hydrophobia in it," I said. I still vaguely recall the exasperating chorus of laughter.

That was only one of my brushes with the silly, unaccountable world of adults. When I asked the inevitable question, "Where did I come from?" I was answered with a piece of nice-Nelly Victorianism in verse: "Where did you come from, baby dear?" / "Out of the everywhere into the here." / "Where did you get that eye so blue?" / "A bit of sky as I came through." / "Where did you get that pearly ear?" / "God spoke and it came out to hear," etc. None of the other poems and stories that were read to me as part of my bedtime ritual ever reached quite such mawkish depths, although there was one other poem, something about a "little blue pigeon with folded wings," that evoked my special disgust.

For the most part, though, my bedtime reading matter was quite entertaining if not altogether enlightening. I liked stories about the processes of the body. One I remember as being entitled *Elizabeth Ann's Tummy,* all about the digestive difficulties of a little girl who ate too much and too unwisely. When Mr. Dill Pickle sat down beside Miss Ice Cream in Elizabeth Ann's tummy, very unpleasant things happened to Elizabeth Ann. I was devoted to a series of articles in one of my mother's household magazines about the Corpies (the name derived from "corpuscle"), little round red men who trotted about inside the body in legions performing various useful duties.

In particular I liked stories about animals. Many of my bedtime stories dated from the Victorian age, and sometimes they had a highly moral tone. One of my earliest enthusiasms was a brief tale about the oyster and the crab. The tiny crab had eyes but no shell to protect it. The much bigger oyster had a strong, roomy shell but no eyes to see when danger was near. So the crab lived with the oyster inside the shell, and when it spied the hungry fish approaching, it gave the oyster a little pinch and the oyster promptly shut its shell tight and both were safe from harm. In a similar way, our conscience lives within us to warn when we are in danger.

The analogy, I fear, was lost on me. I had no more idea about the conscience inside me than I had about the hydrophobia inside the dog, but I loved the story with its illustration of the huge, voracious fish, and I insisted on hearing it so often that my desperate parents finally hid the book to escape from the nightly repetition.

Most of the animals in the books of my childhood were personified. A favorite was Peter Rabbit, whose desperate adventure in Mr. McGregor's garden was described by Beatrix Potter in such precise, tidy prose: " . . . his sobs were overheard by some friendly sparrows, who flew to him in great excitement and implored him to exert himself." Personification served to create empathy. I always wept over Ernest Thompson Seton's sad story of the rabbit that drowned while swimming across a lake to escape from a fox, or perhaps froze to death in the snow while trying to lead the fox away from her burrow—I remember the emotion more than the exact facts in the case.

But personification confused as well as grieved me. In one story I would feel sorry for the fox, pursued by the cruel hunters; in another the fox was the villain and I sympathized with the rabbit, fleeing for its life. In nature it was hard to keep track of the good guys and the bad guys.

When I began to write books for beginning readers, I thought back on my own experience in learning to read. In the first grade I was taught by the phonic method, a system which, in spite of occasional puzzling mispronunciations, gave me a great sense of accomplishment as I unraveled the meaning of the display advertising in my father's newspaper and of the billboards I could see from the streetcar windows. In the formal lessons of the first reader, I always welcomed the words that were repeated. They were familiar islands, already conquered territory requiring no further effort and enabling me to glide over the sentences with increasing speed and assurance.

In the first primers I wrote—the ones about touch and taste, the eyes, the teeth, the skin, and so on—I repeated the vocabulary frequently in varying combinations and restricted the text to short, declarative sentences, avoiding the distraction of dependent clauses as much as possible.

Repetition and simple sentences may be fine for a beginning reader, but for the writer providing those sentences, they can be a frustrating bore. To relieve the monotony of the endless simplicities, I tried mixing in jingles and phonic devices of one sort or another and whenever possible attempted to make a little joke. This had its rewards. In my files I treasure a letter sprawled across the page in laboriously penciled script, the spelling undoubtedly dictated: "My FaVORiTe is tHE tEEth booK wHERE tHE FUNNy pARt IS."

I was less concerned in these early books with the information they contained than with the way they were worded. I wanted to combine a simple vocabulary with recognizable speech patterns, the language ability the beginning reader had already acquired through daily speech. The conversations of my own children were no longer a useful model. They were well past the primer stage. But we lived in the suburbs and had a house and a garden with a swing in it. The swing was a magnet for the kindergarten set in our neighborhood, and when I was preparing to write a book, I would spend time on weekends working in the garden and eavesdropping on the swing crowd, and occasionally even being included in their conversation.

Later, when I sat at my typewriter, I would test each sentence I wrote against my recollection of those conversations. Is this how the kids would have phrased it? If I were talking to them instead of writing it down, is this the way I would say it? After I had moved from the suburbs into a flat in Brooklyn, I kept a well-stocked candy jar on the mantel and a lineup of bric-a-brac in the wall niche. Periodically, my landlord's children had permission from their mother to bring their friends upstairs to raid my candy jar and play with the carved elephants and little wooden owls, and I continued my listening.

I still try to remember the limitations of readers newly introduced to the printed word, but in my later books the emphasis has shifted to content. I have been asked to write about digestion, immunization, heredity, human reproduction, the function of the heart, the muscles, and the brain. This has required a

"Our twins, Paul, Jr. and Kate, when they were about five months old"

certain amount of research, and as the facts have piled up in my notebook, it has become a question of what to use and what to leave out. In this, my guide has been the book report a little girl is supposed to have handed in to her teacher: "This book told me more about crocodiles than I wanted to know."

My editors are not the only source of subjects for my books. My wife, Kay, a child psychologist, suggested several ideas for the early primers. I also had a request from Kathy, the young daughter of one of my friends, for a book explaining what the garbage collectors did with the garbage they collected. My editors liked the idea and I got busy. I wrote about compacters and incinerators and the community that converted its dump into a playground and how New York City had to stop throwing its garbage into the ocean and how garbage and trash keep piling up all across the country. The result was *Where Does the Garbage Go?,* an informative roundup, I felt, for a young generation that would find an even worse situation to be dealt with when it reached voting age.

As soon as I had received my first copies from the publisher, I sent one to Kathy, duly inscribed. Her qualified approval came in a note printed with care on lined notepaper: "Dear Mr. Showers, I liked that book very much but it told where the garbage went in New York." I had failed to take into consideration that Kathy lived in Middletown, New Jersey.

The idea for one of my later books came from my five-months-old grandson. Chris's parents were visiting me that spring, and every night when I came home from work, I would find him lying on a blanket in the living room, fed, bathed, and at peace with the world. I would pick him up, sit on the divan with my feet up on the coffee table (taking my shoes off, of course), and I would prop him against my knees so that we would be facing each other, ready for conversation.

Chris would eye me coolly, and I would smile and give him a kiss and tell him what a fine boy he was. Then, in the same tone I would use with an adult, I would tell him what kind of day I had had at the office, what gossip I had heard, where I had gone to lunch and with whom, what the traffic was like coming home on the bus, etc. Just an ordinary conversation. At first it would be a one-way communication, but as Chris caught my friendly mood, he would react. Never taking his eyes off mine, he would utter little sounds, attempt a momentary smile or fleeting frown and wave his hands about, clearly doing his best to take part in our little chat. It was a happy time for both of us, and he would become so animated I would have to grab his body with both hands to keep him from bouncing off my knees onto the floor.

It was years since I had been so intimately acquainted with a baby, and Chris's readiness to communicate fascinated me. Here, not quite half a year old, was a well-defined, responsive personality eager to make contact but hampered by an apparatus he didn't yet know how to control. I thought of the line of Wordsworth's: "Our birth is but a sleep and a forgetting," and I remembered the image of our astronauts, walking about clumsily in their space suits as they sent back their broadcast from the surface of the moon the previous summer. Chris was our astronaut, newly arrived on earth and just learning to make use of the new body he found himself in.

This was the theme of *The Moon Walker,* an account of the first year in a baby's life, from newborn to toddler. In developing the idea, I wrote for an older child in a family where a baby had just been born. I wanted to put together a kind of chronological guide to help the older child avoid feelings of displacement or resentment by becoming an intelligent observer of the remarkable changes in the first year of human growth.

I was pleased when *Moon Walker* was accepted for publication, but acceptance is not necessarily a happy ending for a manuscript. It wasn't in the case of *Moon Walker.* On the press, two pages somehow got transposed, an accident that didn't improve the slender story line, and I hated the illustrations, which portrayed with clumsy whimsicality a family of shambling grotesques, all focusing on an ugly, snouty infant whose navel was coyly revealed at every opportunity. As is usual in these matters, I knew nothing about the artwork until I saw the finished book, misprints and all. *Moon Walker* is now out of print, and just as well.

This chronicle began in the middle, and it needs a flashback. I was born in 1910 in Sunnyside, a village in the Yakima Valley of the state of Washington. It was the month of April, and Halley's comet was putting on a spectacular show overhead every night. The stories my parents later told me about this display so impressed me that by the time I was ten I had resolved to live until I was seventy-six, so I could get a good look the next time the comet came around.

I reached seventy-six with no difficulty, but Halley's comet was a total washout. Its reappearance in 1986 was largely confined to the southern hemisphere. I had planned to fly to Hawaii in April, when the comet was expected to be clearly visible there on the southern horizon, but I canceled the trip after reading that one lady, who had joined a special tour to the Andes for a better view, had complained about going all that distance to see nothing but "a crummy little fuzz ball."

To be born under a comet is an event that is hard to duplicate, and nothing very remarkable occurred in my life during the years that followed. When I was three, my parents moved east to Muskegon, a small town in Michigan, and in due course I entered kindergarten there. As I remember it, I was eager to go.

In my childhood, there were no preschool sessions, no nursery schools. You simply got bigger and learned to tell time and use a buttonhook to fasten your shoes, and mornings you stood in the front yard and watched the big kids parade past your house on their way to school, swaggering, self-assured, totally ignoring you. To be left behind, to have to stay back with the babies could, at times, induce a state bordering on self-loathing. When at last I reached school-age, I was enrolled in the McLaughlin kindergarten, a full two blocks distant from my home.

Of my two teachers in McLaughlin kindergarten, Miss Pugh stands out more distinctly. When I think of her, she towers over me, nine feet tall, in a long black skirt that descends steeply to the shiny tips of her black shoes. Above the skirt, I see an expanse of white—a ruffled blouse with a stiff net collar that ascends Miss Pugh's long throat clear up to the jawline. This collar helps support folds of skin that dangle from the jaw like the pendants dangling from Miss Pugh's ears farther up. She smiles down at me from the heights, distant but friendly, her rimless eyeglasses poised on her nose nervously, a bird about to take wing. The glasses are anchored to her nose by gold pincers and are secured from falling and shattering on the floor by a gold chain that drops down from one of the lenses, loops itself across Miss Pugh's negligible bosom, and then, through the magic of a mysterious hidden spring, coils up inside a flat gold button the size of a quarter that she wears on her left breast.

As I recall, Miss Pugh had a deep contralto voice and was forever saying, "Now children," gathering us all together in her smile, "let's take hands and make a big circle." And we would start grabbing, fighting to hold the hands of our best friends and shamelessly rejecting the hands of kids we didn't like. Greta was one of these. Nobody ever wanted to hold Greta's hand except Miss Pugh.

Greta's image (in Michigan we said "Greet-a" or just "Greet") is very dim to me. I cannot see her face. I see only a small girl who is incomprehensibly

"On my fourth birthday and on the brink of entering school"

uncooperative. Greeta always holds back. She can never decide what to do. She twists her shoulders and hangs her head and stares at her shoes and keeps us waiting when we are all impatient to begin the next game.

How we disliked Greeta. And how peculiar that Miss Pugh seemed to like her. Miss Pugh was always calling on Greeta to fetch the crayon box or carry the big banner or pass the scissors. She drew Greeta to her side when we joined hands to make the big circle. "Now let's skip," Miss Pugh would say, removing her glasses and letting the chain draw them up to the gold button. She would hoist up her black skirt on either side, revealing the black leather shoes that buttoned halfway up her stout calves, and away she would go, with Greeta right behind her, skipping around the room, her high topknot of gray hair bobbing recklessly. Our Glumdalclitch.

Miss Pugh was one of us. In every group game we played, she was one of us, skipping, hop-hop-hopping, being a tall tree or a busy bee. Though we often tried to play the games *our* way, Miss Pugh's way usually won out. It always won out in "roll the ball," one of the games we liked best. You made a big circle and sat down on the floor with your legs spread apart so your toes touched the toes of the kid on either side. Miss Pugh would walk to the center of the circle, carrying the big green ball, and we would sing a little song. The object of this song was to choose in a democratic way the lucky kid who would be The One Who Rolls the Ball First, and it ended with the line: "And so we roll the ball to ——— dear." This invariably became a noisy, confused chorus as each of us bellowed out our best friend's name or, with special emphasis, our own name. It made no difference. Miss Pugh's contralto, resonant as an organ pipe, always overwhelmed us with " . . . to *Greeta* dear."

Miss Pugh would then squat down and give the ball a shove in Greeta's direction. When it reached her, Greeta would lean over, lock her arms about the ball and become paralyzed by the circle's undivided attention. We would deluge her with the kind of friendly recognition we never showed at any other time: "Hey, Greet," "Come on, Greet," "Me, Greet, *me*!" Greeta would hang her head, her shoulders would writhe in self-conscious indecision and our spurious friendliness would rapidly dissolve into impatience. It was hard to keep up a show of liking Greeta. Once we got the ball away from her, we never rolled it back to her again.

Miss Pee-ross was Miss Pugh's young assistant. She had dark hair and an abrupt way of moving and speaking. I suppose she actually spelled her name "Pierce," for Miss Pugh pronounced it as if it were spelled that way. But those were the days when we were learning to speak only when called on and to raise our hands when we felt we could answer the teacher's question ("Who can tell me where apples come from? What do we buy when we go to the butcher shop?"). For one eager little girl who sat in one of the red chairs at Miss Pierce's long table, raising the hand was never enough. She would brandish her arm frantically in Miss Pierce's direction, at the same time calling out in a husky whisper, "Miss Pee-ross, Miss Pee-ross!"

I liked Miss Pee-ross and I didn't like her. I liked her because she played music for us during rest period. We folded our arms on the table and put our heads down and kept our eyes shut and our lips closed, and Miss Pee-ross would coax soft tones out of the grand piano over in the corner. She favored selections by Nevin, and Rubinstein's "Spring Song," and MacDowell's "To a Water Lily." I liked them all, for I liked music. My father was the conductor of a choral society, and I had dozed happily on a bench at the back of the auditorium through many an evening rehearsal of Handel's *Messiah* and Haydn's *Creation.* During McLaughlin's rest period I especially looked forward to the changing chords of "To a Water Lily," which seemed to me about the most beautiful music I had ever heard.

Miss Pee-ross's disposition, however, did not match her music. She usually took charge of the crayons-and-paper hour, keeping close watch to see that no one lagged behind the rest of the group as we laboriously cut out pieces of colored paper and pasted them on other pieces of colored paper. Sometimes the crude circles we cut out of the red and yellow paper were apples, sometimes they were balloons, and the paste was delicious. It was scooped out of a large jar and served to us on little cardboard trays—smooth, creamy, and flavored with wintergreen.

Pasting was fun but I disliked sewing. Every now and then we were issued two matching pieces of heavy paper with holes punched along the edges. Yarn was stitched through these holes and, thus fastened together, the pieces of heavy paper became usable objects—hats, purses, many other things I have forgotten. What I have not forgotten is the trouble I had threading my long, blunt needle. The yarn was thick and fuzzy, and no matter how much I sucked on it and twisted it into a point as Miss Pee-ross had demonstrated, it would not go through the eye of my needle. Each time, some stray filament of the yarn would catch on the edge of the eye and my twisted point would buckle and splay hopelessly. Threading your needle required spit and patience. I had little of either.

One day we were to make purses. I sat grimly sucking on my yarn, twisting it and trying to thread it through my needle. One by one the other kids at the table finished their sewing and proudly held aloft their handiwork. They compared purses across the table; they filled them with crayons and pieces of paper. Conversation replaced the hush that had enveloped the table during the threading and stitching. A party mood developed, while I remained hunched over my needle, wetting my yarn and desperately trying to poke it through the eye. When at last it was clear that everyone else had finished and I had not yet even begun, I threw down my yarn and needle and glowered. Miss Pee-ross came over and told me to get busy with my work. I refused. She commanded. I froze, unable to speak or move or look at her. Turning to the rest of the group, Miss Pee-ross announced that I would not join in the next project until I had finished sewing my purse.

After that it was war. I sat in unyielding silence until my worried mother appeared in the big front doorway through which all the other children had gone home an hour earlier. Miss Pee-ross was busy at her desk. I sat at the long table from which all of the day's work had been cleared except for my yarn, my needle, and the two halves of my paper purse.

How the combined forces of Miss Pee-ross and my mother resolved this impasse has been blotted from my mind. Since I did not spend the rest of my life sitting at Miss Pee-ross's long table—at least, literally—I assume I was made to capitulate in some disgraceful manner and push that damned piece of yarn through the needle's eye. In those days, no matter how amiable adults might be on occasion, they were firmly committed to authoritarian principles. Whatever else a child might learn, he had to learn to mind.

There may have been thirty children in our kindergarten rooms. I remember only a few—Greeta; Gene, my best friend; Lowell, who could squeak like a mouse. Alice Plowman must have been a member of that group, too, though I didn't become fully aware of her presence until we were in Miss Kapp's spelling class in the second grade. Alice was a dainty little girl with blue eyes and glistening, taffy-colored hair that hung straight as a string in a Dutch bob.

In kindergarten our class had been sequestered in a small stone building at one end of the school grounds, but after we were promoted to first grade, we joined the big kids in the gloomy main building of McLaughlin School, where the lights were turned on all day in its lofty corridors. Miss Collins was our first-grade teacher, a motherly woman with frizzy white hair. In her room we learned to sit up straight in straight rows at little desks and not to whisper or turn around. Miss Collins taught us to read ("Mr. Lock digs for clams") and led us when we had music, beating time with her pitch pipe and singing along with us so enthusiastically that saliva would trickle out of the corner of her mouth and run down her chin.

In second grade we had Miss Hasse for homeroom and reading and Miss Kapp for spelling. Miss Kapp's room was on the second floor, and three times a week we marched up the steep stairs in single file for our spelling lesson. Miss Kapp was tall, wore her black hair in flat pads over her ears, and rarely smiled. We did little whispering in her room, for her voice could be harsh and her frown was terrifying. We sat in anxious silence, waiting for our turns to recite. We always recited in the same order: first, the row of desks nearest the door, beginning with the child in the front seat and on up the row to the rear of the room. Then it was the second row's turn, front to back, and so on.

"Book," Miss Kapp would command, fixing you with her piercing black eyes. You would rise and stand beside your desk while every kid in the room waited to see whether you were going to make it. "Book," you would repeat, "B–O–O–K, book." Then you would sit down and begin to breathe normally again as Miss Kapp's eyes shifted to the luckless kid behind you.

This system was a model of efficiency but it allowed no room for individual variations, which was unfortunate, for Alice Plowman had a special variation that I thought was adorable. She always got "sh" and "ch" mixed up and she was careless about plurals. I loved to hear her talk. One day when Alice's turn came, the word was "sheep."

"Sheep," said Miss Kapp, focusing her disinterested stare on Alice. Alice stood up beside her desk with a bright, confident smile. "Cheeps," said Alice, "S–H–E–E–P, cheeps."

"No," said Miss Kapp, "that's not correct," and her eyes moved on to the boy in the seat behind Alice. "Sheep," Miss Kapp repeated.

I was furious. I watched Alice as the smile vanished from her face and she sat down, close to tears. I still remember my indignation. It was so unfair. This was spelling class and Alice had spelled the word correctly. I wanted to go to her and comfort her, but she sat four seats behind me in the next row, and you didn't leave your seat without the teacher's permission. From that day on, I disapproved of Miss Kapp. She had humiliated Alice before the whole class.

My school days in Muskegon were numbered. My father was a music teacher, always on the lookout for opportunities to improve his meager income. From Muskegon we moved to Park Ridge, a suburb of Chicago, and then to Rochester in upstate New York, and from there back to Michigan and Grand Rapids.

In the years when I was growing up in Muskegon and Park Ridge, I spent summers with my maternal grandparents, who lived in a small farming community on an electric interurban line about sixty miles north of Detroit. More than half a century has now gone by, but Almont still retains its identity in my mind, as green and sunlit as the pastures, orchards, and fields of grain that bordered it on every side. I was a city-bred child, primarily acquainted with streetcars and elevated railroads, and to me, life in the country was full of the most interesting novelties.

There was a creek at the edge of town that wandered through a mint-scented meadow. It was a perfect place for building dams of mud and stones, and for catching tadpoles, which I carried home in rusty tin cans and deposited in a fishbowl so I could keep track of their slow transformation as they lost their tails and sprouted legs and turned into frogs.

At a farm not far from town I had permission to slide down the strawstack and feed the hens and collect their eggs from the long row of nests in the dusty henhouse. In the barn there was the thrill of climbing to the perilously high rafters where the swallows nested and then jumping down into the billowing, sweet-scented hay below; and on every visit I called on the huge, ugly-tempered sow in her high-boarded pen to watch her nurse her impatient, wriggling litter.

Each June, on the first day of my return to Almont, I went downtown as soon as I had finished breakfast to make a tour of inspection. In Almont, "downtown" meant two blocks of business buildings on Main Street, one, two, and three stories high—the butcher shop, the barbershop, the grocery store, the drugstore, the Star Theatre, the Hotel Gould on whose broad verandah the visiting salesmen liked to lounge in the evening, smoking their cigars.

Main Street's brick and wooden facades stared at each other across a wide expanse of hard-packed earth, lined on either side by iron hitching rails and cobblestone gutters. On a hot day, the lumpy roadway smelled of the crude oil that had been soaked into it to keep down the dust. Where the iron rims of wagon wheels had pressed it smooth, the brown roadbed glistened in the sun and burned your feet as you hopped across it barefoot. At the four corners, the crossroads heart of Almont, a flagpole marked the exact center of the intersection.

The crossroads was dominated by the town's yellow-shingled bank building and the dry-goods store, standing on diagonally opposite corners. Up in the bank's shiny, tin-roofed cupola the clock struck the hours resoundingly. In the stillness of midnight, the clock's high baritone could be heard for miles out in the country when the wind was right. The town's municipal drinking fountain, a white porcelain pillar surmounted by a porcelain bowl with a long red stain under the faucet, stood on the corner by the dry-goods store. Even if you weren't thirsty, you automatically paused there for a drink of the tepid water that had a strange flat taste and a strong smell. The product of Almont's artesian well was blessed with an unpleasant overabundance of minerals.

To reach downtown from my grandparents' home, you walked two shady blocks down Main Street under the high-arching box elders until you came to a mustard yellow house with hydrangea bushes growing along the side porch. That was the point where the shade trees ended, the sidewalk widened, and downtown began with a low, one-story building of tottering red brick: The Racket, Sarah Durham, Prop. The Racket was the one store in Almont that hadn't yet converted to electricity and still burned kerosene lamps.

Sarah was not pronounced the way it was spelled. To everyone she was Sairy Durham, a sharp, shriveled little woman, who wore gingham aprons over floor-length black skirts and skinned her gray hair back into a tight bun and squinted at you over her bifocals. Except for a few close acquaintances, no one ever called her Sairy to her face. She was always Miss Durham.

Sairy's shop was organized chaos. To your right, as you came in from the street, lay the only cleared floor space in her domain. Friendly rocking chairs formed a semicircle beside Sairy's rolltop desk and the little iron stove that kept her warm in winter. The rest of the shop was a clutter of display cases and tables piled high with china, tinware, toys, bric-a-brac, sewing materials, yard goods, and household hardware. You had to walk sideways to penetrate the narrow aisles. The farther you penetrated, the darker it got. Except for up front, The Racket was a gloomy cavern, even at midday. Light entered only through the two modest show windows on either side of the recessed doorway, and they admitted very little of it. The window displays were as cluttered as the shop: dusty vases and figurines set amid pyramids of crockery and sheets of flypaper, whose shiny surfaces, the color of maple syrup, were stippled with flies, most of them dead.

Sairy presided over her merchandise with brisk vigilance. Unless she was working over business papers at her desk or waiting on another customer, she met you at the door as you entered, fixing you with a look that went clear through you. "Good morning, young man. What will you have today?" It made no difference who her customers were or what they wanted to buy, Sairy was attentive to them all, especially the younger ones. She was always at your elbow, an alert wren watching closely while you made up your mind. "Now don't touch that! You'll break it. Here, if you want to touch it, let me hold it for you." Or: "Haven't any caps today. I'm all out. Been out since the Fourth of July. How about a water pistol? You can make just as much of a nuisance of yourself with that."

Her manner was the same with adults as with children—abrupt, authoritative, and free from condescension. It was the way Sairy addressed the whole world. Every week she took an ad in the *Almont Herald,* a six-page paper that went to press on Wednesday in the recesses of the *Herald*'s one-story office and print shop, the local news and small ads in hand-set type, the occasional features and large ads in boilerplate. Sairy's ad was two columns wide and about three inches deep, and it stood out on the page because so much of it was given to white space. Some years ago I visited the much-changed Almont and looked up old issues of the *Herald* in the library there. From week to week, Sairy's ad was a model of succinct, no-nonsense communication: "Odds and ends of SOAP, Thursday night, 4¢ per bar. The Racket."

Fancy soap was a specialty of The Racket. So was penny candy. The penny-candy display was the best in Almont. Miniature wax bottles filled with thick, sweet fluid. You bit off the top, drank the pinkish syrup, and then chewed on the bottle for the rest of the day, an enormous, clushy wad enveloping your back molars. And other delicacies. Pink, yellow, and green sugar buttons attached to long strips of oiled paper. Licorice whips. Miniature fruits and vegetables in marzipan. Chocolate-covered marshmallow cigars. Striped candy sticks—lemon, orange, and peppermint.

I was one of Sairy's regular customers. I had been ever since I was young enough to enjoy taking my bath surrounded by floating toys. In those days when I went to The Racket, I squandered an entire dime on one small box of thin brown cardboard filled with sawdust and tied with red string. You dug into the sawdust carefully and extracted four exquisite little yellow ducks with orange beaks, fabricated in Germany out of wax. The ducks were hollow, light as balloons, and mortally fragile. They floated superbly on the lake around my knees, quacking and performing all sorts of dives and realistic splashings when properly handled. When handled carelessly, they broke like bubbles. Hardly a bath went by that one of them didn't lose a head and sink to the bottom.

Sairy sold wax ducks until World War I cut off trade with Germany. By then I had graduated to cap pistols, crayons, and sugar-coated gum balls, which Sairy kept in a large glass globe on a pedestal. You dropped a penny into the slot, yanked the lever and into the little cup dropped a gum ball—white, brown, red, or yellow—you never knew what it was going to be, for the gum balls were all mixed up inside the globe like Aladdin's bowls of pearls and rubies.

In summer, The Racket was open twice a week during the evening, once on Thursday to make up for the Wednesday afternoon closing that was common practice in all the shops during the slack hot-weather months, and again on Saturday, for Saturday night was Almont's night for celebration. All the farmers and their wives and children were in from the country, the men in overalls, the women in long gingham dresses, the barefoot children in hand-me-downs, and everyone in town turned out to meet them. It was practically a carnival.

On either side of Main Street, the sidewalk was a crowded, noisy corridor. Walled in on one hand by the storefronts, on the other by teams of horses and Model T Fords parked side by side at the hitching rail, the visitors and townspeople clustered in little groups, gossiping with friends they had not seen for a week or more.

Downtown had only one streetlight, a big blue arc lamp dangling from a tall pole at the four corners. The rest of Main Street lay in darkness except for the light streaming from shop windows and doorways, shining on the faces of the strollers. As they moved from the shadow into the light and back into the shadow again, the visitors from the country felt a pleasant tension, the excitement of unexpected encounters: "Well, Mildred! How *are* you! Didn't see you last Saturday." The small boys felt the tension powerfully. They raced up and down, dodging in and out, hiding from each other in doorways, getting underfoot. Where space had not yet been occupied by horses or Model Ts, they jumped up on the hitching rail and skinned the cat and then hung there, head downward, enjoying the spectacle of the whole world walking and talking upside down.

Most of the horses at the hitching rail ignored the sidewalk show going on directly in front of their long, doleful faces. They stood with eyelids drooping, some with noses buried in feed bags. Here and there a nervous filly, eyes wild, hitched to a buggy, stamped and whinnied and pulled at her tether, but the older horses had learned to wait patiently on Saturday night, for the farm people were in no hurry to go home. Nor was I. Even when I didn't have a nickel for an ice-cream cone or the William S. Hart cowboy movie at the Star, I liked being part of the crowd that drifted up and down Main Street. The men tended to gravitate to the barbershop for haircuts and talk of crops and the weather; then they moved on to the hardware store or the town garage, a big, dark, barnlike shed where mechanics in greasy coveralls cursed, spat tobacco juice, and tinkered with balky engines, and the blacksmith at his glowing forge by the alley door was busy all evening shoeing horses.

The women gathered in the grocery store and the dry-goods store, and sooner or later they dropped into The Racket to pay their respects to Sairy Durham. The door was open, the depths of the shop were in darkness, and the circle of rocking chairs by the rolltop desk had become a cozy sitting room enveloped in the radiance of half a dozen kerosene lamps. The invitation was irresistible. After being on their feet half the evening, moving from store to store, the women were ready to sit down for a few minutes, and The Racket's great attraction on Saturday night was that people didn't feel obliged to buy anything there if they didn't want to.

On that night Sairy didn't serve her customers, she received them. She wore her best brooch. She did not put on her apron. Her rocking chairs were seldom empty. As a visitor stepped in the door, one of the earlier arrivals usually rose to say farewells to the group and to continue her rounds. If the visitor actually wanted to buy something, Sairy would excuse herself, pick up a lamp, and lead her customer on a brief tour of the shop's dark interior.

Sairy preferred to sit in the swivel chair at her desk, presiding over the continuous conversation just as she presided over her china and her saucepans, with due consideration for all. It was general knowledge that Sairy never dealt in scandalous gossip. If she was asked, she could usually confirm or discredit reports of deaths, births, illnesses, the progress of convalescents, the arrivals and departures of out-of-town visitors, and similar items of legitimate community news. As Miss Durham, she was frequently asked for advice on a variety of proper topics. Her opinions, which came hopping out of her mouth in crisp, abrupt sentences, were received with respect and gratitude.

All evening long Sairy greeted her public. Around ten-thirty, the sidewalk crowds would begin to thin out. Horses at the hitching rail woke up and neighed impatiently. Fords heaved and coughed and burst into savage roars. One by one, Sairy's visitors took their leave and went out in search of their husbands.

When her last guest had departed, Sairy Durham shut up shop, and once she had closed the rolltop desk, blown out her lamps, and locked The Racket's door behind her, it could be said that Saturday night in Almont was officially over.

Throughout my childhood, Almont was the special world to which I escaped each summer from the tedium of blackboards and chalk dust, penmanship lessons and insoluble arithmetic problems. In fact, its rural charms had such an effect on me that for a time I was undecided on whether to be a streetcar motorman or a farmer when I grew up. Then, as a high-school student in Rochester, I discovered another world—the theatre.

Rochester possessed a beautiful relic of Victorian splendor, the Lyceum, all gilt and faded plush. Throughout the winter the Lyceum was a regular stopping point for Broadway companies setting out on tour, and I haunted the hard benches in its gallery. Later, when I was an undergraduate at the University of Michigan, my indoctrination continued in the theatres of Detroit only forty miles away, and by the time I received my A.B. degree from the university, I had decided to be an actor and a playwright.

I graduated in 1931, just as the Great Depression was getting into full swing, and for several years I drifted, with recurrent hopes and few accomplishments. I had little to offer the theatre, and the theatre had even less to offer me. None of the plays I wrote got anywhere, although one did languish in the hands of a New York agent for a year. Most of the theatre troupes that took me on to play small parts suffered from the same complaint: pernicious box-office anemia.

During these lean years, however, I was sustained by a small but steady income. In high school, I had read not only all the plays of Eugene O'Neill as they were published, but every book by Stephen Leacock I could get my hands on, and at the university I was editor of the campus humor magazine. After graduation I did free-lancing, selling verse and short pieces to the three national humor magazines—*Life, Judge,* and *Ballyhoo.*

"About the time I first began writing children's books"

Life had once been a prosperous weekly, its reputation established early in the century by the contributions of Charles Dana Gibson, the famous illustrator—creator of the turn-of-the-century Gibson girl—and inventor of the Gibson cocktail (an onion in place of the olive). For decades, *Life*'s jokes and cartoons had been standard reading matter in doctors' and dentists' offices throughout the country, but by the 1930s, radio had taken over the business of supplying the nation's weekly ration of humor, and *Life* had been cut back to a monthly.

In the spring of 1932, *Life*'s editors were looking for ways to buoy up the circulation, and, among other things, they decided to expand the magazine's small crossword puzzle, a regular monthly feature, into a gigantic "cockeyed" puzzle. Diagram and definitions would cover a two-page spread. (This was some years before the *New York Times* allowed anything so vulgarly entertaining as a big crossword puzzle to appear in its *Sunday Magazine.*)

Life called its puzzle "cockeyed" because the definitions were to be outrageously misleading and, whenever possible, to be funny. Construction was governed by certain restrictions. Two-letter combinations like RA (Egyptian sun-god) and EM (printer's measure) were banned. So, too, were those three-letter standbys of puzzle makers: ERN (sea eagle), ULE (Mexican gum tree), ERG (unit of energy), and GNU (the hartebeest). All words had to be in the average reader's vocabulary; none could be used that required a hunt through the dictionary. This rule was thrown in for the benefit of Westchester commuters, who presumably might buy the magazine at Grand Central and want to work the puzzle while going home on the train, with no dictionary handy.

I had just sold a standard-size puzzle to *Life* when the decision was made to give the readers the biggest puzzle then on the market, and I was offered the job at fifty dollars a puzzle. At a time when T-bone steak was selling for twenty-eight cents a pound, an income of fifty dollars a month held definite potential, and I accepted.

From that moment on, regardless of what else I might be doing, I made crossword puzzles. Filling in the diagram wasn't difficult. In a way it was fun. Thinking up the definitions was the dismaying part. Each month I had to rack my brains for suitably cockeyed definitions for a list of between 250 and 300 words. The only one I can now recall was for a four-letter word meaning "A bender you can take the children on." The answer was KNEE.

Puzzle making, of course, was always a sideline. I worked sporadically in stock companies and strawhat (summer) theatres. I spent a good part of 1934 in Chicago at the World's Fair—"A Century of Progress"—playing bit parts in tabloid versions of Shakespeare's plays. The performances, running forty-five to fifty minutes per play, were presented on the hour, seven times a day (eight on weekends), seven days a week, in a replica of Shakespeare's Globe Theatre that was the pride of the English Village on the fair's midway. The Globe company may have abbreviated the Bard's work almost beyond recognition in a couple of instances, but it was the only troupe I ever belonged to that made money, and when I quit rather than brave a winter season of one-night stands through the Middle West, I had a modest bank account for the first time in my life.

My success in the theatre was distinctly limited, but my crossword puzzles seemed to find favor with *Life*'s readers. In the fall of 1936 I was preparing to join the staff as an associate editor, and then lightning struck. Henry Luce, the publisher of *Time,* rather abruptly bought up *Life* for the use of its name and converted it into a pictorial weekly. Since I had no experience writing picture captions, that put an end to my steady income.

That autumn I happened to be writing another play, this time in a long-distance collaboration with an old college friend, who was working on the copydesk of the *Detroit Free Press.* I would write a scene and mail it to him, and in a month or two he would send it back to me with his notions for improvements. After my career with *Life* evaporated, he wrote and suggested that I move to Detroit and take a temporary job at the *Free Press* so we could continue our collaboration at close range.

In those days the management of the *Free Press* had a policy of filling staff vacancies with totally inexperienced people, paying them minimal wages, and training them either as reporters or copy editors. The city desk paid its beginning reporters twenty dollars a week during the first year, twenty-five dollars a week in the second. The copydesk, which was responsible for checking facts in the reporters' stories, combing out the more preposterous rhetoric ("Last week the city council confronted a hydra-headed dilemma"), correcting the grammar and writing the headlines, was more generous than the city desk. It paid its beginning editors twenty-five dollars a week in the first year and thirty dollars during the second. I had no interest in chasing fire engines or interviewing Important People and I did have great respect for the extra five dollars a week, so I waited until there was an opening on the copydesk and applied for the job.

When I joined my friend on the copydesk, it was my intention to quit as soon as our play was finished. I had never worked for a newspaper and I had never wanted to, and my initial experience did nothing to change my mind. It was a nightmare trying to remember all the stylebook's rules for capitalization, punctuation, hyphenation, abbreviations, when to spell out numbers, when to use numerals, and then to compress the essence of the story into a headline that contained both subject and verb, didn't put prepositions in the wrong place, fit the allotted space, and at the same time made some kind of sense.

To add to my distress, our play bogged down with fatal second-act trouble in the space of six months, but by then I had given up any thought of quitting. I was enslaved by the advantages of a regular paycheck, even if only twenty-five dollars a week, and I lived in continual fear of being fired for obvious incompetence. This unhappy state of mind persisted for about another year until, quite unexpectedly, I began to get the hang of things. Editing and head writing were no longer such a nightly ordeal, and gradually I was overwhelmed by a new dread. I had reached the limits of my life's potential and was doomed to spend the rest of my days from four in the afternoon till one the next morning, writing heads on a copydesk in Detroit.

Altogether I spent three years at the *Free Press,* and when, in 1940, three of my friends on the copydesk quit, one by one, and went to New York to work—one at the *Journal-American,* another at the *Daily News,* and the third at the *Times*—I had to follow them. The opening on the *Herald-Tribune* copydesk wasn't the only thing that lured me to New York. I liked the idea that I would be able to see a Broadway play whenever I wanted to, or hear the Philharmonic at Carnegie Hall or Flagstad and Melchior at the Met.

By that time I was reconciled to being a newspaperman. My name wasn't up in lights on Broadway, but at last I had an occupational identity, like a carpenter or a lawyer or a dentist, which is important in a society where people like to ask, "And what do you do?" and the answer, "I make crossword puzzles," somehow doesn't seem quite adequate.

In World War II, my flatfeet kept me out of the infantry and my newspaper experience eventually led to a sergeant's rating and the copydesk of *Yank.* After the war, copydesk salaries more than doubled, and I

The author, 1988

was finally earning enough money to get married. I worked briefly for the *New York Sunday Mirror* and then settled at the *Times,* editing stories, first for the travel section and eventually for the *Sunday Magazine.* My wife and I considered we had hit the jackpot when we had twins, a boy and a girl, and we had a wonderful time watching them grow up. Once they had gone away to college, we dissolved our marriage and went our separate ways.

I don't know what the numerologists would make of it, but many important events in my life are connected with historic dates. I was born on April 12, the date the Civil War began with the Confederates' attack on Fort Sumter. I went to work for the *Free Press* on February 22, which was always Washington's birthday until the holiday began to be moved around for the convenience of department-store sales. February 22 was also my wife's birthday and the birthday of our twins. At the *Free Press* I handed in my notice in 1940 on the Fourth of July, and in 1976, when the nation celebrated 200 years of independence on July 4, I submitted my resignation from the *Times* to be effective on the same day. It was a once-in-a-lifetime opportunity to make my personal declaration of independence from the newspaper business to work at my own pace as a free-lance writer.[1] That night the occasion was celebrated with a spectacular fireworks display over the Statue of Liberty in New York Harbor.

[1]My most recent children's book, about the mechanics of hearing, is soon to be published. Tentative title: "Ears Are for Hearing."

BIBLIOGRAPHY

FOR CHILDREN

Nonfiction:

Find Out by Touching (illustrated by Robert Galster). New York: Crowell, 1961; London: A. & C. Black, 1964.

In the Night (illustrated by Ezra Jack Keats). New York: Crowell, 1961; London: A. & C. Black, 1971.

The Listening Walk (illustrated by Aliki). New York: Crowell, 1961; London: A. & C. Black, 1963.

How Many Teeth? (illustrated by Paul Galdone). New York: Crowell, 1962; London: A. & C. Black, 1969.

Look at Your Eyes (illustrated by P. Galdone). New York: Crowell, 1962.

Follow Your Nose (illustrated by P. Galdone). New York: Crowell, 1963; London: A. & C. Black, 1967.

Columbus Day (illustrated by Ed Emberley). New York: Crowell, 1965.

Your Skin and Mine (illustrated by P. Galdone). New York: Crowell, 1965; London: A. & C. Black, 1967.

How You Talk (illustrated by R. Galster). New York: Crowell, 1966; London: A. & C. Black, 1968.

A Drop of Blood (illustrated by Don Madden). New York: Crowell, 1967; London: A. & C. Black, 1968.

Before You Were a Baby, with Kay Sperry Showers (illustrated by Ingrid Fetz). New York: Crowell, 1968.

Hear Your Heart (illustrated by Joseph Low). New York: Crowell, 1968.

A Baby Starts to Grow (illustrated by Rosalind Fry). New York: Crowell, 1969.

Indian Festivals (illustrated by Lorence Bjorklund). New York: Crowell, 1969.

What Happens to a Hamburger (illustrated by Anne Rockwell). New York: Crowell, 1970.

Use Your Brain (illustrated by R. Fry). New York: Crowell, 1971.

Sleep Is for Everyone (illustrated by Wendy Watson). New York: Crowell, 1974; London: A. & C. Black, 1975.

Where Does the Garbage Go? (illustrated by Loretta Lustig). New York: Crowell, 1974.

The Bird and the Stars (illustrated by Mila Lazarevich). Garden City, N.Y.: Doubleday, 1975.

The Moon Walker (illustrated by Susan Perl). Garden City, N.Y.: Doubleday, 1975.

A Book of Scary Things (illustrated by S. Perl). Garden City, N.Y.: Doubleday, 1977.

Me and My Family Tree (illustrated by D. Madden). New York: Crowell, 1978.

No Measles, No Mumps for Me (illustrated by Harriett Barton). New York: Crowell, 1980.

You Can't Make a Move without Your Muscles (illustrated by H. Barton). New York: Crowell, 1982.

FOR ADULTS

Nonfiction:

Fortune Telling for Fun and Popularity. New York: New Home Library, 1942; also published as *Fortune Telling for Fun.* Hollywood, Calif.: Newcastle, 1971; and *Fortune Telling for Fun and Profit.* New York: Bell Publishing, 1985.

Joyce Carol Thomas

1938-

Joyce Carol Thomas, 1988

I must have fallen in love with words when I was still in the womb. Probably because my mother fairly lived in the church house while she was pregnant with me.

In that little wooden white chapel on an Oklahoma hillrise even the spoken words were sung with a kind of lilting sweetness, measured in breaths that rose and fell; words, chanted back and forth from the preacher, the deacon, and the female missionaries. In my writing I try to recreate this music on the printed page. Sing the way those people used to speak.

My mother was such an avid churchgoer that one night while she was tarrying on the altar, our house burned down. She didn't get up off her knees to go put out the fire or to try to save any of our worldly possessions. Maybe she already had the fire described in the lyrics by the gospel quartet groups, "Holy Ghost, it's like fire shut up in my bones." She didn't need to look at the flames or try to control the fire. She moved about the world like that, letting things happen; for I think that in her mind, one thing happening was as good or as bad as another. She allowed life. She and my father built another house.

She told me that when she married my father, she owned a rag doll. My father threw the doll in the garbage can. "You want a baby girl, I'll give you a baby girl," he promised.

They had a gang of children. Gave birth to thirteen, nine of us lived. They kept having boys, she wanted a girl. Fifth of the nine, I was born on May 25, 1938. And the first girl. My sister, Flora, born the year after me, was the second and last daughter. More brothers followed.

My mother studied the Bible a lot, reading it silently and aloud, at home and in church. Sitting up under her I learned to follow along when she sang out the words in her perfect-pitch voice for the preacher to repeat and interpret. I learned to read by listening to and looking at what my mother read.

Hers wasn't a singing voice. Even though there was a melody to her words when she spoke. My father was the singer.

He sang with an *a capella* choir at radio station WBBZ on the Sunday morning broadcast. I remember sitting with one ear glued to the cloth-covered speaker at the bottom of the Emerson radio, hugging the long thin mahogany legs of the floor model trying to listen to every bend of the liquid notes that curled and turned this way and that as they flooded the room. It seemed to me that even the plainest lyric sounded sweet when sung in four-part harmony.

We lived in a small Oklahoma town called Ponca City. Although it was called Ponca City, there was no city there. Its size qualifies it as a town. Still the place was the world to me when I was young. It was only later that I understood, through comparison, what a quaint place Ponca City was—and is. Our house at 1028 South Twelfth Street is no longer standing; all that remains is the backyard cottonwood tree I climbed at dusk to hide among its leaves in a game of hide-and-seek, the annoying white cotton from the cottonwood tree falling, getting caught like lint in my black cotton braids.

Ponca City is the setting for much of my fiction, including three of my novels: *Marked by Fire, Bright Shadow,* and *The Golden Pasture.* Although now I live half a continent away from my hometown, when it comes to my writing I find that I am still there.

We stayed in Ponca until I was in the fourth grade.

Our house sat directly across the street from the school. Crispus Attucks School was named after the African-American hero, first soldier to die in the Boston Massacre, 1770. My character Abyssinia Jackson attends a school with the same name.

Although we lived almost in the school's front door, I was forever anxious about getting to class on time. Not so much because I would be scolded, but because I didn't want to miss anything. My mother had all these other children to attend to, my younger sister's hair to braid, for instance. And there I was impatiently hopping from one foot to the other, waiting my turn to bow down, ducking and cringing under Mama's exacting comb as I watched the clock inch up relentlessly to bell time.

Sometimes I'd brush yesterday's braids in place and rush away, much to my mother's chagrin, for she was the hairdresser of the community and here I was looking like a wild child: hair sticking out every which way on my head.

I learned to braid my own hair when I was about seven, freeing my mother of one of her many duties and easing my own anxiety about punctuality. I felt relieved to be seated in my chair before the bell rang. Didn't want to be late for a lesson or catching the school clown wrestling pigs in the school yard or to miss seeing the principal getting thrown out the window by an irate teenager. Thank goodness the ground was only one level away and the window was open!

"Portrait of my mother, Leona Thompson Haynes (seated on right), with her three sisters"

Getting ready for school included not only hair braiding, but also eating a good breakfast. Because we didn't have much money, my mother was a genius at "making do." If times were hard she'd do a head for twenty-five cents in order to buy groceries. ("Doing a head" meant straightening and/or curling one of the Ponca women's hair.)

Every school morning we had hot Quaker oatmeal or Cream of Wheat or Malt-o-Meal for breakfast, with Pet milk poured over the steaming cereal. And homemade biscuits.

"Light bread" (store-bought, white sliced bread) was a luxury to eat. Little did I know that I would yearn many a day for my mother's fragrant home-baked buttermilk biscuits, piping hot from the oven. If there was dough left over, she made a hoecake, fought over by my brothers and cousin. At noon we ate "beans and corn bread." On alternate days the menu changed and we lunched on "corn bread and beans." Changing the order of the words was the only way to give that meal variety, I tell you.

Dinner could be anything, but usually vegetables—corn, tomatoes, okra, sometimes hot-water corn bread. Not much meat.

But Sunday meals were different. A delight. We dined on Wonder bread and Post Toasties cornflakes for breakfast. Dinner, most of it cooked on Saturday night, might be roast chicken and sage dressing, pan gravy, Kentucky Wonder string beans, Sunday yams, and "monkey bread"—so called because these yeast rolls were so feathery light and buttery good you made a monkey of yourself eating too many of them. And the white coconut cake, moist, jump-in-the-mouth tender, was a mouth-watering delicacy with the blackberry jam filling the middle. Add company and the number of desserts increased accordingly. Out-of-town guests? Then nothing would do but to add sweet-potato pies, peach and pear cobblers. Is there any wonder midwestern and southern folks took naps after such a feast?

Many readers have commented about the importance of food in my novels. Food, they say, occupies almost as much of a place as setting. I suppose the food's joyous inclusion and fragrant presence comes from having a mother who was known as the best cook in town and from having seven competing brothers and one cousin who staged eating contests. Because in such a home food was another language for love, my books are redolent of sugar and spice, kale and collards. Having watched my mother, I know what it means to do a thing well, to cook with a loving/knowing hand scooped into a flour barrel so expert at the art of baking that no measuring cup is needed.

In just about all my novels, broom wheat tea is steeped, poured, sipped. When I had a headache or caught chicken pox or measles, my mother would go into the weed fields and pick the tea leaves and serve me a steaming cup from the crushed golden blossoms. "Good for what ails you," she would assert. Once my brother accidentally scalded my leg with a pan of boiling water in which he'd boiled eggs. I zipped out of the kitchen through the house, flew out the front door, and raced around the yard, too pained to scream. Just ran, whistling in pain. A technicolored agony. I didn't think anything could hurt that badly. The burn scar still remains. Perhaps it was my mother's and Mother Nature's loving care that made me better and not the tea. Who knows? They're inseparable. Broom weed tea and caring! When I write it gives me comfort to see this elixir steeped in an imaginary cup and drunk by one of my characters.

Joyce (right), with her only sister, Flora, 1946

The small towns, the rural settings in which I grew up, have affected my life and my writing. I need and like open space. I like trees and flowers and the earth. And so do my characters. The cotton field is an important place for me and my Abyssinian people. At a little place outside of Ponca City, a place called Red Rock, my family and I picked and chopped cotton. To keep us from being economically exploited too much, my mother kept the books. The look and feel of cotton in the early morning when the dew still glistens on it is a memory of my childhood that I will carry forever. My character Abyssinia Jackson was born in the cotton patch. Telling her story lets me go there once again. Not only to the hard work but to the place where the ghost stories were told, to the place where night was so dark my favorite brother ran into a tree and gashed his forehead wide open.

Staunching the blood was not easy and under the candlelight I wanted to bleed for him, his eyes looked so scared. Yet away from electrical lights, the stars sparkled like a sky-sized chandelier. Red Rock is a place where the night sounds were those of crickets, and the night-lights, fireflies. Where soft sounds came from nature and the sound of the Arkansas River, a lulling wonder or an awful thing especially in the years when the floods came to Ponca and drove people out of their houses. The people who lived near the river bottom, beyond Boone's Grocery Store, let things happen. The Arkansas River followed its natural path; in seasons of heavy rains the swollen river forced folks with their chickens and goats and cows to flee to higher ground. Once the flood waters receded, the people moved back home again. To the same place that the river was sure to flood again.

The Ponca people gave themselves over into the hands of Mother Nature. They took what she dished out, waiting to be bopped upside the head by a tree, run off by a flood, or gifted with a harvest of spring peppergrass greens.

And the spiders. One year in the cotton fields my mother was bitten by a black widow spider. She had to keep her leg up so the poison would not go deeper. It took forever to heal. And there was even talk of her losing the leg. Thank goodness they didn't have to cut her leg off. Something so tiny as a black widow spider can be so deadly. A black widow's venom, measure for measure, contains more poison than that of a rattlesnake. Still, spiders fascinated me and there are awesome spiders in my novel *Journey.* Mostly good spiders.

Maybe I wanted those powerful creatures to be on my side.

When we migrated to California (I had my tenth birthday on the train), we moved again to a small town, settling in a rural area five miles out of Tracy. Can't get much more country than that.

Tracy is also the setting for *Water Girl.* In rural Tracy I fished for minnows in the creek, hunted jackrabbits, milked cows, fed chickens, slopped hogs, listened to crickets chirping. When we found another house, we moved a little closer to town, just three miles out—a house full of spiders. We couldn't get rid of them. Black widow spiders stayed under my bed. Every weekend, while cleaning, I would look and the spiders would be nesting under the mattress. The red spot glowing like a badge of danger. They must have affected my sleep. How, I cannot say. Sleeping with the threat of danger is a different kind of slumber, I suspect.

Add to the spiders, wasps. When we were in Oklahoma, one of my older brothers used to frighten me and my sister with wasps. And I think this brother, like many "responsible" siblings, punished us because he resented having to take care of us, maybe for our being younger or girls. And when my sister told our parents about his staying out late or some other devilment, he punished both of us, putting us in a dark closet (with little light trickling in from the outside) that had a wasp nest in the ceiling corner. This was in Oklahoma. I remember the two of us crouched sweating on the closet floor as the wasps swarmed above us. The fear of being stung uppermost in our minds. Hoping, praying, for our parents to return and save us. I never told. My mother often remarked on my fear of hornets and wasps. Sometimes she would say, "Sister, the wasps won't hurt you, but looks like they'll make you hurt yourself just getting out of the way." She said this as she watched me falling over chairs, bruising an arm, twisting a foot, stubbing a toe, leaping out of the way of the worrisome wasps.

I put wasps in *Marked by Fire.* I wanted to write something scary for my character to deal with, so I figured wasps would do it. Two years ago I gave a talk to some Oakland schoolchildren in the library. The librarian was gone and there was no one in the room but me and the students. In the middle of my talk a wasp flew into the room. I stopped, panicked, and was braced to run. Then I realized I was the only adult there. Not everyone could panic. I looked at the wasp, looked at the children, and decided to stand my ground. I then realized the wasp wouldn't hurt me. The wasps of my childhood had been used as an instrument to terrify me. The wasps were innocent. Today, I'm happy to report I can sit in a room with wasps, bees, and hornets. However, I still don't *choose* to go into a room with any stingers.

A book is a safe place to experience fear. Maybe that's why we like to read scary novels too, don't you think?

Well, the spiders that I feared/fear have become my friends. At least in books!

Flowers are safe friends. I am at home with them. I trust them in my yard, on my table. Before I was ten, I remember that our neighbor down the road kept a garden that was so beautiful, I often asked to run errands that sent me by her yard. It was a country of flowers. Of marigolds and hemlocks. Of daffodils and blue irises. Sunflowers and tiger lilies. Now, if I should see the same garden, it probably would not look as immense. But then some of the flowers were taller than I was. Looked like trees of color. I would linger. Smelling all the perfumes mixed-up together. Delighted with delicious color. My senses overwhelmed. The touch of the rose petals, so delicate, so bright, so wonderful. Pure intoxication!

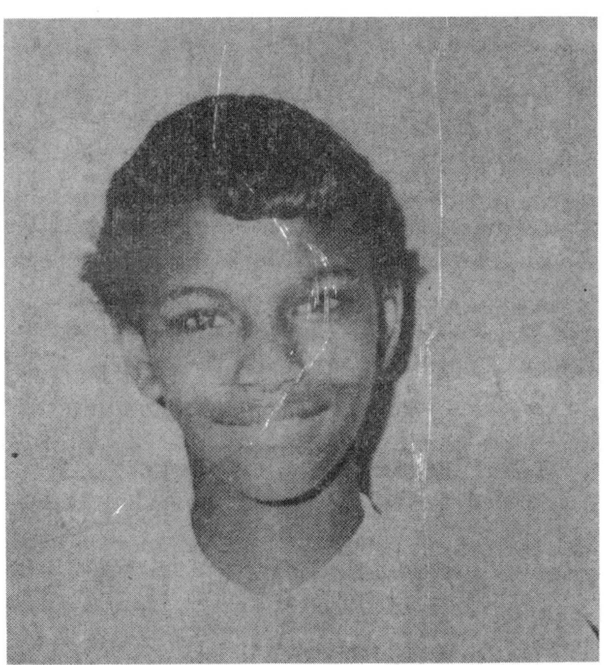

Joyce, age thirteen, as featured in the Tracy Press *after winning the county spelling bee, 1951*

The author (bottom left), in her freshman yearbook photo, about 1954. Joyce was one of the top honor students of the California Scholarship Federation throughout her high-school years.

When we moved to Tracy we continued to harvest crops. This time tomatoes, mainly. And sometimes yellow onions, and the sweet black grapes of the San Joaquin Valley vineyards. I like grapes and especially liked to enjoy their juicy clusters as I worked. But the main summer job was picking tomatoes. Teenagers of all types worked the fields, but our numbers consisted mostly of Blacks and the Mexicans who crossed the California border in the summer to make enough money from the tomato harvest to carry back to Mexico where the money went further. I have never seen anybody work any harder than my workmates, running down the fields with the boxes of red, red tomatoes, working against time, sweat maps on the backs of their shirts. Working with poor people in the fields I have never believed poor people are lazy. I know better. And the mariachi songs, languid, wafting, harmonious, filled the air and made me wonder at the language, at the souls of the people who made such music. I think the music made the work go easier, faster. Much the way the songs in the cotton fields of Oklahoma lightened our loads. And like the people in the church I grew up attending, even when the Spanish speakers talked they seemed to sing.

That language I wanted to know. And so, when I selected foreign languages in high school, I chose Spanish and Latin. I learned the syntax, the spelling, the grammar of the language in school, but I learned the ethos of the language in the fields with the migrant workers. In college too, I majored in Spanish and minored in French. I found foreign languages the language of the church, and that of the Ponca and Tracy people to be a fitting foundation for writing. The music of the word is what I wanted to be able to master in my study of languages. The music of the word is what I want to create in my writing of books.

From this base of languages I taught myself all I know about writing. I have never taken a creative-writing course. My formal education includes a bachelor of arts degree with distinction from California State University, San Jose, graduating with a major in Spanish and a minor in French. And a master of arts degree from Stanford University: education major with an emphasis on Spanish.

I taught foreign language in my first teaching positions in Jordan Junior High and in the middle schools of the Ravenswood City School District. My last teaching positions were as visiting associate professor of English at Purdue University and visiting associate professor of creative writing at the University of California at Santa Cruz.

After I graduated from California State University I took my first trip abroad to Guadalajara, Mexico, where while enjoying my vacation I tested my ability to speak Spanish. Much to my delight, nobody was at a loss to understand my accent when I ordered *enchiladas, arroz còn pollo,* and other culinary delights from the menu. It was Spanish that I spoke *regateando* in the marketplace. And I felt welcome from *la gente.* In addition, I was heartened to find that some of the Mexican people had skin as dark as mine. Others would smile and say, *Que negrita bonita.* I was flattered at the hospitality and goodwill extended to me at every turn. But the phrase I cherished most was *hablas como un loro,* you speak like a native.

That first trip to Guadalajara went so well that over the years I have felt at home in other parts of the world: Nigeria, Hong Kong, Saipan, Rome, Haiti.

Often one of the needs of a writer is the need to be alone. All my life I certainly have had that need. But it was an unfulfilled yearning.

It was not possible to be alone for long in my early years being part of a family of eleven. Especially in our small house where we slept four to a twin-sized bed. Our house in Oklahoma was built a little up off the ground (maybe because of the fear of flooding). Under the house was the only place I could be alone for a spell. I would go there and find some solitude. I made up songs in my head in the rare quiet. And sang them there, clothed them with melodies. Nobody bothered me or asked me questions or commanded me to do anything in my special hideaway.

I could very easily turn into a recluse. Well, almost. Decades later when I was invited to finish up a Pamela Djerassi Fellowship at the Djerassi Foundation in Woodside, I had an entire country house to myself. Nobody came to visit unless I invited them. I wouldn't have houseguests very often. And when friends did come, often I couldn't wait for them to leave. I was ashamed at my delight at being left alone!

This was the first time I had been alone for any extended period of time. Right after high school I had left my huge family to get married and begin to raise a family of my own.

Some of my friends observe that I am alone even in a crowd of people. And that's probably true, too. I think a writer has to be able to go inside herself in order to create. Yet I enjoy talking to students, teachers, librarians, and readers about my work. Perhaps I need the mountains and the multitudes.

I am a nester. My surroundings are important to my spirit. I have created most of my novels here in this house in Berkeley.

My first novel, *Marked by Fire,* was written here. It's a wonderful space in which to meditate and write.

Representing North America in poetry at the International Arts Cultural Festival, Lagos, Nigeria, 1977

There are windows that open to generous light. There is a fantastic water view of the three bridges and the San Francisco Bay from my study. The backyard is a miniforest of pines, avocado, lemon, and apple trees with blackberry and loganberry bushes gracing the landscape. And through the trees I can glimpse the campanile from which the university clock is a time reminder so gentle that if I do not listen carefully, I miss hearing the bells chiming the hour.

Here in my little house I like to think that I have the best of both worlds: my front windows look out onto the front yard and onto the street, with cars coming and going, with sidewalks leading to grocery stores, banks, the cleaners, and the post office. In my backyard the country and in my front yard the city. Until a year ago in the back cottage there lived a dog named Redwood; he was so playful and friendly that I placed him as a character in my fifth novel, *Journey.* I have a cat too, named Smokey, who is the color of smoke; he is a Persian with copper-colored eyes. Other cats, Abyssinian, Himalayan, and Siamese have lived here. I celebrate cats in *Bright Shadow.* In this book the mysterious cat, Opia, reminds Abyssinia that in a world of weeds, flowers are still blooming.

A few summers ago on a trip to Shawnee, Oklahoma, to visit my aunt Mary and uncle Ben who still raise horses for the Boley Rodeo, I saw an Appaloosa who let me ride him. He became the Appaloosa horse named Thunderfoot in *The Golden Pasture.*

I try to remember as I write my fiction that not only do we share the world with other races and nationalities but also with other creatures and critters—horses, cats, dogs, deer, snakes, spiders. So there is the hungry snake in *Marked by Fire,* the dancing deer in *Water Girl,* the mysterious Appaloosa horse in *The Golden Pasture,* the magical cat in *Bright Shadow,* the plotting spiders in *Journey,* and Redwood, the faithful mongrel, also in *Journey.*

I'm often asked about the naming of my characters. How, for instance, did Amber get her name? Amber is a jewel that the sages of ancient time said was a soothing, healing stone. Because Amber is a Black girl, I wanted the dark amber to be the jewel in the mind of the reader, so the epigram to *Water Girl* describes her color and suggests that she is appealing to behold. It reads:

> Amber: the reddish-brown jewel the color of
> mountains in Indian summer, a creation of resin
> from pine trees plunging long ago to the
> bottom of
> the sea, buried there for ages, collecting beauty
> til washed ashore by that ancient midwife
> Water.

Abyssinia, the name used by the shero of *Marked by Fire,* is the old name for Ethiopia. I happen to like Abyssinian cats. And too there are Black churches named Abyssinia, and the name is poetic to me.

I wanted my character to have a name that nobody else had used. It had to be distinctive, arresting, fresh, with a meaning I could embellish. I wanted the original meaning to be shaped by the personality of the character. The person Abyssinia is someone who triumphs over tragedy, who is a healer, a lover and respecter of people and nature. A believer in God. A humanitarian, a sister of light.

The name had to be musical sounding. The five vowels could be the notes to a song, depending upon how they are spoken. *Abyssinia.* I heard them that way and when I read excerpts from the Abyssinian books, I automatically say her name in a way that I hope suggests music. I have always known that words have power and I try to be careful with what comes out of my mouth and with the names I bestow upon my characters. Once when I was writing the fifth draft of *Marked by Fire* I needed to create a sinister, mean, spiteful character. I reached back into my childhood and came upon a man we used to call Trembling Slim. He trembled when he moved and we used to run when he walked the streets. Now I understand that Mr. Slim probably suffered from some devastating illness, but we children were not told this. If I wasn't good, I was told, "All right, we're going to give you to Trembling Slim." Or: "Trembling Slim's gonna get you!" Scared us half to death. So I named this character Trembling Slim. Along about the fifth draft, the character began to talk in a female voice. She said, "My name's not Trembling Slim, this here's Trembling Sally." Okay, I thought, and from that point on Trembling Sally, a fierce, mad woman, made her presence known.

Patience, Abyssinia's mother, got her name from a quality that my mother possessed. Leona Haynes's life mirrored an incomparable patience. I often wonder how she managed to raise nine children and one nephew. A steadfast, sweet-spirited woman, she possessed amazing tolerance. She's gone now but I think of her when life gets trying. It is then that the memory of her fortitude sustains me.

Kaz Tsuruta

"After publishing Bright Shadow," *1983*

Strong, Abyssinia's father, was so named because I wanted to demonstrate his resilience. He made mistakes in the novel; for example, he abandoned his family when they needed him most. Although he made this monstrous error, he was strong enough to turn around and go back home. There is no test if nothing terrible ever happens to us. And there are no perfect situations. We can always act better. As Aretha Franklin sings, "I need a little time to pray. I've been in the storm way too long," then dips between lines ad-libbing, "I know what I'm talking about, I've been there myself." Life is not always sunshine, so when the storms come and lay Strong low, as they do so devastatingly in *Marked by Fire* and in *Bright Shadow,* he pulls himself together, gets on up off the ground, and rises again to meet whatever challenge is laid at his doorstep. Strong is strong enough to understand that when life knocks him down, to get back up, go back home, begin again. Again and again.

More recently, during the writing of *Journey,* another of my characters changed her name. This time I had sent the final draft off to my editor, Jean Feiwel, and proceeded to relax. Eleven drafts and finally done. I had put the manuscript in the mail and sent *Journey* on its journey to New York.

Well, now, about two nights later, I woke up out of a deep sleep. The clock said 2:30 A.M. "What's going on?" I wondered. I'm a sound sleeper. Rarely do I have insomnia.

"My name," said the woman standing at the foot of my bed.

"What?"

"My name is not Margarite. It's Memory."

"Memory?"

She nodded.

I got up. Who wouldn't? Went into the study. Turned on the computer and gave the command that allows me to change a word throughout the manuscript. The machine finds the old word for me and makes the change I type in. The computer found "Margarite." "Change to?" it asked with its green light. "Memory," I typed. And the computer began its search and blinked for me to hit the *Y* (for yes) key for the change to "Memory." I hit *Y* until all the "Margarites" changed to "Memory."

Once this was done, the character started talking. Telling me more. She said I'd left out the part about Meggie's grandmother, whose name was Midnight. I put that in. She went on all through the manuscript. My goodness, by the time she was finished with me I had a new draft. I got on the phone the next day and called my editor. I said, "That last *Journey* draft I sent you? That's not it. Another's on the way."

When she had read the Memory draft of *Journey,* she called back to say, "Why this is incredible!" (She uses incredible to mean amazing.) "Incredible!"

You're telling me, I thought. A visitation is not to be taken lightly.

Names are important.

My own name also. My aunt Mary named me Joyce Carol for joyful song. Everything I write—no matter how gruesome or horrible the conflict, the pain, the suffering—has to turn out with a positive resolution. If there is no joy, I can't use it. I want/need peace and happy endings. Well, I say to myself, I'm the creator. If a happy ending is what I want, I write one.

What wakes up my wit? What triggers my imagination? Why do I choose to pick up a pen to write? I'm not sure what the answers to those questions are. But I know that I write in spite of everything that is going on around me. I have written with tears rolling down my cheeks and with laughter, running through the house like a child. More than once when I was an adolescent I was so intent on scribbling down words that I was absentminded. For example, there's the question of what happened to my father's hat.

I was forever running into difficulty with my imagination. I loved to read and create songs, stories, poems. This enchantment with the written word was sometimes so engrossing that I paid scant attention to some of my household duties. I don't think I was lazy, just obsessed.

On the occasion of my father's hat question, my chore was to clean the kitchen, clear the breakfast table, wash the dishes, wipe off the stove and refrigerator, sweep and mop the floor.

I hurried through these tasks for I was intent upon completing a poem I'd started before breakfast.

Just about the time I'd finished the kitchen and plopped down comfortably on the couch with my pad and pencil, my father came in to announce he could not find his hat. He thought he'd left it on the top of the refrigerator, but it was nowhere to be found.

My mother looked and looked but we could not find the hat. Under the table, no hat. Behind the refrigerator, no hat. In the living room, no hat. In the closet, no hat.

Finally, my father, who would not leave the house without his hat, which he wore everywhere, gave up. Realizing he would be late for work, he decided to brew a nerve-settling pot of coffee. He poured himself a cup and opened the refrigerator to get the Pet milk. Then I heard him yell to my mother, "Come here, Leona, and see what this gal's done!"

Of course I swiftly followed my mother into the kitchen to see what the matter was.

My father was standing glaring into the refrigerator. There, as neatly placed as you please, next to the cream, the butter, the eggs, and the orange juice, sat my father's hat.

Walking around in a daze, dreaming while awake, characterizes my state of mind when I'm writing. Dreams play an important role in my work. My first play, *A Song in the Sky,* started out as a poem, called "Blessing"—the stanzas became the acts. I dreamed the poem about 3:00 A.M. one morning and got up and wrote all the verses down and went right back to sleep. One year later the poem blossomed into a play.

I'm sometimes asked if I'm the same person as my character Abyssinia. Yes and no. Yes, because we share a hometown, elementary school, joys, hurts, recoveries from the myriad sufferings life may offer. No, because Abyssinia can do many things that I wish I could do and can't. She can sing, I can't.

Before I began writing novels I wrote poetry. Another writer remarked that wings are mentioned throughout my work. It is a persistent motif that I had not noticed until she pointed it out to me.

Wings probably mean many things to me. Freedom to fly away, lightness, joy. My son-in-law told me that when he was dating my daughter, he thought he could fly. After leaving her here at the house, he said he would walk up to Holy Hill, a nearby hill of seminaries close to the University of California campus, and be tempted to jump and fly into the sky. Love does that. Makes us feather light. The winged moments of life are like that. Wings, invisible wings, brush my shoulders when I see the flash of wind poppies, look deeply into the dancing eyes of children, watch the sun rise and set, hear Aretha Franklin sing gospel, or listen to the multicolored birds lift their multicolored voices outside my morning window . . . Well, I could go on and on. An artist I met at the Djerassi Foundation painted my portrait once; when I went to the opening of her show at Stanford University, I saw she had sketched, above me where I sat in a chair, just behind my shoulders, an angel woman with wings. I don't think my artist-friend had read any of my poetry at the time. I like her portrait for all the happy reasons I mentioned above.

The prominence of the church in my writing stems from my family's living under the wing of the church. Both literally and figuratively. We lived a half block from the sanctuary and we spent many weekday evenings, as well as almost all day Sunday, in the corner building.

I saw some amazing things there. There was an evangelist, Brother Edwards, who used to travel from town to town, holding revivals. The man could close his eyes and dance the backs of pews from the front of the church to the back, spin around on the shoulder of the back pew, and skip his way back to the front altar without falling.

There his happy acrobatics performed while praising the Lord astonished me, even though I was used to seeing all kinds of strange and wonderful goings-on at the services.

My first published poems happened because the Brother Edwards memory of the 1950s was stirred by a woman shouting a holy dance at a James Cleveland concert at the San Jose Civic Center in 1972. At the time I was a professor at San Jose State University. As I was being transported back in time to an event that many intellectuals would consider unsophisticated, I marveled at the clarity of the connection.

Detail from a painting by Sue Ferguson Gussow entitled "Joyce Carol Thomas and the Angel," completed while the author was working on Water Girl, *1984*

I know a few folks who won't own up to the fact that they're from the backwoods of Mississippi or a long way from Georgia or rural Alabama. They think it marks them as poor and ignorant. They are scared of being thought of as "country bumpkins." I can think of worse things to be.

My background is an ink coloring the rich landscape of my settings, the flightful joys and arduous sufferings of Oklahoma adventures, the starts and turns of the rural California of my fiction.

That woman's shouting (holy dancing) gave rise to three poems in me—"Church Poem," "Shouting," and "The James Cleveland Concert." I mention them here because they were pivotal to my publishing career. They mark my awakening as a woman who willingly and sometimes unwillingly walks the subconscious halls of memory and writes.

Church Poem
(My first published poem)

The smell of sage
mingles with burnt hair
and mama prepares
Sunday dinner
on Saturday night
chicken and dressing
whisper promises in
the ear you hold
with one hand
so your edges
will be straight
as she does your hair

"Bend your head
so you won't
get burnt"
If you bend your head
on Saturday evening
is it the same God
you bend to on
Sunday morning?

Mama, how long
do you beat the cake
"Til your arms
get too sore
to beat some more"
but Betty Crocker
says 4 minutes
"This ain no white folks
cake I aim to bake"

Now line up
with lye soap
and bath towel
pajamas slippers
and robe
sink into the hot
tin tub
scrub off
a week's worth
of dirt
grease down in cold cream
and warm
your backside
by the bubbling fire

On the Sabbath morning
the organ begins
its ascent
choir comes rocking
down the aisle
like so many black notes
stroking the carpet floor
and rising til rested
by Elsa's wanded finger

Sister Elsa's First Sunday
sermon in song
holding a phrase
kneading it like new dough
turning it round
in her head
singing it different
everytime

You can hear her shout
"Take me to the water"
then adding in a whisper
"I know I got religion
I been baptized"

Did you feel
the water riding
riding over your feet
sucking up
the white garment
kissing the breath
from your mouth
when she moaned
"I been baptized?"

I saw a silent
man leap
straight up in the air
sit down
then go striding
across the room
to sit again
understanding
the disciplined notes
in undisciplined song
the unofficial concert

When does
the melody end
and where

does it begin?
YPWW, BYPU, Bible Drill
in shiny legs
and velvet ribbons

Testimony service
and Brother Jackson shouted
then danced
the pewed benches
front row
to back
because I held
my breath
he never, he never missed
a step

Is it the same God
you bend to now
on Sunday morning?
When does the melody
end
and where
does it begin?

"Riding one of the Oklahoma horses that inspired my book The Golden Pasture," *1985*

Instead of feeling the shame that some folks feel about rural southern or midwestern roots, I find cause for celebration. I felt elated after writing that poem. In fact, I felt I could fly!

When the work has gone well I feel an indescribable ecstasy. At the end of an especially good poem or chapter, I say a humble prayer of thanks.

My aunt Corine has a saying that I try to follow: "Children, keep God in your business."

My aunts, Aunt Corine, Aunt Annie Mae, Aunt Birdtee, sisters to my mother, have played supporting roles in my career as writer. Also, my aunt Mary, my father's sister, is a continuing source of inspiration and influence.

I write something every day. My hours are from eight until two in the afternoon, in general. Given other needs, family, speaking engagements, business appointments, the "office" hours may change. Now the characters who wake me up out of sound sleep, I must tell you, are no respecters of office hours either. They come and go when they choose. I am at their mercy and I have been known to write well past my two o'clock closing time. How long does it take me to write a novel? My answer to that is two to three years and all my life. Two to three years of crafting ten to twelve drafts of the novel and all the memories and events that my life holds.

Beyond the writing of the books, the muse still works. Imagination plays a global role in all my storytelling and fiction writing. I was surprised by the persistent subliminal part that imagination played even in the naming of my novels. For me the discovery was a pristine glimpse of the entire vision. A glimmer lodged in the secret wheels of the subconscious mind.

When my fourth novel, *The Golden Pasture,* came in the mail in 1986 I unwrapped it from its crating, studied its cover with the Black boy proudly seated on his horse, and then held this nicely bound edition close to me. Then I lined up the four novels on the stone fireplace mantel, from the first to the fourth, *Marked by Fire, Bright Shadow, Water Girl,* and *The Golden Pasture.* Here were fire, air, water, and earth. A small storytelling miracle. A world of fire, air, water, and earth, shaped by the imagination, illuminated by the muse.

At this writing a musical has been made from my first novel, *Marked by Fire.* How did this happen?

The book, published January 1982, had been out less than a year when I received a letter from Ted Kociolek of New York City. There was something funny about the envelope the letter came in though. It was addressed to Joyce Carol Thomas, San Jose State University, Berkeley, California. Now San Jose State University is located in the city of San Jose, about fifty miles from Berkeley. That I should receive the letter at all was a miracle, but I received it at my desk on campus in San Jose. Mr. Kociolek wrote that he wanted to fly out and talk to me about the possibility of obtaining the dramatic rights to *Marked by Fire.* I called him and asked why he had addressed the letter the way he had. He said he'd tried to reach me through my agent but couldn't and that he'd noticed, in the back of the novel, a short bio that read "the author teaches at San Jose State where she lives in Berkeley." So much for my eastern publishers' understanding of California geography! That error was in one of the first printings.

Ted Kociolek, who was working on another New York show, flew out on an 8:00 P.M. flight and had to return on a twelve midnight flight. Clearly our time was limited. Still I was curious about his ideas. I picked him up at the airport. My first impressions as he walked toward me at Oakland International were: "Here he is, he's so young, he's white, he's redheaded, he's obviously male. What could he possibly know about Abyssinia, a Black girl from Oklahoma?" It turns out he knew quite a lot. Imagine my surprise when we reached my house and he sat down at the piano, pulled out a script with score, and began to play, sing, and act the parts of the characters of a show he'd written based on *Marked by Fire.* You could have knocked me over with a feather. He had risked quite a bit. In the first place, one usually gets permission first on a copyrighted work before making any adaptations. And I could have very easily said, "No thank you." But I was astounded that he had captured the spirit of the book, and I liked the direction in which his musical was leading.

I asked him why he had gone ahead and written the play.

He said he'd found the *Marked by Fire* novel in a Philadelphia bookstore, started reading it, couldn't put it down, and became obsessed with setting it to music. He could not help himself.

I understood. I'd been there myself in my own work. When the muse calls, one simply answers.

Then he added that while working on the musical he had experienced a healing.

I didn't ask him what he meant by that. But whatever it was I looked in his eyes and realized he was telling the truth. I asked him to call my agent, Mitch Douglas, when he returned to New York. He did so, and six years later the musical was on stage, ably directed by the gifted Tazewell Thompson, who moves the story along with subtlety and passion.

The all-Black musical is now titled *Abyssinia* after our central character in *Marked by Fire.* In its showcase and tryout productions in New York and Connecticut the show continues to receive outstanding reviews.

Well, it's a divine play is all I can tell you.

How does it feel to see my words performed on stage? I enjoy looking into the faces of the audiences and feeling their responses. Blacks, Whites, Gentiles, and Jews relate to Abyssinia's story about faith in an emotional heartfelt way. And I suppose that is what we hope for in the arts, that we all share a little bit of the humanity, that we all laugh and cry during the emotional scenes, for life gives us her acts and we, actors and audience, play them as best we can.

It has taken six years for the play to reach where it is today. I don't think the success it's having could have come overnight.

I'm an intuitive person. I rarely go wrong when I follow my "right mind." I'm glad I said Yes to young Ted Kociolek.

I continue to write every day. Poems come between chapters of my fiction. I stop to record them. Characters change their names, in the middle of drafts and in the middle of the night. I enjoy writing. I don't know what else I'd rather be doing. I give it time. The talent part is a gift. When I speak to students I say to them that writing is a process. I don't just sit down and start from page one and type until I reach the end. I think about scenes. I see them. I describe what I see at the time. In later drafts I see more, I write more. I am open to the muse. Sometimes I sit in my study waiting for inspiration to come. Sometimes she lets me sit here. But when she comes I am grateful. Being here in my study is important. When inspiration calls I want to be present. When she calls I answer.

Sometimes ideas don't come in the quiet of the study but they come when I'm driving down the road. Or on an airplane. They rear their heads between speaking engagements. When no pen is in sight and my hands are wet washing dishes, here comes a story. I walk early in the morning to clear my mind before I sit down at my desk. Characters all dressed up in their bright clothing and their country accents walk beside me as I hike up and down the Berkeley hills, inhaling the fresh air. Conversations with my aunts often stir up memories or possibilities. Church services keep my spirits up, especially the singing. Barbershop visits with my son remind me of the rhythms of my deceased father's voice when the men tease each other and gossip. These are the rhythms I hear when my male characters Carl Lee and Strong speak.

I have written this short autobiography in a spiral and not a straight line. Circles within circles, and not straight lines, describe my way of creative thinking and I remember the turning wheels within the middle of a wheel as I tell you something of my life, linking past and present, people and places who have helped and inspired my work.

"At a birthday party in 1983, celebrating the fruit of my family-raising years": from left, granddaughter Maria; son-in-law Herman; Joyce, holding granddaughter Crystal; son Roy; daughter Monica, with granddaughter Aresa

If I had to give advice to young people, it would be that whatever your career choice, prepare yourself to do it well. Quality takes talent and time. Believe in your dreams. Have faith in yourself. Keep working and enjoying today even as you reach for tomorrow. If you choose to write, value your experiences. And color them in the indelible ink of your own background.

And when you come across a book of mine I wish you mainly this: happy reading.

BIBLIOGRAPHY

FOR YOUNG ADULTS

Fiction:

Marked by Fire. New York: Avon, 1982.

Bright Shadow. New York: Avon, 1983.

The Golden Pasture. New York: Scholastic, 1986.

Water Girl. New York: Avon, 1986.

Journey. New York: Scholastic, 1988.

FOR ADULTS

Poetry:

Bittersweet. San Jose, Calif.: Firesign Press, 1973.

Blessing. Berkeley, Calif.: Jocato Press, 1974.

Crystal Breezes. San Jose, Calif.: Firesign Press, 1974.

Black Child (illustrated by Tom Feelings). New York: Zamani Productions, 1981.

Inside the Rainbow. Palo Alto, Calif.: Zikawuna Press, 1982.

Plays:

Look! What a Wonder!, first produced at the Berkeley Community Theatre in Berkeley, Calif., 1976.

A Song in the Sky, first produced at the Montgomery Theatre in San Francisco, Calif., 1976.

Magnolia, first produced at the Old San Francisco Theatre in San Francisco, Calif., 1977.

Ambrosia, first produced at the Little Fox Theatre in San Francisco, Calif., 1978.

Gospel Roots, first produced at California State University in Carson, Calif., 1981.

Garth Williams

1912-

Garth Williams, 1986

I was born in New York City on April 16, 1912. Both my parents were artists. My father, Hamilton Williams, sold his first drawing to *Punch,* England's leading magazine of humor, when he was seventeen. He went to America and worked for several publications in New York. At that time artists illustrated sport pages, stories, and of course there were humorous illustrations, now best found in the *New Yorker* magazine. He also, much later, drew humorous drawings for *Le Rire* in Paris.

My mother was brought up on Barbados in the British West Indies. She was a painter and went to Paris to study art. There she met my father and they were married in London in 1910. After a long honeymoon in France and Spain they went to live on a farm in Caldwell, New Jersey. And that is where my life began.

I was taken to England and introduced to my mother's friends and relations. I was one or two years old and do not remember that visit. But I remember well most of those early years in New Jersey, especially when I was taken by the farmer, our landlord, on his lap to go harrowing or plowing. Or when we went driving out in his two-wheel buggy to Peterson or the Passaic River, crunching along a gravel road or splashing through puddles.

I was a typical Huckleberry Finn, roaming barefoot around the farm, watching the farmer milk the cows by hand, or do his other chores.

One day my father left his studio door open. I entered and found a pile of drawings he had ready to take to New York. I spent a long time looking at them and adding my art to them. I was not punished. "I'm afraid he's going to be an artist," my father said, and removed my additions.

World War I had begun and my mother accepted a teaching job in Barrie, Ontario, at Ovenden, a finishing school for girls run by her old college friends from England.

My sister Fiona had been born in New York when I was three and she was now two so I was no longer alone. I attended the children's class at Ovenden and took care of my sister. I was aware of the war in Europe because I listened to my parents discussing the news, particularly when the German army was very close to Paris. I remember thinking the world was like a big flat dish, about twenty miles across. Where there had been a forest fire in Boonton, New Jersey, I was sure that was the war. If the Germans came to our house in Caldwell, I planned to run past the dairy, to the sea. I would look for a boat and row to England, a few miles out to sea. If the enemy followed, I would row to the edge of the world, where the water poured over. Fortunately the enemy didn't arrive.

I remember the end of World War I. In Canada, airplanes flew over the lake with boxers performing on the upper wing, and it was a very memorable time.

My parents decided to educate Fiona and me in England, so we moved to Sutton, Surrey, when I was ten. I was put into a school with eighteen other boys and six masters. We all came from

Garth (left) and his sister, Fiona (middle), with family friends at Ovenden school, Barrie, Ontario, Canada, 1917

different parts of the world—India, Australia, New Zealand, Canada, or South Africa—and we were being prepared to go into a British public school. I did three years' work in one year and went to a school in London. We lived about fifteen miles south of London. I took the 8:00 A.M. train to London Bridge, then a tram or a bus to my school in the city of London. At 3:15 P.M. I rushed home, catching the 4:00 P.M. train, along with several other boys. We all lived around London. Two brothers lived fifty miles away and had a much longer trip to make. There were one thousand boys in the school.

At seventeen I was prepared to become an architect. I had been working for one on Saturday mornings ever since I was eleven years old. My architect friend was about eighty and had three grown daughters, so I was a stand-in for a son. He taught me to make architectural drawings, hot-air engines, steam-driven model boats, sailboats, gliders, and how to shoot. He was shooting instructor for a regiment of guards. Shooting was easy. His rifle was accurate and I had excellent vision and a very steady hand. I shot the bull's-eye out of the target. He made me demonstrate to the team of guards, which I was proud to do.

When I was fourteen, we had to have target-shooting at school in the Officers Training Corps. When I shot the bull's-eye out, the officer in charge said he wanted me for the school shooting team. That meant I would have to spend my days off going to some distant place to shoot. So the next day I shot the bull's-eye on my neighbor's target and put bullets all over mine. I didn't have to lose my Saturday off. I joined the band and played a fife. We all played jazz as soon as we knew our march.

When the time came for a decision on college, the question of my architectural training had to be decided. My mother took me to see two well-known architects. It was the time of the Depression. They explained they had two fully trained architects helping in their office: one made tea, the other swept the floor. They only did redecoration and house-altering work. The architectural college training took seven years to become qualified. I decided to become an artist, as it required no training. My mother could only afford one three-month term at an art school. After the three months I applied for a scholarship and was given a four-year scholarship to the Royal College of Art in London which paid my living expenses and education. I moved to London.

I won my scholarship as a painter but was very interested in the Design School at the college as I could study every kind of painting and drawing: etching, lithography, mural painting, theatrical scenery. Life-drawing was essential, so I joined the Design School.

When I won special praise for portrait drawing, I decided I must stop drawing and sculpt what I had

In Italy on a Prix de Rome scholarship, 1937

been drawing. I joined Eric Schilsky's sculpture class in the evenings at the Westminster Art School. It took several months before I could control the proportion of my sculpting and produce a very acceptable half-figure. I exhibited it in London at the Royal Academy of Arts annual show and stood next to it to hear what comments people would make. I was amused to hear several say I was an old-time, well-known sculptor who did excellent work. I was being confused with another Williams.

I finished college, put A.R.C.A. after my name, and looked for work. I was selected to be headmaster of an old-time art school outside London. I had to reorganize it into a modern, up-to-date art school. I had an assistant from college to help me. It was an interesting experience but took most of my time, the worst part being the train to and from the town, which lost me two hours travelling each day. I did not return after the first year ended.

Finding myself with two cars but completely broke, I went to Eric Schilsky for advice. He said that the Prix de Rome competition would be judged in six weeks and, though the other contestants had had six months to execute the desired work, I could do it. I explained I had no studio and no money for materials. "If you want it, you can win it, and the Westminster Art School will be glad to lend you studio space and pay the costs of materials and the Italian casters to cast the figures," said Schilsky.

I made my figure at the Westminster and finished the toes while the casters were making the molds on the back of the body. It was delivered as requested, and I won. I was the winner of the 1936 Prix de Rome for sculpture in the British Empire (not the U.S.A. Prix de Rome).

Three very lovely young ladies, all about twenty years old, showed great interest: in my art, of course. I asked a friend, "What can I do? I can't afford to buy them a coffee at this moment, but if one throws her arms around me I'll be lost; I won't be able to say no." They were all from very wealthy families. Needless to say, they didn't throw their arms around me.

In 1936 I went to help the husband of a cousin get elected to Parliament from his constituency in the north of England. It was great fun.

"What do you know about politics?" he asked me.

"Absolutely nothing," I replied.

"You'll learn," he answered.

And I did. Hitler was climbing to power, and England was completely unprepared for a military attack on land, but she did have a navy. The public would not hear of warfare. England would accept visits from Stalin, Hitler, Mussolini; but no war. The English prime minister, Sir Neville Chamberlain, came back from a strange meeting with Hitler where Hitler announced he had no intention of making war on anyone. My friend was elected.

The time was very hectic. I had ended two years in Rome as a scholar. I had met and married a young girl whose mother was a Williams from England and whose father was from a Scotch family originally. She had been brought up in Germany and spoke five languages. Her name was Gunda V. Davidson.

On returning to England I produced a beautiful large poster for the Shell Oil Company. When I took it to them they said, "Alas, we don't have any gasoline for sale, it now belongs to the government and it is called Pool Petrol."

It was 1939: war seemed more imminent every day. It was very hard to find work. My wife, Gunda, found an excellent job as an interpreter for an American firm, for whom she telephoned Spain, Germany, France, Italy, or South America and negotiated for supplies of metals or whatever was required. She spent less than an hour per day on the phone, and read one or two novels and knitted a sweater every week at work. Her pay was very good and mine was next to nothing. Then I had the good fortune to work for Pearson Publications on a newly proposed women's magazine. It was very interesting and I was well paid, but before publication Hitler attacked Poland. War was obviously imminent. Posters in England said "Dig or Die," referring to the need for everyone to help make air-raid shelters.

I had stopped reading newspapers, as it seemed that the end of the world was about to happen every day—not the best climate in which to paint a portrait or poster, or sculpt a portrait, or engage in any other peaceful occupation.

Finally England and France declared war on Germany one Sunday morning in September 1939, and I pushed my drawings off my desk, walked out, and joined the British Red Cross Civilian Defense and St. John's Ambulance Organization, a non-military civilian defense group.

I was posted to Chelsea. There were several actors and artists in the same organization. Sir Lewis Casson, a famous Shakespearean actor, was our chief. We learned our first-aid, our streets, and had our cars (given to us by residents) in perfect condition; but we were not attacked. I was put in charge of cars and drivers at Chelsea Polytechnic. I made the drivers learn the present and past names of all streets and squares, because an elderly person might not recall the latest place name: for example, Chelsea Common

At age twenty-eight, a Red Cross volunteer during the London Blitz, behind a sign that means "air-raid precautions"

had vanished. Our families—those evacuated when war was declared—returned to London. My wife and baby had been evacuated by me to her mother's relations in Wales—Williamses all. It was nice to be together again. My work in the Red Cross demanded twenty-four hours on duty, twenty-four hours off. Every other day I could paint and be an artist.

One year after England declared war on Germany, Hitler attacked London. It was about 4:00 P.M. on a Saturday afternoon. About five hundred planes flew over us and dropped their bombs on the docks and city of London. Clouds of smoke rose like cotton wool over the city. When night came we went onto our roof and sat on the chimney. An area five miles wide by twenty miles long was blazing. The flames were several miles high. Winston Churchill, then prime minister, ordered all the fire engines of England to London. As a line would pass our house on its way to the docks, another line, with their crews black-faced and exhausted, filed out in the opposite direction. This lasted about a week, then bombs started to fall around us. The war had begun.

The next day I was on duty with the Red Cross, in Chelsea. I think about two hundred civilians had been killed or wounded in Chelsea during about thirty-six hours. We were busy. I drove the first squad out to the first bomb incident, as I had to know what reality was like. I found out.

I decided to send Gunda, who was then pregnant with our second child, and our baby daughter, Fiona, to Canada, as the royal family had a cruiser waiting to evacuate them (we were told) if Hitler invaded. I got my family off on a ship to Canada after a few anxious days. London was bombed six or eight times a day and all night long.

Our house in Kensington was shared with a Canadian artist, Julius Griffith, who went through college with me. Griffith joined the Kensington Red Cross and went on duty when I came off, so we never saw each other; we left notes. If something important required us to meet, I ordered one of my Chelsea Red Cross drivers to make a test run to the Kensington depot so that Julius and I could talk for a few minutes.

I had a phone call from Canada: my wife had arrived but Customs refused to let our one-year-old baby into the country, as she had a parent (my wife) born in Germany. My wife was now a British citizen. I called Ovenden, the finishing school in Canada where they were going to live. The headmistress (my mother's great friend who had bought sculpture from me) answered. When she heard our baby had been refused entry into Canada she replied, "The prime minister of Canada is in the garden—wait a minute." Four or five minutes later she spoke again. "It's all settled, she can come into Canada." This was the luckiest moment of my life. If you know officialdom, you know that days, weeks, months, perhaps, of delay were wiped away in less than five minutes. They had arrived safely past enemy submarines: out of danger at last. You must imagine my relief—it is indescribable.

Friends were bombed out, lost their houses or apartments, and came to live in my house; we eventually numbered about a dozen or so.

One night, after about fifteen months of the war, I was walking in a pleasant square in Chelsea while on duty in the Red Cross when a bomb landed by my side. There was no noise, just a blast of air and my eyes were squashed as though in someone's fingers. Next I found myself running about a quarter of a mile from where the bomb had landed. It was probably twenty minutes later. The following morning I couldn't sit up in bed. I felt something had injured me, perhaps a piece of the bomb. I had to pull myself up out of bed by the bedpost. Once standing, I felt broken in half. I reported to the head doctor of our Red Cross branch.

He said, "Nothing has entered your body and nothing has passed out, as there is no wound. Can

From Charlotte's Web *by E. B. White. Illustrated by Garth Williams. (Copyright 1952 by E. B. White. Text copyright © renewed 1980 by E. B. White. Illustrations copyright © renewed 1980 by Garth Williams. Reprinted by permission of Harper & Row, Publishers, Inc.)*

you wiggle your toes and fingers?" I did.

"But I can't lift anything, and when I stand I feel broken at the waist. I can't continue in the Red Cross until I recover."

He suggested I sign a paper of resignation (and receive no pension at the end of the war). I signed and went home to rest. It took weeks before I felt nearly normal. I worked for a Canadian advertising company in London. Then the Americans began to come over.

I thought I might be able to help the Americans in their invasion. I spoke Italian and French and knew those countries very well, and, of course, I knew England extremely well. At this time America was still at peace. I went to see Sir Winston Churchill before volunteering at the American headquarters. When I met Churchill in the House of Commons (the British Parliament) he thought my idea was a good one. We talked about painting (he was also a painter), and then he said, "I am going to give you a letter of introduction to Eleanor and Franklin D. Roosevelt." He did, and I felt very pleased. I went to volunteer in London at the U.S. Embassy.

The American general I saw also thought I had a good idea and that I could be of help in many ways. He mentioned several. Then, when I asked for a commission, he replied that as America was not at war, I would have to go to Washington to collect one. That seemed ridiculous—go to Washington to get a commission and return to England. I had officially been through thirty-six thousand air raids (actually only about two thousand over my head) and I knew much more about the war than the Americans, who came to England for a week and then returned as "experts." What was worse, the Americans, being at peace, could not help me cross the Atlantic.

I went to the representative of a travel agency who could help me get over, and learned I had to be ready to leave at a half-hour's notice.

I packed and said a provisional farewell to all my friends, saying I should not be gone for more than three weeks. I was hoping to return as a brigadier general with a lovely apartment in Mayfair. It seemed many weeks passed. My mother was afraid we would never see each other again. (Tragically, she was killed three years later when she was struck by a car while riding her bicycle.)

The phone finally rang. "Train to Liverpool at 10:45 A.M. tomorrow." Several friends rushed me and my two suitcases to the train. I was off at last. "Tonight I will have a real meal," I said. It was the end of October 1941.

The ship I was to travel on was one of fifty in a convoy. It was an old French refrigeration ship, given to the British when France surrendered, and served as the commodore's ship. I shared a cabin with two American flyers who had brought over a P-36 American fighter plane. We sat with the captain for meals. The captain and officers of the *K.G.5* (I think it was called), the latest British battleship, were on board, but the five of them chose to sit apart in the ship's tiny library. Our captain was most optimistic: "Nobody has ever had their feet wet in any of my crossings."

We passed through a gale: seven knots forward and five knots backward to stern. It lasted two days, and I volunteered to sit in the crow's nest, as I was never seasick; the ship rolled forty-five degrees. The crow's nest was bulletproof; and when we sailed up near the North Pole, the Northern Lights were a view one could never believe.

One month later I reached New York. All lights were on at night; there were no search lights. Food was stacked in the shops; no half a pound of meat a month—if you could find it. I was thirty pounds lighter. The ship had had its food supplies for one week from England. The drinking water of our ship had been on deck in an open vat, and condensed steam from the engine room had deposited oily water into it. The only drink on board had been liquor, brought by the officers of the *K.G.5*. I had tried sea water, and tea made with engine oil plus water; both proved impossible. In New York I ate two pounds of oranges every day to get rid of scurvy.

I phoned my wife and went to Canada to get sunburnt, looking as if I had crawled out of a concentration camp. When I met my two daughters, the war seemed far away.

I was lent a log cabin outside of town, and went there on skis. I slept soundly until a Canadian Pacific train blew its whistle, *coooahoooah,* sounding like an air-raid siren and sending me jumping out of bed at 3:00 A.M.

Three days later I ran out of food and started to ski to town along the flat highway. A milk sled overtook me and the driver said, "Want a ride to town?"

"Sure thing," I replied.

"Well, things are really hopping," said the driver.

"What do you mean?" I asked.

"Have you no radio?" asked the man.

"Nope. I haven't heard or seen the news for a couple of weeks," I said.

"Well, Japan attacked the United States and sank a bunch of ships, battleships."

I hurried to New York. I went to the club where one could volunteer for the U.S. Army and saw the officer in charge.

"I volunteered six months ago in London and am here to pick up my commission. Do you have a letter from General So-and-so, or a list with my name on it?" I asked.

"No, nothing," he said bluntly.

"Should I go to Washington?" I asked.

"You can join the army, the navy, or the air force," he said abruptly, and walked out. That was the rudest reception I had ever had in all my life.

Later I had dinner with two friends, both old Princeton University boys, who were with the O.W.I. (Office of War Information). I told them of my rejection.

"What do you want to go back to the war for?" they asked.

"I only came over to pick up my commission," I replied.

"Well, let us look up your record with the F.B.I."

I took my letter from Sir Winston Churchill to Mrs. Eleanor Roosevelt's office, but could not see her. I was told she was out, but they did take the letter. They then called and informed me that Mrs. Roosevelt would like me to pick out buildings suitable for use as air-raid shelters in downtown Manhattan, in the event of air raids against New York. A limousine and driver appeared in the mornings to drive me everywhere.

I did this for a week. I never was able to meet Mrs. Roosevelt. I felt that perhaps Winston Churchill's letter was considered a probable forgery, because a five-minute "how do you do" seemed the least response I should expect. I pointed out that raids on New York would differ from those on London.

My cousin, who was head of the Anglo-Iranian Oil Company, was in New York. I offered to assist them in camouflage plans if the government required them at some time. I was a fully qualified American camoufleur. They decided it was not necessary, but various oil companies thanked me for alerting them to a possible future problem.

Once again I met with my Princeton University friends to hear what the F.B.I. had said about me, if anything. They were very jovial but could not understand my interest in returning to England and World War II. Once again they asked, "Why do you want to go back to England? You have been badly wounded, and have been in the war for two years since it began."

"What did the F.B.I. say?" I asked.

"They said you are not to be allowed to go to Europe. You are not to be given any commission. You are to be sent to the Pacific."

I was shocked. I could not imagine what could have caused such a report.

That ended my plans very positively.

Franz Berko

Illustrating in his studio, Aspen, Colorado, 1955

Fortunately, I had a great friend in New York, John Sebastian. We had met in Rome, Italy. He was planning to enter the American diplomatic service, but he changed his mind and became a great harmonica player, finally appearing with the New York Philharmonic in Carnegie Hall. He was on his way to the top when I arrived in New York. Since I had arrived from Europe with only one dollar and was now unemployed and penniless, he lent me money every week until I found a job and settled down as a peaceful citizen in New York.

For a while I made high-precision lenses, with plus or minus one millionth of an inch limit, in a New York factory. They had been losing fifty percent of their prisms; I showed them how to reduce their loss to only one or two percent. When I discovered that my lenses cost them less than one dollar and fifty cents, and they were sold at one thousand dollars each to the U.S. Army war effort, I was so disgusted I walked out.

I drew spots for the *New Yorker* magazine and did sample covers. I worked for a new magazine published by Howell Soskin, illustrating stories. Mr. Soskin thought I could make a children's book out of an old English rhyme. I did. It is called *The Chicken*

From Stuart Little *by E. B. White. Illustrated by Garth Williams. (Copyright 1945 by E. B. White. Illustrations copyright © renewed 1973 by Garth Williams. Reprinted by permission of Harper & Row, Publishers, Inc.)*

Book, and was published in 1946.

I had been doing spots and a few gags for the *New Yorker* for over a year so I asked them if I could call myself a *New Yorker* artist. They showed me the conference room with the list of artists on the wall and my name on it.

I looked for advertising work and went to Harper and Brothers with a portfolio of oil paintings, advertising, and *New Yorker* spots, and left it in the children's book department. The editor in chief of that department, Ursula Nordstrom, called me to come up as she had a book I might do. I took my eldest daughter, aged five, who was staying with me from Canada, and went to Harper. Ursula gave me a manuscript and said, "The author wants to know if you like it." It was *Stuart Little.* I read it and said I loved it. Ursula said, "Several other artists are trying to illustrate it, and if you want to try too, give us two or three samples." We returned to my apartment on 14th Street in an old building, now long gone. On my pillow was a mouse. I said to my daughter Fiona: "There's Stuart Little. You must be his friend. Feed him and I hope he stays." I made three sample illustrations: one of him taking a shower, and two others. I got the job, and Stuart the mouse stayed with us until the book was finished. It was published in 1945, three years after I came to New York, and that is how my career as a children's book illustrator began. I have now illustrated over eighty books in the past forty years.

There have been several changes in my private life during all this time, which I will record briefly.

Before the war, when Gunda and I were living near London, we met a young girl named Dorothea whom Gunda said would make me a perfect wife. "Then don't bring her into the house," I had replied. But she did and she was correct. Dorothea would have been a possible wife *if* I were a bachelor. At the time, however, I was still married to Gunda and had no intention of getting a divorce. Dorothea helped my wife take care of our baby daughter.

I recall an incident that occurred more than a year later, after the war had begun, when about twelve people were living in our house. Dorothea went out during an air raid to walk in the snow. I was annoyed (and said so) that several doctors who were sitting with all of us had watched her leave. All of us were in our twenties or thirties. I stopped playing flamenco guitar with two friends and followed her. She came back after half an hour, and I met her and pointed out that she was walking in the snow in open sandals with no socks or stockings. I took her back home, and, with my two guitar-playing friends from the Red Cross, put her to bed, gave her a hot drink, and rubbed her feet and legs with snow, which was the frostbite cure at that time.

Another girl from Germany (or Austria) who was staying in my house was related to L. Frank Baum, the man who wrote *The Wizard of Oz.* She pointed out that Dorothea had been thrown out of school in Austria when she was eleven years old. "What do you think will happen to her when the war ends? She may be twenty with no schooling." She was right. I put Dorothea in a secretarial college near our house in Kensington. She did her homework every night until midnight "because I have to compete with English girls. I don't know the language properly yet," she would say. She finished the two-year course in eight months and found work in a private bank in the stock exchange that had nine clients, all extremely wealthy, for whom the bank invested their money. (One always has to make more, I suppose.)

By this time, I was officially Dorothea's guardian. Dorothea's elder brother, who was an interpreter in the British army when the army invaded Europe, arrived at Buchenwald concentration camp only hours after their father and mother had been killed.

In 1941 I left for America feeling I had a fifty-fifty chance of surviving the war. When I arrived in

From Little House in the Big Woods *by Laura Ingalls Wilder. Illustrated by Garth Williams. (Text copyright 1932 by Laura Ingalls Wilder, renewed © 1960 by Roger L. MacBride. Illustrations copyright 1953 by Garth Williams, renewed © 1981 by Garth Williams. Reprinted by permission of Harper & Row, Publishers, Inc.)*

New York and went to see Gunda in Canada, I was expecting the United States to enter the war about April 1942, giving me six months to get my commission, return, and become established before the invasion of Europe. I explained to Gunda that I might get involved in some dangerous work and become a prisoner, or even lose my life. As, possibly, no one would be able to trace me, we decided that it would be advisable to get a provisional divorce so that she could remarry at any time should she so wish. But as you know, my commission never materialized and I was stranded in New York.

In New York doctors established the fact that my spine had been broken by the earlier bomb explosion at my side in Chelsea Square. With that information and the F.B.I. report, which would prevent me from seeing further action in the war, I decided that perhaps Dorothea, of whom I had grown very fond, would like to marry me. I wrote, and she said, "Yes!" We were separated for four years exactly. I had left England on her seventeenth birthday and she arrived in the United States on her twenty-first birthday.

We were married in Connecticut the next week and lived in New York before returning to England in 1946 with a new post-war Buick. We then lived in a monastery in Tivoli outside Rome for three years, where I illustrated the first Wilder books. We returned to Connecticut where I finished the Wilder books; in 1952 we moved to Aspen, Colorado with our two daughters, Estyn and Jessica.

We all found Aspen great fun; it was then just developing, and everybody knew everybody in town. There was one ski lift, and one T-bar for beginners. We had an old miner's hotel, seven miles up the Castle Creek Valley, that we rebuilt and redecorated. We bought two horses; one for twenty-five and the other for thirty dollars. Mine was the expensive one. The children had Shorty, a small, fat one. We learned to ride. (My father's father and brother had been crack riders. My grandfather only knew about horses: he joined the cavalry and wanted to go to the Boer War in South Africa when he was young, but his family "bought him out of the army." His son, my uncle, was an expert rider and survived World War I in the cavalry.)

In 1962 Dorothea and I went to Puerto Vallarta, in Mexico, on the Pacific, where we fell in love with the land and bought two lots overlooking the town and sea. The town authorities would not give me a certificate to state the lots were within the town

Laura Acosta

View from the main garden at the Williams home in Guanajuato, Mexico, showing the tower with the master bedroom above and the tall window of the living room below

With his five daughters (from left), 1981: Jessica hugging Fiona; Williams (top) and wife, Leticia; Estyn, seated on stairs above Dilys; and Bettina (far right). Also pictured are Estyn's husband (seated on stairs) and various grandchildren.

limits; without that I could lose the lots and any buildings thereon. So I never built there.

In 1963 I was offered lots, with the ruins of an old Spanish silver mine thereon, in Guanajuato, Mexico. I bought them and spent ten years building my home, incorporating the old ruin. I still spend the winters there. The walls are three feet thick, solid stone. One wall is six feet thick and another ten feet thick to support three huge arches.

In the late 1950s, Dorothea started to have slight medical problems as the result of poor blood circulation. Eventually we separated, and she went to England with the children, who were then teenagers, while I went back to Mexico. She had several operations. My lawyer in New York explained that they were drastic operations, and that if they failed she might lose her feet and, later, legs; gangrene threatened her due to lack of circulation. Later he called to say she had died. She was forty years old: it was January 1965.

While we were separated, she had planned to marry another American, a Rhodes scholar whom I had met at Oxford twenty-four years earlier. Dorothea wrote regularly giving me all the news, but the man cancelled their plans because he could not leave his wife, who, it was discovered, had cancer.

I was sure Dorothea would come back to me, and was heartbroken that she never came to see me in Mexico. I felt sure she would love the fascinating ruin which I made my home.

I felt I had reached something like the end of my life. But a bright young girl came to work for me when another American couple left Mexico. Her name was Alicia and she was seventeen. She had a small baby boy. I married her, and life continued.

My eldest daughter, Fiona, took care of her half-sisters, Estyn and Jessica, in England after Dorothea died. We went over to Europe after recovering from "flu," and took Dorothea's children to France and Spain. Fiona had done wonders, and I was greeted at the airport by three grinning, shouting daughters. Alicia had taught herself quite a lot of English and she was accepted by my friends and was very popular.

Alicia and I lived in the big house in Marfil, Guanajuato, and we had a son, Dylan. But Alicia was a girl who couldn't say no! So I waited for one of her boyfriends to carry her off, but finally suggested our marriage wasn't working out. We divorced, and I bought her a house, gave her money for a business—at bloated prices—and paid for our son's needs until

Williams and his only son, Dylan, 1975

he was eighteen years old.

After our divorce I met a lovely girl, age twenty-one. She walked on crutches, which I noticed were not for a broken leg but due to polio. We met at the house of an Englishman who was working in Guanajuato. He wanted me to meet three sisters, Mexicans, because he was engaged to one and thought he should have chosen a different one. He wanted my opinion. I went to the party and said, "You want to marry the one with polio."

"NO!" he said, "I can't make up my mind about the other two sisters."

I asked the one with polio—Leticia—if she could sit for a portrait. She was very beautiful and probably much less active than any other twenty-one year old. She agreed, although I said I was very busy for two months. (I was waiting for my divorce from Alicia to be finalized.)

We met once or twice a week for a lunch or supper. My divorce became final and I asked her to marry me. She said "Yes!" So I said, "I must ask your mother for your hand." She was very frightened. She said her family would hide her. I said I was about the same age as her mother and could not pretend I was only twenty-one.

I met her mother, who asked if I was married.

"I am divorced," I said.

"When were you divorced?" she asked.

"Yesterday," I replied.

She said her eldest son would speak for her. He did. He asked my age.

"I am sixty-one," I replied. "We both have handicaps; Leticia had polio and I am too old."

We eloped to Colorado Springs and were married. We then spent a honeymoon driving through France and going to Switzerland. After three or four months we returned to Mexico.

She is the present, and last, Mrs. Garth Williams. We have a daughter and have been married thirteen years. Leticia has learned to speak very good English and is a very good dress designer, now with a shop and two partners. Our daughter was nine years old in September 1987. Her name is Dilys and she is bilingual.

I am busy illustrating books until I strike a gold mine. I hope to retire and to be able to go back to serious art, painting and/or sculpting, some day soon.

To end this, I will make some comments about illustrating children's books. I shall begin by saying things which have been excellently noted by Maurice Sendak. The first is—we are drawing for children: not for adults, or librarians, or bookstores.

We have noted that our own childhoods remain with us, more so than most people. I feel five years old, easily. We are drawing for ourselves. We try to do better all the time. We are, one might say, drawing for our five-year-old selves.

Sendak has tried to draw and write for very young children—that is most difficult, using a five-year-old's vocabulary.

I also try to see everything with the eyes of the author, as I seldom write a book.

Technical problems of bookmaking I know: I can solve those problems. But to reach the child—I am ready to learn more any day. Once I have decided exactly how I want the illustrations to be, I can start work to produce them. If I fail, I try again, or decide to do them another way.

I hope other people will like them; especially children.

When I started there were about twenty children's book artists. Tenggren and Rojankovsky and the others. Now I think there are two hundred, or two thousand. But never mind, some will always be the best. I hope to be one of those.

With wife, Leticia, at their home in Mexico, 1986

BIBLIOGRAPHY

FOR CHILDREN

Books written and illustrated:

The Chicken Book: A Traditional Rhyme. New York: Howell, Soskin, 1946.

The Adventures of Benjamin Pink. New York: Harper, 1951.

Baby Animals. New York: Simon & Schuster, 1952; London: Publicity Products, 1955.

Baby Farm Animals. New York: Simon & Schuster, 1953; London: Publicity Products, 1955.

The Golden Animal ABC. New York: Simon & Schuster, 1954; London: Publicity Products, 1955. New edition published as *The Big Golden Animal ABC,* 1957.

Baby's First Book. New York: Simon & Schuster, 1955; London: Publicity Products, 1956.

The Rabbits' Wedding. New York: Harper, 1958; London: Collins, 1960.

Books illustrated:

Stuart Little, by E.B. White. New York: Harper, 1945; London: Hamish Hamilton, 1946.

The Great White Hills of New Hampshire, by Ernest Poole. Garden City, N.Y.: Doubleday, 1946.

In Our Town, by Damon Runyon. New York: Creative Age Press, 1946.

Little Fur Family, by Margaret Wise Brown. New York: Harper, 1946; London: Harper, 1947.

Every Month Was May, by Evelyn S. Eaton. New York: Harper, 1947.

The Golden Sleepy Book, by M.W. Brown. New York: Simon & Schuster, 1948.

Robin Hood, by Henry Gilbert. Philadelphia: Lippincott, 1948.

Tiny Library: A Dozen Animal Nonsense Tales, by Dorothy Kunhardt. New York: Simon & Schuster, 1948.

Wait Till the Moon Is Full, by M.W. Brown. New York: Harper, 1948.

Flossie and Bossie, by Eva LeGallienne. New York: Harper, 1948.

The Tall Book of Make-Believe, compiled by Jane Werner Watson. New York: Harper, 1950.

Elves and Fairies (anthology), edited by J.W. Watson. New York: Simon & Schuster, 1951.

Charlotte's Web, by E.B. White. New York: Harper, 1952; London: Hamish Hamilton, 1952.

Mister Dog, the Dog Who Belonged to Himself, by M.W. Brown. New York: Simon & Schuster, 1952; London: Muller, 1954.

Animal Friends, by J.W. Watson. New York: Simon & Schuster, 1953.

My Bedtime Book, by M.W. Brown and J.W. Watson. New York: Golden Press, 1953.

The Sailor Dog, by M.W. Brown. New York: Golden Press, 1953; London: Muller, 1954.

The Friendly Book, by M.W. Brown. New York: Western Publishing, 1954.

The Kitten Who Thought He Was a Mouse, by Mirian Norton. New York: Simon & Schuster, 1954.

The Golden Name Day, by Jennie D. Lindquist. New York: Harper, 1955.

Home for a Bunny, by M.W. Brown. New York: Simon & Schuster, 1956; London: Hamlyn, 1961.

My First Counting Book, by Lilian Moore. New York: Simon & Schuster, 1956.

Three Little Animals, by M.W. Brown. New York: Harper, 1956.

The Happy Orpheline, by Natalie Savage Carlson. New York: Harper, 1957; London: Blackie, 1960.

Over and Over, by Charlotte Zolotow. New York: Harper, 1957; London: Harper, 1979.

Do You Know What I'll Do?, by C. Zolotow. New York: Harper, 1958.

The Family Under the Bridge, by N.S. Carlson. New York: Harper, 1958; London: Blackie, 1969.

Three Bedtime Stories (traditional). New York: Simon & Schuster, 1958.

A Brother for the Orphelines, by N.S. Carlson. New York: Harper, 1959; London, Blackie, 1969.

Emmett's Pig, by Mary Stolz. New York: Harper, 1959; Tadworth: World's Work, 1963.

The Little Silver House, by J.D. Lindquist. New York: Harper, 1959.

The Rescuers, by Margery Sharp. Boston: Little, Brown, 1959; London: Collins, 1959.

Bedtime for Frances, by Russell Hoban. New York: Harper, 1960; London: Faber, 1963.

A Cricket in Times Square, by George Selden Thompson. New York: Farrar, Straus, 1960; London: Dent, 1961.

Miss Bianca, by M. Sharp. Boston: Little, Brown, 1962; London: Collins, 1962.

A Tale of Tails, by Elizabeth H. MacPherson. New York: Golden Press, 1962.

Amigo, by Byrd Baylor Schweitzer. New York: Macmillan, 1963; Tadworth: World's Work, 1975.

The Little Giant Girl and the Elf Boy, by Else H. Minarik. New York: Harper, 1963.

The Sky Was Blue, by C. Zolotow. New York: Harper, 1963; Tadworth: World's Work, 1976.

The Turret, by M. Sharp. Boston: Little, Brown, 1963; London: Collins, 1964.

Bread-and-Butter Indian, by Anne Colver. New York: Holt, 1964.

The Gingerbread Rabbit, by Randall Jarrell. New York: Macmillan, 1964.

The Sailor Dog and Other Stories, by M.W. Brown. New York: Golden Press, 1965.

The Whispering Rabbit and Other Stories, with Lillian Obligado; written by M.W. Brown. New York: Golden Press, 1965.

Miss Bianca in the Salt Mines, by M. Sharp. Boston: Little, Brown, 1966; London: Heinemann, 1966.

A Horn Book Calendar in Honor of Laura Ingalls Wilder. Boston: Horn Book, 1968.

The Laura Ingalls Wilder Songbook, edited by Eugenia Garson and Herbert Haufrecht. New York: Harper, 1968.

Push Kitty, by Jan Wahl. New York: Harper, 1968.

Tucker's Countryside, by G. S. Thompson. New York: Farrar, Straus, 1969; London: Dent, 1971.

Bread-and-Butter Journey, by A. Colver. New York: Holt, 1970.

Lucky Mrs. Ticklefeather and Other Funny Stories, with J.P. Miller; written by D. Kunhardt. New York: Western Publishing, 1973.

Harry Cat's Pet Puppy, by G.S. Thompson. New York: Farrar, Straus, 1974; London: Dent, 1975.

Fox Eyes, by M.W. Brown. New York: Pantheon, 1977.

The Little House Cookbook: Recipes for a Pioneer Kitchen, by Barbara M. Walker. New York: Harper, 1979.

Chester Cricket's Pigeon Ride, by G.S. Thompson. New York: Farrar, Straus, 1981.

Chester Cricket's New Home, by G.S. Thompson. New York: Farrar, Straus, 1983; London: Dent, 1983.

Harry Kitten and Tucker Mouse, by G.S. Thompson. New York: Farrar, Straus, 1986.

Ride a Purple Pelican, by Jack Prelutsky. New York: Greenwillow, 1986.

The Old Meadow, by G.S. Thompson. New York: Farrar, Straus, 1987.

From Little Town on the Prairie *by Laura Ingalls Wilder. Illustrated by Garth Williams. (Text copyright 1941 by Laura Ingalls Wilder. Illustrations copyright 1953 by Garth Williams, renewed © 1981 by Garth Williams. Reprinted by permission of Harper & Row, Publishers, Inc.)*

"Little House" Series:

Little House in the Big Woods, by Laura Ingalls Wilder. New York: Harper, 1953; London: Methuen, 1956.

Little House on the Prairie, by L.I. Wilder. New York: Harper, 1953; Harmondsworth, England: Penguin Books, 1964.

Farmer Boy, by L.I. Wilder. New York: Harper, 1953; Harmondsworth, England: Penguin Books, 1972.

On the Banks of Plum Creek, by L.I. Wilder. New York: Harper, 1953; Harmondsworth, England: Penguin Books, 1965.

By the Shores of Silver Lake, by L.I. Wilder. New York: Harper, 1953; Harmondsworth, England: Penguin Books, 1967.

The Long Winter, by L.I. Wilder. New York: Harper, 1953.

Little Town on the Prairie, by L.I. Wilder. New York: Harper, 1953; London: Lutterworth Press, 1964.

These Happy Golden Years, by L.I. Wilder. New York: Harper, 1953; London: Lutterworth Press, 1964.

The First Four Years, by L.I. Wilder. New York: Harper, 1971; London: Lutterworth Press, 1973.

Cumulative Index

CUMULATIVE INDEX

For every reference that appears *in more than one essay,*
the name of the essayist is given before the volume and page number(s).

INDEX

INDEX

INDEX

INDEX